WESTMAR COLLEGE L
W9-BUT-437

# MARKETING FARM PRODUCTS

# MARKETING

**The Iowa State University Press, Ames, Iowa, U.S.A.**

Geoffrey S. Shepherd
Gene A. Futrell

# FARM PRODUCTS

## –ECONOMIC ANALYSIS

*fifth edition*

GEOFFREY S. SHEPHERD is Professor Emeritus in Agricultural Marketing and Price Policy at Iowa State University. He has specialized in grain, livestock, and dairy marketing and in agricultural price analysis and price policy. His undergraduate training was completed at the University of Saskatchewan and he holds the M.S. degree from Iowa State University and the Ph.D. degree from Harvard University. In addition to his work at Iowa State, he has served in a number of advisory positions in Washington, D.C., West Germany, Japan, Burma, Vietnam, Venezuela, and Peru. His publications include two other books. *Agricultural Price Analysis* and *Farm Policy: New Directions*, as well as numerous bulletins and technical papers. The specialized perodical, *Farm Policy Forum*, was developed under his direction.

GENE A. FUTRELL is Professor and Extension Economist at Iowa State University, where his responsibilities include research and extension teaching in agricultural price analysis, outlook, and agricultural marketing. He holds the M.S. degree from Iowa State University and the Ph.D. degree from Ohio State University. Dr. Futrell is a contributing author to *Human Resources Development* and has written many marketing analysis and outlook newsletters, as well as journal articles, pamphlets, and bulletins.



Composed and printed by
The Iowa State University Press

First edition, 1946

Second edition, 1947

Third edition, 1955
*Second printing, 1958*

Fourth edition, 1962
*Revised printing, 1965*

Fifth edition, 1969
*Revised printing, 1970*

International Standard Book Number: 0–8138–1080–9
Library of Congress Catalog Card Number: 68–17494

# PREFACE

THIS BOOK is ecdysial. It sheds its skin every few years and develops a new one. It has to do this; its body keeps growing and changing, and the old skin is not elastic. But it is still the same creature, only bigger and newer.

My recent work as adviser on marketing and price policy in several countries abroad has taken me out of the mainstream of marketing developments in the United States. Accordingly, I have called upon Gene Futrell, whose work at Iowa State University keeps him immersed in the middle of this stream. We have revised the book extensively and Gene's competent hand appears in many places. It is a pleasure to recognize him as coauthor.

We have completely rewritten several of the chapters, many of the sections, and all of the tables and charts for which more recent data could be found. My experience abroad appears at some points. The structure of the book, however, remains unchanged.

Special appreciation is expressed for the help that Bob Strain provided in the chapters on dairy marketing.

My wife Eleanor edited all the revisions and editions before releasing them into Nancy Schworm's expert editorial hands. This complicated my life—the Chinese symbol for trouble is two women in one house—but the result is a superior product. Eleanor also did the index, a major accomplishment; authors traditionally expire from boredom, if not exhaustion, at that stage.

GEOFFREY SHEPHERD

Lima, Peru
September, 1968

# CONTENTS

# MARKETING FARM PRODUCTS

SECTION 1

# THE ANALYTICAL APPROACH

# 1

# THE THREE BROAD AGRICULTURAL MARKETING PROBLEMS

MUCH IS WRITTEN these days about countries which are in different stages of technological advancement. A good index of how advanced a stage a country has reached is the percentage of income in the country that is spent on food.

In a technologically underdeveloped country, most of the time and energy of the inhabitants is devoted to food production, and most of their income is spent for food. In a more advanced country, a smaller percentage is spent on food. Productivity in agriculture and other lines is high, and a comparatively small percentage of the population can produce enough food for all. This releases manpower and capital for the production of other goods and services, and the fact that food is produced efficiently and cheaply releases income that can be spent to purchase them.

In most countries of the world, food takes first place as the largest item in the average family budget. Even in western Europe, food takes from 25 to 40 per cent of consumers' income; in Russia, it takes about 45 per cent; but in the United States it took less than 22 per cent in 1950, 20 per cent in 1960, and 16 per cent in 1969.

**TABLE 1.1: Relative Importance of the Components of the Consumer Price Index, December, 1963**

| Items in Budget | Percentage Weights |
|---|---|
| Food | 22.4 |
| Housing | 33.2 |
| Apparel | 10.6 |
| Transportation | 13.9 |
| Medical care | 5.7 |
| Personal care | 2.8 |
| Reading and recreation | 6.0 |
| Other goods and services | 5.4 |
| All items | 100.0 |

Source: *The National Food Situation,* USDA, May, 1964, p. 19.

The relative importance of the different items in the family budget is reflected in Table 1.1. This table shows the percentage weights of the different items in the United States Department of Labor *Consumers' Price Index.*

Figure 1.1 shows the data for food in dollars; in recent years, consumers have been spending over $90 billion a year for food. This is less than one-fifth of their total disposable income of over $500 billion a year. This is two-thirds as much money as

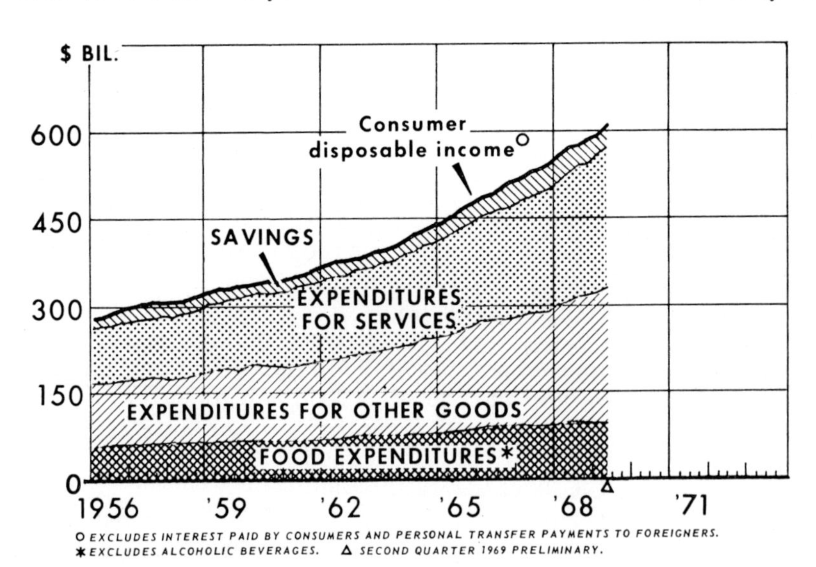


FIG. 1.1—Personal income and expenditures in the United States, 1956–69.

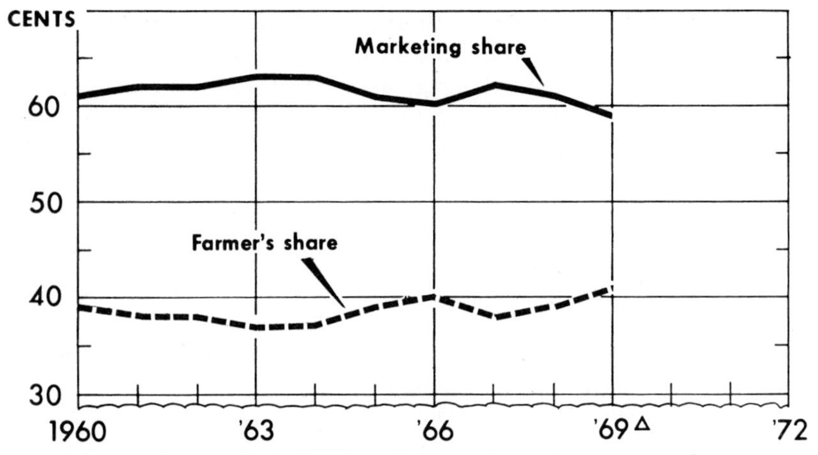


FIG. 1.2—Marketing changes and the farmer's share of the consumer's retail food dollar, 1960–69.

they spend on the first item, housing, and nearly twice as much as they spend on the third item, transportation.

It is difficult to grasp just what billions of dollars mean. Let us put the matter then in terms of dollars per person.

Total personal expenditures for consumer goods and services in the United States per person in 1969 were $2,835. Of that amount, over $511 a year was spent for food. This was $1.40 per person per day. An average family of 3.3 people,[1] therefore, spends over $\$511 \times 3.3 = \$1{,}686$ a year for food, the second biggest item in the average family budget. This means that it costs about $4.62 per day to feed an average family in the United States.

About 80 per cent of the value of farm products marketed in the United States is food. So agricultural production is big business. But agricultural marketing is even bigger. Figure 1.2 shows that the distributive system now receives about 60 per cent of the consumer's food dollar. Getting food from the producer to the consumer costs more than producing the food in the first place. Measured in dollar terms, then, agricultural marketing is a bigger industry than agricultural production.

[1] The average-sized family living together in 1960, according to the 1960 census, was 3.3 persons. On the face of it, this looks as if the average family, consisting of husband and wife and only 1.3 children, was not reproducing itself. But this figure does not include sons and daughters who have grown up and left the family to start households of their own.

Marketing is also bigger than agricultural production measured in labor terms. There are over 8 million workers engaged in agricultural marketing, and about 4.7 million engaged in agricultural production.[2] It takes more men as well as more money to market farm products than it does to produce them. Marketing accounts for three-fifths of the food dollar, leaving only two-fifths or less to go back to the farmer.

Many farmers and consumers feel that this marketing charge is exorbitant. Fifty cents may seem like a lot, but it is accepted on the vague, general, and logically inapplicable basis that share and share alike is fair. But for the marketing system to be getting more than the farmer who produced the food in the first place—this seems unfair.

We shall look into this matter a little later.

## THE CHANGING AGRICULTURAL MARKETING SYSTEM

Agricultural marketing is a turbulent industry as well as a big one. Always on the move, always changing in one way or another, it never seems to settle down.

The structure of the system has been revolutionized in recent years. It has been changing from a primarily centralized marketing system, funneling farm products through a few large central or terminal markets, to a decentralized system where a high proportion of the products short-cuts the central markets and moves instead through decentralized markets in the producing territory. More hogs are sold now in these decentralized markets in Iowa and southern Minnesota alone than in the 12 largest central or terminal markets combined.[3] Processing is being decentralized too. The biggest meat-packing plants now are located in the producing territory, not in the central markets. The biggest meat packers like Swift and Armour who used to be based in "Porkopolis" (that is, Chicago) no longer slaughter hogs at Chicago at all.

The character of the grain business is changing rapidly. The producing territory is dotted with steel bins and wood and concrete local and terminal elevators, built to hold huge governmental storage stocks for stabilization purposes. Grain marketing is becoming less of a merchandising business and more of a storage business. In the area of milk marketing, milkshed boundaries are crumbling under the impact of Grade A ordinances and paper containers: production of skim milk powder

[2] *Agricultural Statistics, 1969,* USDA, p. 442.

[3] 1968 supplement to *Livestock and Meat Statistics,* USDA, 1969, pp. 41–42.

is increasing, rising from 1.2 billion pounds in 1953 to 1.6 billion pounds in 1968;[4] and per capita butter consumption is rapidly declining, falling 50 per cent from 1947–49 to 1969.[5]

Furthermore, there is "high concentration in some segments of the food industry, especially in the various subdivisions of dry grocery manufacturing, and growing concentration in much of it."[6]

At the consumer's end of the system, supermarkets have taken over most of the retail food business. They handle 76 per cent of the total grocery sales in the United States, while "superettes" handle 12 per cent, leaving 12 per cent for small grocery stores.[7] A third of these supermarkets and superettes are operated by chains which go directly to the country for many of their farm products, by-passing both the central markets and the large city wholesale markets. All the way along the route from producer to consumer, technical developments are revolutionizing one marketing practice after another.

These are all physical things. The economic picture also is in a constant state of flux. Both the supply and the demand for farm products are continually changing. On the supply side, big crops and small crops come in unpredictable order and combinations. One year, beef is scarce and pork is plentiful and cheap; the next year, pork is scarce and beef is plentiful. On the demand side, changes in tastes, shopping habits, and food technology keep distributors on the jump. Canned orange juice replaces a substantial share of the demand for fresh oranges; then, within a few years, frozen orange juice replaces a major part of the demand for canned juice. Frozen fruits and vegetables come on the scene in increasing quantity and variety. Milk powder begins to cut into fluid milk sales. Self-service for meat becomes popular, and so on. Continuous study is required to keep abreast of these changes.

## THE ECONOMICS OF AGRICULTURAL MARKETING

In physical terms, agricultural marketing begins when the product is loaded at the farm gate and ends when the goods reaches the consumer's table. It is concerned with such physical things as trucks and refrigerator cars and packing plants and

[4] *Milk Production and Dairy Products,* Annual Statistical Summary, 1968, SRS, USDA, Feb., 1969.

[5] *The National Food Situation,* USDA, Feb., 1969, p. 15.

[6] *Food from Farmer to Consumer,* Report of the National Commission on Food Marketing, June, 1966, p. 93.

[7] "37th Annual Report of the Grocery Industry," *Progressive Grocer,* Apr., 1970, p. 53.

with technological developments in preservation and packaging.

But the economics of marketing takes in more territory. It deals with three separate but related problems: consumers' demands for farm products, the price system that reflects these demands back to distributors and producers and the methods or practices used in exchanging title and getting the physical product from the producer to the consumer in the form that he wants and at the time and place desired.

These three broad agricultural marketing problems can be spelled out more specifically as follows:

### Keeping Abreast of Changes in Demand

The utilities or satisfactions provided by the different farm products create the demand for them. These demands are continually changing. The first agricultural marketing job then is to determine accurately and in quantitative and qualitative terms just what consumer demands are in time, place, and form (the meaning of these terms in this context is elaborated fully in the next chapter) and just what changes are taking place in those demands with the passage of time.

The USDA puts it in these words, addressed to producers, processors, and handlers of farm products:

> You want to find new customers, and you want to get present users to increase their purchases.
>
> But first you must have some sort of an estimate of how many families are now buying your product, and how many haven't yet begun to buy.
>
> "Are there enough potential customers," you ask, "to make it worthwhile to put on a selling campaign?"
>
> "Are most of the people already buying my product? How many potential customers are still to be reached?"[8]

A farmer's job does not begin and end with producing something. Rather, it starts with finding out what potential customers want;[9] producing that product comes next; and the payoff comes from seeing that it reaches the customers in the form they desire.

A good many farmers used to find it difficult to begin their thinking with consumer demands. They were naturally more inclined to begin with what they had produced and to go on from

[8] "Frozen Foods Have Far To Go," *The Agricultural Situation,* USDA, Mar., 1954.

[9] The word "want" is not quite the right word here. A beggar may want a Cadillac, but his want has no economic effect unless he is able to back it up with money on the line. The right word here is "demand"—that is, want or desire, plus purchasing power.

there. They thought that the marketing problem began at the farm gate. Their attitude was "Here's the stuff. We've produced it. Now help us market it as best we can. Look at all this lard. Can't we develop some new uses for it? And look at all this butter. What are we going to do with it?"

Clearly, this was taking hold of the problem at the wrong end. Worse still, it was taking hold of the pig, as it were, after he was full-grown and ready for market and pretty hard to handle. A large share of agriculture's marketing problems arises because the right variety of crop was not planted in the first place or because the right quantity (of butter, for instance) was not produced. To begin with marketing problems at the farm gate is to begin too late, after much of the marketing problem is past solution.

> Often it is hard for the businessman to appreciate the simple fact that the easiest and, in the long run, the surest way to make money is (1) to find out precisely what people want, (2) to make it or buy it, and (3) to sell it to them. Too often his technique was (and still is) to make or purchase what he thought people ought to want and then, by high-pressure salesmanship, to force it upon reluctant customers whose true desires he had misjudged, largely because he had made no intelligent attempt to discover them. The more time, effort, and money a firm spends in carefully, intelligently, and completely planning the product which it will buy or make for sale, the less it is likely to need to spend in the work of selling. There seems to have been a growing appreciation of this fact among marketing managers in recent years.[10]

We used to suppose that the demand for farm products was a very stable thing. In total, and in physical terms, it is. The total demand for food does not change very much because of the fundamental inelasticity of the human stomach. A consumer wants three meals a day pretty regularly, even on holidays. But the economic demand, in money terms, varies a great deal from year to year. Furthermore, the demand for individual farm products varies a great deal over periods of years. Figure 1.3 shows that the per capita demand for poultry rose over 80 per cent from 1950 to 1968, while the per capita consumption of cereal products declined over 10 per cent. And the demand for different kinds and forms of a product—raw, canned, frozen, etc.—varies greatly over short periods.

Consider, for example, the spectacular rise of the broiler

---

[10] Ralph S. Alexander, Frank M. Surface, and Wroe Alderson, *Marketing*, Boston, Ginn and Co., 1949, p. 89. This comment is even more apt today than when it was first written.

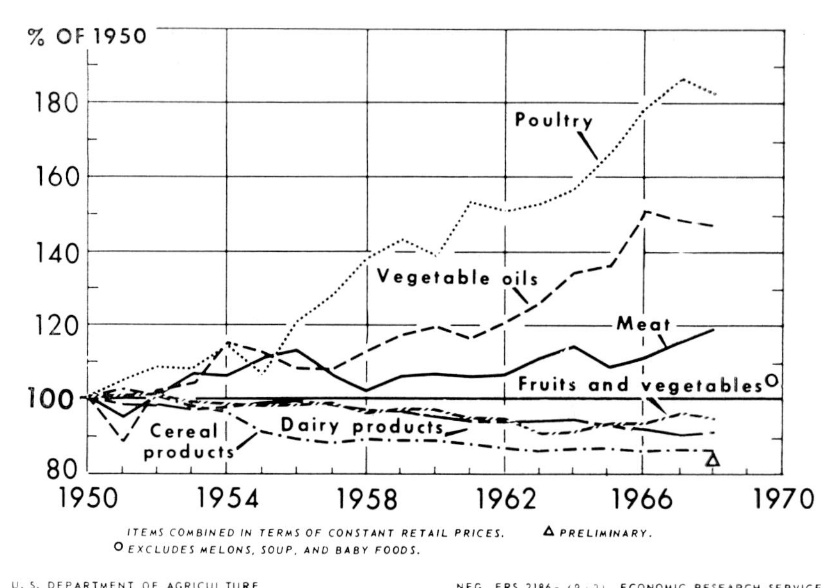


FIG. 1.3—Trends in consumers' eating habits in the United States, 1950–68.

industry. Poultry producers may have thought that their chickens, largely a by-product of the egg-producing industry, were plenty good enough for consumers. But consumers thought differently. They had a latent demand for a younger, smaller, more tender chicken. Some poultrymen began producing what consumers wanted, in factory-type batteries—and the broiler industry was born. Broiler production has increased rapidly, until now it is considerably greater than the production of chickens on farms.

One of the most striking changes in demand that has been taking place is the shift toward more processed foods. Table 1.2 shows how pronounced this shift was over the period from 1947–49 to 1969. In this table, where two forms of a product are shown, it is evident that the processed item has expanded more rapidly than the less highly processed one. For example, for fruits, fresh consumption per person has dropped, while consumption of some processed items has increased. The consumption of fresh fruit per person is down 39 per cent from 1947–49 levels and canned fruit juice consumption has declined 11 per cent, while frozen fruit and juice consumption has nearly tripled.

Other aspects of demand also need exploring. If consumer income increases 10 per cent, how much will that raise the

**TABLE 1.2: Apparent Civilian Per Capita Consumption of Major Food Commodities, Primary Distribution Weight, 1947–49 Averages and 1969**

| Commodity | Average 1947–49 | 1969 |
|---|---|---|
| | *(lbs.)* | *(lbs.)* |
| Meats (carcass weight)—total | 148.5 | 182.3 |
| Eggs (farm basis)—number | 385.0 | 314.0 |
| Cheese | 7.0 | 11.0 |
| Fluid milk and cream | 359.0 | 272.0 |
| Butter, farm and factory | 10.6 | 5.3 |
| Fresh fruits (farm weight) | 132.8 | 81.2 |
| Canned fruit | 18.9 | 24.3 |
| Canned juices | 15.9 | 14.2 |
| Frozen fruit (including juices) | 3.2 | 9.3 |
| Dried fruit | 3.9 | 2.8 |
| Fresh vegetables | 120.5 | 97.4 |
| Canned vegetables | 38.5 | 50.7 |
| Frozen vegetables | 2.8 | 9.3 |

Source: *The National Food Situation,* USDA, Feb., 1970, p. 15.

prices that consumers will pay? If supplies increase 10 per cent, how much will that depress prices? This part of the field of agricultural marketing is concerned with the position, elasticity, curvature, etc., of the demand curve for farm products, at the farm and at retail, and the relation of the curve to consumer income. It involves forecasting how much of the product consumers will take when the producer's goods reach the market and at what prices, measuring what changes are taking place in the demand for different products and for farm products as a whole, and so on. These things are the subject of the USDA and the state university "Outlook" information programs.

### Reflecting Consumers' Demands to Producers

The second broad problem in agricultural marketing is a market price problem.

Consumers' demands are the guides to producers as they lay their production and marketing plans. The chief medium for transmitting consumers' demands to producers is the system of market prices. How accurately do these prices reflect consumer demands? This is the second main problem in the field of agricultural marketing.

When producers meet consumers and sell them the goods face to face, this problem does not arise. Communication is easy. Consumers can tell producers directly just what they want, and why they want one thing rather than another.

But agricultural production in the United States has become

localized in specialized areas, in many cases hundreds of miles distant from consumers. Cotton is grown mainly in the South and Southwest. Oranges are grown in southern California, Texas, and Florida; hogs, mainly in the Corn Belt, and so on. The wide distance and the number of middlemen intervening between producers and consumers creates a producer-consumer communication problem—the problem of keeping producers in touch with consumers' demands and the changes continuously taking place in them.

Producers and consumers who are hundreds of miles apart like this cannot talk directly to each other. Most goods pass through several hands and several changes of ownership on their way from producers to consumers. The demands of consumers have to be passed back by word-of-mouth, as it were, from retailer to wholesaler to processor to local dealer to the producer. And like most word-of-mouth tales, they get distorted in the telling. This is particularly true since the different intermediaries all have different interests—different from each other's, and different from both the consumer's and the producer's.

In this situation, the chief medium of communication is the system of market prices that reaches all the way back from the retail store to the farmer's local market.

This market price system reflects the geographical distribution of consumers over the United States and, for some products, over the world. No traffic cop tells producers where to direct their shipments; the market price system does it automatically. The concentration of consumers in the heavy population areas of the East and Pacific Coast creates a strong demand that raises prices in those areas until they draw shipments of food from surplus food-producing areas. The price system also controls the distribution of goods seasonally as well as over longer periods. And it reflects consumer preferences for the form in which food is presented.

In actuality, as we shall see, the price system for farm products does not work properly in the United States. The price differentials that consumers pay or would be willing to pay for different qualities of a product, in many cases, are not reflected fully through the marketing system to producers; they are narrowed down or eliminated on the way. Producers do not get the right price signals from consumers. The same sort of thing happens over periods of time. Farmers respond to a high price for hogs; and by the time they breed, feed, and market more hogs, other farmers have done the same and hog prices are lower than farmers expected, so they produce fewer hogs—and get more for them than they expected when they reach the market.

It is essential that this price mechanism operate smoothly and accurately, or producers will not produce what consumers want; and the standard of living will not be the highest attainable with the existing level of productive resources and technology. If the price system is working properly, it will tell producers what consumers want, when they want it, and in what form they want it.

It is in this sense that the economics of marketing does not merely begin at the farm gate and end at the housewife's door. It begins long before that, before the seed is planted or the breeding begun. It begins when farmers decide what variety to plant or what kind of livestock to breed and how much—in the light of consumers' demands and their own abilities to produce. It carries on during the growing season, involving questions of farm storage in the case of crops and weight and finish in the case of livestock. Only then does the journey from the farm gate to the housewife's door begin.

### Getting the Goods From Producer to Consumer at the Lowest Cost

The third agricultural marketing problem is getting the goods from producer to consumer at the lowest cost permitted by existing technology.

Marketing costs fall under the three heads of time, place, and form, just as consumer demands and prices do. There are costs of transportation from one place to another, costs of storage from one time to another, and costs of conversion from one form to another. These costs are the economic basis for the time, place, and form differentials in prices that exist in the markets for farm products.

Farmers have sometimes been dubious about the value to them of reductions in marketing costs effected in processors' plants or retail stores. They are inclined to believe that the benefits of these reductions in cost accrue only to the processor or distributor or, at the most, spill over only to the consumer.

This is a misconception. It is true that the benefits of reductions in marketing costs do go first to the particular distributor who introduces them. His profits increase. But soon his competitors adopt his profitable practices. As the use of the new practices spreads, marketing margins are reduced to a new lower level, reflecting the new lower costs. Farm income is equal to the total amount that consumers spend for farm products, minus total marketing costs. For a given amount spent by consumers for farm products in the short run, any reduction in marketing costs adds just that much to farm income. Over the long run, when agricultural production has had time to respond, the benefits of reductions in marketing costs are divided between farmers and consumers. The long-run result is that producers, distributors, and consumers all benefit.

## SUMMARY VIEW

The three major parts of the field of agricultural marketing from an analytical point of view, then, can be described in summary terms:

1. Consumer *demand* for farm products as a group and, separately, by products.
2. The *prices* that reflect these demands more or less accurately to producers.
3. The *costs* of marketing intervening between producers and consumers.

This division of the field of agricultural marketing into three parts is the first step towards a systematic analysis of economic marketing problems. A second and somewhat more technical step is presented in Chapter 2.

# 2

## A FRAMEWORK OF THEORY FOR ANALYZING MARKETING PROBLEMS

THE GENERAL PRINCIPLES of any science are based upon a few fundamental concepts. Real life is too complex to be comprehended by one or two concepts or laws; it must be comprehended bit by bit, by the "one thing at a time" method, "other things being equal" or constant. Accordingly, the scientist searches for a few major uniformities that underlie the complex phenomena of real life, and finding these uniformities necessarily calls for some abstraction. None of these abstract concepts is found in actual life as such, but that is merely because each is overlaid by other phenomena of a less general kind.

The general principles of physics are based upon such abstract concepts as frictionless motion, absolute zero, a perfect vacuum, and so on; those of chemistry, upon pure elements, in terms of atoms, electrons, protons, etc. The general principles of marketing are based similarly upon a few fundamental concepts. One of the most basic of these is the concept of a market.

Markets are variously conceived. *Webster's New International Dictionary*, second edition, unabridged, gives eight different meanings of the word. The first six of these definitions are given below:

1. A meeting together of people, at a stated time and place, for the purpose of traffic (as in cattle, provisions, wares, etc.) by private purchase and sale, and, usually, not by auction; also, the people assembled at such a meeting; as, a *market* is held in the town every week.

2. A public place (as in a town), or a large building, where a market is held; a market place; esp., a place where provisions are sold; as, a city *market;* fish *market.*

3. Buying and selling, or either of the two, as an act or occupation; marketing; a sale or purchase; a bargain. . . .

4. The region in which any commodity can be sold; the geographical or economic extent of commercial demand.

5. Opportunity for selling or buying of commodities, or the rate of price offered for them; also, the phase or course of commercial activity by which the exchange of commodities is effected; as, the *market* is dull, active.

6. A body or group of men associated in, or organized for, the buying and selling of goods. *Market* may be used with reference to goods in general, or of a particular class of goods, expressed or implied, or of those dealing in them; as, the stock *market;* the beef *market.*

Economists themselves use the word with several different and generally vague meanings. In economic literature, one finds the following sample definitions:

"A market in economic parlance is the area within which the forces of demand and supply converge to establish a single price."[1] Another authority considers several definitions and finally chooses this: "A market is the sphere within which price-determining forces operate"—although he apologizes for the vagueness of the word "sphere." One economist has a different idea; he says: "The term 'market' is used here in the sense of funds available for spending rather than in the geographical sense of a market place. It refers to the financial aspect of the market."[2] Another attempts no definition at all but merely classifies markets descriptively as local, central, secondary, jobbing, and retail.[3] Still another economist uses the term to refer both to a market center and to a market sphere; he emphasizes the importance of the sphere.

Under one definition, Chicago, Kansas City, and Liverpool are three wheat markets. Under another definition, they are one market. Under the third, the entire farming and consuming territory of wheat constitutes the market. When the same word

[1] *Encyclopaedia of the Social Sciences,* Vol. 10, 1933, p. 133.

[2] F. A. Harper, "Growth of the Market Among Non-Agricultural People in the United States," *Farm Economics,* Cornell Univ., Nov., 1939, p. 2,839.

[3] Clark and Weld, *Marketing Agricultural Products,* New York, Macmillan, 1932, pp. 49–50.

is used freely and interchangeably in several different senses, it is small wonder that confusion follows.

## MARKET—A GROUP OF BUYERS AND SELLERS

It will simplify matters a good deal if we recognize that a market is neither a place nor a center, an area, or a sphere. A market is a group of men (or women), a group of buyers and sellers with facilities for trading with each other. They may be gathered together at one point, or in one market place, or scattered over a large area—that is only incidental. The important thing which defines a market is the quality of communication among those in it.

This was clearly stated, although not emphasized, by Marshall:

> When demand and supply are spoken of in relation to one another it is of course necessary that the markets to which they refer should be the same. As Cournot says, "Economists understand by the term Market, not any particular market place in which things are bought and sold, but the whole of any region in which buyers and sellers are in such free intercourse with one another that the prices of the same goods tend to equality easily and quickly."* Or again as Jevons says:—"Originally a market was a public place in a town where provisions and other objects were exposed for sale; but the word has been generalized, so as to mean any body of persons who are in intimate business relations and carry on extensive transactions in any commodity. A great city may contain as many markets as there are important branches of trade, and these markets may or may not be localized. The central point of a market is the public exchange, mart or auction rooms, where the traders agree to meet and transact business. In London, the Stock Market, the Corn Market, the Coal Market, the Sugar Market, and many others are distinctly localized; in Manchester, the Cotton Market, the Cotton Waste Market, and others. But this distinction of locality is not necessary. The traders may be spread over a whole town, or region of country, and yet make a market, if they are, by means of fairs, meetings, published price lists, the post office or otherwise, in close communication with each other.†"[4]
>
> * *Recherches sur les Principes Mathématiques de la Théorie des Richesses,* Chap. IV.
>
> † *Theory of Political Economy,* Chap. IV.

Marshall seems to have said the last word on the subject. We have not observed any more recent pronouncements on it by other authors.

In modern times, with the improvements that have taken

[4] Alfred Marshall, *Principles of Economics,* 8th ed., London, Macmillan, 1925, pp. 324–25.

place in communication facilities, the market center is giving way to the broad decentralized market. The prices of innumerable local buyers and sellers are now kept in line, not by reference to a central market but by more nearly direct reference to each other, through a large number of small markets over the producing and consuming area. The men in these small markets, distant as they are from each other physically, are yet in such close communication that they constitute a market, the same as though they were gathered together in one place.

## THE PERFECT MARKET

The definition of a market given above is analogous to a physicist's definition of a vacuum. And just as the physicist defines the *abstract* concept of a vacuum as a perfect *vacuum* or of no heat as absolute zero, the economist may adopt the term "the perfect market" as the abstract concept of a market.

The necessary conditions for a perfect market are that all the buyers and sellers in it have perfect knowledge of demand, supply, and prices and act rationally upon that knowledge. In the simplest case, all the buyers and sellers of a particular commodity are located at a single point in space and are doing business at a single instant of time. The distinguishing feature of such a market is that a uniform price prevails.[5]

In the definition just given, three elements are involved: (1) a particular commodity, (2) a point in space, and (3) an instant of time. These three factors require some elucidation.

### Space

The buyers and sellers who constitute the market for a particular commodity are usually scattered over a considerable territory. This does not preclude the application of the concept of a perfect market; the concept is merely broadened. The uniform price which distinguishes a perfect market is uniform over the area, plus or minus any necessary transportation and handling charges between buyers and sellers in different parts of the territory.

The idea of a "price surface" is helpful here. Where the market covers a considerable territory, the price surface is seldom flat like the surface of an ocean. The surface is highest at

[5] "Thus the more nearly perfect a market is, the stronger is the tendency for the same price to be paid for the same things at the same time in all parts of the market; but of course if the market is large, allowance must be made for the expense of delivering the goods to different purchasers; each of whom must be supposed to pay in addition to the market price a special charge on account of delivery." *Ibid.*, p. 325.

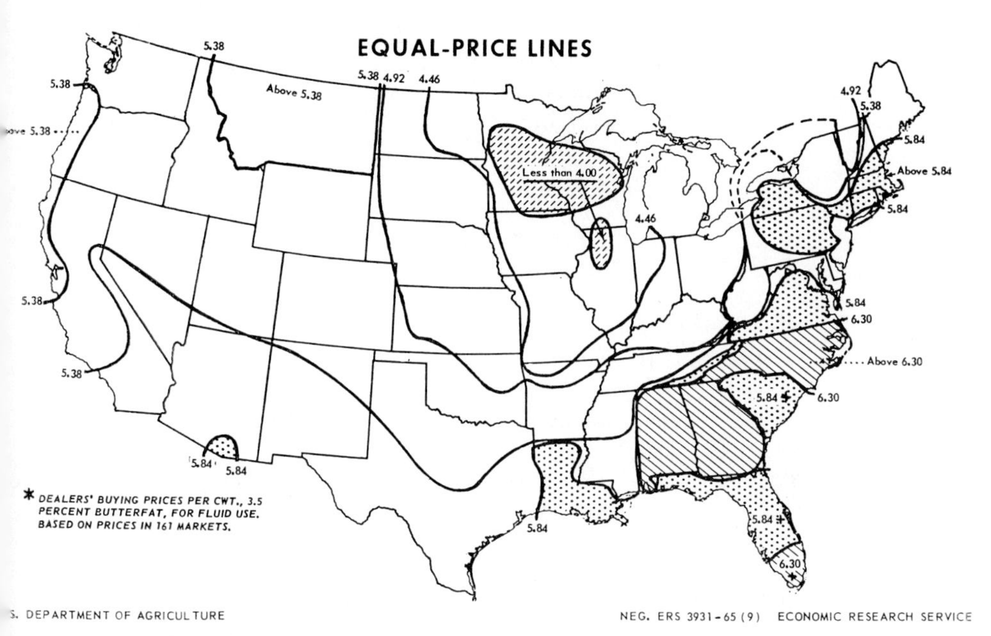


FIG. 2.1—Price structure for milk, July, 1964–June, 1965.

the points where the local demand is greatest relative to the local supply. But so long as the high point does not get higher, by more than a transportation and handling charge, than prices in the nearest surplus territory, the market is still perfect. The price surface for milk in the United States, based on 1964–65 prices, is shown in Figure 2.1.[6] The low point in this price surface lies in the Minnesota-Wisconsin area where the price is below $4 per 100 pounds. This is a heavy milk-producing area and is a supply source for some milk-deficit points; it is also an area of substantial production of manufactured dairy products. The price peaks, ranging up to $6.30 or more, are in the states along the Atlantic coast.

The difference from the low to the high price points corresponds roughly with the costs of transportation and handling. About 75 per cent of the price variation between the different areas is associated with distance. This relationship between milk prices and distance from Wisconsin is shown in Figure 2.2.

The expansion of the concept of a market to cover a geographical area does not introduce any complications into the theory of price determination, other than the transportation-

[6] Floyd A. Lasley, *Geographic Structure of Milk Prices 1964–65*, USDA, ERS-258, Sept., 1965.

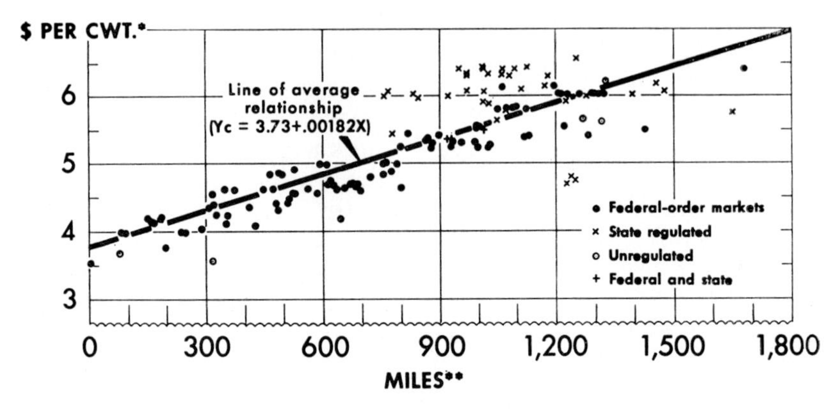


FIG. 2.2—Fluid milk prices related to distance from Wisconsin (in 136 markets east of the Rockies), July, 1964–June, 1965.

cost differentials mentioned in the preceding paragraph. The group of buyers and sellers may be concentrated at one point, or at several points, or it may be widely scattered. Prices are determined by the whole group in either case. For example, all the trading in butter might take place in one room in New York, with prices posted currently on a blackboard where all the buyers and sellers could see them. This would approach a perfect market (that is, it would reflect supply and demand conditions accurately), since all buying and selling prices would be known to all the buyers and sellers, and the prices that would just move the existing supply into consumption would be continuously and accurately determined.

If because of overcrowding, another office were opened up across the street, or for that matter several hundred miles away in Chicago, with prices and orders handled telegraphically, there would be no change in the situation, economically speaking. There is no reason why prices (adjusted for transportation charges) would be different from what they were before. If each buyer and seller knew accurately what the buying and selling prices of the others were, they would act the same as if they were all together in one room. The thought may be carried further. If many offices were opened in a large number of small towns with only one or two buyers and sellers in each town but all well provided with current price information, the situation would still be unchanged. Prices still would be determined in the same manner and would be the same as before.

The point may be generalized as follows: When a group of buyers and sellers are all together, trading in one room with prices and other information posted where everybody can see them, the requirements of the perfect market are approximated. If the group is widely scattered but the market knowledge possessed by traders is unimpaired, the market is equally good. Each buyer or seller has an effect on the market price proportional to the volume of his purchases or sales, but no more; Smith's 1,000 bushels added to the supply cut the demand curve at a lower point to the same extent as the sum of ten other farmers' 100 bushels each; no one buyer or knot of sellers or buyers can "set the price" in the one case more than in the other. Fundamentally, competition is just as good in the scattered market as in the concentrated market. For competition does not depend upon having all buyers in one room, or in one stockyard, so that they can rub elbows. It depends upon buyers and sellers being in touch with each other's prices, not with each other's persons. If buyers and sellers do not know each other's prices, it does not matter how close to each other they are physically; and if they do know each other's prices, by radio or telegraph or any other means, it does not matter how far apart they are physically.

The abstract concept of the perfect market is useful in that it provides a standard, a sort of sea-level point from which to measure aberrations in prices over the area where buyers and sellers are scattered. If prices at one point are more than transportation and handling charges above prices at another point, then the prices at the one point are too high, or are too low at the other. Which point is out of line, and by how much, can be determined by comparison with still other points in the area.

### Time

The buyers and sellers in a market usually do business, not at one point of time, but in the form of a series of transactions over a period of time. The concept of the uniform price may be broadened not only geographically, to cover an area, but also chronologically, to cover a period of time. The price is uniform over a period of time, plus or minus the storage charges involved in carrying some of the commodity over from periods of relative abundance to periods of relative scarcity.

That is to say, the standard of the perfect market used in appraising market prices over an area of geographical *space* can be applied also to appraising market prices over a period of *time*. This element of time is most important in the case of durable goods. If manipulation, squeezes, false rumors, etc., drive prices at any one point of time out of line with prices at another point of time (that is, more than a carrying charge above or below them), the extent of the aberration can be measured; and we can say that prices were too high or too low at this or that point of time.

This broadening of the concept of a perfect market to cover a period of time is not explicitly set forth in the literature, like the geographical broadening of the concept by Cournot, Jevons, and Marshall. But it is clear that a market should be perfect in time as well as in space. It is as faulty to have corn prices at Chicago 3 cents lower today than yesterday (if no change has taken place in fundamental demand and supply conditions) as it is to have Des Moines prices 3 cents lower than a shipping charge to Chicago today.

The test of the uniformity of prices over a period of time (plus or minus carrying charges) can be applied separately to the central market, the local market, or the whole market of primary producers and consumers, conceivably with different results in each case. At the central market for beef cattle, for example, receipts may be heavy for a few days and prices may fall. A few days later, receipts may fall off and prices rise, perhaps 50 cents per 100 pounds. We will assume that the demand remained constant throughout. If the time elapsing between the low and high price points were five days, and it cost 10 cents per 100 pounds per day to carry cattle at the central market, then that market would have done as perfect a job of equilibrating prices over time as physical conditions permit. It would have reduced price fluctuations to a carrying charge from the low price point to the high.

But by the same test the producer and consumer market as a whole would be adjudged defective. A farmer ordinarily feeds his beef cattle to the point of maximum net returns. If he sends his cattle to market before that point, he will net slightly less; if he holds them past that point, he will also lose. But the point is more like a rounded hilltop than a sharp mountain peak. The effect on the farmer's net returns of selling his cattle a few days earlier or later is negligible; his carrying charge for a few days is practically zero. Accordingly, if an adequate market-reporting system had been available to farmers, the heavy runs of cattle would not have taken place, and prices would not have had to fall at the terminal market. The marketing system did not provide the primary producers with enough market information.

The problem of market perfection over a period of time is also complicated by the fact that even after a market has done a perfect job of discounting the (predictable) future, unpredictable events may change the picture later on.

### Form

Modern economic theory has drawn our attention to the difficulty of defining "a commodity" or "a product."[7] Strictly speaking, every lot of "a commodity" being exchanged in a market is different from every other lot, just as every leaf on a tree is different from every other leaf. Each lot is a separate commodity, and the uniform price for "a commodity" that distinguishes a perfect market ceases to have meaning; there is only one lot of each commodity. But under actual conditions, goods, like leaves, have certain similarities which permit them to be divided into broad categories—hogs, wheat, corn, etc.—each of which may be spoken of as "a commodity."

This primitive degree of market classification served for centuries in history, where cattle, for example, were not only considered as "a commodity" but even were used as money (the word "pecuniary" is derived from the Latin word *pecus* for cattle). But as markets became more and more important in economic life, greater accuracy in definitions of commodities became desirable. Some cattle were worth more in exchange than other cattle. In order to give some recognition to these differences within a commodity, each became subdivided into market classes. Hogs, for instance, were divided into butcher hogs, packing sows, stags, etc.; wheat into winter, spring, hard, and soft; and corn into flint corn, dent corn, and so on. This still left a good deal of diversity even within classes. It meant that market quotations still had to be expressed in price ranges, not in single prices. A further subdivision then followed. The market class, butcher hogs, for example, was subdivided by weight and, finally, by grade.

This process of classification and subclassification permits a wider and more accurate application of the concept of market perfection. The price for 92 score butter, for example, at one point in space or time can be closely compared with the price for 92 score butter at another point because there is very little difference between the values of different lots of 92 score butter. The pricing process also becomes more objective because the classification of goods into classes and grades reduces the "higgling and bargaining" in the market place concerning what the particular lot of goods is worth.

We saw earlier that a perfect market would result in a

[7] Edward Chamberlin, *The Theory of Monopolistic Competition*, Cambridge, Harvard Univ. Press, 1957, Chap. IV.

price that would be uniform (plus or minus storage costs) at any one market over a period of time, when fundamental demand and supply remained unchanged. We now extend the concept further to recognize that a perfect market would result in a uniform price for "a commodity" (for example, wheat) plus or minus appropriate price differentials for different classes and grades within that "commodity."

That is, No. 1 Hard Red Winter wheat in a certain market might be worth 2 cents more per bushel to the consumer than No. 2 wheat. But if the market were paying the producer 3 cents per bushel more, or only 1 cent per bushel more, the market would be just as inaccurate or imperfect as if differences existed in prices at various geographical points or different points of time. A packer, buying butcher hogs (of given weights) pretty much at a "flat" price when actually the cutout values of those hogs might vary over a range of 50 cents or $1 per 100 pounds, would be operating an imperfect market with respect to form.

It is in this sense that the market in all the different commodities may be regarded as one vast all-embracing market. We commonly regard the different markets for the different grades, weights, and classes of beef cattle (with their relationships determined by their differences in form) as the beef cattle market. Similarly, in a broader view, the markets for different kinds of livestock (cattle, hogs, sheep, poultry, etc.) make up the livestock market. The livestock market is one element in the general food market and cannot get very far out of line with other foods in that broad market. And so on to other groups of commodities.

## EQUIVALENCE OF PRICES WITH COSTS

In a perfect market, the price differentials in time, place, and form would be equivalent to the corresponding differences in costs.

Prices at any one time, therefore, would be uniform over geographical areas, plus or minus the cost of getting supplies from surplus to deficit areas. The price of fresh pork loins, for example, in New York City would be the same as the price in Chicago plus transportation and handling charges from the one city to the other.

Prices in a perfect market also would be uniform at any one point over periods of time, plus or minus the costs of storing from one period to another (or the costs of producing at different times). The price of cotton, for example, would rise after harvest by an amount equal to the costs of storage. A comparison of the seasonal rise in the prices of the different grains shown in Chapter 11 with the costs of storage shows that there is fairly close agreement between them.

Finally, the prices for different grades of a product in a perfect market at any one point of time would be uniform, plus or minus the costs of converting the product from one grade or form to another or plus the relative costs of producing the different grades. The price of choice steers, for example, would exceed the price of good steers by the difference between the costs of producing the one or the other. And the price of beef at retail would be the price at wholesale plus the costs of operating the retail market.

This concept of the perfect market is a measuring stick or criterion or standard of reference, analogous to the physicists' concept of the perfect vacuum, or frictionless motion—never attainable in actual life but nevertheless an essential standard or reference in scientific study.

These three criteria of market perfection correspond with the orthodox division of utilities in economic theory into space, time, and form utilities. And the criterion of the perfect market, in which differences in prices equal differences in costs, is merely a specialized part of the criterion that is generally accepted for the whole field of economic theory—the equivalence of marginal revenues to marginal costs. In a perfectly competitive market (with horizontal demand curves for the products of individual producers) the equivalence of marginal revenues and costs leads to an equivalence of average revenues and costs, and this maximizes production from a given set of resources, given the existing distribution of income.

The concept of the perfect market as a criterion or tool for analyzing and appraising market performance can be integrated now with the analytical breakdown of marketing into the three interrelated problem areas, demand, prices, and costs, that were outlined in Chapter 1. The nature of this integration is indicated in Table 2.1.

## BREAK WITH TRADITIONAL FUNCTIONAL APPROACH

This analytical breakdown of marketing into its economic elements, arranged in systematic relation to one another in a sort of periodic table, represents a clean break with the traditional functional approach to marketing. The functional approach was analogous to the early classificatory work of the botanist, which classified plants according to their physical characteristics preparatory to studying them.

**TABLE 2.1: Integration of the Concept of the Perfect Market With the Analysis of Marketing Problems**

| *Utilities* That Create Demand | *Prices* That Reflect Demand to Producers | *Costs* of Getting Goods From Producer to Consumer |
|---|---|---|
| Time | Price movements over long, medium, and short periods of time. | Costs of production at different times, and costs of storage from one time to another. |
| Place | Price differentials between different places. | Costs of production in different places, and costs of transportation from one place to another. |
| Form | Price differentials between different grades or forms. | Costs of production of different grades or forms, and costs of processing the product into different grades or forms. |

The traditional functional approach in marketing merely attempted to classify and describe marketing services according to the "functions" they performed. These were first conceived as "functions of middlemen." But presently it became clear that they were really "functions of marketing," rather than of middlemen, since they "have to be performed in getting goods from producer to consumer regardless of who performs them." This idea was valid, but it resulted in the word "functions" being carried over into a phrase where it did not quite fit and where its meaning was not very clear.

These functions of marketing (jobs to be done) were differently conceived by various authors.[8] There was no agreement like the agreement reached by botanists on Linnaeus' system of classification in botany. H. C. Taylor listed as functions: grading, packing, assembling, processing, selling, transporting, storing and warehousing, financing and risk-taking, and dispersing. Clark and Weld disagreed with this list.

> To the authors . . . it seems that processing is really manufacture and so not marketing at all; finance and risk-taking are really separate functions. Dispersing is a marketing process involving all of the marketing functions and, if narrowed in its meaning, dispersing is primarily assembly looked at from the selling rather than the buying point of view. Another possible function, market news, could be included, but this seems rather an essential element in selling and buying.

[8]The specific sources of the quotations given on this page and the next several pages may be found in: G. Shepherd, "The Analytical Problem Approach to Marketing," *The Journal of Marketing* (Oct., 1955), p. 175.

Clark and Weld held that marketing consisted of three major processes—concentration, equalization, and dispersion—and seven marketing functions:

1. Assembling
2. Storing
3. Financing
4. Assumption of risks
5. Standardization
6. Selling
7. Transportation

A later author listed three main functions: (1) assembly, (2) processing (which Clark and Weld considered to be neither a function nor a part of marketing at all), and (3) dispersion (which Clark and Weld regarded as involving all of the marketing functions, or as assembly). Secondary services include packaging, grading, demand creation, etc. A still later author, Kohls, classified all marketing activities into three major processes, as Clark and Weld and Thomsen did (though Thomsen called them functions), but differed from them all in that he considered the major processes to be:

1. Assembly (which Clark and Weld regarded as a function, not a process—whatever the difference is).
2. Equalization (which Thomsen considered to be neither a process nor a function, nor for that matter anything else, since he ignored the term completely and used the concept only as incidental to the secondary service of storage).
3. Dispersion (which Clark and Weld regarded as a process, but which Thomsen regarded as a function—again, whatever the difference may be).

He then gave, as shown below, what he alleged to be a fairly widely accepted classification of functions:

A. Exchange Functions
   1. Buying (assembling)
B. Physical Functions
   2. Storage
   3. Transportation
C. Facilitating Functions
   4. Standardization
   5. Financing
   6. Risk Bearing
   7. Market information

Thus each author had his own list of functions. This was confusing and unscientific. Even if a solid basis of classification could have been found, the whole approach was merely descriptive and classificatory. At the most, it showed only why marketing was needed. It did not show how to go to the root of marketing problems and to work out solutions to them. The analytical approach we develop in this book is more analogous to the geneticist's approach to botanical problems, a study which penetrates to the genetic constitution of plants and shows how to breed better ones. The analytical approach used here does not describe and classify the function of demand creation, for example; rather, it breaks marketing problems down into their economic elements and measures demand to determine whether demand creation is needed in the first place, or whether, instead, a change in the form or quantity of the good is needed to meet the demand—something that is not included in any list of functions.

## DIAGNOSTIC AID

The analytical economic approach used in this book is crystallized in the structure of concepts set up in Table 2.1. This structure of concepts can be used as a diagnostic aid in appraising a marketing system as a whole, in locating particular problems, and in solving them. It can also be used to place a given specialized problem or research project in a broad context, helping the student see his problem in relation to others.

A national livestock marketing advisory committee, for instance, could use the table as a basis for appraising livestock marketing, for locating weak spots, and in developing recommendations for improvements. The committee would be able to deal with its assignment in a systematic analytical way. It would start with the *demand* for meat: Is the demand increasing, or decreasing, or changing in any other way over *time*? And is the demand for beef, for example, changing in a different way from the demand for pork? Next, is the demand changing with respect to *place*, including the location of packing plants as well as consumers? And then, is the demand changing with respect to *form*, that is, the weight and grade of cuts, lean or fat pork, self-serve or service retailing, fresh or frozen, and so on?

The second step then would be to appraise the *price* system for livestock and meats. Is it reflecting consumers' preferences on the one hand and producers' and distributors' costs on the other, again under the headings of time, place, and form? Are prices variable enough to keep supplies moving through to the consumer without surpluses or shortages occurring? Are they too variable to provide reliable guides to producers?

The third step would be to consider the *costs* of marketing as such and how they might be reduced. Are there too many small, high-cost marketing units to permit maximum efficiency? What is the optimum size of marketing units, taking costs of procurement as well as costs of processing and handling in the plant into account? If the optimum size is large relative to the market, so that the number of units is small and monopolistic rather than atomistic competitive conditions prevail, what needs to be done?

Other questions follow. Are the costs of storage over time being reduced to the minimum? Would a change in form permit further reductions? Are transportation costs the lowest permitted by existing technology?

The systematic research approach outlined above provides a structural framework for appraising markets and market performance. It provides a basis for integrating separate studies horizontally and vertically. And it helps to locate the problems and state them clearly and it points the way to their solution. This approach is used in these ways throughout this book.

IN SECTION I of this book we set up the conceptual framework to apply to the analysis of marketing problems. In Section II we use this framework with those overall marketing problems common to agriculture as a whole, cutting across commodity lines. In Section III we narrow the field of view, turn our microscope up to a higher power, and examine separately those specialized commodity marketing problems that differ from one commodity to another.

# SECTION 2

# OVERALL MARKETING PROBLEMS

We organize our study throughout along the lines laid out in Section I. In each case we begin with the first part of the field, the *demand* for the product, and proceed thereafter to study *prices* and then *costs*. Within each of these three parts, we deal with time, place, and form. Our objective is to maximize producers', distributors', and consumers' real incomes of goods and services. Our viewpoint and method makes use of the problem-solving viewpoint and method of science.

We study the situation in the United States because that is of more interest to most of our readers than the situation in other countries. But the same general approach can be applied to any country where adequate statistics are available.

The first chapter in this section deals briefly with the theory of demand, to help us understand and interpret the facts and relationships presented in the subsequent chapters.

# 3

# ELEMENTARY THEORY OF DEMAND

THE ELEMENTARY THEORY of demand is relatively simple.

After a product has become well established in the market, the more of the product that is offered for sale, the lower the price must be to move all of it into consumption. This can be stated in formal terms as the *law of demand:* The larger the quantity produced, the lower the price (and conversely, the lower the price, the larger the quantity that can be sold). This can be put in a single phrase: Price varies inversely with quantity supplied.[1]

There are several reasons why larger quantities have to be sold at lower prices.

One reason is *physiological.* We get a good deal of satisfaction out of a helping of ice cream for dessert. We get less satisfaction, however, out of a second helping. If we were willing to pay 20 cents for the first helping, we perhaps would pay only 10 cents for the second. We would give nothing at all for a third. The more we have of almost anything, the less satisfaction we get out of the last unit we consume at a sitting. Since

[1] Correspondingly, the law of supply can be stated thus: The larger the quantity demanded, the higher must be the price to induce the production of that larger quantity (and conversely). In a single phrase: Price varies directly with quantity demanded.

The two statements together constitute the law of supply and demand: Price varies inversely with supply and directly with demand.

the first helping of ice cream we would eat at 20 cents is indistinguishable at the retail store from the second helping we would take only at 10 cents, the price of all ice cream drops to 10 cents per helping if there is that much to be sold.

The second reason why prices vary inversely with supplies is *physiological and cultural*. People differ in their physiological makeup and in the tastes that they have cultivated. One man loves spinach; a second will eat it only if it is cheap; and a third may not like spinach at all. Spinach has to be sold at a moderately low price to induce the second man to buy it and at a very low price to induce the third.

The third reason is *economic*. The distribution of income is uneven—a rich man and a poor man, though they have the same tastes, will not buy the same amounts of steaks or olives. Prices have to be low before the poor man can buy at all.

## EQUILIBRIUM FOR THE INDIVIDUAL

The law of demand follows from the fundamental characteristic of demand that consumers can substitute one commodity for another to a considerable extent, according to the relative prices, quantities, and want-satisfying power of the different commodities. If beef is plentiful and cheap, consumers will buy more of it and buy less pork and pay less for it, for example, than if beef were scarce and high priced.

Each individual buys more and more of different products until the addition to the total satisfaction he gets from the last small unit of each one (the "marginal unit") is proportional to its price. Thus if cabbage is 10 cents a pound and lettuce, 20 cents, the consumer will buy enough of each until he gets twice as much additional satisfaction from the last pound of lettuce as he does from the last pound of cabbage. The same thing is true with respect to bananas and other foods, and indeed all other goods and services. The consumer allocates his income among the different goods and services he buys until he gets the same additional satisfaction from the last nickel spent on each one.[2]

## EQUILIBRIUM FOR THE MARKET

The law of demand can be seen at work every year, and every day and hour too, for that matter, in agricultural markets. Big crop—low price; small crop—high price. That is the law of demand, and it works automatically. The price rises or falls

[2] The consumer's behavior in this matter, and the reasons for differing elasticities of demand, can be explained in technical terms with the aid of indifference curves showing the marginal rates of substitution between two products. This explanation is given in most textbooks on the principles of economics, and in any case need not detain us here.

**TABLE 3.1: Quantities and Associated Prices for Strawberries (Hypothetical Data)**

| Period I | Million Boxes | Price Per Box |
|---|---|---|
| | 1.1 | $ .80 |
| | 0.9 | $1.20 |
| Period II | | |
| | 1.2 | $ .80 |
| | 1.0 | $1.20 |

and rations the commodity among those who have the strongest demand for it, until nobody who is willing to buy at that price goes away empty-handed, and all of the commodity is sold. Under those conditions the market is said to be in equilibrium. The equilibrium is a moving equilibrium, like that of a man riding a bicycle.

## THE ELASTICITY OF DEMAND

The law of demand in the market place is illustrated in the upper part of Table 3.1, which shows hypothetical data for strawberries. Round numbers are used to keep the arithmetic simple. The table shows that strawberries sold for 80 cents per box one year and $1.20 per box the next year. The table shows also that the production of strawberries decreased from 1.1 million boxes the first year to 0.9 million boxes the next year.

These price and production data are plotted in Figure 3.1. In the case of a perishable product like strawberries, which cannot be stored from one year to the next,[3] the quantity produced is the same as the quantity consumed. The quantity produced and consumed is plotted along the bottom of Figure 3.1, while the price is plotted up the side. When we connect the two points of intersection, we get a straight line that slopes downward to the right. This is shown as the solid line in Figure 3.1.

This line represents the demand for strawberries. The demand for a product is not something that you can represent by a single figure, or by a single point. Demand is defined as a series of figures—the series or schedule of different quantities that consumers will take at a series of different prices. Normally, consumers will take larger quantities only at lower prices.

In this case, an increase in strawberry production (and consumption) of 20 per cent resulted in a decrease in price of 40 per cent. Or to put it the other way around, a decrease in price

[3] Strawberries can be frozen and sold in that form later in the season. But the frozen strawberries are not stored and carried over to a later year; they are all consumed in the same year they were produced.

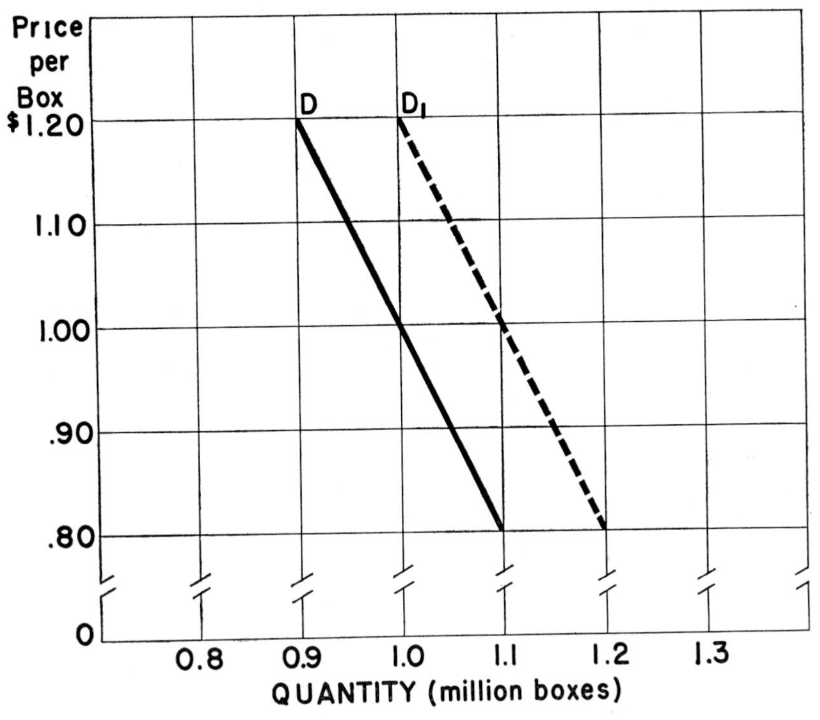


FIG. 3.1—Hypothetical demand curves for strawberries.

of 40 per cent was needed to move the 20 per cent increase in quantity into consumption. The response of consumption to the change in price was small. We say then that the demand for strawberries is inelastic. If the percentage change in consumption is less than the percentage change in price, the demand is called inelastic.

The general formula for computing elasticity is

$$\text{Elasticity} = \frac{\text{percentage change in quantity}}{\text{percentage change in price}}$$

and the elasticity may be defined numerically as the change in quantity associated with a 1 per cent change in price. Thus, in the example above, a 20 per cent change in quantity is associated with a 40 per cent change in price; the elasticity is $20/40 = 0.5$.

Strictly speaking, this figure should be preceded by a minus sign because an increase in quantity (represented by a plus sign) is associated with a decrease in price (represented by a minus sign) and a plus divided by a minus yields a minus quantity.

### Elasticity and Total Revenue

The elasticity of the demand has a direct effect upon the total revenue from the sale of different-sized crops. If the demand for a crop is inelastic, then the bigger the crop, the smaller the total revenue. The increase in the size of the crop causes a more than proportional decrease in the price per unit.

Thus, in the example given above, the small crop of 0.9 million boxes sold for $1.20 per box; the total revenue was $108 million. The large crop of 1.1 million boxes, however, sold for only 80 cents per box; the total revenue then was only $88 million. The large crop was worth less than the small crop. When the demand is inelastic like this, a large crop brings not only a lower price per unit but a lower total revenue for the whole crop as well.

### Elasticity of Demand for Food

The demand for any one food is more elastic than the demand for food as a whole. It is easier to substitute one food for another than it is to substitute something else for food as a whole. The elasticity of the demand for pork at retail in the United States is about —0.7, and for beef, about —0.9.[4] But for all meat together, it is about —0.6. The elasticity for food as a whole in the United States is about —0.25.

### Elasticity at Farm and Retail Level

The elasticity of the demand at the farm is usually less than the elasticity at the retail level because middlemen's charges are relatively fixed, so most of a change in prices at retail is passed back to the farmer. If we assume for the moment, for purposes of clarity, that middlemen's charges remain completely fixed in cents and that half of the consumer's food dollar gets back to the farmer, then a change in a retail price of say 10 cents (10 per cent of a dollar) shows up as a change of 10 cents at the farm level (which is 20 per cent of the 50 cents the farmer gets). The percentage change in price (the denominator in the elasticity formula) at the farm is twice as great as at retail, so the elasticity of demand is only half as great as at retail.

---

[4] George Brandow, *Interrelations Among Demands for Farm Products*, Pa. State Univ. Bul. 680, 1961, p. 17.

## CHANGES IN DEMAND

Changes in demand can be measured by measuring the changes that take place in consumption and prices.

We may refer again to the upper part of Table 3.1 and the solid straight line in Figure 3.1. The table and figure show that strawberries sold for 80 cents per box one year and $1.20 per box the next year.

The lower part of Table 3.1 shows that in some later period, at the same prices as in the two earlier years shown in the upper part of the table, producers could sell 120 and 100 million boxes instead of 110 and 90 million. The whole demand curve in Figure 3.1 moved to the right, from the position shown by the solid line to the position shown by the dashed line. When this happens, we say that the demand increased.

It is only when the whole curve shifts like this that we say the demand has changed. A change from 80 cents one year to $1.20 the next, merely because production dropped from 110 million boxes to 90 million, does not mean that the demand had changed. It only means that the *supply* changed and cut the demand curve at a different point. It is only when the whole curve changes its position that we say the demand has changed.

The effect of a change in demand upon the price of a product depends upon the extent of the shift in the position of the demand curve and upon the elasticity of the demand. It also depends upon the elasticity of the supply. This will be shown in Chapter 9 on the theory of prices.

The chief factors that cause changes in demand are three:

1. Changes in total population and in the age composition of the population.
2. Changes in income per capita and in its distribution.
3. Changes in tastes.

### Changes in Population

The relation between changes in population and demand, other things being equal, is simple; a change in population causes a proportional change in demand.

Other things of course never do remain exactly equal. The composition of the population by age groups is always changing. This affects the total demand. A population with a high proportion of babies and small children eats less than a population heavily weighted by adults. The composition of the population, however, changes only slowly and by small amounts from year to year; for our purposes here, it can be considered only a minor factor.

**Changes in Income**

The relation between changes in income and changes in demand is not so simple.

Around the middle of the nineteenth century Ernst Engel studied consumer's budgets in Belgium and Saxony to determine the relation between income and expenditures for food. His work showed that high-income groups spend more per capita for food than low-income groups; but the high-income groups spend a smaller *proportion* of their incomes for food than the low-income groups. A number of statistical studies since Engel's time have revealed similar relations between income and expenditures for food in other countries.

A typical income-food expenditure curve for the United States is shown in Figure 3.2.[5] The upper part of the chart (Section A) shows that high-income groups spend more money for food than low-income groups. The straight line drawn through the dots shows that, on the average, a man with 1 per cent more income than another did not spend 1 per cent more money for food; he spent only 0:44 per cent more. The income-elasticity of expenditures for food, then, was about 0.44.

The lower part of Figure 3.2 (Section B) shows that, although high-income groups spend more money for food than low-income groups, what they spend is a smaller percentage of their incomes. The general rule is this: The bigger the income, the smaller is the per cent spent on food.

The percentage spent on food by the high-income groups would be still lower than it is were it not for the fact that the high-income groups have larger families than the low-income groups. Of the families included in the 1955 food consumption survey, the average family size of the highest-income group ($10,000 and over) was 3.80 persons; the lowest-income group families (under $2,000) averaged 2.88 persons. Average family size in the $3,000–$7,999 income groups was about 3.60 persons.

It used to be said that "the rich get rich and the poor get children." This does not appear to be borne out by the 1955 survey data or by the 1965 food consumption survey data shown in Table 3.2. The high-income groups have larger families, however, not because high incomes are conducive to fertility, but because income and family size both increase with the passage of time. Normally, a young couple begins their married

[5] Basic data from "Food Consumption of Households in the United States," *Household Food Consumption Survey, 1955*, USDA, Rept. 1, p. 11.

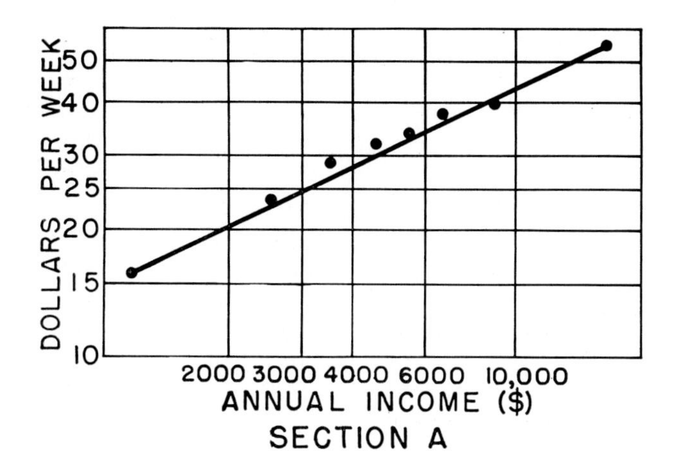


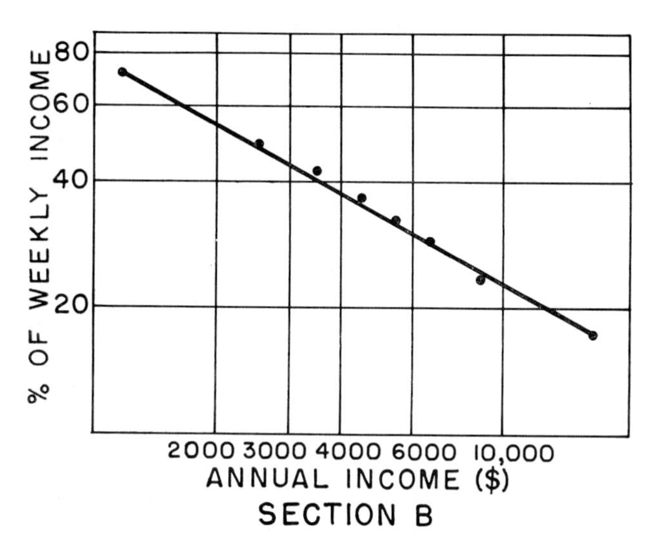


FIG. 3.2—Weekly food expense, April–June, 1955, by income groups: (A) in dollars; (B) as per cent of income.

life at the bottom of the ladder with a small income and a small family. Bigger pay checks and more children often come along together during the next several years.

Preliminary data from the 1965 Food Consumption Survey in Table 3.2 show the same kind of income-food expenditure relationship revealed in the 1955 survey.[6] The money value of

[6] "Money Value of Food Used by Households in the United States, Spring, 1965," *Food Consumption Survey, 1965–66*, USDA, Sept., 1966.

**TABLE 3.2: Money Value of Food Used Per Housekeeping Household Per Week, Spring, 1965, United States**

| Urbanization and 1964 Money Income After Taxes | Household Size* | All Food | Money Value of Food Used at Home | | | Expense for Meals and Snacks Away From Home |
|---|---|---|---|---|---|---|
| | | | All† | Bought | Home produced | |
| (1) | (2) | (3) | (4) | (5) | (6) | (7) |
| *(dollars)* | *(persons)* | *(dollars)* | *(dollars)* | *(dollars)* | *(dollars)* | *(dollars)* |
| *All urbanizations* | | | | | | |
| All households‡ ..... | 3.29 | 35.01 | 28.91 | 26.95 | 1.27 | 6.11 |
| Under 3,000 ....... | 2.57 | 19.62 | 17.82 | 15.10 | 1.79 | 1.80 |
| 3,000–4,999 ........ | 3.39 | 30.20 | 26.23 | 23.91 | 1.60 | 3.98 |
| 5,000–6,999 ........ | 3.59 | 37.48 | 31.52 | 29.71 | 1.18 | 5.96 |
| 7,000–9,999 ........ | 3.60 | 43.09 | 34.79 | 33.45 | .78 | 8.30 |
| 10,000 and over .... | 3.63 | 54.16 | 40.01 | 38.42 | .98 | 14.15 |
| *Urban* | | | | | | |
| All households‡ ..... | 3.10 | 35.51 | 28.74 | 27.83 | .31 | 6.77 |
| Under 3,000 ....... | 2.26 | 18.39 | 16.58 | 15.39 | .36 | 1.81 |
| 3,000–4,999 ........ | 3.19 | 28.77 | 24.60 | 23.79 | .26 | 4.17 |
| 5,000–6,999 ........ | 3.44 | 37.20 | 30.93 | 30.02 | .32 | 6.27 |
| 7,000–9,999 ........ | 3.53 | 43.17 | 34.42 | 33.63 | .26 | 8.75 |
| 10,000 and over .... | 3.56 | 55.20 | 40.06 | 39.10 | .42 | 15.15 |
| *Rural nonfarm* | | | | | | |
| All households‡ ..... | 3.50 | 33.32 | 28.63 | 25.77 | 1.93 | 4.69 |
| Under 3,000 ....... | 2.85 | 19.72 | 17.98 | 14.35 | 2.40 | 1.74 |
| 3,000–4,999 ........ | 3.70 | 32.26 | 28.73 | 25.29 | 2.30 | 3.53 |
| 5,000–6,999 ........ | 3.90 | 37.70 | 32.33 | 29.71 | 1.89 | 5.37 |
| 7,000–9,999 ........ | 3.80 | 42.75 | 35.73 | 33.81 | 1.32 | 7.02 |
| 10,000 and over .... | 3.83 | 50.83 | 40.06 | 37.81 | 1.35 | 10.77 |
| *Rural farm* | | | | | | |
| All households‡ ..... | 3.99 | 35.68 | 31.85 | 21.32 | 9.80 | 3.82 |
| Under 3,000 ....... | 3.81 | 27.76 | 25.82 | 15.43 | 9.73 | 1.94 |
| 3,000–4,999 ........ | 4.00 | 35.19 | 31.42 | 20.76 | 9.97 | 3.77 |
| 5,000–6,999 ........ | 4.16 | 40.20 | 35.84 | 25.36 | 9.71 | 4.36 |
| 7,000–9,999 ........ | 3.95 | 42.65 | 37.08 | 26.83 | 9.41 | 5.57 |
| 10,000 and over .... | 4.41 | 47.90 | 40.18 | 28.86 | 10.31 | 7.72 |

Source: "Money Value of Food Used by Households in the United States, Spring, 1965," *Food Consumption Survey, 1965–66,* USDA, Sept., 1966.

* Total number of meals served from home food supplies divided by 21.

† Includes money value of food federally donated and received as gifts and pay.

‡ Includes households not classified by income.

food used at home increased at each higher level of household income. This was true for each urbanization category. Expenditures for meals eaten away from home rose sharply as household income increased. The income-food expenditure relationships for all households included in the 1965 survey are shown graphically in Figure 3.3.

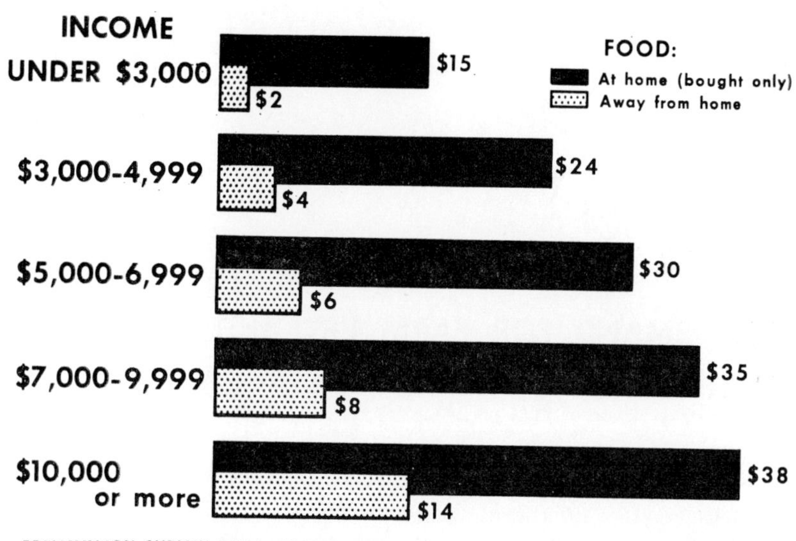


FIG. 3.3—Money value of food used per household per week, spring, 1965, United States.

# 4

# THE DEMAND FOR FARM PRODUCTS IN THE UNITED STATES

HAVING REVIEWED the elementary theory of demand in the preceding chapter, we are ready now to analyze the facts of the demand situation in the United States.

The great bulk of farm production in the United States consists of food,[1] and the demand for food is more homogeneous than the demand for all farm products (including textiles, for example) taken together. In this chapter, therefore, we will concentrate mostly on the demand for food. The demand for the chief nonfood items, such as cotton, is considered later in the commodity section of this book.

Nearly all the food consumed in the United States is produced in the United States. And nearly all of the food produced in the United States is consumed there also. The source and distribution of food in this country during recent years is shown in Table 4.1.

[1] Cotton and tobacco are the two chief nonfood items. The value of the cotton crop amounts to about $1.5 billion, and the value of the tobacco crop amounts to about $1.2 billion. Wool is worth about $75 million. The total receipts from the sale of all farm products since 1965 have averaged above $39 billion annually. On the whole, farm products, used directly or indirectly for food, account for about 90 per cent of the value marketed. *Agricultural Statistics, 1968*, USDA, 1969, pp. 60, 101, and 474.

**TABLE 4.1: Net Supply Utilization of Farm Food Commodities, 1947–49 and 1957–59 Averages, 1950, and 1955 Through 1969 (Percentage of Net Utilization in Each Year)**

| | | | | Domestic Use | | | Exports |
|---|---|---|---|---|---|---|---|
| | | | | Food | | Net | and |
| | Net Produc- | Net Im- | Stock | Civil- | Mili- | non- | Ship- |
| Year | tion* | ports† | Change‡ | ian | tary§ | food‖ | ments |
| 1947–49 ...... | 90.7 | 11.2 | —1.9 | 86.4 | 3.8 | 4.1 | 5.6 |
| 1957–59 ...... | 91.6 | 11.4 | —3.0 | 86.3 | 1.6 | 3.2 | 8.8 |
| 1950 ......... | 89.5 | 12.0 | —1.5 | 88.2 | 2.1 | 4.3 | 5.4 |
| 1955 ......... | 91.4 | 10.6 | —2.0 | 87.4 | 1.9 | 3.5 | 7.2 |
| 1956 ......... | 90.4 | 10.6 | —1.0 | 85.9 | 1.8 | 3.4 | 8.9 |
| 1957 ......... | 90.6 | 10.7 | —1.3 | 85.9 | 1.7 | 3.2 | 9.2 |
| 1958 ......... | 94.4 | 11.3 | —5.7 | 86.9 | 1.6 | 3.2 | 8.3 |
| 1959 ......... | 89.8 | 12.3 | —2.1 | 86.2 | 1.6 | 3.2 | 9.0 |
| 1960 ......... | 91.8 | 11.4 | —3.2 | 85.4 | 1.4 | 3.0 | 10.2 |
| 1961 ......... | 88.4 | 11.9 | — .3 | 84.9 | 1.6 | 2.9 | 10.6 |
| 1962 ......... | 87.3 | 11.7 | 1.0 | 84.2 | 1.6 | 2.9 | 11.3 |
| 1963 ......... | 88.3 | 11.4 | .3 | 83.4 | 1.5 | 2.9 | 12.2 |
| 1964 ......... | 86.6 | 9.9 | 4.0 | 82.0 | 1.5 | 2.9 | 13.6 |
| 1965 ......... | 90.6 | 9.9 | —0.5 | 82.4 | 1.8 | 3.0 | 12.8 |
| 1966 ......... | 87.0 | 10.4 | 2.6 | 81.8 | 1.8 | 2.9 | 13.5 |
| 1967 ......... | 93.0 | 10.3 | —3.3 | 83.4 | 1.9 | 2.8 | 11.9 |
| 1968 ......... | 91.3 | 11.3 | —2.6 | 83.7 | 1.8 | 2.7 | 11.8 |
| 1969 ......... | 91.0 | 10.4 | —1.4 | 84.8 | 1.5 | 2.8 | 10.9 |

Source: *The National Food Situation,* USDA, Feb., 1970, p. 9.

The term "net" in this table means that commodities used for feed and seed are excluded to avoid double-counting. Developed from quantitative data on supply and use of processed and unprocessed farm products, valued in terms of constant farm prices. For description of basic procedure see *Measuring the Supply and Utilization of Farm Commodities,* USDA, Agr. Handbook 91, on a 50-state basis since 1962.

* Excludes feed and seed used from domestic production.

†Excludes imports for seed and feed use; includes shipments from U.S. territories.

‡ Includes farm and commercial stocks and holdings under government programs. Negatives indicate increases in stocks from beginning to end of year; positives signify withdrawals from stocks.

§ Includes civilian feeding in areas occupied by our Armed Forces.

‖ Excludes feed and seed; includes some waste and loss at farm level.

This table shows that about 10 per cent of the food we consume in the United States is imported from other countries. It shows also that exports of food have risen from about 6 per cent of U.S. production in 1947–49 to about 11 per cent in 1969. The nation as a whole is about 90 per cent self-sufficient with respect to food. On balance, it is a slight net exporter of food in most years.

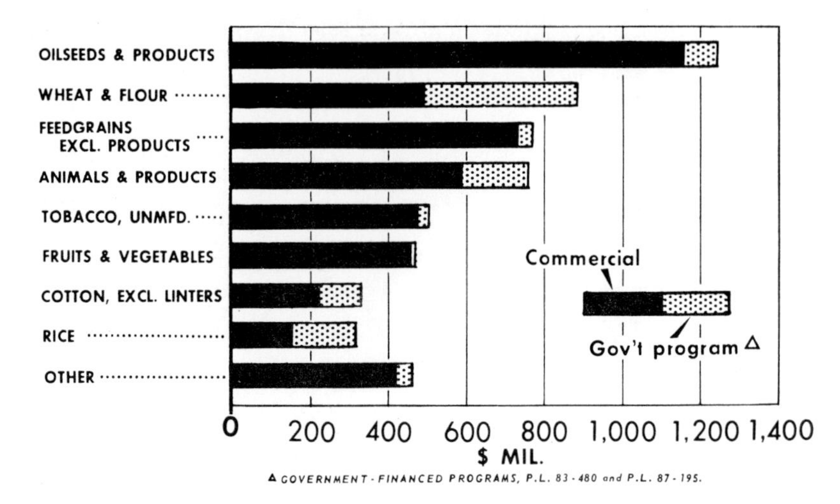


FIG. 4.1—Value of U.S. farm exports, 1969 (year ending June 30).

The figures above refer only to *food.* When cotton, tobacco, and other nonfood items are taken into account along with food, the United States is a slight net exporter.

Figure 4.1 shows that nearly half of our agricultural exports consists of wheat, feed grains, and oilseeds. The exports of wheat increased enormously after the end of World War II. Exports of cotton also increased after the war, but declined in the 1960's. The largest export gains have been for feed grains and oilseeds. In 1968–69, wheat exports equaled over one-third of the annual production, while exports took about two-fifths of U.S. output of tobacco, soybeans and soybean products, hides and skins, and tallow. About one-eighth of the corn crop was exported, one-fourth of the cotton, and three-fifths of the rice. The export market demand has become increasingly important to the producers of these and other products. For some farm products, however, exports are a secondary matter.

The domestic demand for food and fiber in the United States in the future will depend upon the three chief factors discussed in the preceding chapter—population, income, and tastes. These factors are considered in turn below.

## UNITED STATES POPULATION PROSPECTS

The chief factor affecting the demand for farm products is the rate of population growth in the United States. Population grew at such a steady rate that until about 1920 forecasts of population growth to the year 2,000 were made with consider-

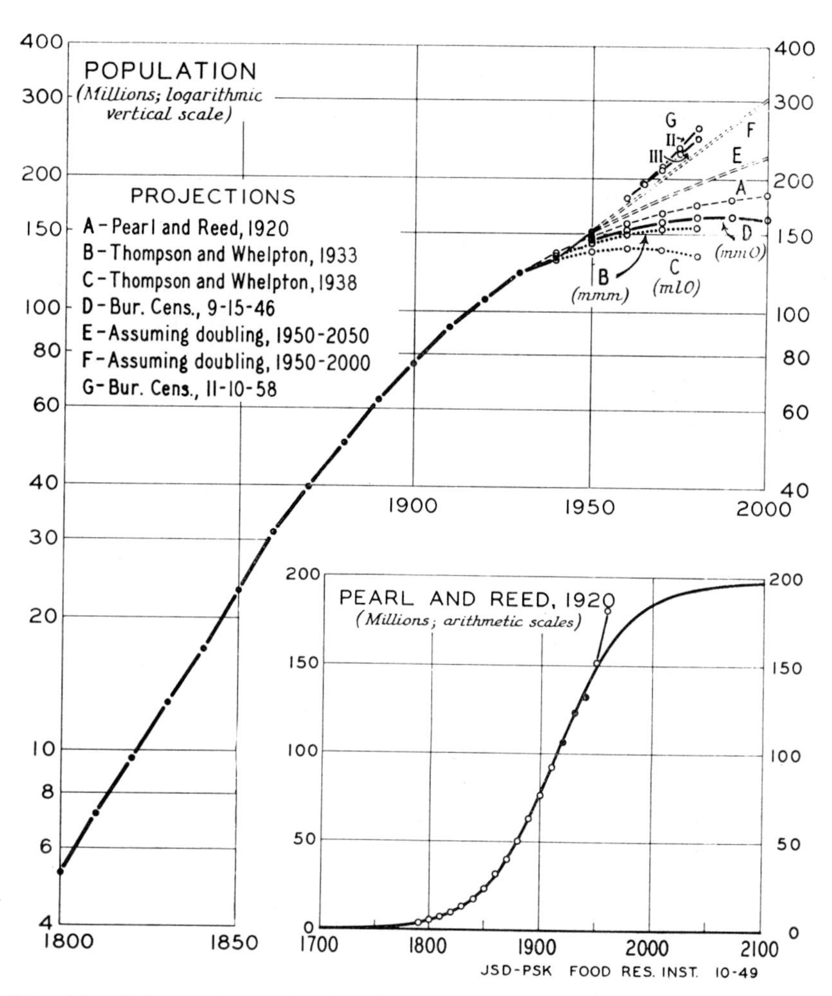


FIG. 4.2 — U.S. population by decades, 1800–1960, with selected projections.

able confidence. One such forecast is marked A in Figure 4.2.

After 1920, however, immigration and birth rates decreased and the rate of population growth began to slow down. Population experts then began to revise their estimates. The decline in the rate of growth accelerated during the 1930's to about 0.7 per cent per year. Projections were made then by responsible population experts[2] to show that the decline in the rate of growth would continue until the population would level out at about 140 million by 1965 and would actually begin to decline thereafter.

[2] W. S. Thompson and P. K. Whelpton, "The Problems of a Changing Population," *Report of the Committee on Population Problems to the National Resources Committee*, May, 1938, p. 24.

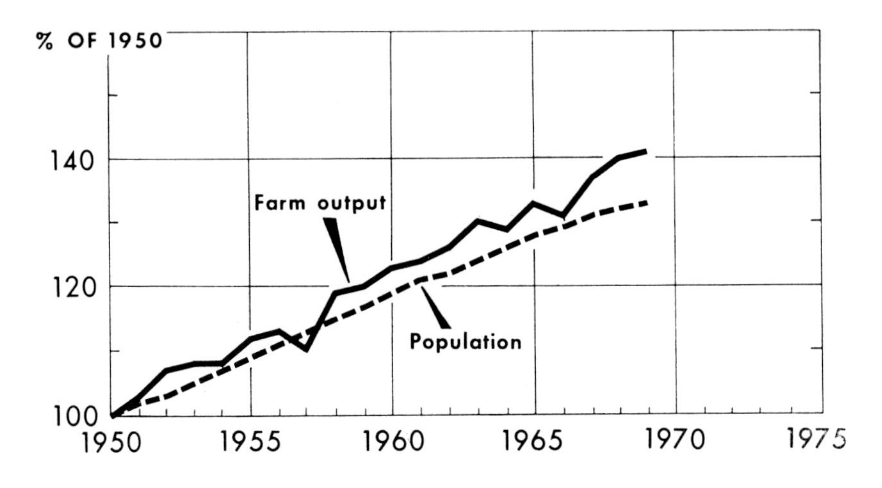


FIG. 4.3—U.S. population and farm output, 1950–69.

This projection is shown by the curve marked C as shown in Figure 4.2.[3] Comparisons were made with the logistic curve shown in the lower part of the chart. O. E. Baker of the USDA and others made many speeches about the dismal prospect for the United States and especially for U.S. agriculture.

These projections might well have been borne out if the depression conditions of the 1930's had continued. But the life of the forecaster is hard. In actuality, World War II and the prosperity that came with it reversed the decline in the birth rate and forced the experts to revise their projections upward. At first they merely raised the level at which the population would level out and postponed the date about 100 years. Some of these more recent projections are shown in the upper part of the chart. The actual growth by 1950 and 1960, at the rate of about 1.8 per cent per year, is shown by the short straight line in the lower part of the chart.

Figure 4.3 shows that U.S. farm output increased at a little faster rate than total U.S. population from 1950 to 1969. In 1969, output was 8 points higher than population.

## INCOME-ELASTICITY AND DEMAND FOR FOOD

The income-elasticity of the demand for food derived from a nation-wide consumer survey taken in 1955, for the nation as

[3] Joe Davis, "Implications of Prospective United States Population Growth in the 1960's," *Milbank Memorial Fund Quarterly,* Vol. 2 (Apr., 1961).

**TABLE 4.2: Consumer Income and Expenditure, United States, 1939–68***

| Year | Disposable Personal Income | Personal Consumption Expenditures | | | |
|---|---|---|---|---|---|
| | | Total | Food | Other goods | Services |
| | | *(billion dollars)* | | | |
| 1939 ....... | 70.3 | 66.8 | 15.7 | 26.1 | 25.0 |
| 1940 ....... | 75.7 | 70.8 | 16.6 | 28.2 | 26.0 |
| 1941 ....... | 92.7 | 80.6 | 19.2 | 33.3 | 28.1 |
| 1942 ....... | 116.9 | 88.5 | 23.3 | 34.4 | 30.8 |
| 1943 ....... | 133.5 | 99.3 | 27.4 | 37.7 | 34.2 |
| 1944 ....... | 146.3 | 108.3 | 29.9 | 41.2 | 37.2 |
| 1945 ....... | 150.2 | 119.7 | 33.2 | 46.7 | 39.8 |
| 1946 ....... | 160.0 | 143.4 | 39.0 | 59.1 | 45.3 |
| 1947 ....... | 169.8 | 160.7 | 43.7 | 67.2 | 49.8 |
| 1948 ....... | 189.1 | 173.6 | 46.3 | 72.6 | 54.7 |
| 1949 ....... | 188.6 | 176.8 | 44.8 | 74.4 | 57.6 |
| 1950 ....... | 206.9 | 191.0 | 46.0 | 82.6 | 62.4 |
| 1951 ....... | 226.6 | 206.3 | 52.1 | 86.3 | 67.9 |
| 1952 ....... | 238.3 | 216.7 | 54.7 | 88.6 | 73.4 |
| 1953 ....... | 252.6 | 230.0 | 55.5 | 94.6 | 79.9 |
| 1954 ....... | 257.4 | 236.5 | 56.5 | 94.6 | 85.4 |
| 1955 ....... | 275.3 | 254.4 | 58.1 | 104.9 | 91.4 |
| 1956 ....... | 293.2 | 266.7 | 60.4 | 107.8 | 98.5 |
| 1957 ....... | 308.5 | 281.4 | 63.9 | 112.5 | 105.0 |
| 1958 ....... | 318.8 | 290.1 | 66.6 | 111.5 | 112.0 |
| 1959 ....... | 337.3 | 311.2 | 68.4 | 122.5 | 120.3 |
| 1960 ....... | 350.0 | 325.2 | 70.1 | 126.4 | 128.7 |
| 1961 ....... | 364.4 | 335.2 | 72.1 | 128.0 | 135.1 |
| 1962 ....... | 385.3 | 355.1 | 74.4 | 137.7 | 143.0 |
| 1963 ....... | 404.6 | 375.0 | 76.5 | 146.1 | 152.4 |
| 1964 ....... | 438.1 | 401.2 | 80.5 | 157.4 | 163.3 |
| 1965 ....... | 473.2 | 433.1 | 85.8 | 171.4 | 175.9 |
| 1966 ....... | 511.9 | 466.3 | 92.0 | 185.7 | 188.6 |
| 1967 ....... | 546.5 | 492.3 | 93.6 | 194.5 | 204.2 |
| 1968 ....... | 590.0 | 536.6 | 99.4 | 214.4 | 222.8 |

* Data published quarterly in *Survey of Current Business,* Department of Commerce.

a whole, was found to be 0.37. Can we use this figure to project the demand for food in the future? If, for instance, per capita income rises 3 per cent per year, will per capita expenditures for food rise about $0.37 \times 3 = 1.11$ per cent per year?

Let us see first whether this sort of thing has been happening in the recent past.

## Percentage of Consumers' Income Spent on Food

Table 4.2 shows expenditures for food in the United States, for other goods, and for services from 1939 to 1968. The table shows that consumer disposable income and expenditures have risen every year since 1939. The changes from 1956 to 1969 were shown in Figure 1.1 in Chapter 1.

The chart and table show that expenditures for food have been rising; but they have not been rising as rapidly in percentage terms as consumer disposable income. Thus income rose from an average of $182.5 billion in 1947–49, just after World War II, to $590.0 billion in 1968; this was a rise of about 223 per cent. Expenditures for all food increased by 121 per cent in the same period.

This situation can be put another way: In 1947–49, consumers spent 24.6 per cent of their disposable income for food, but in 1968 they spent only 16.8 per cent. Food has been losing ground in the competition for the consumer's dollar.

### Farmer's Share of Food Dollar

This shows only a part of the picture. A breakdown of the food expenditures shows that consumers have been spending a smaller percentage of their incomes for food; in addition, farmers have been getting a smaller percentage of consumers' expenditures for food. They have been getting a smaller percentage of a smaller percentage.

The total retail cost of the domestic farm food products sold by farmers and consumed by civilian consumers in the United States since 1940 is shown in Table 4.3.[4] Figure 4.4 shows the same thing since 1957. The figure also shows the farm-to-retail marketing bill for this food and the farm value (the money that farmers received).

The table shows that consumers' expenditures for domestic farm foods increased 106 per cent from 1947–49 to 1968, and the farm-to-retail marketing bill increased 147 per cent, while the payment to farmers rose 53 per cent.

In summary, then: Consumers' disposable income from 1947–49 to 1968 rose 223 per cent; their expenditures for domestic farm-produced food, however, rose only 106 per cent (up

[4] The total expenditures for food bought by consumers are compiled and published by the U.S. Department of Commerce. The total retail cost, for domestic farm food products only, is compiled by the USDA. This total retail cost shown in Table 4.3 and Figure 4.4 is smaller than the total expenditures for food because it does not include imports, seafoods, food consumed on farms where produced, nor food for the Armed Forces.

The USDA also compiles another series, similar to its retail cost series but including the estimated extra cost of food consumed in restaurants (over what the cost would be if the food had been purchased in retail stores) and the estimated lower cost of food for institutions, etc., bought at less than retail price. This series is entitled "Civilian Expenditures for Food." The reasons for needing three different series and their characteristics are given in some detail by K. E. Ogren, *The Farmer's Share: Three Measurements*, Vol. VIII, No. 2, USDA, pp. 43–50, and by M. Burk in *The Marketing and Transportation Situation*, USDA, Nov., 1958, pp. 20–25.

**TABLE 4.3: The Total Marketing Bill, Farm Value, and Consumer Expenditures for Domestic Farm Food Products Bought by Civilians, United States, 1940, 1945, 1947–49 Average, and Annual 1950–68**

| Year | Total Marketing Bill* | Farm Value | Civilian Expenditures for Farm Foods |
|---|---|---|---|
| | *(billion dollars)* | *(billion dollars)* | *(billion dollars)* |
| 1940 .......... | 9.1 | 5.6 | 14.7 |
| 1945 .......... | 14.9 | 12.6 | 26.8 |
| 1949 .......... | 26.0 | 17.4 | 43.4 |
| 1947–49 av. .... | 24.5 | 18.9 | 43.4 |
| 1950 .......... | 26.0 | 18.0 | 44.0 |
| 1951 .......... | 28.7 | 20.5 | 49.2 |
| 1952 .......... | 30.5 | 20.4 | 50.9 |
| 1953 .......... | 31.5 | 19.5 | 51.0 |
| 1954 .......... | 32.3 | 18.8 | 51.1 |
| 1955 .......... | 34.4 | 18.7 | 53.1 |
| 1956 .......... | 36.3 | 19.2 | 55.5 |
| 1957 .......... | 37.9 | 20.4 | 58.3 |
| 1958 .......... | 39.5 | 21.5 | 61.0 |
| 1959 .......... | 42.2 | 20.9 | 63.1 |
| 1960 .......... | 44.2 | 21.7 | 65.9 |
| 1961 .......... | 45.1 | 22.0 | 67.1 |
| 1962 .......... | 46.9 | 22.4 | 69.3 |
| 1963 .......... | 48.9 | 22.6 | 71.5 |
| 1964 .......... | 51.2 | 23.4 | 74.6 |
| 1965 .......... | 52.1 | 25.5 | 77.6 |
| 1966 .......... | 54.7 | 28.1 | 82.8 |
| 1967 .......... | 57.5 | 27.3 | 84.8 |
| 1968 .......... | 60.6 | 28.9 | 89.5 |

Source: *Marketing and Transportation Situation,* USDA, Aug., 1969, p. 13.

* Difference between civilian expenditures and farm value except that federal processor taxes have been deducted for 1933–35 and allowances for federal government payments to processors have been added for 1943–46.

Estimates in this table do not cover Alaska and Hawaii because of inadequate data.

121 per cent on all food); and farmers' receipts for the food rose only 53 per cent.

Why did these things happen? And is the same sort of thing likely to continue in the future?

## DECLINE IN PERCENTAGE OF CONSUMERS' INCOME SPENT FOR FOOD

If Engel's law had the same effect over periods of times that it has at a given point of time, after 1947–49 would not consumers' expenditures for food have risen $223 \times 0.37$ per cent, or 83 per cent? Why did they rise more than this—by 121 per cent?

Thus the question is not, why did the percentage of consumers' income spent for food decline so much after 1947–49, but why did it decline so little?

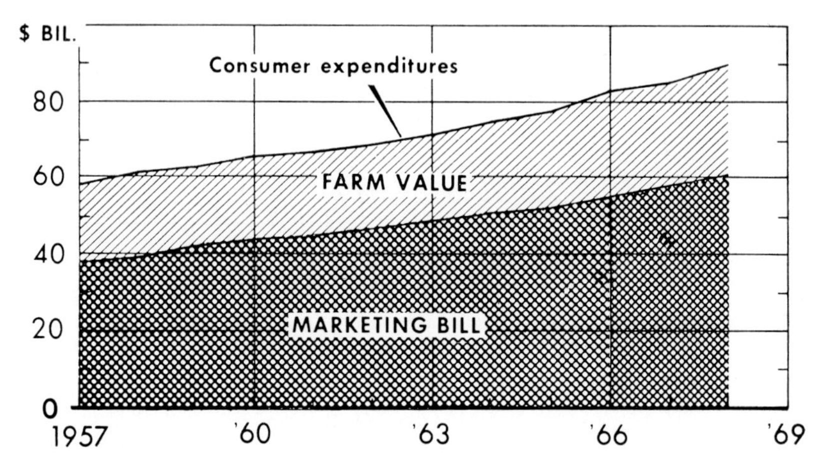


FIG. 4.4—Farm value and total marketing bill for farm foods, 1953–68.

There are several reasons:

1. Part of the rise in consumers' income from 1947–49 to 1968 was not a rise in real income, but a rise in monetary income only, the result of inflation. From 1947–49 to 1968, the consumer price index rose from 100 to 149, a rise of 49 per cent. Adjusting 1968 consumer income by the rise in the consumer price index (590.0 ÷ 149) indicates 1968 consumer income was $396.0 billion when expressed in 1947–49 dollars. Thus, consumers' real income rose not 223 per cent but 117 per cent (396 ÷ 182.5 = 217 − 100 = 117). So the percentage spent on food declined less than it would have if the rise in consumers' money income had all been in real income.
2. Another part of the rise in consumers' income was simply the result of an increase in the number of consumers. The population of the United States grew 37 per cent from 1947–49 to 1968. If all the increase in consumers' income had been due to the increase in population, one would not have expected the percentage of income spent for food to decline at all. Engel's law applies to per capita income, not to total national income.

   Table 4.4 shows the data in per capita form. The table shows that *per capita* money income rose 135 per cent from 1947–49 to 1968.
3. Table 4.4 also shows another reason why the percentage of consumers' income spent for food declined on a per capita basis. The percentage actually spent declined from 24.6 per

**Table 4.4: Per Capita Food Cost and Expenditure Related to Disposable Personal Income, United States—Average 1935–39, 1947–49, 1950, and Annual 1955–69**

| Year and Quarter | Disposable Personal Income | Total Expenditure for Consumer Goods and Services | Food Expenditure | | | Cost to Consumer of Fixed Quantities of Food Representing 1935–39 Average Annual Consumption Per Person | |
|---|---|---|---|---|---|---|---|
| | | | | Percentage of— | | | |
| | | | Actual | Disposable income | Total expenditure for goods, services | Actual | Percentage of disposable income |
| | *(dollars)* | *(dollars)* | *(dollars)* | *(per cent)* | *(per cent)* | *(dollars)* | *(per cent)* |
| 1935–39 | 514 | 493 | 118.6 | 23.1 | 24.0 | 118.6 | 23.1 |
| 1947–49 | 1,244 | 1,161 | 306 | 24.6 | 26.4 | 248 | 19.9 |
| 1950 | 1,364 | 1,259 | 303 | 22.2 | 24.1 | 245 | 17.9 |
| 1955 | 1,666 | 1,539 | 352 | 21.1 | 22.9 | 266 | 16.0 |
| 1956 | 1,743 | 1,585 | 359 | 20.6 | 22.6 | 268 | 15.5 |
| 1957 | 1,801 | 1,643 | 373 | 20.7 | 22.7 | 277 | 15.5 |
| 1958 | 1,831 | 1,666 | 382 | 20.9 | 22.9 | 288 | 16.0 |
| 1959 | 1,905 | 1,758 | 386 | 20.3 | 22.0 | | |
| 1960 | 1,937 | 1,800 | 388 | 20.0 | 21.6 | 286 | 15.0 |
| 1961 | 1,983 | 1,824 | 392 | 19.8 | 21.5 | 289 | 15.0 |
| 1962 | 2,064 | 1,902 | 399 | 19.3 | 21.0 | 292 | 14.0 |
| 1963 | 2,136 | 1,980 | 404 | 18.9 | 20.4 | 296 | 14.0 |
| 1964 | 2,280 | 2,088 | 419 | 18.4 | 20.1 | 300 | 13.0 |
| 1965 | 2,432 | 2,225 | 441 | 18.2 | 19.9 | 308 | 13.0 |
| 1966 | 2,600 | 2,368 | 467 | 18.3 | 19.9 | 324 | 12.0 |
| 1967 | 2,745 | 2,474 | 470 | 17.1 | 19.0 | 327 | 12.0 |
| 1968 | 2,933 | 2,668 | 494 | 16.8 | 18.5 | 338 | 12.0 |
| 1969 | 3,098 | 2,835 | 511 | 16.5 | 18.0 | 354 | 11.0 |

Sources: *U.S. Food Consumption,* USDA, Stat. Bul. 364, 1965, p. 184; *Consumption of Food in the United States, 1909–52,* USDA, Handbook 62, 1961, pp. 46–48; and *Marketing and Transportation Situation,* USDA, (selected issues).

**TABLE 4.5: Food Consumption; Index of Per Capita Consumption (1957–59 = 100) United States, 1910–69 (Retail Weights)**

| Year | Index | Year | Index |
|---|---|---|---|
| 1910 ........ | 87 | 1956 ........ | 102 |
| 1920 ........ | 86 | 1957 ........ | 100 |
| 1930 ........ | 90 | 1958 ........ | 99 |
| 1940 ........ | 95 | 1959 ........ | 101 |
| 1945 ........ | 101 | 1960 ........ | 101 |
| 1946 ........ | 104 | 1961 ........ | 100 |
| 1947 ........ | 101 | 1962 ........ | 100 |
| 1948 ........ | 98 | 1963 ........ | 101 |
| 1949 ........ | 98 | 1964 ........ | 102 |
| 1950 ........ | 99 | 1965 ........ | 101 |
| 1951 ........ | 98 | 1966 ........ | 103 |
| 1952 ........ | 100 | 1967 ........ | 104 |
| 1953 ........ | 101 | 1968 ........ | 106 |
| 1954 ........ | 100 | 1969 ........ | 106 |
| 1955 ........ | 101 | | |

Source: *The National Food Situation,* USDA, Feb., 1967, p. 2, and Feb., 1970, p. 13. This index is a physical-volume, price-weighted index, in terms of 1947–49 retail prices through 1954 and 1957–59 retail prices thereafter.

cent in 1947–49 to 16.8 in 1968. But the quantity and composition of the food changed over this period. If it had remained unchanged from the 1935–39 period, the percentage would have declined much more.

4. The percentage of farmers in the population declined over the period from about 17 per cent in 1947–49 to about 5 in 1969. People spend more for food when they take an urban job than when they were on the farm; their home-produced food on the farm is valued in the series used above at farm prices, but when farmers take a job in town they pay retail prices, which are more than twice as high as farm prices.[5]
5. More "built-in maid service" was included in many foods. Apparently, however, this did not increase expenditures for foods much. A pilot study indicated that the average housewife pays less than 1 per cent more for these convenience foods than for the less-processed kind.[6]
6. People "ate out" more. It costs more to eat in a restaurant than it does to eat at home.
7. Another force was acting in the opposite direction to those listed above—the rate of increase in the demand for food

[5] Since the mid-1930's the use of purchased farm foods has risen almost twice as much as the use of farm foods from all sources. In the mid-1930's home production supplied about 20 per cent of civilian consumption of all farm foods. In 1957 the proportion was down to about 8 per cent and by 1969 was probably only 2–3 per cent.

[6] R. C. Harris and P. B. Dwoskin, *Convenience Foods and Their Cost to Consumers*, USDA, 1958.

relative to the rate of increase in supply. If everything else remained constant, but the demand for food increased relative to the supply of food, the percentage of consumers' disposable income spent for food would rise because the demand and supply of food are both inelastic.

What actually has been happening in recent years? Has the population been pressing on the food supply, or has the food supply been pressing on the population?

Table 4.5 shows the per capita consumption of food from 1910 to 1969 which indicates that per capita consumption has been increasing; the food supply has been pressing on the population. This in itself would reduce the percentage of consumers' income spent on food. Fluctuations in the amounts of different commodities consumed are shown in Table 4.6.

These are the chief reasons why the percentage of consumers' income spent for food changed differently over time, in relation to consumer income, from the way it differed among income classes at the one point of time in 1955. Not only are the rates different in themselves, other things being equal; in addition, other things did not remain equal; a million other things were changing with the passage of time.[7]

## DECLINE IN FARMERS' SHARE OF CONSUMERS' FOOD DOLLAR

Why did the farmers' share of the consumers' expenditures for food decline from 1947 to 1968? Why did food expenditures and marketing costs rise so much and payments to farmers rise so little?

The chief components of the rise in marketing costs are shown in Figure 4.5. This figure shows that the chief reason for the rise in marketing costs was the rise in labor, transportation, and other costs. Profits were only a small item, and they did not change much in any case. Further light is thrown on this matter by Figure 4.6. It shows that the farmers' share of the consumers' retail-store food dollar did not decline *from* normal during the 1950's; it declined *to* normal. Since 1960, it has ranged from 37 to 41 per cent—just about the same as it was in the 1930's before World War II.

It seems likely that the changes reported above will continue in the future. The prospects are that farmers will continue to receive a smaller share of a smaller percentage of consumers' expenditures.

---

[7] A detailed technical discussion of the reasons for the differences between cross-section and chronological income-food relationships is given in M. C. Burk, "Some Analyses of Income-Food Relationships," *Jour. of the Am. Stat. Assn.*, Vol. 53, No. 284 (Dec., 1958), pp. 905–27.

**TABLE 4.6: Apparent Civilian Per Capita Consumption of Major Food Commodities, Primary Distribution Weight, Calendar Year, 1947–49, Average and Estimates for 1969, With Percentage Comparisons***

| Commodity | Average 1947–49 | 1969 Preliminary | 1969 as a Percentage of 1947–49 |
|---|---|---|---|
| | *(pounds)* | *(pounds)* | *(per cent)* |
| *Meat* (carcass weight)—Total | 148.5 | 182.3 | 123 |
| Beef | 65.6 | 110.7 | 169 |
| Veal | 9.7 | 3.4 | 35 |
| Lamb and mutton | 4.8 | 3.4 | 71 |
| Pork (excluding lard) | 68.4 | 64.8 | 95 |
| *Fish* (edible weight)—Total | 10.7 | 11.0 | 103 |
| Fresh and frozen | 5.9 | 6.2 | 105 |
| Canned† | 4.2 | 3.9 | 93 |
| Cured | .6 | .5 | 83 |
| *Poultry products* | | | |
| Eggs (farm basis)—Number | 385.0 | 314.0 | 82 |
| Chicken (ready-to-cook) | 18.7 | 39.4 | 211 |
| Turkey (ready-to-cook) | 3.3 | 8.2 | 248 |
| *Dairy products* | | | |
| Total milk fat solids | 29.5 | 20.7 | 70 |
| Total nonfat milk solids | 42.9 | 41.4 | 97 |
| Cheese | 7.0 | 11.0 | 157 |
| Condensed and evaporated milk | 20.1 | 8.2 | 41 |
| Fluid milk and cream | 359.0 | 272.0 | 76 |
| Ice cream (product weight) | 18.7 | 18.1 | 97 |
| *Fats and oils* (fat content‡)—Total | 42.4 | 51.6 | 122 |
| Butter, farm and factory (actual weight) | 10.6 | 5.3 | 50 |
| Margarine (actual weight) | 5.6 | 10.8 | 193 |
| Lard | 12.4 | 5.1 | 41 |
| Shortening | 9.6 | 16.9 | 176 |
| Other edible fats and oils | 7.3 | 16.6 | 227 |
| *Fruits* | | | |
| Fresh (farm weight)—Total | 132.8 | 81.2 | 61 |
| Citrus | 54.8 | 28.5 | 52 |
| Apples (commercial) | 25.5 | 17.1 | 67 |
| Other (excluding melons) | 52.5 | 35.6 | 68 |
| Processed | | | |
| Canned fruit | 18.9 | 24.3 | 129 |
| Canned juices | 15.9 | 14.2 | 89 |
| Frozen (including juices) | 3.2 | 9.3 | 291 |
| Dried | 3.9 | 2.8 | 72 |
| *Vegetables*§ | | | |
| Fresh | 120.5 | 97.4 | 81 |
| Canned (excluding potatoes and sweet potatoes) | 38.5 | 50.7 | 132 |
| Frozen (excluding potatoes) | 2.8 | 9.3 | 332 |

**TABLE 4.6:** (continued)

| Commodity | Average 1947–49 | 1969 Preliminary | 1969 as a Percentage of 1947–49 |
|---|---|---|---|
| | *(pounds)* | *(pounds)* | *(per cent)* |
| *Potatoes and sweet potatoes* | | | |
| Potatoes (fresh equivalent) | 113.8 | 115.9 | 102 |
| Sweet potatoes (fresh equivalent) | 13.0 | 5.8 | 45 |
| *Dry edible beans* | 6.7 | 6.6 | 99 |
| *Melons* | 27.4 | 22.3 | 81 |
| *Sugar* (refined) | 95.2 | 99.7 | 105 |
| *Grains* | | | |
| Corn products | | | |
| Cornmeal and flour | 12.9 | 5.5 | 43 |
| Corn syrup and sugar | 14.1 | 19.3 | 137 |
| Wheat | | | |
| Flour‖ | 137.0 | 110.0 | 80 |
| Breakfast cereals | 3.2 | 2.9 | 91 |
| Rice (milled) | 4.9 | 8.3 | 169 |
| *Other* | | | |
| Coffee (green beans) | 18.2 | 14.7 | 81 |
| Tea | .58 | .73 | 126 |
| Cocoa beans | 4.0 | 3.9 | 98 |
| Peanuts (shelled) | 4.4 | 5.9 | 134 |

Source: *The National Food Situation,* USDA, Feb., 1970, p. 15.

* Quantity in pounds except for eggs which are stated in number. Data on calendar-year basis except for dried fruits, which are on pack-year basis; fresh citrus fruits, dry field peas, and peanuts on a crop-year basis; and rice on August 1 year. All years begin in the year indicated except for fresh citrus, which begins in October of the previous year, and rice, which begins in August of previous year. Population estimates used to obtain per capita consumption figures are official census estimates of civilian production.

† Includes canned food products containing small quantities of fish, such as clam chowder, etc.

‡ Computed from unrounded data.

§ This series covers total commercial production for sale as fresh, both for shipment to distant markets and for local markets. Excludes farm garden output for farm household use.

‖ Includes white, whole wheat, and semolina flour.

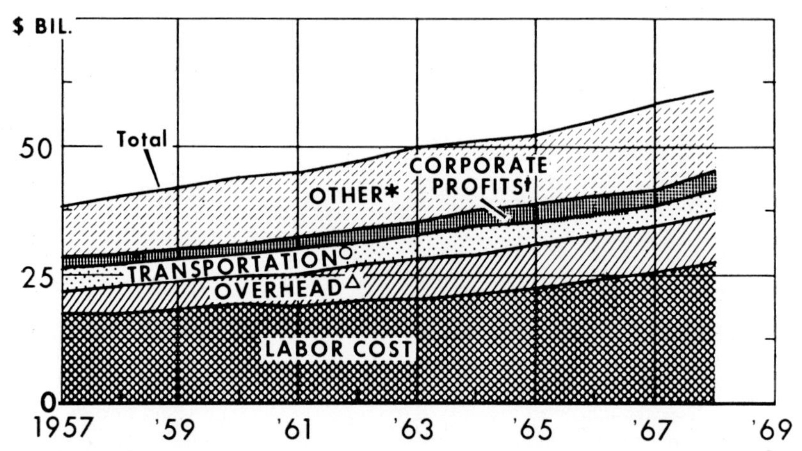


FIG. 4.5—Components of the farm food marketing bill, 1953–68.

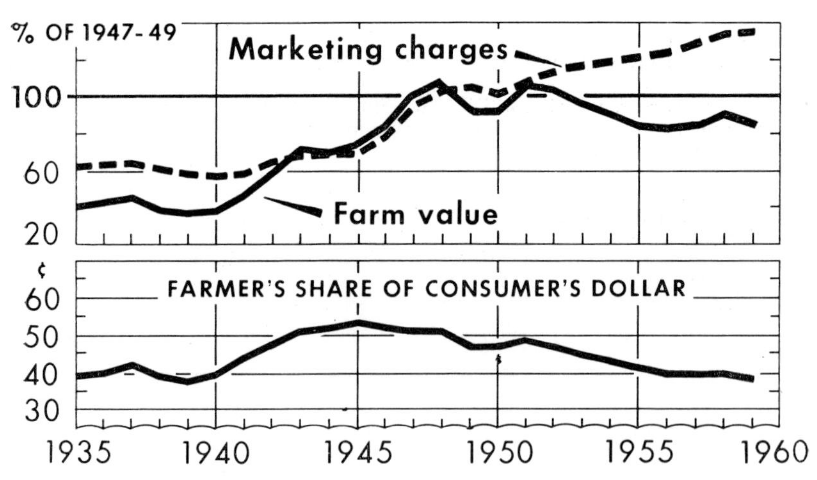


FIG. 4.6—Marketing charges and farm values for market basket. (After 1959 this chart was not kept up to date. It was replaced by one that extended back only to 1950, and therefore was unintentionally misleading.)

# 5

## ARE WE WELL FED?

FIGURE 1.3 (page 10) shows how the per capita consumption of different foods has changed in recent years. It is like a movie, showing developments with the passage of time and bringing the audience up to the present.

Now we would like to stop the projector and study the last scene in the movie in greater detail. Figure 1.3 shows the average per capita consumption data only as a single figure for each food item for the United States as a whole. Each average figure covers a wide range of dispersion. Some people eat more total food than the average; some people eat less; and some people eat more of some foods and less of others.

Table 5.1 shows how the per capita consumption of various foods differs by income groups, separately for each kind of food. Well-to-do consumers eat more of some foods per capita than consumers with small incomes, eating nearly 60 per cent more fresh fruit, about 25 per cent more dairy products, and 33 per cent more meat. High-income families also eat more fresh vegetables, more processed fruits and vegetables, more bakery products, and more than twice as much fruit and vegetable juices as those with the lowest income. Some foods are eaten in smaller quantities by the more prosperous groups; they use less than half as much flour and other cereals as the lowest income families.

**TABLE 5.1: Consumption Per Person of Selected Foods in U.S. Households, by Income Group, in a Week, Spring, 1965**

| Annual Income | Meats | Poultry | Dairy (excluding butter)* | Eggs | Fats and Oils† | Flour and Cereals | Bakery Products | Fresh Fruits | Fresh Vegetables‡ | Frozen and Canned Fruits and Vegetables§ | Fruit and Vegetable Juices‖ | Potatoes and Sweet Potatoes¶ |
|---|---|---|---|---|---|---|---|---|---|---|---|---|
| | *(lb.)* | *(lb.)* | *(qt.)* | *(no.)* | *(lb.)* | *(lb.)* | *(lb.)* | *(lb.)* | *(lb.)* | *(lb.)* | *(lb.)* | *(lb.)* |
| *United States* | | | | | | | | | | | | |
| All households . | 3.36 | 0.85 | 4.07 | 7.0 | 0.82 | 1.43 | 2.32 | 2.49 | 2.23 | 1.58 | 1.21 | 1.63 |
| Under $3,000 ... | 2.78 | 0.84 | 3.62 | 6.4 | 0.86 | 2.15 | 1.96 | 2.06 | 2.19 | 1.24 | 0.78 | 1.52 |
| $3,000–$4,999 ... | 3.15 | 0.88 | 3.77 | 6.6 | 0.84 | 1.64 | 2.19 | 2.11 | 2.04 | 1.49 | 0.90 | 1.74 |
| $5,000–$6,999 ... | 3.47 | 0.84 | 4.16 | 6.8 | 0.82 | 1.28 | 2.38 | 2.47 | 2.13 | 1.67 | 1.16 | 1.66 |
| $7,000–$9,999 ... | 3.57 | 0.83 | 4.34 | 6.6 | 0.81 | 1.15 | 2.56 | 2.70 | 2.29 | 1.73 | 1.41 | 1.69 |
| $10,000 and over | 3.71 | 0.91 | 4.48 | 8.1 | 0.77 | 1.01 | 2.52 | 3.25 | 2.58 | 1.72 | 1.89 | 1.50 |

Source: *Food Consumption of Households in the United States, Spring, 1965,* USDA, ARS62-16, 1967.
* Milk equivalent, nutrient basis.
† Including butter.
‡ Excluding potatoes and sweet potatoes. Including quantities canned or frozen at home.
§ Commercially processed. Excluding canned juices.
‖ Including, on a single-strength basis, commercially processed fresh, frozen, canned, and powdered juices.
¶ Including fresh and processed, on a product-weight basis.

## DIFFERENCES IN EXPENDITURES FOR DIFFERENT FOODS BY INCOME GROUPS

Table 5.2 shows the same sort of information as Table 5.1, with one important difference. Table 5.1 shows the relation between income and pounds of food consumed. Table 5.2 shows the relation between income and *expenditures* for food. The one table shows pounds eaten or drunk; the other shows dollars spent.

Table 5.2 shows that food expenditures rise uniformly with income for nearly all foods. The chief reason why the middle- and high-income groups spend more for food is that they buy more expensive foods (as well as a larger quantity of some foods, as shown in Table 5.1). They probably waste more food too. They buy more steak, for instance, and less chuck roast, and leave more on the plate.

The preceding tables show the per capita consumption of different foods, and the per capita expenditures for different foods, by different income groups in the United States. They do not answer the question, however, whether people in the United States are getting as much of the right kinds of food as they need from a nutritional point of view, nor whether they are eating better than in former years.

## TRENDS IN DIETARY LEVELS

Diets in the United States have shown a considerable improvement since a large-scale survey in the 1930's classified a third of the diets as "poor." Based on the standards used in the earlier period, diets today probably could be called "poor" in less than 10 per cent of the households. However, based on current standards, the percentage is estimated to be somewhat higher than this.

Some information bearing on this question is given in Table 5.3, which shows that the nutritional makeup of the average American diet has changed significantly since 1947–49. The average consumption of foods in pounds has increased slightly, and the calorie intake shows a slight increase, from 3,230 in 1947–49 to 3,240 in 1969. Calcium and ascorbic acid consumption have both declined 6 per cent; vitamin A, 10 per cent; and thiamin, 5 per cent. Consumption of riboflavin has shown a slight decline, while supplies of other nutrients are moderately above the 1947–49 period.

Much of this improvement arises from a bread and flour enrichment program initiated in 1941. Economic conditions, newer developments in the marketing of foods, and nutrition education have also had a part.

**TABLE 5.2: Expenditures Per Person for Food Consumed at Home in U.S. Households, by Commodity Group and Income, in a Week, Spring, 1965**

| Annual Income | Total for All Food | Meats | Dairy Products* | Poultry and Eggs | Fats and Oils† | Fruits‡ | Vege-tables‡ | Sugar and Sweets | Cereal and Bakery Products | Other§ |
|---|---|---|---|---|---|---|---|---|---|---|
| | *(dollars)* | *(dollars)* | *(dollars)* | *(dollars)* | *(dollars)* | *(dollars)* | *(dollars)* | *(dollars)* | *(dollars)* | *(dollars)* |
| All United States ..... | 8.79 | 2.33 | 1.10 | 0.59 | 0.30 | 0.50 | 1.05 | 0.27 | 1.02 | 1.63 |
| Under $3,000 .... | 6.93 | 1.66 | 0.90 | 0.55 | 0.27 | 0.40 | 0.90 | 0.26 | 0.89 | 1.10 |
| $3,000—$4,999 .... | 7.74 | 1.99 | 0.99 | 0.58 | 0.28 | 0.42 | 0.96 | 0.27 | 0.94 | 1.31 |
| $5,000—$6,999 .... | 8.78 | 2.37 | 1.12 | 0.58 | 0.30 | 0.50 | 1.04 | 0.26 | 1.03 | 1.58 |
| $7,000—$9,999 .... | 9.66 | 2.63 | 1.21 | 0.57 | 0.32 | 0.56 | 1.13 | 0.28 | 1.12 | 1.84 |
| $10,000 and over . | 11.02 | 2.98 | 1.31 | 0.66 | 0.33 | 0.66 | 1.26 | 0.28 | 1.18 | 2.36 |

Source: *Food Consumption of Households in the United States, Spring, 1965*, USDA, ARS62-16, 1967.

* Excluding butter.

† Including butter.

‡ Including both fresh and processed commodities. Vegetables include potatoes and sweet potatoes, tomato catsup, chili sauce and tomato relishes, pickles, and olives.

§ Including nonalcoholic beverages, fishery products, nuts, soups, commercially prepared puddings, seasonings, and leavening agents.

**TABLE 5.3: Nutrients Available for Civilian Consumption Per Capita Per Day, 1947–49 Average, and Preliminary Estimates for 1969, With Percentage Comparisons***

| Nutrient | Unit | Average 1947–49 | 1969 Preliminary | 1969 as a Percentage of 1947–49 |
|---|---|---|---|---|
| Food energy | cal. | 3,230 | 3,240 | 100 |
| Protein | gm. | 95 | 99 | 104 |
| Fat | gm. | 141 | 153 | 109 |
| Calcium | gm. | .99 | .93 | 94 |
| Iron | mg. | 16.7 | 17.0 | 102 |
| Vitamin A value | I.U. | 8,700 | 7,800 | 90 |
| Thiamin | mg. | 1.91 | 1.82 | 95 |
| Riboflavin | mg. | 2.28 | 2.25 | 99 |
| Ascorbic acid | mg. | 113 | 106 | 94 |

Source: *The National Food Situation,* USDA, Nov., 1969, p. 28.

* Data computed by Consumer and Food Economics Research Division, ARS, on the basis of estimates of apparent per capita consumption (retail basis), including estimates of produce of rural and urban home gardens, supplied by the Economic and Statistical Analysis Division, ERS. No deduction has been made in nutrient estimates for loss or waste of food in households or for destruction or loss of nutrients during the preparation of food. Data for iron, thiamin, riboflavin, and niacin include the amounts of those nutrients added to flour and cereal products; quantities of Vitamin A value added to margarine and milk; and quantities of ascorbic acid added to fruit juices and drinks.

Most of the improvement, however, took place in the period between the mid-thirties and the early postwar period. Relatively little improvement in dietary levels has taken place since a food consumption survey was made in 1948. In fact there is some indication that diets have become less adequate nutritionally in recent years. A survey made in 1955 showed that about the same proportion of urban household diets as in 1948 furnished recommended amounts of calcium, vitamin A, thiamin, and riboflavin —nutrients often in shorter than desirable supply.[1] Protein, iron, and niacin levels improved; but ascorbic acid levels were somewhat lower. A similar survey in 1965, however, showed a smaller percentage of diets providing recommended allowances of calcium, vitamin A, thiamin, and ascorbic acid than in 1955.[2]

Protein, iron, and niacin levels have improved chiefly because of greater consumption of meat, poultry, and fish. In the spring of 1965, U.S. families consumed, per person, about 4.6 pounds of these foods a week, compared with a little over 3

[1] "Dietary Levels of Households in the United States," *Household Food Consumption Survey, 1955,* USDA, Rept. 6, Mar., 1957.

[2] *Dietary Levels of Households in the United States, Spring, 1965* (preliminary report), USDA, ARS62–17, Jan., 1968.

pounds in 1948. The lower ascorbic-acid levels resulted chiefly from a decrease in the household consumption of potatoes and green vegetables. Quantities of milk, fats and oils, and grain products used are all below those of the earlier period.

Food expenditures of city families in a week in the spring of 1965 averaged $34.04, including money spent for meals away from home. This was 33 per cent more than a similar period in 1948 and 15 per cent more than in the spring of 1955. Higher food prices account for most of the increase between 1955 and 1965, since the index of retail food prices also rose by 15 per cent in that period. Higher prices account for much of the total change since 1948. But some of it results from a shift toward more expensive types of foods and includes the cost of services received with meals eaten away from home.

## ARE WE WELL FED?

Is the present diet adequate?

Some answers to this question are provided by the 1965 food consumption survey.[3] Food supplies on today's markets in the United States are more than adequate in quantity and variety to provide everyone with more than the amounts of nutrients recommended by the National Research Council if they were evenly distributed. But the 1965 survey showed that the diets in a considerable number of the households in the United States did not meet the recommended levels. The percentages are shown in Table 5.4.

The table shows that more families were short of calcium, vitamin C (ascorbic acid), and Vitamin A than any other nutrients. Thirty per cent of the households had diets that provided less calcium than the allowances recommended by the National Research Council. Twenty-seven per cent had less than recommended amounts of ascorbic acid (vitamin C), and 26 per cent were below recommended levels of vitamin A. Somewhat smaller proportions had less riboflavin, thiamin, protein, and iron than the allowances specify. Viewed from the overall nutrient level, 20 per cent of the households in the 1965 survey were considered to have "poor" diets, compared with 15 per cent in 1955. Diets were considered to be "poor" if they provided less than two-thirds of the recommended allowance for one or more nutrients.

Milk is the principal source of calcium; and vegetables and fruits, especially citrus, are the chief source of vitamin C. It is estimated that if everyone in this country whose food intake was deficient in these two nutrients had a diet that met nutritional

[3] *Ibid.*

**TABLE 5.4: Percentage of Households Using Food at Home in a Week, Spring, 1965, That Did Not Furnish Recommended Amounts of Seven Nutrients***

| Annual Income After Income Taxes for Households of Two or More Persons | Protein (under 70 mg.) | Calcium (under 0.8 gm.) | Iron (under 10 mg.) | Vitamin A Value (under 5,000 I.U.) | Thia-mine† (under 1.2 mg.) | Ribo-flavin† (under 1.7 mg.) | Ascorbic Acid† (under 70 mg.) |
|---|---|---|---|---|---|---|---|
| | *(per cent)* | *(per cent)* | *(per cent)* | *(per cent)* | *(per cent)* | *(per cent)* | *(per cent)* |
| All Households | 5 | 30 | 10 | 26 | 8 | 6 | 27 |
| Under $3,000 | 12 | 36 | 11 | 36 | 10 | 10 | 42 |
| $3,000–$4,999 | 5 | 35 | 10 | 26 | 8 | 6 | 33 |
| $5,000–$6,999 | 4 | 29 | 10 | 24 | 8 | 5 | 24 |
| $7,000–$9,999 | 2 | 26 | 8 | 20 | 6 | 4 | 20 |
| $10,000 and over | 2 | 24 | 8 | 18 | 6 | 3 | 12 |

Source: *Dietary Levels of Households in the United States, Spring, 1965* (preliminary report), USDA, ARS62-17, Jan., 1968.

* Recommended dietary allowances set by the Food and Nutrition Board of the National Academy of Sciences—National Research Council.

† Cooking losses deducted.

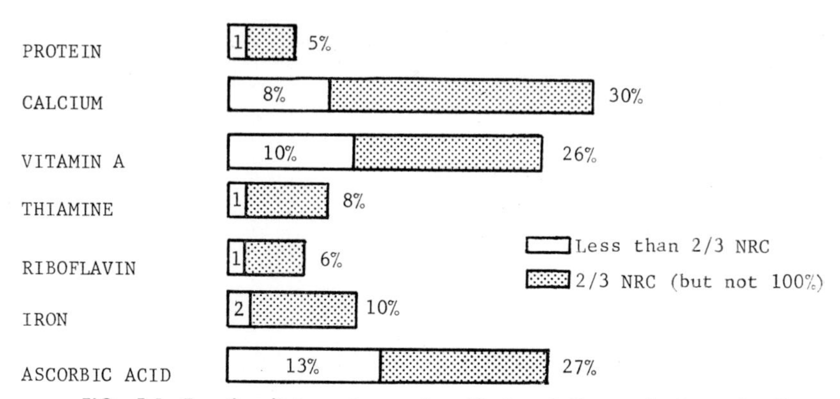


FIG. 5.1—Family diets not meeting National Research Council allowances, 1955. (Source: Based on data in **Dietary Levels of Households in the United States, Spring, 1965,** preliminary report, USDA, ARS62-17, Jan., 1968.)

recommendations, about 9 per cent more milk would be used by households and about 6 per cent more fruits and vegetables.

The table also shows some inverse relation between dietary deficiency and income. In general, more low-income households had deficient diets than high-income households.

This does not mean that large proportions of the population were suffering from malnutrition. The recommended allowances of the National Research Council provide a considerable margin of safety over average needs. The margin varies for the different nutrients. Figure 5.1 shows that relatively few households scored very low (less than two-thirds of the recommended levels) for the nutrients studied.

The data from the survey, however, show the amounts of nutrients in the food that came into household kitchens for consumption, not the amounts that were eaten. How much food was discarded either as plate waste or during or after preparation was not reported. Hence the amounts of nutrients in the food actually eaten may be smaller than the amounts shown in tables and charts of the study. Losses in terms of calories may be especially high.

## PROMOTION AND ADVERTISING

Can the demand for food be increased by advertising and other promotional means?

One misconception concerning this question needs to be cleared up at the outset. Many people discuss this question as if

**TABLE 5.5: Estimated Funds Expended and Number of Agricultural Groups, United States, 1963**

| Type of Organization | Number of Promoting Organizations | Expenditures |
|---|---|---|
| | | *(1,000 dollars)* |
| Voluntary producer-processor groups .......... | 469 | 32,802 |
| Cooperatives .................................. | 534 | 30,017 |
| Commissions, councils, boards, institutes, etc., established under enabling legislation ........ | 134 | 26,121 |
| State departments of agriculture ............... | 32 | 1,570 |
| Others and unidentified ........................ | 63 | 1,553 |
| | 1,241 | 92,063 |

Source: Carl R. Twining and Peter L. Henderson, *Promotional Activities of Agricultural Groups,* USDA, Marketing Res. Rept. 742, 1965.

nothing, or very little, were done to advertise farm products. This is far from the truth. Over 1,200 groups in the United States were engaged in the promotion of agricultural products in 1963, when they spent about $92 million, as shown in Table 5.5.

In addition to the money spent by these groups, it is estimated that roughly 20 per cent of the total of $12 billion spent on advertising of all kinds in the United States was directed to the promotion of food and food products.

The effectiveness of promotional and advertising programs for farm commodities is the subject of much debate. Considering the stability of total food consumption, it appears probable that an increase in the consumption of one product occurs at the expense of another product or products. Thus, advertising by one segment of the industry might result in competitive advertising by other segments. The net result may be that no change takes place in consumption, but all the groups have less income after advertising costs are deducted.

Although no precise appraisal of a particular advertising program for farm products can be made here, this much can be said: The answer to the question of whether the program will expand the demand for a product sufficiently for the increase in returns to more than cover the advertising costs requires that certain criteria be met:

1. The advertised product must be identifiable.
2. The product must be such that advertising can convince persons that a difference in quality exists between advertised and unadvertised supplies.

3. Advertising must be backed up by a coordinated program of distribution and favorable display in all stores.
4. Advertising must be concentrated sufficiently to make an impression on consumers.

Giving consideration to the above criteria, it appears that most state and regional advertising of a portion of the total output of unprocessed commodities would likely have little effect on the total demand for those commodities and on the total demand for food.

## WOULD IMPROVED DIETS EXPAND DEMAND?

The argument is often made that if low-income families could increase their consumption of food, they would "eat up the surplus" represented by food stocks and unused productive capacity.

Food consumption surveys throw some light on this question. While the diets of many people in the United States are short of specific nutrients, indications are that on an average diets are more than adequate in calories. Table 5.4 indicates that among families with incomes of $3,000 or less, the diets of 12 per cent of the families did not furnish the recommended amounts of protein.[4] For other nutrients, diets were below recommended levels in the following percentages of families: calcium, 36 per cent; iron, 11 per cent; thiamin and riboflavin both 10 per cent; vitamin A, 36 per cent; and ascorbic acid, 42 per cent. At the same time, average daily calorie intake per person was 3,115 for these low-income families, compared with an average of 3,211 for all families and the present recommended daily allowance of from 2,600 to 2,900 calories for men from 18 to 55 years of age. Considering that the recommended calorie intake for women, girls, and small children is much lower than for men, these results indicate that more than adequate calorie levels exist on the average—even among low-income families.

Even so, some families are deficient in calories while others overeat. But there is no way readily to balance the effects of overconsumption and underconsumption among individuals for estimating the net impact on total food demand if all diets were at the recommended level. While the problem of inadequate levels of specific nutrients is probably more serious, this does not appear to be entirely a matter of income and ability to be properly fed. Survey results show that the diets of some families in all income groupings are below recommended levels for specific

[4] *Dietary Levels of Households in the United States, Spring, 1965,* (preliminary report), USDA, ARS62-17, Jan., 1968.

nutrients. The 1965 survey, for example, showed that among families with incomes of $10,000 and over in all urbanization categories, diets were below recommended levels for calcium in 24 per cent of the cases; for vitamin A, 18 per cent, for vitamin C, 12 per cent; and for iron, 8 per cent.[5]

While diets have not improved during recent years in terms of nutrient content, the nutrients for adequate nutrition for all are available in our food supply. The number of persons in the United States with diets containing less than recommended calorie levels is probably quite small. The following statement regarding the food-demand expansion potential of improving U.S. diets is probably still quite applicable.

> The people of the United States, in general, are well fed. Improving consumer diets through increasing food consumption will not result in even moderate increases in total food consumption. However, welfare considerations may be of equal or greater importance than elimination of surpluses. Demand expansion proposals simultaneously attack both problem areas. Therefore, the extent to which demand expansion efforts can reduce the agricultural surplus mainly depends on how seriously the public views the problem of nutritional shortages and the amount it is willing to spend to remedy this problem.[6]

Even the continued rise in per capita income that is forecast for the future in the United States is not expected to increase the consumption of food very much. Most of the increase will result from population growth. We are already so well off that most of any further increases in incomes will be spent for goods other than food. Figure 5.2 shows that the 45 per cent increase in per capita income since 1950 has led to only a small increase in per capita food consumption. Further increases in income will have still less effect.

## DOMESTIC PROGRAMS TO EXPAND FOOD DEMAND AND IMPROVE DIETS[7]

Several government programs in operation are aimed at improving the diets of low-income families as well as providing better nutrition for school children. These include direct commodity distribution, the Food Stamp Program, the National School Lunch Program, the Special Milk Program, and the Child

[5] *Ibid.*

[6] John M. Wetmore, Martin E. Abel, and Elmer W. Learn, *Expanding the Demand for Farm Food Products in the United States,* Minn. Agr. Exp. Sta. Bul. 456, June, 1961, p. 16.

[7] *Farm Commodity and Related Programs,* USDA, Agr. Handbook 345, 1967.

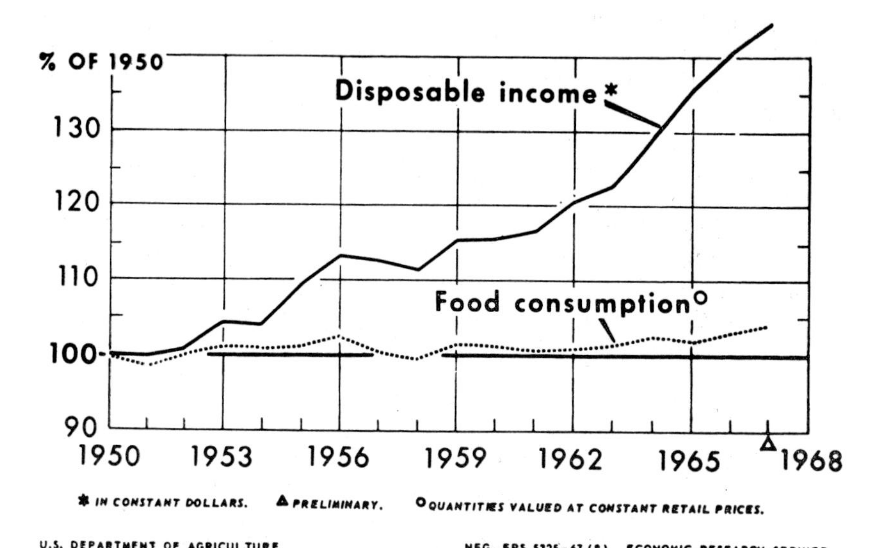


FIG. 5.2—Per capita disposable income and consumption of food, 1950–67.

Nutrition Program. While these programs have limited demand expansion effects, their major objective is better nutrition.

The present Food Stamp Program was first initiated on a pilot basis in 1961 and was extended by the Food Stamp Act of 1964. In this program, eligible low-income families purchase low-cost food stamps that can be used to buy food in participating retail stores. The cost of the food stamps to the individual family varies according to family income, size, and other circumstances. The cost may range from nothing for very low-income families to half or more of the retail value of the stamps for families with higher income. In 1969 approximately 2.9 million persons were participating in the Food Stamp Program.

Under the commodity distribution program, food products acquired by the USDA under price support and surplus removal operations are distributed directly to needy families, charitable institutions, and schools. During fiscal 1969, food donations under this program were received by 3.6 million persons in family units. In addition, approximately 2.5 million adults and children in charitable institutions and summer camps and 21 million school children benefited from direct food donations under other programs.

The National School Lunch Program, the Special Milk Program, and the Child Nutrition Program are all designed to improve the nutrition of the nation's school children. The School Lunch Program, first established in 1946, provides cash assistance to participating schools for the purchase of food items as well as direct donation of certain foods for use in school lunches. The Special Milk Program, initiated in 1955, helps provide milk at low cost to schools, camps, and child-care institutions to encourage fluid milk consumption by children. This is done by reimbursing participating schools for a portion of the cost of the milk served. In fiscal 1969, approximately 71,000 schools participated in the School Lunch Program, involving 20 million children during the peak month. In the same year, approximately 95,000 schools, camps, and nonprofit child-care institutions participated in the Special Milk Program.

A relatively new food assistance program was authorized under the Child Nutrition Act of 1966. Main provisions of this program are (1) to provide financial assistance to schools in low-income areas for purchase of food service equipment and (2) to provide nutritious breakfasts to school children when needed because of low-income situations or because they must travel long distances to school.

# 6

# THE SUPPLY OF FARM PRODUCTS

AGRICULTURE IN THE UNITED STATES is a diverse industry; it has become highly specialized within itself. With the passage of time, the production of each farm product gradually has become localized in the areas where it can be produced at the lowest opportunity cost. If a new lower-cost area is opened, its product undersells the product from the previous area; eventually the new area partly or completely replaces the old.

## DEVELOPMENT OF SPECIALIZATION

Today, the great staple crops are produced primarily in the specialized areas shown in Figure 6.1. Greater detail for wheat is given in Figures 27.2 and 27.3 in Chapter 27, and for livestock, in Figures 23.1, 23.2, and 23.3 in Chapter 23. Cotton is grown in the South, the Southwest, and California. Tobacco, rice, and flax are grown in the limited areas shown in Figure 6.2. The production of the less important "specialty" crops is still more localized; citrus fruit production is highly concentrated in small areas of California, Florida, Texas, and Arizona; and the product is shipped thousands of miles to population areas throughout the country. In 1969 over 50 per cent of the potato crop was grown in four states, much of this in only a few counties. The spotty nature of the production areas is shown in Figure 6.3.

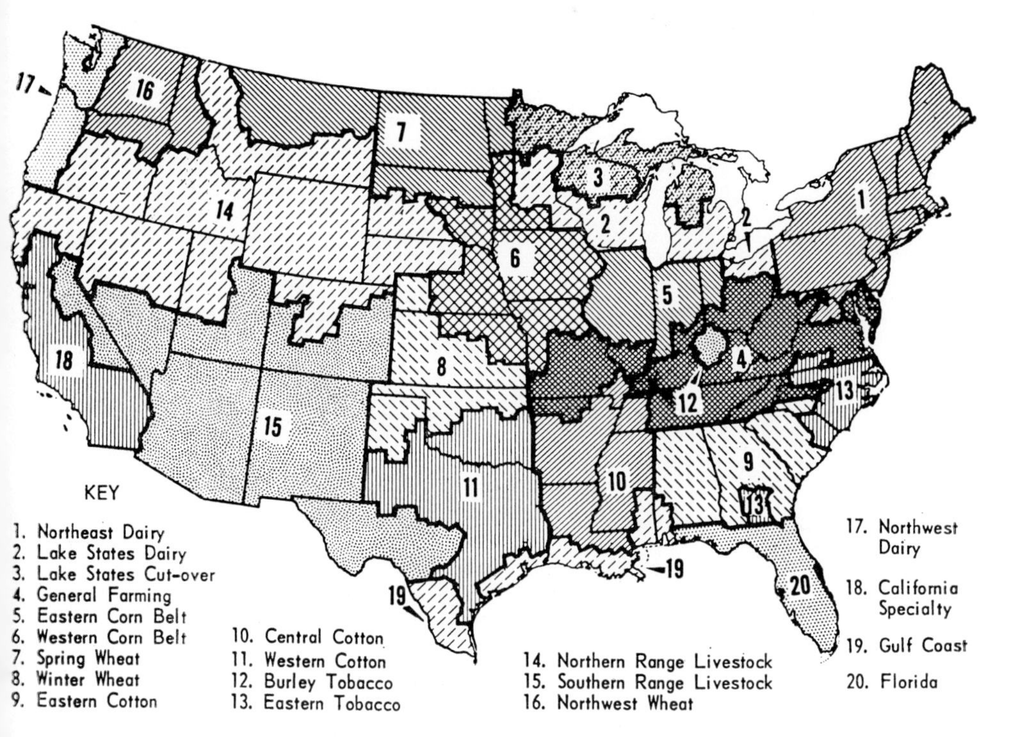


FIG. 6.1—Agricultural regions in the United States.

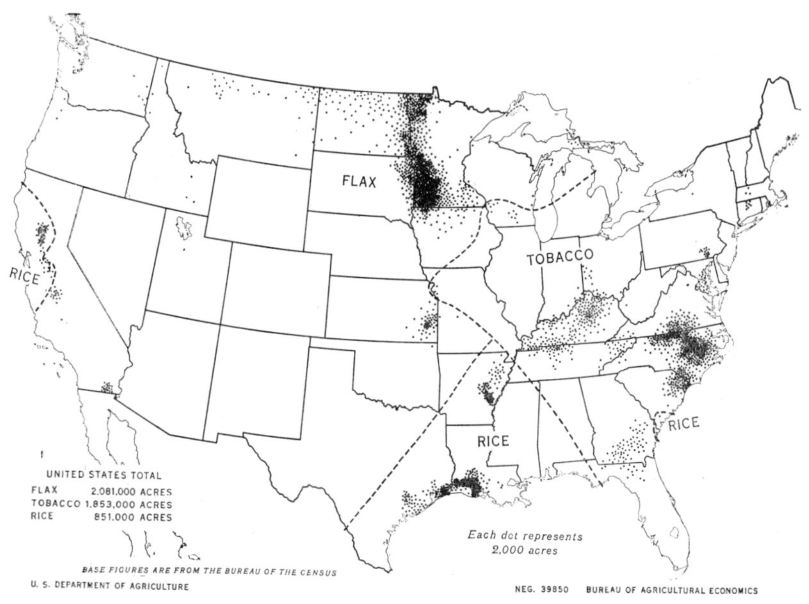


FIG. 6.2 — Tobacco, rice, and flax producing areas in the United States.

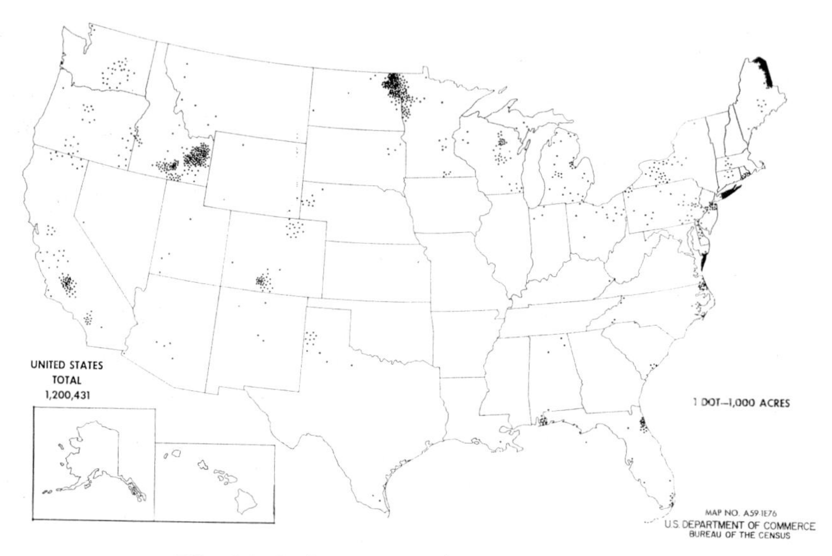


FIG. 6.3—Irish potato producing areas, United States.

The localization of production in the areas where each product can be produced most cheaply is a continuous process. The areas shift as new varieties are evolved, as new inventions or methods lower transportation costs or improve services, as irrigation projects are developed, or as movements in population take place. The extension of the railroads westward in the 1870's and the perfection of the refrigerator car are old and familiar examples. The shipment of perishable fresh fruits by airplane is a more recent development. Shifts in the location of the producing areas for different products are still proceeding. This is true even for such staple products as wheat and cotton.

Technological developments in production practices have proceeded at a rapid pace for many years. One example is the adoption of hybrid corn. In Iowa about 95 per cent of the farmers made this change in about ten years. Fertilizer use provides a more recent illustration. Use of the principal plant nutrients (nitrogen, phosphorus, and potassium) more than doubled from 1960 to 1969, and 1969 usage was four and one-half times as great as in 1950.

Rapid changes have also occurred in the relative importance of different agricultural products and in the geographic location of production. The number of beef cows on U.S. farms and ranches increased by 41 per cent between 1955 and 1969, while milk-cow numbers declined by 40 per cent. The number of stock sheep in the United States dropped by nearly one-third in the same period, but turkey production went up sharply—from 65.6 million birds in 1955 to 106.4 million in 1969. Commercial broiler production provides perhaps the most dramatic example of all. From an annual production of only 143 million broilers in 1940, volume rose to nearly 1.1 billion in 1955 and to 2.8 billion in 1969.

There have been equally important changes in crop production. The harvested acreage of soybeans rose from 13.8 million in 1950 to 40.9 million in 1969, reflecting a rapid growth in demand for soybean meal and soybean oil. At the same time, oat acreage dropped from 39.3 million in 1950 to 18.0 million in 1969.

The egg and cattle industries provide good illustrations of shifts in geographic specialization in the production of particular agricultural products. In 1955 the north central states accounted for 48 per cent of U.S. egg production while the south Atlantic and south central states combined produced 22 per cent of the total. By 1969 the proportion produced in the north central states had declined to 27 per cent, and the two southern regions increased to 42 per cent of the total.

The wider geographic distribution of the nation's beef cows is another example. The eleven western states accounted for 32 per cent of the beef cows on U.S. farms and ranches in 1940; by 1969 the proportion had dropped to 21 per cent. In the same period the proportion of the nation's beef cows in the south central states went from 25 to 37 per cent and in the north central states from 27 to 33 per cent.

There are other broader results of the change in production technology. Average farm size has increased as the number of farms has declined. And farms have become more specialized in most cases. Capital has been substituted for labor at a rapid rate in agricultural production. As a result, employment in agricultural declined from 9.5 million workers in 1940 to 3.6 million in 1969, or from 20 per cent of the labor force to less than 5 per cent. Output per man-hour in agriculture increased an amazing 3.1 times between 1950 and 1969.

The net result of all these changes has been a sharp rise in the efficiency of the nation's agricultural plant. Considering all agricultural production inputs, output per unit of input increased by 27 per cent in this period.

## LONG-RUN INCREASES IN U.S. FOOD SUPPLY

A USDA study of the farm production potential of the United States by 1980 in relation to needs investigated whether the supply of farm products was likely to keep up with the demand.[1] The study proceeded on the basis of demand levels developed from the following assumptions:

1. That U.S. population will be 245 million by 1980.
2. That the U.S. economy, as measured by gross national product, will expand at an annual rate of about 4 per cent, and real per capita disposable income will rise by 2.3 per cent per year.
3. That per capita consumption of farm products in total will show little change.
4. That exports will increase at the same rate as in the 1950–60 decade.

On these assumptions, the study concluded that the productive capacity of U.S. agriculture is more than sufficient to meet the projected 1980 needs of the U.S. population for food and fiber and to provide for a relatively high level of exports at the same or lower relative prices than in 1959–61. Total cropland harvested would be only a little above the 1959–61 level under the projections of yield and utilization that were made. Substantial adjustments in crop acreages, however, would be required—less oat and hay acreage, for example, and more soybeans and wheat.

An alternate assumption in the study was that all cropland currently diverted from production under various government programs would be planted to crops in 1980. This would mean about 30 million more acres in cropland than in 1959–61. Projected output under this assumption was more than 10 per cent above projected levels of use in 1980.

Another study of 1980 food needs and production potential considered alternate levels of exports and different farm program alternatives.[2] Domestic demand was assumed to increase with gains in population and per capita income and was projected at the same level under each of the various export-farm program alternatives. One set of projections was based on a free-market assumption, with exports at the 1950–65 trend level. An alternate assumption with a free market was that all available cropland would be in production in 1980 and that the excess over domestic needs would be exported. The results of these free-market projections were summarized as follows:

[1] R. F. Daly and A. C. Egbert, "A Look Ahead for Food and Agriculture," *Agricultural Economics Research,* USDA, Vol. 18, No. 1, Jan., 1966.

[2] Earl O. Heady and Leo V. Mayer, *Food Needs and U.S. Agriculture in 1980,* National Advisory Commission on Food and Fiber, Tech. Papers, Vol. 1, Washington, D.C., Aug., 1967.

"Excess capacity will remain a significant factor facing the agricultural sector unless the nation adopts a policy of exporting all available quantities of agricultural commodities. This excess capacity will approximate 50 million acres of available cropland by 1980 if exports follow trends established over the period 1950–65."[3]

Three other projections were made in the same study, assuming alternately:

1. Continuation of voluntary land retirement programs for feed grains and wheat similar to those in effect during 1965 and 1966 and continuation of exports at the 1950–65 trend level.
2. Mandatory acreage controls with strict quotas on wheat, feed grains and cotton, and exports at the 1950–65 trend level.
3. Mandatory acreage controls but lower export levels due to cessation of export subsidies.

In each case, projected 1980 demands could be met with substantial cropland left out of production. Excess capacity under the three alternatives, measured by idled cropland, was projected at 48, 38, and 71 million acres, respectively. This would compare with 56 million acres retired under government programs in 1965.[4]

In general then, current projections imply that considerable acreage will still need to be held out of production in 1980 to prevent overproduction of farm products. If acreage is not controlled, the prospects are that agricultural production will continue to be excessive; and this will exert downward pressure on agricultural prices.

Only time can confirm or reject the accuracy of these projections. However, past projections of U.S. agricultural yields and output have typically been too conservative. For example, projections of 1975 crop yields made in a 1960 USDA study were reached by the mid-sixties for many crops. Exports of agricultural products have also expanded more rapidly than projected.

## INSTABILITY OF PRODUCTION OF INDIVIDUAL FARM PRODUCTS

The total volume of agricultural production remains remarkably stable from year to year. Figure 6.4 shows that the trend of agricultural production rises at the rate of about 2 per cent per year, but the fluctuations from one year to the next seldom exceed 3 or 4 per cent.

[3] *Ibid.*
[4] *Ibid.*

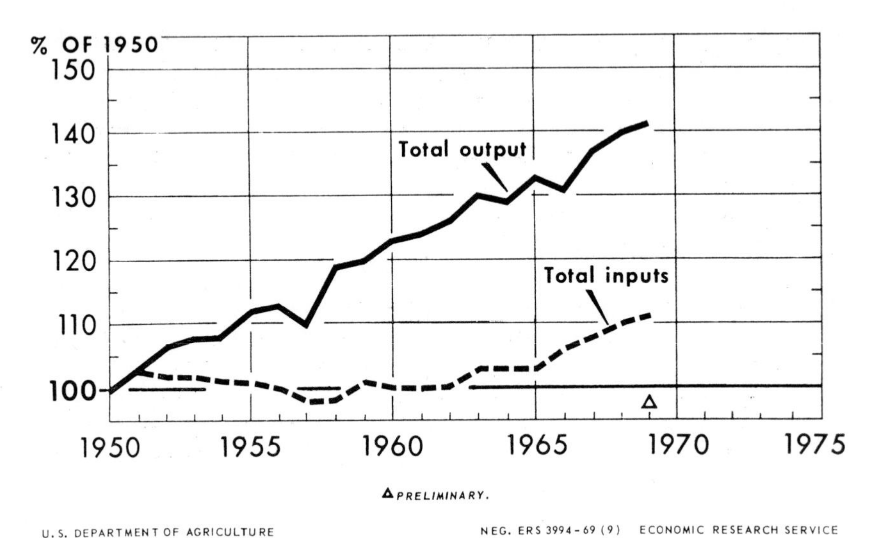


FIG. 6.4—Production and inputs in agriculture, United States, 1950–69.

The relative stability of total agricultural production, however, masks an extreme instability in the production of individual farm products, considered separately.

Most crops and products are subject to the hazards of drouth and flood, hail and wind, cold and heat, insects, disease, and occasional erratic changes in individual farmers' plans. Changes in government programs also may cause large year-to-year variations in production of individual crops. For example, the corn crop dropped from 4.0 billion bushels in 1963 to 3.5 billion in 1964; then jumped to 4.1 billion in 1965.[5] Cotton production dropped from 15 million bales in 1965 to less than 10 million bales in 1966; then to 7.5 million bales in 1967 and back to 10.1 million bales in 1969.[6]

In addition to the irregular fluctuations in production that take place from year to year, cyclic fluctuations occur in the production of some farm products. Hog production has a marked tendency to move in cycles. When hog prices are high, hog production will increase for about two years, until that increase in production lowers hog prices; these low prices discourage hog production, and this decrease in production raises hog prices; these high prices increase hog production, and so on.

Finally, most farm products are produced seasonally. They come on the market in greatest volume in certain seasons of the

[5] *Crop Production, 1969 Annual Summary,* USDA, 1969, p. 37.
[6] *Ibid.,* p. 38.

year and and in only small volume, or not at all, in other seasons. If the crops are durable, such as cotton or wheat, they can be put into storage and sent to market fairly evenly through the year; if they are perishable, like most fruits, they must either be canned, frozen, or otherwise made less perishable, or else consumed heavily at the time of harvest and in smaller quantities during the rest of the year.

Total agricultural production remains stable in spite of these violent fluctuations in the production of individual crops, because the United States is large, and the weather varies in different parts of the country. One crop grows well under favorable weather in one area, while another crop in a different part of the country is struck by drought or other adverse weather. Ordinarily, the fluctuations in the production of the different crops cancel out to a large extent.

### Effects of Unstable Production

Consumers, therefore, fare pretty well from year to year so far as total food intake is concerned. The total consumption of food closely follows the total production of food. It has to. Consumers cannot eat more than is produced, nor will farmers sell less, except for some storage of durable crops. Total production remains fairly stable from year to year, so total consumption does too. A shortage of one food is usually offset by a surplus of another, and foods are interchangeable enough so that no great damage is done to consumers' diets or palates.

Farmers, as producers, are affected most by fluctuations in individual crop production. They are pretty well specialized as producers; each farmer raises only one product, or a few related products, and a partial or complete failure of that particular crop directly affects the quantity that he can sell.

The effects on a farmer's total income, however, are different from the effects on the quantity that he sells. Fluctuations in yield ordinarily cause opposite fluctuations in prices. When production goes down, the price goes up. The effects of this inverse relation between production and price differs from crop to crop.

When the demand remains stable, a reduction of 20 per cent in the size of the corn crop, for example, puts corn prices up about 30 per cent. The total income from this small crop, therefore, is $(80 \times 130)/100 = 104$ per cent of the income from an average crop. That is, a crop that is 80 per cent of average size is worth 4 per cent more than an average crop.

A large corn crop, however, is worth a good deal less than an average crop. The total income from a crop 20 per cent larger than average size is $(120 \times 70)/100 = 84$ per cent of the income from an average crop. Thus in the case of corn the inverse relation between changes in production and price keeps the total income from small crops almost the same as for an average crop. But a large crop *decreases* the total income by almost the same percentage as the increase in the size of the crop.[7] The same thing is true of hogs, which consume nearly half of the corn fed to livestock.

The normal inverse relation between production and prices, therefore, only partially stabilizes total income and applies only to the total income received by the producers of a crop as a group. It applies to individual farmers' incomes only if the yields on all the farms producing a given crop varied alike. The rub comes in the fact that yields on all farms do not do this. One farmer may have a good yield in a year when most other farmers have poor yields, and he can cash in on his high yield at good prices; next year the situation may be reversed. The inverse relation between production and prices helps to stabilize incomes to the producers of a crop as a group, but it leaves the individual farmer still exposed to an uncertain yield and income on his individual farm.

Since 1933, the Commodity Credit Corporation has been engaged in commodity loan and storage programs designed to stabilize the market supplies and prices of the so-called "basic" products—cotton, wheat, corn, tobacco, rice, and peanuts. While details of specific programs have varied, the objective has been to remove the excess over average production from the market in good crop years and put it into storage. These quantities can be taken out of storage to add to supplies later in poor crop years.

To the extent that these programs attain their objectives, they stabilize prices from year to year against fluctuations in production. This, however, does not stabilize incomes. Without a program of this sort, as shown above, big crops are worth less than average crops. With the program, big crops are worth more than average crops, and small crops are worth less.

With or without a price stabilization program, individual farmers' incomes are still affected by variations in the crop yields on their individual farms. One farm or group of farms

[7] The relation between changes in production and price is called the elasticity of the demand. This elasticity is computed by dividing the percentage change in quantity by the percentage change in price. Thus the elasticity of the demand for corn is $20/30 = 0.66$. Other products have other elasticities; and changes in production, therefore, have other effects on total income. The technical, statistical, mathematical, and economic problems involved in measuring elasticity are discussed fully in Geoffrey Shepherd, *Agricultural Price Analysis*, Iowa State Univ. Press, Ames, 1968.

may be struck by drouth, hail, or flood in the same year when other farms are blessed by timely rains. In order to protect farmers against this kind of income instability, federal crop insurance programs have been set up for cotton, wheat, and corn. These programs offer insurance to individual farmers against variations in crop yields on their farms.

## BRIDGING THE GAP BETWEEN PRODUCER AND CONSUMER

We have on the one side, therefore, a fairly stable *need* for farm products in the United States, but a very unstable demand. And on the other side, we have a fairly stable *total production* of farm products, but a very unstable production of individual crops and livestock products, varying irregularly in some cases and cyclically in others. The United States is like a vast market hall, with hungry consumers at one end shouting their orders for food and continually changing their minds about the prices they can afford to pay; and at the other end of the hall, harried producers dashing in and continually dumping varying kinds and quantities of goods for sale on the counters. All the elements of bedlam are here. Yet somehow the goods move through the market, producers get their money, and consumers get their food.

To bridge the tremendous distances between agricultural producers and consumers in the United States, to smooth out the irregular flow or to keep a succession of irregular flows of different products meshing in with one another over periods of time, and to set and reset prices continually so that consumers will never lack supplies at those prices, and vice versa, a huge and complicated marketing system has developed over the years. This system is not the sort of thing that gradually improves until it reaches perfection. Rather, it goes through a continuous evolutionary process in an environment that is continually and rapidly changing. As fast as the system changes to adapt itself to a change in the environment, the environment already is changing to something else again. The system is always a jump or two behind, in a stage of transition from what was needed yesterday to what is needed today.

A description and appraisal of a marketing system, therefore, needs to be phrased not merely in terms of the present but in terms of the recent past that gave the system its present form. An analysis of the present agricultural marketing system of this sort is given in Chapter 7.

# 7

# THE MARKETING SYSTEM THAT BRINGS SUPPLY AND DEMAND TOGETHER

THE AGRICULTURAL MARKETING SYSTEM has been rapidly changing. No doubt it will continue to change, perhaps even more rapidly, in the future. There is nothing mysterious about the causes of these changes. They result from technological developments in transportation, communication, and preservation.

## THE TRADITIONAL LOCAL AND CENTRAL MARKET SYSTEM

The agricultural marketing system that developed as the railroad opened up the West after 1850 was based upon the methods of transportation and communication that existed then. The team and wagon was an efficient unit for handling small loads for short distances over poor country roads. Its small size and low speed, however, made it inefficient for long trips. These physical characteristics of the horse and wagon set the pattern of the country markets. They were *local markets,* small in size but large in number, located in small country towns. Each local market served a territory with a radius of only a few miles.

The railroad was an efficient unit for hauling large loads for long distances at higher speeds. The markets that developed as a result were the *central markets,* large in size and few in number, located at large cities and strategic transportation points.

The local markets and central markets complemented each other to form a fairly efficient system for getting farm products from producer to consumer. The local markets in the country assembled small quantities of farm products into carload lots for shipment to the central markets. The central markets concentrated those small quantities from the local markets into large quantities, for milling, packing, and so forth, and for dispersion to smaller wholesale and retail markets in the consuming areas.

The prices in the central markets were linked to one another, so that relative prices would not fluctuate (except for short intervals) by more than the cost of transporting goods from supply areas to the different markets. For some durable commodities such as wheat, having high specific value and therefore low transportation costs, the central market system covered the globe.

The central markets were and still are often hundreds of miles away from the local markets that supply them, and the producer or local dealer seldom accompanies his goods. The great bulk of produce that flows to the central markets is consigned there to commission men who represent the seller. They make the best sale they can, deduct their commission from the proceeds, and remit the remainder to the farmer or local dealer who consigned the goods to them.

One of the shortcomings of the traditional system is the congestion that results from the concentration of commodities at the central markets. The vast area, the quantity of equipment, and the manpower involved in the Union Stockyards at Chicago, for example, illustrate the complexity of a large central market and afford some idea of the cost. This concentration of physical products facilitates price making but is an expensive operation.

## CHANGES IN THE STRUCTURE OF THE AGRICULTURAL MARKETING SYSTEM

Before World War II, new developments in transportation and communication began to reduce the advantage of concentrating physical products at central markets. These new developments were (1) the great improvement that was made in motor trucks (largely resulting from the perfection of the heavy pneumatic tire), (2) the rapid extension of concrete highways over the countryside, and (3) the wide use of radio.

The first two changes reduced the cost and improved the speed and reliability of the short-haul movement of goods to market, until it became as fast and efficient as the long haul by railroad. Goods could be assembled and dispersed at the markets in small towns or cities, in large enough volume for efficient processing, more cheaply and rapidly than at the great terminal or central markets in metropolitan areas. From the physical point of view, the marketing and processing job could be done as well in a small city like Enid, Oklahoma, or Waterloo, Iowa, as in a large metropolis like Chicago or Kansas City; and it could be done more cheaply. Accordingly, buyers and sellers began to short-cut the central market in considerable numbers and to do their buying and selling directly at interior markets. The traditional central market began to give way to a more decentralized system.

In addition to improvements in trucks and highways, changes in freight rates favoring shipment of carcass meat had a decentralizing effect upon the slaughter (and therefore upon the marketing) of one important commodity, livestock. However, marketing has become as much or more decentralized for other commodities as well—grain, apples, truck crops, and so forth—for which changes in freight rates were unimportant.

The truck and the paved highway made decentralization of the handling of products physically possible. At the same time, the increasing use of radio made that decentralization economically feasible. In its field, communication, radio was a perfect parallel to the other two advances in their field, transportation; for it was a perfect instrument for disseminating market news to the decentralized market. The use of trucks and concrete highways scattered "the market" over the whole producing area; radio similarly scattered *market news* over the whole area, right into the producer's homes. The one perfectly complemented the other.

The radio would not have been much use if there had been no market news to broadcast. The federal government, aware of the market decentralization that was taking place and alive to the potentialities of radio, vastly expanded its news-reporting service, using all three agencies—the press, the telegraph and telephone, and the radio. Every effort was made to decentralize market news step by step with the decentralization of physical marketing.

The federal government marketing services also made great strides in commodity standardization. Reporting of prices is not useful unless there is a common language in which the different grades of the commodities can be described. It does not help a country seller much to tell him that cattle are selling from $20 to $30 per 100 pounds at Chicago, or even to tell him that "good" cattle are selling from $26 to $28 if his idea of what "good" means differs from the reporter's idea. Along with the growth in the volume of market reports, therefore, went an increase in the accuracy and uniformity of the descriptions of different grades of the commodities whose prices and quantities were reported.

Thus, as the result of specific technological developments in transportation and communication, a new intermediate type of market has partially replaced the traditional local and central market. In these intermediary markets, not only do the physical goods short-cut the central markets but the market news and the process of price determination short-cut them also. The new intermediate markets, instead of being articulated vertically with the central markets (both in flow of goods and prices) are articulated horizontally with each other; they are now as likely to lead the central markets as to follow them. The concentration, equalization, and dispersion of the physical goods, as well as the price-determining and title-transferring process, that took place at the central markets is now spread throughout the country.

### Livestock Marketing

The extent of the change in livestock marketing in the United States from 1923 to 1951 is shown in Figure 7.1. The percentages of the different kinds of livestock sold on the terminal markets differ, but they all declined substantially. Collection

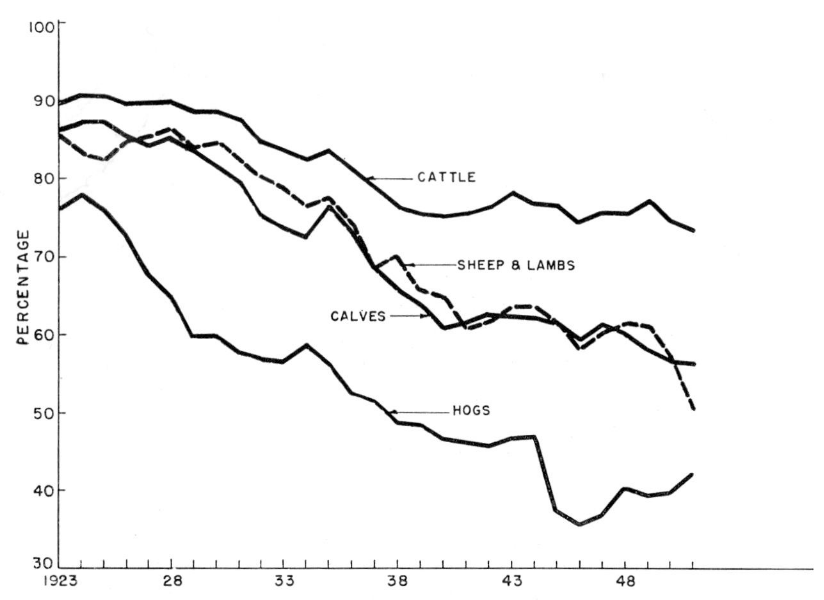


FIG. 7.1—Percentages of livestock sold through terminal markets in the United States, 1923–51. (Data discontinued after 1951.)

of this particular set of data was discontinued in 1951. Later comparable data on the sources of livestock purchased by packers indicate that the decline in the relative volume at terminal markets continued after 1951. In 1968 only 25 per cent of the cattle, 14 per cent of the calves, and 19 per cent of both hogs and sheep purchased by packers were obtained at terminal markets.[1]

Another significant development in the marketing system was the rapid growth of the livestock auction market from 1930 to 1950. Auctions have continued to be an important market outlet for the nation's livestock, especially for feeder cattle, feeder lambs, feeder pigs, and slaughter cows and calves. Eighteen per cent of packer purchases of cattle for slaughter in 1968 were bought at auctions, along with 52 per cent of the calves, 14 per cent of the hogs, and 15 per cent of the sheep.[2]

In contrast to large public markets which receive some livestock from considerable distance, many auction markets draw their supplies largely from the communities in which they are located. These auction markets are in some respects comparable with terminal markets, in that they bring several buyers physically together in the same ring. They are relatively good outlets for small lots and odd weights or grades of livestock.

Figure 7.2 shows the growth in number of livestock auctions from 1900 to 1955. Auction markets developed rather slowly through the 1920's; they were then largely concentrated in the north central states, extending from Kentucky through Iowa, Nebraska, and Oklahoma. About 200 auctions are estimated to have been operating by 1930. The first complete count made in 1937 indicated that 1,345 auctions were operating in the United States. Another count showed 2,472 operating in 1949. The peak in numbers was reached in 1952, when over 2,500 different livestock auctions were holding sales. Another complete count in 1955 showed that auction numbers had declined to 2,322.[3] Indications are that the number of livestock auctions has declined somewhat since 1955. In the north central states, for example, the number of livestock auctions dropped from an estimated 1,035 in 1956 to 899 in 1964.[4]

### Grain Marketing

A somewhat similar change has taken place in grain marketing, as a smaller proportion of the grain sold passes through

---

[1] *Packers and Stockyards Resume*, USDA, Packers and Stockyards Administration, Vol. 7, No. 13, Dec., 1969.

[2] *Ibid.*

[3] V. B. Phillips and G. Engelman, *Market Outlets for Livestock Products*, USDA, Marketing Res. Rept. 216, Mar., 1958, pp. 5, 7, 8.

[4] *Organization and Competition in the Livestock and Meat Industry*, National Commission on Food Marketing, Tech. Study 1, June, 1966, p. 129.

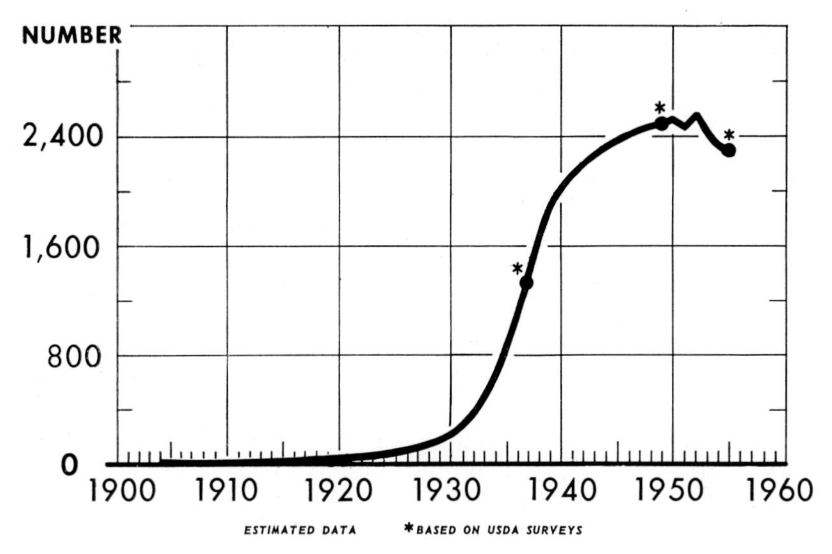


FIG. 7.2—Estimated growth curve of the number of livestock auctions in operation in the United States, 1900–55.

large terminal markets. A major development has been the growth of subterminal elevators which combine the functions of the country elevator and the terminal. Usually the subterminals are substantially larger than the typical country elevator and receive grain either directly from farmers or from smaller elevators. While local country elevators continue to be the largest single primary market for off-farm sales of grain, the number of such elevators has declined and more grain is moving directly to subterminal points. From there it is sold to terminal elevators, to processors, or to exporters.

### Poultry and Egg Marketing

In poultry and eggs, there has been a major shift to more decentralized channels of marketing. Increased demand for high-quality products; rising processing and handling costs at central markets; larger and more specialized production units; and a shift in the location of egg-grading and cartoning operations to chain stores, assembler-shippers, and producer-shippers have been important factors in the change.

The marketing channel for many eggs consists of farm pick-up by an assembler-shipper who ships in truckload lots to wholesale distributors, who in turn sell to retailers. Other eggs are shipped directly from large producer-distributors to wholesale distributors and then to retailers. An increasing volume of eggs moves directly from assembler-shippers or producer-distributors to retail chains or other retailers. Egg prices typically are based on wholesale levels in New York, Chicago, Boston, or Los Angeles, with local prices adjusted from this base to reflect transportation cost, quality, and handling costs.

In the case of broilers and turkeys, much of the volume goes directly from processing plants to retailers, bypassing wholesale distributors. However, prices in major terminal markets for ready-to-cook poultry are often the base for determining prices at processing centers in producing areas.[5]

### Wholesaling-Retailing Changes

The process of decentralization in farm product marketing has been accelerated by the growth of corporate and voluntary food chains as the predominant outlet for retail distribution. Through centralized large-volume buying to meet the needs of many stores, it has become feasible and more economical to bypass the wholesale distributor at the terminal market or other location in many cases. This has been true for fruits and vegetables, poultry products, and meats, although the extent to which distribution channels have been shortened varies somewhat. In fruit and vegetable marketing, it is reflected in movement of produce directly from shipping points to chain warehouses. Movement of poultry and eggs directly from both assemblers and producers to retailers has become common. In the meat industry, aided also by federal grades or other specifications that facilitate purchase without personal inspection, much of the product moves directly from packing plants to retail chains.

In this process of decentralization, producers or assemblers have taken over some of the marketing functions, such as grading or packaging, that were done previously at the wholesale market. Other wholesaling functions have been assumed by the retailer at the other end of the system. This shortening of marketing channels improves marketing efficiency and results in some reduction in marketing costs as well. Products shipped direct from country points or processing plants to the chain warehouse do not incur all of the handling and commission costs that exist when products move through a separate wholesaler. However, the savings are likely to be less than the margins of the separate wholesaler or jobber, since shippers and retailers may incur some added costs in picking up these middleman's functions.

---

[5] *Agricultural Markets in Change,* USDA, Agr. Econ. Rept. 95, July, 1966.

In another context, it used to be true that the great wholesale reservoirs performed an indispensable equalizing process. But nowadays the major part of the stream of agricultural commerce bypasses those reservoirs; it flows more directly from producer to consumer. Numerous smaller reservoirs upstream from the central reservoir now take care of most of the floods, and in so doing reduce the size of the job. Less concentration and dispersion are needed, for much of the water is dispersed before it ever reaches the central reservoir; the traditional central market structure is giving way to the decentralized market structure of modern times.

## PRICE MAKING IN THE DECENTRALIZED MARKET SYSTEM

The evolution of the price-making process appears in perspective as a gradual process of reducing the time and energy spent or wasted in price determination and of increasing the accuracy of the prices.

It is obvious that a great amount of time and energy was wasted in "higgling and bargaining" in the primitive markets of early times. Even now in a primitive eastern market a buyer and seller may spend hours bickering over a price that in modern markets would be struck in an instant.

In the more modern central market, the waste of time is reduced. The job is concentrated into a few expert hands, and central market prices and receipts information is readily available. But central markets are handicapped by the high cost of the transportation and handling associated with the tremendous physical concentration of the goods in small congested areas. Less energy is spent in price determination, but more is spent in the concentrating of the physical goods.

In the modern decentralized market, the costs of transportation and handling are less because the degree of physical concentration of the goods is less. But until the advent of radio, the cost of the "higgling and bargaining" (by telephone) was high; or, if slower methods of communication were used, the effectiveness of the process was impaired. The radio, however, permits broadcast of market information to producers at no cost to themselves (other than the cost of the receiving set, which they buy partly for entertainment anyway) and thereby reduces the cost of the trading considerably. It also reduces the necessity for "higgling and bargaining" because the market information is broadcast in considerable detail; and the more comprehensive the market news is, the less need there is for argument about the price of particular lots.

In the most highly developed type of decentralized market, the waste of energy in trading is still further reduced. The commodity is graded and standardized so that the price-making process for each lot of goods is reduced more or less completely to a grade-determining process. The more objective these grades are, the more this process of grade determination is expedited. Perhaps the most expeditious method of all is to place the grading process in the hands of an impartial third party, such as a government grader. There is then only one part of the whole trading process left to be argued about. That part is the determination of the price for the commodity in general, that is, "today's price" for hogs, or corn, or whatever the commodity is. And if this is posted publicly at the market place, there is not much room for argument left; the seller simply brings his product in or takes it somewhere else.

### The Price Committee System

The final step in the elimination of wasted energy is the price committee system.

When a price committee system is put into effect, the determination of the price of the commodity is taken out of the hands of the individual traders altogether. It is turned over to a central committee which determines not what prices are being paid by dealers, but what prices dealers must pay.

When a price-determining committee is set up, no change takes place in the structure of the market, but the machinery for price determination is changed. Prices are set not by the unregulated forces of supply and demand operating through the interplay of hundreds of buyers and sellers all over the market, but by a single committee, representing the buyers and sellers, brought together in one room.

The committees in some cases merely set a price for the coming week which will in their judgment clear the market. In those cases the price is the same as the unregulated supply and demand price, but with the small day-to-day fluctuations taken out. In other cases, the committee goes further. It controls the supply by various means—sliding-scale tariffs, production regulations quotas, and the like—as in the case of the Norwegian government grain monopoly. In some of the British marketing schemes, the committee sets the price at some other level than the unregulated supply and demand price. The price committee system then results in what may be called "negotiated prices."

In the United States, the price committee system has found its greatest expression in the field of milk marketing, where it functions much as it does in Europe. The committee exerts some influence on supply by setting up inspection provisions, quotas, and the like. The price committee system is also being used in California with various specialty crops.

The price committee system is a great saver of time and energy. It removes the last source of "higgling and bargaining" in the market place—the determination of today's price for the commodity. The committee does not eliminate this determination, but merely removes it from hundreds of scattered points in the decentralized market to one focal point, eliminating the hundreds of inexpert, unequal combats all over the decentralized market territory and concentrating them in a few expert hands. In the cases where it is practicable, the price committee system reduces to an absolute minimum the amount of gasoline, telegrams, telephone calls, and argumentation that otherwise would be spent in the price-making process. Instead of hundreds of buyers and sellers driving or telephoning and telegraphing here and there (each trying to outsmart the other and to buy cheap or to sell dear) half a dozen men meet in a committee room once a week and the job is done.

This price committee system is well suited to hogs (actually, to hog carcasses) in Denmark. The marketing system is decentralized, but the area is comparatively small and homogeneous, the product is standardized, and most of it moves to one outlet (the British export market). These conditions are favorable to the price committee system. Where wide areas are involved, as in the United States with regional variations in local supplies from year to year and place differentials that are continually changing, the system would be more difficult to administer. The job would be still more complicated if grade differentials fluctuated irregularly. In addition, the price committee requires adequate safeguards to keep it from being misused. It should not be a quotations committee of dealers, for such a committee may misrepresent prices, but it should be an impartial, quasipublic body with the public adequately represented.

The open competitive system may not be able to do a satisfactory job of price determination in some of our decentralized agricultural markets; a price committee system, made flexible enough to fit the needs of the decentralized markets and adequately safeguarded against abuse, may be required. In the case of some crops and products, some progress has in fact been made along these lines as an incidental feature of the commodity loans and price floors instituted by the USDA. Some of these loan rates for durable products originally were geographically flat (that is, they were uniform all over the country) and the commodities piled up in storage mostly in the normally low-price areas. Later, the rates were changed to conform to normal geographical differentials. Grade differentials were also introduced. Local surpluses or shortages resulting from these fixed differentials (fixed throughout the season) were handled by local storage and unstorage operations.

In the case of price floors for perishable products that cannot be stored, however, more flexible area and grade differentials are needed. The geographical and grade differentials need to be changed frequently as local changes in supply and demand take place, for these changes cannot be taken care of by storage operations. This problem still awaits solution.

# 8

# PRODUCTION AND MARKETING INFORMATION REQUIRED

THE PRECEDING CHAPTERS have outlined the physical and economic supply and demand environment in which farmers have to plan each year what and how much to produce. The situation can be summarized in a few sentences. The need for farm products is stable, but the demand is highly unstable, varying from year to year in a manner that is difficult to predict accurately very far ahead of time. The supply of most farm products fluctuates from year to year, partly on account of unpredictable fluctuations in yields due to weather, and partly because of variations in crop acreages. Each farmer can determine how much he will plant, but he can only guess how much others will plant and has no way of knowing how much the weather will affect yields nor what the total production will be when the crop is all in.

The fluctuating demand for farm products, therefore, is met by a fluctuating supply. The marketing system attempts to correlate the two as best it can, by storage from times of surplus to times of scarcity and by frequent and sometimes violent fluctuations in prices.

A farmer in this environment has a difficult job. He is like a man with imperfect eyesight shooting with an inaccurate rifle through a fog at an erratically jumping jackrabbit. It is obviously difficult or impossible for any one farmer alone to gather the current national and world economic information that he needs each year to enable him to produce what the market will want by the time his products are ready for sale. About the best that any one farmer could do would be to plan his next year's production according to this year's prices. This would not be much better than forecasting tomorrow's weather to be the same as today's. A central agency, the Weather Bureau, is needed to forecast the weather on the basis of information from all over the country and several miles up in the sky. A similar central agency is needed to gather and interpret economic market information for farmers.

Accordingly, the USDA has been providing the two types of current information required: (1) basic supply and demand information that will help farmers lay their production plans each year and (2) month-to-month and day-to-day market reports that will help them market their products after they are produced.

## DEVELOPMENT OF "OUTLOOK" INFORMATION

The depression in the early 1920's convinced many leaders, both inside and outside agriculture, that some means must be found for planning the production and marketing of farm products on a more intelligent basis. They believed that economic research should be used more and more as a guide to future developments.

Beginning in 1922, the USDA moved beyond the old boundary which had confined it to developing improved techniques of production only. It began to gather and disseminate economic information which would enable individual farmers to make changes in their acreages of crops and production of livestock in the light of prospective domestic and foreign demands. It also worked out methods for obtaining information from farmers about their production plans—how much of each crop or product they intended to produce.

When the Bureau of Agricultural Economics (BAE) was set up in 1922, the attempt was made to get the results of economic research out to farmers in such form as to serve as a useful guide to their production and marketing the following year. As one of its first steps along this line, the BAE issued reports on farmers' "intentions to plant" for a number of different crops.

The suggestion was made that this information would be more useful to farmers if it were interpreted in the light of the general economic conditions expected during the coming year. A group of nationally known economists and statisticians from outside the USDA were called together to analyze the "intentions" report and show farmers whether or not these intentions were in line with prospective demand. The first "Outlook" conference of this character was held in April, 1923. Another similar meeting was called in July to comment on the special pig survey in June and on the July estimates of the wheat crop.

The second "Outlook" report in 1924 was so well received that the outlook work was organized thereafter on a permanent basis. The work has been expanded steadily since that time, in the extent of the research on which it is based and in the wide dissemination of the results through regional and state meetings. Today, nearly all states conduct agricultural outlook programs, including the adaptation of national agricultural outlook information to fit local conditions.

As the outlook work progressed, it developed into a spring program in which the emphasis was placed on production plans and a fall program in which major attention was given to marketing. This, in turn, gave way to a year-round service. Separate reports for about a dozen different commodities were developed and issued monthly in mimeographed form.

These reports, now in printed form, have become a permanent feature of USDA informational work, although most of them are no longer issued every month. They include *The Livestock and Meat Situation,* issued six times a year; also, *The Feed Situation, The Fats and Oils Situation, The Poultry and Egg Situation, The Dairy Situation,* and *The Cotton Situation,* all issued five times a year; others include *The Fruit Situation, The Vegetable Situation, The Wheat Situation, The Wool Situation, The Demand and Price Situation, The Farm Income Situation, The Marketing and Transportation Situation,* and *The National Food Situation,* all published four times a year. In addition, *The Tobacco Situation* is published three times a year, *Farm Real Estate Market Developments* twice a year, and *The Agricultural Finance Outlook, The Farm Cost Situation* and *The World Agricultural Situation* each once per year. These reports may be obtained free of charge upon request from the Division of Information, Office of Management Services, USDA, Washington, D.C. 20250.

In addition to these outlook and situation reports, the Statistical Reporting Service of the USDA releases a large number of reports containing estimates of crop and livestock production, inventory, and stocks. These include monthly crop reports of field crops during the growing season, quarterly grain stocks reports, quarterly reports on sow farrowings and pig crop, quarterly (and for some states monthly) reports on the number of cattle on grain feed, calf and lamb crop reports, January 1 estimates of livestock and poultry numbers, and many others. A listing of these reports is given in a USDA pamphlet published annually, *Periodic Reports of Agricultural Economics,* available from the Statistical Reporting Service, USDA, Washington, D.C. 20250.

With the passage of time, the "Outlook" conferences, both in Washington and in the state and county meetings, have been held more frequently throughout the year and have been incorporated into a wide variety of farm meetings. "Outlook" information thus has become less of an annual affair and is available more continuously for use by farmers on a year-round basis.

The agricultural colleges also publish outlook reports on the products that are important in their states. *Economic and Marketing Information for Indiana Farmers,* printed monthly by Purdue University, contains many articles that are "outlook" in character. The same publication also regularly carries brief outlook statements on a variety of products. *Economic Information for Ohio Farmers,* issued by Ohio State University, and *The Oklahoma Agricultural Outlook and Market Analysis,* published by Oklahoma State University, are other examples. *Iowa Farm Science,* published monthly by Iowa State University, regularly contains two pages of "Farm Outlook." Other states, too numerous to mention, publish similar reports.

A few of the universities publish weekly or biweekly outlook or market analysis reports. Examples include the *Illinois Farmers' Outlook Letter,* published weekly by the University of Illinois, and *Iowa Farm Outlook,* issued twice a month by Iowa State University.

The early annual outlook forecasts made by the USDA had a rather good record. A study of the first six annual outlook reports credited them with 84 to 94 per cent accuracy. A later study reached similar conclusions, crediting the USDA outlook forecasts over a 30-year period with an accuracy of 75 per cent.

When we recall all the jokes made at the expense of the weather man, in spite of the high accuracy of his forecasts, it is not surprising that price forecasting of equal or less accuracy has come in for its share of ribbing.

#### Statistical Bases of Forecasts

In recent years more adequate statistics have been developed. Economic forecasting has become less of an art and more of a science.

The annual "Outlook" forecast for agriculture, prepared by the USDA in October or November each year, is formulated in three stages: (1) a forecast of the general level of economic activity in the United States, together with a forecast of the level of foreign demand for goods and services from this country; (2) a translation of this forecast into its meaning for agriculture as a whole, that is, in terms of the anticipated general level of agricultural prices and of farm income; and (3) a more detailed forecast of the impact of the general level of demand for agricultural products and estimated supplies on the prices to be received or the income to be obtained from the sale of individual crops and livestock products.[1]

The first stage is based on estimates of demand from four broad areas of spending: (1) consumer expenditures; (2) private investment in business facilities, equipment, and inventories and in residential housing; (3) government (state, local, and federal) purchases of goods and services; and (4) net foreign exports.

These estimates provide the basis for estimating consumers' disposable income, which exerts an important influence on the demand for farm products and therefore upon farm product prices. The next step is to estimate foreign demand. The outlook for the various individual farm products is then developed, reflecting total demand conditions and the supply situation for each product.

### Selling What Has Been Produced

After farmers have made their decisions as to what to produce and the products are ready for market, the problem remains of selling them at the time, in the place, and in the form that will bring in the highest net returns.

The durable staples, for example cotton, wheat, corn, etc., can be sold early or late in the season, or for that matter held over for later seasons. A certain amount of flexibility is possible in the timing of livestock sales; livestock can be fed for longer or shorter periods (to heavy or light weights). In addition, some latitude in market selection—selection of the place of sale—is possible for many products. And there is some flexibility in the form in which products can be sold.

The buyers of farm products usually represent large firms—millers, meat packers, etc. These firms usually cover a good deal of territory. Through their buyers and salesmen at numerous points they can keep themselves posted on market conditions all over the country. Some of these firms carry on a good deal of market research; Swift's Agricultural Research Department and Wilson's Livestock Service are two examples.

The individual farmer is obviously too small to provide out

[1] For greater detail, see G. Shepherd, *Agricultural Price Analysis*, Iowa State Univ. Press, Ames, 1968, Chap. 2.

of his own pocket the market information possessed by the buyers of farm products. The federal government, therefore, has undertaken to provide farmers not only with the broad annual and monthly production and demand information that will help farmers plan their production, as described above, but also with current week-to-week and day-to-day market reports that will help them market the goods that they produce.

## FEDERAL MARKET NEWS

The federal market news service has grown to its present stature from a humble beginning in 1915, when the first report was issued on strawberries at Hammond, Louisiana. Today daily reports are issued by about 220 market news offices connected by leased wire and located in the major producing and distributing centers. The service covers the movement, market supplies, quality, and price trends and quotations on livestock, meats, wool, fruits, vegetables, dairy and poultry products, grain, hay, seeds, feedstuffs, cotton and cottonseed, tobacco, rice, honey, peanuts, and other products.[2]

Before the service was established and developed on a nation-wide scale, only a relatively few producers could get the market information they needed in time for it to be of practical value—if they could get it at all. And all too frequently the information that did reach them was colored to the advantage of unscrupulous persons who were seeking to profit by it.

Procuring the information which goes into these market reports is a complex job. Reporters on the markets and in producing areas interview buyers and sellers during trading hours and also inspect records made available by these trade interests. They observe actual transactions and make an appraisal of the quality, grade, or condition of the commodities, since these are important factors in determining whether the established prices are actually higher, lower, or unchanged from previous trading sessions. Such appraisals can be made because the reporters are commodity specialists. Reports on shipments from producing centers and arrivals at terminal markets are received from railroads and boat lines. Reports of truck unloadings at certain large cities, and warehousemen's reports of stocks in storage also are collected. Numerous contacts with other groups are made for essential news.

With the increased movement of farm products from producing areas directly to processors or retailers, market news from major terminal or wholesale markets alone is no longer

[2] For details, see *Federal-State Market News Report*, USDA, C&MS-21, 1966.

adequate. To keep pace with these changes, market news is now reported in many major producing areas of the country for livestock, dairy and poultry products, fruits and vegetables, and grains. This expansion in market news reporting in decentralized markets will probably continue.

### Cotton

Daily cotton price quotations cover the principal cotton markets. Weekly reviews of cotton market conditions are released from Atlanta, Memphis, Dallas, and Phoenix. The various reports are distributed directly by mail and indirectly through the press. The radio also is used extensively to keep farmers and others currently informed of changes occurring on the major cotton markets.

Market news work and cotton classification (grading) are closely coordinated. Weekly reports on cotton quality are issued during the harvest season, covering the major producing areas. Special arrangements have been made to help farmers obtain local market prices through representatives selected by organized producer groups. This service for farmers, when coupled with official cotton classification, strengthens their bargaining power. It encourages the production of better quality cotton and improves the efficiency of the cotton-marketing system generally.

Reports from Atlanta, Memphis, Dallas, and Phoenix also show prices and grades of cottonseed sold in the various areas.

### Dairy and Poultry Products

Market information about poultry products includes market receipts, deliveries to breakers, cold-storage movements and stocks, movements into retail channels, and prices in producing areas at processing and shipping points and at major wholesale markets. Most of the price information on broilers is on a ready-to-cook basis, reflecting the high proportion of the supply that is produced under contract with processors or feed suppliers. Turkey prices are reported on both a live and a ready-to-cook basis in various markets.

In addition to data on terminal market receipts, information is also collected and distributed on receipts at country points in different areas where eggs and poultry are assembled or processed. These data show supplies available for trading and to some extent indicate current production, particularly in the case of eggs.

The quantities of dairy and poultry products arriving at a particular market may be used for local consumption, storage, or shipment to other markets. Therefore, information on receipts alone does not give a complete picture of the supply of the various items currently moving into consumption. Accordingly, information on movements into retail channels is compiled from reports received from representative groups of retail distributors. Since retail distributors carry stocks for short periods, this information closely measures the rate at which these products move into consumption. Daily and weekly reports of cold-storage stocks in selected markets provide a basis for estimating total U.S. stocks.

In the past, wholesale prices in the terminal markets were the chief basis for butter and cheese market reports. Owing to changes in marketing practices—such as the increase in direct marketing (especially to retail distributors by cooperative associations), direct buying in the country by large retail distributors, and mergers of the markets resulting from large-scale organization—the volume of business through wholesale channels has declined sharply. Accordingly, the methods of reporting the dairy produce markets have been adapted to these changing practices. The emphasis in some markets has been shifted from the reporting of wholesale selling prices to the reporting of prices received in processing areas.

### Fruits and Vegetables

The market news service on fruits and vegetables makes extensive use of the USDA's teletype circuits, which link the major terminal markets of the country as well as many of the major producing areas. This provides a rapid interchange of information on available supplies, demand, movement, and prices.

Reports showing daily carlot shipments, rail and truck receipts, market trends, and prices in the terminal markets as well as in major producing areas are compiled and disseminated by the market news offices in both terminal markets and shipping areas. The information is distributed by mail, wire, telephone, press, and radio to growers, shippers, railroads, truckers, and receivers. It is also made available to every segment of the distributive trade and to governmental, educational, and research institutions.

At some markets special broadcasts, made by the market newsmen early each morning, provide growers and shippers with a summary of market activities and trading to that time. In some other offices market news is broadcast later in the day. At several markets special broadcasts are made which include information of interest to consumers. Permanent offices are maintained in 42 of the major receiving markets and shipping points, with seasonal offices operating from 1 to 8 months in about 26 other producing areas.

Weekly reports on peanuts and a monthly honey report are issued from Washington. Altogether, approximately 10 million daily reports are mailed each year to about 60,000 growers, shippers, wholesalers, and others.

In a number of states cooperative agreements in which the states pay a part of the cost of the service permit a broader service than could be maintained with federal funds alone.

### Grain, Feed, and Hay

Market news on grain is reported by the USDA's market news service at the principal markets, in most cases on a weekly basis. Price information is also obtained at country elevator points in several states. In addition to price information, weekly reviews of the grain market provide information on the underlying factors that determine crop prices, including foreign market conditions.

Among the principal grain reports are those from Minneapolis on rye, barley, flaxseed, oats, corn, soybeans, and wheat; from Chicago on wheat, corn, soybeans, barley, and oats; from Kansas City, Mo. on corn, winter wheat, oats, grain sorghums, soybeans, and barley; from Los Angeles on grain sorghums and barley; and from Portland, Oreg., on wheat and barley. A weekly summary of all grain market information and statistics is released by the USDA from Independence, Mo.

Although not a part of the USDA's market news service, daily price information is available to farmers and others from such major grain exchanges as those in Chicago, Minneapolis, and Kansas City. Most newspapers include cash-grain and futures quotations regularly on their market pages and many radio stations broadcast futures quotations each day.

Market reports on feed ingredients are available to feeders and others from several markets. These reports include prices of all by-product feeds, information about their supply and distribution, and the areas of greatest demand. Commercial correspondents and federal field offices furnish information on the prices of such by-product feeds as wheat-mill feeds, cottonseed meal, soybean meal, meat meal, fish meal, and dehydrated alfalfa meal. In addition to reports from Chicago, Minneapolis, Kansas City, Los Angeles, and other locations, a weekly summary of feed market news for all major markets is released from Hyattsville, Md.

The market news service on hay is especially important to

producers and shippers. Hay market information is collected and disseminated from Kansas City, Mo., and several points in California, including El Centro, Los Angeles, Fresno, and Sacramento. In southern California news on hay is reported daily.

### Livestock, Meats, and Wool

Daily livestock market news includes information on supply, price trends, demand conditions, detailed quotations on the day's sales, and the estimated receipts for the following day.

The market news day in livestock begins about 6 A.M. At this hour the market news office at each major livestock terminal assembles a report on livestock receipts or the salable supply. This is exchanged by direct wire so that within a few minutes each major market knows the estimated supply situation at all markets.

Shortly after 8 A.M. the market news reporters at terminal markets start their rounds to interview buyers, shippers, and commission men. Reporters covering such decentralized markets as the interior Iowa-southern Minnesota area also begin to make telephone contacts with packers, shippers, and others. Between 8 A.M. and 9:30 A.M. the first price report—the opening or flash—is issued. This gives the tone of the market—weak, strong, or steady—and quotations on any early sales. The first opening report is usually on hogs, with flashes on the cattle and sheep markets released somewhat later.

Sometime between 9:30 A.M. and 11 A.M. the "51" or midmorning report is issued, including information on market activity, price trends, and price quotations. Next comes the advance estimates of supplies for the following day. Finally, a closing report is issued between 11 A.M. and 2 P.M.

Not every one of the livestock market news offices follows exactly this pattern. The services provided are designed to meet local market needs and methods of operations, and yet to be sufficiently uniform to be usable and understandable in all livestock-producing and marketing centers.

Market news on livestock is now collected and disseminated from about 30 public markets, and from several large producing areas such as Iowa, where direct trading is especially important and has considerable influence on price trends.

### Dissemination of Market News

Market information collected at any one market or market area is made available to the public by means of radio, the press, television, telephone, mail, and bulletin board. It is also distributed widely over leased and commercial telegraph wires to all important trading centers, through trade and farm publications, commercial and financial institutions, and other agencies. The leased wire and radio system of the market news service is shown in Figure 8.1.

Daily market reports, issued by market news offices, are mailed to a large number of farmers, buyers, and other commercial interests. This service is available on request from many markets without cost. Most newspapers—particularly in farming areas—carry market news as a regular feature. A disadvantage of these methods of market news dissemination is that the information is ordinarily a day or more late. On the other hand, considerable detail can be included; and these reports provide a good way to keep in general touch with market developments.

Farmers and others need more current means of getting market information, however, if it is to be of much value in day-to-day marketing and buying decisions. Radio is one of the most important ways of disseminating and receiving market news quickly. In 1960, the number of radio stations carrying market news reports in the United States was nearly 1,600. This was about 45 per cent of the radio stations in the country. A number of stations supply facilities that enable the reporters to broadcast directly from the market. Some of these stations provide three to five scheduled broadcasts a day.

A study of farm market news dissemination in Iowa provides another indication of the importance of radio in getting market information to farmers. Ninety-six per cent of the farmers surveyed listed the radio as a source of farm market news; and 66 per cent said it was the most frequently used source of farm market news.[3] These and other results of the study are shown in Tables 8.1 and 8.2.

Television has also become an important means of disseminating farm market news. In 1960 farm market information was carried by 169 television stations in the country, about half of the total number. In the market news study cited earlier, over half of the farmers surveyed obtained some market information from television.

A development that is making market news still more readily available to farmers and others is the use of telephone recordings of current market information. Brief market reports are taped on telephone-answering equipment which can be called

[3] Joe M. Bohlen and George M. Beal, *Dissemination of Farm Market News and Its Importance in Decision-Making,* Iowa Agr. and Home Econ. Exp. Sta. Res. Bul. 553, July, 1967.

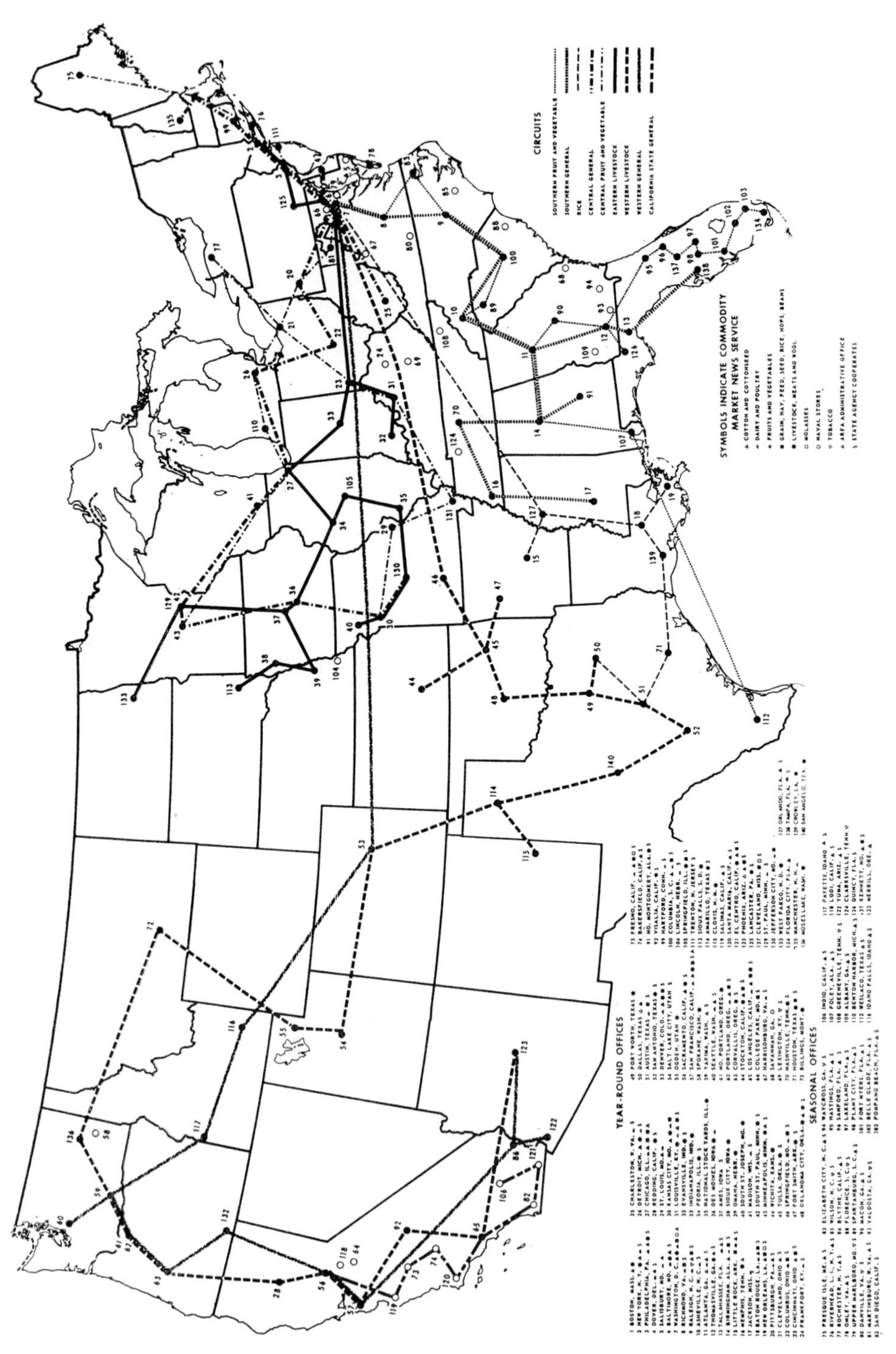

FIG. 8.1—Marketing news offices and Teletype system of the Consumer and Marketing Service, USDA, April, 1967.

**TABLE 8.1: Sources of Farm Market News**

| Source | No. Farmers | % of 147 |
|---|---|---|
| Radio | 141 | 95.9 |
| Newspaper | 86 | 58.5 |
| Television | 63 | 42.9 |
| Magazines and journals | 33 | 22.4 |
| Buyer (telephone buyer; buying station; livestock dealer; packer) | 27 | 18.4 |
| Commission man; commission firm | 9 | 6.1 |
| Commission report; producers' market sheet; feeders' report | 7 | 4.8 |
| Neighbor; hired man | 4 | 2.7 |
| Elevator | 2 | 1.4 |
| Trucker | 1 | 0.7 |
| Farm Bureau | 1 | 0.7 |

at any time of the day or night. The information may be updated several times a day, depending upon the particular kind of market, and can be obtained at any time by simply dialing the proper number.

Fruit and vegetable market news is available through these telephone-answering devices in several producing areas of Arizona, California, Texas, Idaho, and Florida. Similar service is available for livestock market news in Colorado and for dairy, poultry, and grain market news in several states. Market news specialists at Iowa State University provide current "code-a-phone" market news reports of three minutes each on grains, slaughter livestock, and feeder cattle, and these can be obtained at any time by telephone.

One way that the dissemination of market news to farmers and others could be made more effective would be to have a market news interpreter or analyst in each state or marketing area. This person could summarize the available market information and translate it into language that would tell farmers quickly what they want to know—without their reading or listening through several different reports from several different markets. The summary information could be disseminated to users by radio, television, or by telephone-answering equipment.

**TABLE 8.2: Perception of Various Sources of Farm Market Reports**

| Source | Use Most Frequently | Most Accurate | Most Timely | Most Understandable | Most Complete |
|---|---|---|---|---|---|
| Radio | 67.4 | 53.3 | 66.0 | 41.8 | 46.1 |
| Buyer | 14.8 | 29.6 | 14.8 | 40.7 | 14.8 |
| Television | 14.3 | 14.3 | 20.6 | 34.9 | 19.0 |
| Newspaper | 12.8 | 18.6 | 9.3 | 22.1 | 33.7 |
| Magazines and journals | 0.0 | 3.0 | 0.0 | 15.2 | 15.2 |

Greater localization in the dissemination of market reports is needed too. It is not sufficient merely to report the central market prices and leave each farmer to subtract a fixed differential from those markets to convert them into prices at his local market. The actual market price differentials between the central markets and the local markets fluctuate from day to day and from month to month. The only way to report local market prices to farmers is to gather and disseminate them on a local or small-area basis.

This is not an easy thing to do, for the number of local or small-area markets is large. The problem is discussed further at the end of Chapter 14.

# 9

# ELEMENTARY THEORY OF PRICES

PRICES PERFORM essential functions in an economic free-enterprise system. First of all, they tell producers what and how much to produce. High prices for beef during the early 1950's told ranchers and feeders to produce more beef cattle. They did. It takes several years to breed more cows and get more beef cattle on the market, and it takes several months more to stop them if the increase is too large. Ranchers and feeders marketed 18 per cent more cattle (pounds live weight) in 1953 than in 1952, and that big increase depressed the price of beef cattle 33 per cent. This slowed down and nearly stopped the increase in beef cattle production in its tracks. Again in 1963 and 1964, beef production increased more rapidly than beef demand. Cattle marketings increased by 13 per cent in the two-year period and prices declined by 15 per cent.

Over time, these movements of prices automatically keep supplies coming forward approximately in line with consumers' demands. They ration or allocate productive resources—acres of land, bushels of feed, tons of hay, manpower, machinery, and so forth—to the production of the goods and services that consumers demand.

Prices also perform an internal rationing and allocating function within each producing farm. The prices of the productive resources or factors of production mentioned above, subsumed in economists' language under the headings *land, labor, capital,* and *entrepreneurship,* tell farmers how to combine them in proportions that will keep their costs at a minimum and result in the most efficient production. This is the province of farm management.

After the goods and services desired by consumers are produced, prices guide them through the channels of trade so that they end up where consumers want them, when they want them, and in the form they want them. And finally, prices ration the goods and services to those who demand them most urgently and in proportions that will all be consumed.

In this automatic price system, every consumer and producer sits in on the price committee, as it were, and casts his dollar vote as to what should be produced and consumed and what prices are needed to do the job of allocating and rationing.

## AGRICULTURAL PRICES ARE VARIABLE

What are the mechanics of this price system?

In Chapter 3, dealing with the elementary theory of demand, we show that a change in demand is represented by a shift to the left or right in the position of the demand curve.

The effects of a change in demand upon prices and consumption depend upon the elasticity of the demand. They also depend upon the elasticity of the supply.

Figure 9.1 shows what happens in the short run when the size of the crop is fixed—that is, when the supply is absolutely inelastic and the supply curve is a vertical straight line. The 10 per cent increase in quantities shown for Period II in the lower part of Table 3.1 (p. 32) moves the demand curve 10 per cent to the right.

This 10 per cent shift to the right in the position of the demand curve causes the price to rise 20 per cent. Prices rise twice as much as the demand increases, much as an iceboat sailing across the wind can go faster than the speed of the wind. If the elasticity of the demand curve were 1.0, instead of 0.5, the price would have risen only 10 per cent.

The 20 per cent rise in price, however, resulted from the inelasticity of the supply as well as of the demand. If the supply were completely elastic, as represented by the horizontal line shown in the chart, then the price would not rise at all, no matter how inelastic the demand might be. All that would happen would be that the consumption would increase 10 per cent, the same as the increase in demand—much as an iceboat can only go as fast as the wind in the same direction as the wind, not any faster.

These two extremes, absolutely elastic supply and absolutely

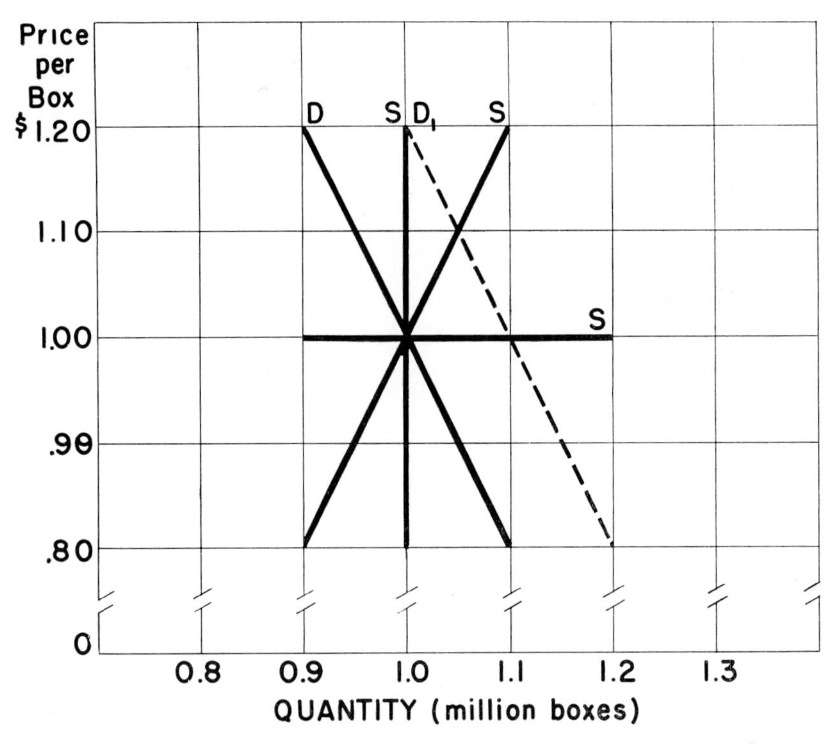


FIG. 9.1—Hypothetical demand and supply curves for strawberries.

inelastic supply, never exist in real life. Even with a fixed crop, farmers can always cull a little more or less and carry over a little less (or more in the case of durable crops) in response to different prices. And from year to year there is still more elasticity, since farmers then have time to plant more or fewer acres or to breed more or less stock.

Let us consider what the response of production to price might be in the case of a specific crop like strawberries.

If an increase in the price of strawberries of, for example, 10 per cent (10 cents a box) would induce strawberry producers to increase their production by less than 10 per cent, we would say that the supply was inelastic. If producers increased their production only 5 per cent, the elasticity of the supply, computed by the use of the same formula that was used for demand, would be

$$\frac{\text{Percentage increase in quantity}}{\text{Percentage increase in price}} = \frac{5}{10} = 0.5$$

Note that the sign of this coefficient is positive.

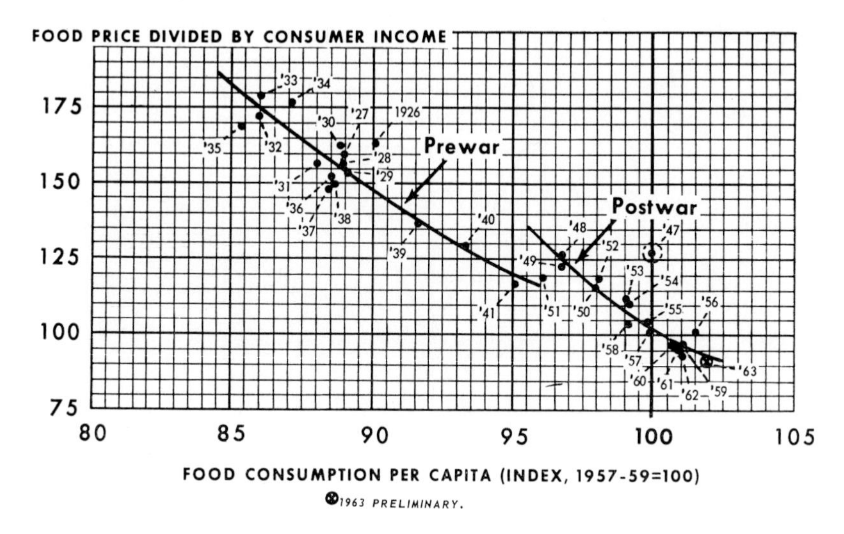


FIG. 9.2—Aggregate food demand curves, United States. (Source: Frederick V. Waugh, **Demand and Price Analysis,** USDA, Tech. Bul. 1316, 1964.)

With an elasticity of supply of 0.5, the price would rise from $1 to $1.10. The consumption would increase from 100 to 105 million boxes. If the supply curve were more elastic than this, the price would rise less, but the consumption would rise more.

For agricultural products as a whole, the demand is less elastic than for any one product. If only one, say pork, is scarce, consumers can substitute beef for pork to a considerable extent. The same is true of supply. Farmers can produce more soybeans and less oats, etc., in response to changes in their relative prices. But the demand for *food* is pretty inelastic; if food is scarce, consumers cannot substitute something else for food very easily, nor can farmers immediately produce much more or less food in response to rising or declining prices. Figure 9.2 shows demand curves for food, derived from empirical data, in the pre-World War II and postwar periods. They are highly inelastic.

## INELASTIC DEMAND AND SUPPLY

The elasticity of the demand for food in the prewar period shown in Figure 9.2 is about —0.27. That is, a change in price of 1 per cent is associated with an inverse change in consumption of only 0.27 per cent. In the postwar period, the relationship is even more inelastic, about —0.17.

Corresponding supply curves for all food are extremely inelastic. The elasticity of the supply of any one farm product (the responsiveness of the production of that product to changes in its price when the prices of other farm products remain unchanged) is considerably greater than the elasticity of the supply of farm products as a group. If the price of soybeans, for example, rises while the prices of other farm products remain unchanged, farmers will take some acres out of other crops and plant more soybeans. Soybean production will increase, perhaps more than proportionally to the increase in prices. That is, the supply curve for a single crop such as soybeans may be more elastic than unity.

The elasticities of the supply of some individual farm products have been estimated empirically, although this problem is made difficult by such things as changing technology and variations in weather conditions that affect production. At a particular time, the elasticity of supply varies with the rate at which farmers' costs rise as they increase the production of the crop.

Hogs are one of the products for which the supply elasticity has been estimated empirically. One study, based on data for 1949–60, estimated the average supply elasticity at 0.82.[1] This was derived from a regression equation that measured the relationship of the spring pig crop (December–May farrowings) to the prices received by farmers for hogs, corn, and beef cattle in the preceding October–December quarter and the annual production of oats, barley, and grain sorghum.

The hog-corn price ratio has also been used as an indicator of changes in hog production. In these computations, the average ratio of the United States average farm price of hogs to the price of corn (the hog-corn price ratio) during the breeding season (October–February) is plotted against the number of sows farrowing the following spring. In the pre-World War II period, this type of analysis indicated an equilibrium point in production when the hog-corn price ratio was around 12. Above 12, production increased while lower hog-corn price ratios resulted in decreased farrowings. More recent indications are that this relationship has changed as the cost structure in hog production has changed, and nonfeed costs have made up more of the total costs in hog production. From 1962 through 1967, farrowings increased only in periods following hog-corn ratios of 16.0 and above.

This is shown simply and clearly in Figure 9.3. In this

[1] Arthur A. Harlow, *Factors Affecting the Price and Supply of Hogs*, USDA, Tech. Bul. 1274, 1962.

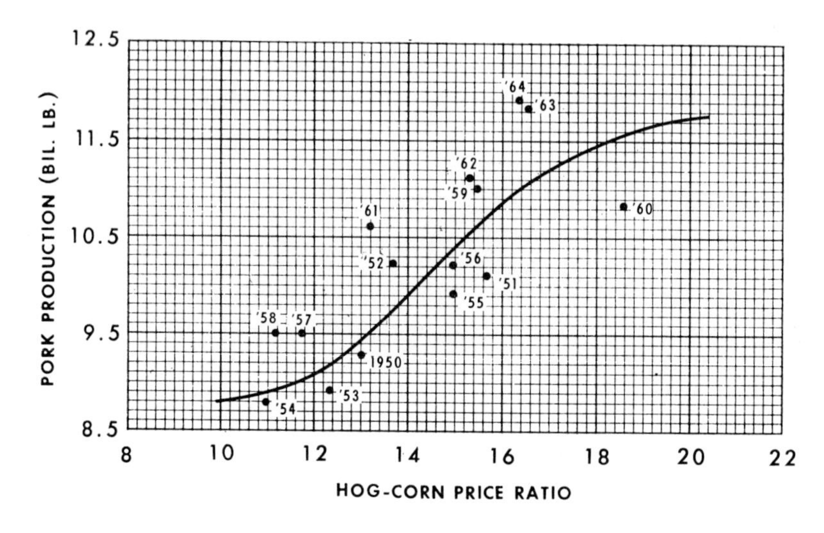


FIG. 9.3—Relation between the hog-corn ratio and pork production two years later. (Source: Frederick V. Waugh, **Graphic Analysis: Applications in Agricultural Economics,** USDA, Agr. Handbook 326, 1966, p. 35.)

chart, annual pork production is plotted against the hog-corn price ratio two years earlier. The chart also shows that the elasticity of supply in the central part of the curve was 0.7 for the 1953–64 period shown; this was a little lower than the elasticity of 0.82 shown for the earlier period 1949–60 in the Harlow study.

Note that in this chart production is plotted up and down the side rather than in the usual position along the bottom, for the good reason that the supply in this case is the dependent variable (the one we want to explain), whereas most charts showing the elasticity of demand and supply are designed to explain prices. Note also that in the case of Figure 9.3, the supply curve becomes less elastic in the high hog-corn price range; increased production then becomes more difficult.

A knowledge of relations of this sort is essential for the intelligent operation of government farm price programs. It is essential also for individual farm operation. It is evident that the effects of a change in demand on prices and consumption depend upon the elasticities of demand and supply. Since the elasticities of demand and supply in agriculture are both low, small changes in demand and supply cause violent changes in agricultural prices. Conversely, large changes in agricultural prices cause only small changes in agricultural production and consumption.

The response of agricultural prices to changes in demand and supply is not only violent but in the case of some commodities, it is cyclic because there is an inherent time lag in the response of production to a change in the price of the product. The reasons for this cyclic behavior and the nature of the cycles in two specific products, hogs and beef cattle, are examined in some detail in Chapter 10.

## EFFECTS OF CHANGES IN DISTRIBUTION COSTS

The foregoing discussion shows how prices are determined by the interaction of consumer demand and producer supply. For purposes of clarity, the marketing charges intervening between the producer and the consumer were not accounted for.

We saw earlier that these marketing charges are large, usually larger than the share of the consumer's dollar that gets back to the farmer. Our next step, then, will be to take these marketing charges into account. We will show how they intervene between producer and consumer and to what extent it is true that "Mrs. Consumer sets the price the farmer gets." We will also show whether changes in marketing charges are passed back to the producer or forward to the consumer.

It should be recognized from the first that this problem concerns not one market, but two different markets.[2] These are definitely related to each other, but they are two distinct markets with respect to place. The one is the producer's market, where the farmer sells the goods to the middleman; the other is the consumer's market, where the middleman sells the goods to the consumer.

The exposition will be clearer if made in terms of some specific commodity whose costs of distribution have increased. Beef cattle may be used as an illustration. No pure consumer's or producer's market for beef cattle exists, of course; but New York, the heaviest consuming state, can be used as a representative consumer's market.

We may assume that the shipping charges for beef cattle from Iowa to New York were roughly $1 per 100 pounds in

[2] The use of the term "market" here is restricted to the place or area aspect. Fundamentally, the two markets are one and the same market; the prices in one depend directly upon the prices in the other; the two markets are hooked up "in series," separated only by the transportation and handling charges required to bridge the distance between them. But it is precisely this separation by the amount of the transportation charges that is the object of this study.

Period I and increased to approximately $2 per 100 pounds in Period II. The average farm price of beef cattle in Iowa may be taken as $17 per 100 pounds in our example. To carry through the reasoning in the simplest terms, we shall assume that all of the beef cattle are produced in Iowa and all of them are consumed in New York.[3]

Each of these markets has its own pair of demand and supply schedules. The two pairs are similar; the series of quantities are the same at both markets. The only difference is that the prices in the New York schedules are all $1 per 100 pounds higher than those of the Iowa schedules. If a graph of the New York schedules were superimposed on a graph of the Iowa schedules, the New York curves would both lie $1 higher in the graph than the Iowa schedules; otherwise, the two pairs of curves are identical.

At each market only one schedule is a basic or primary schedule; the other is derived from the corresponding schedule at the other market. In the Iowa market, for example, the supply schedule is basic or primary. It is based directly upon the costs of raising different quantities of beef cattle in Iowa. It is not affected by changes in the cost of getting beef cattle to New York. Changes in this cost will affect the *demand* curve for beef cattle in Iowa, and the new demand curve will cut the Iowa supply curve at a lower point. The quantity of beef cattle demanded will change. The position of the *supply* curve at the Iowa market will not be affected, for it is based on the costs of producing different quantities of beef cattle in Iowa, and nothing has happened to change these costs.[4] But the demand schedule at the Iowa market is not a primary schedule. It is a derived schedule, derived from the demand schedule at New York simply by deducting the cost of moving beef cattle from Iowa to New York from the prices at New York. It is directly and fully affected by changes in the cost of transportation.

At New York, the demand schedule is basic or primary. It

[3] After the argument has been worked through on this basis, this assumption can be removed and the reasoning applied to the more complex situation actually existing in the United States, in which beef cattle are produced and consumed all over the country, with intervening distances ranging from nothing to more than a thousand miles between producer and consumer. This application would not change the essential nature of the reasoning here laid down.

[4] We are speaking here of supply curves, not cost curves. A supply curve is the locus of the intersection points of different quantities of beef cattle with the different marginal costs of producing them. It should be clearly distinguished from a cost curve, which simply shows the costs of different producers for a given total quantity at a given instant of time, not the different marginal costs of producing different total quantities. See Marshall, *Principles*, pp. 810–12.

**TABLE 9.1: Supply and Demand Schedules for Beef Cattle, Elasticities Equal (Hypothetical Data)**

*Iowa*

| Demand Schedule | | | Supply Schedule | |
|---|---|---|---|---|
| Prices* Period I | Quantities† | Prices Period II | Prices | Quantities |
| $19 | 15 | $18 | $15 | 15 |
| 18 | 16 | 17 | 16 | 16 |
| 17 | 17 | 16 | 17 | 17 |
| 16 | 18 | 15 | 18 | 18 |
| 15 | 19 | 14 | 19 | 19 |

*New York*

| Demand Schedule | | Supply Schedule | | |
|---|---|---|---|---|
| Prices | Quantities | Prices Period I | Quantities | Prices Period II |
| $20 | 15 | $16 | 15 | $17 |
| 19 | 16 | 17 | 16 | 18 |
| 18 | 17 | 18 | 17 | 19 |
| 17 | 18 | 19 | 18 | 20 |
| 16 | 19 | 20 | 19 | 21 |

* Prices in dollars per 100 pounds live weight.
† Quantities in billions of pounds.

is based directly upon the desires and purchasing power of the beef consumers located there. Changes in the cost of moving beef cattle from Iowa to New York do not affect the New York demand schedule because these changes do not affect the factors on which that schedule is based. But the New York *supply* schedule is not a primary schedule. It is derived from the basic Iowa supply schedule by adding the cost of getting beef cattle from Iowa to New York and is therefore directly affected by changes in that cost.

The schedules showing the situations in Periods I and II are shown in Table 9.1. The data are purely hypothetical. They are represented graphically in Figure 9.4.[5] Equilibrium for Period I is reached at a quantity of 17 billion pounds and a price of $17 per 100 pounds in Iowa and $18 in New York.

In Period II, shipping charges increased from $1 per 100 pounds to $2. This has no effect upon either of the two primary schedules—the supply schedule for beef cattle in Iowa and the

[5] These curves have slopes of −1 for the demand curves and +1 for the supply curves. The demand does not represent conditions of unit elasticity (except close to the center). Such curves would be concave from above on an arithmetic scale like the one used in the chart. But the actual demand curve for beef cattle has an elasticity of −0.68. (See G. E. Brandow, *Interrelations Among Demands for Farm Products and Implications for Control of Market Supply*, Coll. of Agr., Pa. State Univ., 1961, p. 59.)

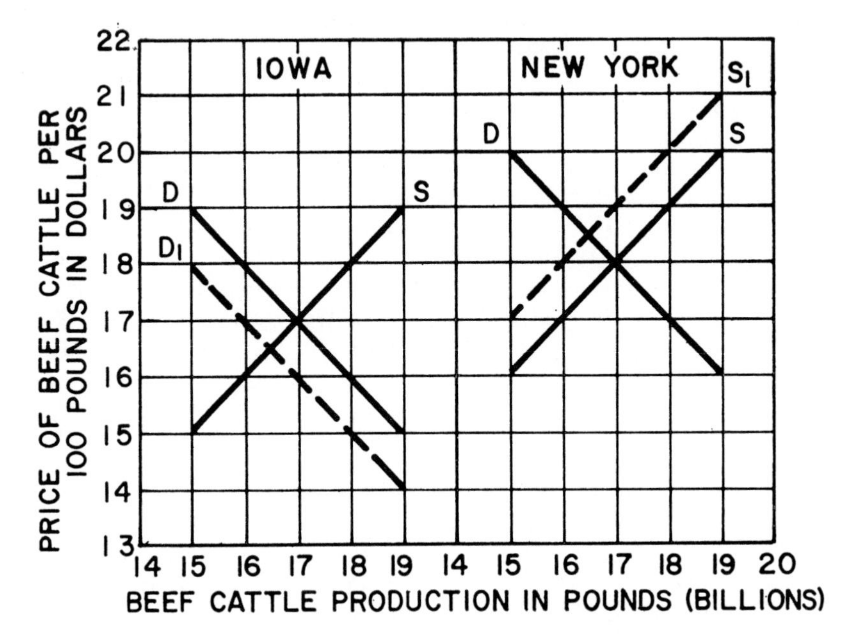


FIG. 9.4—Demand and supply curves for Iowa and New York.
D Period I demand curve — S Period I supply curve
$D_1$ Period II demand curve — $S_1$ Period II supply curve
Period I shipping charge, $1 per 100 lbs. Equilibrium reached at a production of 17 billion lbs., with a price of $17 in Iowa and $18 in New York.
Period II shipping charge, $2 per 100 lbs. Equilibrium reached at a production of 16.5 billion lbs., with a price of $16.50 in Iowa and $18.50 in New York.

demand for beef cattle in New York. The cost of raising different quantities of beef cattle remains the same in Iowa, the series of prices that consumers will pay for different quantities in New York are unchanged.

But the derived schedules are directly affected. The supply prices for beef cattle in New York go up by the full amount of the increased shipping charges. It now costs $1 per 100 pounds more to deliver beef cattle in New York than it did before the change was made. The new supply schedule for New York is shown in the third column of the New York supply schedule. The prices in it are all $1 higher than the prices in Period I.

A similar but opposite change has taken place in the demand for beef cattle in Iowa. Consumers at New York previously would pay $18 per 100 pounds when 17 billion pounds of beef were produced. This meant that they would pay $17 per 100 pounds—that is, $18 minus $1 shipping charge—in Iowa. But now shipping charges have gone up to $2 per 100 pounds; so $2 instead of $1 per 100 pounds is clipped from the New York price. New York consumers now pay only $16 per 100 pounds in Iowa for the same quantity for which they previously paid $17. Other quantities in the schedule react similarly. This is shown by the third column in the Iowa demand schedule.

If we plot these new demand and supply schedules for Iowa and for New York, we find that the equilibrium point on both markets is reached at a quantity of 16.5 billion pounds, with a price for that quantity of $16.50 per 100 pounds in Iowa and $18.50 per 100 pounds in New York. The burden of the increased middleman's charges has been divided equally between the producer and the consumer, and the production and consumption of beef have decreased from 17 to 16.5 billion pounds.

The reason that the burden was divided equally between the producer and the consumer is that the demand and supply curves both have the same elasticity, namely unity. The burden would have been just as equally divided if the elasticities of the supply and demand curves had been some other figure, but equilibrium would have been reached at a different quantity from

**TABLE 9.2: Supply and Demand Schedules for Beef Cattle, Elasticities Unequal (Hypothetical Data)**

*Iowa*

| Demand Schedule | | | Supply Schedule | |
|---|---|---|---|---|
| Prices* Period I | Quantities† | Prices Period II | Prices | Quantities |
| $21 | 15 | $20 | $15 | 15 |
| 19 | 16 | 18 | 16 | 16 |
| 17 | 17 | 16 | 17 | 17 |
| 15 | 18 | 14 | 18 | 18 |
| 13 | 19 | 12 | 19 | 19 |

*New York*

| Demand Schedule | | Supply Schedule | | |
|---|---|---|---|---|
| Prices | Quantities | Prices Period I | Quantities | Prices Period II |
| $22 | 15 | $16 | 15 | $17 |
| 20 | 16 | 17 | 16 | 18 |
| 18 | 17 | 18 | 17 | 19 |
| 16 | 18 | 19 | 18 | 20 |
| 14 | 19 | 20 | 19 | 21 |

* Prices in dollars per 100 pounds live weight.
† Quantities in billions of pounds.

that just worked out. With an elasticity of —.5 for the demand curve and +.5 for the supply curve, equilibrium would be reached at 16.75 instead of 16.5 billion pounds.

The case is different, however, when the elasticities of the demand and supply curves are unequal. Then the burden is unequally divided between the producer and consumer. This can be shown by replacing the demand schedule just employed with one of —.5 elasticity. Under these conditions, a reduction in quantity of 1 billion pounds causes a rise in price of $2 per 100 pounds instead of $1. This situation and the effects of an increase in shipping charges from $1 to $2, are shown in Table 9.2 and Figure 9.5.

This time the new equilibrium is reached not at 16.5 billion

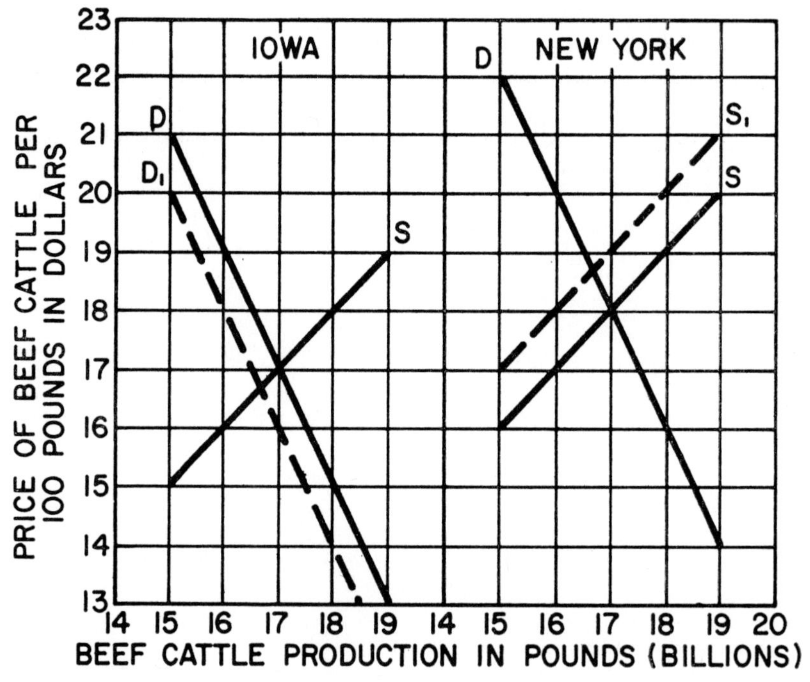


FIG. 9.5—Demand and supply curves for Iowa and New York—inelastic demand.

D Period I demand curve — S Period I supply curve

$D_1$ Period II demand curve — $S_1$ Period II supply curve

Period I shipping charge, $1 per 100 lbs. Equilibrium reached at a production of 17 billion lbs., with a price of $17 in Iowa and $18 in New York.

Period II shipping charge, $2 per 100 lbs. Equilibrium reached at a production of 16.66 billion lbs., with a price of $16.66 in Iowa and $18.66 in New York.

pounds but at 16.66 billion, and at a price of $16.66 in Iowa and $18.66 in New York, instead of $16.50 and $17.50, respectively. The production of beef cattle, therefore, has been reduced less than in the former case. More of the burden of the increased shipping charges is borne by the consumer and less by the producer.

## CONCLUSIONS

This chapter can be summarized in these words (the statement is put in terms of a decrease in middleman's margin; the effects of an increase in middleman's margins is the converse of this): A decrease in middleman's margins (1) increases production and consumption (by the same amounts, since what is produced is consumed, no more and no less), and (2) both lowers prices to consumers and raises prices to producers by amounts which added together equal the decrease in the middleman's margin. The division between the producer and consumer depends upon (is inversely proportional to) the relative elasticities of their supply and demand; the one with the more elastic curve gets the smaller share.

# 10

# CYCLIC MOVEMENTS IN AGRICULTURAL PRODUCTION AND PRICES

THE FIRST agricultural marketing problem is to determine as accurately as possible each year, before seeding or breeding time, what the demand, supply, and price for each product is likely to be by the time the product is ready for market.

If the demand, supply, or price of a product exhibits a strong periodic or cyclic movement, the job is easier. The cyclic movement can be projected with some assurance into the future, and the first step toward a forecast can be taken on that basis.

The production of most crops—wheat, cotton, corn, etc.—fluctuates markedly from year to year. These fluctuations are highly irregular; they are chiefly determined by the weather, which in the main is not cyclic in its changes. For anything more than a few days ahead the weather remains almost completely unpredictable. There seems to be no cyclic movement, at least no predictable cyclic movement, in crop yields.

The production and prices of the major kinds of livestock also fluctuate greatly from year to year, and there is a good deal of irregularity in these fluctuations too. But some of the prices also show, running through these irregular movements, a more or less marked cyclic movement, with each cycle extending over a period of several years. These movements are usually referred

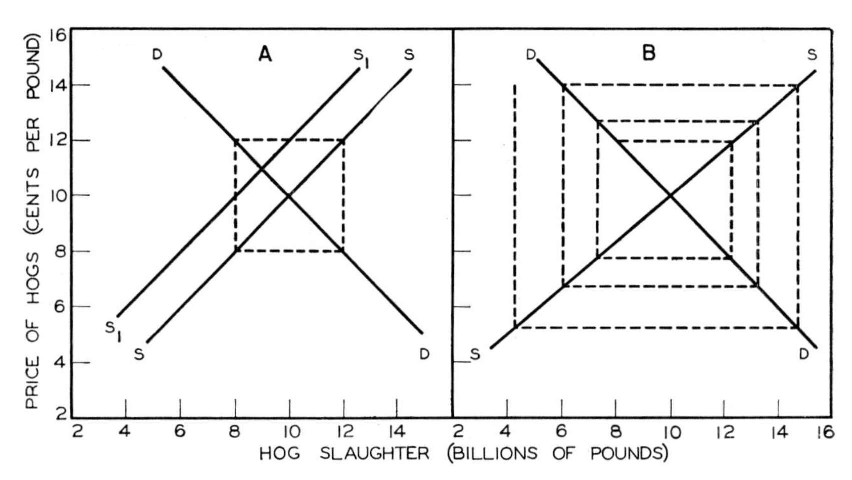


FIG. 10.1—Hypothetical demand and supply curves for hogs, illustrating the "cobweb theorem."

to as cycles, but this word is not exactly the right one. It implies a more fixed regular periodicity than the movements actually show. The word *oscillations* would convey the idea better. The term *cycles* is so firmly established in the literature of the subject, however, that we shall use it here, with the understanding that it refers to movements that are not rigorously periodic in character, but show some irregularity.

## THE "COBWEB THEOREM"

A generalized explanation of the inherent cyclic characteristics of the production system of some commodities has been given the name "cobweb theorem."[1]

The law of supply and demand explains how prices reach an equilibrium at the point of intersection of the demand and supply curves. The cobweb theorem explains how, in the case of some commodities, the price does not settle at this equilibrium point but fluctuates about it.

In the case of commodities where the amounts demanded and supplied can be instantly adjusted to the price, cycles do not occur. Thus, as in Figure 10.1A, the price would reach equilibrium at 10 cents per pound, with production and consumption at 10 billion pounds.

If the commodity were hogs and production and consump-

[1] M. J. B. Ezekiel, "The Cobweb Theorem," *Quarterly Journal of Economics,* Vol. 52, Feb., 1938, p. 255. This was the pioneering paper on this subject. For a later exposition, see A. A. Harlow, *Factors Affecting the Price and Supply of Hogs,* USDA, Tech. Bul. 1274, 1962, pp. 27–37.

tion responded to price instantly, a sudden drouth, reducing corn supplies, would affect hog production and prices in the manner shown by the new supply curve $S_1$ $S_1$ in Figure 10.1A. The drouth would reduce the supply of hogs by 2 billion pounds, let us say (i.e., it would reduce each amount in the supply schedule by 2 billion); and the price would rise toward 12 cents. But as prices rose, that would reduce consumption. If production and consumption adjustments could be made rapidly, the price could not rise above 11 cents because at any price above this more would be produced than could be sold, and the excess would pull prices down. The price would rise, therefore, only to 11 cents, the amount supplied would be 9 billion pounds, and at those figures a new equilibrium would be attained. The next year, if corn supplies returned to normal, the supply curve would return to its original position, as would price and production. There would be no cyclic movement of hog production and prices resulting from the initial short corn crop disturbance.

But actually it takes a year or two for hog production to change in response to prices in the manner shown by the curves in Figure 10.1A. In the simplest terms, the short-time (one year, let us say) supply curve for hogs is a vertical line. A drouth causing a reduction in the supply of hogs of 2 billion pounds (i.e., a shift in the vertical supply curve from 10 on the quantity axis to 8) would raise the price to 12 cents. Then, when corn supplies returned to normal the next year, farmers would look at the high 12-cent price and increase their hog production, not merely back to normal, but *above it,* for the 12-cent price cuts the supply curve at 12 billion pounds, not at 10 billion pounds.

Then what would happen? That large supply of hogs would reach the market the next year and depress the price to 8 cents, as Figure 10.1A shows (a quantity of 12 billion pounds cuts the demand curve at 8 cents). This low price would lead farmers to reduce their production of hogs the next year to 8 billion pounds; this would raise the price to 12 cents; they would increase production next year to 12 billion pounds, and so on.

The difference between this and the simple equilibrium case results fundamentally from the lag of one year between the price and adjustment of production to that price. Other contributing conditions are that farmers are influenced more heavily by current prices than by prospective prices, and each producer's production is so small an item in the total production of hogs that he ignores the effect of his own production on prices.

It can easily be shown that if the supply curve is more elastic than the demand curve, the cycles, instead of merely continuing, would get larger and larger. This is shown in Figure

10.1B; the "cobweb" appearance of this sort of chart is clear. Similarly, it can be shown that where the supply curve is less elastic than the demand curve, the cycles get smaller and smaller. The price fluctuations converge toward an equilibrium point, instead of diverging from it as in the previous case.

The lag in the case of hogs actually is about two years rather than one, resulting in a cycle that averages about four years in length. In the case of beef and dairy cattle, the lag is much greater than two years. It takes longer to get in and out of production or to change the level of production for cattle than for hogs.

This illustration shows how the law of supply and demand works out when there is a lag in production response, so that producers cannot respond instantly to changes in price, but do respond to present prices rather than to prospective prices when their supply will reach the market. The fundamental law is still at work in the same way as ever, but its results are overlaid by the results of an additional law working along with it, just as the retarding action of air upon a falling body will keep its rate of fall from accelerating beyond a certain point, or the upward thrust of air upon an airplane's wings offsets the downward pull of gravity; the law of gravity in these cases is not repealed, any more than the law of supply and demand is repealed in the case of price cycles.

## HOG PRICE AND PRODUCTION CYCLES

Figures 10.2 and 10.3 show that hog prices follow a fairly regular cyclic pattern, first going up for about two years, then down for about two years. (The prices shown in Figure 10.2 were each divided by the corresponding index of the general price level, in order to remove as much as possible the effects of changes in the general price level.) Sometimes it takes three years from one high to another, sometimes as long as five, or even six, but the general outline of a cycle averaging about four years in length has persisted through at least the past 50 years. Furthermore, the cycles are divided into alternate major and minor cycles. High peaks are usually followed by a lesser peak. The major cycles are four to six years long; the minor ones are three to four years long. The average of all of them is about four years. During the 55 years from 1890 to 1945 there were 14 hog price cycles; eight of them were major, and each was followed by a minor one. World War II interrupted the cyclic movement, but by 1950 it had reestablished itself. The cycles since 1958 are shown in a different way in Figure 10.3.

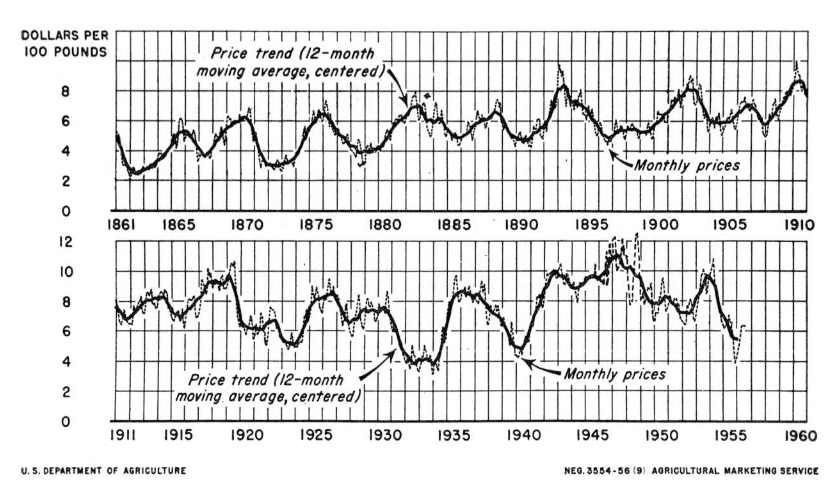


FIG. 10.2—Heavy hogs: prices at Chicago by months, 1861–1956 (adjusted to 1910–14 price level).

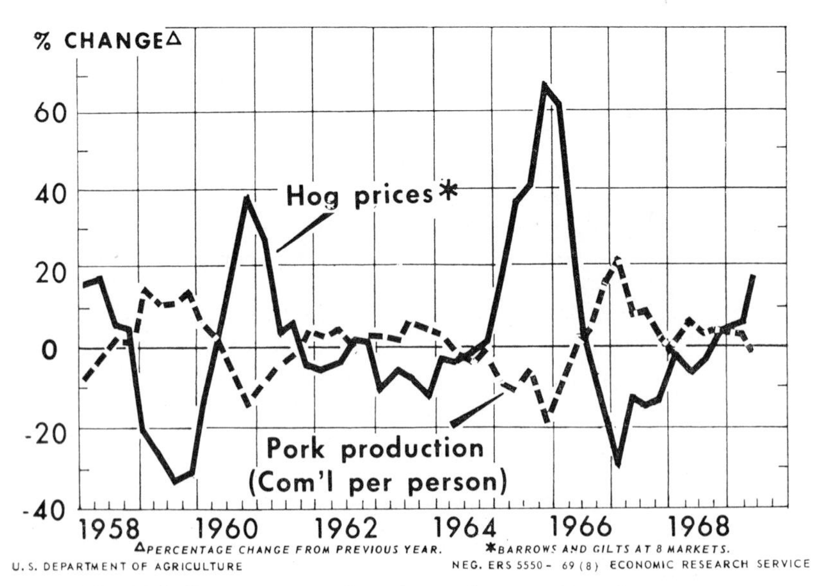


FIG. 10.3—Hog prices and pork production, United States, 1958–69.

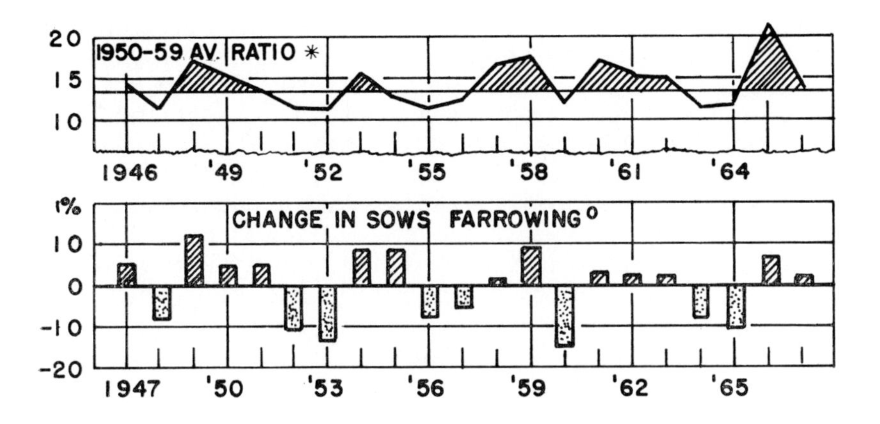


FIG. 10.4—Influence of the hog-corn price ratio in the fall on the number of sows farrowing the next spring, 1947–67.

#### What Causes Hog Price Cycles?

The internal mechanism of the hog price cycle is also shown in Figure 10.3. A high price for hogs one year stimulates increases in the pig crops during the next year or two. These larger pig crops show up as increased pork production a few months later. The high level of pork production concurrently depresses the price of hogs. This low price of hogs decreases the size of the pig crops during the next year or two; this decreases hog slaughter and concurrently raises hog prices—and off we go again on another cycle.

A clearer view of part of the mechanism is shown in Figure 10.4. This shows that it is not merely the price of hogs that causes cycles in hog production, but the ratio between the price of hogs and the price of corn—the hog-corn ratio.

The relation or ratio between corn prices and hog prices is an important factor in influencing hog production. Hog prices may be low, but this factor may be offset by a still lower corn price. The relation between the two prices is the important thing. This relation is termed the hog-corn price ratio. It represents the price of hogs per 100 pounds divided by the price of corn per bushel; it may be thought of as the number of bushels of corn that it would take to buy 100 pounds of live pork. It does not represent the number of bushels of corn that it takes to produce 100 pounds of pork.

When the hog-corn price ratio is higher than usual, hog

feeding is more profitable than usual. Farmers generally respond to this situation by breeding and feeding more hogs. During the period from 1949 to 1955, for example, the hog-corn price ratio, computed from Chicago prices for hogs and corn, averaged about 13 to 1. When the hog-corn price ratio was above this level, farmers increased their production of hogs; when it was below, farmers decreased their production.

In recent years, the average level of the hog-corn price ratio has risen to about 16 to 1. This is now the level above which farmers increase their production of hogs, and below which they reduce it.

The chief reason for this rise in the general level of the hog-corn price ratio is the change that has taken place in the structure of the costs of producing hogs—that is, in the relative costs and quantities of the things that make up the costs of production. The costs of feed are relatively less than they used to be; and such nonfeed costs as labor, buildings, and equipment make up a larger proportion of the costs than formerly. Thus a higher hog-corn price ratio is needed to make hog production profitable, and the hog-corn price ratio is a less adequate indicator of the profitability of feeding hogs.

Furthermore, the hog-corn price ratio is not an accurate indicator of the *amount* of change. This is due in part to the changing cost structure mentioned. In addition, price support and storage programs for corn provide farmers an additional alternative for corn (storage under price support loan). This means that all of a large corn crop, for example, is not used to expand hog production; a major part of it is put into storage. Actual hog prices and the hog price outlook now are more important influences on hog production changes than previously.

The effect of the changing hog-corn ratios in the fall on the number of sows farrowing the next spring is shown in Figure 10.4. The upper part of the chart shows the hog-corn ratios drawn above and below the average line, with the portions above the average shaded and the portions below the line unshaded. The lower part of the chart shows the changes in sows farrowing the next spring.

Comparison of the upper part of the chart with the lower shows how a period of larger than average hog-corn ratios causes an increase in hog marketings a year or two later, while a period of smaller than average ratios causes a decrease in marketings a year or two later.

The hog-corn price ratio may change because of a change either in corn prices or in hog prices, or both. Corn prices fluctuate from year to year, in relation to the general price level, in a random, irregular manner. This is because they fluctuate with changes in corn production which in turn result chiefly from changes in the weather. These irregular fluctuations in corn prices cannot explain the regular (cyclic) changes in hog prices. They may start hog prices swinging, as we start a tuning fork ringing with a single blow; but once started, the system of hog prices and production swings with its own inherent periodicity, as a tuning fork vibrates with its own inherent frequency. The cycles in hog prices, therefore, while perhaps set in motion by shocks from outside (such as large or small corn crops), are kept going by certain characteristics inherent in the hog production system—the ease of expansion and contraction of the hog enterprise, the length of time from breeding to market maturity, the tendency for hog producers to respond to present prices rather than prospective prices, and so forth.

## BEEF-CATTLE PRICE AND PRODUCTION CYCLES

Beef-cattle numbers on farms, slaughter, and prices also move in cycles. They are another example of unstable equilibrium.

Figure 10.5 shows that the cycles in numbers on farms and in slaughter (production) run from 10 to 15 years in length. The

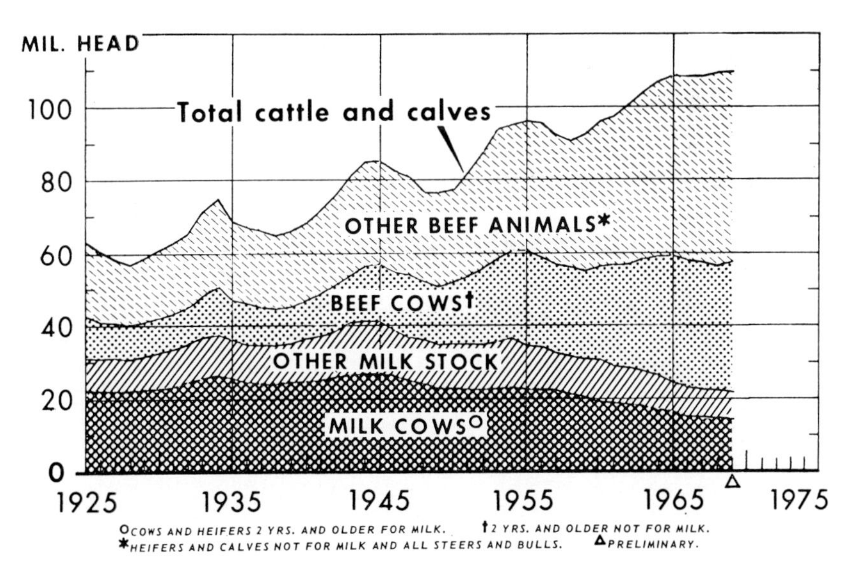


FIG. 10.5—Cattle on farms, January 1, 1925–69.

cycles in slaughter (production) follow the cycles in numbers on farms.

When beef slaughter is high and beef prices are depressed, beef producers get depressed too. They send a higher proportion of their breeding stock to market, thus increasing market receipts and slaughter and reducing prices further. Beef-cattle numbers on farms decline. Within a few years this causes a decline in market receipts and slaughter, and prices begin to rise. The beef-cattle business begins to look up. Farmers and ranchers begin to hold back more cows and heifers to build up their herds. The unstable equilibrium then begins to work upward instead of downward. The retention of some breeding stock reduces market receipts, and this reduction in slaughter raises prices further. This continues until the build-up on farms and ranches begins to approach the limits of carrying capacity, and market receipts from the larger herd become large enough to halt the rise in prices or turn it downward. Farmers and ranchers then send a higher than normal proportion of their breeding stock to market to cash in on the high prices. Receipts increase further and drive prices lower. This induces further liquidation and further price reduction. This reaction may be drastic, such as it was in 1953, when beef slaughter increased 30 per cent over 1952 and beef-cattle prices decreased about 30 per cent also.

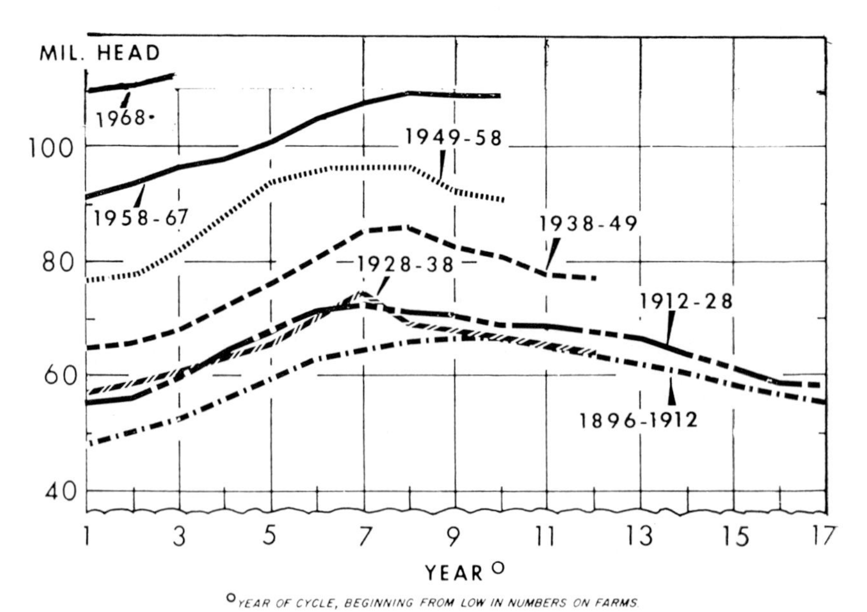


FIG. 10.6—Cattle on farms, by cycles, United States, 1896–1970.

Figure 10.6 shows that the last three cattle cycles were shorter than the earlier cycles. The cycle from 1928 to 1938 lasted only 11 years; the cycle from 1938 to 1949 was 12 years; the 1949–58 cycle only 9 years; and the cycle that began during 1958 lasted 10 years. By contrast, the earlier cycles lasted about 17 years.

## OTHER CYCLIC MOVEMENTS

Production and prices of eggs also follow a fairly regular cyclic pattern. Relatively profitable egg prices are typically accompanied by larger hatchings of egg-type chicks for replacement and addition to laying flocks. This continues until the increased hatch is reflected in a larger laying flock, increased egg production, and lower prices. After a period of unprofitable prices, hatchings are cut back and the laying flock becomes smaller. This results in a lower level of egg production and higher prices. Since it takes only five months from hatch until chicks are in egg production, this whole process (from one period of profitable prices through a complete cycle to another period of profitable prices) can take place in about three years.

Sheep and lamb production formerly followed a fairly definite cyclic pattern, varying in response to price and profit conditions in the industry. Figure 10.7, however, shows that a general downtrend in sheep and lamb numbers in the United States has persisted, even through periods of relatively favorable prices.

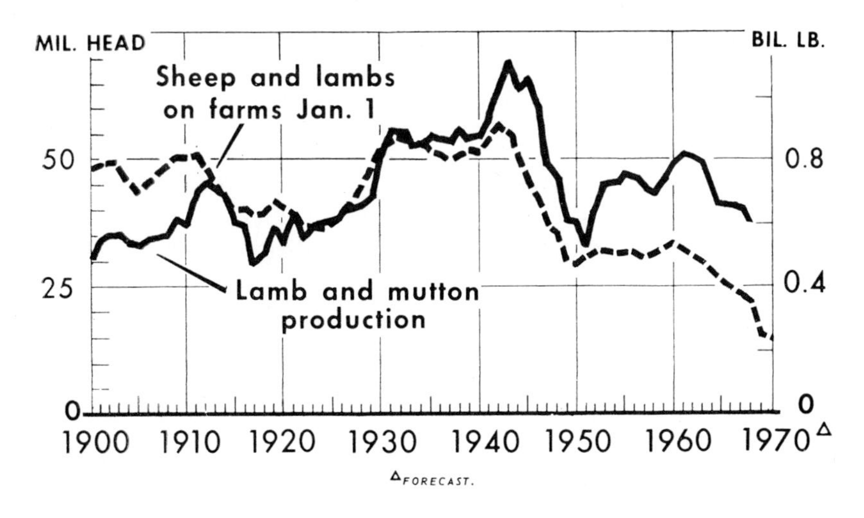


FIG. 10.7—Sheep and lambs on U.S. farms, January 1, and lamb and mutton production, United States, 1900–69.

## CONCLUSIONS

Cyclic movements in the prices of certain farm products are an evidence of imperfection in the functioning of the market over periods of time. They cause alternate periods of overcrowding and underutilization of productive equipment, thereby increasing costs. They result chiefly from imperfect forecasting of prices on the part of producers.

Producers forecast prices imperfectly partly because these prices are affected by unpredictable factors—large and small crops, upheavals and depressions in demand, etc.—as well as by predictable ones. The price of the product may be high now not merely because it is at the top of the cycle but also because a sustained increase in demand is under way. In that case, if the cyclic swing is the more important factor, production should be reduced because lower prices are expected in a year or two; if the increase in demand is the more important, production should be increased. More market information is needed in cases like this to help the farmer make the right decision.

Furthermore, a very large corn crop may make it more profitable for a man to raise more hogs (even though it may require selling those hogs in the downswing of prices), than to keep his hog production constant, since he has to sell on the same downswing of prices in either case. It may be only the subsequent swings in the cycle that are uneconomic. The question quickly gets into all sorts of complications related to the particular setup on each farm, but two general conclusions stand out:

1. To the extent that cyclic price movements result from imperfect market knowledge on the part of the producer, that knowledge needs to be strengthened by increased price analysis research and "Outlook" extension work.
2. To the extent that cyclic price movements result from unpredictable forces affecting the sizes of crops, federal programs for stabilizing crop supplies and prices are helpful.

# 11

## SEASONAL PRICE MOVEMENTS

UP TO THIS POINT we have been studying price movements that extend over a period of several or many years. We turn now to consider short-time movements of prices within the year, or what are usually called seasonal price movements (movements of prices within the season, usually about a year in length).

The prices of most farm products do not remain constant through the season; they follow some regular seasonal pattern. This is not necessarily an evidence of imperfection in the market with respect to time. The price of a product can be expected to run higher in some months than in others for several reasons. Field crops usually cost less to market straight from the field than later in the season. Accordingly, most field crops come to market heavily at harvest time, when their costs of production plus costs of storage are lowest (since storage costs at harvest time are zero). These heavy sales depress prices until they reach the point where the seasonal rise in price thereafter corresponds roughly with differences in the costs of storage from one part of the year to another.

Livestock and many other perishable agricultural products are produced the year round, but the level of production may vary seasonally because of biological factors in the production process, weather patterns, and seasonal differences in production costs. As market supplies vary within the year for one or more of these reasons, prices also follow seasonal patterns that are often fairly consistent from year to year. Seasonal variations in the demand for a particular product can also affect the seasonal price pattern.

The prices of perishable crops can be expected to fluctuate seasonally more than the prices of the more durable (storable) crops, unless their production is usually uniform throughout the year. A crop like strawberries cannot be withheld from the market during periods of heavy shipments and low prices and stored for several months until shipments become lighter and prices rise. At the other extreme, durable commodities like wheat, cotton, etc., can be stored at comparatively low cost, so that the seasonal fluctuations in their prices are comparatively small. Whenever their prices fall slightly below the levels that are expected to be realized later in the season, the operators of storage warehouses buy up the excess of current supplies over current needs and put them into storage until later in the season. The truth of this is illustrated in the case of most of the great agricultural staples where the bulk of the speculative risk can be shifted to professional speculators in futures contracts; the men who do the actual storing are content to earn a modest but more certain "carrying charge."

The question to be investigated in this chapter, therefore, is this: Do the seasonal price patterns for different farm products correspond with the costs of producing the product at (or storing it to) different times of the year? If so, the market is perfect in this particular respect; if not, it is imperfect.

Average seasonal price patterns are only a rough guide to the behavior of prices in any one year. Before average seasonal price movements can be of much use, they must be supplemented by a study of changing trends and erratic forces at work each year, separately for each commodity. This is too big a job for the space available in the present chapter; it is big enough for a book in itself. Accordingly, only a few products will be studied here—eggs, hogs, beef cattle, and the most important grains—representing the great classes of agricultural products. Even for these products, the analyses will be only preliminary in nature, not exhaustive.

## THE SEASONAL BEHAVIOR OF EGG PRICES

The seasonal variation in egg prices has been decreasing slowly and has shifted somewhat within the year. In the early 1930's the peak price (reached then in January) was about twice as high as the average during the three low months, March, April, and May. From 1955 through 1960 prices averaged high-

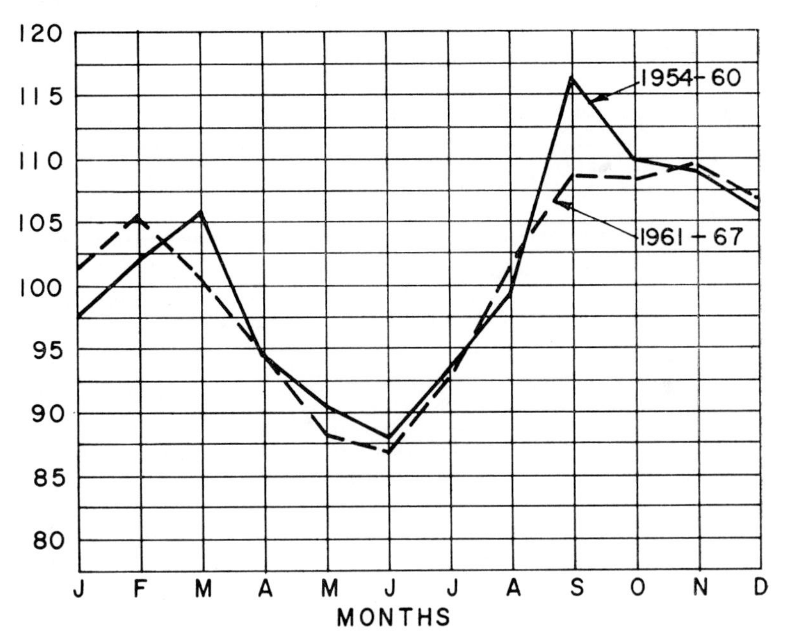


FIG. 11.1—Seasonal index of egg prices, Iowa, 1954–60 and 1961–67. (Source: Allan P. Rahn, Iowa State University, unpublished research.)

est during September and were 31 per cent above the two lowest price months of May and June (Figure 11.1). During the 1961–67 period prices averaged highest in November, although September and October prices were nearly as high. Prices in this three-month period were 24 per cent above the two low months of May and June.

This reduction in seasonal price variation results from the technological changes that have been taking place in egg production and the growth of larger, more specialized egg operations. The hatch of egg-type chicks during the last half of the year has increased sharply in recent years. As a result, pullet replacements are added to many flocks in a more uniform pattern during the year so that layer numbers and rate of lay also show less variation. This is especially true of larger, commercial egg operations which try to maintain production as uniformly as possible throughout the year.

The average seasonal variation in egg prices at retail and at the farm and the farm-retail spread for the 1947–58 period is

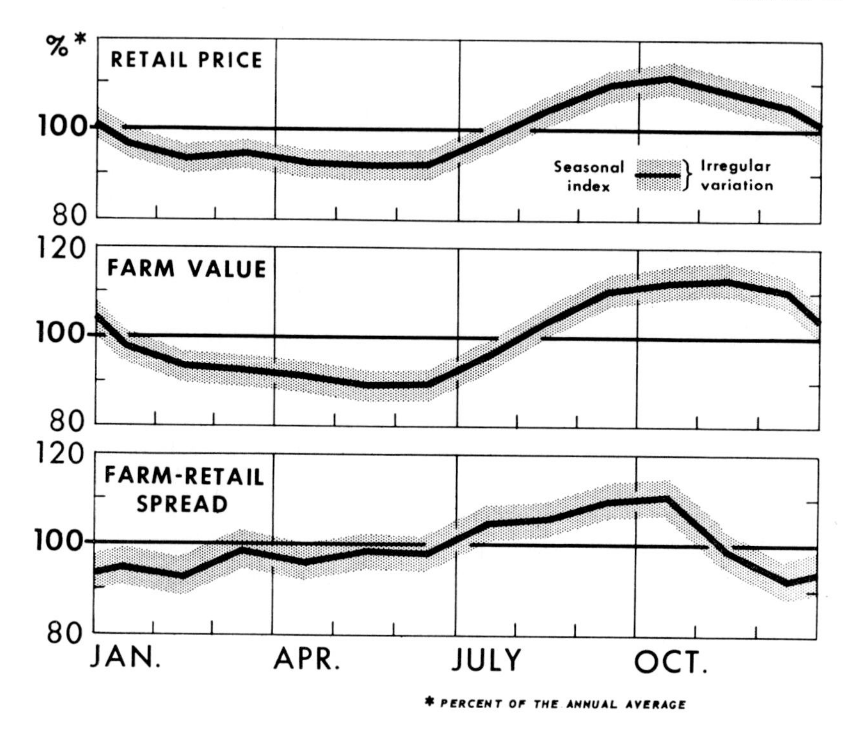


FIG. 11.2—Seasonal indexes of U.S. average retail egg prices, farm value, and farm-retail spread, average, 1947–58.

shown in Figure 11.2. The seasonal pattern of farm prices is very similar to that shown for more recent years in Figure 11.1. Retail prices follow approximately the same seasonal pattern as farm prices. The seasonal index of the farm-retail spread moved in the same general direction as prices, indicating that unit costs of marketing eggs tend to increase with decreases in the volume of eggs marketed.

## THE SEASONAL PATTERN OF HOG PRICES

Farm prices of hogs have a more definite seasonal pattern than farm prices of the other meat animals (Figure 11.3). Wholesale and retail prices of pork follow a seasonal pattern that is similar to live prices. However, the changes are usually smaller and tend to lag live price changes by about a month as shown in Figure 11.4. Seasonal patterns of both farm and retail values of pork are inverse to the seasonal pattern of hog production. Hog prices typically advance during the spring and early summer, when marketings are approaching the seasonal low, and

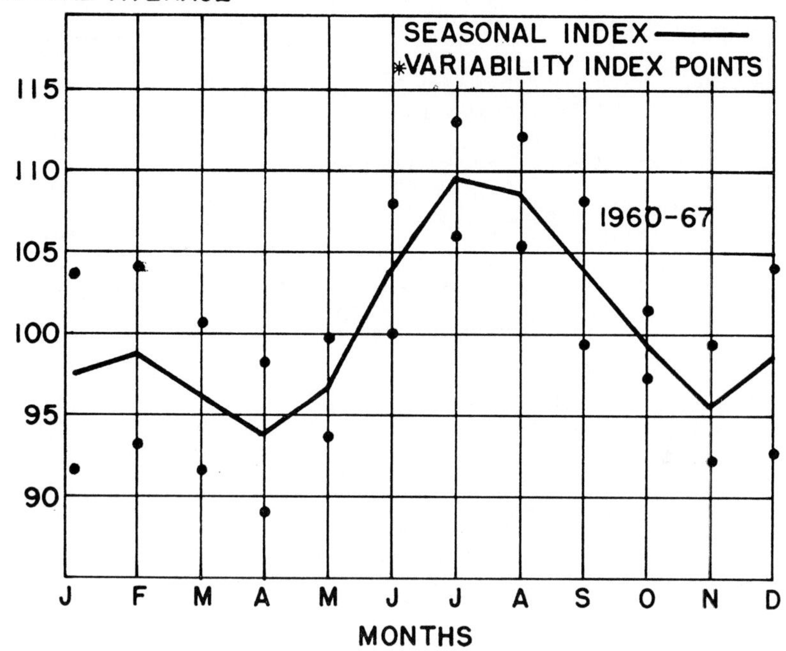


FIG. 11.3—Seasonal index of hog prices, average of barrows and gilts at eight markets (Chicago, Sioux City, Omaha, Kansas City, St. Louis National Stockyards, South St. Paul, Indianapolis, and South St. Joseph), 1960–67. (*Variability index points represent the possible range that the price index for a particular month will be 95 per cent of the time.) (Source: Allan P. Rahn, Iowa State University, unpublished research.)

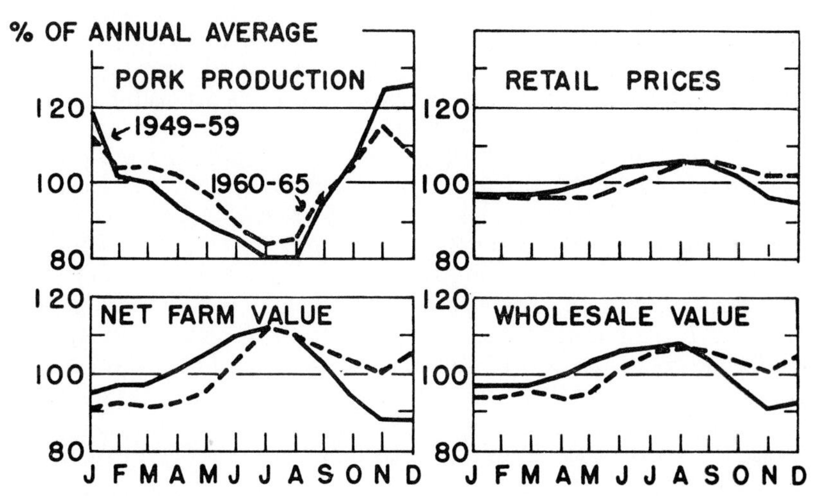


FIG. 11.4—Seasonal variation in pork production and prices. (Source: J. Bruce Bullick, Richard Eisenberg, and Duane Hacklander, **Price Spreads for Pork,** USDA, Misc. Publ. 1051, Jan., 1967, p. 8.)

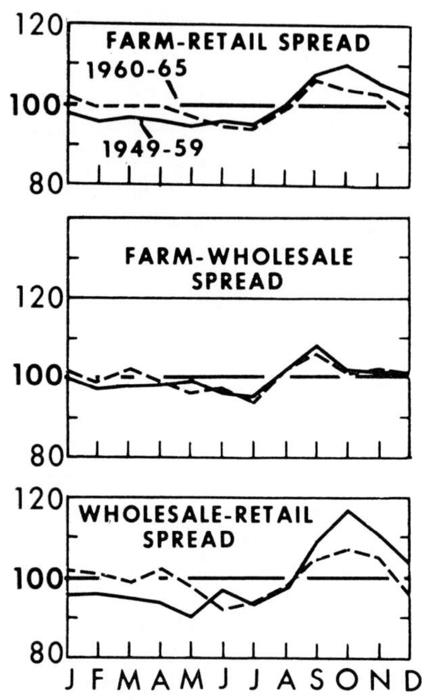


FIG. 11.5—Seasonal variation in price spreads for pork. (Source: J. Bruce Bullick, Richard Eisenberg, and Duane Hacklander, **Price Spreads for Pork**, USDA, Misc. Publ. 1051, Jan., 1967, p. 8.)

decline in response to sharp increases in marketings during the fall. A more even monthly distribution of sow farrowings during the year has moderated these production and price patterns somewhat in recent years. However, more sows are still farrowed during the March–May period than in the other months, while farrowings are smallest during the October–January period.

The farm-retail spread for pork tends to be inversely related to hog prices and retail pork prices, but this relation was not as evident in the 1960–65 period as in 1949–59 (Figure 11.5). As hog marketings drop seasonally, farm prices increase faster than retail prices, and the farm-retail spread narrows. A part of this seasonal contraction in the spread is due to factors affecting the wholesale-retail portion of the over-all farm retail spread. These factors can be explained in two ways: As there is a rather fixed and inflexible supply of hog-marketing services during the short run in terms of plant facilities and labor supply, (1) a dwindling supply of hogs causes sharply increased buying competition among packers, not matched by a similar increase in competition among retailers for pork or (2) diminishing demand for hog-marketing services forces packers to take a lower margin—or price—for their processing and wholesaling services. Conversely, when hog marketings are increasing seasonally, hog prices drop and the farm-retail spread widens. During these seasons, packers compete less actively with one another as the demand for their hog-marketing services increases. Lags in adjustments between farm and wholesale prices and between wholesale and retail prices also contribute to the expansion of the farm-retail spread when prices are dropping and to the contraction when prices rise.

The major change that has taken place in the seasonal pattern of pork prices and of the farm-retail spread is the gradual reduction in the price variations. This has been due largely to corresponding changes in the seasonal pattern of hog marketings. Earlier farrowings and feeding for faster gain have shifted the marketing pattern. A more nearly equal balance between fall and spring pig crops and some tendency toward more year-round farrowings have smoothed seasonal variations in marketings.

### Seasonal Changes in Price Differentials

The seasonal changes in the price differentials between light and heavy hogs directly reflect the seasonal changes in the price differentials between light and heavy wholesale pork cuts.

The changes in differentials between light and heavy pork cuts result chiefly from seasonal changes in the percentages of sows and of hogs of different weights in the run—that is, from changes in what is called the "consist" of the receipts of hogs at the market.

The prices of hogs of the lighter weights turn up and down earlier than the prices of heavier hogs. Hogs of 180–200 pounds, for instance, touch their summer peak in July and then decline, while 240–270-pound hogs ordinarily are highest about mid-August and do not go down much until September. Seasonal price changes come first for light hogs simply because market receipts of the young, lighter hogs are in advance of those for heavier hogs.

### Relations Between Hog Price Movements and Weights

The differences in price trends for hogs of various weights are important to marketing programs of producers. A producer will gain if, without too much extra cost, he can prepare his hogs for marketing in a high-price period and if he can make good use of a knowledge of seasonal trends in deciding at what weight to sell his hogs. At some seasons it pays to hold hogs to heavier weights. At other times more is gained by selling light.[1]

In making these decisions, producers can compare seasonal price behavior for successive weight groups. A hog held an extra week or two moves into a heavier weight classification. Thus, the market price for a 190-pound barrow on September 1st may be compared with the price for a 220-pound hog on September 15th or a 250-pound hog on October 1st if the daily gain is 2 pounds.

A method of making such comparisons is provided in Table 11.1. Normal seasonal variations in prices for hogs of each of three weights are shown in dollars per 100 pounds, based on an assumed average of $20 for 200–220-pound hogs for the entire year. This is an arbitrary figure chosen for illustration. Any other base price could be used, with all values raised or lowered in proportion. Prices for hogs lighter and heavier than 200–220 pounds range up or down according to 1947–53 average price ratios by weights.

A distinctive feature of the table is that it allows comparisons across weight groups. With arrows as guides, a "normal" price for hogs of one weight can be compared with a "normal" price for hogs 30 pounds heavier 2 weeks later, and for hogs 60 pounds heavier 4 weeks later. Moreover, the price difference is converted into the value per 100 pounds of the added weight gain. Thus, a 190-pound barrow that on January 1 could be sold for $18.80 would normally be slightly lower priced as a 220-pound barrow on January 15—at $18.75. In taking this small price loss, the producer is paid at the rate of $18.50 per 100 pounds for the 30 pounds added.

An example will show how the calculations are made. A 190-pound hog at $18.80 is worth $35.70. A 220-pound hog sold for $18.75 two weeks later brings $41.25. The increase in value for the 30 pounds is $5.55, which amounts to an $18.50 rate per 100 pounds. This price for added weight is lower than either the original or final price of the entire hog because it reflects the price loss of 5 cents taken on the entire weight.

These calculated values for added weight gain show how well a producer profits by holding hogs to heavier weights in a season of rising prices and how much he gains by selling light ahead of a price downtrend. In the May–July price uptrend, values of $23.80 to $27.70 (based on an annual average price of

[1] Part of this section is based on a report by Harold F. Breimyer, "Seasonal Variation in Prices of Barrows and Gilts," *The Livestock and Meat Situation*, USDA, May, 1954, pp. 24–28.

**TABLE. 11.1: Normal Relationships Between Prices of Hogs of Three Weights and Value of the Weight Gained by Holding Two Weeks**

| Date | 190-Lb. Hogs Per 100 Lb. | Value of Weight Gain | | 220-Lb. Hogs Per 100 Lb. | Value of Weight Gain | | 250-Lb. Hogs Per 100 Lb. |
|---|---|---|---|---|---|---|---|
| | | 30 lb. | Per 100 lb. | | 30 lb. | Per 100 lb. | |
| | *(dollars)* | *(dollars)* | *(dollars)* | *(dollars)* | *(dollars)* | *(dollars)* | *(dollars)* |
| January 1 | 18.80 | | | 18.35 | | | 17.95 |
| | | 5.55 | 18.50 | | 5.35 | 17.85 | |
| January 15 | 19.30 | | | 18.75 | | | 18.25 |
| | | 5.35 | 17.85 | | 5.13 | 17.10 | |
| February 1 | 19.55 | | | 19.10 | | | 18.55 |
| | | 5.19 | 17.30 | | 4.73 | 15.75 | |
| February 15 | 19.70 | | | 19.25 | | | 18.70 |
| | | 5.10 | 17.00 | | 4.57 | 15.25 | |
| March 1 | 19.50 | | | 19.35 | | | 18.75 |
| | | 5.30 | 17.65 | | 4.32 | 14.40 | |
| March 15 | 19.10 | | | 19.25 | | | 18.75 |
| | | 5.44 | 18.15 | | 3.97 | 13.25 | |
| April 1 | 18.55 | | | 18.95 | | | 18.55 |
| | | 5.84 | 19.45 | | 4.05 | 13.50 | |
| April 15 | 18.30 | | | 18.65 | | | 18.30 |
| | | 7.14 | 23.80 | | 5.70 | 19.00 | |
| May 1 | 18.65 | | | 19.05 | | | 18.70 |
| | | 7.76 | 25.85 | | 6.29 | 20.95 | |
| May 15 | 19.30 | | | 19.65 | | | 19.30 |
| | | 7.66 | 25.55 | | 6.39 | 21.30 | |
| June 1 | 19.90 | | | 20.15 | | | 19.85 |
| | | 7.84 | 26.15 | | 6.75 | 22.50 | |
| June 15 | 20.70 | | | 20.75 | | | 20.45 |
| | | 8.01 | 26.70 | | 7.25 | 24.15 | |
| July 1 | 21.60 | | | 21.50 | | | 21.15 |
| | | 8.31 | 27.70 | | 7.66 | 25.55 | |
| July 15 | 22.50 | | | 22.45 | | | 22.00 |
| | | 7.39 | 24.65 | | 6.45 | 21.50 | |
| August 1 | 22.80 | | | 22.80 | | | 22.35 |
| | | 6.53 | 21.75 | | 5.76 | 19.20 | |
| August 15 | 22.50 | | | 22.65 | | | 22.35 |
| | | 6.44 | 21.45 | | 5.79 | 19.30 | |
| September 1 | 21.95 | | | 22.35 | | | 22.25 |
| | | 6.35 | 21.15 | | 5.63 | 18.75 | |
| September 15 | 21.30 | | | 21.85 | | | 21.90 |
| | | 5.82 | 19.40 | | 4.75 | 15.85 | |
| October 1 | 20.50 | | | 21.05 | | | 21.10 |
| | | 5.16 | 17.20 | | 3.73 | 12.45 | |
| October 15 | 19.70 | | | 20.05 | | | 20.00 |
| | | 4.35 | 14.50 | | 2.94 | 9.80 | |
| November 1 | 18.85 | | | 19.00 | | | 18.80 |
| | | 4.17 | 13.90 | | 3.30 | 11.00 | |
| November 15 | 18.10 | | | 18.15 | | | 18.05 |
| | | 4.75 | 15.85 | | 4.27 | 14.25 | |
| December 1 | 17.95 | | | 17.80 | | | 17.70 |
| | | 5.39 | 17.95 | | 5.04 | 16.80 | |
| December 15 | 18.30 | | | 17.95 | | | 17.70 |
| | | 5.54 | 18.45 | | 5.39 | 17.95 | |
| January 1 | 18.80 | | | 18.35 | | | 17.95 |

Source: Harold F. Breimyer, "Seasonal Variation in Prices of Barrows and Gilts," *The Livestock and Meat Situation,* USDA, May, 1954.

$20 for medium-weight hogs) are returned for the extra weight between 190 and 220 pounds, and $20.95 to $25.55 for the weight between 220 and 250 pounds. But holding hogs at the middle of the fall price decline can return as little as $13.90 or $9.80 for the two extra weights.

The data in Table 11.1 should be used with regard to two other factors: (1) the cost of putting on added gain and (2) the uniformity of the "normal" seasonal price trends.

The cost of additional gain can be calculated approximately from prices of corn and other feed prevailing at any time. The cost naturally is much greater when feed is high in price than when it is lower. Quantities of feed required can be estimated by a producer from his own experience. He can also refer to data on average feed requirements as guides. Generally, about 4.1 bushels of corn or its equal in other feeds are required to take a 200-pound hog up to 250 pounds. Around 5.5 bushels of corn or its equal in other feed are needed to put 50 pounds of gain on a 250-pound hog.[2]

Feed is usually around two-thirds of the total cost of raising hogs. You would just about break even if you got a return of $1.45 for each $1 worth of feed you put into them.

These data can be used to estimate costs of 30 pounds of gain at different prices of corn. Calculations are given in Table 11.2. These costs can be compared directly with the figures in boxes in Table 11.1.

An obvious observation is that hogs profitably can be held longer and to heavier weights when prices of corn are low in relation to the price of hogs than when corn prices are higher. Corn at $1.30 would bear about an average relationship to $20 hogs. At that price, the gain between 190 and 220 pounds would cost approximately $15.07 per 100 pounds and that between 220 and 250 pounds would cost $15.70. At this normal price relationship between hogs and corn it pays to hold hogs to 220 pounds at nearly all seasons in an average year, but at fewer times to hold to 250 pounds. At a lower price of corn—$1 or $1.10—hogs can more often be fed to heavier weights. At a higher corn price, feeding to a heavier market weight is profitable only at particular seasons such as late spring and summer.

Normal seasonal trends in prices of hogs are followed more regularly at some seasons of the year than at others. Prices usually rise from mid-December to mid-January. They also usually rise in January–February, April–May, May–June, and June–July. They almost invariably decline in October–November and typi-

[2] John T. Larsen and Robert L. Rizek, *The Costs of Feeding to Heavier Weights*, USDA, ERS-371, Feb., 1968.

**TABLE 11.2: Cost of Putting 30 Pounds of Gain on Hogs Weighing 190 and 220 Pounds at Several Assumed Prices for Corn**

| | Total Cost of Gain* | | | |
|---|---|---|---|---|
| | 190-lb. hog fed to 220 lb. | | 220-lb. hog fed to 250 lb. | |
| Price of Corn, Per Bushel | Cost of 30 lb. | Cost per 100 lb. | Cost of 30 lb. | Cost per 100 lb. |
| *(dollars)* | *(dollars)* | *(dollars)* | *(dollars)* | *(dollars)* |
| 1.00 .......... | 3.48 | 11.60 | 3.63 | 12.10 |
| 1.10 .......... | 3.83 | 12.77 | 3.99 | 13.30 |
| 1.20 .......... | 4.18 | 13.93 | 4.35 | 14.50 |
| 1.30 .......... | 4.52 | 15.07 | 4.71 | 15.70 |
| 1.40 .......... | 4.87 | 16.23 | 5.08 | 16.93 |
| 1.50 .......... | 5.22 | 17.40 | 5.44 | 18.13 |

Source: Derived from data in John T. Larsen and Robert L. Rizek, *The Costs of Feeding to Heavier Weights,* USDA, ERS-371, Feb., 1968, pp. 27–28.

* Calculated on the basis that 2.4 bushels of corn or its equivalent are required to raise a hog from 190 to 220 pounds, and 2.5 bushels from 220 to 250 pounds. An extra 45 per cent is added to the cost of feed as the approximate costs other than feed.

cally fall in September–October, November–December, and March–April. Trends between other pairs of months are less consistent. Conditions in some years cause marked departures from normal seasonal trends and from normal differences by weights.

In general, producers will profit by assuming that prices will follow a normal seasonal pattern instead of disregarding seasonality entirely. They will profit even more if they will use outlook information to guide them in anticipating how seasonality for each weight and the price differentials between weights may differ from normal in a given year.

In a year when hog prices are on a long uptrend, seasonal upswings will be prolonged and downswings curtailed. It is usually more profitable to feed to heavier weights than in an average year. When prices are declining, the downswings are longer and upswings shorter, and marketing at lighter weights than usual is often a profitable practice.

Thus we can combine these general rules into a summary statement: In a year when hog prices are high or rising, it generally pays to hold hogs a little longer than usual. When prices are low or on a long downtrend, selling early and at lighter weights is better.

## SEASONAL PATTERNS IN BEEF-CATTLE PRICES

The average seasonal variation in beef-cattle prices for the years 1960 through 1967 is shown in Figure 11.6. These sea-

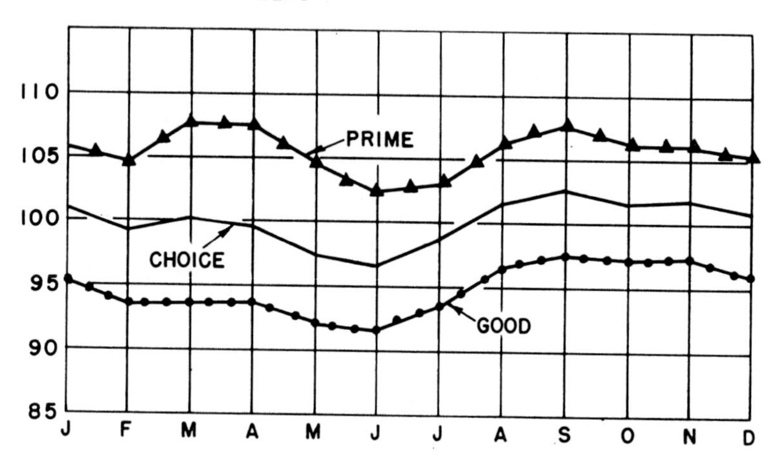


FIG. 11.6—Seasonal variation in slaughter steer prices at Chicago, 1960–67. (*Monthly averages for 1960–67 as a per cent of the 1960–67 average for all Choice steers at Chicago.)

sonal changes in price have become more moderate in recent years. In addition, the seasonal pattern of price changes has become less uniform from year to year.

Several developments in the cattle industry have contributed to the more moderate and less consistent pattern of seasonal price changes. One is the growth of many large commercial feeding operations that follow a year-round program of placing cattle in feedlots and of marketing fed cattle. Along with this has been a trend to shorter feeding programs, an increase in the relative number of heifers that are grain-fed before slaughter, a continued uptrend in the proportion of calves grain-fed, and a general upward trend in the proportion of the total beef supply that is from grain-fed cattle. This is in contrast to earlier years when a higher percentage of the cattle to be grain-fed were placed on feed during the fall months and were kept on feed or roughage for a longer period before slaughter.

The seasonal price patterns for different grades of cattle vary slightly due to differences in the relative number of each grade marketed during the year. These differences are shown in Figure 11.6. Prices on Choice steers average highest in September. Prime steer prices are also seasonally high in September but are usually equally high during March and April.

As a result of the differences in seasonal price patterns among different grades of cattle, the price spreads between grades tend to vary seasonally. The price spread between Prime

**TABLE 11.3: Monthly Grade Distribution of Slaughter Steers Sold at Seven Terminal Markets, 1960–67 Average***

| Month | Per Cent of Total Receipts | | |
|---|---|---|---|
| | Prime | Choice | Good |
| January | 4.7 | 54.7 | 35.2 |
| February | 5.1 | 54.2 | 35.2 |
| March | 4.2 | 53.7 | 36.3 |
| April | 3.4 | 54.6 | 35.8 |
| May | 3.4 | 57.4 | 33.6 |
| June | 3.8 | 60.7 | 30.6 |
| July | 4.4 | 61.5 | 29.9 |
| August | 5.2 | 61.7 | 29.1 |
| September | 5.3 | 62.3 | 28.5 |
| October | 5.5 | 62.2 | 28.2 |
| November | 7.8 | 63.3 | 25.1 |
| December | 5.9 | 59.3 | 30.3 |

Source: *Livestock, Meat, Wool Market News* (Weekly Summary and Statistics), USDA, selected issues, 1960–68.

* Chicago, Omaha, Sioux City, Kansas City, St. Louis National Stockyards, South St. Joseph, and Denver.

and Choice grades of slaughter steers is normally greater during the March–May period than at other times. The spread between Choice and Good grades is more uniform, but tends to be widest during the first four months of the year.

The reason for these changes in price spreads is shown in Table 11.3. The proportion of Prime steers in the market supply is smallest during the March–June period when the price spread is greatest. Good grade steers are in relatively smaller supply during the last half of the year and consequently sell somewhat closer to the Choice grade than during the early months when supplies are relatively larger. A higher proportion of Choice steers in the supply during the summer and fall also narrows the spread between Choice and Good.

### Feeder Cattle

Figure 11.7 shows the seasonal price pattern for feeder calves at Kansas City. Average seasonal price changes in the 1960–67 period were quite moderate. Prices averaged highest during March and April and were lowest in August and December. This is largely a result of the seasonal variation in the volume of cattle shipped to markets or directly to feeders. Marketings normally increase during the fall months, with calf supplies especially large during the October–December period.

## SEASONAL PATTERNS IN LAMB PRICES

Prices on slaughter lambs are usually highest in June, as shown in Figure 11.8. Prices decline during the summer and

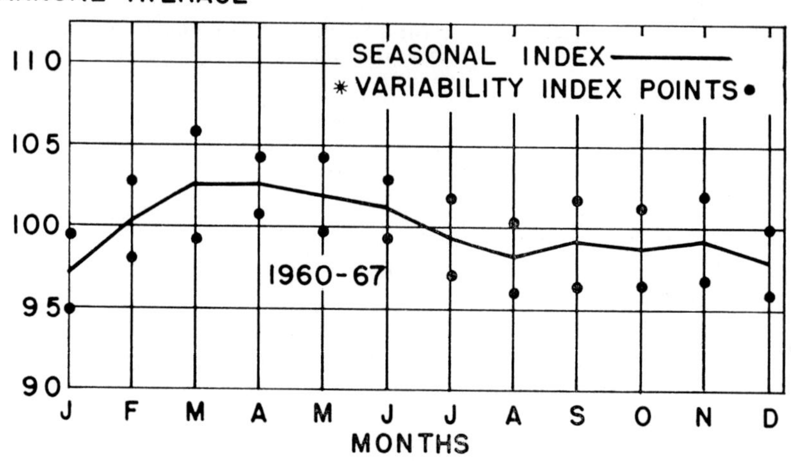


FIG. 11.7—Seasonal index of feeder calf prices, Good and Choice grades, Kansas City, 1960–67. (*Variability index points represent the possible range that the price index for a particular month will be 95 per cent of the time.) (Source: Allan P. Rahn, Iowa State University, unpublished research.)

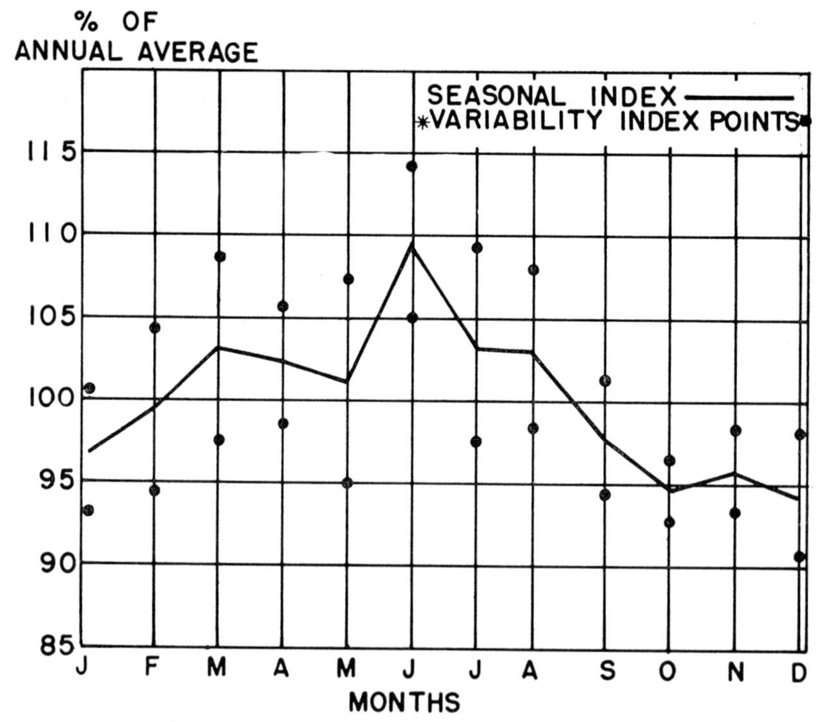


FIG. 11.8—Seasonal index of slaughter lamb prices, Choice and Prime, Omaha, 1960–67. (*Variability index points represent the possible range that the price index for a particular month will be 95 per cent of the time.) (Source: Allan P. Rahn, Iowa State University, unpublished research.)

average lowest during the final quarter of the year. While this is the average pattern of price movements, it is not highly consistent from year to year. This is indicated by the fairly wide range of variability attached to most of the monthly indexes.

## SEASONAL PRICE MOVEMENTS FOR GRAIN

A man has more latitude in the sale of his grain than he has in the sale of his livestock because it can be held for several months or years, whereas livestock usually has to be sold within a few weeks.

Figures are sometimes published showing the price rise from the low month of the harvest period to the highest month during the subsequent marketing season. The inference then is drawn that the difference between these low and high prices shows the gain that farmers could have made from storing their grain. Data of this sort are shown in Table 11.4. It shows that price differences from November to July on corn during the period from 1955–56 to 1968–69 ranged from 25 cents per bushel down to minus 2 cents. The average November to July price change for the entire period was 14 cents per bushel. These data can be misleading. They imply that farmers could have realized these price gains. While this is correct, they could have done so only if they had been omniscient, and could have told *at the time* when the price had reached its highest point for the season. It is easy to look back after the end of the season and

**TABLE 11.4: Price Change on Corn From November to July, Iowa, 1955–56 to 1968–69**

| Marketing Year | November–July Price Change |
|---|---|
| | *(¢/bu)* |
| 1955–56 | +25 |
| 1956–57 | –01 |
| 1957–58 | +17 |
| 1958–59 | +20 |
| 1959–60 | +12 |
| 1960–61 | +21 |
| 1961–62 | +07 |
| 1962–63 | +22 |
| 1963–64 | +06 |
| 1964–65 | +12 |
| 1965–66 | +21 |
| 1966–67 | –02 |
| 1967–68 | +07 |
| 1968–69 | +14 |
| Average, 1955–56 to 1968–69 | +14 |

**TABLE 11.5: Average-Season Price Rise for Corn, Oats, Wheat, and Soybeans in Iowa**

| Commodity | Low Month | High Month | Price Rise, in Cents Per Bushel 1948–53 | Price Rise, in Cents Per Bushel 1955–69 |
|---|---|---|---|---|
| Corn . . . . . . . . . | November | July–Sept. | 15 | 14 |
| Oats . . . . . . . . . | August | Dec.–Jan. | 13 | 6 |
| Wheat . . . . . . . | August | March–May | 12 | 13 |
| Soybeans . . . . . | October | May–June | 35 | 36 |

put your finger on the highest prices for that season, but it is very difficult to do this at the time. During the 1955–69 period, peak prices occurred during seven different months, although most often within the May–September period. It is very unlikely that farmers would have hit the high point every year.

Table 11.5 shows the average seasonal price rise for corn, oats, soybeans, and wheat during two periods—1948–53 and 1955–69. It is evident that "the" average seasonal price rise depends to some extent on how far back you go in computing your average. You may go back five years and get one answer. If you go back to 1940, you get another because that period includes years when prices were rising rapidly, which makes the average seasonal price rise high.

Figure 11.9 shows the average seasonal price patterns on corn and soybeans at Chicago for the years 1955–67. Seasonal price movements on corn are fairly consistent from year to year. Highest prices usually occur during the May–July period, with the low point typically in November during the harvest. Prices normally rise from the harvesttime low by enough to cover storage costs, although the rise in some years may be greater or less depending upon current supply-demand conditions and production prospects.

Seasonal price variation in soybeans is less consistent than in the case of corn and averages somewhat less as well. The low point in prices normally comes in October during harvest. On the average, prices are highest during April and May; however, the seasonal indexes for these months have a fairly large variability range.

Seasonal price movements for oats and wheat are shown in Figure 11.10, based on prices received by Iowa farmers during the 1955–67 period. Seasonal price movements are quite similar for the two grains. In both crops the seasonal price changes closely reflect the harvest-storage pattern, with lowest prices during the harvest season. This is usually followed by rising prices in the fall. Oats prices tend to peak by January and remain fairly steady until late spring. Wheat prices, however, normally rise to a peak in April, then decline until the harvest low.

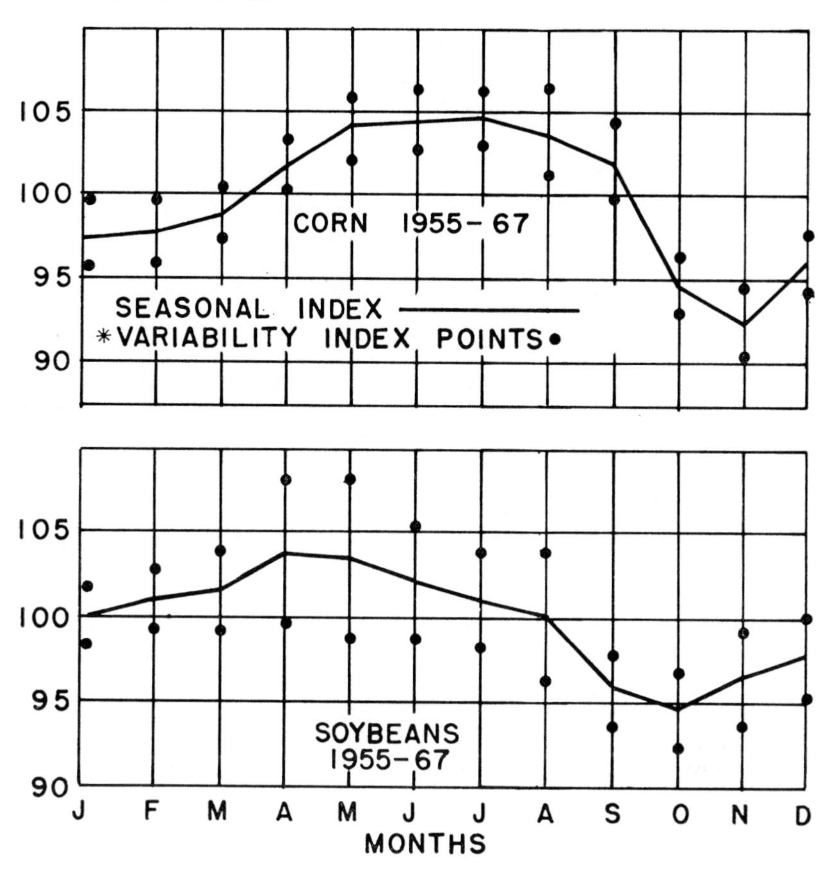


FIG. 11.9—Seasonal price indexes for No. 3 yellow corn and No. 1 soybeans, Chicago, 1955–67. (*Variability index points represent the possible range that the price index for a particular month will be 95 per cent of the time.) (Source: Allan P. Rahn, Iowa State University, unpublished research.)

However, the difficulty with seasonal price movements is that they are not followed closely each year. Prices rise much more than average some years, and rise much less than average or actually decline some other years. We need to remember what happened to the statistician who tried to wade across the river that was only 3 feet deep *on the average.*

Can we do better than merely accepting the average seasonal price rises given in Table 11.5 and shown in Figure 11.9 and 11.10?

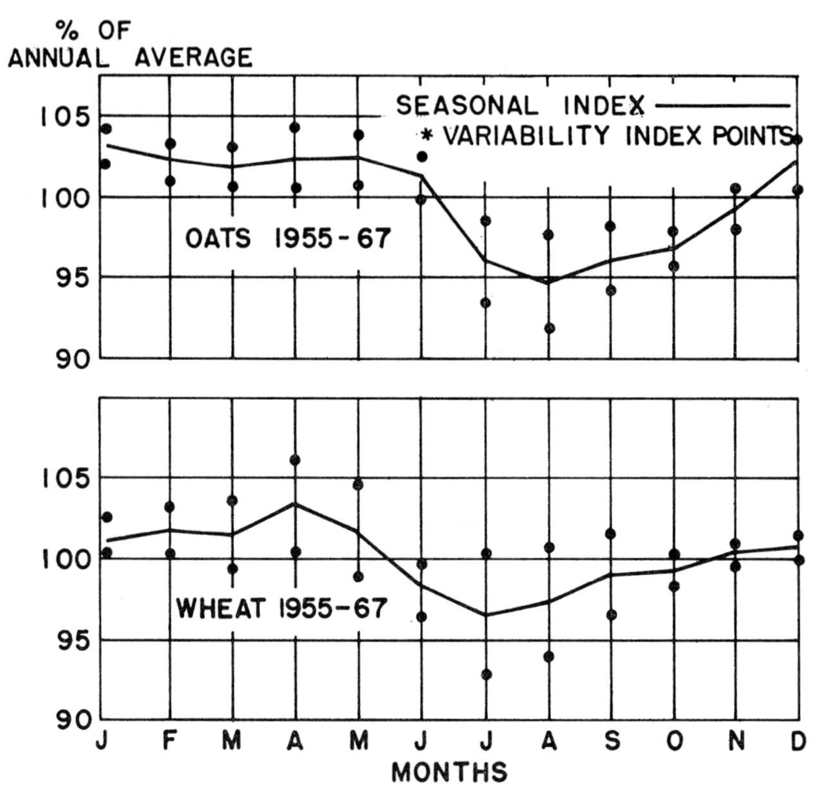


FIG. 11.10—Seasonal price indexes for oats and wheat, price received by farmers, Iowa, 1955–67. (*Variability index points represent the possible range that the price index for a particular month will be 95 per cent of the time.) (Source: Allan P. Rahn, Iowa State University, unpublished research.)

We can isolate some of the factors that will make the price rise more or less than usual, or bring the peak earlier or later than usual. We used to be able to say: After a big crop, store until late in the season, for the next year's crop is likely to be smaller; the effect of that smaller crop on price will show up before the new crop is harvested and will boost the price you can get from the old crop. Conversely, for opposite reasons, after a small crop sell soon after harvest; next year's crop probably will be larger and pull down the price before the old crop season is over.

The rule does not work out in quite so clear-cut a fashion now, because the Commodity Credit Corporation puts a floor under the large crops, retarding the decline in prices, although not arresting it. And short crops do not force the price as high as they used to because the excess supplies that were withdrawn from the market in good crop years are returned to the market in seasons of short supply. But the rule is still worth keeping in mind.

Another way of assessing whether or not to store is to regard the whole matter simply as a gamble, where the odds are, say, 2 out of 3 that the seasonal rise in price will be enough to cover the costs of storage, and 1 out of 3 that it will not. Or maybe the odds are only 1 to 3 that storage will pay, and 2 to 3 that it will not.

Whether it will be profitable to store grain depends upon the costs of storage, at the farm or in local or terminal elevators, as well as on the rise in prices. These costs are examined in detail in Chapter 28 on grain storage costs.

# 12

## HEDGING IN FUTURES CONTRACTS

IN THE CASE of certain products a distinctive method of meeting price fluctuations is available. This method is the practice of "hedging"; that is, of executing opposite sales or purchases in the "futures market" to offset the purchases or sales of physical products—grain, butter, etc.—made in the "cash" market. These terms, and the whole setting of "futures trading," require some explanation before the technique of hedging can be explained and its effects analyzed.

Futures markets represent a system of trading in futures contracts (contracts calling for the delivery of specified kinds and amounts of the physical commodity at a specified time and place). For many years, futures markets existed mainly for certain durable and readily storable products such as grains, cotton, and wool. To a lesser extent, futures trading was also conducted in some perishable, though storable, commodities such as butter and eggs. In November, 1964, futures trading was extended to live meat animals for the first time, when the Chicago Mercantile Exchange initiated futures trading on live beef steers. Futures trading in live hogs was added about a year and a half later.

The general principles underlying this system are the same for the various products. For the sake of concreteness, our discussion will be phrased in terms of wheat or corn, but it applies almost equally well to the other products.

The volume of trading in futures contracts is large relative to the volume of the actual grain. In the case of wheat, it is about ten times the volume of trading in the physical commodity itself. More than 90 per cent of all the trading in grain futures in the United States is conducted on the trading floor of the Chicago Board of Trade.

The trading floor of the Chicago Board of Trade is divided by an imaginary line into two parts. In the one part are the tables at which samples of physical (cash) grain are exposed, and the cash grain is bought and sold on the basis of those samples; in the other part are the "pits"—depressions in the floor, like bomb craters, each lined with a series of concentric circular steps so that traders standing on the steps in any pit can all see and hear each other. No physical grain is sold in the pits—nothing but paper contracts. These contracts call for delivery of physical grain at some future date, but in actuality less than 1 per cent of them ever mature and involve delivery of cash grain. More than 99 per cent of the futures contracts are closed out by the exchange of offsetting contracts before the delivery date.

The trade in futures contracts is not confined to the terminal markets where the pits are located. That is where the trades are executed, but a large proportion of them originate out in the country and are flashed to the pits by an extensive system of private telephone and telegraph wires connecting branch offices with the head offices of numerous commission firms located in Chicago or New York. A man in any small country town can keep in almost minute-to-minute touch with the market by radio and, if he wants to sell or buy a futures contract, can usually have his order executed in the pit and receive confirmation within five minutes.

Futures trading has been the center of a good deal of popular attention and at times attack, because of the speculative nature of most of the transactions in futures and because of the effect that the trading in futures may have on the prices of the physical commodity. We will examine the nature of trading in futures contracts in this chapter and deal with the effects of this trading on the prices of the commodity in the next chapter.

## TRADING IN FUTURES CONTRACTS

Trading in futures contracts consists of two kinds; or rather, there is only one kind of trading, but it is conducted for two different purposes. The one is "hedging," and the other is purely speculative.

When a farmer sells a load of corn at the local elevator, he usually receives payment at once; he can go home with the money in his pocket. The elevator man then sells the grain by either one of two methods. He loads it into a car and consigns the carload to a terminal market where it will be sold for his account by a commission man; or, he sells it direct to some cash grain buyer, on the basis of an "on-track" bid at his local elevator siding or a "to-arrive" bid based on delivery at the buyer's point.

If the local elevator man follows the first method of sale, about a week will elapse before the corn he bought from the farmer can be put through his elevator, loaded on a car, shipped to a terminal market, and finally sold there. During this week that elapses between the time the local elevator man buys the corn from the farmer and the time he sells it at the terminal market, the price of corn may decline, perhaps 5 or 10 cents a bushel. The elevator man would thereby lose $50, $100, or more on his carload of corn. He might continue buying and selling like this, hoping that on the next carload the price would rise so that he would recoup his losses. But many local elevators do not have a very big financial margin to run on. If they happened to strike a succession of 5- or 10-cent losses on many carloads of corn, they might go broke.

Local elevator men can protect themselves against this sort of difficulty by hedging their purchases of grain. That is, whenever an elevator man buys 5,000 bushels of corn, he can immediately sell a 5,000-bushel corn future. Then when he sells the corn a week or so later on the terminal market, he can buy back his future. If the price of cash corn has fallen 5 cents, he loses 5 cents on his cash corn; but the future will in most cases have fallen about 5 cents also, and he will gain on the future transaction as much as he lost on the cash. He will therefore break even; the hedge will have protected him against loss.

The hedge will also have "protected" him against any gain. If the price of corn had risen 5 cents, he would have profited on his cash corn, but the future would have risen too and he would have lost an equal amount there. In other words, by hedging, the elevator man avoids making any speculative losses or gains and derives his entire income, as he should, from his physical grain-handling operations.

The procedure for hedging can be conveniently summarized in a tabular form like that in Table 12.1. This shows a case of a declining market. In this illustration no allowance has been made for local elevator handling charges (usually 2 or 3 cents a bushel), freight charges, or other minor charges. Their inclusion would only complicate the presentation. We will assume that the elevator man bought the grain at a price that would cover freight and other handling charges and leave him 2 cents a bushel for his local elevator handling charge. The hedge shown above pro-

**TABLE 12.1: Hedging Transactions**

| Cash Grain Transactions | Futures Transactions |
|---|---|
| Dec. 12—Buys 5,000 bu. corn @ $1.50 | Dec. 12—Sells 5,000 bu. May future @ $1.54 |
| Dec. 19—Sells 5,000 bu. corn @ $1.45 | Dec. 19—Buys 5,000 bu. May future @ $1.49 |
| Loss on cash grain = 5¢ a bushel | Gain on futures = 5¢ a bushel |
| Net gain or loss* = 0 | |

* In these examples the cost of the hedge (the sale and purchase of the futures) which is 3/8 cent per bushel for the "round turn" (the sale and purchase together) is ignored, for simplicity in presentation. If it were included here, the elevator man would have a net loss of 3/8 cent per bushel, instead of breaking even.

tects this 2-cent local handling charge and enables him to confine his operations to his legitimate field, handling grain, without becoming involved in speculative activities.

## CHANGES IN SPREAD BETWEEN CASH AND FUTURES PRICES

In the explanation above, the assumption was made that cash and futures prices moved up or down together, that is, by roughly the same amount. That is what usually happens. Sometimes, however, the spread between the cash and futures prices may widen or narrow 1 or 2 cents, or even more.

Figure 12.1 shows that the futures prices for wool move

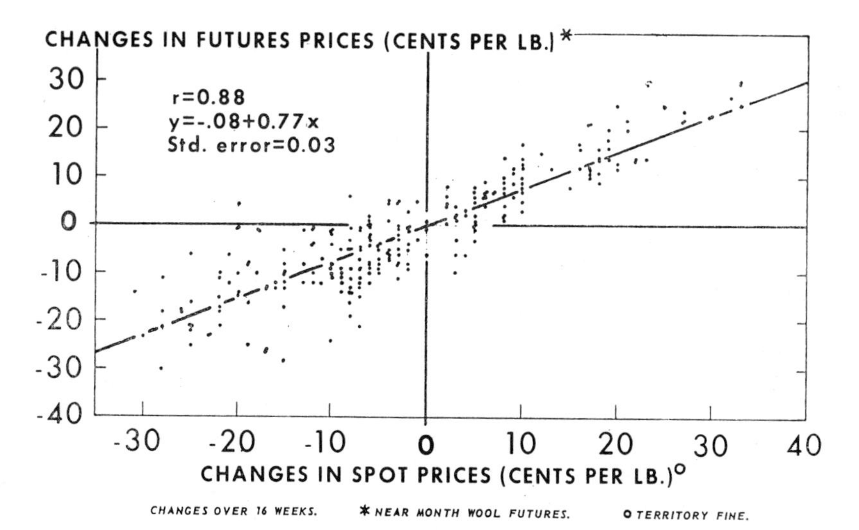


FIG. 12.1—Changes over 16-week periods in cash prices of Territory Fine Staple wool in Boston and in prices of wool futures contracts for the near month in New York, Apr., 1955 to Mar., 1960.

fairly closely with the spot prices over 16-week periods, but that the correlation is not perfect. If the correlation were perfect, the dots in the chart would all fall on the sloping line which shows the nature of the relation between spot and futures prices. But the chart shows that there is a good deal of scatter about the line. The correlation coefficient ($r$) is only 0.88 (perfect correlation would be represented by 1.0).[1]

Moreover, the chart shows that futures prices changed less than spot prices—a change of 1 cent in spot prices was associated, on the average, with a change of only 0.77 of a cent in futures prices.

Under these conditions, the hedge, no matter how well placed, does not give perfect protection. The hedger may lose, or gain, by the amount of the change in the spread.

If the spread narrows, will the hedger gain, or will he lose? This can be figured out by visualizing the relations between the different prices. A reference to the tabular presentation in Table 12.1 may help. The spread between cash and futures when the hedging operation began was 4 cents. Let us suppose that the futures fell more rapidly than the cash, and that when the transaction was completed, the futures price stood at $1.48 instead of the $1.49 given in the table. The gain on the futures would then have been 6 cents instead of 5, and the entire hedging operation would have yielded the hedger a net gain of 1 cent. Conversely, if the cash price had fallen more rapidly than the futures, the hedger would have lost. Small changes in the spread between cash and futures prices occur frequently, so hedging does not give complete protection against price changes.

## LONG-TIME HEDGING

We have described one type of hedging—short-time hedging, the purpose of which is to protect the owner of grain from changes in price while the grain is in transit. Another type of hedging, for a different purpose, can also be employed to advantage. This is long-time hedging, in which the hedging operation extends over a period, not of a week, but of several months or a year.

To understand this type of hedging, we need first to understand the normal relationship of the cash price to the futures prices in a free market uncomplicated by the effects of government loan and stabilization operations.

When the new corn crop begins to move to market in heavy volume, the cash price is usually several cents below the price of

[1] L. D. Howell, *Analysis of Hedging and Other Operations in Wool and Wool Top Futures*, USDA, Tech. Bul. 1260, Jan., 1962, p. 18.

the next or "nearby" future. That is, in January the price of cash corn is usually several cents below the price of the May future. The price of the May future, in turn, is usually a few cents below the price of the July future.

A heavy run of grain to market may at times depress the cash price further than usual below the future. The spread between the cash and the futures prices, however, cannot at any time be greater than the cost at the terminal market of carrying cash corn from that time to the delivery month. For if it were, say, 2 cents wider, operators of terminal storage elevators would buy up cash grain, hedge it, put it in store, and hold it until the delivery month (when the prices of cash and futures have to come together,[2] because the two are then interchangeable). They would then deliver the grain and make a net profit, of 2 cents a bushel in this case, after paying the storage charges.

Accordingly, the cash price, within the crop-moving season, ordinarily runs below the futures, but not further below than the amount of the storage charge to the delivery month. The situation in the simplest case is shown in Figure 12.2.

In this figure, the futures prices are represented by horizontal lines. This assumes that on the average the speculators forecast fairly accurately what prices will be later on as the delivery month approaches. This assumption appears reasonable, since if it appeared at any time that prices in the delivery month would be higher than the present price of the futures, more buyers than sellers of that future would appear and the price of the future would be bid up to equality with the expected price in the delivery month.

Figure 12.2 represents only the general principles of the relationships between cash and futures prices. An actual illustration, taken directly from the market prices of cash corn prices and futures prices at Chicago in 1960–61, is shown in Table

[2] Actually, in the delivery month the cash price usually runs slightly above the futures price. There are several reasons for this. First, a buyer of cash grain gets the grain just when he wants it; but the buyer of a futures contract who wishes to convert it into grain must stand ready to receive the grain any day in the delivery month ("at the seller's option"). This makes futures contracts a fraction of a cent less valuable than cash grain of a similar grade. Second, No. 2 cash grain may grade anywhere between just barely No. 2, and almost No. 1, and usually grades well up in some factors (weight, moisture content, color, etc.) if not in all, but grain delivered on futures contracts is usually "skin grade"—grain that has been mixed with other grain until it just barely qualifies as No. 2 in most or all grade factors, and accordingly is worth less than "country-run" or "virgin" cash grain.

A good discussion of the relation between cotton cash and futures prices is given in A. B. Cox, *Cotton; Demand, Supply, Merchandising,* Austin. Tex., Hemphill's, 1953, Part V.

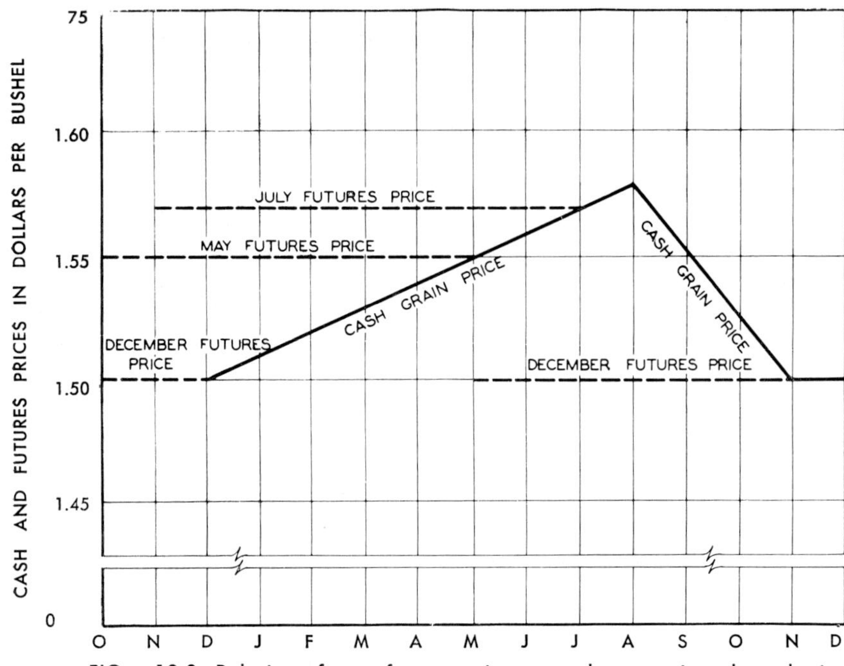


FIG. 12.2—Relation of corn futures prices to cash corn prices, hypothetical data.

12.2 and Figures 12.3 and 12.4. Figure 12.4 is the same as Figure 12.3 except that the prices of the July future were set at zero, appearing therefore as a straight line in Figure 12.4, and the differences between these prices and the other prices were plotted above and below that straight line.[3]

It is evident from these charts that the actual behavior of cash corn and futures prices follow the general pattern laid down in Figure 12.2. The various futures prices were above the cash prices nearly all of the time, and the different prices were related to each other by approximately the costs of storage.

Departures from the normal or average behavior of cash and futures prices resulted from the specific features of the corn harvest in 1960. As harvest time approached,

> . . . it became apparent that the crop was larger than expected, so there would be a substantial crib overrun to be sold and stored off farms. The crop was also wet, further complicating the storage problem. The entire price structure declined. It should be especially noted that three things happened: the price went down, the spreads among the futures increased, and the cash discount under the fu-

[3] *Uses of Grain Futures Markets in the Farm Business*, Ill. Agr. Exp. Sta. Bul. 696, Sept., 1963, pp. 26, 27.

**TABLE 12.2: Prices of Cash Corn at Country Elevators, Cash Corn To Arrive Chicago; and December, March, May, and July Futures, Weekly, 1960–61***

| Date | East-central Illinois Farm Price | No. 2 Yellow To Arrive Chicago | Dec. | March | May | July |
|---|---|---|---|---|---|---|
| 1960 | | | | | | |
| Sept. 2 ....... | 96 | 107½ | 110½ | 114½ | 116¾ | 118½ |
| 9 ....... | 96 | 109¼ | 110¼ | 114⅛ | 116¾ | 118½ |
| 16 ....... | 96 | 108¼ | 109¼ | 113⅝ | 116¼ | 118¼ |
| 23 ....... | 95½ | 108 | 109⅜ | 113⅝ | 116⅝ | 118¾ |
| 30 ....... | 96 | 109¼ | 109¼ | 113½ | 116½ | 118¾ |
| Oct. 7 ....... | 95 | 107½ | 108⅝ | 112½ | 115¼ | 117⅝ |
| 14 ....... | 94 | 107 | 108 | 112 | 115 | 117½ |
| 21 ....... | 94 | 107¾ | 109¼ | 113⅞ | 116⅜ | 118¾ |
| 28 ....... | 92 | 102¾ | 107⅛ | 112¼ | 115¼ | 117½ |
| Nov. 4 ....... | 90½ | 102¼ | 107¼ | 112⅜ | 115⅞ | 118 |
| 11 ....... | 96½ | 99 | 105⅝ | 110½ | 114⅜ | 117⅛ |
| 18 ....... | 82 | 91 | 100⅞ | 106¼ | 110⅛ | 113 |
| 25 ....... | 83 | 95½ | 102⅜ | 107⅞ | 111¾ | 114¾ |
| Dec. 2 ....... | 88 | 99 | 103⅜ | 108½ | 112⅛ | 114¾ |
| 9 ....... | 93½ | 101¼ | 104¼ | 109¼ | 112¾ | 115½ |
| 16 ....... | 95½ | 103¾ | 104 | 108¾ | 112⅜ | 114⅞ |
| 23 ....... | 98 | 107½ | | 109¾ | 113¼ | 115⅞ |
| 30 ....... | 99 | 108¼ | | 109¼ | 113 | 116 |
| 1961 | | | | | | |
| Jan. 6 ....... | 100½ | 110½ | | 112 | 115⅝ | 118⅝ |
| 13 ....... | 100 | 110¾ | | 111¾ | 115⅜ | 118¾ |
| 20 ....... | 100½ | 111¼ | | 111½ | 115½ | 118¼ |
| 27 ....... | 103 | 114¼ | | 114 | 117⅞ | 120½ |
| Feb. 3 ....... | 107½ | 117¼ | | 117¼ | 121⅛ | 125 |
| 10 ....... | 105½ | 115½ | | 115½ | 119⅝ | 123 |
| 17 ....... | 103 | 112½ | | 113⅝ | 117½ | 121½ |
| 24 ....... | 105 | 113¼ | | 114¼ | 118⅝ | 122¼ |
| March 3 ....... | 104 | 114½ | | 114 | 117⅞ | 121⅞ |
| 10 ....... | 105 | 117 | | 118⅛ | 118⅛ | 121⅝ |
| 17 ....... | 104 | 116 | | 113½ | 116¾ | 119⅞ |
| 24 ....... | 103½ | 112 | | | 115½ | 119⅛ |
| 31 ....... | 95½ | 105½ | | | 109⅛ | 112⅝ |
| April 7 ....... | 97 | 108 | | | 109⅜ | 113½ |
| 14 ....... | 100 | 108½ | | | 108⅞ | 112¾ |
| 21 ....... | 102 | 113½ | | | 111⅜ | 115⅛ |
| 28 ....... | 103 | 114¾ | | | 111⅞ | 116½ |
| May 5 ....... | 102 | 113¼ | | | 111⅞ | 115½ |
| 12 ....... | 103½ | 114½ | | | 114 | 117⅝ |
| 19 ....... | 103 | 113½ | | | 112⅞ | 116 |
| 26 ....... | 103½ | 114¼ | | | | 115⅜ |
| June 2 ....... | 104½ | 116 | | | | 116¾ |
| 9 ....... | 103 | 114 | | | | 115 |
| 16 ....... | 101 | 112¾ | | | | 113¼ |
| 23 ....... | 101 | 113¾ | | | | 113¾ |
| 30 ....... | 102 | 113½ | | | | 113⅝ |
| July 7 ....... | 102 | 115½ | | | | 113⅞ |
| 14 ....... | 104½ | 115½ | | | | 114⅛ |
| 20 ....... | 103 | 115¼ | | | | 113⅜ |

* Source: *Uses of Grain Futures Markets in the Farm Business,* Ill. Agr. Exp. Sta. Bul. 696, Sept., 1963, p. 26.

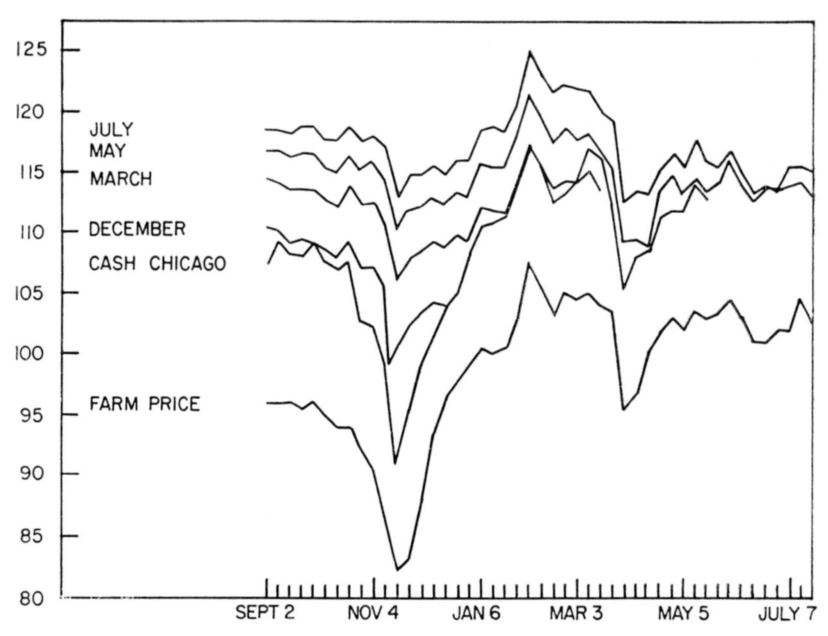


FIG. 12.3—Prices and price relationships for corn during the 1960–61 crop season. Figures shown are cash corn to arrive at Chicago, and futures for December, March, May, and July. (Source: **Uses of Grain Futures in the Farm Business,** Ill. Agr. Sta. Bul. 696, Sept., 1963, p. 27.)

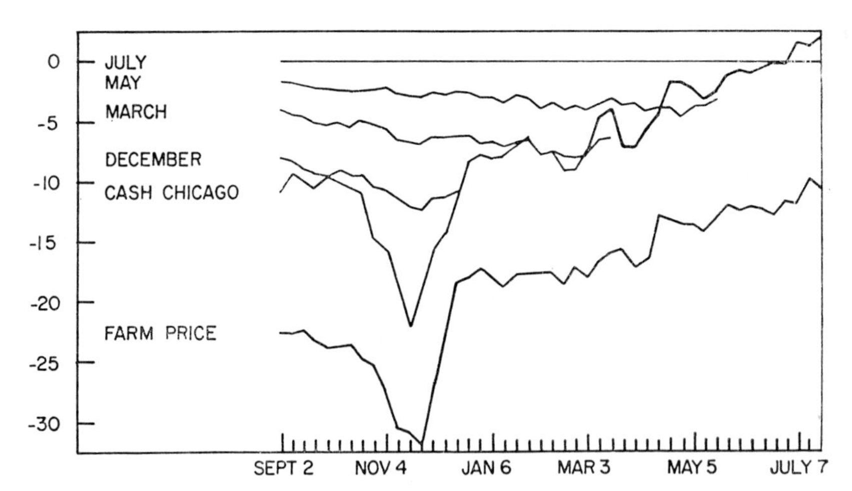


FIG. 12.4—Prices and price relationships for corn during the 1960–61 crop season. The information given is the same as that in Fig. 12.3 except that the July future was set at zero and the other prices were plotted in relation to it. (Source: **Uses of Grain Futures in the Farm Business,** Ill. Agr. Sta. Bul. 696, Sept., 1963, p. 28.)

tures increased. The decline in the price of July corn was the same as the decrease in level of prices, or 5½ to 6 cents. The widening of the spreads and the decrease in cash prices in excess of 5½ to 6 cents was really an increase in the going market price of storage. Put differently, the farm price decrease was 14 cents, of which about 6 cents was a decrease in price and 8 cents was an increase in the price of storing corn.

After the harvest low, the price level of corn varied considerably, but the price interrelationships were fairly consistent with the theoretical patterns.[4]

The relationships shown in Figures 12.3 and 12.4 also differ from year to year as well as among the different futures. For instance, if the supplies of grain are so great that all the available storage space is filled, the cash-future spreads may widen by more than the carrying charge. When this happens, anyone who can buy actual corn and put it into storage at a lower cost than the spread between the cash and futures prices can cinch a profit by buying corn, putting it in storage, and hedging it by an opposite sale of the same amount of futures contracts. This is not a speculation; no risk is involved; the cash and futures prices have to come together in the delivery month. At that time (in the delivery month) the operator can sell his actual corn and buy back his hedge, profiting by the excess of the original cash-future spread over his carrying costs.

It need hardly be said that this result is entirely unaffected by whether the price of cash and futures rises, remains constant, or falls during the months while the operation is being carried on. The hedge not only permits the operator to earn the carrying charge but also protects him, like any other hedge, against a decline in price. It is also obvious that not only elevator men but any others—farmers, for instance—with empty storage space available can follow this practice of long-time hedging whenever the cash-future spreads are wide. The exposition above is phrased in terms of corn, but it applies equally well to wheat, oats, or any other durable commodity for which futures contracts are available.

## SPECULATION TO AVOID STORAGE COSTS

Many grain farmers like to speculate a bit with their crops. For example, they may decide to hold their wheat, hoping for a higher price sometime during the season before the next crop comes on. Most of them hold the physical grain, but some sell their wheat crop right after harvest and buy an equal amount of

[4] *Ibid.*, p. 25. (This bulletin gives an excellent treatment of the subject.)

futures in its place. They then hold the futures instead of the cash grain. They reason that by so doing they escape the storage costs that are incurred in the holding of actual grain.

This belief is probably based on the assumption that cash and futures prices move parallel to each other. They do seem to move that way from day to day. Divergencies exist, however, even in these short-time movements; and over the storage period from one harvest to the next, the price of cash grain usually rises relative to the futures, as shown earlier in this chapter. A farmer who sells his wheat and holds futures instead escapes the storage costs of holding the grain, but he "escapes" the relative rise in the price of the cash grain too.

Actually, this practice of holding the futures instead of the cash grain is nothing but the opposite of the operation "storing to earn the carrying charge" described in the preceding section. If that operation (buying cash grain and selling the future against it) results in a profit, the opposite operation (selling wheat and holding futures instead) would result in a loss. Instead of a blanket condemnation of this practice as unprofitable, however, a better statement would be this: On the average, it does not pay a farmer to sell his wheat crop after harvest and hold futures instead. The only time it would pay him to do this is when the futures price is above the cash price by less than his storage costs to the delivery month; in that case the future is cheap relative to the cash.

## A FEEDER'S HEDGE

A practice followed by some Corn Belt feeders may also be examined. Some cattle feeders, feeding more corn than they grow themselves, may find their neighbors unwilling to sell corn in the winter because they believe they would get a higher price if they held their corn until the next summer. In that case, the feeder may offer to buy the corn for immediate (winter) consumption but agree to pay the farmer the going price any day the farmer cares to select between then and September 1. That sounds fair enough. Many sales are consummated on that basis. The feeder takes the corn, immediately buys the same amount of futures against it, feeds his cattle, and perhaps sells them before the farmer comes over, say in July, and demands that day's price for his corn. The feeder then merely sells his future and pays the farmer that day's price, and everyone is satisfied. If the price is substantially higher then than it was in the winter, the farmer gains; and the feeder does not lose because he benefits from the accompanying rise in the price of futures.

In this whole operation, however, the feeder holds the same place as the wheat farmer, described in the preceding section, who sells his wheat and holds the future instead. He loses by whatever excess he had to pay for his future over the price of cash grain plus the costs of storing that grain. In his case, however, this loss may be more than offset by the fact that if he could not have bought the cash corn locally, except under the arrangement described, the extra cost of importing it from some distance away might have been more than the cost of using the futures market.

## APPRAISAL OF HEDGING

Viewed in the light of the criterion of the perfect market, hedging appears as a practice by which individual farmers and dealers resign themselves to market imperfection with respect to fluctuations in prices over short periods of time, a year or less in length, and attempt merely to neutralize the fluctuations by executing offsetting contracts in the futures markets. These futures contracts are available only for some agricultural products, and hedging neutralizes only part of the fluctuation in their prices, not all of it.

Historically, futures markets have been more widely used by dealers and processors than by farmers; they typically have been used to provide price protection on purchases of products for shipment, storage, or processing. The newer futures markets in livestock, however, appear to be more adaptable to hedging use by livestock producers and feeders than by processors or dealers. They offer a way of removing much of the uncertainty due to price changes during the production or feeding period for cattle and hogs. Futures markets in grains and certain other products can also be used by farmers in the same way—also to hedge products during storage and to hedge feed costs. While farmer use of futures markets has been limited in the past, interest among farmers and feeders in both grain and livestock futures as a management tool is increasing.

While hedging has its uses, it does not go to the heart of the trouble (unstable prices) and correct it. It is a palliative to neutralize the effects of the disease, not a cure to remove the disease itself.

# 13

## EFFECT OF SPECULATION IN FUTURES CONTRACTS UPON GRAIN PRICES

HEDGING is a useful device for partially protecting buyers and sellers of grain against the uncertainties that result from unstable grain prices. The large volume of speculation in futures contracts that makes hedging possible, however, may have some undesirable effects on the prices of cash grain: (1) It may increase the spread between the prices farmers receive for their grain and the prices consumers pay for it—that is, it may lower the whole level of cash grain prices received by farmers and/or raise the prices paid by consumers. (2) It may increase fluctuations in cash prices; if so, hedging merely protects against price fluctuations which the speculation that goes with hedging itself (partly) creates. It is conceivable that if there were no hedging and speculation, there would be less need for hedging.

Are these real possibilities, or are they just pure imagination? The question cannot be answered by a direct appeal to a few simple statistics. It requires first of all a clear grasp of the principles that underlie the operation of the futures market. These principles differ according to the length of time involved. The discussion accordingly will be divided into two parts: (1) the effect of speculation in futures contracts upon cash grain prices over periods of several months, an entire season, or longer and

(2) the effect of speculation for shorter periods of time, such as from day to day or week to week.

## EFFECTS OF SPECULATION OVER PERIODS OF SEVERAL MONTHS

Are futures prices at any time determined by the current prospects for cash prices in the delivery month? Are they a forecast (based on current knowledge) of what cash prices will be in the delivery month? If so, that would mean that futures prices are based upon (prospective) cash prices.

Many people would not accept this conclusion. They believe that the line of causation runs the other way—that cash prices are based upon futures prices or at least are greatly affected by futures prices. That belief is inherent in the title of the present chapter. Is this belief entirely false? Do futures prices actually have no effect upon cash prices?

### Effects of Futures Prices on Cash Prices

Futures prices, even though they are determined by the prospects for cash prices in the delivery month, can under certain conditions affect the current prices of cash grain. These conditions exist (1) whenever futures prices are more than a carrying charge above current cash prices and (2) during squeezes. These squeezes are discussed later under the heading of short-time fluctuations. Here we will deal only with the carrying-charge condition.

In the preceding chapter, it was shown that whenever the price of cash grain falls more than a carrying charge below the price of futures, grain dealers will buy the cash, sell the future against it as a hedge, and hold the cash grain until the delivery month arrives. In the delivery month the price of cash grain must be at least as high as the future (it is in fact usually a cent or more above it), so the grain dealer who hedged when the spread between cash and futures was wider than his carrying charges can be sure of making a profit by selling the grain and buying back the future when the delivery month arrives.

Whenever the price of cash grain falls more than a carrying charge below the futures, therefore, grain dealers buy the cash and sell the future in such quantities that their actions raise cash prices, or depress futures prices, or both, until the spread between them narrows to the point where it barely covers storage charges. In fact, as long as storage space is available, the spread between cash and futures prices cannot be greater than the carrying charge to the delivery month. As soon as the spread becomes slightly greater than the carrying charge, the action of grain dealers in taking advantage of it keeps the spread from getting any wider. The cash price, then, cannot fall more than a carrying charge below the future. It can rise to any height above the future but it cannot fall more than a carrying charge below the future.

When grain dealers buy the cash and sell the future, the cash rises, or the future falls, or both. Which of these is likely to happen? On the face of it, one might think that the cash would rise and the future would fall by about equal amounts, since the amount of buying of the one would be equal to the selling of the other. But it must be remembered that the futures prices are based solidly on the prospects for cash prices in the delivery month. If nothing has happened to change those prospects, the price of the future will fall only slightly, perhaps not at all, when "hedging pressure" is put on it. For if speculators still believe that the prospects for cash corn are such that it will be worth 95 cents in December, they will buy the December future whenever it falls below 95 cents; the downward hedging pressure on the December future will depress prices only slightly, enough to call forth purely speculative support. The December future will remain at, or close to, 95 cents, and the narrowing of the spread between cash and futures prices will be accomplished almost entirely by a rise in the cash prices.[1]

It is only through the hedging mechanism that this supporting of cash prices would be effected. If no storage space were available to potential hedgers, for instance, no amount of volume of futures trading by itself would support cash prices. The support that is actually effected through the hedging mechanism has been exaggerated in some of the literature. If there were no futures trading at all, and cash corn prices fell for the hypothetical reason given above or for any other reason, cash grain

[1] Paul Mehl, formerly with the Commodity Exchange Authority, comments on this point, "Any pressure, speculative or hedging, can depress prices temporarily even in the face of bullish factors. I have seen the price of futures depressed in the face of bullish new crop conditions due to heavy liquidation of an old crop future. The selling pressure of the old crop futures was greater than the buying of the new crop futures." This is no doubt correct, but it is a short-time phenomenon, not a long-time matter. If the volume of hedging sales orders coming in, to be executed "at the market," is greater than the volume of buying orders at that time, some of the hedgers have to offer to sell at ⅛ or ¼ of a cent below the going price to get their orders executed at all. This lowers the going price ⅛ or ¼ of a cent, or more, until this lowering evokes enough speculative buying orders to equal the volume of sales orders. Because market knowledge is not perfect in the grain market, even though more perfect than in some other commodity markets, the going price has to fall temporarily in order to call forth additional speculative buying (or covering of previous speculative sales). This is a matter of institutional friction, not of price-determining principles.

dealers would buy cash corn whenever its price fell more than a carrying charge below the prospective price in later months. The only additional support that can be attributed to the futures market is that with it the cash grain dealers can hedge their position; without it, they would have to carry the risks themselves instead of loading them on to the futures speculators' shoulders.

Some preliminary conclusions may now be drawn. They refer only to long-time (seasonal and annual) price determination; short-time (week-to-week and day-to-day) price fluctuations are dealt with in the next section. The major conclusion is that futures prices do not determine cash prices; things work the other way around—cash prices determine futures prices. More accurately, the prospects for cash prices in each delivery month determine each of the current futures prices.

The minor conclusion is a sort of amendment to the major conclusion given above: Futures prices set a floor below which cash prices cannot fall by more than a carrying charge to the delivery month. This effect of futures prices on cash prices works through the hedging mechanism and is comparatively small.

## SHORT-TIME PRICE FLUCTUATIONS

The preceding conclusions apply to the broad movements of grain prices from one season to the next and from one year to another. The small, short-time perturbations of prices from hour to hour and day to day are another story.

Some observers have argued that speculation cannot cause short-time price fluctuations. Any speculator, they say, who attempts to sell the future down out of line with fundamental price conditions has to buy back the same future before long, and the fundamental price conditions will have helped to pull prices back up when he buys, so that he is likely to suffer a net loss rather than gain from his operations.

But this argument leaves out of account two things—"follow the leader" trading and "stop-loss" orders. Some of the trading in futures contracts is done by traders who try to size up what the larger speculators are doing and to go along with them. If they believe that a large speculator is offering futures in considerable quantities, they will sell (in smaller quantities) too. If the large speculator is selling because of advance information or more accurate interpretation of current events than the interpretations of others, they will benefit from his foresight. If he is merely seeking to unsettle the market, they will help him; his large sales, unsettling on account of their size, will be reinforced by their small sales.

"Stop-loss" orders are also a factor, especially in very active markets. (A speculator who has bought at 75 and seen prices rise to 81 may protect his profits by putting in a "stop-loss" order —an order to sell if the price falls to 80 or 79 cents.) A considerable amount of stop-loss orders on the market complicates things. A large speculator, sensing the existence of stop-loss orders at 79 cents when the current price is 81 cents, might test the market to satisfy himself there was not much latent buying power in it and then throw half a million bushels of futures on the market. If the market is nervous, it may break through these stop-loss orders at 80 and 79 cents. Then he gets help. The stop-loss orders are uncovered and are thrown on the market regardless of the effect they may have on prices. Under their weight, the price may drop another 1 or 2 cents; if the market uncovers further stop-loss orders on the way down, it may go still lower. "The market," the reporter will say in the evening papers, "was honeycombed with stop-loss orders. Prices broke several cents, once they started down." The initial sale of half a million bushels of futures may have resulted in the dumping on the market of several times that volume of other speculators' contracts. Then the large speculator, whose half a million bushels have been sold at an average price of 80 cents, can buy them back at a lower price and pocket his profits.

This illustration has been phrased in terms of declining prices, but the mechanism works just as well the other way around. Stop-loss orders can be used to protect shorts against rising prices, and in that case they may contribute to a rise started by a large speculator's buying. Regulations, instituted during the past few years, which limit the amount of trading that can be conducted by any one speculator have reduced the effects of the operations described above.

### "SQUEEZES"

Another source of short-time price fluctuations is "squeezes."

The volume of futures trading in wheat, for example, is ordinarily about ten times greater than the volume of trading in the actual grain itself. At any one time, the volume of futures contracts outstanding (the "open contracts") is large relative to the volume of actual grain in the market.[2] Usually more than 99 per cent of the bushels represented by the futures contracts are closed out by offsetting futures contracts, so that very little grain is actually delivered on any of them.

But the contracts specify actual delivery of the grain unless

[2] There are several reasons for this, one of them being that the bulk of the trading in futures is entered in Chicago, but only a small part of the visible supply of grain is stored there and only a small part of the grain in the country passes through Chicago.

both buyer and seller accept offsetting contracts. A large market operator may see an opportunity, in years when deliverable grain is scarce, quietly to buy large quantities of futures and also to buy most of the supplies of deliverable grain as they come on the market during the delivery month. As the end of the delivery month approaches, the "shorts" (the speculators, who have sold futures contracts expecting to "get out of the market" by making offsetting purchases of contracts before the end of the delivery month, and any bona fide hedgers, whose grain is "out of deliverable position," that is, stored in elevators in the country or in other contract markets, or whose grain is of nondeliverable grade) find that there is a "congestion" in the futures market; they cannot close out their trades by offsetting contracts without paying an exorbitant price for them to the "squeezer." They are caught. As the last trading day of the delivery month approaches, if there is not enough time to get more grain in from the country, the "shorts" finally have to pay the "squeezer" his price or default on their contracts. The price of cash grain may rise 12 or 14 cents in the last few days of trading.

The Chicago Board of Trade has put through several measures designed to make it difficult or impossible to conduct a squeeze. During the last three business days of the delivery month, the delivery of grain on contracts is permitted in cars anywhere within switching distance of Chicago. Other grades of grain than the basic contract grade are deliverable at stated premiums or discounts; trading in the expiring future is not permitted during the last seven days of the delivery month, giving the "shorts" the rest of the month to bring grain in from the country or from other terminals. And finally, definite limits have been put upon the number of bushels of futures contracts that any one trader may hold, and upon the volume of trading that he may conduct.[3] These measures, however, have not been entirely successful in preventing "squeezes."

They occurred even during World War II. General Foods

[3] The Commodity Exchange Act specifies the following trading limits:

*Position Limits.* 1. The limit on the maximum net long or net short position which any person may hold or control in any one grain on any one contract market, except as specifically authorized by paragraph 2 hereof, is: 2,000,000 bushels in any one future or in all futures combined.

2. To the extent that the net position held or controlled by any one person in all futures combined in any one grain or any one contract market is shown to represent spreading in the same grain between markets, the limit on net position in all futures combined set forth in paragraph 1 hereof may be exceeded on such contract market, but in no case shall the excess result in a net position of more than 3,000,000 bushels in all futures combined nor more than 2,000,000 bushels in any one future.

*Daily Trading Limits.* 3. The limit on the maximum amount which any person may buy, and on the maximum amount which any person may sell, of any one grain on any one contract market during any one business

Corporation and some individuals, including Phillip O'Brien, a former president of the Chicago Board of Trade, cornered the May rye futures on the Chicago Board of Trade in 1944. Beginning in December, 1942, General Foods built up a long position in rye futures and physical grain. In December, 1943, it took delivery on 1,880,000 bushels of December, 1943, rye futures. This brought its holding of rye grain in Chicago to 7,230,000 bushels, about 76 per cent of the total deliverable supply in Chicago at that time.

The business conduct committee of the Chicago Board of Trade ordered General Foods to acquire no more rye futures or grain; but the other gentlemen mentioned above, on their own or as authorized agents for the company, continued operations in rye during 1944. Canadian as well as other rye began to be drawn out of position to Chicago. The group extended its operations to Winnipeg. On May 27, 1944, it held 11,805,000 bushels of deliverable rye in Chicago—89 per cent of the total deliverable supply there—occupying about 50 per cent of the total public grain storage space in the city and congesting transportation facilities at a time when they were needed for more important war purposes.[4]

A complaint issued under the Commodity Exchange Act, on May 26, 1945, charged the General Foods Corporation, Charles W. Metcalf, Daniel F. Rice, Daniel F. Rice and Company, Phillip R. O'Brien, and Lawrence J. Ryan with cornering and manipulating the price of rye and rye futures contracts on the Chicago Board of Trade in May, 1944, and prior thereto. After much litigation, the group was cleared of the charges by the United States Circuit Court of Appeals in October, 1948.

Controversy over the effects of futures trading on commodity prices was touched off again in 1957, when a wave of

---

day, except as specifically authorized by paragraph 4 hereof, is: 2,000,000 bushels in any one future or in all futures combined.

4. To the extent that purchases or sales of any one grain on any one contract market during any one business day made by any person are shown to represent spreading, or the closing of spreads, in the same grain between markets, the limit set forth in paragraph 3 hereof may be exceeded on such contract market, but in no case shall the excess result in total purchases of more than 3,000,000 bushels, or total sales of more than 3,000,000 bushels, and in no event shall such person's total purchases or total sales, during any one business day, in any one future exceed 2,000,000 bushels.

The foregoing limits upon position and upon daily trading shall not be constructed to apply to bona fide hedging transactions as defined in paragraph 3 of section 4a of the Commodity Exchange Act.

[4] United States Department of Agriculture Before the War, Food Administrator, In re *General Foods Corporation, Charles W. Metcalf, Daniel F. Rice and Company, Daniel F. Rice, Lawrence J. Ryan, and Phillip R. O'Brien. CE-A Docket No. 34. Complaint and Notice of Hearing Under Section 6(b) of the Commodity Exchange Act* (mimeo.), USDA, undated.

speculation in onion futures swept the price of onions up from about $1.20 per 50-pound sack to over $2 for a few days, after which they subsided to less than $1. Hearings were held, and futures trading in onions was prohibited by law.[5]

## EFFECT OF VOLUME OF FUTURES TRADING ON PRICES

Opinions differ concerning the effect of a large volume of futures trading on cash grain. Many farmers believe that the cost of the large volume of futures trading exacts a toll from the physical grain in the channels of trade. "Every bushel of grain is sold about ten times over in the pit," they say, and go on to reason that the cost of this trading is borne by the physical grain; it shows up either in lower prices to the producer, or higher prices to the consumer, or both. This opinion is not endorsed by members of the Board of Trade. They hold quite an opposite view. Let us examine the farmers' beliefs first, and then turn to the opposing opinions.

### Every Bushel Is Not "Sold Ten Times Over"

It is true that the volume of futures trading in wheat is about ten times the volume of the cash trading in the terminal markets.[6] But it is not true that "every bushel of wheat is sold ten times over"; neither is it true that the average bushel of wheat is sold ten times over; far from it.

This becomes apparent if we trace a carload of wheat from the farm through the local elevator to the terminal market and the ultimate buyer. Let us suppose that an exporter located at Minneapolis is offering $1.70 a bushel for wheat at the Minneapolis market. He appears on the floor of the Minneapolis Grain Exchange and a commission man to whom a carload of wheat has been consigned from a local elevator man at, let us say, Brookings, South Dakota, sells him a carload of wheat at $1.70. The commission man takes the exporter's check for the wheat, deducts his commission of 1½ cents a bushel, and remits the rest to the local elevator man at Brookings. The local elevator man thus receives $1.68½ a bushel for his wheat, minus freight and inspection charges. The "cost of speculation" does not enter in anywhere along the line between the price paid by the consumer for cash grain and the price received by the farmer.

---

[5] This episode, and the effects of futures trading in general, are discussed at several points in *Futures Trading Seminar, History and Development*, Vol. I, Madison, Wisc., Mimir Press, 1960.

[6] Inspected receipts of wheat at 107 markets in the 1966–67 marketing year totaled a little over 1.3 billion bushels, about the same as the total 1966 U.S. wheat crop. The total volume of trading in wheat futures in the same period was 10.4 billion bushels (see *Commodity Futures Statistics, July, 1966–June, 1967*, USDA, Stat. Bul. 414, p. 2).

Then where does the money come from if not from the physical commodity? It comes from the futures speculators and hedgers themselves. This is also made clear by tracing through a specific transaction, in this case in the futures market. A speculator buys, let us say, 10,000 bushels of July futures at $1.80. He puts up 15 cents per bushel margin with his broker. The man from whom he bought may have been a hedger, selling a future to hedge a purchase of cash grain; he puts up a margin also. A week later, the price rises, and the original buyer now sells his 10,000 bushels at $1.85. For simplicity, we will suppose that the original seller (the hedger) also closes out his trade, too. What happens? The original buyer's broker sends him a check for 19⅝ cents per bushel (that is, the margin of 15 cents plus the gain of 5 cents, minus the ⅜-cent brokerage fee for executing the sale and purchase); the original seller's broker sends him a check for 9⅝ cents per bushel (that is, the margin of 15 cents *minus* the loss of 5 cents, minus ⅜-cent brokerage fee for executing the purchase and sale; in his particular case the loss would have been offset by a corresponding rise in the price of the cash grain he owned). The cost of futures speculation came from the two futures traders themselves, not from the physical grain. The conclusion can be generalized to cover the whole body of futures trading.

### Does a Large Volume of Trading Support Prices?

Some proponents of futures trading believe that a large volume of trading raises the price of cash grain. Some of them phrase their argument merely in terms of the volume of trading. Others concentrate on the buying involved; a large volume of buying, they say, raises prices in any market for futures contracts as well as for physical commodities.

We can for the moment overlook two obvious weaknesses in the buying argument: (1) The large volume of buying referred to is buying of futures contracts, not of physical cash grain and (2) if there is a large volume of buying in the futures market, there is an exactly equally large volume of selling there too, since every purchase is bought from somebody who sold, and the supply of futures contracts is virtually unlimited.

The thing that raises the prices of futures contracts is not the volume of trading but the willingness of traders to pay higher prices. That willingness, expressed in actual payment of higher prices, results in higher prices regardless of volume. It may induce an increase in volume, but that volume is an effect of the rising prices, not a cause. If we want to explain the reasons for rising prices, we have to search for the factors that induce traders to pay higher prices, not for the factors that increase volume.

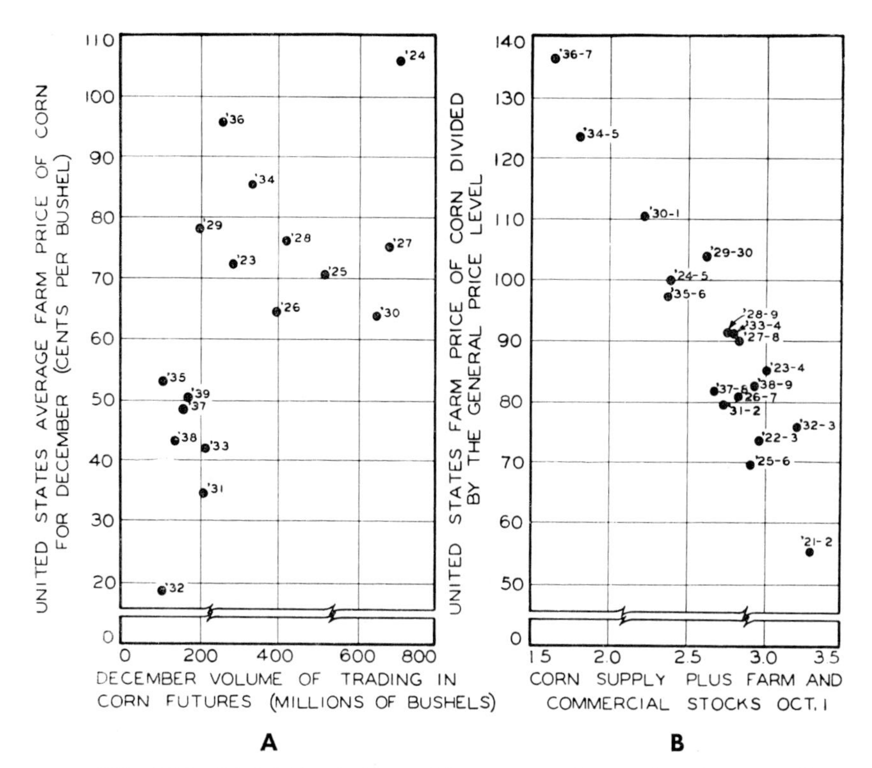


FIG. 13.1—(**A**) Relation between U.S. average farm price of corn on Dec. 15 and the total volume of trading in corn futures in Dec., 1923–38. (**B**) Relation between adjusted U.S. average farm price of corn, Oct.–Sept., and U.S. corn production, 1921–38. The corn price in section **B** is deflated by the Bureau of Labor Statistics index of all commodity prices at wholesale. (Source: **Agricultural Statistics,** USDA, 1931 and 1939; and **Feed Statistics,** USDA, mimeo., Feb., 1940, p. 37.)

The U.S. average price of corn at the farm in December is plotted against the volume of trading in corn futures for the same month each year from 1923 to 1938 in Figure 13.1A. This chart shows a fairly high positive correlation between the volume of trading in corn futures and the price of cash corn. (The correlation has been reduced since the operations of the Commodity Credit Corporation have become so important in the grain trade.)

But one must always be on guard in drawing conclusions from statistical correlations. Correlation does not show causation nor its direction. Prices were high in certain years shown in Figure 13.1A, not because the volume of futures trading was high, but because the size of the corn crop in those years was small. Prices were low in other years, not because the volume of trading was low, but because the corn crop was large. This is shown in Figure 13.1B, where the size of the corn crop is plotted

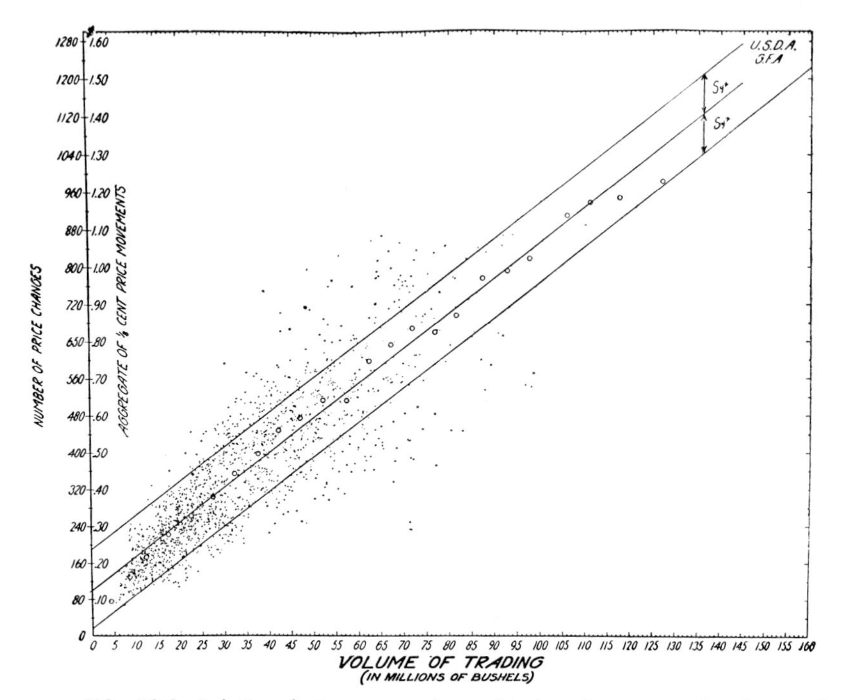


FIG. 13.2—Relation between number of price changes and volume of trading in futures, Jan. 2, 1924, to Dec. 31, 1931. (Courtesy of Commodity Exchange Authority.) (More recent studies are not available.)

along with the seasonal average price each year. The negative correlation between the two is evident. It is well known that high prices attract attention to the speculative market, and low prices chill speculative fervor. The real sequence of causation, then, is not (C) large volume of futures→ (B) high corn prices, but (A) small crop of corn→ (B) high prices→ (C) large volume of futures trading.

### Does Speculation Stabilize Prices?

That brings us to the final question—Is there any statistical evidence that speculation stabilizes prices?

We have touched on this question before. A chart provided by the Commodity Exchange Administration (now Commodity Exchange Authority) (CEA) sheds some light on this question, even though the data is not recent. Figure 13.2 shows the number of price changes each day and the volume of trading on the same day, over a period of 2,069 days from January 2, 1924, to December 31, 1931, excluding 1926 and part of 1925 when "old" and "new" style futures were being traded in. Each dot represents the volume of trading for one day and the number of ⅛-cent price changes that occurred on the same day. The hollow circles represent averages of the individual dots by 5 million-bushel class intervals. The correlation is positive, showing that a large volume of trading is associated with numerous changes in price, not with stable prices. The correlation between the daily price range (difference between the low and high price for the day) and the daily volume of trading is similarly high. It is 0.8.

Care needs to be taken here in interpreting this correlation, the same as with the preceding charts. One cannot conclude merely from study of the chart that a large volume of trading causes unstable prices; nor can one conclude that the causation runs the opposite way. Whatever conclusions are drawn will have to be based on a knowledge of futures trading and on economic reasoning, plus the statistical information shown in the chart. But at least, in view of this chart, one is not likely to accept uncritically the argument that a large volume of trading and stable prices go together.

A more recent study of the influence of speculation on the price behavior of grain futures reached these general conclusions:

> Original, objective analyses show that speculation explained part of short-term price ranges or changes in most of the market situations for which estimating procedures were developed. The relative importance attributable to speculation, compared with other explanatory variables, varied widely, as did its absolute price effect.
>
> Rigorous analysis of price ranges over longer intervals, however, required the introduction of many supply and consumption ratios into multiple regression equations. These explanations suggest that most price behavior during short-term periods (one or several weeks) primarily reflects logical, objective market response to important new commodity statistics. While these factors, singly and jointly with the extent of divergence of market price from the effective loan level, were of prime importance in explaining inter-day price variance, price behavior also reflected the transactions by speculators and others.[7]

More specific conclusions relative to price changes on corn futures for the period from 1956–65 were as follows: "Comparisons between levels of speculative positions and the degree of price fluctuations indicated quite convincingly that monthly

[7] *Margins, Speculation and Prices in Grains Futures Markets*, USDA, Dec., 1967, pp. 4–5. (Unnumbered report prepared for ERS by Robert R. Nathan Associates, Inc., Washington, D.C.)

price ranges were not related to levels of speculative positions during this nine-year period."[8]

Another argument that is sometimes made—that for every sale in the futures market there must be a corresponding purchase, so futures trading can have no effect on futures or cash prices—warrants attention only because it is used so frequently. The considered opinion of the administrator of the CEA on this question is worth quoting here:

> We have never agreed with the thought that inasmuch as for every sale in the futures market there must be a purchase it follows that futures trading can have little if any price effect. We have always considered that immediate changes in futures prices are brought about by the attitude of buyers and sellers using the market. Thus, when buyers are aggressive and sellers hesitant, a higher quotation is registered; when sellers are insistent and buyers hold off, a lower quotation. Back of the immediate causes of price change are the many reasons for the attitude of buyers and sellers. Trade gossip, the uneven flow of orders to buy or sell, depletion of margins, the type of orders, and the touching off of stop-loss orders are common reasons for the fluctuation of futures prices over a short period of time.
>
> Of somewhat longer-term effect are the occasional instances where a large number of speculative traders are induced to come into the market by the fact that some particular situation is being widely publicized. We think it is clear that such waves of speculative activity have resulted in prices being temporarily forced up or down from their normal level, with the inevitable corrective reaction in which the prices will temporarily deviate from normal in the opposite direction. Of course, basic economic factors in the form of available supplies and effective demand are pervasive forces in shaping futures as well as cash prices in the long run.[9]

Another considered opinion runs in somewhat broader terms:

> Data on changes in cash prices and in prices of futures contracts show that anticipated changes in the demand-and-supply situation, particularly from one crop-year to another, were more clearly indicated and were somewhat more accurately discounted in prices of futures contracts than in prices of the cash commodity. These data along with other available information indicate that futures trading usually tends to lessen the seasonal fluctuations in prices of grain and to reduce the extent of price changes from one season to another. But futures markets, by facilitating trading, no doubt in-

[8] *Ibid.*, p. 38.

[9] Personal communication, Aug. 21, 1959.

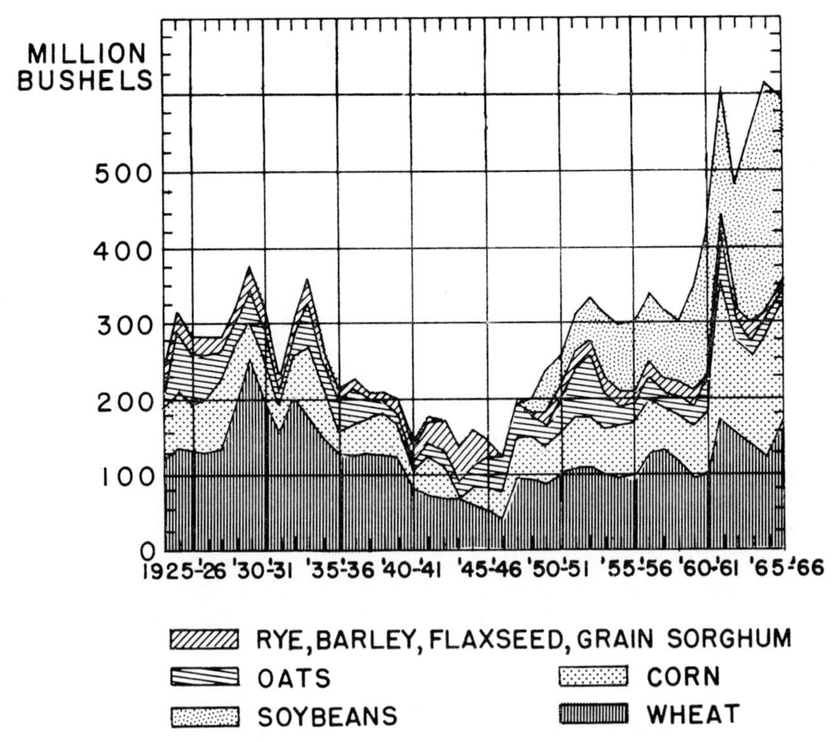


FIG. 13.3—All grain futures: average month-end open contracts on all contract markets, United States, July, 1923–66.

crease the frequency of changes in grain prices and may at times increase the amounts of these changes over relatively short periods.[10]

## APPRAISAL

It seems evident that the futures trading on the large terminal markets merits neither the blame that has been heaped upon it for causing large fluctuations nor the praise that has been bestowed upon it for its alleged stabilizing force. Actually, it appears to have very little effect either one way or the other, except perhaps to accentuate small, short-time fluctuations. Various technical internal features of the futures market operation have deserved and received correction, partly voluntary and partly enforced by the government. Hedging probably narrows the grain-handling margin by enabling the grain operator to shift most of his price risk to others. Occasional "squeezes" still

[10] L. D. Howell, *Analysis of Hedging and Other Operations in Grain Futures*, USDA, Tech. Bul. 971, Aug., 1948, p. 65.

occur, and small short-time (hour-to-hour or day-to-day) fluctuations may be accentuated by speculation. But except for these things the effect of futures trading on prices is not very great.

There has been some feeling that futures markets in grains and related products would become less important because of the stabilization programs of the federal government. This was expressed even before World War II when the magnitude of these programs was smaller than in recent years. The price support loan and purchase programs of the Commodity Credit Corporation (CCC) are a direct attack on the problem of unstable prices. Hedging provides some protection against fluctuations in prices, but the operations of the CCC are designed to reduce the fluctuations. To the extent that they succeed, hedging and speculation become less necessary or advantageous. Figure 13.3 shows how the volume of futures contracts open at the end of the month—a good measure of the use being made of the futures market—declined substantially from 1930 to 1945. After 1945, the postwar price inflation carried grain prices upward, fluctuating freely above the CCC loan rates most of the time. Speculative activity increased. Figure 13.3 shows that the average month-end open contracts for wheat increased considerably from 1945 to the mid-sixties, moving back to the levels of the 1930's. Open contracts in corn and soybeans have risen sharply, while the other grains have shown a decline. Total open contracts during the 1960–65 period were by far the largest in history. And the number of open contracts on these grains increased further during the 1966–69 period. So it is evident that pre-World War II expectations of a continued decline in futures trading were, as Mark Twain said of reports of his death, greatly exaggerated.

# 14

# THE PRICE SURFACE IN DECENTRALIZED MARKETS

THE FOUR preceding chapters were all concerned with changes in prices over periods of time. The present chapter deals with a different sort of problem—price changes in *place;* that is, changes in prices at one point relative to prices at other points. The price of a product at one market point may rise at a time when prices at other markets may remain constant or decline. It pays to select the highest net market point in place as well as in time.

The rise of decentralized markets discussed in earlier chapters has accentuated this problem of place. It has confronted farmers with two new marketing problems: (1) the job of picking out the highest net price point in the decentralized market area and (2) the problem of determining the effect of direct marketing on the general price level of the commodity. These two problems will be dealt with in order. The first one is discussed here; the other, in Chapter 15.

## SELLING IN A DECENTRALIZED MARKET

Under the early local and central market system, the problem of market selection was simpler than it is now. Farmers merely had to choose between selling to a local buyer or consigning to the nearest terminal market. The short-time (day-to-day) shipping time problem could scarcely be handled at all; current market news was so scarce and the distances to the terminal markets were so great that it was almost impossible for farmers to respond quickly to short-time (day-to-day) changes in prices.

The situation is different today. Farmers now can choose among many outlets for their livestock. The present-day decentralized marketing system offers farmers access not only to the distant terminal markets but also to numerous local markets close at hand. Usually, several of these local concentration points and interior packing plants are located within easy trucking radius of any one point, while the more distant markets can be reached by rail, as before, either directly by individual farmers or through a local dealer or a cooperative shipping association. The plentiful market news now available enables farmers to keep more or less in current touch with these numerous local markets within the broad decentralized market that covers the whole country.

The price surface over the broad nation-wide market is of course not flat. There is a good deal of geographical specialization of livestock production, and the heavy livestock-producing areas do not coincide with the heavy meat-consuming areas. Two-thirds of the cattle, for example, are produced west of the Mississippi, but only one-third of the beef is eaten there; the other two-thirds is shipped to the high-consumption areas in the East. The price surface is therefore flat plus or minus transportation charges from the surplus to the deficit areas.

Figure 14.1 illustrates the nature of the price surface for hogs. The map shows in somewhat generalized form the average prices by areas for 1965–66. There is a spread of 50 cents to $1 per 100 pounds between the heavy hog-producing areas of the Corn Belt and parts of eastern United States. The spread between the western Corn Belt and the West Coast area is around $1 per 100 pounds. These price differences are roughly equal to the cost of shipping hogs from one area to the other, including transportation and other costs.

The lowest points on the price surface were in the Maine-Vermont-New Hampshire area and parts of Wyoming and Nevada. Prices were also relatively lower in the Arkansas-Louisiana area and in North Dakota. None of these states are major hog-producing states. The lower price levels probably reflect in part the sparseness of hog production and a lack of hog-processing facilities. There may be some quality differences between areas as well.

At the other extreme, price levels in both Hawaii and Alaska

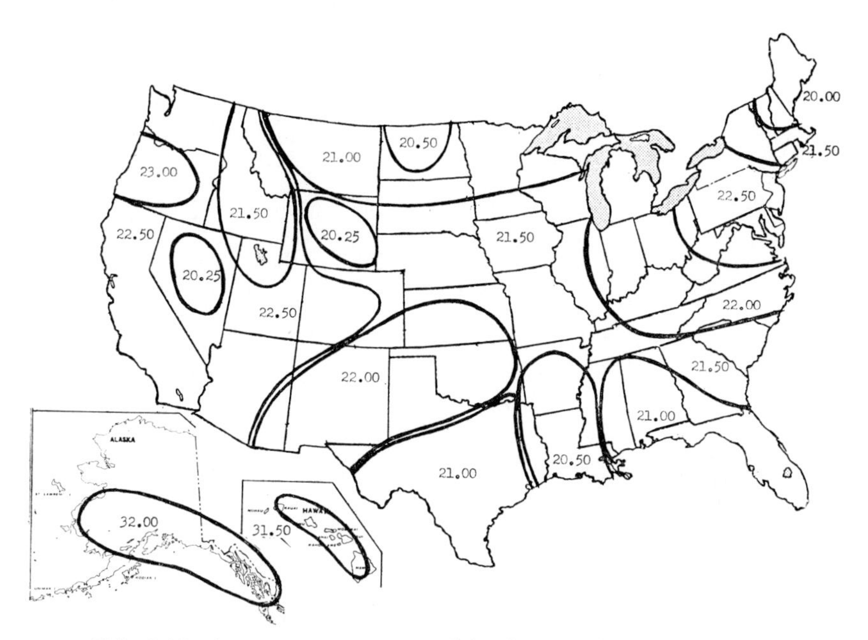


FIG. 14.1—Average prices received by farmers for hogs, in dollars per 100 pounds, 1965–66. (Source: Based on data in **Agricultural Prices,** USDA, annual issues, June, 1966, and June, 1967.

reflect the very large costs involved in transporting pork from the Corn Belt to these distant states. Average prices in Alaska and Hawaii in 1965–66 were around $32 per 100 pounds, over $10 above the general average in the Corn Belt.

## RELATIONSHIP OF MARKET PRICE FLUCTUATIONS

Perfection with respect to place in the market represents only the average behavior over a period of ten years. For shorter periods of time—from month to month or day to day—the situation is different. The water in the ocean averages flat over a period of time, but for short periods tidal movements raise some areas above and depress other areas below the average level, storms sweep across the tidal movements, and ripples ride the surface of the waves. So it is with the prices at the local markets over the country. The price surface heaves and sinks, billows and ripples; it is never still.

This is shown clearly in Figure 14.2 by the behavior of corn prices in the different regions of the United States.[1] In this

[1] *Changes in Spatial Grain-Price Patterns in the United States and in the North Central Region, 1946–1958*, Ill. Agr. Exp. Sta. Bul. 663, 1960.

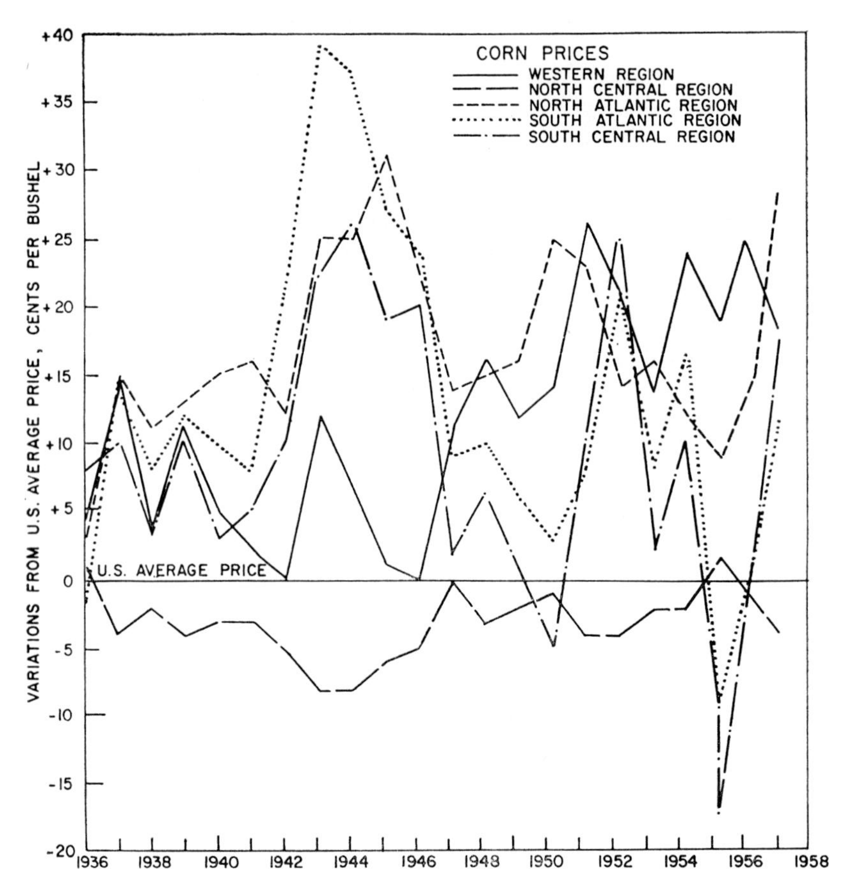


FIG. 14.2—Differences between U.S. average price and regional corn prices, 1936–58.

chart, the difference between the farm price of corn in each region and the U.S. average farm price of corn is plotted as so much above or below the straight horizontal line running across the chart at 0. The differences change from approximately plus 40 cents to minus 10 cents—a range of nearly 50 cents—in the case of the South Atlantic Region. These changes took place even though corn prices were being supported at loan rates that varied relative to each other very little or not at all.

The annual variations in winter wheat prices, by states, are shown in a similar manner in Figure 14.3. The range of differences in this case covers about 30 cents (the geographical area is smaller than in the case of corn shown in Figure 14.2).

The same sort of thing is true for hog, beef-cattle, and other

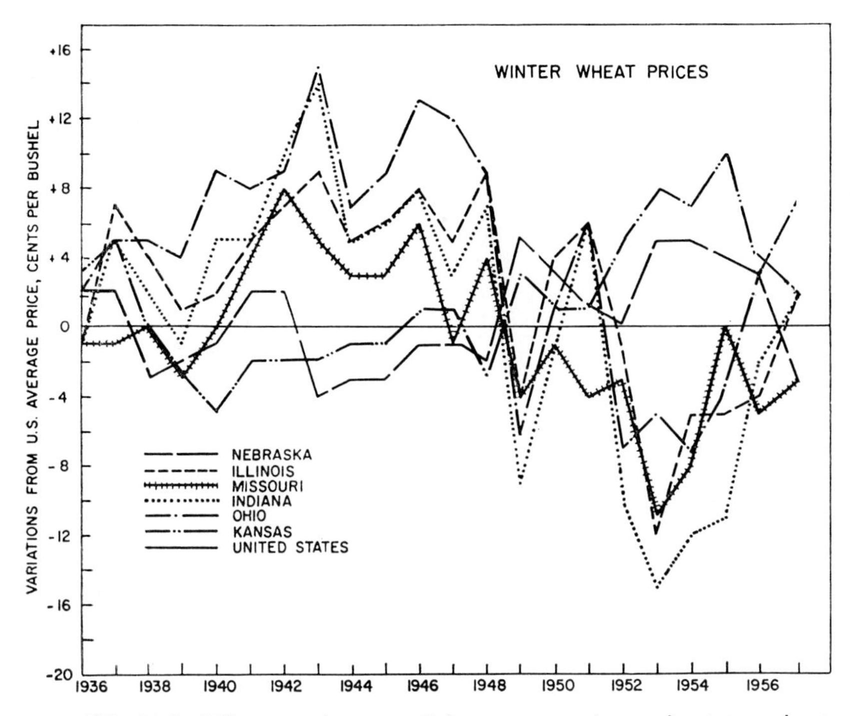


FIG. 14.3—Differences between U.S. average price and winter wheat prices in six states, 1936–57.

livestock prices. And it is true from week to week and day to day as well as from year to year.

The prices at different markets fluctuate in relation to each other because of the fluctuations in local supply and demand at each point. The packer's sales of his pork products, which are the basis of his demand for hogs, fluctuate from day to day and from week to week. His receipts of hogs fluctuate in response to changes in local supply conditions. The only way he can keep the supply of hogs adjusted to his demand for them is to raise or lower his prices relative to the prices at other markets. When the packer wants more hogs, he raises his price; when he has too many, he lowers it.

It makes a great difference, therefore, which market the farmer chooses. Some days one market will net 10 or 20 cents higher than another; some days it will net 10 or 20 cents lower.

## Medium- and Long-Time Movements

Hog price differentials change not only from day to day, but also from month to month and year to year. There are tides and

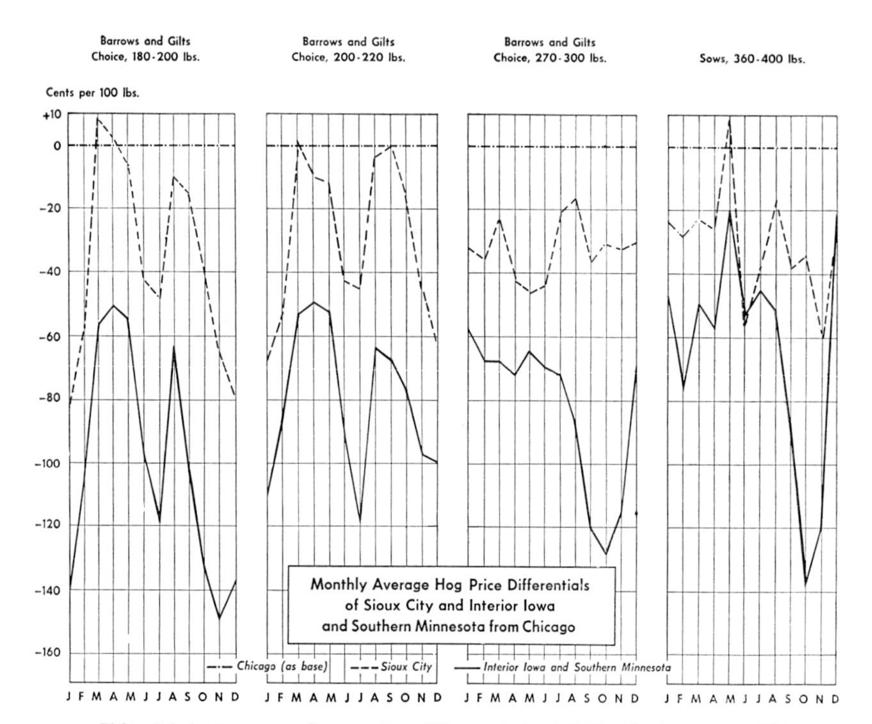


FIG. 14.4—Average hog price differentials, 1949–51, between Chicago, Sioux City, and interior markets. Prices at Chicago are represented by the horizontal line at zero. (Source: Sam Thompson, "Choosing Right Hog Market Can Increase Returns," **Iowa Farm Science**, Iowa State Univ., Nov., 1962, p. 456.)

long swells as well as waves and ripples on the price surface.

The average differentials from month to month between hog prices at several midwestern markets, 1949–51, are shown in Figure 14.4.

Wholesale meat market price differentials behave much the same as livestock market price differentials.

In 1949, the weekly prices of fresh pork loins, 8–12 pounds average at New York, for example, varied all the way from $4 per 100 pounds above the corresponding prices at Chicago, to $3 below the price at Chicago. A more recent check in 1969 showed New York prices ranging from $2.30 per 100 pounds above Chicago prices to 15 cents below. A differential of from $1.50 to $2.00 per 100 pounds, New York over Chicago, was quite common, although during several weeks the difference was less than $1.00.

It is not clear, on the face of it, why packers would ship fresh pork loins to New York at times to sell at only slightly more than the Chicago price; or why they would let a differential of $2 or more of New York over Chicago persist for several weeks at a time. Yet this sort of thing happened, both for pork loins and for other pork and beef items as well. Here is an interesting field for further study.

## CAUSES OF SPATIAL IMPERFECTION

The broad market for hogs covering the heavy hog-producing and consuming areas apparently falls short of perfection with respect to place. The price surface is swept by ripples, waves, and tidal movements. The short-time imperfections result partly from lack of information and partly from time lags in supply responses. The terminal markets have an excellent price-reporting system, but much of their trade territory is several hundred miles away, and adjustments of supply and demand involve time lags of a day or more. The interior markets are free from this distance-and-time handicap, but their price-reporting system is not as specific as the system at the terminal markets.

There has been a weak link at the end of the market news dissemination chain, at the final stage of getting the information to farmers, but this is being strengthened. At each terminal market the market reports are handed to messengers for the press and radio wire news services—AP, AP-Radio, UPI, and Western Union's CND (Commercial News Dispatch). Each market news office also posts mimeographed reports of prices and receipts at other markets, as well as at the market concerned, for the information of the trade at the local exchange. The final daily summary is then mailed to publishers for their market news columns and to others who have requested the service.

The federal-state market news service in Des Moines collects market information on several livestock and poultry products in the decentralized Iowa-southern Minnesota area. Its daily coverage includes hogs, sheep and lambs, chickens, eggs, and turkeys. The beef-cattle market is reported twice weekly. The hog report, for example, covers 20 packing plants and 13 shipping points in the area.

The Iowa State University broadcasting station at Ames, WOI, plays an important role in disseminating this market information to farmers and others. The market news is received by teletype at WOI where it is assembled, interpreted, and summarized for broadcast on radio and television. This station broadcasts market news at 15 different times during the day and includes coverage of major terminal markets as well as the Iowa-southern Minnesota area. (See Chapter 8 for further discussion of dissemination of market news.)

This more extensive market news system should enable

farmers to keep better track of relative livestock price movements at different markets and to adjust shipments to take advantage of price differences. This potentially could bring the broad livestock market over the country closer to the conditions of a perfect market, with uniform prices plus or minus appropriate differentials in time, place, and form.

The objective is not to keep prices more uniform than they have been in the past, with local supplies and demands continuing to fluctuate. Those variations in prices were all that kept the fluctuations in local supplies and demands within bounds. The objective, rather, is to bring the market news system closer to perfection, so that variations in local prices resulting from variations in local supplies and demands will be spotted quickly and will be responded to so rapidly by changes in shipments that the price variation will be kept smaller than in the past.

Progress in this direction is limited by the fact that the language in which the market news is expressed falls short of accuracy because it is difficult to describe livestock on the hoof accurately by grades. The market news system broadcasts prices by grades—U.S. No. 1 barrows and gilts, for example, by specified weight ranges—and each grade covers rather a wide range of values. The prices for each grade therefore are reported in rather wide ranges. It is difficult for a farmer to tell whether a bid of 10 cents higher at one market than at another actually would bring him 10 cents more for his load of hogs.

If the basis of the sale of livestock at some time in the future were changed from live weight to carcass weight and grade, certified by government graders in the packing plants as discussed in Chapter 22, substantial further improvement would be possible. Government reporters at the plants could ensure accuracy in the individual plant's price broadcasts, making them comparable with the terminal market reports; and government carcass weighers and graders would ensure accuracy and impartiality in weighing and grading the carcasses. Farmers then would not need to telephone, bargain, or dicker at all. They simply would compare the reports from the different points, choose the highest, and take their hogs there, much as the housewife now compares prices at different stores, by reading the advertisements in the local paper, and then proceeds to buy or order from this or that store without attempting to bargain or dicker about the price.

This would bring the market close to the competitive ideal. A market should be a place where all the buyers and sellers are equally well informed and full publicity is given to all transactions, and the object is not to take advantage of others' ignorance, but to play the game with the cards face up on the table. The advantage in such a game goes to the man with the best cards. That is, the advantage goes to the most efficient plant operator and distributor, as it should, not to the best bluffer or to the one who knows best how to take advantage of the other players' less adequate information.

This kind of a market lacks the color and sparkle that comes from the clash of different personalities in rough-and-ready economic combat. It operates merely in the plain white light of full publicity, where personalities count for little, and only the facts prevail.

# 15

# INFLUENCE OF DECENTRALIZED MARKETING ON THE PRICE LEVEL OF A COMMODITY

DOES DIRECT MARKETING have any effect on the general price level of the product?

There are two ways in which it might have an effect. In an industry where the buyers and sellers are comparatively few, they may prefer to enter into more or less permanent contracts with each other, using prices that are not bargained for afresh at the time of each sale, but are set once and for all at so much under or over the basic central market price, whatever that price may be. In such a case, if the volume of direct sales becomes large and the volume of terminal market sales small, the price at the terminal market may not be as representative of total demand and supply conditions as it should; yet being used as the basic settlement price, it may affect the prices for most of the total supply.

In cases where the buyers and sellers are numerous and do not trade on the basis of continuing contracts, some observers feel that the growth of direct marketing might affect the price level by reducing the competition at the central markets, weakening the price there and thus weakening the price structure over the whole market area.

These two situations are well illustrated in actual life—the first in the butter trade and the second in the livestock trade. They are taken up in this chapter in that order.

## EFFECTS OF DECENTRALIZED MARKETING ON BUTTER PRICES

In the centralized market of an earlier day, most creameries in the United States sold their butter through commission men in the wholesale market. Today the situation is reversed. Most of the butter bypasses the central markets entirely, moving instead directly from creamery to distributor.

There were several reasons why the volume of trading at the central markets has declined. Butter quality became more uniform, storage facilities were improved, rail service became faster and more reliable, and the danger of deterioration in transit declined. Buyers were able to depend on the quality of butter remaining high if it was high when made. They began to establish direct contacts with creameries in order to develop their own regular sources of supply. Many creameries found it profitable and convenient to make long-time arrangements to sell their butter direct to these buyers, to avoid the brokerage and other charges at the central markets and to reduce the trouble of locating the best buyer for each shipment.

Later, chain stores, butter marketing cooperatives like Land O'Lakes, and large dairy corporations distributed increased quantities of butter directly from creameries to retail stores and institutional users. They also bypassed the central market. Table 15.1 shows that, by 1965, the percentage of total U.S. butter production sold on the Chicago Mercantile Exchange and the New York Mercantile Exchange had declined almost to the vanishing point.[1]

Thus the physical marketing system for butter is almost completely decentralized, but wholesale butter prices all over the country are still determined by what goes on in the two central market butter exchanges. A survey of butter plants by the University of Minnesota in November and December, 1965, showed that the bulk butter prices of manufacturing plants in that part of the country were based almost exclusively on either the Chicago or New York Mercantile Exchange prices; almost 100 per cent of the bulk butter sales were based on these quotations. The prices determined in the sale of 0.1 per cent of the butter in the two exchanges determine the prices for the other 99.9 per cent throughout the butter-producing areas.

[1] The discussion of the mercantile exchanges is condensed from *Organization and Competition in the Dairy Industry*, National Commission on Food Marketing, Tech. Study 3, June, 1966, pp. 283–85.

**TABLE 15.1: Butter Traded on Chicago and New York Mercantile Exchanges as Per Cent of U.S. Butter Production, Selected Years 1947–65**

| Year | Per Cent of Butter Production |
|---|---|
| 1947 | 0.7 |
| 1951 | 0.6 |
| 1960 | 0.2 |
| 1965 | 0.1 |

Source: Calculated from data in: March, Robert W. and Herrmann, Louis F., *The Establishment of Central Market Butter Prices at Chicago and New York,* USDA, Marketing Res. Rept. 53, June, 1953, pp. 43–44; *Dairy Statistics Through 1960,* USDA, Stat. Bul. 303, and supplement for 1963–64, Table 224; and *Dairy and Poultry Market News,* USDA, Consumer and Marketing Serv. Rept., 1965.

Trading on the Chicago and New York Exchanges is conducted by voice on the exchange floor. Offers to sell or bids to buy are posted along with grade and quantity. When an offer matches a bid and a sale is made, the price is posted on the sales board.

Exchange prices are reported by Urner-Barry publications and by the market news service of the USDA for use by the trade in buying and selling butter. They are published for both the New York and Chicago markets and include bids and offers when no sales are made.

Both of the reporting services use the same method of determining price quotations. The quoted daily price for each grade is the latest sale, bid, or offer. In the case of a bid, it will not change the quotation from the previous day unless it is a higher price. If it is an offer, it will not change the quotation from the previous day unless it is a lower price. Thus, the quotation may vary from day to day even though no trades are taking place on the exchanges.

The bypassing of the central markets might mean nothing more than that the bulk of the butter today moves by the most direct route from producer to consumer and avoids the charges ranging up to half a cent a pound at New York as well as the necessity for immediate or 24-hour delivery in New York or Chicago. But actually these reductions in cost are only one of the effects of direct movements of butter. The other most important effect is on butter prices.

The effect on prices could be pronounced because of the method by which creameries sell their butter. Most creameries sell on the basis of a sales agreement with a receiver of butter, which may run unchanged for months or years at a time. This agreement generally provides that the creamery will be paid, not so many cents per pound, but such-and-such a premium over the commercial price quotation on the Mercantile Exchange at Chicago or New York on the day of arrival. Thus the less than 1 per cent of butter sold on these exchanges establishes the price for the bulk of the butter that is sold direct without going through the exchanges.

It is paradoxical but nonetheless true that the direct sales agreement system, which requires that there be a reliable central market price quotation on which to base the sales agreements, itself reduces the volume of trading at the central markets and thus undermines the reliability of the central market quotation.

The reliability of the quotation has been questioned on two scores:

1. The volume of trading and the number of traders is so small and the market so thin that prices are unduly susceptible to manipulation by one or a few traders dealing in relatively small quantities.
2. The bulk of the sales agreements provide for premiums over the commercial exchange quotation. Therefore, either the exchange prices do not reflect supply and demand accurately (the prices are too low) or the price reports underquote the market.

Butter traders generally defend the market on the first score (thinness). They take the position that when butter is moving freely, with no surpluses or shortages, this is evidence that prices on the exchange are at the right level, in line with supply and demand. It is not necessary for the volume of trading to be large; in principle, there is no need at such times for any trading at all to take place on the exchange. At other times, if butter is not moving freely and surpluses or shortages develop, traders will sell or buy on the exchange in an attempt to bring prices in line with supply and demand. It may not even be necessary, actually, to sell or buy at lower or higher prices, but only to offer to do so. A large volume of trading is not needed in any case.

Butter traders also defend the market on the second score (underquoting). Butter of known characteristics within the grade, bought direct, is worth a premium over butter on the exchanges that is not available for inspection before sale. Creamery managers, they say, know the situation and use the quotation as a basing price rather than an average price.

A third feature of the decentralized marketing system is the extent to which it accurately reflects price differentials for quality.

On this score, the record is not so good. Upgrading, particularly in times of butter shortage, is widespread. This practice of paying for low-grade butter on the basis of a higher grade reduces the incentive to produce the higher grades and discourages quality programs. In addition, different creameries receive different prices for the same grade of bulk butter. Since the prices received by creameries are not reported by the market news service and are not made public, this situation makes it difficult for a creamery manager to tell whether he is getting the full market value for his butter or not.

*An overall appraisal* of the whole butter pricing system and of the arguments pro and con may be put in the following terms:

1. The reductions in costs achieved under the decentralized butter marketing system are such that traders are likely to continue to use it.
2. The effects on the level and stability of prices are controversial. It appears probable that an increase in the volume of trading on the exchange would be beneficial. Certain changes in the rules of the Wisconsin Cheese Exchange have been notably successful in increasing the volume of trading in cheese there.

   In addition, it would be helpful if bimonthly or quarterly reports could be issued, showing country creamery price differentials from the exchange quotations.
3. The accuracy of the price differentials received by creameries for quality could be improved, and the whole butter-marketing system made more coherent, if the butter market reporting were decentralized in line with the decentralization that has taken place in the marketing system. This has been done for hogs. It needs to be done for butter. These decentralized butter market reports would report the prices received by creameries in the country, not the prices received by wholesalers in Chicago or New York.

## EFFECTS OF DECENTRALIZED MARKETING ON LIVESTOCK PRICES

The marked increase in the direct buying of livestock that has taken place over the past few decades was shown in Figure 7.1.

The decline in the volume of livestock sales at the terminal markets that resulted from the increase in direct buying of livestock hit the terminal commission firms hard. It also began to create an insecure feeling in farmers' minds with respect to the determination of prices. Previously, many farmers had looked to Chicago, approvingly or otherwise, for price leadership. It seemed to them that prices at the local market depended on Chicago prices. If the decline in volume of sales at Chicago and the other terminal markets continued, perhaps to the point of complete disappearance, what would happen to local prices? Would not the whole price-determining system go to pieces?[2]

The livestock commission men at the terminal markets, who see their volume of business and therefore their income sharply reduced by the growth of direct buying, are naturally opposed to direct buying. The packers, who have expanded their direct buying presumably because it pays them to do so, just as naturally defend their practices. On the sidelines, livestock growers watch the combat with mixed feelings. Many are suspicious of the packers. Sellers are always inclined to believe that buyers are getting the best of them, especially when the buyers are large and powerful corporations. They are more inclined to listen to the commission men, who are their sales agents, than to the packers.

The arguments against direct packer buying are many and various. They may be summarized, however, under three separate heads.

1. Direct packer buying at interior country points takes the cream of the crop. The rest of the hogs—the lower grade—go to the terminal markets and establish low prices there. These low prices in turn are reflected in low country prices, and all hog prices decline.
2. The terminal markets are competitive markets; where there are numerous buyers at one market, there is active competion. But when hogs are bought direct, there is usually only one buyer. There is no competition. Hog prices suffer accordingly.
3. When packers buy a substantial proportion of their hogs direct, in the country, that reduces competition (i.e., demand) at the terminal markets and results in lower prices there; and since hog prices are based on terminal prices, this lower price at terminals reduces prices over the whole producing area.

### Does Direct Buying Take the Cream of the Crop?

This first argument is probably the least important and will be dealt with first. While recent research on this question is not available, an early USDA study of the direct marketing of hogs

[2] The sale of hogs was discontinued at the Chicago Union Stockyards in May, 1970. Subsequent development may help answer this question in the case of hogs.

investigated the question of grades of hogs sold at different markets rather thoroughly. A group of qualified hog graders visited various markets in the course of this study and graded nearly 200,000 hogs, at 132 markets distributed over the 15 leading hog-producing states. The results of their grading showed that the grades of hogs purchased at the two kinds of markets, the public terminal markets and the interior (direct-buying) markets, in percentage form were as follows:[3]

| | Choice *(per cent)* | Good *(per cent)* | Medium *(per cent)* | Cull *(per cent)* |
|---|---|---|---|---|
| Public markets | 15.4 | 50.7 | 30.4 | 3.5 |
| Interior markets | 15.6 | 51.1 | 30.9 | 2.4 |

Because of the outstanding importance of the Chicago market, a special check was made of the grades of hogs received as direct purchases and for sale at the public stockyards at that market where 56,051 hogs were graded, of which 36,150 were public market hogs and 20,901 direct purchases. The percentage distribution of these was:

| | Choice *(per cent)* | Good *(per cent)* | Medium *(per cent)* | Cull *(per cent)* |
|---|---|---|---|---|
| Consigned for sale | 19.3 | 41.7 | 33.8 | 5.2 |
| Bought direct | 15.5 | 40.9 | 40.9 | 3.7 |

The results of this study showed that the interior markets did not take the cream of the crop at that time. There does not appear to be any readily apparent evidence that the situation has greatly changed.

#### Does Direct Buying Reduce Competition?

The second argument, that there is no competition when hogs are bought direct, implies that competition exists only where several buyers are physically present. But competition—that is, offers to buy or sell—is not restricted only to those who are physically present. If a buyer comes to my farm and offers $17 per 100 pounds for my hogs, and if I pick up my telephone and get a bid of $17.50 from another buyer, 50 or 100 miles or more away, or listen to my radio and hear that prices are higher at other points, there is competition for my hogs right on

[3] *The Direct Marketing of Hogs*, USDA, Misc. Pub. 222, 1935, pp. 18–19. (Grade designations are those in effect at the time the research was conducted and have since been replaced by the designations U.S. No. 1, U.S. No. 2, and U.S. No. 3.)

my farm, just as if the buyers were physically present. In fact, I am in a stronger position with my hogs on my farm than if they were at a distant public market.

At public markets, the competition is for a supply of hogs that is physically present, largely out of the control of the producers, and under the necessity of early sale. At interior buying points it is a competition to draw hogs, that are still under the control of the producer, to different points. Competition at public markets is more apparent than at interior points since relatively large numbers of buyers and sellers in personal contact are readily observable at the former, while at the latter the chief evidences of competition are the posted prices and the telephone or personal requests being received for bids on hogs. But to the producer at home, with hogs for sale, the latter competition is more useful since he is in a stronger position opposite the buyer with his hogs still at home than he would be if they were at a public market and had to be sold.[4]

### Does Direct Buying Reduce Price Levels?

The third argument, that direct packer buying reduces the demand and therefore the prices at the terminal markets and thereby reduces the general level of hog prices, is more difficult to evaluate in simple and concrete terms. If it is considered against a background of economic theory, however, the outlines of the elements involved stand out more clearly. The economic theory involved deals with price determination in present-day markets. And this requires a clear understanding of just what is "the market" in which hog prices are determined.

In Chapter 2, which deals with the concept of the perfect market, it is shown that economists, as well as others, are guilty of some confusion in defining a market. Some define it as the place where a commodity is bought and sold. In that sense, "two women and a goose make a market," and the Chicago Board of Trade is a market. Other economists define a market as the total of the several markets that deal in the same commodity. Still others regard the market as an area or sphere over which price-determining forces work; it may be local, as in the case of bricks, or it may be world-wide, as in the case of wheat or U.S. government bonds.

It was shown in Chapter 2 that these definitions do not get at the economics of the matter and a more useful definition of a market is: a group of freely competing buyers and sellers with facilities for trading. The group of buyers and sellers may be concentrated at one point, or at several points, or it may be widely scattered. Prices are determined by the whole group in

[4] *Ibid.*, p. 17.

either case and will be the same and determined in the same manner in the one case as in the other, provided that the trading facilities are as good in the one case as in the other.

Looked at in this light, the arguments given above as to the effect of direct buying on the price of hogs are seen to miss the point. They assume that a terminal market sets the price of hogs. This is not true. Many more hogs are bought in Iowa than in any single terminal.[5] It would be more accurate to say that Iowa sets the price of hogs than to say that some terminal sets it. Actually, neither is correct. The price of hogs is set by the whole group of buyers and sellers all over the country and, for that matter, all over the world. In a centralized market it makes no difference to the level of prices whether the bulk of the trading is done on the east side of the pit in the case of wheat (or of the stockyards in the case of livestock) or whether it is done on the west side. And in a decentralized market it makes no difference whether most of the trading is done in the eastern part of the trading territory, or on the west side, or in a little knot in any one part, or all over the territory—provided that the facilities for trading are as good in the decentralized market as in the centralized market.

This may sound like a very nice theory, unconfirmed by any empirical test. Empirical tests have been made, however, by several different economist-statisticians, and they all tell the same story—there is no factual evidence of any depressing effect of direct buying on the price of hogs.

The authors of a 1961 study of this subject, which employed multiple correlation methods, concluded with these observations:

> That terminal prices are not sufficiently high to compensate producers in typical country market areas for transportation costs to the terminal carries an implication that is rather clear: Transportation costs to a terminal center appear to serve as one basis for determination of minimum distances between terminal and country market locations. That a terminal may provide a convenient price-registering service because of the news reporting facilities established at such centers is plausible. That the terminal may serve to establish prices for a specified area is also plausible, but this appears only to occur within a distinct area, the limits of which are determined by the maximum transportation cost that a terminal can compensate pro-

[5] About 20 million hogs are produced annually in Iowa, and more than 70 per cent of these are sold direct. Thus more than 14 million hogs are sold direct in Iowa. Sioux City, the terminal with the largest hog volume in 1969, had sales of 1.9 million head. *Livestock Meat Wool Market News*, USDA, Vol. 38, No. 4, 1970, p. 81.

ducers for; and country markets proved generally to be located beyond these limits. Such conditions would provide the terminal with a natural locational advantage in space, but this limited spatial advantage is no different from that enjoyed by any market place. There may be one further implication: As long as the level of transportation costs remains rather stable, it tends to specify a market area that is relatively static in size. This may serve as an additional, though fragile, basis for the continuing tendency for terminal markets to receive a declining share of total marketings as livestock populations rise.

The study disclosed a striking similarity in the geographic distribution of country and terminal shipments of Indiana hogs over a large eastern segment of the United States. Moreover, the study provided evidence of (1) a rapid exchange of information bearing upon price, (2) a uniform spatial price pattern in which differences were too small to permit adjustments for transportation costs between markets in a territory which therefore was apparently only a portion of a larger market area, and (3) a significant relationship between prices of live hogs at Indiana markets and wholesale pork prices quoted on a national basis.

While the results of the investigation cannot be regarded as conclusive, they do tend to provide empirical support for the concept of a national market for slaughter hogs and to support hypotheses permitting (1) no price advantage to patrons of individual markets and (2) no privilege of price domination by individual markets beyond the small area in which they enjoy a locational advantage.[6]

## AVOIDING THE DANGERS IN DIRECT PACKER BUYING

The danger from direct buying is not that it may substantially lower the price of hogs by undermining Chicago prices or some other assumed basic price. The danger lies in the extent to which the actual situation in hog marketing falls short of the proviso that "a scattered market is as good as a concentrated market, provided that the trading facilities are as good in the one case as in the other."

### Need for Adequate Market News

It is evident that if the trading facilities are not good, individual sellers (or buyers) may suffer. If some seller who has not put himself in touch with the best bids available accepts $17.50 per 100 pounds for his hogs when he could have received $17.75 somewhere else, he loses 25 cents per 100 pounds. He would do better to pay a commission man to do his selling for him (provided that the price thus obtained was higher than the other by

[6] Thomas T. Stout and Richard L. Feltner, "A Note on Spatial Pricing Accuracy and Price Relationships in the Market for Slaughter Hogs," *Journal of Farm Economics*, Vol. 44 (Feb., 1962), pp. 218–19.

more than the commission and other charges). If market facilities are poor, direct buying may lose the seller more money than the commission charges he avoids by selling direct.

This puts the responsibility squarely upon the packers and the farmers to provide first-class market facilities for direct buying if farmers are to be protected from potential bad effects of the practice. The most important of these market facilities is a stream of current, accurate, and detailed market news as to livestock prices at all available points in the general market for livestock.

### Need for Adequate Grading System

A second important need is for a uniform and relatively fine-grained system of grades and an accurate way of determining where individual hogs or lots of hogs fall in that system. It would do a farmer very little good to hear over the radio that hogs at a certain point were selling at from $16 to $18 per 100 pounds if he could not tell where his hogs would fall in that price range. The situation improves greatly if the market news is refined and standardized, so that a farmer can hear that U.S. No. 1 and 2 butcher hogs from 200 to 220 pounds are selling for $18 to $18.15 per 100 pounds. Even then the farmer may not get full value for high-quality hogs, for that grading system does not specifically include dressing percentage. That is left to the final bargaining between the seller and buyer, with the likelihood that both high- and low-quality hogs will be sold at prices closer to the average than their true cut-out value.

### Need for Knowledge of Packers' Buying Practices

A third important need is a thorough study of packers' competitive practices in the decentralized markets compared with those in the terminal markets. So little is known about either that all that can be done here is to raise one or two questions. Direct packer buying might lead to geographical division of market territory and thus to lower prices at the farm; this is unlikely in view of the heterogeneous nature of the competition in the area, but more needs to be known about the methods by which interior packers establish their prices from day to day. Or, direct packer buying might lead to a breakdown of central market volume-sharing schemes (if they did exist in actual fact) and thus result in higher prices at the farm. It might intensify the duplication of packer buying and selling services and thus widen middleman's costs; or it might enable buyers, sellers, and product to get together with lower costs than those involved in using the central markets.

Pending the results of such studies, only tentative conclusions can be reached. The judgment as to the good or evil effects of direct buying depends upon how good the market news is, how good the grading system is, and how fully competitive the packers' buying system is. If market news is inaccurate, not detailed, and not available currently, and farmers do not use even what is available, then direct buying of hogs could have adverse effects upon hog prices. If market news and market grades are adequate, direct buying permits farmers to escape some of the costs of selling hogs on terminal markets; this could result in a net gain, divided between farmers and packers. A program of action to deal with the direct packer buying question, therefore, calls for steps to improve market news and market grades to the highest possible accuracy and timeliness.

# 16

## GRADES, VALUES, AND PRICES

In the primitive single-market systems of earlier days, the buyers, the sellers, and the physical goods themselves were concentrated at one point. The buyers and sellers passed from one lot of goods to another, comparing, contrasting, and making up their minds what each lot of goods was worth. An endless amount of time was spent in "higgling and bargaining" and in bringing the goods to the market in the first place and hauling them away afterwards; but since the physical goods, buyers, and sellers were all present at the same spot, the necessary comparisons of goods, bids, and offers could be made without recourse to verbal description. The eye and the hand were adequate for appraising the different lots of goods, and the tongue and the ear were all that were needed to make and receive or reject the price of "this lot" or "that lot." The goods were sold by the primitive time-proved method of personal inspection, and no description other than "this" or "that" was needed.

After the industrial revolution and the invention of the railroad, steamship, telegraph, and telephone, the single-market fairs were replaced by a system of local and central markets. The prices at these different markets could be compared by means of the telegraph and telephone, but there was no way of comparing the goods for which these prices were paid. The markets were often hundreds of miles apart. The buyers and sellers could not move from market to market inspecting the goods in person as they used to move from lot to lot in the old-fashioned single-market fair. Nor could the goods be moved from market to market; the distances were too great.

## NEED FOR STANDARDIZED GRADE SPECIFICATIONS

Unless the markets were to remain isolated single markets, with goods selling at one price in one market and at another price in another market, some way had to be found to describe the different lots of goods in words that could be conveyed over the telegraph or telephone along with the prices. Ever since the advent of trucks, paved roads, and radios the need for the concentration of the physical goods at central or terminal markets has lessened, and the need for a more and more accurate language for describing goods at a distance has still further increased. If Mahomet could not go to the mountain, nor the mountain to Mahomet, some way had to be worked out to describe the various mountains to the various Mahomets in words that they could all understand. When distances become too great for buyers to inspect the different lots of goods in person, sale by inspection has to give way to sale by description; and that requires that a uniform and accurate descriptive language be evolved. The prices can be broadcast to all buyers and sellers, enabling price comparisons over the entire market area. The goods themselves cannot be broadcast, but their descriptions can.

What is needed is the development of an accurate and intelligible trade language, so that consumers can tell producers what they want by means of words, numbers, or other symbols that can be used at a distance, independent of the presence of the physical goods. Then consumers and producers can talk intelligibly to each other even though they are hundreds of miles apart.

Obviously a million different lots of goods cannot be described individually, lot by lot. They must be classified into a small number of classes and described merely by reference to their place in this classification. This requires, first, that the most important value-determining characteristics of each kind of good (cotton, or wheat, etc.) be determined and, second, that a set of specifications of these several characteristics be set up in such a way that each lot of goods can be placed somewhere in that set of specifications.

The set of specifications for each product starts with the attributes that give the product the greatest value in the market. It ends with those that give the product the least value. The set as a whole is divided into perhaps half a dozen, or some such small number, divisions; each division is called a grade and is given a number or word. This saves words, for buyers and sellers can then refer to "No. 1" or "No. 2" instead of listing the full description of each grade.

The use of this set of grade specifications enables a local elevator man, for example, to classify loads of wheat into different groups (grades) according to the attributes given in the specifications. His job thus becomes a matter of determining physical characteristics. If a load of wheat grades No. 2 (has the attributes laid down in the specifications for No. 2), then it is worth so many cents a bushel less than a load that grades No. 1; how many cents less is shown by reference to the prices quoted that day for the different grades.

This illustration has been phrased in terms of the buyer, but it is evident that grading equally simplifies the job of the seller. This is particularly true if the buyers all agree to use one uniform set of specifications. In that case the seller can directly compare the prices for each grade quoted by one buyer with the prices quoted for the same grades by another buyer.

If the set of specifications is phrased in such terms as "heavy," "damp," etc., the grading depends to a large extent on the judgment of the grader. It is subjective; that is, it depends upon the judgment of the subject who is doing the grading. If, however, the specifications are laid down in definite objective numerical terms—"60 pounds to the bushel" instead of "heavy," or "15 per cent moisture content" instead of "damp"—the grading then becomes objective; it depends only upon the attributes of the object. If there is any difference of opinion as to the grade of a load of grain, it can be settled by objective measurement tests, not by argument over a matter of opinion.

Many commodities have attributes which cannot be measured objectively, and in any case there is always a question whether the buyer, an interested party, can be expected to do the grading strictly impartially. So in some cases it has been found advisable to put the grading in the hands of an impartial third party, such as a government grader. This promotes satisfaction all along the line. The seller then knows that if he has canvassed the available bids and selected the highest price, he is getting the full value of his load. If it was graded No. 2, it was actually No. 2, not merely called No. 2 by the local buyer in order to enable him to buy it cheaply. He and the distant buyer have been able to talk the same trade language, agree on prices, and exchange goods with the minimum of wasted energy and the maximum of accuracy and efficiency.

## MARKETING EFFICIENCY AND GRADING[1]

Economists are interested in efficiency within a marketing process. They divide these efficiencies into two types.

One of these is "operational efficiency." Here they are concerned with the efficiency of conducting the various physical activities during the marketing process, the movement, the processing, and the distribution of livestock and meats. They want this entire job to be done with as much output per man-hour as possible.

The other type of efficiency is called "pricing efficiency." Here they are concerned with how freely and how effectively prices arise during the marketing process and make themselves known to various interests in the marketing and distribution trade. They are concerned with the accuracy, the precision, and the speed with which prices are established and reflected through the marketing system from consumer to producer or from one level of trading to the other.

### Operational Efficiency

1. Grading has eliminated much of the time and expense in the bargaining process caused by arguing about the level of quality of the product being traded. Grading provides a more precise definition of the commodity and permits bargaining to settle down quickly to the basic price issues which relate to supply and demand.
2. Increased selling by description has helped to reduce the relatively costly branch house distribution system in which each carcass was inspected before purchase. This has moved the wholesale marketing system toward more direct movement of meat to the ultimate retail outlets. In 1929, 54 per cent of the meat we produced moved through packer-owned branch houses. By 1948 this figure had dropped to 26 per cent, and in 1963 it was 14 per cent.
3. Grading has increased specialization of slaughter. Some slaughterers specialize in chain store beef, other slaughterers specialize in cow and calf slaughter. This specialization has probably increased operational efficiency also.
4. Grading has reduced the expense of competitive brand advertising and high-pressure salesmanship. Grading provides a widely known and highly acceptable brand which becomes a common denominator for trading over the entire country.
5. The enlarged market area for both buyers and sellers, which

[1] Adapted from G. Engelman, *Issues in Grading Livestock and Meats*, USDA, Dec., 1961.

grading provides, encourages a more efficient movement of meat to ultimate outlets, thus minimizing transportation costs.

All these factors tend to increase the efficiency of the marketing process and exert a downward pressure on marketing costs. These various effects can be readily recognized in the industry. Buying on description and by specification has increased. Distribution territories of packers as well as the procurement territories of large-volume buyers have greatly widened in the last few years. Branch houses have greatly decreased in number. The slaughtering industry is becoming more specialized.

#### Pricing Efficiency

1. Grading provides a more accurate language for price quotations. Buyers and sellers can understand each other more easily. They know what they are talking about. Grading makes market news much more meaningful and enables it to be transmitted more effectively by radio, telephone, teletype, or in the press. By enlarging the area of informed decision making in the marketing process, grading makes the pricing system a more articulate means for communicating consumer preferences to producers.
2. Grading increases buying and selling by description. In the case of meat, for example, this has reduced much of the need for inspecting each carcass before purchasing. Instead of looking at the carcasses for sale in a number of packinghouse coolers, a chain store buyer in Chicago can negotiate for several carloads of beef for Washington stores one minute, and ten minutes later he can buy several carloads of beef for stores in New York. This enlarges the area of the market in the meat trade. It puts buyers in contact with more sellers and puts sellers in contact with more buyers.
3. Grading increases the level of competition in the market. This follows in part from selling by description. The improved accuracy of pricing intensifies price competition. Grading opens up distant outlets for small packers. They can sell in national outlets that were formerly preempted by the large national packers with their extensive branch house systems and nationally advertised brands. A federal grade is a national brand known equally well over all the country. Furthermore, this national brand is not a private franchise. It is accessible to all packers, both large and small. The net result is a higher level of price competition in the marketing and distribution industries.

4. Grading enables the market place to allocate more systematically the available supplies of each kind and quality of meat among the various demands to the highest order of use for each. For example, Prime grade is probably too wasteful for the mass market retail trade. When the fat is trimmed away, the lean portions come at too high a price for most retail store customers. The hotel and restaurant customers, however, like Prime grade because it is a more consistent indicator of eating quality; they are not nearly as much concerned about the price. The Prime grade provides a useful service in getting the fatter beef out of the way of the retail customer, at the same time directing this beef to the market that will pay the highest price for it—the hotel and restaurant trade.

   In the same way, Canner, Cutter, and Utility grades are directed into processed meats. These grades may provide some very economical meat. They may be more nutritious from the standpoint of the essential amino acids which are contained in meat. Nevertheless, they do not seem to give the eating satisfaction of the higher grades and, therefore, are directed into the various kinds of lower-priced processed meats.

   The other grades, particularly Choice and Good, are directed to the fresh meat retail trade. The grading system helps each retail store to buy the particular kind and quality of meat it thinks most suitable for its own clientele.
5. Grading helps in achieving a measure of standardization and quality control in the merchandising process. One of the important food-merchandising lessons learned since World War II has been standardization. When a customer buys a can of applesauce, she expects and wants that can of applesauce to taste exactly the same as the can she bought two weeks ago. The food processing industries have spent millions of dollars in achieving quality control and standardization of the products they sell. In fresh meat, quality control is not possible in the same degree that it is available in processed food products. Nevertheless, grading provides the most effective available means to get as much quality control as possible in fresh meats.

## OBJECTIVE GRADING FOR GRAIN

The principal factors that determine the commercial grade of grain are test weight per bushel, moisture content, damaged kernels, freedom from foreign materials and other grains or other classes of the same grain, and "condition"—that is, whether the grain is cool and sweet or whether it is musty or sour, heat-

**TABLE 16.1: Official U.S. Grade Standards for all Classes of Wheat Except Mixed Wheat**

| | Minimum Test Weight Per Bushel | | Maximum Limits of— | | | | | | |
|---|---|---|---|---|---|---|---|---|---|
| | | | Defects | | | | | Wheat of other classes* | |
| Grade | Hard Red Spring wheat | All other classes | Heat-damaged kernels | Damaged kernels (total) | Foreign material | Shrunken and broken kernels | Total | Contrasting classes | Total |
| | *(pounds)* | *(pounds)* | *(per cent)* | *(per cent)* | *(per cent)* | *(per cent)* | *(per cent)* | *(per cent)* | *(per cent)* |
| 1 .... | 58.0 | 60.0 | 0.1 | 2.0 | 0.5 | 3.0 | 3.0 | 1.0 | 3.0 |
| 2 .... | 57.0 | 58.0 | 0.2 | 4.0 | 1.0 | 5.0 | 5.0 | 2.0 | 5.0 |
| 3 .... | 55.0 | 56.0 | 0.5 | 7.0 | 2.0 | 8.0 | 8.0 | 3.0 | 10.0 |
| 4 .... | 53.0 | 54.0 | 1.0 | 10.0 | 3.0 | 12.0 | 12.0 | 10.0 | 10.0 |
| 5 .... | 50.0 | 51.0 | 3.0 | 15.0 | 5.0 | 20.0 | 20.0 | 10.0 | 10.0 |

Sample grade: Sample grade shall be wheat which does not meet the requirements for any of the grades from No. 1 to No. 5, inclusive; or which contains stones; or which is musty, or sour, or heating; or which has any commercially objectionable foreign odor except of smut or garlic; or which contains a quantity of smut so great that any one or more of the grade requirements cannot be applied accurately; or which is otherwise of distinctly low quality.

Source: *Official Grain Standards of the United States,* USDA, SRA-AMS-177, May, 1964.

* Red Durum wheat of any grade may contain not more than 10.0 per cent of wheat of other classes.

ing, or hot. In the case of wheat, the protein content is also important. These are the factors of prime importance for commercial trading purposes.

The official specifications for the different grades of wheat cover eight printed pages, for wheat is divided into six classes for purposes of grading, with detailed specifications within each grade. The essential grade requirements for Hard Red Spring wheat are reproduced in Table 16.1 as an example.

The grading of grain used to be largely subjective. Moisture content, for example, was determined by touch. Inspectors would judge by the feel of the hand whether grain was dry, "tough," or damp. Today the grading is almost completely objective. When federal standards for grain were first put into effect, an objective moisture tester was developed by means of which the water was distilled from the sample of grain and measured in a graduated container. The method was slow, however, and not always accurate. In recent years, a new moisture tester has been invented, which measures the resistance to an electric current as it passes through a sample of grain. This method has now been made official. It takes only 30 seconds to determine the moisture content of grain with this tester, whereas the old distilling method required 40 minutes.

Wheat with a high gluten content often commands a substantial premium (sometimes as much as 40 cents a bushel) over wheat of low gluten content. A quick, simple sedimentation test of the gluten content and quality of wheat—the bread-baking qualities of the grain—was developed by the USDA and applied on a commercial scale to exports in 1960.[2]

## LIVESTOCK AND MEAT GRADING

The job of working out a set of grade specifications for livestock and meats is considerably more complicated than for grain.

Both products pass through the same general marketing machinery: (1) the producers' local or regional farm market (the local elevator in the case of grain and the local or packer buyer, or commission man, in the case of livestock); (2) the wholesale or processing market (the miller in the case of grain, the packer in the case of livestock); and (3) the retail market (the butcher and baker).

In the case of grain the same set of specifications is used in the producer's local market and the wholesale or processing market, and by the time the product reaches the retail market it is so transformed (into bread, for example) that no *grain* grades can be applied at all.

In the case of livestock the product appears in three different forms as it passes through the marketing machinery. It is a live animal in the producer's local or regional market, and the grades must be live animal grades; it is a carcass or a large wholesale cut in the wholesale or processing market, and the grades must be carcass or wholesale cut grades; and it is a small cut of meat—a steak, a roast, etc.—in the retail meat market, calling for grades adapted to that product in that market.

The problem of livestock and meat grading, then, is really three problems, each complicated enough by the nature of the product, but all complicated further by the problem of correlating the three sets of specifications for the three products—the live animal, the carcass, and the retail cut.

---

[2] *Agricultural Marketing,* USDA, Feb., 1961, p. 3.

The test is based upon the fact that gluten in a water suspension swells enormously and takes up water rapidly when the proper concentration of lactic acid is added. In the test, a small sample of flour is obtained from wheat ground for two minutes. This flour is sifted and put into a water suspension in a graduated glass cylinder. Lactic acid is added. The level to which the swollen gluten settles after a given interval is measured. Both the quantity of the gluten and its quality, as shown by its ability to absorb water, are indicated quickly.

There is a close relation between sedimentation test indications and bread-baking quality of wheat as judged by comparative loaf volume and baking scores obtained in experimental bread-baking tests.

The sedimentation test is a better indicator than the usual protein test of inferior gluten quality of such wheats as Chieftan and Red Chief. The protein test does not reflect differences in gluten quality.

## Grades for Beef Cattle

The history of beef-cattle grading is similar in main outline to the history of grain grading. Grade names at first were vague general terms like "Native," "Good Native," "Western," "Fed Western," "Improved," "Texan," etc.—generally based more on the locality where the livestock was produced than on the characteristics of the product from the standpoint of the consumer. Furthermore, the terms meant different things in different localities. "Native" meant one thing in one market and another thing in another. In the dressed meat trade each slaughterer had, and to a considerable extent still has, his own system of grades. Beef that would be called "Good Native" by one wholesaler might be called "Fed Western" by another.

In 1917 the Department of Agriculture set up a standard uniform classification for livestock and meats and used it in reporting prices, demand, and supply when the livestock market news reports were inaugurated in 1918. Both the original grades and the revisions made since were based on extended consultation and research. These grades pay no attention to the breed nor to the locality where the animal was produced. They are the basis for the livestock market reports but are not universally used as the basis for trading. In most cases, each of the different packers and dealers still retains his own private system of grades, different from the system used by his competitors.

## Beef Carcass Grading

The grading of beef *carcasses* has been carried a step further than the grading of beef *cattle*. In 1923 the federal government began the official grading of beef, not merely for market reporting purposes, but as the basis for purchases of beef as a special service to the United States Steamship Lines. Since that time a number of steamship lines, hotels, hospitals, and other institutional buyers of beef in large quantities have come to specify that the beef they buy must have been graded and stamped by an official federal grader.

This system spread to everyday commercial transactions in 1927. A grade-stamping machine was devised with a wheel in the head that imprints the grade in a long ribbon down the carcass. This stamp remains visible in the retail cuts and therefore carries through to the consumer. In 1928 this sort of grading and stamping was put on a service basis and made available to anyone who wanted to pay for it. The cost is $8.20 per hour, which amounts to about 15 cents per carcass. In February, 1968, about 450 government meat graders were located in 49 states. Government carcass grading was made compulsory for all beef slaughtered under federal inspection during World War II.

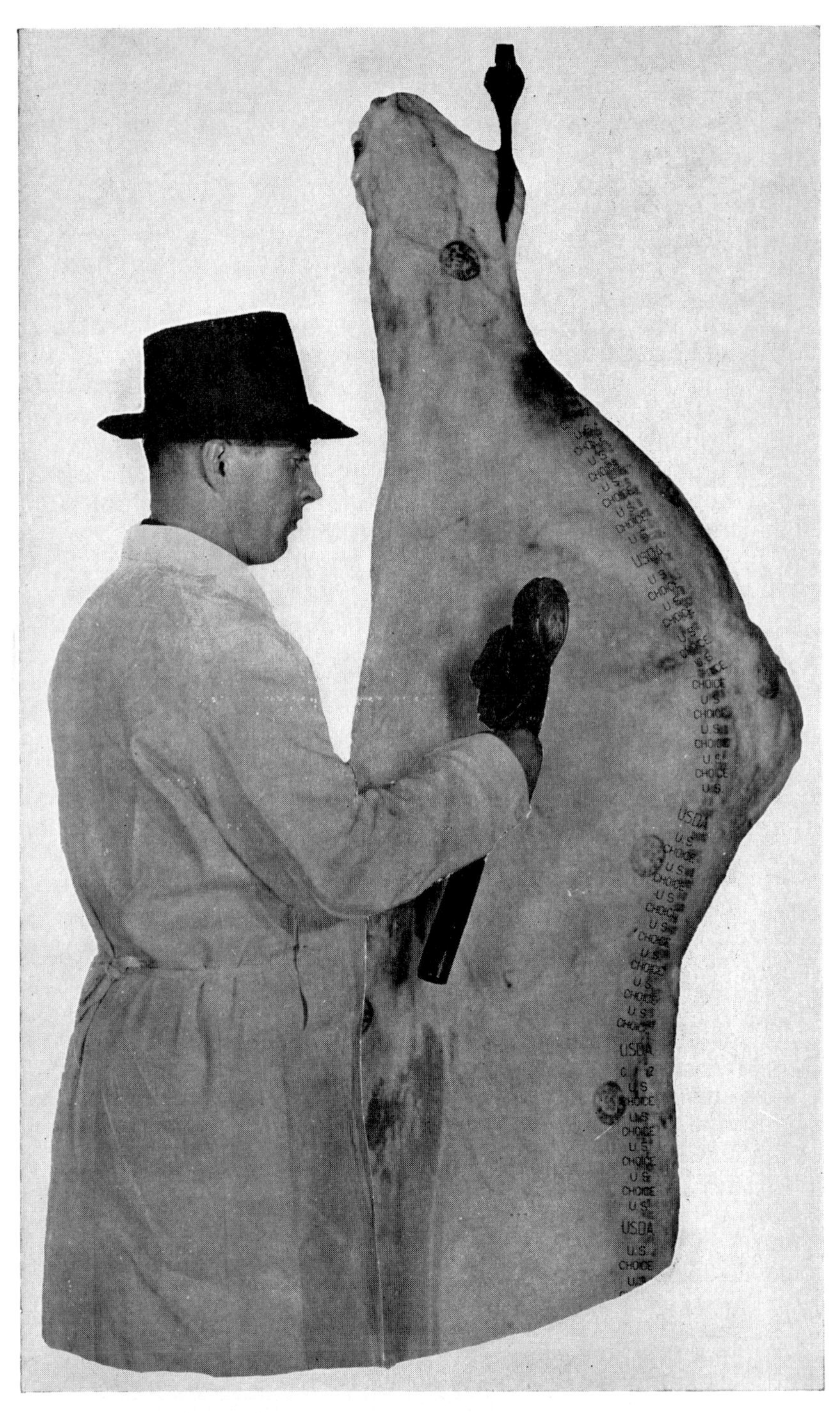


FIG. 16.1—U.S. government grader demonstrating the use of the official grading stamp. (Courtesy of the USDA.)

There are eight official grades for beef (carcasses). They are:

| | |
|---|---|
| U.S. Prime | U.S. Commercial |
| U.S. Choice | U.S. Utility |
| U.S. Good | U.S. Cutter |
| U.S. Standard | U.S. Canner |

These grade names leave much to be desired on the score of clarity. The consumer has to memorize their relative positions, which are not obvious from the names themselves as they would be if the grades were numbered No. 1, No. 2, etc. The grade specifications are still subjective like the early grades for grain. It is difficult to work out objective specifications for beef grades.

The number of pounds of beef graded annually since 1930 is shown in Table 16.2. These quantities are also expressed as percentages of federally inspected production and total commercial production.

Grading facilitates trade and enables sale by description instead of inspection. Prior to the introduction of beef grading, about two-thirds of the meat was wholesaled through branch houses or independent wholesale houses where each carcass was sold to the retailer on the basis of personal inspection—a relatively costly system of distribution. Less than one-third of U.S. meat is now wholesaled in this manner. The remainder is distributed by more direct and presumably less costly methods. These direct channels are made possible by sale by description. Grade standards have particularly facilitated the development of mass merchandising methods by chain stores. From his office in Denver, a chain store buyer can buy carcasses in Chicago for retail stores in Washington. Ten minutes later he may negotiate in San Francisco for deliveries on the West Coast. Without grade standards this type of mass procurement and its associated economies obviously would not be possible. The use of federal grades also has opened new and distant outlets for small packers. These opportunities were formerly monopolized by the large packers with their extensive branch house systems and privately advertised brands. Rather than enhancing the monopolistic gains of large processors, in this instance at least, the federal grading system has tended to raise the level of competition in meat distribution.

## DUAL GRADING SYSTEM FOR BEEF CARCASSES

Since July of 1962 the livestock and meat industry has been trying a new approach to beef grading—a dual grading system

**TABLE 16.2: Quantity of Beef Graded or Certified as Complying With Specifications by the USDA, With Ratios to Federally Inspected and Total Commercial Production, 1930–68***

| Year | Quantity Graded | Percentage of— Federally inspected production | Commercial production† |
|---|---|---|---|
| | *(1,000,000 pounds)* | *(per cent)* | *(per cent)* |
| 1930 | 69 | 1.6 | 1.2 |
| 1935 | 268 | 5.8 | 4.2 |
| 1940 | 578 | 11.7 | 8.3 |
| 1945 | 9,177 | 126.8 | 92.4 |
| 1950 | 2,262 | 31.4 | 24.4 |
| 1955 | 6,050 | 59.3 | 44.6 |
| 1960 | 7,058 | 61.8 | 49.1 |
| 1961 | 7,439 | 61.9 | 49.8 |
| 1962 | 7,399 | 61.7 | 49.6 |
| 1963 | 8,312 | 63.3 | 51.8 |
| 1964 | 10,053 | 66.6 | 55.7 |
| 1965 | 10,295 | 66.8 | 56.2 |
| 1966 | 12,037 | 74.2 | 61.8 |
| 1967 | 12,728 | 75.6 | 63.7 |
| 1968 | 13,082 | 73.3 | 63.3 |

Source: *The Livestock and Meat Situation,* USDA, May, 1950, p. 17. Data for 1950–56 from *Livestock Market News Statistics,* USDA, 1956, p. 71. Data for 1957–65 from *Livestock and Meat Statistics,* USDA, Stat. Bul. 333, supplements for 1960, 1965, and 1968.

* Quantities graded, based on estimated weight of carcasses and meat products. From December 16, 1942 to October 16, 1946 (except for July and August, 1946), all grades of beef except Cutter and Canner were required to be graded by a U.S. official grader.

† Federally inspected slaughter and other wholesale and retail slaughter, excluding farm slaughter.

for beef carcasses. The dual grading system provides for two separate grade identifications on beef carcasses: (1) a quality grade, which indicates palatability of meat—reflecting factors associated with tenderness, juiciness, and flavor—and has been widely used for over a quarter-century and (2) a yield grade, reflecting the "cutability"—the percentage of salable meat which the retailer can cut from the carcass. These two grades are represented by the two symbols shown in Figure 16.3.

The older grading system based on quality factors alone has also been continued and remains the most widely used. The volume of yield-graded beef has been increasing and in 1969 amounted to around 20 per cent of the total volume of beef

FIG. 16.2—(By permission of **The New Yorker**, copyright, the F-R. Publishing Corporation.)

FIG. 16.3—The quality grade of dual-graded beef will be identified by of ribbon-type imprint of the quality name. The cutability grade will be stamped on each quarter of the carcass. Both will appear in red ink. However, the cutability grade, mainly of interest to the trade, will not necessarily show up on retail cuts.

officially graded.[3] The new program, if generally adopted, would provide greater dollar-and-cents incentive, through the private marketing system, for cattlemen to produce the type of beef that consumers want.

In today's market both quality and cutability strongly influence the ultimate value of the beef carcass. The new grading system takes them both into account. Dual grading provides a more precise market identification for beef carcasses and is also applicable to live cattle. It therefore furnishes the means for a more accurate reflection of consumer preferences back through the marketing channels to the producer.

This should result in the producer being paid for his cattle on the basis of their value at the retail-consumer level. More important, it would encourage the production of meat-type cattle with carcasses that combine high-quality meat with thickness of muscling and a minimum of excess fat.

## Grades for Hogs and Hog Products

The problems involved in grading hogs and hog products have also been receiving attention.

Tentative standards for grades of pork carcasses and fresh pork cuts were issued by the U.S. Department of Agriculture in 1931. These tentative standards were slightly revised in 1933 and published in Circular No. 288.[4]

[3] *Livestock Market News Statistics,* USDA (weekly issues), 1966.

[4] The next two pages are adapted from *Official United States Standards for Grades of Pork Carcasses (Barrow and Gilt),* Title 7, Chap. I, Pt. 53, Sections 53.140–53.143 of the Code of Federal Regulations, issued Sept., 1952, reprinted, with amendments, July, 1955 and March, 1968.

New standards for grades of barrow and gilt carcasses were proposed by the U.S. Department of Agriculture in 1949. These standards represented the first application of objective measurements as guides to grades for pork carcasses. Slight revisions were made in the proposed standards prior to promulgation by the Secretary of Agriculture as the official U.S. standards for grades of barrow and gilt carcasses effective September 12, 1952.

The official standards were amended in July, 1955, by changing the grade designations Choice No. 1, Choice No. 2, and Choice No. 3 to U.S. No. 1, U.S. No. 2, and U.S. No. 3, respectively. Two other grades, Medium and Cull, were used to designate underfinished carcasses and those otherwise lacking in quality. In addition, the back fat thickness requirements were reduced for each grade and the descriptive specifications were reworded slightly to reflect the reduced fat thickness requirements and to allow more uniform interpretation of the standards.

These standards remained in use until April, 1968, when further revisions were made in grade standards for barrows and gilts. Standards for other classes of hogs were not changed at that time. The 1968 revisions were made to reflect improvement in pork carcasses, especially with respect to yield of trimmed major wholesale cuts. The present grade designations for barrows and gilts are U.S. No. 1, U.S. No. 2, U.S. No. 3, U.S. No. 4, and U.S. Utility. Requirements for U.S. No. 2, 3, and 4 grades are similar to the former U.S. No. 1, 2, and 3 grades; yield requirements for the present U.S. No. 1 grade are higher than any that existed under the former standards. The grade, U.S. Utility, replaced the former Medium and Cull grades. The barrow and gilt standards are discussed in more detail in the next section.

The official standards for pork carcasses provide for segregation according to (1) class, as determined by the apparent sex condition of the animal at the time of slaughter and (2) grade, which reflects quality of pork and the relative proportion of lean cuts to fat cuts in the carcass.

The five classes of pork carcasses, comparable to the same five classes of slaughter hogs, are barrow, gilt, sow, stag, and boar carcasses.

## GRADES OF BARROW AND GILT CARCASSES

Differences in barrow and gilt carcasses due to sex condition are minor, and the grade standards are equally applicable for grading both classes.

Barrow and gilt carcasses are graded primarily on the basis of (1) quality-indicating characteristics of the lean and (2) expected combined yields of the four lean cuts (ham, loin, picnic shoulder, and Boston butt). The grades are divided into two broad groups on the basis of quality. Grade designations U.S. 1 through 4 apply to carcasses with characteristics which indicate that the lean in the four lean cuts will have acceptable quality. Carcasses with characteristics which indicate that the lean will be of unacceptable quality are graded U.S. Utility. If quality is determined to be acceptable, the specific grade is based upon the expected yield of the lean cuts.

When possible, the quality evaluation is made by observing the characteristics of the lean in a cut surface of the carcass, preferably the loin eye at the tenth rib. If necessary, other major muscle surfaces can be used for the evaluation instead. When observation of a cut surface in the carcass is not possible, indirect evaluation of the quality of the lean is made on the basis of firmness of the fat and lean, amount of feathering between the ribs, and color of the lean. Evaluation of quality is also based on the suitability of the belly for the production of bacon, with thickness of the belly the main factor considered.

Estimation of yield of lean cuts is based on the relationships between actual average back fat thickness and the carcass weight and length. The expected yield requirements for the different grades, based on the four lean cuts and chilled carcass weight, are as follows:

| Grade | Yield |
| --- | --- |
| U.S. No. 1 ......... | 53 per cent and over |
| U.S. No. 2 ......... | 50–52.9 per cent |
| U.S. No. 3 ......... | 47–49.9 per cent |
| U.S. No. 4 ......... | Less than 47 per cent |

The required back fat measurements for different carcass lengths and weights, as shown in Table 16.3, provide objective guides for determining the carcass grades.

The U.S. No. 1 grade combines characteristics indicative of acceptable quality with an expected yield of the four lean cuts of 53 per cent or more. Similarly, grades U.S. No. 2, 3, and 4 combine indications of acceptable quality with the yield expectations indicated above for each grade.

U.S. Utility includes all carcasses that have characteristics that indicate unacceptable lean quality, or which do not have acceptable belly thickness. Also included in this grade are all carcasses that are soft and oily, regardless of other quality-indicating characteristics.

While carcass measurements furnish a reliable general guide to grade, the final grade of borderline carcasses may vary from that indicated by measurements due to consideration of

**TABLE 16.3: Weight, Length, and Measurement Guides to Grades for Barrow and Gilt Carcasses**

| Carcass Weight or Carcass Length* | Average Back Fat Thickness (Inches)† by Grade | | | |
|---|---|---|---|---|
| | U.S. No. 1 | U.S. No. 2 | U.S. No. 3 | U.S. No. 4 |
| 120–164 pounds or 27–29.9 inches ....... | 1.3–1.4 | 1.6–1.7 | 1.9–2.0 | 2.0 or more |
| 165–204 pounds or 30–32.9 inches ....... | 1.4–1.5 | 1.7–1.8 | 2.0–2.1 | 2.1 or more |
| 205–255 pounds or 33–36 inches ........ | 1.5–1.6 | 1.8–1.9 | 2.1–2.2 | 2.2 or more |

* Either carcass weight or length may be used with back fat thickness as a reliable guide to grade. The table shows the normal length range for given weights. In cases where length and back fat thickness indicate a different grade than weight and back fat, the grade shall be determined by using length. Carcass weight is is based on a chilled, packer-style carcass. Carcass length is measured from the forward point of the aitch bone to the forward edge of the first rib.

† Average of measurements made opposite the first and last ribs and last lumbar vertebra.

other characteristics such as degree of muscling and fat distribution. However, application of these additional factors is limited to borderline carcasses, and in no case may the final grade be more than one grade different from that indicated by carcass measurements. The standards describe carcasses typical of each grade, and no attempt is made to describe the nearly limitless number of combinations of characteristics that may qualify a carcass for a particular grade.

The detailed specifications for the grades of barrow and gilt carcasses define the term "acceptable quality" and discuss more fully the measurements given in Table 16.3. They include such terms as "moderately full and thick," but no quantitative or numerical objective specifications other than those given in the table.

### GRADES OF SLAUGHTER SOW CARCASSES

Official standards for grades of slaughter sow carcasses were established on August 18, 1956. The objective specifications are not set out by carcass weight or length as the specifications for barrow and gilt carcasses are. They are simply given in terms of average back fat thickness, as shown below:

| Grade: | Average Back Fat Thickness* |
|---|---|
| U.S. No. 1 ........................... | 1.5 to 1.9 inches |
| U.S. No. 2 ........................... | 1.9 to 2.3 inches |
| U.S. No. 3 ........................... | 2.3 or more inches |
| Medium ............................. | 1.1 to 1.5 inches |
| Cull ................................ | Less than 1.1 inches |

* Average of three measurements, skin included, made opposite first and last ribs and the last lumbar vertebra.

These back fat thicknesses run a little higher than the thicknesses for the heaviest or longest barrow and gilt carcasses.

### GRADES FOR HOGS

It should be clearly understood that the grade standards and specifications given above refer to hog *carcasses*. They provide a basis, however, for grades for hogs. Official grades for slaughter barrows and gilts correspond directly to the carcass standards and the grade designations are the same—U.S. No. 1, U.S. No. 2, U.S. No. 3, U.S. No. 4, and U.S. Utility. These grades are widely used in market news reporting, in futures trading for live hogs, and for other marketing purposes. Figure 16.4 shows typical price quotations for hogs at several midwest markets. The quotations are generally given by 20-pound weight ranges for butcher hogs (barrows and gilts) and by wider weight ranges for sows.

## TOBACCO GRADING

In the case of some products, it has been recognized that more is needed than the setting up of grades and standards. In addition, some governmental action is advisable to get these standards applied, and applied where they will do the grower the most good.

In the early 1930's for example, it became apparent that something needed to be done to set up standards against which tobacco quality might be measured and recognized. Something needed to be done to apply these standards on behalf of the tobacco growers at the time of sale. Something needed to be done to see that each grower might have the opportunity to know the current market value of tobacco according to grade. And something needed to be done to help growers prepare their tobacco better for market because poor preparation was costing some of them plenty.

To help solve these problems the Tobacco Inspection Act of 1935 was passed, supplementing the Tobacco Stocks and Standards Act of 1929.

### Standardization

Today government-developed tobacco standard grades and standard-type classifications are the basis of tobacco inspection, market news, stock reports, crop estimates, commodity loans, training courses, farm demonstration work, and many other government tobacco activities. These standards of type and grade are used by certain tobacco cooperative marketing associations as a basis for receiving, packing, selling, and settling with their members. When shown on warehouse receipts issued under the U.S. Warehouse Act, the types and grades give bankers

# LIVESTOCK MARKETS

(Federal-State Market News Service)

## HOG RECEIPTS

| | Tuesday (Estimate) | Wk. Ago | Yr. Ago | This Wk. to Date | —Corr. Period— Last Wk. | Last Yr. |
|---|---|---|---|---|---|---|
| *Interior Iowa-So. Minn. ...... | 65,000 | 84,000 | 111,000 | 101,000 | 163,000 | 171,000 |
| 12 Public Markets (Salable) ... | 46,100 | 42,300 | 48,400 | 103,000 | 109,000 | 111,000 |

*Monday receipts, 36,000.

## SHEEP RECEIPTS

| | Tuesday (Estimate) | Wk. Ago | Yr. Ago | This Wk. to Date | —Corr. Period— Last Wk. | Last Yr. |
|---|---|---|---|---|---|---|
| **Interior Iowa-So. Minn. ...... | 2,300 | 2,200 | 1,800 | 4,000 | 3,400 | 4,800 |
| 12 Public Markets (Salable) ... | 5,600 | 6,100 | 6,400 | 12,000 | 13,000 | 13,000 |

**Monday receipts, 1,700.

## HOG QUOTATIONS

| Barrows, gilts | Int. Ia. So. Minn. | —Terminal Markets— Chicago | Sioux City | Omaha | E. St. Louis |
|---|---|---|---|---|---|
| **U.S. No. 1** | | | | | |
| 200-220 lb .......... | $.... .... | $.... .... | $.... .... | $.... .... | $25.50-25.50 |
| **U.S. No. 2** | | | | | |
| 200-220 lb .......... | 24.00-25.00 | 25.50-26.00 | 25.25-25.50 | 25.25-25.50 | .... .... |
| 220-240 lb .......... | 23.75-24.75 | 25.25-25.75 | 25.00-25.50 | 25.00-25.50 | .... .... |
| **U.S. No. 3** | | | | | |
| 200-220 lb .......... | 23.75-24.75 | .... .... | 25.00-25.25 | 24.75-25.50 | .... .... |
| 220-240 lb .......... | 23.50-24.50 | 24.50-25.25 | 24.75-25.25 | 24.50-25.25 | .... .... |
| 240-270 lb .......... | 22.50-24.25 | 23.50-24.75 | .... .... | 23.75-24.75 | .... .... |
| **U.S. No.** | | | | | |
| 270-300 lb .......... | .... .... | .... .... | .... .... | 22.00-23.75 | .... .... |
| **U.S. No. 1 & 2** | | | | | |
| 180-200 lb .......... | .... .... | 25.00-26.00 | 25.25-25.50 | 25.25-25.75 | .... .... |
| 200-220 lb .......... | 24.25-25.25 | 26.00-26.25 | 25.00-25.50 | 25.50-25.75 | 25.25-25.50 |
| 220-240 lb .......... | 24.00-25.00 | 25.50-26.00 | 25.00-25.50 | 25.25-25.75 | 24.75-25.25 |
| **U.S. No. 2 & 3** | | | | | |
| 180-200 lb .......... | .... .... | 24.50-25.50 | 25.00-25.25 | 25.00-25.50 | .... .... |
| 200-220 lb .......... | 23.75-25.00 | 25.25-25.75 | 25.00-25.25 | 25.00-25.50 | 25.00- |
| 220-240 lb .......... | 23.50-24.75 | 24.75-25.50 | 24.75-25.25 | 24.75-25.25 | 24.50-25.00 |
| 240-270 lb .......... | 22.75-24.50 | 24.00-25.00 | 24.00-25.00 | 24.25-25.00 | 23.50-24.50 |
| **U.S. No. 3 & 4** | | | | | |
| 240-270 lb .......... | 22.50-24.00 | 23.50-24.50 | 24.00-25.00 | 23.75-24.50 | 22.75-24.00 |
| 270-300 lb .......... | 21.50-23.25 | 22.75-23.50 | 22.50-24.25 | 22.00-23.75 | 22.00-22.75 |
| **U.S. No. 1-3** | | | | | |
| 180-200 lb .......... | .... .... | 24.75-25.75 | 25.00-25.50 | 25.00-25.50 | .... .... |
| 200-220 lb .......... | 23.75-25.00 | 25.50-26.00 | 25.00-25.50 | 25.25-25.50 | 25.00-25.25 |
| 220-240 lb .......... | 23.75-24.75 | 25.25-25.75 | 25.00-25.25 | 25.00-25.50 | 24.50-25.25 |
| **U.S. No. 2-4** | | | | | |
| 240-270 lb .......... | 22.75-24.25 | 23.50-24.75 | 24.00-25.00 | 24.00-24.75 | 23.00-24.25 |
| **Sows—U.S. No. 1 & 3** | | | | | |
| 270-330 lb .......... | 20.50-21.25 | .... .... | .... .... | .... .... | 21.00-21.25 |
| 330-400 lb .......... | 19.75-20.75 | 20.50-21.25 | 20.75-21.00 | 20.75-21.50 | 20.25-21.25 |
| 400-550 lb .......... | 18.00-20.25 | 19.50-20.50 | 20.25-20.75 | 20.25-20.75 | 19.25-20.25 |

*Receipts of hogs cover direct purchases by 23 packing plants within the interior area and Southern Minnesota and direct purchases for out-of-state shipments by 8 major shipping organizations.

**Prices on sheep and lambs in the accompanying report on Interior Iowa and southern Minnesota markets are based on the sale of animals originating in the area and sold at 2 plants in Iowa and one in southern Minnesota and some order buyers.

FIG. 16.4—Hog prices at interior Iowa and southern Minnesota packing points and selected terminal markets. (Des Moines **Register**, May 6, 1970.)

and others reliable information about the character and value of the tobacco covered by the receipts offered as collateral for loans. They are used also by tobacco experiment stations in evaluating the effect of different fertilization and culture methods.

Six major classes of tobacco have been designated by the USDA to cover the different types of tobacco grown in the United States.[5] Three of the classes are based on the method used in curing—flue-cured, fire-cured, and air-cured. The other three classes are based on the use for which the tobacco is grown. These are cigar-filler, cigar-binder, and cigar-wrapper. A final

[5] *Tobacco in the United States,* USDA, Misc. Publ. C&MS-867, Oct., 1966.

designation, miscellaneous domestic, is used for tobaccos that do not fall under one of the major classes. Flue-cured and air-cured tobaccos make up the bulk of the U.S. production, accounting for approximately 60 per cent and 33 per cent, respectively, of the total.

Within the major classes there are 24 important commercial types of tobacco. Official standards have been established for each of these types. Standards were established first to cover flue-cured tobacco produced in Virginia, North Carolina, South Carolina, Georgia, Florida, and Alabama; fire-cured tobacco produced in Virginia, Kentucky, and Tennessee; light air-cured (burley) tobacco produced in Kentucky, Tennessee, Ohio, Indiana, Missouri, Alabama, Virginia, West Virginia, and North Carolina; and dark air-cured tobacco produced in Virginia, Kentucky, Tennessee, and Indiana.

Grade standards were established more recently on Pennsylvania seedleaf tobacco, Ohio and Puerto Rican cigar-filler type, Connecticut Valley and Wisconsin cigar-binder tobacco, and shade-grown tobacco from the Connecticut Valley, Georgia, and Florida.

### Hazards of the Public Auction Market

Even more so than for most other commodities, farmers have found it difficult to learn and understand the system that buyers use to appraise the grade and quality and to determine the price they will pay for tobacco. Most of the tobacco grown in the United States (about 95 per cent) is sold at loose-leaf auction markets. The buyers represent the large tobacco manufacturing companies and leaf dealers, each of which has private grades and grade symbols. These are subject to change. The sale is conducted by warehouse operators, commission men for the growers. Sales are recorded only to the extent necessary for computing the gross sale amount for each grower in settling accounts.

Several hazards confront tobacco growers when they sell their tobacco at a public auction market:

1. Buyers understand the technical considerations involved in the quality of tobacco for specific uses, but many growers (sellers) do not. The tobacco of any type includes an extraordinary range of qualities, characteristics, and values based on technical considerations. As a result, the grade designation that the buyer places on a lot of tobacco at the time of sale has little, if any, meaning to most farmers. Yet prices for the various grades on a single day's sale may range from 3 to 50 cents a pound.

2. Because most lots of tobacco are sold very rapidly—at a rate as high as 600 or more an hour—bids are based on snap judgments of quality, which often are bad.
3. Very often these snap judgments result in bids of prices that are considerably below the current average price paid for tobacco of similar quality. For example, changes in the quality of daylight, which may affect accurate evaluation of quality, are such that in many sales growers cannot get prices corresponding to the value of their tobacco on the prevailing market.
4. In the absence of inspection service, growers have no systematic way to learn what their tobacco is worth. In addition, very much tobacco is inefficiently prepared for market.

### Tobacco Inspection Act

Avoidable losses to growers from the above causes can be sizable. That is what the grower is faced with. And that is where the Tobacco Inspection Act comes in. Among other things, this act authorizes the Secretary of Agriculture to establish standards for tobacco by which its type, grade, size, condition, or other characteristics may be determined; to demonstrate these standards; and to designate certain auction markets for inspection service after determining by referendum that two-thirds of the voting growers favor designation. Any tobacco offered for sale on these designated markets must be inspected and certified without fee by authorized inspectors.

With specific information on grade and on current selling prices, the grower can arrive at the approximate value of his tobacco and decide whether the auction bid price is fair and reasonable in the light of existing market conditions. When the bid price is substantially lower than the current average for the grade, the farmer may immediately reject the sale and demand a resale. Since auction sales of tobacco are conducted at a very rapid rate, as mentioned above, errors of judgment leading to unreasonably low prices are numerous.

To make price information available, federal market reporters follow the sale and record required data from the basket tickets. These tickets contain all the information essential for price reports—the grade, number of pounds, and price. Records are obtained from the different markets that sell the same type of tobacco, and they are combined and compiled in field offices for the publication of mimeographed daily and weekly reports covering each type area. These reports are furnished to growers on the auction floors and further disseminated by press and radio. In addition, season market reviews are issued covering the types of tobacco sold at auction. These reviews include average prices for each grade, average prices for the markets, the total quantity sold on each market, statistics to show the percentage distribution of the crop according to quality factors, and other related market information.

Therefore, because on all auction markets the grower has the privilege of rejecting a sale and calling for a resale, this information service goes to the heart of the principal weaknesses of the auction marketing system. Through the services provided under the act, farmers have an opportunity to learn to put their tobacco in better condition for marketing. Then when the tobacco is sold at auction the farmer can look at the government grade on each lot of his tobacco, look at the price that has been offered, and look at the prevailing price published for each particular grade. If the price offered is significantly below the prevailing price for a particular grade of tobacco, the farmer has a right to reject the sale on that grade and to resell the tobacco later.

For example, assume a Georgia tobacco grower offered 172 pounds of tobacco for sale on the Pelham, Georgia, market. The price offered originally was 40 cents a pound. The market quotation for the particular government grade of tobacco was 55 cents a pound. Next day, on resale of the same lot of tobacco, the grower received 55 cents a pound. That meant $25.80 (or 37.5 per cent) more for this amount of tobacco than he was originally offered.

It goes without saying that sometimes farmers reject a sale of tobacco and upon resale of that tobacco receive a price lower than the original offer. But on the average, farmers who take advantage of this grading and market news service gain substantially. And on the other side of the picture, farmers who use this information frequently will refrain from rejecting a sale when they can see they have received a fair price.

Inspection and market news services now exist for all tobacco auction markets.

## FRUITS AND VEGETABLES

Grades and standards are widely used at shipping-point and wholesale levels for a number of fruits and vegetables. In 1970 official grades were in effect for 83 fresh fruits and vegetables, as well as 39 fruits and vegetables for processing. Consumer grade standards have also been established for a limited number of fresh fruits and vegetables but are not widely used at retail. The inspection and grading processes for fruits and vegetables are closely related. A part of the inspection procedure, for example, is certification that the product is within prescribed quality tolerances for the grade.

The use of the federal-state inspection service and official U.S. grading standards facilitates trading between shippers and buyers. The standards furnish a basis for contracts between shippers and buyers, and the federal-state inspection certificate indicates compliance and noncompliance with quality provisions of contracts. The certificate discourages receivers from making unwarranted rejections of shipments in the markets. It also aids in the settlement of disputes between shippers and buyers, and the detailed description of the shipment facilitates the settlement of any damage claims against transportation agencies. Federal-state inspection certificates are prima facie evidence in all U.S. courts and in most state courts.

## APPRAISAL

The grading systems for the different agricultural products considered in this chapter have reached different stages of adequacy. The markets for grain have reached a fairly high stage of accuracy in establishing uniform and objective grade specifications and in allocating different lots of grain in groups according to those specifications. The markets for livestock and for some livestock products, however, appear to be still in a rather primitive stage. Consumers' preferences are not accurately reflected back to the producer. In many cases, differences in value are not well recognized, and too nearly a "flat price" is paid for good, bad, and indifferent products. This offers very little incentive for producers to raise high-quality products and thus has a depressing effect on the average quality of the product and therefore on its consumption.

One reason for this is the greater difficulty of working out and applying objective specifications to livestock and livestock products. Yet adequate specifications have been worked out for most of these products, and others are in the process. The difficulty is to get them applied. The main obstacle to improvement along these lines is the inertia of old habits and customs on the part of producers, dealers, processors, distributors, and consumers.

# 17

# GOVERNMENT PROGRAMS TO CONTROL AGRICULTURAL PRICES

AGRICULTURAL PRICE POLICY in the United States has gone through a most interesting evolution since the 1920's. The evolution proceeded in three steps or stages.

In the first stage, the traditional open competitive market was accepted as the arbiter of prices. The objective of agricultural price policy was to improve the working of the open market by providing better market news, reducing economic friction, overcoming lags, and making the markets for farm products as sensitive and accurate reflectors of supply and demand as possible.

In the second stage, the traditional *long-run* open-market prices were still accepted, but *short-run* month-to-month and year-to-year open-market price variations were called into question. Storage programs were developed to control supply and demand, smooth out the short-run variations in supplies, and stabilize prices about the long-run trend.

In the third stage (partly concurrent with the second stage), the traditional long-run open-market prices were called into question, as well as the short-run variations. The long-run level of agricultural prices was believed by many observers to be low, because the traditional market was not open in the first place; it was open on the farmer's side but more or less closed (monopolized) on the other side.

These three steps are outlined stage by stage in this chapter.

## PERFECTING THE OPEN COMPETITIVE MARKET

During the early stages of the development of agricultural price policy, the open competitive market was accepted as the regulator of production and consumption. The objective was to make the competitive market as free and sensitive as possible—to bring it closer to perfection.

Perfect competition (with a large number of small producers, each unable to affect price appreciably and possessing perfect information[1]) is in practice unattainable, as in the field of physics a perfect vacuum is in practice unattainable. But perfect competition can be approached, as in physics a perfect vacuum can be approached; an objective is a useful thing even if it cannot be fully attained.

The USDA recognized that open competition requires abundant market information before it can be effective. The buyers (the large processors and distributors) had reasonably good market information, but the sellers (individual farmers) by themselves did not. So one of the first objectives of agricultural price policy was the provision of accurate crop reports and daily, weekly, and monthly market news. The purpose here was to enable the open market to function more perfectly. The USDA built up an extensive system of crop reports and market news, designed to help farmers keep up to date on what had happened and what was happening.

But this was not enough. There is a time lag of weeks, months, or years in most agricultural production. Farmers need to know not only what has happened and what is happening but they need to know as accurately as existing information permits what is going to happen by the time their products reach the market, several months or years after their production decisions have been made.

Chapter 8 explained how the outlook work of the USDA was designed to provide this advance information. The objective of outlook work was to improve the open competitive market still further—to make the market more perfect by increasing farmers' knowledge about what supply, demand, and prices *would be* when their products reached the market. The open market was still accepted as the regulator of production and consumption; the objective was merely to reduce friction and make the market as free and sensitive a reflector of supply and demand as possible.

---

[1]E. H. Chamberlin, *The Theory of Monopolistic Competition,* Cambridge, Harvard Univ. Press, 1946, pp. 6–7.

At the same time the federal government was working from another direction. Through the Federal Trade Commission and the Department of Justice, it was endeavoring to make the markets more open and competitive throughout the whole economy by a general attack on monopoly. Examples of specific actions under this program with respect to agriculture were the Packer Consent Decree of 1920, the Grain Futures Act of 1922, and the Perishable Agricultural Commodities Act, 1930, whose purpose was to reduce monopsonistic elements on the buying side of the market for agricultural products.

This acceptance of the open competitive market was part of the general economic tradition going back at least as far as Adam Smith. The work of general economic theorists in recent decades has provided a more rigorous and objective confirmation of the traditional acceptance of the open competitive market. Their work uses an impressive apparatus of budget lines, indifference surfaces, isoproduct contours, block diagrams, etc., and proceeds on the assumption that consumers aim at maximizing their satisfaction and producers aim at maximizing their profits. It demonstrates that with a given distribution of income on the one hand and a given stage of productive technique on the other, perfect competition in product and factor markets is efficient in maximizing satisfaction or welfare, in the sense that no change in the distribution of products is possible that would increase the satisfaction of one individual or group without decreasing the satisfactions of others, and no change in resource use is possible that would increase the production of one producer without decreasing the production of another.[2]

## STABILIZATION: "INTERFERENCE" WITH THE OPEN MARKET

During the late 1920's and early 1930's agricultural price policy in the United States and many other countries was carried a significant step further. It went beyond reducing friction in the working of the open market and undertook to affect the supply and demand for the products and *modify* the working of the open market. Whereas previously the objective had been to render the open market as accurate and sensitive a reflector of changes in supply and demand as possible, now a new and additional objective was sought. That objective was to regulate (control) the supply and demand so as to stabilize prices.

This objective was sought through the stabilization operations of the Federal Farm Board from 1929 to 1933, and the similar activities of the Commodity Credit Corporation (hereafter referred to as the CCC) since that time.

---

[2] See, for example, Tibor Scitovsky, *Welfare and Competition*, Homewood, Ill., Irwin, 1951, p. 59.

To some extent the original drive for stabilizing prices was really a drive only for "stabilizing them upwards"—that is, only for raising prices when they were low, not also for depressing them when they were high. But, in actual fact, stabilizing prices by putting products into storage in order to raise prices when they were low also involved stabilizing prices by taking those products out of storage in later years in order to depress prices when they were high. The stabilization worked both ways. In most cases (a perishable crop like potatoes being an exception) "stabilizing them upwards" turned out to mean stabilizing them downwards, too. This was true with respect to the effects of variations in demand as well as in supply. Price ceilings were placed on farm products to hold them down when they were too high, just as price floors were put under them when they were too low.

This stabilization involves direct governmental interference with the open competitive market when prices are too low or too high. What is the economic basis for this interference? What does "too low" or "too high" mean?

The basis for interfering with the open market (which previously had been endorsed as the regulator of production) is that the short-time variations are confusing rather than helpful guides to producers. A rise in the price of corn relative to wheat of, let us say, 30 per cent that persisted for five or ten years probably would be a reliable guide to producers that they should put more acres into corn and less into wheat. But a rise of 30 per cent that resulted merely from a short crop of corn due to bad weather and lasted only for one year, would require merely a small and temporary increase in corn acreage; good weather the next year, in fact, might rectify the shortage without requiring any increase in acreage.

The short-time variations in prices that result from variations in general demand similarly go further than necessary to guide producers toward changes in production. Beyond that necessary point, they have a disorganizing effect on production in agriculture and the rest of the economy. During the first few years of the depression of the 1930's, for example, both total agricultural acreage and production increased rather than decreased, with the decrease in demand. And as the depression continued, long-run farm ownership and operation plans were disrupted with distressing results to the farm families concerned. Similarly, the rise in agricultural prices during World War II, if unchecked by ceilings, would have had disruptive effects and reduced production in the whole economy.

Briefly, then, the economic basis for short-run price stabilization is the improvement in resource allocation, the increase in total production, and the reduction of farm family distress that such stabilization brings. What is needed is not complete stabilization, which would freeze the allocation of resources and have other harmful effects, but partial stabilization to remove most if not all of the short-run variations and to keep prices at about the long-run open-market levels that reflect fundamental changes in production technology and consumer demand. The objective is to retain the allocative guidance provided by long-run open-market price levels and to remove the confusion caused by short-run variations about those levels.

The agricultural price and income stabilization programs, then, may be regarded as an attempt to bring the open competitive market still closer to perfection than the provision of market news and outlook information can. The objective is to reduce or remove the variations in price that result from erratic and unpredictable variations in supply and demand (such as those due to the weather) which do not represent the mutual adjustment of producers and consumers to each other.

We may summarize the two stages of the development of agricultural price policy in these terms: (1) To the end of the 1920's open competitive market prices were accepted as the most efficient means to the end of maximizing production and consumer satisfaction, and the objective of agricultural price policy was to bring the market closer to perfect competition. (2) Then, from about 1929 on, short-run open-market prices were considered too variable to be efficient, and attempts were made to reduce or smooth out short-run variations about long-run levels. These long-run levels were accepted as the most efficient means to the end of maximizing production and consumer satisfaction.

### Does the Open Market Really Exist?

Along with this move to stabilize agricultural prices about long-run open-market levels went a conflicting current of thought that sought to raise those long-run levels because they were really not open-market levels in the first place.

According to this view, the open market was only a fiction. It did not exist in actual life. The market was open on the farmer's side, but monopolistic on the other side. During the depression of the 1930's agriculture maintained or, in fact, actually increased its production (from an index of 97 in 1929 to 101 in 1932). Agricultural prices fell 57 per cent (from an index of 138 in 1929 to 61 in 1932), while industrial production was reduced

47 per cent (from 110 in 1929 to 58 in 1932) and industrial prices fell only 23 per cent (from 113 to 87). Competition in industry was less open (atomistic) than in agriculture.

Furthermore, in the case of certain specific commodities, competitive farmers were directly up against monopsonistic or oligopsonistic buyers in what was clearly not an open market. Milk was a prominent example of this; in each large milkshed several hundred or thousand milk-producing farmers would be pitted against perhaps only half a dozen large milk distributors.

To meet farmers' desires to stabilize supplies and prices and develop what has been called countervailing power in dealing with monopolies, three different kinds of programs were developed:

1. Stabilization programs designed to stabilize the market supplies of storable crops by government storage operations. These were undertaken first by the Federal Farm Board in 1929 and, after its demise in 1933, by the CCC.
2. Acreage control programs designed to reduce production in line with reduced demand. These were undertaken by the AAA, beginning in 1933.
3. Marketing agreements designed to develop countervailing power in specific cases such as milk and a few specialty fruits. These were undertaken by separate commodity groups under the supervision of the USDA, beginning also in 1933.

The first of these three programs (the stabilization program) is examined briefly below. A brief discussion of acreage control programs follows. Marketing agreements, used chiefly with milk, are discussed in Chapter 24.

## STABILIZING SUPPLIES BY STORAGE OPERATIONS

The Federal Farm Board's attempt to stabilize the prices of farm products from 1929 to 1933 ended in failure primarily because of the severe industrial depression that took place after 1929. The CCC then was set up to do the job in a somewhat different fashion. It engaged in storage operations for a number of durable (storable) crops, designed to withhold most of the excess over average supplies in good crop years and return them to the market in poor crop years.

Corn is a relatively durable commodity and can be stored for several years without serious deterioration if it was in good condition to begin with. Stabilizing the market supplies of corn and other feed grans should reduce the instability in livestock production that results from the year-to-year variation in feed pro-

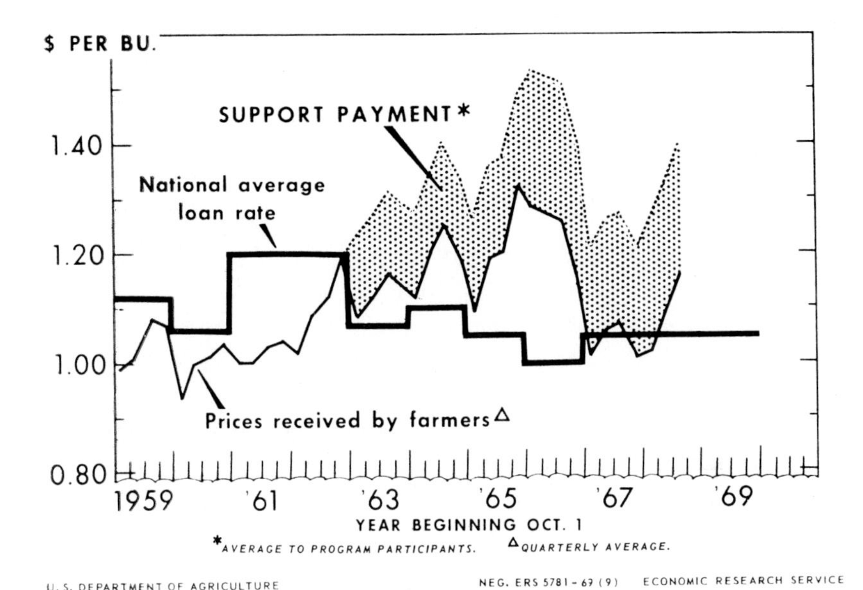


FIG. 17.1—Corn prices, loan rates, and support payments, 1959–69.

duction. The CCC stabilizes the market supplies of corn and other feed grains by underwriting nonrecourse commodity loans to farmers on corn and other feed grains that they hold under seal in cribs on their farms. The loan rates, support levels, and prices of corn, 1959–69, are shown in Figure 17.1.

It is evident from this chart that the storage operations for corn have only partially stabilized corn prices, even in recent years when the program was fully developed, with the use of support payments to supplement the loans. Indeed, in the 1950's the program became overdeveloped. The totals placed under price support loans each year were more than necessary for price stabilization purposes; and stocks of feed grains, consisting mostly of corn, grew to an alarming size—to a peak of nearly 2 billion bushels in 1961.

The nature of the problem is shown in Figure 17.2. Not until the voluntary feed-grains adjustment program was adopted in 1961 was it possible to arrest and reverse the build-up in stocks. The same type of program was continued during the 1962–65 period and was extended for an additional four-year period by the Food and Agriculture Act of 1965. During the period from October 1, 1961, to October 1, 1967, total feed-grain carryover stocks were reduced from 85 to 37 million tons, but increased moderately to 50 million tons by October 1, 1969.

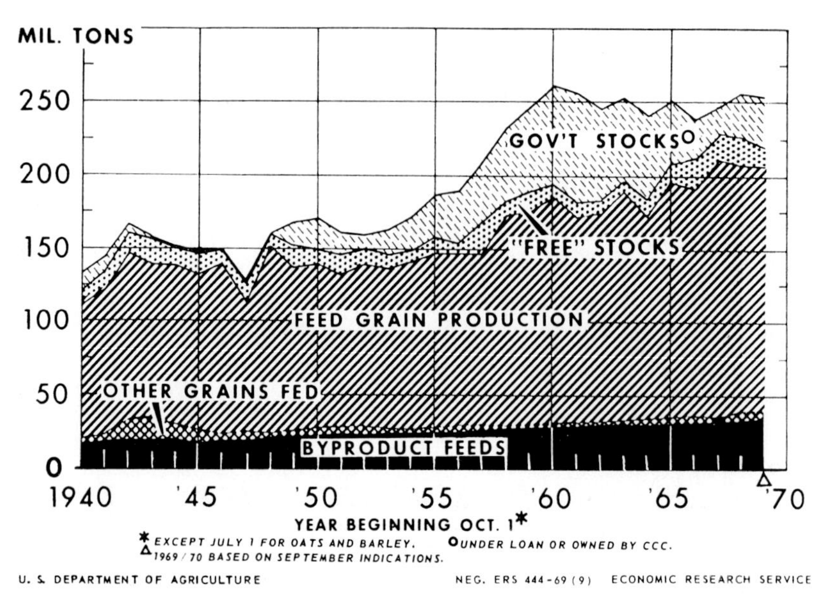


FIG. 17.2—U.S. government and other feed-grain stocks in relation to production, 1940–69.

The same sort of thing happened with wheat. The build-up of stocks to a record level of nearly 1.5 billion bushels in 1961 and the subsequent decline to less than half a billion bushels are shown in Figure 17.3. Stocks rose, however, to over 800 million bushels in 1969.

## STABILIZING WHEAT AND COTTON PRICES

Wheat and cotton, dissimilar in most of their physical characteristics, are considered together here because they are similar in several important economic characteristics.

Both of them are export commodities; that is, substantial percentages of the crop are sold abroad. In recent years, about half the U.S. wheat and cotton crops have been exported. The prices of these crops, therefore, are strongly influenced by conditions in countries other than the United States.

In addition, the wheat and cotton milling industries based on these two crops are not much affected by variations in the prices of the crops. Livestock production based on corn is much affected by year-to-year variations in the price of corn, but wheat-flour and cotton-textile production and consumption are very little affected by variations in the prices of wheat and cotton. Stabilizing corn prices tends to stabilize hog production and

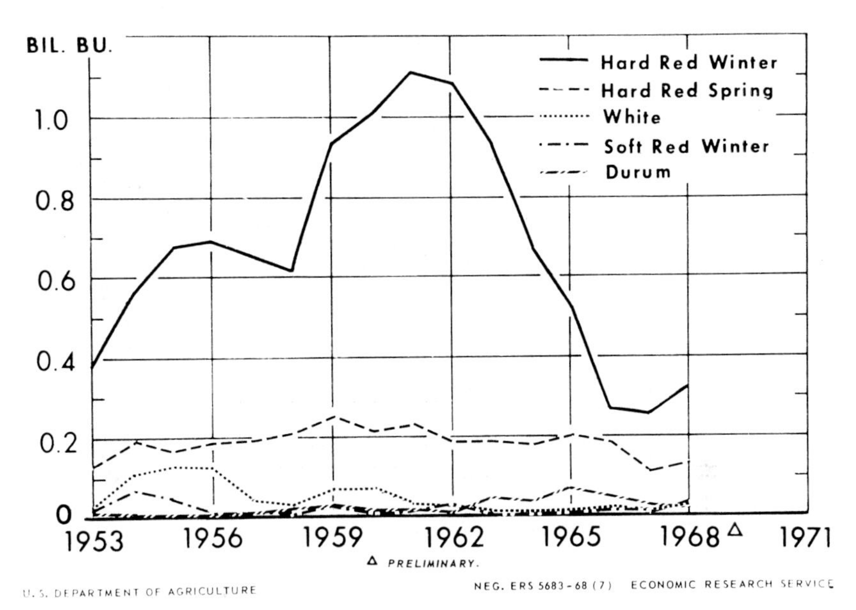


FIG. 17.3—Carryover of wheat by class, 1953–68.

prices, but stabilizing wheat and cotton prices would have very little stabilizing effect on wheat-flour and cotton-textile production and prices, for they are not much affected by variations in wheat and cotton prices in the first place.

For the reasons, then, that (1) wheat and cotton are export crops and (2) variations in their prices do not disturb the industries based upon them, price supports that vary inversely with the total U.S. supply each year would be more appropriate than fixed price supports. Price supports with this sort of flexibility would be lower in big crop years and would increase exports in those years; conversely, higher price supports in short crop years would decrease exports. In addition, the flexible price supports would tend to stabilize wheat and cotton producers' incomes; the effect of variations in crop size would be more or less completely offset by the opposite variations in prices.

Flexible price supports of this nature were written into the Agricultural Act of 1949 in the form of "sliding scales" of loan rates varying inversely with the total supply. The sliding scales are reproduced in Table 17.1. The scales for cotton and peanuts are similar, but started with a supply percentage of 108 instead of 102. Amendments to the 1949 act resulted in only limited use of flexible supports during the 1949–54 period. The Agricultural Act of 1954 also established flexible price supports on basic com-

**TABLE 17.1: "Sliding Scales" for Loan Rates**

| For tobacco (except as otherwise provided herein), corn, wheat, and rice if the supply percentage as of the beginning of the marketing year is: | The level of support shall be not less than the following percentage of the parity price: |
|---|---|
| Not more than 102 | 90 |
| More than 102 but not more than 104 | 89 |
| More than 104 but not more than 106 | 88 |
| More than 106 but not more than 108 | 87 |
| More than 108 but not more than 110 | 86 |
| More than 110 but not more than 112 | 85 |
| More than 112 but not more than 114 | 84 |
| More than 114 but not more than 116 | 83 |
| More than 116 but not more than 118 | 82 |
| More than 118 but not more than 120 | 81 |
| More than 120 but not more than 122 | 80 |
| More than 122 but not more than 124 | 79 |
| More than 124 but not more than 126 | 78 |
| More than 126 but not more than 128 | 77 |
| More than 128 but not more than 130 | 76 |
| More than 130 | 75 |

modities. Flexible support provisions on some commodities have since been eliminated by later legislation, although they remain in effect for certain others.

The loan rates and prices of wheat since 1960 are shown in Figure 17.4.

## ACREAGE CONTROL PROGRAMS

The Agricultural Adjustment Act (AAA) acreage control programs in the 1930's were partially successful in reducing acreage, but their effects on their real objective—production—were small. Many farmers did not take part in the program. Those who did took out their poorest acres and used more fertilizer on the reduced acreage so that yields per acre increased. Most of the acres taken out of production of one crop were put into the production of other crops, and the effect on total production was negligible.[3] Acreage controls were discontinued during the 1940's but were invoked again in the 1950's.

One program which included acreage controls on a comprehensive scale was the Soil Bank program, which rented part or whole farms from farmers for a number of years (up to ten) and kept them out of production. The acreage taken out of production under this program rose to 27 million by 1960, but crop production continued to increase.

[3] *Effect of Acreage Allotment Programs*, USDA, Rept. 3, June, 1956; and Geoffrey Shepherd, *Appraisal of the Federal Feed-Grains Program*, Iowa Agr. Exp. Sta. Res. Bul. 501, Jan., 1962.

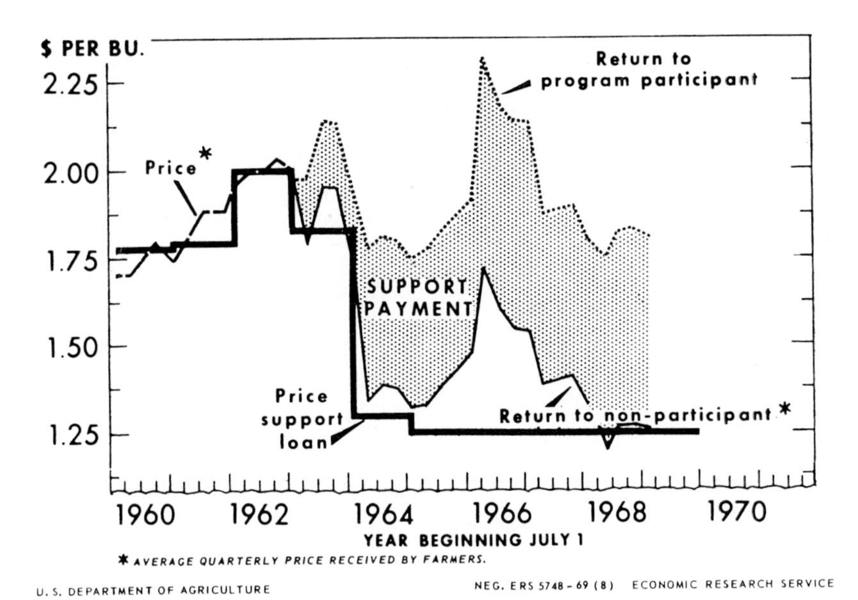


FIG. 17.4—U.S. average wheat prices and loan rates, 1960–69.

Another effort was the emergency 1961 feed-grains program, under which farmers were paid for diversion of acreage from feed-grain production. A similar program was put into effect for wheat. Both programs were continued in 1962 and again in the Agricultural Act of 1965.

Even if acreage reduction programs can reduce production, they may have undesirable economic effects. They tend to freeze production patterns and prevent, or at the least retard, the changes in acreage that farmers make in response to new technological developments—changes that should be adapted to the particular farm and farm operator.

Furthermore, reductions in acreage, if effective, merely benefit acreage. Within a very few years, they no longer benefit farmers. The higher returns are simply capitalized into the value of the land, or into rents, so that new buyers and renters are no better off than before.

This has been demonstrated empirically. Production control has met with some success in tobacco. The chief effects there, however, have been to bid up the price of land (a tobacco allotment is reported to add $1,000 or more per acre of allotment to the value of a farm). This is a benefit only to the present landowner. Once the land has been sold to another owner, there is no more benefit to anyone. There is in fact only harm to young people starting to farm, as they find it more difficult to raise the amount of capital required for ownership.

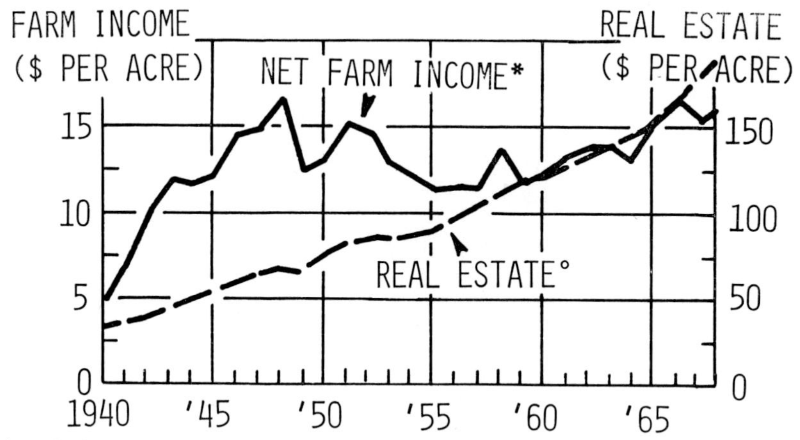


* Includes interest paid on farm mortgage debt and net rents to nonfarm landlords.

° Farmland and buildings, value per acre, March 1 of the following year.

FIG. 17.5—U.S. average value of farmland and buildings per acre and net farm income per acre, 1940–68.

The effects of production control programs on a national scale are difficult to isolate, since many different things were happening to different crops at the same time—the technological revolution in production practices, changes in domestic and foreign demand, and so forth. But the net effect of them all on farm incomes and land values is shown in Figure 17.5. This shows that farm income per acre from farm sources declined after World War II then rose to the earlier level; the value of land per acre, however, more than tripled.

Experience with acreage controls has demonstrated these principles: The prices of farm products can be supported above open-market levels only if market supplies are reduced accordingly. Reduction of market supplies requires destruction of part of the supply already produced, or reduction of production. These things are difficult to accomplish. In cases where production has been reduced by acreage reduction, the benefit has naturally gone to the factor that is reduced—to acreage, that is, to land. But the fundamental purpose of agricultural policy is to benefit men. The purpose is to increase income per farmer. That requires a reduction in the number of farmers, not a reduction in the number of acres.

Labor unions are effective in raising wage rates, because they have monopolistic control of the number of men employed at the particular job. They exercise this power by preventing the employer from employing men below the wage rate accepted by the union. This wage rate, higher than the "open" (one-sided) market rate, cuts the employer's demand curve for labor at a higher point. So the employer hires fewer men. Those who are hired get the benefit of the higher wages.

Agricultural monopolistic policy will not increase income per farmer unless it is backed up, as the power of union labor is backed up, by reduction in the number of farmers. This is a far more difficult problem than the reduction of the number of union laborers.

Raising the union wage rate *reduces* the number of laborers who will be employed at that rate. But raising farm income increases the number of farmers—by reducing the incentive for young farmers to migrate from the farm to better-paying industrial jobs.

### THE LEVEL OF PER CAPITA FARM INCOME

A program to raise the level of per capita income per farmer can succeed over a period of years only if it reduces the number of farmers dividing up the total agricultural income. This process of reduction in the number of farmers, far from being a radical and alarming idea, is something that has been going on for years, with beneficial results all around. Figure 17.6 shows that the farm population declined from 30.5 million in 1940 to 10.5 million in 1968. If the same number of persons had remained on farms in 1968 as were there in 1940, the income per person would have been about one-third as large as it actually was in

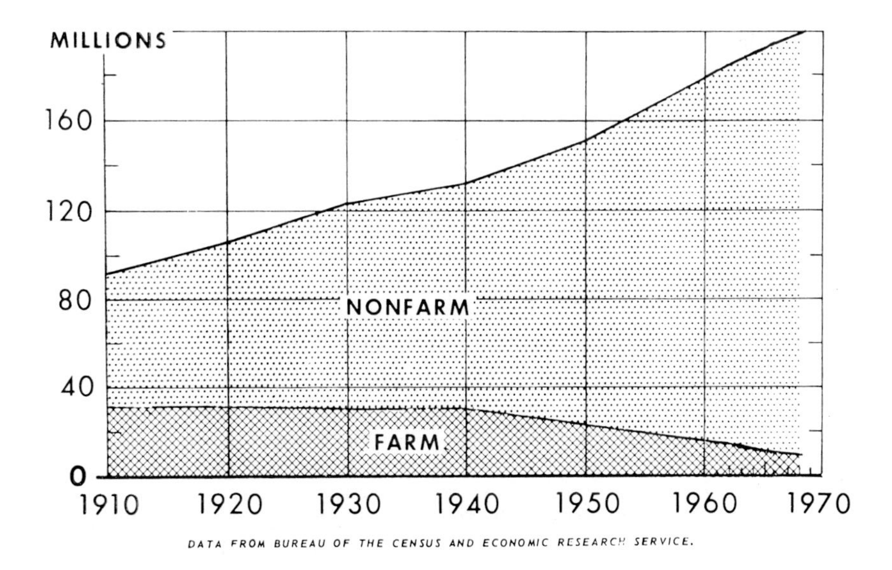


FIG. 17.6—Decline in farm population, United States, 1910–68.

1968. And nonfarm industry would have suffered from a shortage of workers.

The birth rate in agriculture is higher than necessary to maintain a constant farm population. In contrast, the urban birth rate is too low to maintain the increasing urban population that is needed to produce the increasing quantity of goods and services that make up an increasing level of living. The birth rate in agriculture is so high that about half a million persons per year have been moving off farms and into jobs in urban centers where the birth rate is lower.

The level of money income (adjusted for any differences in psychic or nonmoney income) per capita in agriculture is depressed by the continuing excess of farmers on a national basis to the point where it must be lower than nonagricultural income by an amount reflecting the money and other costs of moving from a farm to a nonfarm job.

Thus the "open" competitive market in agriculture results in lower per capita incomes than open competitive market levels. The reason for this is that the "open" market is only partly open on one side (the monopolized side) while it is excessively open on the other (the farmer-entry side).

An increase in *per capita* farm income is needed, not in *total* farm income. The way to increase per capita farm income is to reduce the factor whose remuneration you want to increase. The thing to do is to reduce the number of farmers. The smaller number of farmers then will cut the total agricultural income pie into larger pieces per farmer.

This reduction cannot be brought about the way labor unions do it—by, in effect, reducing entry into the trade. The feasible solution is to reduce the continuing excess of farmers—not by reducing the number born, but by expediting the emigration of the excess boys and girls off the farm into urban jobs. The goal is to raise per capita incomes on farms as closely as possible to equality with incomes for comparable ability in town. This can be done by providing training for farm boys and girls that will fit them to compete with urban boys and girls for urban jobs and by providing a nation-wide employment service that will put farm boys and girls in touch with urban jobs.

The whole field of agricultural price policy is discussed fully in several books to which the interested reader is referred.[4]

[4] G. Shepherd, *Farm Policy; New Directions*, 1964; and *Agricultural Price Analysis*, 1962, Ames, Iowa State Univ. Press. See also his *Appraisal of the Feed-Grains Programs*, NCR Regional Pub. 128, Iowa Agr. Exp. Sta. Res. Bul. 501, Jan., 1962, and *Controlling Agricultural Supply by Controlling Inputs*, Univ. of Mo. Agr. Exp. Sta. Interregional Bul. 798, June, 1963.

*An Adaptive Program for Agriculture*, Committee for Economic Development, New York, 1962.

*Food and Agriculture—A Program for the 1960's*, USDA, March, 1962.

# 18

## ELEMENTARY THEORY OF COSTS

THE THEORY OF COSTS, involving fixed costs and variable costs, average, total, and marginal costs, and several other varieties, is quite complex. Even an elementary treatment requires several chapters. The subject is well handled in most general economics books, and we will not attempt to duplicate it here. We will focus attention on one aspect that is most relevant to marketing problems—the "economies of scale," that is, the relation of costs to scale of operations, as measured by volume of business or by capacity.

The relation of costs to scale can be considered on two different levels (1) the macroeconomic, where the unit is a whole industry and (2) the microeconomic, where the unit is a single firm. We analyzed the relation of costs of scale on the macroeconomic level in Chapter 9 on the elementary theory of prices; we will deal with it on the microeconomic level here.

The relation between costs and volume of business is a crucial relation for any business firm. Farmers, processors, and distributors need to know what size of farm or processing plant or store will be most efficient, that is, will operate at lowest cost.

The same principles apply to farms, processing plants, and stores. We will leave the application of the principles to farms to specialists in farm management and focus our attention on the application to processing plants and stores. Is a two-churn creamery, for example, more efficient than a one-churn cream-

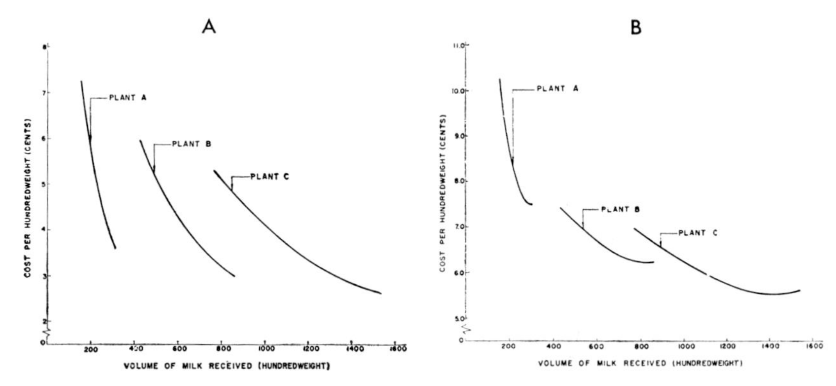


FIG. 18.1—(**A**) Fixed costs and (**B**) variable costs, per 100 pounds of milk received in three different-sized plants.

ery? What size of cotton gin operates at the lowest cost? What size grain elevators? What size of retail store?

## FIXED AND VARIABLE COSTS

Operating costs may be divided into two broad categories—fixed and variable.

Fixed costs do not vary with volume in the short run. The cost of the physical plant is a fixed cost. So is the cost of a piece of equipment. These fixed costs continue, whether the plant and equipment are used or not. If the volume of business is small, the fixed cost per unit could be high. Double the volume, and you halve the fixed cost per unit. Treble it, and you reduce the fixed cost by two-thirds. The fixed costs per unit decline (although at a decreasing rate) as volume expands, until the limits of the capacity of the building or piece of equipment are reached.

Figure 18.1A shows the fixed costs of milk-receiving operations per unit of volume (called average fixed costs for short) for milk plants of three different capacities: 31,000 pounds, 86,000 pounds, and 154,000 pounds.[1] The curves show the relation of costs to the capacity of the plant as well as to the volume of business in that plant.

Variable costs, as the name implies, vary with the volume of business. As volume increases, the total of the variable costs increases too. The variable costs per unit of business may decline, remain constant, or decline up to some point and rise beyond that point, according to the nature of the business. Figure 18.1B shows the average variable costs per unit for the same three

[1] E. L. Baum, R. D. Riley, and E. E. Weeks, *Economies of Scale in the Operation of Can and Tank Milk Receiving Rooms, With Special Reference to Western Washington*, Wash. State Univ. Tech. Bull. 12, May, 1954.

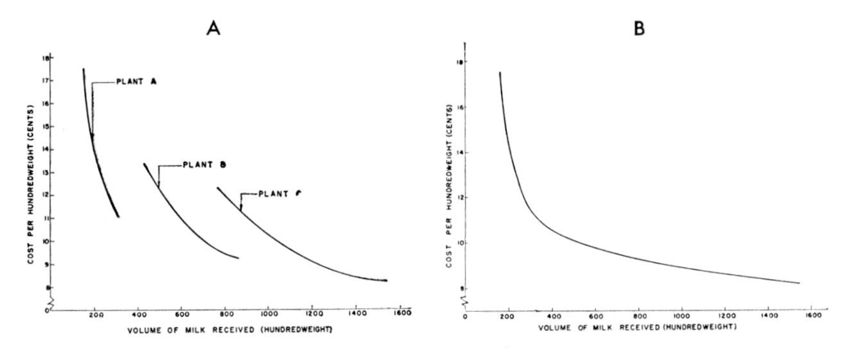


FIG. 18.2—(**A**) Total cost per 100 pounds of milk received in three different-sized plants and (**B**) long-run "envelope" or "planning" curve.

plants for which the fixed costs are shown in Figure 18.1A. The curves level out or even turn up at the right-hand end as the volume of business approaches the limits of the capacity of the plant.

The sum of the fixed and variable costs per unit decline with increasing volume, but not so rapidly as the fixed costs alone; and they usually level out, or begin to rise, as the volume approaches the capacity of the plant. Figure 18.2A shows the sum of the fixed and variable costs (called average total unit costs) for the same three plants. The curve for the largest plant becomes almost horizontal at the right-hand end, at about 1 cent lower cost than the medium-sized plant and at nearly 3 cents lower cost than the small-sized plant.

Additional curves could be drawn in on Figure 18.2A, intermediate between the three curves shown, for plants of intermediate capacities. The lower points of the curves could then be joined by a single line. If the capacities formed a discrete series due to indivisibilities of equipment, the curve would have a scalloped or sawtoothed appearance. If not, it would be smooth, as shown in Figure 18.2B. This curve is called an "envelope" curve. Another name is "planning" curve. This name is apt, because the curve is a long-run cost curve showing the economies of scale and can be used by businessmen in planning how large a plant to construct.

## FOOD STORE OPERATING COSTS[2]

A detailed analysis of many stores indicates that (1) store *size* has little effect on store costs but that (2) store *utilization*

[2] This section is based upon *Organization and Competition in Food Retailing,* National Commission on Food Marketing, Tech. Study 7, June, 1966, pp. 140–43.

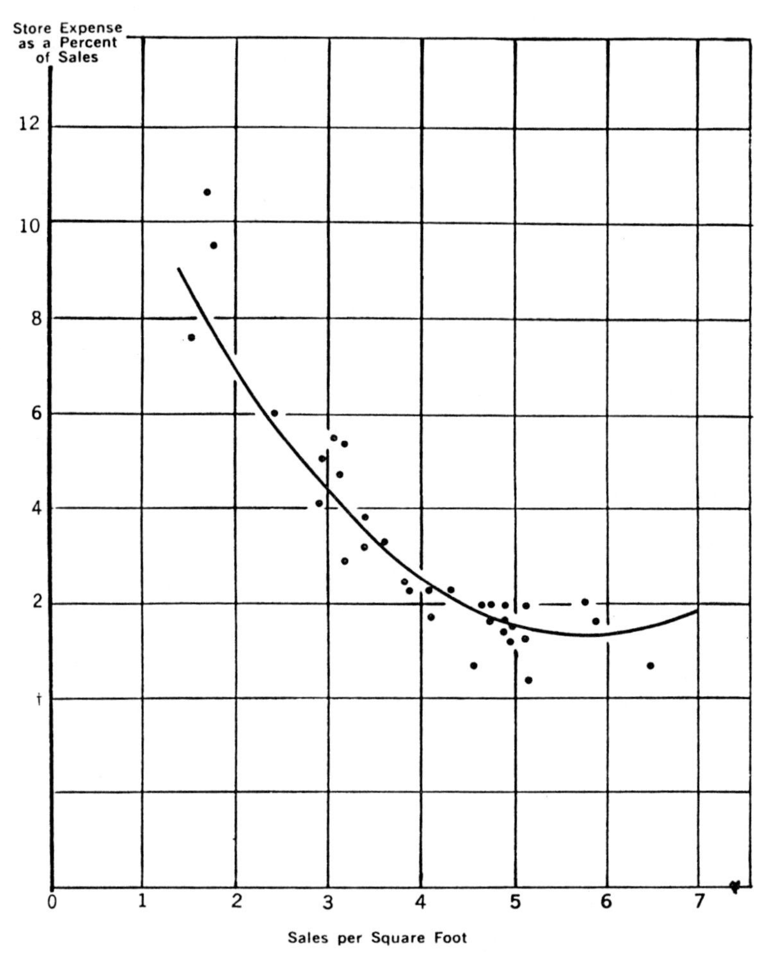


†All costs are shown in relation to an arbitrary base to avoid disclosure.

FIG. 18.3—Scatter diagram of store expense and sales per square foot, for stores of 7,000 to 8,000 square feet, corrected for variation in wage rates. (Source: **Organization and Competition in Food Retailing,** National Commission on Food Marketing, Tech. Study 7, June, 1966, p. 141.)

(that is, the extent to which a store's capacity is used) has a very significant effect.

The basic analysis of store size amounts to a comparison of the costs of smaller stores with the costs of similar larger stores. Similarly, costs of stores utilized at one rate are compared with costs of stores operating at a different rate.

Figure 18.3 is an example of the type of comparison included in this analysis. In this figure, store costs are measured as a per cent of sales on the vertical axis. Different rates of utilization are measured by sales per square foot of selling area on the horizontal axis. The points indicated on Figure 18.3 show that for low rates of utilization, the costs are fairly high and, as utilization increases, costs decline first and then begin to flatten out.

The line going through these points is fitted statistically. It shows the average relationship between utilization and cost. This average relationship does not explain all the variation in costs, as some of the points are not very close to the line. In this particular case, the line explains about 85 per cent of the variation in costs. This analysis does not explain all the variation in costs because it does not take into account the skill of the store manager and the individual setting in which each store operates. On the other hand, it is useful to know how variation in costs can be explained by size and utilization of stores.

The analysis of the effect of store *size* upon costs was conducted similarly to the utilization analysis. Results of one of these tests are given in Figure 18.4. The per cent of cost variation "explained" by the variables used ($R^2$), the average size of

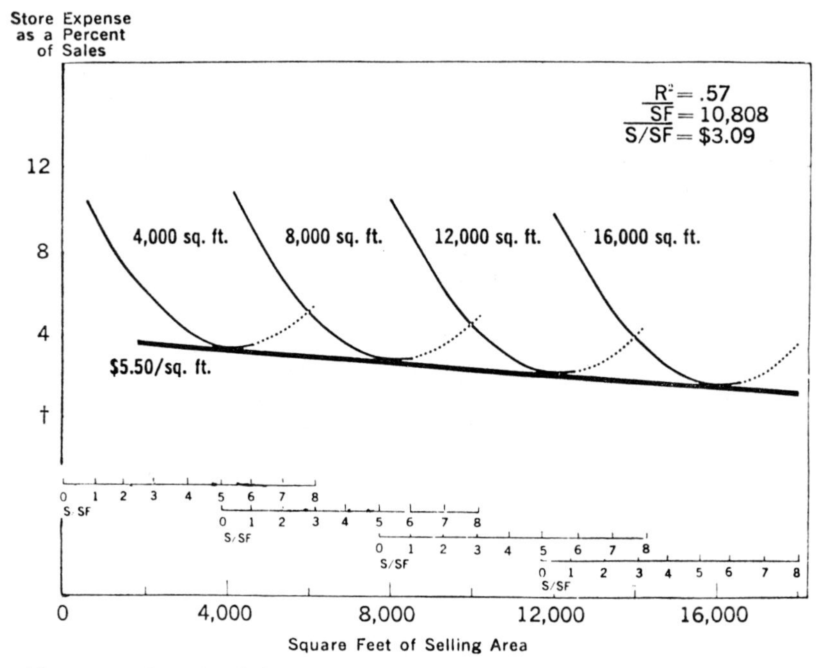


†All costs are shown in relation to an arbitrary base to avoid disclosure.

FIG. 18.4—Relationship between retail store costs and store size. (Source: **Organization and Competition in Food Retailing,** National Commission on Food Marketing, Tech. Study 7, June, 1966, p. 142.)

store observed (SF), and the average rate of utilization (S/SF) are indicated on the figure. On the average, about 70 per cent of the variation in cost was explained by this analysis. Variations in the cost levels from one test to another result primarily from variations in accounting procedures used. Some variation may also be the result of different sizes of stores and different rates of utilization from one test to another.

This figure shows cost behavior in two dimensions. The fishhook-shaped lines identified by 4,000 square feet, 8,000 square feet, 12,000 square feet, and 16,000 square feet show the way in which costs vary as sales per square feet vary in each of four sizes of store. (These sizes of store refer to selling area.) Connecting the lowest points of these "short-run cost curves" is a line which usually slopes down to the right. This shows the way cost varies as the size of store is increased, keeping the sales per square foot constant at the level which gives minimum cost.

This general relationship is similar in all the tests. The short-run curves identifying the relationship between sales per square foot and costs are always curvilinear, while in most cases the long-run curves are straight. The variation in costs attributable to size of store is about 2 cents. The variation attributable to utilization, however, often is more than a 10-cent change (or 10 per cent of the sales dollar).

Through most of the range of the cost curve relating sales per square foot and store costs, a 20 per cent increase in *volume* lowers costs by about 1 cent, or 1 per cent of sales. Even though this effect is not spectacular, it still constitutes a tremendous force in the competitive behavior at the retail level. This means that if for every five customers a sixth one can be added, costs will be reduced 1 cent. In view of the narrow profits as a per cent of sales in the food-retailing industry, this cost situation encourages extensive promotion to increase volume and thereby to bring costs into line and improve profits.

In considering the economics of *size* of store, the total range of variation typically covers somewhat less than 2 cents from stores of 4,000 square feet of selling area to stores of 16,000 square feet. When the comparison is drawn between a store of about 10,000 square feet and a store of 16,000 square feet, the differences are quite small. In fact, some of the tests showed a slight tendency for the cost level to begin increasing again after reaching a low point of about 10,000 to 12,000 square feet. For this reason, no particularly strong incentive for building very large stores grows out of cost behavior alone.

Butter-manufacturing cost curves, based on a sample of Iowa creameries, are shown in Figure 25.2 in Chapter 25 on butter. The curve to the left in that figure shows the relation of cost to volume for one-churn creameries. The curve to the right shows the relation for creameries with two or more churns. These curves show that the larger creameries with two or more churns operate at lower cost than the smaller creameries but at approximately half a cent lower cost than one-churn creameries operating at the volume of maximum efficiency.

Cost curves for two kinds of meat-retailing methods—service and self-service—are shown in Figure 23.14 in Chapter 23 on livestock.

Further discussion of costs involves the relations among average, total, and marginal (addition-to-total) costs. These relations are well handled in most general economics books. We will offer only a brief exposition here.

## TOTAL, AVERAGE, AND MARGINAL COSTS

Marginal cost is not the cost of producing the last unit; it is the *addition to total cost* when one more unit is produced. These two things are quite different concepts.

Similarly, marginal revenue is not the same thing as the revenue from the sale of the last unit. It is the addition to total revenue when one more unit is sold. And this usually is quite different from the revenue obtained from selling one more unit. For offering one more unit may reduce the price received for all the other units. Marginal revenue can in fact even be negative.

Marginal costs are independent of the amount of the total fixed costs. The amount of the total fixed costs affects the average costs per unit, but not the marginal costs. This follows directly from the definition of marginal costs (the difference between successive total costs); since if the fixed costs remain constant, as they must by definition, the differences between successive total costs are the same whether the fixed costs (which enter alike into all the total costs, and therefore cancel out in the subtractions or differences) are $1,000, $100, or zero. The significance of this will become apparent later.

It is clear from these definitions that a man will increase his production all the time that his marginal revenue is greater than his marginal cost. That is, if producing one unit more than before adds 50 cents to his total cost but selling one unit more adds 60 cents to his total revenue (that is, if his marginal cost is 50 cents and his marginal revenue 60 cents), he will produce and sell that one unit more, for it will add 10 cents to his total profit. He will as a matter of fact keep on expanding his production until his marginal cost becomes as great as his marginal revenue. That maximizes his total profits.

**TABLE 18.1: Cost and Revenue Schedule (Hypothetical Data)**

| | Cost Data | | | Revenue Data | | |
|---|---|---|---|---|---|---|
| Quantity | Total cost | Average cost | Marginal cost | Total revenue | Average revenue | Marginal revenue |
| 1 ..... | 64 | 64 | 64 | 20 | 20 | 20 |
| 2 ..... | 83 | 41.5 | 19 | 40 | 20 | 20 |
| 3 ..... | 101 | 33.7 | 18 | 60 | 20 | 20 |
| 4 ..... | 118 | 29.5 | 17 | 80 | 20 | 20 |
| 5 ..... | 134 | 26.8 | 16 | 100 | 20 | 20 |
| 6 ..... | 149 | 24.8 | 15 | 120 | 20 | 20 |
| 7 ..... | 163 | 23.3 | 14 | 140 | 20 | 20 |
| 8 ..... | 176 | 22.0 | 13 | 160 | 20 | 20 |
| 9 ..... | 188 | 20.9 | 12 | 180 | 20 | 20 |
| 10 ..... | 200 | 20.0 | 12 | 200 | 20 | 20 |
| 11 ..... | 213 | 19.4 | 13 | 220 | 20 | 20 |
| 12 ..... | 227 | 18.9 | 14 | 240 | 20 | 20 |
| 13 ..... | 242 | 18.6 | 15 | 260 | 20 | 20 |
| 14 ..... | 258 | 18.4 | 16 | 280 | 20 | 20 |
| 15 ..... | 275 | 18.3 | 17 | 300 | 20 | 20 |
| 16 ..... | 293 | 18.3 | 18 | 320 | 20 | 20 |
| 17 ..... | 312 | 18.4 | 19 | 340 | 20 | 20 |
| 18 ..... | 332 | 18.4 | 20 | 360 | 20 | 20 |
| 19 ..... | 353 | 18.6 | 21 | 380 | 20 | 20 |
| 20 ..... | 375 | 18.8 | 22 | 400 | 20 | 20 |
| 21 ..... | 398 | 19.0 | 23 | 420 | 20 | 20 |
| 22 ..... | 422 | 19.2 | 24 | 440 | 20 | 20 |

A table showing the average, total, and marginal *costs* of producing various quantities in one part, and average, total, and marginal *revenues* from the sale of various quantities in another, can be used to show where equilibrium will be reached. Hypothetical cost and revenue data of this sort are shown in the two parts of Table 18.1. The marginal cost in each case is simply the difference between two successive total costs; the same thing holds with marginal revenues.

It takes only a moment to determine from this table that production will be carried out to 18 quantity units, for at that point marginal costs are equal to marginal revenues; they are both $20.

The location of this equilibrium point is particularly simple in this case, for the marginal revenues are the same ($20) for all quantities. The reason for this is that average revenues remain constant (this is a case of perfect competition). No matter what quantities are produced, the sale of one more unit always brings in another $20; so the marginal revenue (addition to total revenue) is always $20.

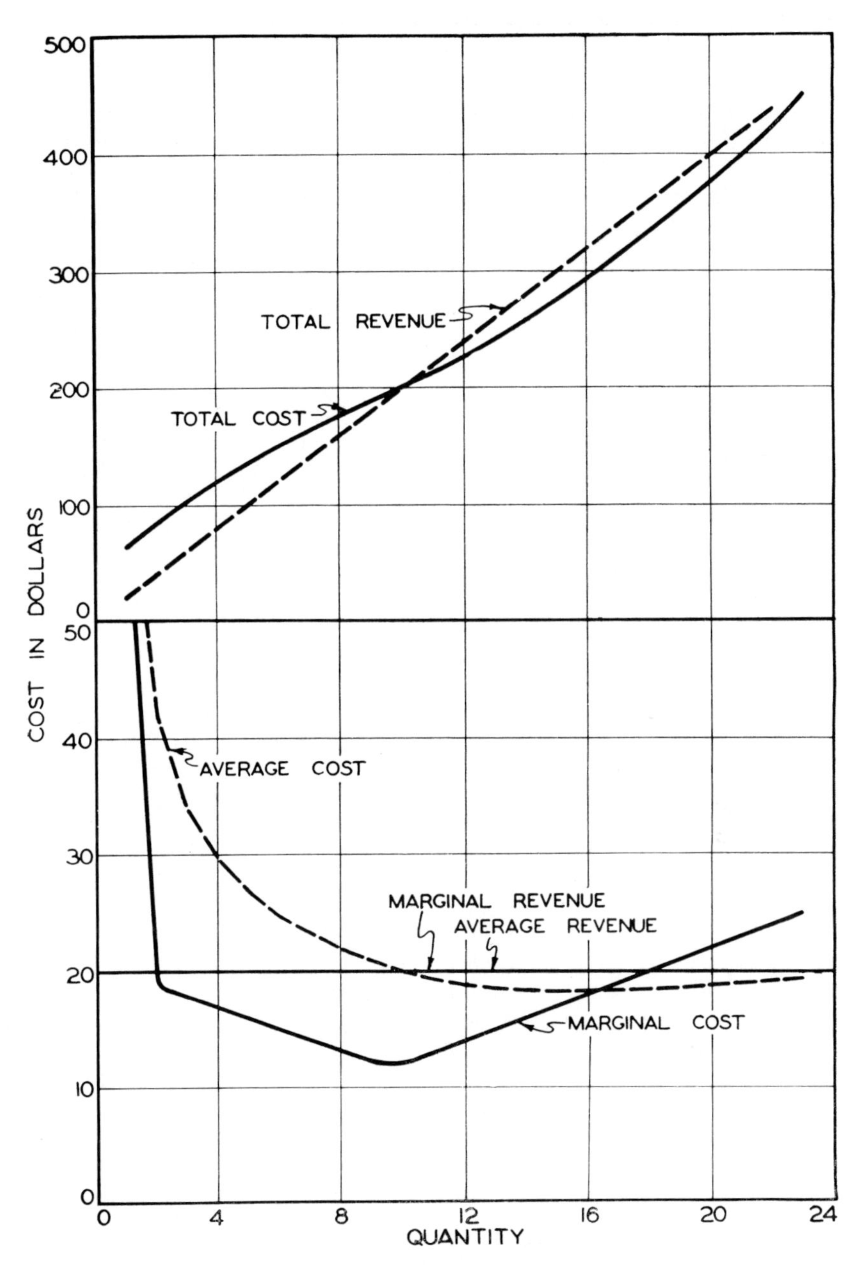


FIG. 18.5—Effect of quantity produced upon total, average, and marginal revenue and cost. Hypothetical data.

A little more light is thrown on the subject if the data shown in Table 18.1 are plotted in graphic form. This is done in Figure 18.5. This figure shows how the marginal cost curve at first falls, and then rises, to cut the average cost curve at its lowest point. It must necessarily do this because a very small section of the average cost curve at its lowest point may be regarded as a horizontal straight line, and we saw (in connection with average and marginal revenue curves) that where the average curve is a horizontal straight line, the marginal values are necessarily the same as the average values.

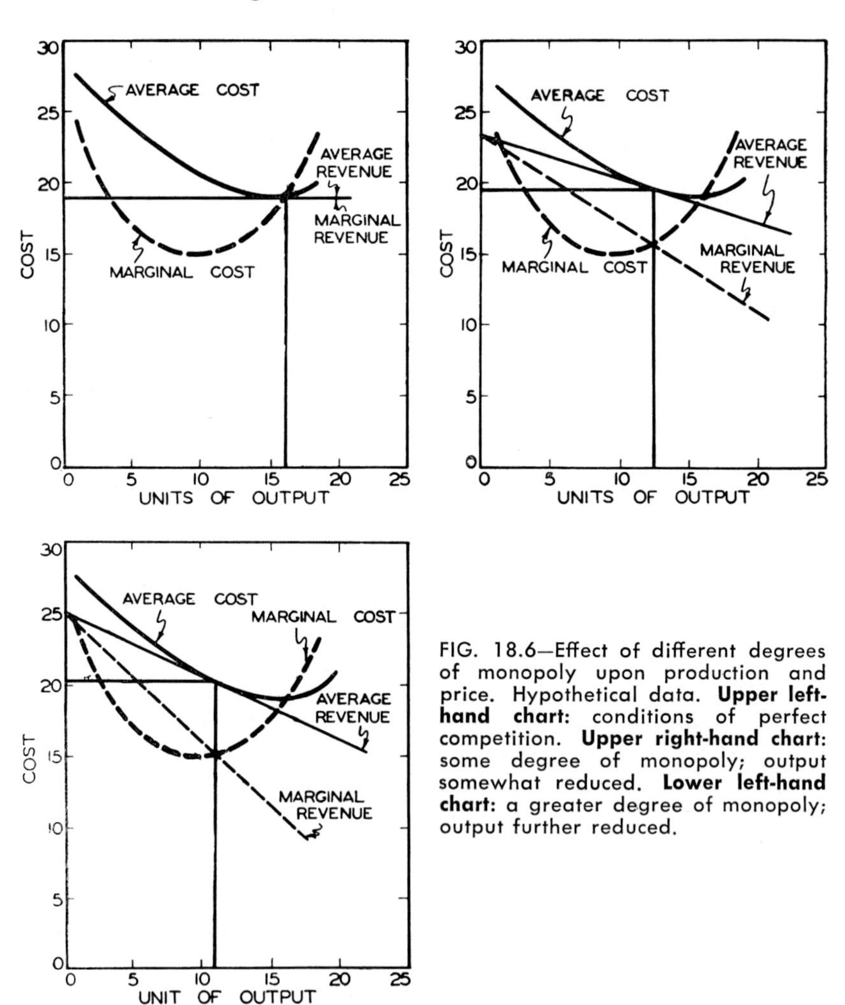


FIG. 18.6—Effect of different degrees of monopoly upon production and price. Hypothetical data. **Upper left-hand chart:** conditions of perfect competition. **Upper right-hand chart:** some degree of monopoly; output somewhat reduced. **Lower left-hand chart:** a greater degree of monopoly; output further reduced.

The figure also shows that, at the point where the marginal cost equals the marginal revenue, the total revenue rises to its greatest height above the total cost. That is, the difference between the total revenue and the total cost (i.e., the profit) is the greatest at that point. This also is necessarily true.

Finally, the figure shows that under conditions of perfect competition the average revenue and marginal revenue curves coincide throughout their length. It shows, furthermore, that production is carried on at the lowest possible average cost—almost. The reason for the "almost" is that prices in the illustration used here exceed average costs, at the point to which production is carried, and profits (in excess of wages of management, interest on capital, and all other normal costs) exist. If these profits induced others to enter this field of production, as they would under perfect competition, supplies would increase and prices would fall to equality with the lowest point on the average cost curve.

Under perfect competition, each producer sells so small a part of the total production of a commodity that his actions have a negligible effect upon the price; his sales curve is a horizontal straight line.

Under monopoly, however, a producer's sales curve has a negative slope, approaching the slope of the demand curve for the product as a whole. The steepness of the slope depends upon the degree of monopoly. The marginal revenue curve then lies below the average revenue curve, as shown in Figure 18.6. The marginal revenue curve, therefore, intersects the marginal cost curve to the left of the lowest point on the average cost curve. Prices may be higher than under perfect competition unless the larger scale of production of the monopolistic producer permits his cost curve to run substantially lower than the curve for a small producer.

Thus one effect of a monopoly, other things being equal, is a lower production and a higher price than would exist under free competition (the prices shown in Figure 18.6 are less than 20 for free competition but more than 20 for monopoly).

But if the whole cost curve of the monopoly runs substantially lower than the cost curves of small producers (because the monopoly is large) that would permit the intersection of the monopoly's marginal cost and marginal revenue curves to lie lower and farther to the right—perhaps farther than the intersection under free competition. This larger quantity of production then would sell at a *lower* price than the price under free competition. Each case, therefore, needs to be examined on its own merits.

# 19

## THE OVERALL COSTS OF MARKETING FARM PRODUCTS

THE USDA COMPUTES each month the retail cost of what it calls a farm food "market basket." This is defined as the average quantity of farm food products purchased per wage-earner and clerical-worker family in the United States.

The make-up of the market basket, a matter of some interest in itself, is given in considerable detail in Table 19.1. The importance of each product in the market basket is shown in percentage terms. The percentage figures in the table show, for instance, that meat is the biggest food item. Fruits and vegetables come next, followed by dairy products and by bakery and cereal products.

The USDA also computes the shares for the division of the money that consumers spend for the items in this market basket between the marketing system and the farmer who produced the food. These shares are shown in Table 19.2. The shares vary from year to year. Sometimes the farmer gets about half of the consumer's food dollar; sometimes he gets only a little more than a third. In recent years, the farmer's share has been running at about 39 per cent. That is, only about 39 cents of the consumer's dollar spent for food gets back to the farmer.

Why should it cost more to get the food from producer to consumer than it does to produce it in the first place? Many

**TABLE 19.1: List of Priced Items Included and Relative Importance of Each Item in the Retail Cost of the Market Basket of Farm Foods***

| | (per cent) |
|---|---|
| *Market Basket* | *100.0* |
| Meat Products | 27.9 |
| Beef, all | 15.3 |
| Lamb | .7 |
| Pork | 10.8 |
| Veal | 1.1 |
| Dairy Products | 17.8 |
| Butter | 1.6 |
| Cheese, American process | 2.3 |
| Evaporated milk | 1.3 |
| Fluid milk | 10.5 |
| Ice cream | 2.1 |
| Poultry and Eggs | 8.6 |
| Chickens, frying | 4.2 |
| Eggs | 4.0 |
| Turkeys | .4 |
| Bakery and Cereal Products | 15.7 |
| Bread, white | 4.8 |
| Bread, whole or cracked wheat | .6 |
| Cake, layer with icing | 2.8 |
| Cookies, sandwich | 1.4 |
| Corn flakes | 1.7 |
| Cracker meal | .5 |
| Flour, white | 2.5 |
| Pretzels | .7 |
| Rice | .7 |
| All Fruits and Vegetables | 21.8 |
| Fresh fruits and vegetables | 9.8 |
| Apples | 1.3 |
| Grapefruit | .3 |
| Grapes | .1 |
| Lemons | .1 |
| Oranges | 1.4 |
| Orange juice, chilled | .3 |
| Strawberries | .2 |
| Watermelons | .2 |
| Cabbage | .3 |
| Carrots | .4 |
| Celery | .4 |
| Cucumbers | .2 |
| Lettuce | 1.1 |
| Onions | .4 |
| Peppers, green | .3 |
| Potatoes | 1.6 |
| Spinach | .2 |
| Tomatoes | 1.0 |
| Processed Fruits and Vegetables | 12.0 |
| Canned | 6.6 |
| Fruit cocktail | .6 |
| Peaches | 1.2 |
| Pears | .4 |
| Beets | .3 |
| Corn | 1.3 |
| Peas | 1.1 |
| Pickle relish | .9 |
| Tomatoes | .8 |
| Frozen | 4.4 |
| Broccoli | .3 |
| French fried potatoes | 1.3 |
| Lemonade | .2 |
| Orange juice concentrate | 2.1 |
| Peas | .5 |
| Dried | 1.0 |
| Beans | .3 |
| Potatoes, instant | .7 |
| Fats and oils | 3.5 |
| Margarine | 1.5 |
| Peanut butter | .5 |
| Salad and cooking oil | .8 |
| Vegetable shortening | .7 |
| Miscellaneous | 4.7 |
| Canned spaghetti | 1.9 |
| Grape jelly | 1.8 |
| Sugar | 1.0 |

Source: *Farm-Retail Spreads for Food Products,* USDA, ERS-226, Apr., 1965, pp. 5–6.

* Relative weights as of Dec., 1963.

farmers and consumers suspect that it must be because the marketing system is grossly inefficient or distributors are making exorbitant profits.

But this belief does not stand up under investigation.

## SIGNIFICANCE OF WIDE OR NARROW MARGINS

The significance of wide or narrow marketing margins may easily be misunderstood.

**TABLE 19.2: Farm Food Products: Farmer's Share of the Retail Cost, 1915–69**

| Year | Farmer's Share | Year | Farmer's Share |
|---|---|---|---|
| | *(per cent)* | | *(per cent)* |
| 1915 | 44 | 1950 | 47 |
| | | 1951 | 48 |
| 1920 | 43 | 1952 | 47 |
| | | 1953 | 45 |
| 1925 | 42 | 1954 | 44 |
| 1930 | 39 | 1955 | 41 |
| 1935 | 39 | 1956 | 40 |
| 1936 | 40 | 1957 | 40 |
| 1937 | 42 | 1958 | 40 |
| 1938 | 39 | 1959 | 38 |
| 1939 | 38 | | |
| | | 1960 | 39 |
| 1940 | 40 | 1961 | 38 |
| 1941 | 44 | 1962 | 38 |
| 1942 | 48 | 1963 | 37 |
| 1943 | 51 | 1964 | 37 |
| 1944 | 52 | | |
| 1945 | 53 | 1965 | 39 |
| 1946 | 52 | 1966 | 40 |
| 1947 | 51 | 1967 | 38 |
| 1948 | 50 | 1968 | 39 |
| 1949 | 46 | 1969 | 41* |

Source: *The Marketing and Transportation Situation,* USDA, Feb., 1970, p. 6; also earlier issues.
* Preliminary.

There is a general preconception that wide margins mean high prices to consumers and low prices and incomes to producers. According to this view, the narrower the margin, the more efficient the market.

This view will not stand up. If individual farmers marketed their products directly, in person, to individual consumers at their homes, the prices paid by consumers and the prices received by farmers would be identical. The marketing margin would be zero. But "the market," far from being efficient because the margin was low (zero in this limiting case), would be exceedingly inefficient.

This kind of market would clearly be very inefficient if each farmer peddled his produce from house to house, or if each consumer bought her goods by shopping from farm to farm. In either case, a great deal of time would be spent in the marketing process.

A step forward in efficiency would be taken if a farmers' market were set up, where farmers and consumers could meet at the same place. This in effect has been done in many countries.

But this is only one step forward in efficiency. The products in these markets are heterogeneous in quality and ungraded. Each consumer has to spend time doing two things: (1) selecting the quality she wants from among a number of different farmers' lots by direct inspection and (2) bargaining about the price.

In addition, this kind of market is still inefficient as far as the farmer is concerned. For each farmer has to spend a considerable share of his time hauling his little load to the market and selling it there during the hours when the market is open.

The efficiency of a market, therefore, cannot be measured simply by the width of the margins, either in percentage form or in absolute amounts.

## MIDDLEMEN IN THE MARKET

The significance of the number of middlemen in a market may also be misunderstood.

There is a general preconception that the presence of many middlemen means that they force apart the prices paid by consumers and the prices received by farmers. According to this view, the fewer middlemen, the more efficient the market.

This view is not valid. In the case where farmers distribute the products directly to consumers, the number of middlemen would be zero. But as indicated above, the market then would be exceedingly inefficient.

Unless farmers valued their time spent in marketing at close to zero, one trucker could haul the produce of several or many farmers at a fraction of the cost involved if every farmer hauled his own; the operations of these truckers would reduce costs and make the market more efficient. Furthermore, one retailer could sell to consumers the loads brought in by several or many truckers more efficiently than the truckers could themselves; the introduction of this additional middleman (the retailer) would lower costs further.

Note that these middlemen could not come between farmer and consumer and force their prices apart. If they tried to widen the margins by charging more than their services were worth, they would get no business; the farmer would refuse to pay their charges; and the truckers would soon disappear from the market if it were competitive.

This is clearly true of the numbers of middlemen "in series" in the marketing links between the farmer and the consumer. It is less clear but equally true of the numbers "in parallel" at one link in the chain. If two retailers can do the job at lower cost than one (in terms of consumer convenience as well as money), both will find a useful place in the marketing system; consumers will patronize them both. But if one retailer can do the job more cheaply than two (including the cost of consumer's time), one will soon disappear.

## AN ACCURATE MEASURE OF EFFICIENCY

Then what is an accurate measure of the efficiency of a market?

An accurate measure is the total cost, estimated in man-hours and other costs (gasoline, tires, etc.), spent on the marketing process by all the middlemen involved and by the producers and consumers of the products. This total cost, divided into the total value of the products sold, provides a percentage figure which accurately measures the efficiency of the market.

This is the same concept of efficiency that is used in engineering, where the efficiency of a gasoline engine, for example, is computed by dividing the actual output of power by the theoretical maximum output if all the energy of the gasoline were converted into power. The formula is:

$$\frac{\text{Actual power} \times 100}{\text{Theoretical maximum}} = \text{efficiency}$$

This formula provides a coefficient that measures the efficiency of the engine. The higher the figure, the higher the efficiency. Because of the inescapable loss of some energy by heat, friction, etc., this coefficient cannot be higher than 100; in actual present-day engines, it usually runs well below 50.

In an analogous manner, market efficiency can be computed by the formula:

$$\frac{\text{Value added by marketing} \times 100}{\text{Cost of marketing services}} = \text{efficiency}$$

Thus, if in one market the total marketing costs incurred by all participants (producers, marketers, and consumers) were \$5,000 and the value added by marketing were \$10,000, the efficiency of the market could be measured as

$$\frac{10{,}000 \times 100}{5{,}000} = 200$$

If in another market the figures were

$$\frac{10{,}000 \times 100}{8{,}000} = 125$$

the efficiency of this second market would be lower than the efficiency of the first market, as the coefficient indicates.

This might better be considered a measure of the productivity of the resources engaged in marketing. The important point here is that in measuring efficiency or productivity, the measure of costs covers not only the costs incurred by the marketers (otherwise the most efficient market would be one where producers sold their goods themselves directly to consumers) but by producers, consumers, and marketers all together.[1]

## CAUSES OF HIGH MARKETING COSTS

The fact that more than half of the consumer's dollar now goes for marketing costs does not necessarily mean that "something must be wrong with our distributing system." It is primarily an evidence of important changes that have been taking place in the whole agricultural producing and marketing system over a long period.

### Place

The most obvious change of this sort is a matter of geographical space. Along with the development of the resources of the United States has gone an increasing specialization in production, which increases marketing costs, but this may decrease production costs more than enough to offset that increase.

Today, for example, grapefruit is grown in Florida and Texas; lemons mainly in California; oranges in California, Florida, and Texas; and lettuce in California and Arizona; they are then shipped across the continent and sold by the carload in New York. The marketing costs are high. But the costs of production are so low in these areas that the total cost of production and marketing combined is lower than the cost of similar produce raised anywhere else. The existence of high marketing costs in itself does not necessarily mean that something is wrong. Generally, it means only that the product is being grown in the most efficient low-cost producing area, and that the total cost (of production and marketing) is less to the consumer than if the product were grown close at hand and the proportion of marketing costs were low.

The localization of production in areas far from the market reduces production costs, but it increases marketing costs. A product that was raised close to market at a cost of 70 cents may have cost only 30 cents to market, thus selling for $1 to the consumer. If a new more distant area is opened where the

[1] We are indebted to William C. Motes, USDA, for his suggestions which led to the reformulation of the original ideas in the preceding paragraph and formula.

product costs, say, only 40 cents to produce, marketing costs may rise, to perhaps 40 cents because of the greater distance to be covered. At first, the product continues to sell for $1, and the producers in the new area get $1 — 40¢ = 60¢ for their product, which cost them only 40 cents to produce. They make high profits which induce expanded production in the new area until that expansion in production lowers prices, say, to 80 cents. Marketing costs now have risen from 30 per cent of the consumer's dollar to 50 per cent. But consumers are better off than before, for they can now buy for 80 cents the product that used to cost them $1. And producers are better off too, for reductions in the cost of food permit reductions in the costs of manufactured products that farmers buy.

Lettuce is a good example. Only 34 cents of the consumer's dollar spent for lettuce gets back to the farmer; the other 66 cents goes to the marketing system. Lettuce marketing costs are high. Why are they high? Not because lettuce marketing is less efficient than the marketing of other farm products, nor because much processing of the product is required. Marketing costs are high because lettuce is bulky and perishable and is produced so far from the consumer. More than three-fifths of the lettuce acreage in the United States is located in California. Most of this lettuce is shipped across the continent to the heavy population areas in the East. Yet the costs of production in the efficient producing areas in California are so low that the combined costs of production and marketing from there are less than the costs from eastern areas close to the consumer.

Thus high marketing costs do not necessarily mean inefficiency. They may mean merely that production costs are so low in areas far from market that they more than offset the high costs of marketing. They therefore permit the commodity to be produced at lower total cost than if it were raised close to market, where marketing costs would be low.

The high proportion of the consumer's dollar that goes to cover marketing costs does not necessarily mean that "there are too many middlemen between producer and consumer," any more than it means that the producer and consumer are too far apart geographically. A middleman only comes between the producer and consumer in the first place by getting the goods from the one to the other more cheaply than they can without his help. In that case eliminating the middleman would be a step backward in marketing efficiency, not forward. A middleman who persists in a situation that has so changed that he can no longer earn his keep is soon eliminated by lack of business.

**Time**

A second change in the marketing system is the increasing amount of time utility embodied in consumers' goods. Many foods that were consumed only in certain seasons of the year are now available to consumers the year around. The development of producing areas in warmer and sometimes wetter (irrigated) southern and western areas, where many fruits and vegetables can be grown "out of (northern and eastern) season," is one reason for this; but the development and improvement of refrigeration and other kinds of storage have contributed also. Butter, eggs, poultry, pork, and more recently, fruits and vegetables handled by "quick-freezing" methods, are examples of this storage over periods of time. The increase in canning, formerly done mainly in the home but now chiefly in factories, is another example. (Canning involves a change in form too and is discussed under that heading in the next section.) All of these things, while desirable and economic (in the sense of being worth more than they cost), cost money and widen the spread between the producer and the consumer.

**Form**

A third change in the marketing system has arisen from considerations of consumption rather than production. It is a matter, not of place or time, but of form. Consumers under the pressures of urbanization have been demanding that their products be packaged in more and more finished form—that is, more nearly ready to eat.

Today we buy foods in small quantities, and they require a minimum of "processing" in the home. We buy little flour except for occasional use. We buy almost all our bread and a good share of our cookies and cakes ready-made. We buy much of our food in cans, all cooked and ready to serve. Frozen foods are widely used. Our bacon is already sliced and wrapped. The goods our parents bought were only part way along toward the finished form; in those days we carried them the rest of the way in our kitchen and sewing room. The goods we buy today are ready to eat or wear, and it is only natural that the extra costs involved in (1) processing them to this more finished form, (2) handling them in much smaller units, and (3) wrapping them in expensive packages widen the margin between what we pay and what the producer gets.

All this means that we have been shifting more and more of the processing of our goods from the home to the factory or processing plant. We spend less money for seamstresses and cooks and kitchen maids around the house and more money for the processors' services embodied in the goods we buy. We also get less unpaid household labor from our women and children. Our kitchens have shrunk from the large and bustling rooms of colonial days; they have become compact labor-saving mechanized "kitchenettes." The widening of our marketing margins represents not so much a social loss as a social transfer of much activity from the home to the factory. In view of the greater efficiency of the factory, this may represent a net social gain.

For example, not only has the consumption of cake risen compared with the consumption of bread but the form in which cake ingredients are purchased has changed also. Housewives are now buying cake mix rather than the separate ingredients: eggs, flour, etc. The cake mix is more convenient. And the use of mix may result in a higher average quality of cake.

## CHANGES IN MARGINS OVER PERIODS OF TIME

Table 19.2 shows that the percentage of the consumer's food dollar that gets back to the farmer changes from year to year. When retail prices decline or rise, most of the impact of that change falls upon farm prices. The change is not distributed equally or proportionately between the marketing margin and the farmer; the marketing margin remains comparatively stable. When retail prices fall, margins in dollars and cents fall less than prices; in percentage terms they rise.

During World War II, in 1945, the farmer's share of the consumer's food dollar rose to a peak of 53 per cent. By 1963 it had declined to 37 per cent, but in 1969 it moved up to 41 per cent. The lowest percentage of all, 32, was reached in 1932 at the bottom of the industrial depression of the 1930's.

The precise nature of the relation between retail prices and farm prices is shown in Figure 19.1. The pattern illustrated for the market basket in this figure shows the fitted line of relationship lying about halfway between the line representing a fixed margin in terms of dollars and the line representing a fixed-percentage margin in terms of ratio to retail cost or ratio to farm value. In this chart the size of the margin is measured by the height of any point above the zero margin line. The fitted average pattern of relationship suggests that the food-marketing margin for the total market basket consists of elements of which about 50 per cent are stable, failing to reflect variation in response to price changes; and 50 per cent vary in direct proportion to changes in retail and farm prices.

Patterns of relationship estimated for several of the important commodity groups show considerable variation in the

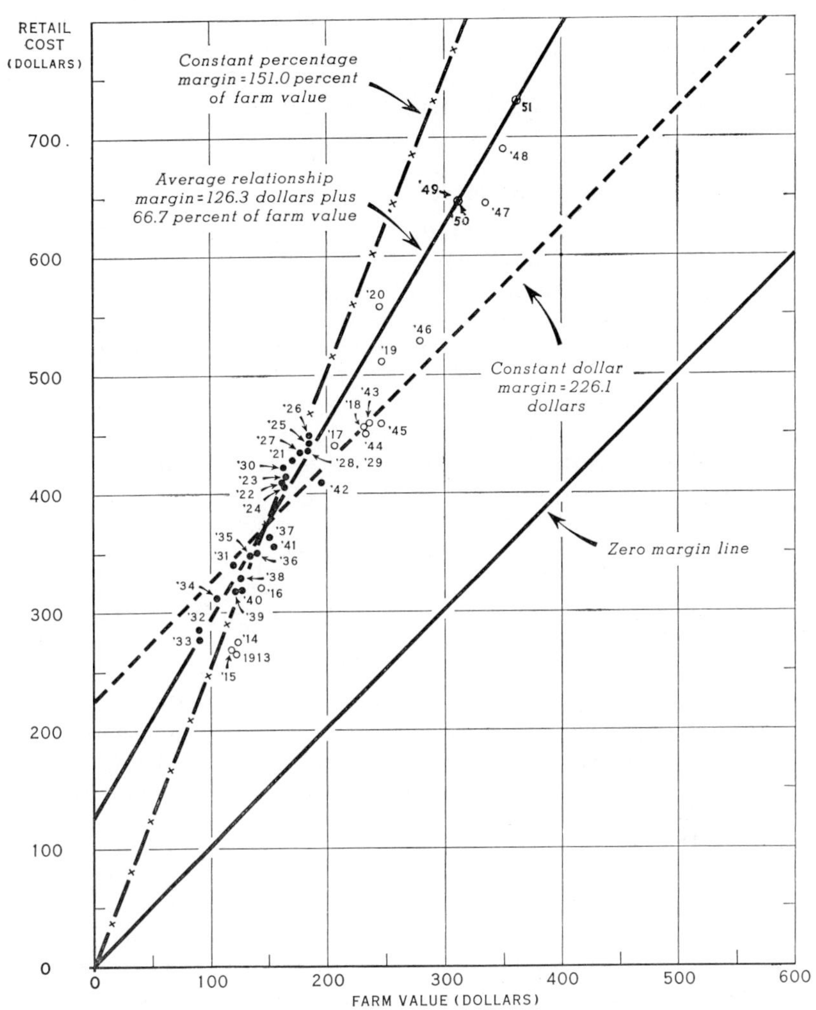


U. S. DEPARTMENT OF AGRICULTURE NEG. 43743A BUREAU OF AGRICULTURAL ECONOMICS

FIG. 19.1—Market basket farm food products—relation of retail cost of 1935–39 average annual family purchases to farm value, 1913–51.

character of the fitted relationship when compared to the fixed-dollar margin and the constant-percentage margin. The fitted-margin line for the meat-products group falls very close to the fixed-dollar margin line and apparently contains only minor elements which vary proportionally to prices. On the other hand, the margins for fruits and vegetables and for the poultry and eggs group conform more closely to the constant percentage margin, indicating that marketing charges for these groups vary widely with fluctuations in prices at retail and at the farm. The pattern for dairy products is rather similar to that shown for the entire market basket.

### Marketing Margins More Stable Than Prices

The relative stability of marketing margins in comparison with the variation of retail prices is a matter of great importance in determining the influence of the food-marketing margin structure upon prices and incomes received by farmers. If margins were always a fixed proportion of retail prices or farm prices, then percentage changes in retail and farm prices would be identical and farm incomes would fluctuate to the same degree as fluctuation of consumer expenditures. However, the apparent tendency of marketing margins toward greater stability than that observed in retail prices and the existence of numerous rigidities in the market system have an unfortunate cumulative effect upon prices and incomes of farmers during periods of business recession. A perfectly stable margin equivalent to a constant-dollar margin would multiply the variation in retail prices and in consumers' expenditures into much wider relative fluctuation in terms of the prices and incomes received by farmers. This may be illustrated by meat products for which the marketing margin is rather close to a fixed-dollar margin, as indicated in the preceding paragraph. Beginning with a period during which the farmers received 50 cents out of the consumer dollar spent for meat products and assuming that the meat-marketing margin was constant in terms of dollars per unit, a 25 per cent decline in the retail price would produce a 50 per cent decline in prices received by farmers and would reduce the farmer's share from 50 per cent to 33 per cent. So extreme an example seldom occurs in fact, but the tendency toward stability in marketing margins has this type of effect when retail prices decline—accentuating the decline in farm prices and reducing the farmer's share of consumers' expenditures.

Marketing margins are more stable than prices because some of the elements of cost on which they are based remain comparatively constant. Transportation costs, store rentals, taxes, etc., change only slowly and to a small extent over time. If these costs (and profits) remained absolutely constant in dollars and cents, to that extent marketing margins would remain constant in dollars and cents also. The flexibility that marketing margins do have results chiefly from the flexibility that exists in

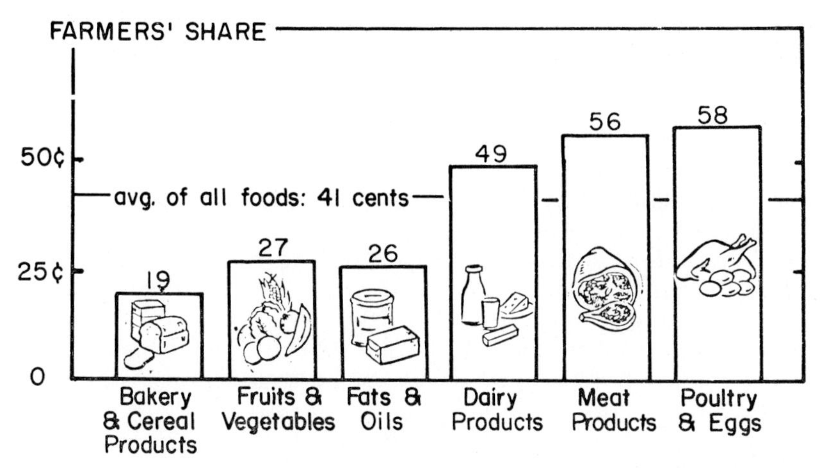


FIG. 19.2—Farm food products—farmer's share of retail cost, Oct.–Dec., 1969.

the labor costs per unit of farm food products marketed. Hourly earnings vary directly almost as much as retail food prices vary.

## MARKETING SHARES FOR DIFFERENT PRODUCTS

The shares into which the consumer's food dollar is divided between the marketing system and the farmer differ greatly from product to product. Table 19.3 shows the shares separately by individual products in 1969.

The table shows that in 1969 the farmer's share ranged from over 55 per cent for meat products and poultry and eggs down to about 20 per cent for bakery and cereal products. The farmer's share of the retail cost of individual food products varied over an even wider range.

Figure 19.2 shows only the division of the consumer's dollar between the marketing system and the farmer. The share of the consumer's dollar spent for poultry and eggs that gets back to the farmer is large; his share of the grain-products dollar is small. But this has nothing to do with the efficiency of the marketing systems for the two groups of products. Grain marketing is as efficient as poultry and egg marketing, or more so. The chief reason why the grain farmer gets so small a share of the consumer's dollar is the large amount of processing the product goes through before it reaches the consumer. Eggs reach the kitchen in the same form that they left the hen; but grain has to be ground, and the flour baked, and the bread sliced and wrapped before it reaches the consumer, and this processing costs a lot of money.

### Marketing Margins Vary

Farmers become exasperated when the price of the product they sell declines but the price of the product at retail does not come down correspondingly.

A situation of this sort happened during 1963. The price of steers shown near the bottom of Figure 19.3 declined about $7 per 100 pounds from November 1962 to March 1963. But the price of beef at retail, shown by the solid line in the upper part of the chart, remained practically unchanged until February and then declined only a few cents per pound by March.

A 1,000-pound steer makes about 450 pounds of beef in the retail store (the "dressing percentage" is only 45). One would expect, therefore, that a decline of $1 per 100 pounds in the price of steers would soon show up in a change of 2¼ cents per pound in the price of beef in the retail store. But Figure 19.3 shows that the change in the price of beef at retail was much *less* than the change in the price of steers. The decline in the price of beef at retail that would have taken place if the decline in the price of steers had been fully reflected in the retail price is shown by the dashed line in the upper part of the chart, where it falls below the actual price.

The reasons why retail prices are sluggish like this are not fully known. Figure 19.3 shows, however, that it works both ways—when prices are going up as well as when they are going down. In the latter half of 1962 the price of steers rose substantially, but the price of beef at retail rose only a few cents. The price at retail that would have fully reflected the rise in the price of steers is shown by the dashed line in the upper part of the chart, where it rises above the actual price. Farmers do not mind when this sort of thing happens; it is only when prices are declining that they feel hurt.

## RETAILING AND PROCESSING COSTS

Farmers have often complained about the costs which are most apparent to them—the margins taken by local dealers, freight rates, terminal marketing charges, and so forth. It is natural for a man to attack a difficult and complicated problem at the points that are closest to him. But the greatest part of the costs of marketing is incurred, not at the farmer's end of the marketing machinery, but at two other points—in the processor's plant and in the retail store.

**TABLE 19.3: Farm Food Products: Farmer's Share of Retail Cost, Oct.–Dec., 1969**

| Product* | Farm Equivalent | Retail Unit | Farmer's Share |
|---|---|---|---|
| | | | *(per cent)* |
| Market basket | Farm produce equivalent to products bought per urban wage-earner and clerical-worker household in 1960–61 | Average quantities purchased per urban wage-earner and clerical-worker household in 1960–61 | 41 |
| Meat products | | | 56 |
| Dairy products | | | 49 |
| Poultry and eggs | | | 58 |
| Bakery and cereal products† | | | |
| All ingredients | | | 19 |
| Grain | | | 14 |
| All fruits and vegetables | | | 27 |
| Fresh fruits and vegetables | | | 33 |
| Fresh fruits | | | 27 |
| Fresh vegetables | | | 36 |
| Processed fruits and vegetables | | | 21 |
| Fats and oils | | | 26 |
| Miscellaneous products | | | 17 |
| Beef, Choice grade | 2.25 lb. Choice grade cattle | Pound | 60 |
| Lamb, Choice grade | 2.33 lb. lamb | Pound | 57 |
| Pork | 2.00 lb. hogs | Pound | 58 |
| Butter | Cream and whole milk | Pound | 73 |
| Cheese, American process | Milk for American cheese | ½ pound | 45 |
| Ice cream | Cream, milk, and sugar | ½ gallon | 34 |
| Milk, evaporated | Milk for evaporating | 14½-ounce can | 48 |
| Milk, fresh | | | |
| Home delivered | 4.39 lb. Class I milk | ½ gallon | 45 |
| Sold in stores | 4.39 lb. Class I milk | ½ gallon | 51 |
| Chickens, frying, ready-to-cook | 1.37 lb. broiler | Pound | 46 |
| Eggs, Grade A large | 1.03 dozen | Dozen | 70 |
| Bread, white | | | |
| All ingredients | Wheat and other ingredients | Pound | 14 |
| Wheat | .877 lb. wheat | Pound | 11 |
| Bread, whole or cracked wheat | .708 lb. wheat | Pound | 10 |
| Cookies, sandwich | .528 lb. wheat | Pound | 9 |
| Corn flakes | 2.87 lb. yellow corn | 12 ounces | 8 |
| Flour, white | 6.8 lb. wheat | 5 pounds | 35 |
| Apples | 1.04 lb. apples | Pound | 29 |
| Grapefruit | 1.03 grapefruit | Each | 21 |
| Lemons | 1.04 lb. lemons | Pound | 34 |
| Oranges | 1.03 doz. oranges | Dozen | 20 |
| Cabbage | 1.08 lb. cabbage | Pound | 36 |
| Carrots | 1.03 lb. carrots | Pound | 41 |

**TABLE 19.3:** (continued)

| Product* | Farm Equivalent | Retail Unit | Farmer's Share |
|---|---|---|---|
| | | | *(per cent)* |
| Celery | 1.08 lb. celery | Pound | 33 |
| Cucumbers | 1.09 lb. cucumbers | Pound | 35 |
| Lettuce | 1.88 lb. lettuce | Head | 43 |
| Onions | 1.06 lb. onions | Pound | 34 |
| Peppers, green | 1.09 lb. peppers | Pound | 45 |
| Potatoes | 10.42 lb. potatoes | 10 pounds | 26 |
| Tomatoes | 1.18 lb. tomatoes | Pound | 43 |
| Peaches, canned | 1.60 lb. Calif. cling peaches | No. 2½ can | 18 |
| Pears, canned | 1.85 lb. pears for canning | No. 2½ can | 18 |
| Beets, canned | 1.24 lb. beets for canning | No. 303 can | 7 |
| Corn, canned | 2.495 lb. sweet corn | No. 303 can | 12 |
| Peas, canned | .69 lb. peas for canning | No. 303 can | 15 |
| Tomatoes, canned | 1.84 lb. tomatoes for canning | No. 303 can | 17 |
| Orange juice, concentrate, frozen | 3.77 lb. oranges | 6-ounce can | 47 |
| French fried potatoes, frozen | 1.38 lb. potatoes | 9 ounces | 18 |
| Peas, frozen | .70 lb. peas for freezing | 10 ounces | 17 |
| Beans, navy | 1.00 lb. Mich. dry beans | Pound | 31 |
| Margarine | Soybeans, cottonseed, and milk | Pound | 25 |
| Peanut butter | 1.33 lb. peanuts | 12-ounce jar | 35 |
| Salad and cooking oil | Soybeans, cottonseed, and corn | Pint | 22 |
| Vegetable shortening | Soybeans and cottonseed | 3 pounds | 29 |
| Sugar | Sugar beets and cane | 5 pounds | 40 |
| Spaghetti with sauce, canned | Wheat, tomatoes, cheese, sugar | 15½-ounce can | 11 |

Source: *The Marketing and Transportation Situation,* USDA, Feb., 1970, p. 23.

* Product groups include more items than those listed in this table. For example, in addition to the products listed—Choice beef, lamb, and pork (major products except lard)—the meat products group includes lower grades of beef, the minor edible pork products, and veal.

† For the bakery products group and the individual wheat products, gross farm value, by-product allowance, net farm value, and farmer's share are based on the market price of wheat received by farmers plus the cost of the marketing certificate to millers. This cost equals the value of the domestic marketing certificate received by farmers complying fully with the wheat program.

### Processor's Share

The processor's share in 1914 was only 12 per cent. It then rose to 21 per cent in 1939 and has continued at about that level ever since. This rise in processing costs is not something that the marketing system has forced on the consumer; it is something that the consumer has forced on the marketing system. And she has done it for good reasons. When she buys food in finished forms, she does not have to spend time squeezing oranges, for example, or shelling peas. She opens a can of frozen orange

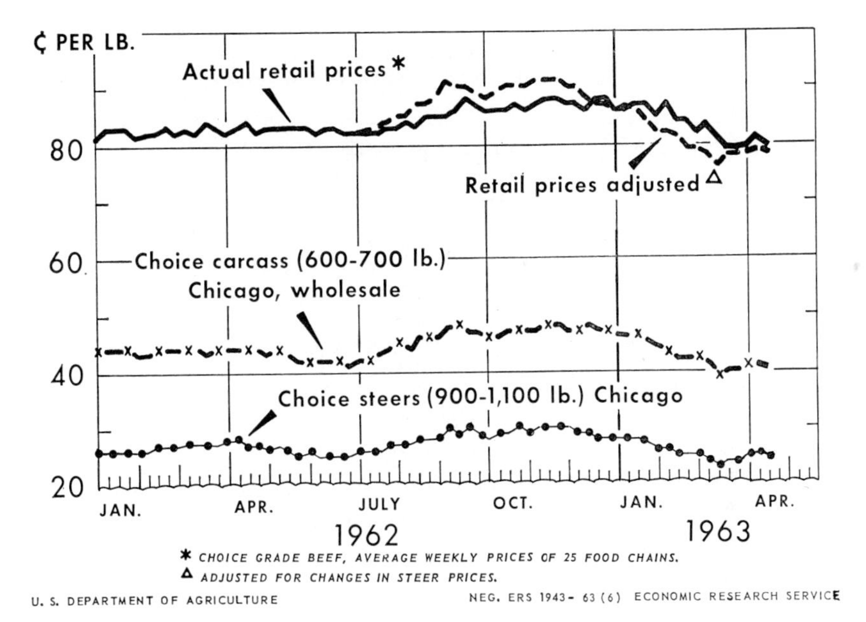


FIG. 19.3—Relationship of actual retail price of beef to fluctuations in market price of beef, 1962–63.

juice concentrate, dilutes it with water, and pours it directly into the glass; she opens a package of frozen peas and puts them directly into a saucepan. This increases processing costs, but it saves her time. Housewives used to buy flour and fresh produce and hire maids to bake bread and to prepare food for the table. Now those who would be maids get good jobs in business offices and factories; consumers find it cheaper and more satisfactory to buy bread baked in bakeries and vegetables processed and frozen in plants where the "maids" can work more efficiently than they can in the family kitchen. Consumers are not capricious or irrational in asking for expensively processed food. They are simply adjusting intelligently to technological, economic, and sociological changes that have been taking place throughout our whole economy.

**Profits**

Profits take only a small percentage of the consumer's food dollar—about 5 per cent, as indicated earlier in Figure 4.5.

The profits of some of the leading groups of food corporations are shown in Table 19.4. The profits are shown after federal taxes in two different ways—in terms of percentage of investment (stockholders' equity) and in terms of rate on sales.

In most cases, profits as a percentage of stockholders' equity

**TABLE 19.4: Net Profits (After Taxes on Income) as a Percentage of Stockholders' Equity and as a Percentage of Sales, Food Manufacturing and Retailing Companies, Annual 1957–68**

| Year | Profits as Percentage of Stockholders' Equity* | |
|---|---|---|
| | Food manufacturing companies | 15 retail food chains |
| | *(per cent)* | *(per cent)* |
| 1957 | 8.8 | 14.9 |
| 1958 | 9.2 | 14.5 |
| 1959 | 9.6 | 13.4 |
| 1960 | 9.2 | 13.0 |
| 1961 | 9.4 | 12.0 |
| 1962 | 9.2 | 11.7 |
| 1963 | 9.3 | 11.4 |
| 1964 | 10.4 | 11.5 |
| 1965 | 11.0 | 11.3 |
| 1966 | 11.5 | 11.4 |
| 1967 | 11.1 | 10.3 |
| 1968 | 10.9 | 10.3 |
| | Profits as Percentage of Sales | |
| 1957 | 2.1 | 1.3 |
| 1958 | 2.1 | 1.3 |
| 1959 | 2.3 | 1.3 |
| 1960 | 2.2 | 1.3 |
| 1961 | 2.2 | 1.2 |
| 1962 | 2.2 | 1.2 |
| 1963 | 2.2 | 1.2 |
| 1964 | 2.5 | 1.3 |
| 1965 | 2.6 | 1.2 |
| 1966 | 2.5 | 1.2 |
| 1967 | 2.4 | 1.1 |
| 1968 | 2.4 | 1.1 |

Source: *The Marketing and Transportation Situation,* USDA, Nov., 1969, p. 17.

* Ratio of net profits to average of stockholders' equity at the beginning and end of the year. Stockholders' equity is excess of total balance sheet assets over liabilities. Compiled from *Moody's Industrial Manual* and company annual reports.

were high during and immediately after World War II. Profits as a percentage of sales, however, were relatively constant.

A distributor, looking at these figures showing profits as a percentage of sales, might consider them low. Consumers might consider them high. Farmers, looking at the profits as a percentage of stockholders' equity (in the upper part of the table), might consider them high. What do we as impartial economists say?

We recognize that profits as a percentage of sales are a matter of interest to the consumer, showing him where his money goes; but these figures may leave some misleading impressions.

They are to a considerable extent a function of the rapidity of the turnover of goods in the industry. An industry with a slow turnover of goods has to receive a larger profit per item than an industry with a rapid turnover to get the same profit per dollar of stockholders' equity (per dollar of investment). And it is profit per dollar of investment that counts from an operational point of view.

We recognize that in our primarily private-enterprise economy, profits must be high enough to induce a flow of capital into the industry (or permit the industry to finance itself) sufficient to maintain its equipment as a going concern.

The profits as a percentage of stockholders' equity shown in Table 19.4 are higher than the 6 or 7 per cent which is sometimes quoted as a fair average figure to cover pure interest plus the element of risk for all but the wholesale food distributing group. Profits as a percentage of sales, however, are small.

The fact that middlemen's profits take only a small percentage of the consumer's dollar has led some people to conclude that the width of the spread between producers' and consumers' prices cannot be appreciably reduced. This conclusion, however, is not valid. Half a dozen milk dealers might be handling milk distribution in a city, making no profits at all. This would not mean that margins could not be reduced; the dealers might be making no profits because the whole system of milk collection, plant operation, and delivery was inefficient. Reorganization of the plants or of the collection or delivery system might permit reductions in margins and an increase in profits and, eventually, reductions in prices to consumers.

The fact that middlemen's profits are small merely shows that most of the charges intervening between producer and consumer are not profits, but costs. Even if profits were wiped out entirely, that would reduce middlemen's margins only to a small extent. But reduction in the *costs* of marketing would have a substantial effect on margins and farm and retail prices. This is the area where the greatest progress can be made.

# 20

# REDUCING MARKETING COSTS BY COOPERATION

A CONSIDERABLE PART of the agricultural marketing system in the United States is owned and operated by farmers themselves. Farmers' cooperative elevators, farmers' cooperative creameries, etc., are familiar examples of local farmer-owned marketing units. Some cooperative marketing agencies are state-wide or regional in scope; the California Fruit Growers' Exchange, Land O'Lakes Creameries, Inc., etc., occupy important positions in their trades.

These local, regional, and national cooperatives are marketing agencies. They sell their members' farm products. Other cooperative agencies, called purchasing associations, operate in the reverse direction; they *buy* farm supplies for their farmer members.

Taken all together, these agricultural cooperative marketing and purchasing associations add up to an impressive total. In 1967–68 there were 7,940 cooperative agricultural marketing and purchasing associations active in the United States. Of that number 4,929 were engaged primarily in marketing farm products, 2,835 were farm supply cooperatives, and 176 provided services. In addition to these cooperative commodity marketing and purchasing associations, in 1967–68 about 1,250 mutual fire insurance companies were serving 3 million members. More than 900 rural electric cooperatives provided service to over 5 million members, and more than 200 rural telephone cooperatives supplied farm families with telephone service. In the field of finance, 652 federal land bank farm loan associations, 451 farm production credit associations, and 775 rural credit unions provided credit to farmers. There were also 1,310 livestock improvement associations—sire, dairy herd improvement, and artificial insemination groups and 7,729 mutual irrigation companies.[1]

Since 1929–30 the number of marketing associations has declined steadily. The total decline by 1967–68 was more than 5,000. During the same period, the number of farm supply associations increased by 1,400.

The total dollar volume of business in 1967–68 by marketing associations was $13.2 billion (77 per cent of the total). Farm supply or purchasing cooperatives had business volume totaling $3.5 billion. The total, including $316.0 million for services, was $17.0 billion. This was about eight times as large as the prewar figures and compared with $8.1 billion in 1950–51. A substantial part of the increase, however, reflects the rise in agricultural price levels since 1939.

The volume of business done by the various commodity groups and the purchasing groups is shown in Table 20.1. The relative importance of cooperatives in marketing farm products and in the farm supply business is shown graphically in Figures 20.1 and 20.2.

## WHAT IS A COOPERATIVE?

How are cooperatives any different from regular private business concerns? (The term "private" is not very apt, but is widely used. Cooperatives are private businesses too.)

The fundamental difference is that the cooperative is operated in the interests of its *patrons* as an agency for marketing their products, while the private business concern is operated in the interests of the stockholders or other *owners* as a means of

[1] *Statistics of Farmer Cooperatives,* 1967–68, USDA, FCS Rept. 11, May, 1970.

The number of cooperatives of all kinds in existence in other countries is truly astounding. Europe leads, with U.S.S.R. and Asia following. Most of these are agricultural cooperatives. For a brief interpretive history of agricultural cooperation in the United States see H. E. Erdman, "Trends in Cooperative Expansion 1900–1950," *Journal of Farm Economics,* Vol. 32 (Nov., 1950).

**TABLE 20.1: Number of Cooperatives Handling Specified Items and Estimated Business Volume, by Products Marketed, Supplies Purchased, and Services Provided, 1967–68***

| Item | Cooperatives Handling | | Gross Volume (includes intercooperative business) | | Net Volume (excludes intercooperative business) | |
|---|---|---|---|---|---|---|
| | *(number)* | *(per cent)*† | *($1,000)* | *(per cent)* | *($1,000)* | *(per cent)* |
| Products Marketed: | | | | | | |
| Beans and peas (dry edible) | 54 | 0.7 | 54,060 | 0.2 | 34,364 | 0.2 |
| Cotton and cotton products | 571 | 7.2 | 475,933 | 2.1 | 413,259 | 2.4 |
| Dairy products | 1,129 | 14.2 | 5,404,561 | 24.3 | 4,454,516 | 26.4 |
| Fruits and vegetables | 553 | 7.0 | 1,981,346 | 8.8 | 1,645,221 | 9.6 |
| Grain, soybeans, and soybean meal and oil | 2,567 | 32.3 | 4,583,002 | 20.4 | 2,899,313 | 17.0 |
| Livestock and livestock products | 425 | 5.4 | 1,961,011 | 8.7 | 1,856,390 | 10.9 |
| Nuts | 68 | 0.9 | 232,499 | 1.0 | 223,052 | 1.3 |
| Poultry products | 353 | 4.4 | 598,759 | 2.7 | 488,105 | 2.7 |
| Rice | 57 | 0.7 | 363,510 | 1.6 | 285,630 | 1.7 |
| Sugar products | 69 | 0.9 | 538,697 | 2.4 | 537,838 | 3.2 |
| Tobacco | 28 | 0.4 | 282,714 | 1.3 | 282,714 | 1.7 |
| Wool and mohair | 204 | 2.6 | 22,953 | 0.1 | 22,951 | 0.1 |
| Miscellaneous‡ | 161 | 2.0 | 57,575 | 0.3 | 53,893 | 0.3 |
| Total farm products | 5,552§ | 69.9 | 16,556,620 | 73.9 | 13,179,246 | 77.5 |
| Supplies Purchased: | | | | | | |
| Building materials | 2,164 | 27.3 | 187,038 | 0.8 | 133,646 | 0.8 |
| Containers and packaging supplies | 1,080 | 13.6 | 89,784 | 0.4 | 32,478 | 0.2 |
| Farm machinery and equipment | 1,563 | 19.7 | 167,966 | 0.7 | 109,123 | 0.6 |
| Feed | 4,228 | 53.2 | 1,654,294 | 7.4 | 1,169,377 | 6.9 |
| Fertilizer | 4,338 | 54.6 | 1,243,618 | 5.5 | 664,736 | 3.9 |
| Meats and groceries | 730 | 9.2 | 101,798 | 0.5 | 76,700 | 0.4 |
| Petroleum products | 2,745 | 34.6 | 1,207,527 | 5.4 | 785,150 | 4.6 |
| Seed | 3,986 | 50.2 | 185,064 | 0.8 | 129,223 | 0.8 |
| Sprays and dusts (farm chemicals) | 3,551 | 44.7 | 215,272 | 1.0 | 128,095 | 0.7 |
| Miscellaneous supplies‖ | 4,841 | 61.0 | 488,964 | 2.2 | 292,606 | 1.7 |
| Total farm supplies | 6,368§ | 80.2 | 5,541,325 | 24.7 | 3,521,134 | 20.6 |
| Services Provided: | | | | | | |
| Trucking, cotton ginning, storage, grinding, locker plants, miscellaneous | 5,329§ | 67.1 | 316,014¶ | 1.4 | 316,014¶ | 1.9 |
| Total business | 7,940§ | 100.0 | 22,413,959 | 100.0 | 17,034,395 | 100.0 |

Source: *Statistics of Farmer Cooperatives, 1967–68,* USDA, FCS Rept. 11, May, 1970.

* Preliminary.

† Number of cooperatives handling each commodity group is computed as a percentage of the total number of 7,940 cooperatives listed.

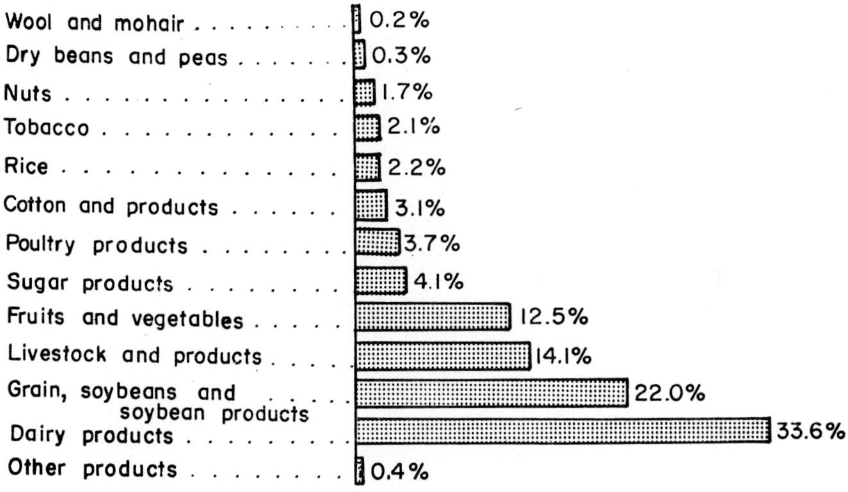

Wool and mohair . . . . . . . . . . 0.2%
Dry beans and peas . . . . . . . 0.3%
Nuts . . . . . . . . . . . . . . . . 1.7%
Tobacco . . . . . . . . . . . . 2.1%
Rice . . . . . . . . . . . . . . 2.2%
Cotton and products . . . . . . 3.1%
Poultry products . . . . . . . . 3.7%
Sugar products . . . . . . . . 4.1%
Fruits and vegetables . . . . . 12.5%
Livestock and products . . . . 14.1%
Grain, soybeans and soybean products . . . . . 22.0%
Dairy products . . . . . . . . . 33.6%
Other products . . . . . . . . 0.4%

**Based on net marketing business of 13.2 billion.**

FIG. 20.1—Relative importance of major farm products marketed by cooperatives, 1967–68. (Source: **Statistics of Farmer Cooperatives, 1967–68,** USDA, FCS Rept. 11, May, 1970.)

making profits on their capital investment. The cooperative is run by and for those who use it, rather than by those who own it.

In a private concern the patrons usually are not the owners. By contrast, in a cooperative most patrons are owners. But the cooperative is run in the interests of the owners as patrons, not in their interests as owners who want to make a profit on their investment.

In order to insure that the cooperative association will be run in the interest of its patrons rather than in the interest of its owners, the by-laws of the association usually include some of the "Rochdale principles of cooperation." These principles were established by one of the early associations, begun by a small group of poverty-stricken flannel weavers at Rochdale,

‡ Includes coffee, forest products, fur pelts, hay, hops, seed marketed for growers, nursery stock, tung oil, and other farm products not separately classified.

§ Because many cooperatives do more than one type of business, these totals are less than the number that would be obtained by adding the number of cooperatives handling individual items or performing individual services.

|| Includes plant equipment, automotive supplies, hardware, chicks, and other supplies not separately classified.

¶ Charges for services related to marketing or purchasing but not included in the volume reported for these activities.

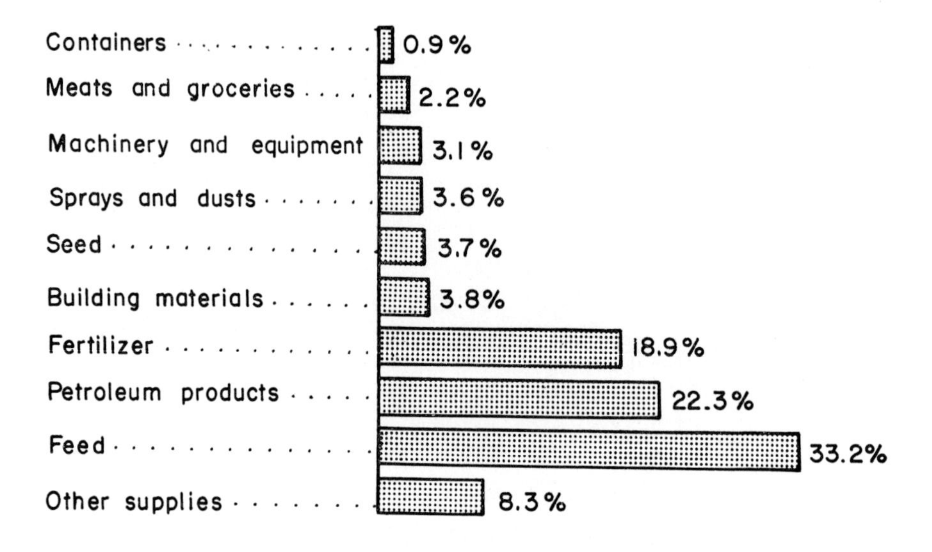


FIG. 20.2—Relative importance of major farm supplies handled by cooperatives, 1967–68. (Source: **Statistics of Farmer Cooperatives, 1967–68,** USDA, FCS Rept. 11, May, 1970.)

England in 1844.[2] The three most important of these principles are described below.

### One Man, One Vote

In order to keep the control in the hands of the patrons rather than those who put up the capital, control is allocated on the principle of "one man (member), one vote," not, as in a private concern, one share of stock, one vote.

This principle was adopted 100 years ago, at a time when the wider extension of political democracy was a prominent public question; it reflects the influence of those times. From a strictly economic point of view, "one dollar of patronage, one vote" would be better. Where the patrons contribute approximately equal volumes of business, the results are about the same; and the "one man, one vote" procedure saves a lot of computation.

[2] The Rochdale Pioneers probably have been given too much credit for these principles. Other associations used some or all of them before the Rochdale Pioneers did, and important modifications of the principles have been made since 1844. But the name has become firmly established in the literature of cooperation.

### Limited Returns on Capital

The return on capital in most cooperatives is limited to a modest percentage, usually between 5 and 8 per cent. Thus capital is paid for its hire but has no voice in the management.

The early cooperatives adapted private industry's capital stock as their instrument for raising capital. More recently, many cooperatives are using certificates of indebtedness, which automatically are issued to new patrons in return for deductions from their checks and automatically retired by payments from a revolving fund from those who cease to be patrons.

### Patronage Dividends

In a private organization any excess of revenues over costs is distributed among the shareholders at the end of the quarter, year, or other accounting period in proportion to their holdings of shares. The excess is distributed as dividends on capital stock. In a cooperative the excess is distributed among the patrons in proportion to their patronage. It is distributed as patronage dividends per dollar of business done.

Most cooperatives pay the "going price" for the products they handle and then pay the patronage dividend at the end of the year or at the end of the quarter, much as ordinary dividends on capital stock are distributed. Some cooperatives, however, pool their returns and pay their patronage dividends along with the payment for the products sold. For example, a cooperative milk plant simply might pay the patrons for their milk at regular biweekly or monthly periods, all that was received for the milk, minus expenses; the patronage dividend is not set out as such but is merely part of the check for milk.

It would be interesting and instructive to trace the development and present status of cooperative marketing in the various commodity and purchasing groups. The story of the struggles, accomplishments, and failures of cooperation reads like a historical novel. It teaches many lessons in economics, business, psychology, and politics. That story, however, is too long even for a whole book. It already has been told by many authors in many books over the past 100 years. A partial bibliography is afforded by the footnote references in the rest of this chapter. Here we will present only the essential principles of cooperation, analyze the place and purpose of cooperation, and show what it can and can not do to reduce the costs of marketing.

## COOPERATIVE MARKETING ASSOCIATIONS

Farmers set up their own cooperative marketing associations because they want them to be run in their interest as patrons, rather than in their interest as owners and contributors of capital. They want marketing done in the interest of the producers, rather than of the middlemen who own the regular private marketing business.

This is rather a general objective. Specifically, what do farmers expect to accomplish when they set up and run their own cooperative marketing agencies?

The original objectives of cooperation in the early days in England, from the time of Rochdale (consumers') cooperation in 1844, were "production for use" and "the elimination of private profit." The consumer cooperators set out to reform or reconstruct the entire capitalistic system with consumers, through their cooperatives, reigning supreme.[3]

Some consumer cooperative leaders in the United States still retain this view. Agricultural cooperative leaders, however, hold quite different views. These views were clearly defined during the period between World Wars I and II when the movement was maturing.

### Farmers' Seek Larger Profits

Farmers are essentially capitalistic. Their pride of ownership is strong. This is true even of most tenant farmers. Their chief complaint against the established order is that it has not enabled them to be better capitalists—to own more.

Their reason for cooperative endeavors, whether buying or selling, is not to eliminate private profit, but to get more profit for themselves. They attempt to do this on the one hand by buying supplies cheaper; on the other by getting a greater net return from what they produce.

This distinction in ideology is so marked that many European cooperative spokesmen refuse to classify farm cooperation as real cooperation at all. They say it is merely a modified form of capitalism, and as such they do not like it.[4]

Other opinions by agricultural cooperative leaders are equally simple and clear. "It should be apparent that to the farmer cooperation is business. Farm cooperatives are business institutions."[5] "The main purpose of the cooperative association is to make money for its members. For this purpose any lawful policy which is profitable is right and any policy which is un-

---

[3] Sidney and Beatrice Webb, *The Consumers' Cooperative Movement,* London, Longmans, Green and Co., 1921.

[4] C. V. Gregory, "The Distinction Between Producer and Consumer Cooperatives," *American Cooperation, 1937,* Washington, D.C., American Institute of Cooperation, p. 139.

Sidney and Beatrice Webb, *op. cit.,* pp. 414–20, say: "Agricultural cooperation . . . forms . . . no rightful part of the consumers' cooperative movement."

[5] Robin Hood, "Lessons We Have Learned," *Cooperative Journal,* National Cooperative Council (Sept.–Oct. 1936).

profitable is wrong."[6] And most bluntly of all, "I regard a farmer-owned, farmer-controlled cooperative as a legal, practical means by which a group of self-selected, selfish capitalists seek to improve their individual economic positions in a competitive society."[7]

### Marketing Services at Cost

The objective of agricultural cooperation, therefore, is not to eliminate profits as such, but to divert them from the owners to the patrons. This in effect provides farmers with marketing services at cost.

This objective usually is limited to the diversion of middlemen's profits to farmer patrons. As shown above, most farmer cooperative leaders object to the extension of the principle to the diversion of distributors' *and producers'* profits to ultimate consumer patrons.

In a perfectly competitive economy, profits would continually tend to zero, and the part that cooperation could play would be small. Its objective—marketing services at cost—already would be attained.

Precisely because many parts of our existing economy are *not* perfectly competitive, however, cooperation has a useful part to play. In many cases, the size of the most efficient unit is so large relative to the size of the market that the business becomes concentrated in the hands of a few large and efficient operators. The laws of atomistic competition do not have a chance to work, and charges remain considerably higher than costs.

Most local markets for farm products, for example, are small. One buyer in each market could handle the job more efficiently (at lower cost) than several buyers dividing up the business among themselves. Yet one buyer would have some degree of monopoly control and naturally could be expected to try to keep most of the benefits of his efficiency for himself rather than passing them on in the form of low margins. Thus a single buyer would try to charge nearly as much for his services as the total charged by several buyers. He might charge more.

In that situation, farmers prefer to have more than one buyer on the market to establish some semblance of competition. Yet this is not a satisfactory solution. For if the number of buyers is small, they are likely to follow a policy, if not of actual collusion, at least of "live and let live"—something considerably

[6] Frederick V. Waugh, "Grades—What the Public Wants and Can Pay For," *News for Farmer Cooperatives* (Jan., 1941), p. 10.

[7] H. E. Babcock, "Cooperatives, the Pace-Setters in Agriculture," *Journal of Farm Economics*, Vol. 17 (Feb., 1935), pp. 153–56.

These quotations seem to have settled the matter. The authors know of no more recent discussions.

short of competition; while a large number of buyers divides up the business so much that the small volume results in high costs, often made still higher because of the time and money each buyer spends in soliciting business away from the other buyers.

A better solution is for farmers to set up a marketing agency of their own, charge the going rate, and return the excess of that rate over costs to its patrons in the form of patronage dividends. That gives them marketing services at cost.

### Reducing Costs

The greatest opportunities for cooperatives, however, lie not in the field of diverting profits, but in the field of reducing costs.

In most cases, profits are minimal; where they are large, they are usually fleeting. It was indicated in Chapter 19 that total profits all along the line from producer to consumer amount to only about 5 cents of the consumer's food dollar. But costs are about 60 per cent.

Furthermore, a considerable share of what is usually called profits actually is costs. American Telephone and Telegraph, for example, made a net profit of $2.2 billion in the year ending December 31, 1969. At that time they had over 90 million telephones in service. Does that mean they could have paid a patronage dividend of about $24 per telephone It does not, because a good share of the so-called "profit" was actually a cost. It was interest on investment. If a company makes a "profit" of 10 per cent on its investment, that 10 per cent cannot all be paid in patronage dividends, because nearly half of it is interest on the money invested in the business. If prospective investors could not expect any return on their investment, they would not put their money into the business. It could run on borrowed money (bonds), but in that case it certainly would have to pay interest on the bonds as a cost. Even if cooperators agree to put up the money and get no return on it, that simply means that a good share of the patronage dividends they receive is interest on their investment and not patronage dividends at all.

In any case, the greatest opportunities for cooperatives lie not in the small area of profits, but in the large area of costs. A reduction of 10 per cent in costs would amount to far more than the complete elimination (diversion) of middlemen's profits.

How can cooperatives reduce costs? They have to pay a manager and other hired help, as any other business. They have to pay rent, heat, light, and other bills. How can they operate at any lower cost than competing private concerns?

Many cooperatives have found that they cannot operate at lower cost than private business. They found that a large share of what they called profits was really costs, which they could not reduce.

In most cases, however, cooperatives are in a good position to reduce costs, for two or three specific reasons. Their costs of advertising and other forms of solicitation should be lower than those of private businesses. Cooperatives also are in a position to reduce costs by handling products in larger volume than their private competitors. Farmers can see the advantage of patronizing their own agency when that patronage increases volume and reduces costs, and those lowered costs are passed directly on to them in the form of patronage dividends. In a situation where the volume of business required for efficient operation is large relative to the size of the market, monopoly or oligopoly is likely to result. Cooperation is one of the few ways by which such situations can be rendered harmless. Cooperation can divert the profits being made by private agencies and can also cut costs substantially by reducing competitive wastes and by virtue of the large volume of business that a cooperative can build up—a larger volume than would be safe in the hands of a private agency.

### Improving Marketing Practices

Finally, there are many marketing situations in which dealers can make the most money by following practices that are adverse to farmers' interests. Some dealers, for example, believe that they can make more money buying eggs on an ungraded basis and sorting and grading them for their trade than they can by buying eggs on grade from the farmer in the first place. Perhaps they are right. But when no incentive is offered to farmers for high-grade produce, the quality of the product is low and farmers' interests suffer. Again, grain growers' interests might be better served if the identity of different grades or even carlots of grain were preserved from the farm to the miller. But if grain dealers can make more money by mixing and blending grain, they will proceed to do so regardless of the farmers' interests in the matter. And if feed mixers or fertilizer companies can make more money by certain practices which are of no value to or are actually deleterious to farmers' interests, there is no assurance that they will not follow them. But farmer cooperatives set up in these fields can be made to operate in farmers' interests.

Cooperation, therefore, is one simple, effective, nongovernmental means for preventing or reducing monopoly, for reducing costs that monopolistic situations usually entail, and for controlling exploitive practices on the part of the trade.

In effect, farmers who set up marketing or purchasing cooperatives integrate those marketing services with their production operations on the farm, much as Ford integrates its sales organization and parts of its raw materials procurement with its manufacturing operations. Ford does this as an individual corporation because its business is big enough to permit it to do so; farmers have to cooperate among themselves in order to get a big enough volume of business to permit their marketing organization to operate at an efficient size. The family-size farm is an efficient size for production, but not for marketing. Private marketing businesses are usually large enough to operate efficiently; and if they do the job properly from the farmer's point of view, he has no need to get into their field. But if they do not, he can bring together a large enough volume of business, by cooperation, to do his own marketing.

### THE LEGAL STATUS OF COOPERATION IN THE UNITED STATES

When the Sherman Anti-Trust Act was passed in the United States in 1890, some of the legislators foresaw that it might be used, in a manner that was not intended, to break up cooperative associations and labor unions as "combinations in restraint of trade." Senator Sherman even proposed an amendment to his bill exempting these two groups from action under his bill. But the bill was finally passed without any exemptions.

It was not long before farmers' cooperatives began to have trouble with the Sherman Act. In 1895, a milk producers' association of 1,500 farmers in the Chicago territory was indicted under the Illinois state antitrust law of 1891 and declared by the state court to be a combination in restraint of trade and therefore unlawful. Again, in 1913, a local livestock shipping association in Iowa was in trouble because its members agreed to ship all their hogs through the association or to pay a "maintenance fee" of 5 cents per 100 pounds to the association for any hogs they shipped through any other agency. Action was brought against the association by a local private dealer and sustained finally by the Iowa Supreme Court. From 1895 to 1910, cooperatives were indicted in five states under state antitrust laws, and in Louisiana under the Sherman Act.

By 1914, agricultural cooperatives had become numerous, and the act had caused them so much trouble that the Clayton Amendment was passed. This amendment exempted from the Sherman Act "labor, agricultural, or horticultural associations, instituted for the purposes of mutual help, and not having capital stock or conducted for profit."

This amendment represented a distinct step forward, but it was unsatisfactory on two counts. In the first place, it was phrased in terms of the definition of the purposes, financial set-up, and membership of the association, not in terms of the practices followed. The amendment therefore did not protect a farmers' association from being brought to court because of its actions, but only protected it from being prosecuted on the basis of its type of organization.

In the second place, the Clayton Amendment protected only cooperative associations "not having capital stock." This may have been unintentional, or it may have been done to restrict the amendment to what was considered the "purest" (nonstock) type of cooperative. But many perfectly good cooperatives had capital stock, and they accordingly were not protected by the amendment.

In 1922, therefore, the Capper-Volstead Act was passed, exempting associations of

> . . . persons engaged in the production of agricultural products, as farmers, planters, ranchmen, dairymen, or fruit growers . . . corporate or otherwise, with or without capital stock. . . . *Provided, howver*, that such associations are operating for the mutual benefit of the members thereof as such producers and conform to one or both of the following requirements: first, that no member of the association is allowed more than one vote because of the amount of stock or membership capital he may own therein; or, second, that the association does not pay dividends on stock or membership capital in excess of 8 percentum per annum.

The associations, however, were permitted to deal in the products of nonmembers to an amount equal to those handled for members.

The act states further:

> If the Secretary of Agriculture shall have reason to believe that such association monopolizes or restrains trade to such an extent that the price of any agricultural product is unduly enhanced by reason thereof, he shall serve upon such association a complaint stating his charge in that respect, to which complaint shall be attached or contained therein, a notice of hearing, specifying a day and place, not less than thirty days after the service thereof, requiring the association to show cause why an order should not be made directing it to cease and desist therefrom. An association so complained of may at the time and place so fixed show cause why such order should not be entered. The evidence given on such a hearing shall be reduced to writing and made a part of the record therein. If upon such hearing the Secretary of Agriculture shall be of the opinion that such association monopolizes or restrains trade to such an extent that the price of any agricultural product is unduly enhanced thereby, he shall issue and cause to be served upon the association an order reciting the facts found by him, directing such association to cease and desist there-

from. . . . The Department of Justice shall have charge of the enforcement of such order.

Thus the act is designed both to protect agricultural cooperatives from unwarranted prosecution under the Sherman Anti-Trust Act and to protect consumers from any misuse of their new powers by the cooperatives.

**Federal Tax Exemptions**

As early as 1898 a federal corporate tax law stated that the tax did not apply to agricultural organizations operated only for the mutual benefit of members. The Income Tax Law of 1916 also exempted farm cooperatives. These exemptions have been continued and made clearer in the income tax laws which are in effect today.

Section 101 (12) of the Internal Revenue Code now provides for the exemption of duly qualified farmers' cooperative associations from the payment of corporation income taxes, the stamp tax on capital stock, and the excess profits tax. The requirements which farmer cooperatives must meet to qualify for exemptions under these tax laws are similar to those of the Capper-Volstead Act. Cooperatives are not automatically exempt under these tax laws. They must apply to the Bureau of Internal Revenue for exemption status. If this application is approved, after their case has been scrutinized, they receive a "letter of exemption," under which they do not have to pay corporation income taxes.

Some private business leaders have objected to this exemption of cooperatives from the payment of corporation income taxes. They contend that patronage dividends are the same as profits, differing only in that they are paid to patrons instead of owners (on capital), and that they should be taxed the same as profits.

To this charge, the cooperatives have one effective answer. They say that patronage dividends are not profits at all, but merely refunds of overcharges paid at the end of the year instead of in the form of lower charges at the time the service is rendered. They say that the word "exemption" is a misnomer; cooperatives pay no income taxes because they have no income to tax.

In those cases where patronage dividends are distributed currently, in the form of higher prices for products sold or lower prices for goods purchased through the association, which is common practice in "pooling" cooperatives, the question of taxability does not arise at all. If the present exemption law were changed and patronage dividends were taxed, other cooperatives could pay their dividends currently in the form of higher or lower prices for the products they handle. This would intensify rather than reduce price competition and displease rather than please those who now object to cooperative exemption from income taxation.

Cooperatives can sum up their case in these words: They distribute everything above costs to their patrons. Let private industry do the same, and it will not have to pay any corporate income taxes.

## AGRICULTURAL COOPERATION VERSUS CONSUMER COOPERATION

Agricultural cooperation as a method for reducing the costs of marketing farm products is subject to one important limitation. It is applied mostly to the part of the marketing system that is closest to the farmer—to local creameries, local grain elevators, local livestock marketing associations, etc. But the marketing costs at the farmer's end of the marketing system take a relatively small part of the consumer's dollar. As shown in Chapter 19, the biggest share of the consumer's dollar goes to the retailer.

Farmers directed most of their early cooperative activities to selling. More recently they have also been active in purchasing, especially of supplies used in production—concentrate feeds, fertilizer, fencing, tractor and truck fuel, etc. Farmers have not done much cooperating as ordinary consumers of household products; that part of the field has been left mostly to urban consumer cooperatives, whose philosophy, as shown above, is different from and in some respects opposed to that of farmer cooperatives.

Is agricultural cooperation going to be concentrated on local selling and handling activities? To what extent will it increase its retailing? Is it going to remain aloof from consumer cooperation or antagonistic to it?

These are interesting questions to speculate upon. They come to a sharp focus at present only in connection with farmers' cooperative purchasing associations, but they loom in the background of the marketing cooperatives also.[8]

Farmers' purchasing associations handle a good deal of gasoline, oil, and other petroleum products. Private distributors of those products have fought back by slashing their prices (in many cases from 3.5 to 4 cents less than the price at filling stations). This leaves barely enough to cover costs. The oil com-

[8] See Joseph Knapp, *Seeds That Grew—A History of the Cooperative Grange League Federation*, Hinsdale, N.Y., Anderson House, 1960. See also his *Farmers in Business*, Washington, D.C., American Institute of Cooperation, 1963.

panies can do this so long as they have the profits from the filling station trade, refining, pipelines, etc., to keep them going. The farmers' purchasing cooperatives have entered the filling station business themselves in some cases, having already gone into refining, drilling, and pipelines. Similar conditions exist with respect to other goods handled by purchasing cooperatives —lumber, fertilizer, feeds, etc.

The need for a broader base for cooperative action is less evident in the case of farmers' marketing cooperatives. But even there, the steady trend away from self-sufficiency in agriculture is making farmers more consumer-minded. For as they no longer "grow their own wool and wear it" but buy their clothes and most of their food from the store, they are steadily becoming more like urban consumers. Farmers who have done well with purchases of fuel and other farm supplies on a cooperative basis are not likely to turn a blind eye upon purchases of food and clothing. This would require cooperation with urban consumers even more than a cooperative filling station would. It seems likely that the future lies with cooperation between producer and consumer groups rather than with conflict between them.

## SOURCES OF INFORMATION ON COOPERATION

Those who are interested in the field of cooperation can keep in touch with current developments by subscribing to *News for Farmer Cooperatives* and the bulletins published by the Farmer Cooperative Service of the USDA.

Another good source of information is the American Institute of Cooperation, 1616 H St., N.W., Washington, D.C. 20006. The institute maintains a list of references on the subject of cooperation, such as the American Cooperation Yearbooks, several books or pamphlets on legal problems, and bulletins (some of them free). These publications, along with those published by the state agricultural universities, provide a good foundation for thorough study of the field.

# 21

## REDUCING THE COSTS OF RETAIL DISTRIBUTION

THE RETAIL MARKET is located at the far end of the marketing system from the farmer. Farmers frequently overlook it or give it very little attention because it is so remote. But retailing is the most important of all marketing functions. It takes from 20 to 25 per cent of the consumer's food dollar; this is nearly half the total marketing margin all the way from producer to consumer.

Ordinarily, retailing takes a larger share out of the consumer's dollar than any other marketing function; in many cases it takes a larger share than all other marketing costs combined. The retail margins for most fresh fruits and vegetables, for example, usually range between 28 and 30 per cent of the retail price.

The large size of the retailer's margin has led some observers to conclude that retailing must be inefficient, or retail profits exorbitant, or both. This is an error. The size of the margin in itself does not necessarily show anything of the kind. It does show, however, that retailing is a costly operation, and that any significant reductions that can be made in retailing costs will represent an appreciable proportion of the consumer's dollar.

Reductions in marketing costs at the retailing end of the

distributive system eventually benefit farmers as much as reductions at their own end of the system. The sequence of events is something like this: Some enterprising retailer figures out a new method of handling beans, for example, in a way that reduces his handling cost by 10 per cent of the retail price. At first, he can keep that 10 per cent saving to himself. Bean producers and consumers both continue to pay and receive the same prices as before.

Sooner or later, however, things will begin to happen. Either the retailer will reduce the price of beans to the consumer, on his own initiative, in order to increase his sales (mostly by taking business away from his competitors, for the demand for the beans that he handles is more elastic than the demand for the beans in the city as a whole), or his competitors will begin to adopt his more efficient methods, eventually cutting prices until the margin on beans is reduced about in line with the margins on other comparable products.

At those lower prices, they will sell more beans than before. They will then pay higher prices in the wholesale markets or country markets in order to get more beans. If the supply of beans is about as elastic as the demand, the original 10 per cent reduction in cost will be divided 50–50 between higher prices paid to farmers and lower prices charged to consumers. If the supply is less elastic than the demand, farmers' prices will rise more than consumers' prices fall, and conversely.

## MASS RETAILING OF FOOD PRODUCTS

Chain stores occupy a prominent place in retail food distribution in the United States. In 1941 chain stores handled about 41 per cent of the total sales of food at retail. During World War II, the great demand for goods of all kinds relative to supply and the OPA price ceilings reduced the influence of prices on quantities sold; gas rationing reduced most consumers' shopping range to the local corner grocery, and sales in chain stores did not increase as rapidly as sales in independent stores. The proportion handled by chain stores declined to a low of 31 per cent by 1945. After the war, however, the percentage rose again. It reached 39 per cent in 1959 and rose to 41 per cent in 1962.[1] In 1969 the proportion of sales increased to a little over 43 per cent.[2] Thus chain stores in the United States handle a slightly higher percentage of the total retail food business now than they handled before World War II.

---

[1] "Facts in Grocery Distribution," *Progressive Grocer* (1963), p. 3.

[2] "37th Annual Report of the Grocery Industry," *Progressive Grocer* (Apr., 1970), p. 53.

The five leading grocery chains in the United States in order of size are the Atlantic and Pacific Tea Company, the Safeway Stores, The Kroger Company, Food Fair Stores, and the Acme Stores Company. The volume of business per store in these chains is now more than ten times as large as it was before World War II, but the number of stores has been cut approximately in half. The data for recent years are given in Table 21.1.

**TABLE 21.1: Sales in Millions of Dollars and Number of Stores Operated by Each of the Five Largest Food Chains, 1947–69**

| Year | A & P Tea Co. | Safeway Stores | The Kroger Company | Acme* Stores Co. | Food Fair Stores |
|---|---|---|---|---|---|
| | | | *Sales* | | |
| 1947 ...... | $2,545 | $1,111 | $ 754 | $ 388 | $ ... |
| 1950 ...... | 3,180 | 1,209 | 861 | 469 | 206 |
| 1953 ...... | 3,989 | 1,751 | 1,059 | 604 | 348 |
| 1956 ...... | 4,482 | 1,989 | 1,492 | 737 | 545 |
| 1960 ...... | 5,049 | 2,469 | 1,870 | 889 | 840 |
| 1963 ...... | 5,311 | 2,650 | 2,102 | 1,081 | 1,105 |
| 1965 ...... | 5,080 | 2,939 | 2,555 | 1,161 | 1,205 |
| 1967 ...... | 5,459 | 3,361 | 2,806 | 1,294 | 1,372 |
| 1969 ...... | 5,763 | 4,100 | 3,477 | 1,646 | 1,793 |
| | | | *Number of Stores* | | |
| 1947 ...... | 5,108 | 2,401 | 2,516 | 1,921 | ... |
| 1950 ...... | ... | 2,084 | 2,054 | 1,505 | ... |
| 1953 ...... | 4,200 | 2,037 | 1,810 | 1,132 | ... |
| 1956 ...... | 4,252 | 2,117 | 1,437 | 831 | ... |
| 1960 ...... | 4,276 | 2,207 | 1,372 | 810 | 404 |
| 1963 ...... | 4,501 | 2,059 | 1,366 | 862 | ... |
| 1965 ...... | 4,625 | 2,170 | 1,459 | 902 | 587 |
| 1967 ...... | 4,724 | 2,240 | 1,483 | 891 | 630 |
| 1969 ...... | 4,700 | 2,250 | 1,488 | 890 | 633 |

Sources: National Association of Food Chains and "Facts in Grocery Distribution," *Progressive Grocer* (1962), p. 25 and (1963), p. 31; "37th Annual Report of the Grocery Industry," *Progressive Grocer,* Apr., 1970, p. 67. Data for 1960–65 from *Supermarket Merchandising* (Apr. issues, 1960–66).

* Formerly American Stores Company. Name changed in 1962.

The smaller sectional and local chain stores together handle more business than the total handled by the large national chains.

### Cooperatives and Voluntary Chains of Independent Retailers

Another phase of large-scale retailing is the organization of voluntary and cooperative chains of independent retailers. Such chains are of two types: (1) the wholesaler-sponsored chain in which the wholesaler takes the initiative in bringing about a closer merchandising affiliation with a group of independent retailers, and (2) the cooperative chain wherein the independent retailers own and operate a wholesaling enterprise on a cooperative basis. In both types the objective is fundamentally the same, namely, to integrate the wholesaling and retailing functions more closely and to provide the independent enterpriser in the grocery field with whatever advantages there may be in large-scale buying and wholesaling operations.

Voluntary and cooperative chains differ greatly in the character of their operations and the services which they render to their member stores. Some of them are closely knit, coordinated organizations which provide the retailer with nearly all his grocery stocks and assist him actively in the management and operation of his store. In organizations of this sort the methods of wholesaling and retailing take on many of the characteristics of the corporate chains.

The movement has gone so far that by now the vast majority of the grocery stores in the United States are either members of chains or of some kind of cooperative or voluntary group. The traditional independent grocery is becoming a rarity.

### The Supermarket

The term "supermarket" means a retail unit which aims toward a reduction of retailing costs by means of a large volume of business and a minimum of service to consumers.

The increase in the importance of the supermarket during the last 35 years has been no less than phenomenal. Within two or three years after their first appearance in 1933, thousands had been established in all parts of the country. They have continued to grow since that time. By 1969 supermarkets, defined as stores with annual sales of $500,000 or more, were doing 76 per cent of the total grocery store business. "Superettes," with annual sales between $150,000 and $500,000, were doing 12 per cent. Small stores, below $150,000, were doing only 12 per cent. The percentages for selected years back to 1952 are shown in Figure 21.1. The data for 1969 are given in Table 21.2.[3]

### Discount Retailing[4]

The rise of discount stores and discount merchandising was one of the important developments in food retailing during the 1960's. Discount stores are somewhat like the early supermarkets in that they offer a minimum of "frills." Discount merchandising

[3] *Ibid.*, p. 7.

[4] This section is based largely on Martin Leiman, *Food Retailing by Discount Houses*, USDA, Marketing Res. Rept. 785, Feb., 1967.

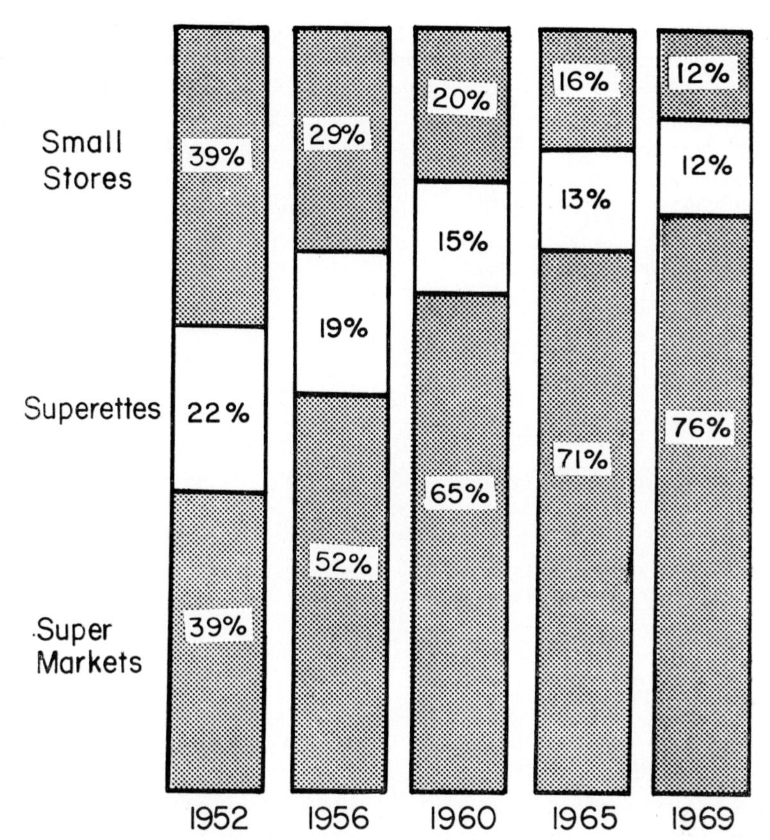


FIG. 21.1—Share of grocery store sales by size of store, 1952–69. (Source: National Association of Food Chains and **Progressive Grocer,** 1962, p. 25; 1963, p. 31; and 1970, p. 7.)

When chain and independent stores are combined and grouped according to volume class (supermarkets, superettes, and small stores), one sees a decided trend toward supermarket dominance. Since 1960, however, the trend has slowed down considerably due to natural causes —the supermarkets' share has reached a very high level beyond which sharp increases are more difficult, and a steadily declining number of desirable sites exist for new stores. A new factor has recently strengthened the superette and small-store classes—the growth of convenience, sometimes called bantam or drive-in, stores that now approach 4,000 in number.

has also extended into the operations of some of the larger chains and independent food retailers. In 1969 discount pricing programs were employed by 60 per cent of the retail food chains and by 27 per cent of the leading independents. By eliminating some services and using simplified display and pricing methods, margins are often reduced by 2.5 to 3.0 percentage points.

**TABLE 21.2: Grocery Store Sales by Size and Ownership, 1969.**

| Type of Store | Number | Per Cent of Total | Sales (billions) | Per Cent of Total |
|---|---|---|---|---|
| *All Stores* | 219,330 | 100 | 82.205 | 100 |
| *Supermarkets* | 37,180 | 17.0 | 62.500 | 76.0 |
| Chain Supermarkets | 19,700 | 9.0 | 36.120 | 43.9 |
| $500,000 to $1,000,000 | 4,600 | 2.1 | 3.780 | 4.6 |
| $1,000,000 to $2,000,000 | 9,200 | 4.2 | 15,395 | 18.7 |
| Over $2,000,000 | 5,900 | 2.7 | 16,945 | 20.6 |
| Independent Supermarkets | 17,480 | 8.0 | 26.380 | 32.1 |
| $500,000 to $1,000,000 | 9,100 | 4.1 | 7.630 | 9.3 |
| $1,000,000 to $2,000,000 | 5,580 | 2.6 | 8.850 | 10.8 |
| Over $2,000,000 | 2,800 | 1.3 | 9.900 | 12.0 |
| *Superettes* | 31,000 | 14.2 | 10.180 | 12.4 |
| Chain Superettes | 5,000 | 2.3 | 1.280 | 1.5 |
| $150,000 to $300,000 | 3,700 | 1.8 | 0.755 | 0.8 |
| $300,000 to $500,000 | 1,300 | 0.5 | 0.525 | 0.7 |
| Independent Superettes | 26,000 | 11.9 | 8.900 | 10.9 |
| $150,000 to $300,000 | 13,800 | 6.4 | 3.455 | 4.2 |
| $300,000 to $500,000 | 12,200 | 5.5 | 5.445 | 6.7 |
| *Small Stores* | 151,150 | 68.8 | 9.525 | 11.6 |
| Chain Small Stores | 6,150 | 2.8 | 0.725 | 0.9 |
| Under $100,000 | 1,200 | 0.5 | 0.050 | 0.1 |
| $100,000 to $150,000 | 4,950 | 2.3 | 0.675 | 0.8 |
| Independent Small Stores | 145,000 | 66.0 | 8.800 | 10.7 |
| Under $100,000 | 130,000 | 59.2 | 6.850 | 8.3 |
| $100,000 to $150,000 | 15,000 | 6.8 | 1.950 | 2.4 |

Source: "37th Annual Report of the Grocery Industry," *Progressive Grocer* (Apr., 1970).

Many questions have been and continue to be raised about food discounting. Is it an innovation as significant as the introduction of the supermarket? Do discount food stores have economies of scale that conventional food stores do not? Is the variety and assortment of merchandise carried by discounters as complete as will be found in conventional food stores? Are some discount-house food departments operated at a loss in order to increase customer traffic? If so, are these losses subsidized by other departments of the discount houses? Are discount food prices lower than those in conventional food stores? Have the operators of conventional food stores made substantial changes in store operations to meet this new type of competition? What effect will food discounting have on food distribution?

A study of these questions, published in 1967, led to the following conclusions:

Discount food stores had significantly higher average weekly sales and were open fewer hours during the week than conventional food stores.

The discounters' gross margins on selling prices were significantly lower than those of the conventional food stores, as were "other costs" (defined as all costs except labor costs). The discounters' labor costs as a percentage of sales were also significantly lower, although their wage rates were not significantly different from those paid by conventional retailers. Discounters' sales per man-hour and per full-time-equivalent employee averaged higher than for conventional retailers. These differences were not wholly attributable to differences in sales size, indicating that the discounters made more efficient use of employees.

The discounters also had both a higher customer count and a higher average sale per customer, yet they offered their customers a smaller variety of merchandise. An examination of prices for 30 identical items showed that the discounters' prices were significantly lower. The discounters had larger stores, both in terms of total store and selling area, and also had larger parking lots.

All the stores in the sample advertised. The chains and discounters had identical advertising costs as a percentage of sales, yet their media-use patterns differed, as did their patterns of buying merchandise for resale.

Some of the chain respondents said that their stores had been affected by discounters' competition. However, both for those stores affected and for those not affected by discounting, management took similar actions to meet the threat of this new competition. The most common reactions to the threat of discount competition were reduced prices and increased advertising and promotional activity. A smaller percentage of the independent food stores indicated that they had felt the impact of competition from discount food stores. Their actions to meet the competition of discounters were similar to those taken by chain stores.

### Vertical Integration by the Grocery Chains

Another important aspect of mass distribution from the standpoint of marketing efficiency is the fact that mass distributors have tended to integrate successive marketing functions within a single organization. Grocery chains are commonly thought of only in connection with the retailing of food products. Their enterprises, however, reach into all phases of food processing and distribution, and in many cases they bridge the entire span between producer and consumer. More than any other type of large-scale food concern, they furnish examples of vertically integrated and diversified enterprises.

Virtually all these large grocery chain store systems operate their own warehouses for servicing their retail units with stocks of goods. The Atlantic and Pacific Tea Company operates about 37 warehouses and processing plants in the larger cities of the country. The function performed by these warehouses is essentially the same as that which the specialized wholesaler performs for the independent retailer. Consequently, the corporate chains purchase almost nothing from, and virtually have no dealings with, the specialized grocery wholesaler.

Today there are few food-processing industries into which some chain has not integrated. Some leading examples are meat packing, cheese, condensed milk, ice cream, fluid milk, bakery products, coffee roasting, soft drinks, soaps and bleaches, salad dressing, and canned fish. It is easier to cite the exceptions—certainly tobacco products and most cereals are the outstanding holdouts. But even these holdouts may go.

In addition to vertical integration through ownership, many food retailers have become tied—through contracts or informal agreements—with their suppliers. The familiar result here is the so-called "captive supplier."

Vertical integration by food retailers into food processing is possible because they have developed their own brands which are acceptable to consumers. Consequently, chains can easily overcome what is perhaps the main barrier to successful entry into food processing, the difficulty of developing acceptable brands. Moreover, because they have access to substantial financial resources, capital outlays are not serious barriers to entry in many fields. Finally, they can quite easily overcome the other main barriers to entry, technical and business know-how, by buying out going concerns.

The chains also have gone a long way toward the displacement of the various middlemen engaged in the handling of fresh fruits and vegetables. The larger systems have set up their own subsidiaries for handling these commodities and, wherever possible, buy direct from growers and shippers rather than from the regular terminal wholesale markets.

Vertical integration reduces the number of bargaining transactions and ownership transfers necessary to move goods from producer to consumer. The importance of this is commonly overlooked. A considerable part of the total cost of distributing food products is incurred for the purpose of bringing about ownership transfers at various stages in the marketing process.

Brokers' fees, wholesalers' commissions, salesmen's salaries, advertising expenditures—all are partially chargeable to the efforts of sellers and manufacturers to find retail outlets for their goods. Obviously the greater the number of such buyers and sellers and the more functionally specialized they are, the greater the number of ownership transfers necessary to move the commodity forward toward the consumer.

## COMPONENTS OF THE COST OF RETAILING

Since the major function of grocery retailing is of a combined distributive-service nature, it is a rather labor-intensive industry. Figure 21.2 shows that store labor alone accounts for nearly two-fifths of all operating expenses. Since other expense categories such as administrative expense are also partially composed of labor, it is likely that this factor alone accounts for about 50 per cent of total operating expenses.

The third most important expense category, behind store labor and administrative expense, is "rent and real estate." For most chain organizations, this expense is in the form of periodic lease payments. A fairly small percentage of the new supermarkets opened in recent years were owned by the operator, either outright or through a subsidiary.

The expenses of advertising and promotion (including trading stamps) follow in relative importance. Expenditures for trading stamps have declined in recent years as the number of food retailers using stamps has declined. In 1969 trading stamps were used by 37 per cent of the local and regional chains and by 27.5 per cent of the independent supermarkets and superettes. This compared with 42.5 and 32.0 per cent, respectively, only two years earlier.

In order of their importance, the other major expense items are services purchased, miscellaneous expenses, equipment depreciation and rental, store supplies, taxes and licenses, utilities, interest, repairs, and insurance.

### Gross Margins By Department[5]

Figure 21.3 shows that the major departmental gross margins have all exhibited a rising tendency over the period 1953–64, grocery and produce margins increasing at a slightly faster rate than meat margins.

As these figures suggest, there is a considerable variation in

[5] This section is based in part on *ibid.*, p. 221.

gross margin among departments. Of the three major departments, produce has the highest margin, followed by meat and groceries in that order. Table 21.3 provides gross margins for three conventional retail grocery store departments, as measured

| PERCENT OF SALES | | PERCENT OF EXPENSES |
|---|---|---|
| 0.5 | Insurance | 2.4 |
| 0.5 | Repairs | 2.4 |
| 0.7 | Interest | 3.3 |
| 0.7 | Utilities | 3.3 |
| 0.9 | Miscellaneous | 4.3 |
| 0.9 | Supplies | 4.3 |
| 0.9 | Equipment Depreciation & Rental | 4.3 |
| 0.9 | Taxes & Licenses | 4.3 |
| 1.2 | Services Purchased | 5.8 |
| 1.5 | Advertising & Promotion | 7.2 |
| 1.6 | Property Rentals | 7.7 |
| 2.6 | Administrative | 12.4 |
| 8.0 | Store Labor | 38.3 |
| 20.9% | | 100.0 |

FIG. 21.2—Retail operating expenses as a per cent of sales and of total operating expenses, 1968–69. (Source: Based on data in "37th Annual Report of the Grocery Industry," **Progressive Grocer**, Apr., 1970, p. 62.)

in various studies conducted by the National Commission on Food Marketing. The variation in gross margin between departments is traceable to many factors, including variations in expense levels, regular and special pricing policies, and tradition.

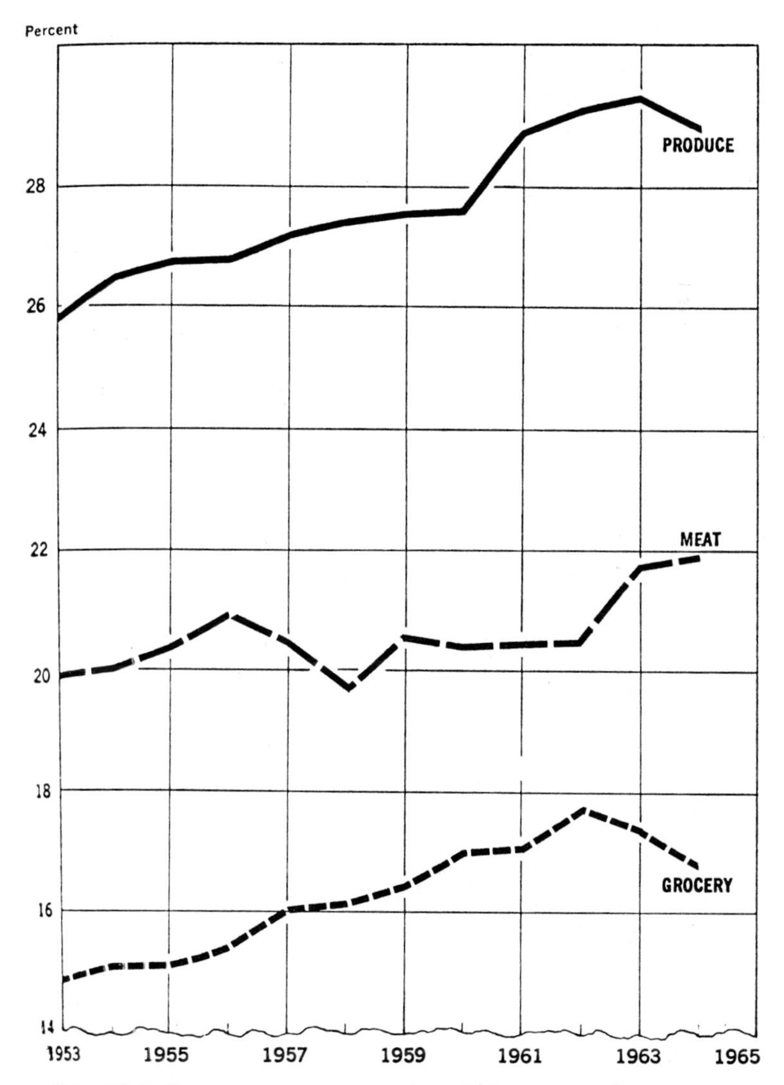


FIG. 21.3—Department gross margins within supermarkets as a per cent of sales, 1953–64. (Source: **Figure Exchange,** Super Market Institute, 1953–64. Data for years since 1964 not available from published sources.)

**TABLE 21.3: Gross Margin as a Per Cent of Sales by Major Department, 1953–64***

| Year | Grocery | Produce | Meat | Entire Firm |
|---|---|---|---|---|
| 1953 ....... | 14.87 | 25.83 | 19.96 | .... |
| 1954 ....... | 15.11 | 26.55 | 20.02 | 17.37 |
| 1955 ....... | 15.12 | 26.76 | 20.42 | 17.76 |
| 1956 ....... | 15.38 | 26.79 | 20.96 | 17.94 |
| 1957 ....... | 16.03 | 27.20 | 20.51 | 18.11 |
| 1958 ....... | 16.12 | 27.46 | 19.70 | 18.12 |
| 1959 ....... | 16.36 | 27.45 | 20.59 | 18.26 |
| 1960 ....... | 17.04 | 27.62 | 20.38 | 18.64 |
| 1961 ....... | 17.05 | 28.98 | 20.43 | 18.83 |
| 1962 ....... | 17.44 | 29.32 | 20.46 | 19.46 |
| 1963 ....... | 17.44 | 29.51 | 21.78 | 19.75 |
| 1964 ....... | 16.80 | 29.00 | 21.90 | .... |

Source: *Organization and Competition in Food Retailing*, National Commission on Food Marketing, Tech. Study 7, June, 1966, p. 224.

* Data for 1953–57 and 1964 are simple averages of quarterly data. Data for remaining years are annual. Table taken from **Figure Exchange,** Super Market Institute, 1953–64.

### Gross Margin Trends

Gross margin as a per cent of sales has gradually risen since the mid-fifties. The gross margin levels of single-unit and multi-unit types of firms reflect this rise. The multiple-store firms had consistently higher margins. This is largely due to the warehousing and transportation operations carried on by some of the larger multistore firms. It may also stem in part from variations in product mix. The disparity between the two types appears to have widened slightly, particularly since 1960. The extent to which the increase in disparity is caused by the larger firms assuming additional functions may be judged better by comparing firms within the multistore category by sales volume.

Since the smaller-firm category contains very few if any warehouse-integrated retailers, the margin may be considered an almost strictly retail one. The larger-firm classification is known to contain a number of establishments operating their own warehouses. The more rapid advance of the gross margins of the larger firms suggests that a portion of the increase is explained by the assumption of additional functions by the firms in this size group.

## DECLINING STORE NUMBERS AND CONCENTRATION IN FOOD RETAILING

The over-all picture in food retailing is one of declining store numbers and increasing store size and concentration.

Between 1948 and 1963, the number of grocery stores dropped from 378,000 to 231,000, or about 10,000 per year. The decline in store numbers has been slower since 1963, however, with about 219,000 grocery stores in 1969. Accompanying the drop in store numbers has been considerable growth in store size and volume. While larger stores have been the general trend, there has also been a rapid increase in small "convenience" stores in urban areas. These stores carry a smaller number of items but offer convenient access and quick selection and checkout. The number of these stores increased from only 500 in 1957 to around 11,600 in 1969.[6]

But these change are not by any means the most crucial changes occurring in the structure of food retailing. The really significant change is the increasing market concentration.

We have long had some large food chain firms. As early as 1930, A & P did 37.5 per cent of the food chain business and 12.3 per cent of all food store business. And in 1940, the four largest chains did 60 per cent of all food chain business and 22 per cent of all food store business.

But contrary to much popular opinion, the big change in market structure of food retailing in recent years is not that the traditional giants are growing in relative importance. On the contrary, the four largest chains do a smaller part of the food retail business today than they did in 1940—about 17 per cent in 1969.

Are we to infer from this that there have been no significant structural changes in food retailing other than the greater degree of specification buying, etc., that we hear so much about? Not at all. It's just that we must look elsewhere for the changes.

First, between 1948 and 1969 the share of all business done by food chains (11 or more stores) has increased quite regularly —from 34 to about 43 per cent—and this trend may well continue.

Second, although the top four chains do a smaller share of total chain business than in 1940, concentration is increasing within the chain part of food retailing. Not only is the number of chains declining—due to mergers—but a fairly large number of significantly sized chains have emerged since 1940, thus joining the traditional giants. By 1969 the country's top 20 food chains accounted for about 78 per cent of all food chain business and about 34 per cent of all food store business.

But again, this is only part of the story. Independent food stores still do much of the grocery business—about 50 per cent in 1969. But big changes have occurred here too. More often than not independents have become affiliated with "volun-

[6] *Ibid.* p. 7.

tary and cooperative chains"—either wholesaler-sponsored voluntary groups or retailer-sponsored cooperatives. They have done so to achieve some of the advantages of buying and merchandising enjoyed by chains. Although such organizations date from before 1900, they have become increasingly important, and by 1969 around 85 per cent of the sales of independents were funneled through members of "voluntary chains." Some of these voluntaries rival the largest chains in size.

Moreover, these voluntary and cooperative chains are offering more and more wholesale services. Over 90 per cent are supplying their members with frozen foods; over 50 per cent, fresh meats; and about 40 per cent, milk and dairy products.

**Implications of Changing Market Structure to Competition**

First, although the market structure of all food-processing industries departs greatly from that of a highly competitive industry like agriculture, the market structure of nearly all the food industries seems to encourage much keener competitive behavior—by any measure of competition—than that found in many other parts of the economy. Certainly, compared to the steel, chemical, auto, petroleum-refining, and many other leading industries, the food-processing industries are relatively competitive. They have more firms, lower concentration, lower barriers to entry, and often less product differentiation. But while they may be relatively competitive, they may not be considered competitive enough by farmers—especially in buying from farmers. As a result, continued pressure for integration into these industries by farmers through their cooperatives may be expected.

Second, and perhaps more important, the net effect of recent structural changes in many food industries seems to favor intensification of competition in their selling behavior, if not in buying. Much of the credit, or blame, for this—depending on your point of view—must go to food retailers. It is important that we recognize exactly what it is about food retailing today that tends to intensify competitive behavior in processing.

There is much vague talk these days about the *increasing market power* of food retailers. Some credit it to the increasing size of individual supermarkets and others seem to imply that specification buying—which is now called a kind of integration —somehow places suppliers of food retailers at a competitive disadvantage.

Much of this talk is nonsense. There is not much inherently new about the procurement policies of large chains. Rather, we merely have more large chains and voluntary chains than ever before. The traditional giants have long done what is becoming so commonplace today.

### The Changing Balance of Power

The changing balance of power between food processors and retailers may be explained by the structural considerations mentioned earlier. Whereas in the 1930's food processors faced only a few very large chains and organized independents, in the 1970's the bulk of their sales must be to these groups. The greatest single force intensifying competition in food processing is that food retailers are in the unique position of being able to *neutralize* much of any market power which processors may have achieved.

The word *neutralize* is emphasized because, as we review the available evidence, the so-called "buying power" of food chains does not give them much real monopoly power in the usual sense of the word. There are still so many food retailers (about 250 chains, 800 voluntary and cooperative chains, and about 190,000 unaffiliated independents) that in buying, no one —or even a few—can push prices below competitive levels for long, except in quite localized markets. However, because so many retailers are now able to sell under their own brands or labels and can easily enter many fields of processing, they have the effect of forcing many food industries into behaving like quite keen competitors. Large food retailers are able, in effect, to enter these industries and rob them of some of their market power; sometimes the threat to do so is enough. The result? Prices are pushed down toward costs—or in the short run even below costs.

This distinction between neutralizing the market power of others and having market power yourself, may seem like quibbling over terms. And if your power is being neutralized you will not much care what it is called. But from the point of public policy this distinction is important—making it clear why we (society) have a stake in maintaining a competitive food-retailing industry. The increases in concentration wrought by mergers in food retailing—which have averaged around 400 stores a year since 1952—certainly should make those interested in preserving competition concerned over their impact on the future structure of food retailing.

Consequently, if our public policy is really one of maintaining competition, and if we are correct in concluding that the present structure of food retailing is playing a leading role in making competition more effective throughout the food industries, then public policy should be directed toward preventing the structure of food retailing from becoming excessively concentrated. Also, we must have a vigorously enforced antitrust policy aimed at striking at discriminatory practices wherever they appear.

It certainly could be an unhappy day for farmers, processors, and consumers if an industry as important to public welfare as food retailing were to become so concentrated that the bulk of all purchases and sales were funneled through a dozen or two national and voluntary chains. Impossible? Some authorities are convinced it could happen in this generation. However, recent merger decisions in other industries suggest that our antitrust laws, vigorously enforced, may be an effective deterrent to such concentration.

THE PRECEDING PART dealt with certain marketing problems common to all farm products or to large groups of farm products. The present part deals with marketing problems that differ from one farm product to another. Thus they need to be taken up separately, product by product.

The products could be taken up in the order of the difficulty of their marketing problems, the stage of development of the system, or some other basis.

# SECTION 3

# COMMODITY MARKETING PROBLEMS

But it would be difficult to get much agreement on this order. Accordingly, they are taken up here in an order that makes economic sense and that can be measured objectively: in the order of the value of the sales of these products for the United States as a whole. This value, of some interest in itself, is given in Table 22.1.

The discussion for each product is organized along the analytical lines set out in Chapter 1. It begins with measurements of the demand for the product, then appraises the accuracy of the price system that reflects this demand to the producer, and ends with suggestions for reducing marketing costs.

# 22

# LIVESTOCK AND MEAT: DEMAND AND PRICES

MEAT ANIMALS bring in more income to farmers in the United States than any other product group. They yield more than twice as much income as the second most important item, dairy products—15.4 billion dollars in 1968, compared with 6.0 billion for dairy products. Beef cattle alone brought in more than 11 billion dollars. These comparisons are shown in Table 22.1.

Similarly, meat is the biggest item in the family food budget. Table 19.1 in Chapter 19 shows that it takes 28 per cent of the consumer's expenditure for food.

## GEOGRAPHICAL PATTERNS OF MEAT CONSUMPTION AND PRODUCTION

The geographical pattern of meat consumption in the United States is very similar to the geographical pattern of human population. A 1965 survey of household use of foods indicates that per capita consumption of meat, poultry, and fish combined was about the same in each of the four major regions of the country.[1] There were differences in the per capita use of different kinds of meat, however. Per capita consumption of

[1] *Food Consumption of Households in the United States, Spring, 1965*, USDA, ARS62-16, Aug., 1967, p. 4.

**TABLE 22.1: Cash Receipts by Commodity Groups, United States, 1968***

| Commodity | Value in Millions of Dollars | Percentage of All Commodities |
|---|---|---|
| All commodities: | 44,386 | 100.0 |
| Livestock and products | 25,539 | 57.5 |
| Crops | 18,846 | 42.5 |
| Commodity groups: | | |
| Meat animals | 15,407 | 34.7 |
| Dairy products | 5,962 | 13.4 |
| Poultry and eggs | 3,827 | 8.6 |
| Feed crops | 4,134 | 9.3 |
| Food grains | 2,337 | 5.3 |
| Cotton | 1,385 | 3.1 |
| Vegetables | 2,835 | 6.4 |
| Fruit and nuts | 2,055 | 4.6 |
| Oil crops | 2,847 | 6.4 |
| Tobacco | 1,176 | 2.6 |
| All other crops | 2,077 | 4.7 |
| Miscellaneous livestock | 344 | 0.8 |

Source: *Farm Income,* USDA, FIS-214 Suppl., Aug., 1969, p. 85.

* The receipts for cattle and calves were $11,271 million; for hogs, they were $3,820 million.

beef, for example, is greater in the West than in the South; and the quantity of pork used per person is somewhat larger in the South and North Central regions than in the West and Northeast.

The pattern of meat production is shown in Figure 22.1. The chart shows that livestock production is concentrated chiefly in the Corn Belt states. Texas, California, Oklahoma, and Colorado are other major producing states. In recent years, livestock production and feeding has increased considerably in the southern and southwestern states as well as in the western Corn Belt.

It is evident from Figure 22.1 that most livestock or meat has to be shipped long distances from the heavy-producing areas to the heavy-consuming areas.

## CHANGES IN THE DEMAND FOR MEAT

Figure 22.2 shows that the long-run trend of the per capita annual consumption of "red meat" in the United States rose from about 125 pounds in the 1930's to about 182 pounds in 1969. The trend in pork consumption remained practically horizontal, while the trend for beef and veal rose from about 60 pounds in the 1930's to over 110 pounds in 1969. The increase in total meat consumption resulted almost entirely from this increase in the consumption of beef. The per capita consumption of the different kinds of meat annually since 1955, is given in Table 22.2

Figure 22.3 shows the percentage of consumers' disposable income spent for beef and pork. It shows that the value of meat

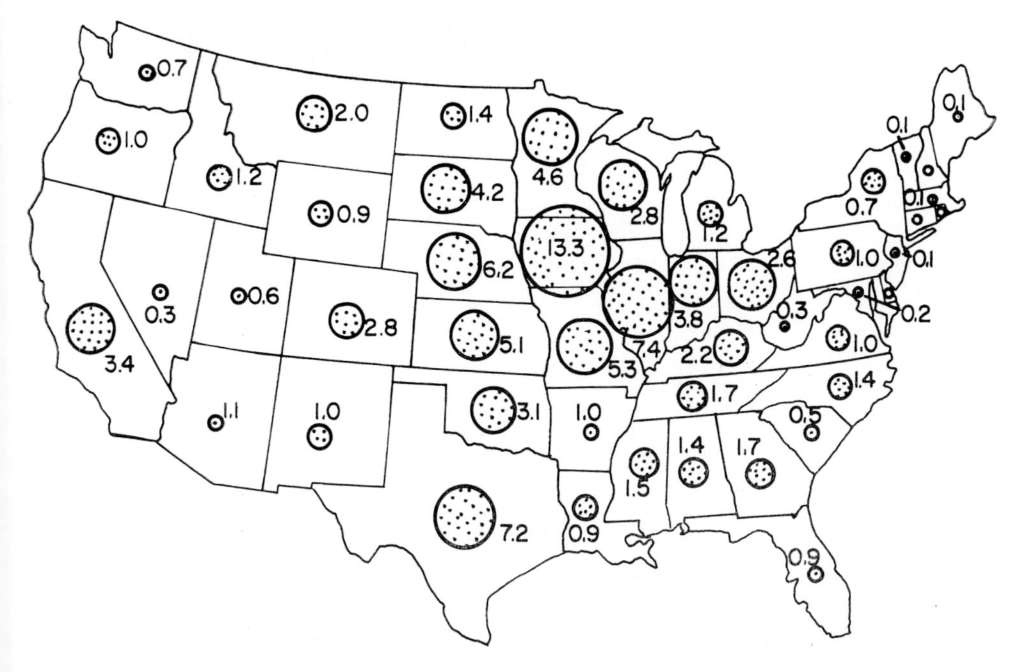


FIG. 22.1—Farm production of meat animals, live weight, 1969. Percentage of U.S. total produced in each state.

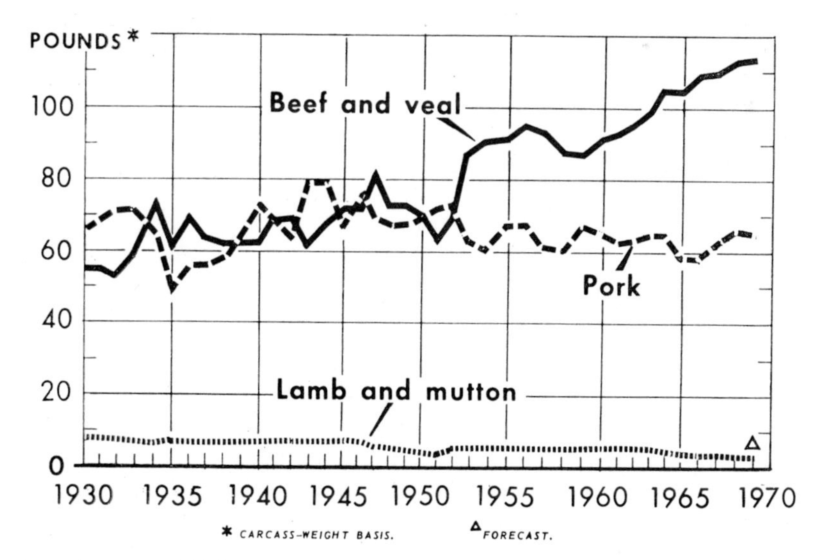


FIG. 22.2—Per capita annual consumption of red meat in the United States, 1930–69.

**TABLE 22.2: Consumption Per Person of Red Meat and Poultry, United States, 1955–69**

| Year | Beef | Veal | Lamb and mutton | Pork | Total | Poultry | Red meat and poultry |
|---|---|---|---|---|---|---|---|
| | Consumption Per Person (in pounds) | | | | | | |
| 1955 ....... | 82.0 | 9.4 | 4.6 | 66.8 | 162.8 | 26.3 | 189.1 |
| 1956 ....... | 85.4 | 9.5 | 4.5 | 67.3 | 166.7 | 29.6 | 196.3 |
| 1957 ....... | 84.6 | 8.8 | 4.2 | 61.1 | 158.7 | 31.4 | 190.1 |
| 1958 ....... | 80.5 | 6.7 | 4.2 | 60.2 | 151.6 | 34.1 | 185.7 |
| 1959 ....... | 81.4 | 5.7 | 4.8 | 67.6 | 159.5 | 35.2 | 194.7 |
| 1960 ....... | 85.0 | 6.1 | 4.8 | 64.9 | 160.8 | 34.1 | 194.9 |
| 1961 ....... | 87.7 | 5.6 | 5.1 | 62.0 | 160.4 | 37.4 | 197.8 |
| 1962 ....... | 88.8 | 5.5 | 5.2 | 63.5 | 163.0 | 36.9 | 199.9 |
| 1963 ....... | 94.3 | 4.9 | 4.8 | 65.3 | 169.3 | 37.5 | 206.8 |
| 1964 ....... | 99.8 | 5.2 | 4.2 | 65.3 | 174.5 | 38.3 | 212.8 |
| 1965 ....... | 99.3 | 5.2 | 3.7 | 58.5 | 166.7 | 40.8 | 207.5 |
| 1966 ....... | 104.0 | 4.5 | 4.0 | 58.0 | 170.5 | 43.8 | 214.3 |
| 1967 ....... | 105.9 | 3.8 | 3.9 | 63.9 | 177.5 | 45.7 | 223.2 |
| 1968 ....... | 109.4 | 3.6 | 3.7 | 66.0 | 182.7 | 45.0 | 227.7 |
| 1969* ..... | 110.7 | 3.4 | 3.4 | 64.8 | 182.3 | 47.6 | 229.9 |

Source: *Livestock and Meat Statistics,* USDA, Nov., 1961, p. 5; and *The National Food Situation,* USDA, Nov., 1967, p. 14 and Feb., 1970, p. 15.
* Preliminary.

consumed has declined since 1920 in relation to disposable income. Before 1935, the retail value of meat ran between 6 and 7 per cent of disposable income. The percentage declined under price controls and rationing during World War II, rebounded

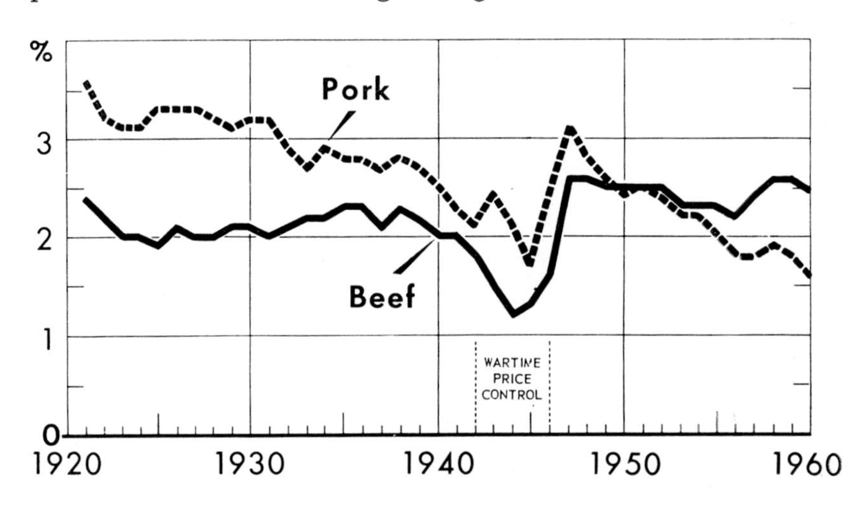


FIG. 22.3—Percentage of consumers' disposable income spent for beef and for pork, 1920–61.

**TABLE 22.3: Retail Value of Meat as Percentage of Disposable Income**

| Year | Beef | Pork | All Meat |
|---|---|---|---|
| | | (*per cent*) | |
| 1950 | 2.5 | 2.4 | 5.5 |
| 1951 | 2.5 | 2.5 | 5.5 |
| 1952 | 2.5 | 2.4 | 5.4 |
| 1953 | 2.5 | 2.2 | 5.3 |
| 1954 | 2.4 | 2.2 | 5.1 |
| 1955 | 2.4 | 2.0 | 4.8 |
| 1956 | 2.4 | 1.8 | 4.6 |
| 1957 | 2.5 | 1.8 | 4.7 |
| 1958 | 2.7 | 1.9 | 5.0 |
| 1959 | 2.7 | 1.8 | 4.9 |
| 1960 | 2.7 | 1.7 | 4.8 |
| 1961 | 2.7 | 1.7 | 4.7 |
| 1962 | 2.7 | 1.7 | 4.7 |
| 1963 | 2.7 | 1.6 | 4.6 |
| 1964 | 2.5 | 1.5 | 4.3 |
| 1965 | 2.5 | 1.4 | 4.2 |
| 1966 | 2.5 | 1.5 | 4.3 |
| 1967 | 2.4 | 1.4 | 4.0 |
| 1968 | 2.4 | 1.4 | 4.0 |
| 1969 | 2.5 | 1.4 | 4.1 |

Source: *The Livestock and Meat Situation,* USDA, May, 1963, p. 26. Data for 1965–69 derived from consumption retail price and income data published in current issues of *The Livestock and Meat Situation* and *The Marketing and Transportation Situation,* USDA.

after the war, and then declined to only a little above 5 per cent during the early 1950's. It declined below 5 per cent in the early 1960's and was down to slightly over 4 per cent in 1969. The percentages for the past years since 1950 are given in Table 22.3.

### Changes in the Demand for Beef and Pork[2]

The decline in the demand for meat has all been due to the decline in the demand for pork. Consumers in America now spend less of their income for pork than they used to.

This has been going on for quite awhile, but it has become dramatically evident since the end of World War II. During the 1920's, consumers spent a little over 3 per cent of their disposable income for pork. Spending for pork slipped gradually during the 1930's, until in 1940 consumers were spending about 2.5 per cent of their income for pork. After World War II consumer spending for pork rose to about 3.1 per cent in 1947. Since that time it has dropped rather steadily to about 1.4 per cent in 1969. This is less than half of the spending rate for the postwar high

[2] This section is adapted largely from Gerald Engelman, *Issues and Problems in Grading Hogs,* USDA, Dec., 1961.

in 1947. It is also less than half the spending rate that pork enjoyed during the 1920's.

Beef has enjoyed a more favored position among consumers. During the 1920's, consumers were spending only about 2 per cent of their income on beef. Spending for beef has gone up gradually. In the years from 1947 to 1969, spending for beef has been fairly constant at about 2.5 per cent of consumers' disposable income.

Several explanations may have a bearing on this shift in consumer purchases, this declining demand for pork and increasing demand for beef. Urban people on the average eat more beef than rural people, and the country has become more urbanized. Beef has a considerable income elasticity. By that we mean that beef purchases tend to increase with rising incomes (they "stretch more"). Pork purchases, on the other hand, are only slightly affected by differences in income. Per capita income has been rising steadily since World War II.

Another factor which should not be overlooked, however, is the dislike consumers have for pork that carries excess fat. In recent years, more of the leaner kind of pork has been available in retail markets, and there are indications that this may be arresting the decline in demand for pork.

The general rise in money income that took place over the past 25 years obscured the changes that were taking place in the demand for beef and pork separately. These changes can be revealed more clearly if the retail prices of beef and pork each year are divided by the consumer price index that year, and then plotted against per capita consumption. This is done for beef, pork, lamb, veal, and chicken in Figure 22.4.[3] The data are given in Table 22.4.

The dots in the pork section of Figure 22.4 cluster about two different lines. This appears to indicate that the demand for pork declined suddenly from 1952 to 1954.

The dots in the beef section of the figure also fall about two different lines. This appears to indicate that the demand for beef increased at one jump, from 1957 to 1958, and remained high thereafter.

### Reasons for Changes in the Per Capita Demand for Pork

The sudden decrease in the per capita demand for pork from 1952 to 1953 and 1954 shown in the pork section of Figure 22.4 cannot be explained by a sudden increase in the per capita

[3] This figure is adapted from F. V. Waugh, *Demand and Price Analysis*, USDA, Tech. Bul. 1316, 1964, p. 41.

**TABLE 22.4: Retail Prices Divided by the Food Component of the Consumer Price Index (1957–59 = 100) and Per Capita Consumption (Lbs. Carcass Weight)**

| Year | Pork | | Beef | | Lamb | | Veal | | Chicken | |
|---|---|---|---|---|---|---|---|---|---|---|
| | *(pounds)* | *(cents)* | *(pounds)* | *(cents)* | *(pounds)* | *(cents)* | *(pounds)* | *(cents)* | *(pounds)* | *(cents)* |
| 1948 ...... | 67.8 | 64.22 | 63.1 | 78.76 | 5.1 | 73.91 | 9.5 | 73.24 | 18.3 | 71.63 |
| 1949 ...... | 67.7 | 60.27 | 63.9 | 74.77 | 4.1 | 80.75 | 8.9 | 74.19 | 19.6 | 70.36 |
| 1950 ...... | 69.2 | 59.01 | 63.4 | 86.27 | 4.0 | 82.26 | 8.0 | 79.23 | 20.6 | 66.44 |
| 1951 ...... | 71.9 | 57.51 | 56.1 | 85.41 | 3.4 | 82.28 | 6.6 | 83.13 | 21.7 | 62.63 |
| 1952 ...... | 72.4 | 54.61 | 62.2 | 81.39 | 4.2 | 82.15 | 7.2 | 82.24 | 22.1 | 61.94 |
| 1953 ...... | 63.5 | 61.33 | 77.6 | 64.54 | 4.7 | 68.25 | 9.5 | 66.98 | 21.9 | 61.23 |
| 1954 ...... | 60.0 | 62.49 | 80.1 | 62.88 | 4.6 | 69.65 | 10.0 | 64.55 | 22.8 | 55.33 |
| 1955 ...... | 66.8 | 54.22 | 82.0 | 62.76 | 4.6 | 68.52 | 9.4 | 66.34 | 21.3 | 58.29 |
| 1956 ...... | 67.3 | 51.40 | 85.4 | 60.90 | 4.5 | 68.30 | 9.5 | 63.60 | 24.4 | 50.40 |
| 1957 ...... | 61.1 | 57.72 | 84.6 | 63.23 | 4.2 | 70.04 | 8.8 | 65.63 | 25.5 | 47.70 |
| 1958 ...... | 60.2 | 59.77 | 80.5 | 71.14 | 4.2 | 73.21 | 6.7 | 75.19 | 28.2 | 45.25 |
| 1959 ...... | 67.6 | 53.43 | 81.4 | 74.18 | 4.8 | 70.44 | 5.7 | 80.76 | 28.9 | 41.90 |
| 1960 ...... | 64.9 | 52.48 | 85.0 | 71.60 | 4.8 | 68.75 | 6.1 | 79.12 | 28.2 | 42.10 |
| 1961 ...... | 62.0 | 54.15 | 87.7 | 69.39 | 5.1 | 64.31 | 5.6 | 78.54 | 30.3 | 37.59 |
| 1962 ...... | 63.5 | 53.80 | 88.8 | 70.99 | 5.2 | 68.24 | 5.5 | 80.85 | 30.2 | 39.26 |

Source: F. V. Waugh, *Demand and Price Analysis,* USDA, Tech. Bul. 1316, 1964, p. 41.

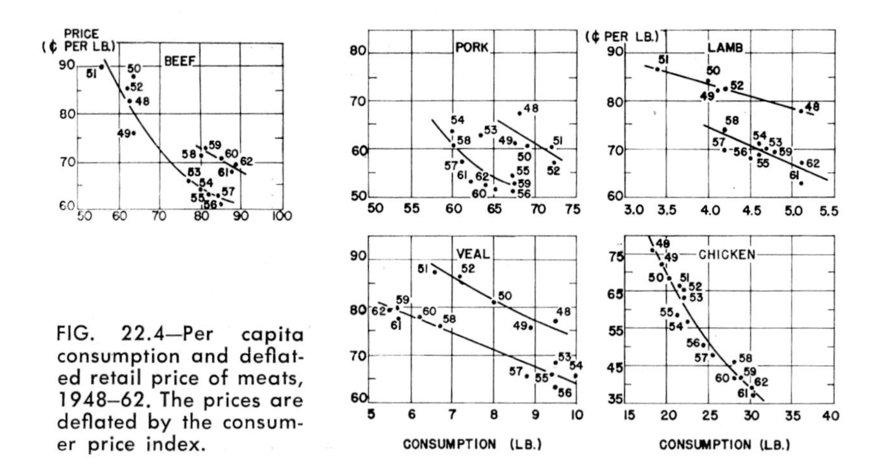


FIG. 22.4—Per capita consumption and deflated retail price of meats, 1948–62. The prices are deflated by the consumer price index.

demand for beef, for that increase came at a different time—from 1957 to 1958. But further analysis shows that most of it can be explained by changes that took place in the per capita production and therefore *consumption* of beef.

The beef section of Figure 22.4 shows that from 1952 to 1953, beef *consumption* suddenly increased 23 per cent, from 62.2 pounds to 77.6 pounds; after 1953 consumption continued to increase, although more slowly. This increase in consumption resulted from an increase in the supply of beef; the supply curve moved to the right. The increase in consumption was not initiated by consumers; they merely reacted to an increase initiated by producers. This increase in production, causing an increase in consumption, explains most of the sudden decline in the demand for pork from 1952 to 1954, and the continued but slower decline thereafter. Consumers found beef suddenly more plentiful and cheaper than before. They bought and ate more of it. They had less room left for pork; their demand for pork suddenly decreased.

This increase in beef production and consumption also explains the sudden decline that took place in the demand for veal and for lamb, shown in Figure 22.4. Even the demand for chicken declined to a small extent at that time; thereafter, increasing production of chicken merely cut the stationary demand curve for chicken at lower points.

The sudden decrease in the demand for pork from 1952 to 1953 and 1954, then, can be explained by the sudden increase that took place in beef production and consumption at that time. But after 1954, the demand for pork continued to decline, more slowly than before but more steadily. How can this slow and steady decline in the demand for pork be explained?

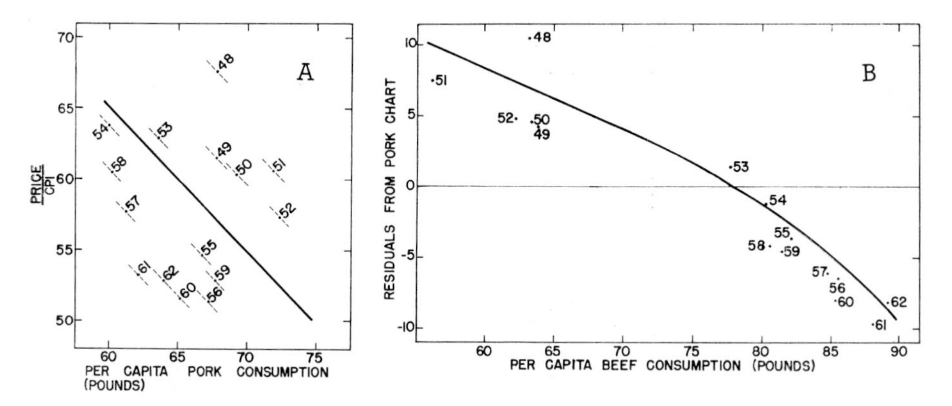


FIG. 22.5—Section **A**: U.S. average deflated retail price of pork plotted against U.S. per capita consumption of pork. Section **B**: Residuals from Section **A** plotted against U.S. per capita consumption of beef.

The decline from 1954 to 1956 can be explained by a further increase in beef production and consumption that took place, slowly but steadily, from 1954 to 1956. After 1956, however, beef production and consumption declined for two years, and the demand for beef suddenly increased. The first chart in the pork section of Figure 22.4 shows that during those years, the demand for pork ceased to decline and even increased a little. The changes in beef could logically be considered the reason for these changes in pork.

Still later, after 1958, the production and consumption of beef began to increase again. Correspondingly, the demand for pork began to resume its decline. The increase in beef production and consumption could logically be the cause of the decline in the demand for pork in this case, as in the earlier years from 1952 to 1954.

This analysis is given some statistical confirmation in Figure 22.5. The left-hand section of this figure is the same as the pork chart in Figure 22.4, but one single line is drawn in instead of two. The short, dashed lines help to show how the demand curve moved to the left with the passage of time. The residuals (the vertical deviations of the dots above or below the single line) from this chart are plotted against beef consumption in the right-hand section of Figure 22.5. The dots fall fairly closely about a negatively sloping line, which shows how the demand for pork decreases as the consumption of beef increases.

## Changes in the Demand for Different Cuts of Pork

Changes also have been taking place in the demand for different cuts of pork.

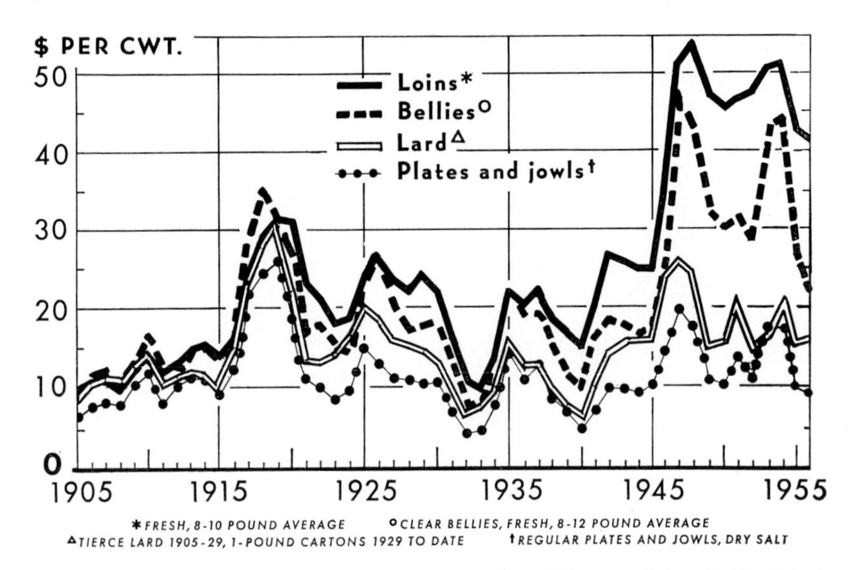


U. S. DEPARTMENT OF AGRICULTURE NEG. 658-57 (11) AGRICULTURAL MARKETING SERVICE

FIG. 22.6—Wholesale pork prices, Chicago, 1905–56.

Figure 22.6 shows the wholesale prices at Chicago for fat and lean pork cuts from 1905 through 1956. In the early years, loins, bellies, lard, and plates and jowls all sold at nearly the same price. Since about 1940, loins, one of the four lean cuts, have been in greater demand; and their prices have been higher than lard and the fat cuts. Prices for hams, butts, and picnics—the remaining lean cuts—have followed the trend for loins. This relationship between prices of the lean and fat cuts of pork has continued in recent years.

Before 1920, the prices of lard and the fat cuts which are readily converted into lard were held up by a relatively strong export demand and rather strong domestic demand. In the early part of this period, lard commanded a higher price than any other pork item; today it is the cheapest major pork product. It is worth less than one-fourth the price of most of the lean cuts.

Bellies, which are sold primarily as bacon, are in an intermediate position. Bacon prices have not increased as much as the prices of the lean cuts over the years, but more than lard prices. There has been a rather consistent widening of the gap between prices of lean cuts and fat from the beginning of the century up to the present. Lean cuts now are worth more than twice as much as live hogs. But fat is worth less than half as much as live hogs, pound for pound.

## HOGS[4]

One of the problems in pork is the fact that price incentives have not played their important role in our free-market pricing system nearly as effectively as they have for beef and beef cattle. Beef-cattle grades were developed in the mid-twenties and were widely accepted and effectively used after World War II. Grades for live hogs and hog carcasses were developed in the late 1940's. They were officially promulgated in 1952, but their use has not been nearly as widely accepted.

### How Do Our Hogs Grade?

Because grades are not widely used in marketing hogs, it has been difficult to say where we stand in producing different grades. However, two special studies made by the USDA provide estimates of the level of and recent change in hog quality.

In 1960 and 1961 a USDA hog grading specialist spent a year traveling from plant to plant grading hog carcasses. Sixty-one pairs of visits (six months apart) were made to 56 federally inspected plants across the country. Virtually all the larger plants were included in the sample. About 45,000 barrow and gilt carcasses were graded during this period. The estimated U.S. average grade distribution for the year from September, 1960, through August, 1961, was:

33.4 per cent U.S. No. 1,
38.6 per cent U.S. No. 2,
25.9 per cent U.S. No. 3,
2.0 per cent Medium, and
0.1 per cent Cull

A similar study was conducted during the period from April, 1967, through March, 1968, to provide a later estimate of the quality of hogs produced.[5] The study covered 121 full-day hog kills in 56 federally inspected plants, representing all regions of the country and all seasons of the year. A total of 57,000 barrow and gilt carcasses were graded. The preliminary results of the 1967–68 study were as follows:

49.0 per cent U.S. No. 1,
36.0 per cent U.S. No. 2,
12.0 per cent U.S. No. 3, and
3.0 per cent Medium and Cull

---

[4] Adapted largely from Gerald Engelman, *The Economics of Marketing Meat-Type Hogs,* North Central Livestock Marketing and Production Specialists Regional Extension Conference, Austin, Minn., May 12, 1954, p. 9.

[5] Donald B. Agnew, "Farmer's Provide . . . Leaner, Meatier Pork," *The Farm Index*, USDA, July, 1968.

The study was completed before the revision in grade standards for pork carcasses became effective in April, 1968 (see Chapter 16). So both studies reflect identical grade standards. The results of the 1967–68 study show considerable improvement in hog quality from 1960–61 to 1967–68. The large increase in the proportion of U.S. No. 1 hogs and the decrease in the proportion of U.S. No. 3 hogs represent significant progress by the pork industry.

The average grade distribution for earlier years is unknown. Nevertheless, it is generally agreed there was considerable improvement in the quality of slaughter hogs between 1950 and 1960. Improvement during this period was suggested by lighter average slaughter weights on hogs and by barrow show and testing station carcass and cutout records which showed increases in the percentage of lean cuts.

## How Hogs Grade in Canada

Canada does a much better job of quality hog production than the United States. In October, 1957, the relationship of U.S. grade standards to the Canadian grade standards was studied to determine how they compared—to determine the equivalent ranges for given grades under the separate U.S. and Canadian grading systems. The Canadians have grade consist records on their hogs going back to 1930. On the basis of this comparison of U.S. and Canadian grades, it was estimated that the grade consist for Canada in terms of our grade standards would have been about as follows in 1957:

71 per cent U.S. No. 1,
26 per cent U.S. No. 2,
2 per cent U.S. No. 3, and
1 per cent Medium

Canada produced over twice the proportion of U.S. No. 1's that we produced during the 1960–61 year. The proportion of U.S. hogs grading U.S. No. 1 in 1967–68 was still well below the level in Canada ten years earlier. Canada has almost eliminated the hogs that would grade U.S. No. 3. In 1957 only 2 per cent of such hogs were marketed in Canada. In the United States, however, 26 per cent were No. 3's in 1960–61 and 12 per cent in 1967–68.

Several factors account for this difference. The Canadian government pays a premium for each A grade carcass (the Canadian A grade is roughly equivalent to the top half of U.S. No. 1). Canadian packers have also consistently paid wider differentials between grades than packers have in the United States. Furthermore, oats and barley, the principal grain concentrates fed in

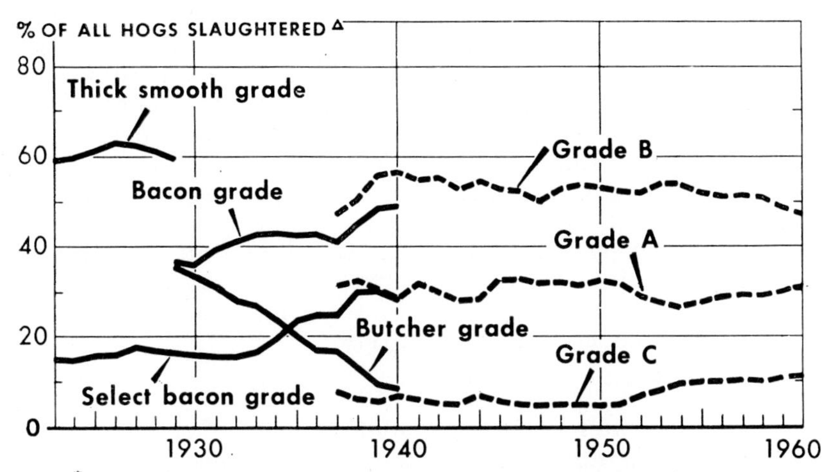


FIG. 22.7—Barrows and gilts slaughtered in Canada, by grade, 1923–60.

Canada, have a higher fiber content and a lower energy rating than corn. This difference in ration may account for a longer feeding period for the same equivalent gain, more growth of lean muscle tissue and less deposition of fat.

But another factor should not be overlooked. For more than 30 years all hogs in Canada have been graded by uniform standards, either alive or in carcass form. Canada developed and refined their live grades in the 1920's and their carcass grades during the 1930's. By 1930 all live hogs in Canada were graded. By 1940, all hogs were graded and sold on a carcass basis, the standard system since that time.

It is interesting to note in Figure 22.7 that substantially all progress in grade consist was made during the period between 1930 and 1940, the first ten years that all hogs in Canada were graded.

Canadian grade A hogs and most of the grade B hogs are equivalent to U.S. No. 1's.[6] The rest of Grade B and almost all of the grade C hogs are about the same as U.S. No. 2's. This means that by 1940, a year when we had scarcely begun to think about grading hogs or carcasses, Canada was already producing about 70 per cent of its hogs equivalent to U.S. No. 1's.

With every shipment of hogs under the Canadian system,

[6] Based on U.S. pork standards in effect prior to revisions made in March, 1968.

the producer gets an invoice showing the number of grade A, grade B, and grade C carcasses he delivered. The invoice also shows the total pounds for each grade and the price for each grade. In this way the producer has a rather complete report on his own performance so that he can appraise the progress of his own breeding, feeding, and management programs. This is one big advantage he has over his American counterpart. His marketing system speaks to him with a more accurate and a more articulate language. Every producer receives a full grade report and sees the price differentials between each grade. The Canadian marketing system carries the price incentive all the way down to the producer rather effectively.

### Indicators and Attributes of Hog Carcass Merit

Although the federal grade standards have not been widely used, their mere existence has raised criticism about their effectiveness, particularly in hog-marketing circles. This is understandable. None of us likes to have changes forced upon us by circumstances beyond our own control. The mere existence of grade standards carries an implication that changes in the operation of marketers and buyers might be desirable. So it should not surprise us that the standards have been termed "inadequate" or "inaccurate," because they do not meet the ideal objective of making a perfect sort.

Another criticism has implied that the federal grade standards are not based on "cutability"—the cutout value. They *are* based on cutability. In fact, hog carcass standards, as revised in 1968, are based heavily on the yield of major lean cuts. Some have said that federal grades encourage the so-called "meatless wonder," a hog that is reported to measure well, but yields little meat. This "meatless wonder" is a rare occurrence, hardly worth the fuss that has been made over him. But the federal grade specifications call for placing such hogs in the U.S. Utility grade. Most of the real "meatless wonders" are extremely fat hogs at the outer range of the No. 3 grade.

Most criticisms seem to arise from confusion about the concepts of *indicators* and *attributes* in grading. The *indicators* are the visible, physical factors a grader sees and evaluates in placing a given carcass in a particular grade. In hog carcass grading we have some objective factors somewhat comparable to those for the dual grading for beef. The objective factors are backfat, length, and carcass weight. Subjective factors such as the apparent muscling in the carcass are also considered. These external indicators are highly related with a continuous variable, the per cent of lean cuts in the carcass. This per cent of lean cuts then becomes a quality *attribute*. It is an important attribute to processors because lean cuts provide the most valuable cuts of the hog carcass.

The indicators are used to predict the percentage of lean cuts in the carcass. The scale of the indicators is a continuous variable and can be segmented, but this does not result in a segmented scale of the quality attribute, the percentage of lean cuts. Within each grade there is a distribution which approaches what we call the normal curve. And the curve for each grade overlaps the curve for other grades. This means that some of the hogs with indicators that would predict a grade 2 might actually cut out as though they should have been placed in grade 1. All this says is that the grade standards are not perfect. We will demonstrate, however, that they do an eminently satisfactory job. Perfection is not required in grading hogs or beef effectively, or grain or fresh vegetables for that matter.

## Value Differentials Between Grades

The differences between the values of different grades of hogs, based on the prices of wholesale cuts at Chicago in 1957, are shown in Table 22.5.

The table shows the differences in the yields of all the pork items, the lean cuts, the bellies, the fat, and the other miscellaneous items. When these cuts are all priced at a flat figure regardless of grade, the differences between grades are 80 cents per grade, per 100 pounds of carcass. The differences per 100 pounds live weight are about 50 cents.[7]

The differences in value between grades arise from the quantitative differences in the yields of the different cuts, exclusive of any differences in the grades of the cuts. In calculating the value differences between grades, it was assumed that all the cuts sold at the same price regardless of the grade. That is, it was assumed that the hams from the meaty hogs sold for the same price as the hams from the overfat kind, regardless of the excess fat they might carry.

Although consumers dislike the excess fat in their pork cuts, they have very few opportunities to pay a premium for selected leaner, meatier kinds of pork cuts. This is a case in which consumers cannot effectively demonstrate their preferences for leaner pork in the market place. They don't get an opportunity to call their price signals very well. The free-market pricing system does not operate as effectively as it would if consumers could demonstrate a prefer-

[7] The differences per 100 pounds live weight would be more like 56 cents so far as the effect of average yield (about 70 per cent) is concerned (80 cents times .70 = 56 cents), but the fatter hogs usually yield a little better than the leaner hogs, and this reduces the differences between the values of the different grades of live hogs to about 50 cents per 100 pounds live weight.

**TABLE 22.5: Carcass Cutting and Value Yields for Different Grades of Hogs at 220 Pounds Live Weight, and Wholesale Prices at Chicago, 1957***

| Wholesale Cut | Average Price† | U.S. No. 1 | | U.S. No. 2 | | U.S. No. 3 | |
|---|---|---|---|---|---|---|---|
| | | Percentage yield, carcass basis | Value | Percentage yield, carcass basis | Value | Percentage yield, carcass basis | Value |
| | *(dollars)* | *(per cent)* | *(dollars)* | *(per cent)* | *(dollars)* | *(per cent)* | *(dollars)* |
| Four lean cuts: | | | | | | | |
| Skinned hams, 12–14 lbs. | 42.83 | 19.4 | 8.31 | 18.2 | 7.79 | 17.0 | 7.28 |
| Loins, 10–12 lbs. | 43.39 | 14.7 | 6.38 | 13.9 | 6.03 | 13.1 | 5.68 |
| Picnics, 6–8 lbs. | 24.26 | 9.9 | 2.40 | 9.4 | 2.28 | 8.9 | 2.16 |
| Boston butts | 34.03 | 8.0 | 2.72 | 7.5 | 2.55 | 7.0 | 2.38 |
| Subtotal, four lean cuts | | 52.0 | | 49.0 | | 46.0 | |
| Bellies, square cut, 10–12 lbs. | 34.07 | 15.0 | 5.11 | 15.6 | 5.32 | 16.2 | 5.52 |
| Pork trim, 50 per cent lean | 21.09 | 5.0 | 1.06 | 4.5 | .95 | 4.0 | .84 |
| Jowl butts | 14.36 | 3.5 | .50 | 3.8 | .54 | 4.1 | .58 |
| Spareribs—3 lbs. down | 38.07 | 2.5 | .95 | 2.3 | .87 | 2.1 | .79 |
| Neck bones | 9.74 | 2.0 | .19 | 1.8 | .17 | 1.6 | .15 |
| Feet | 2.62 | 3.1 | .08 | 2.8 | .07 | 2.5 | .06 |
| Tails | 11.75 | 0.2 | .02 | .2 | .02 | .2 | .02 |
| Fat for lard | 10.05 | 16.7 | 1.68 | 20.0 | 2.01 | 23.3 | 2.34 |
| Value per 100 pounds carcass weight | | | 29.40 | | 28.60 | | 27.80 |
| Dressing percentage | | 67.5 | | 68.0 | | 68.5 | |
| Value per 100 pounds live weight | | | 19.84 | | 19.44 | | 19.04 |

Source: G. Engelman and R. Gaarder, *Marketing Meat-Type Hogs*, USDA, Marketing Res. Rept. 227, 1958, p. 13.

* Carcass yields of 220-pound hogs with dressing percentages of 67.5, 68.0, and 68.5 per cent, respectively, and average backfat thickness of 1.4, 1.7, and 2.0 inches, respectively. Cutting yields are developed from research data reported in: Gerald Engelman, A. A. Dowell, E. F. Ferrin, and P. A. Anderson, *Marketing Slaughter Hogs by Carcass Weight and Grade,* Univ. of Minn. Agr. Exp. Sta. Tech. Bul. 187, Apr., 1950.

† Fresh carlot wholesale prices at Chicago from the *National Provisioner,* Dec., 1956–Nov., 1957. Price of fat for lard—80 per cent of price for prime steam lard, loose. (Average lard yield of fat cuts is approximately 80 per cent.)

ence in terms of price. What could happen if this price difference could be carried all the way back to the farmer?

Suppose we could get an extra nickel a pound for just the hams and loins from the No. 1 carcasses over the hams and loins from No. 2 carcasses. What would a nickel a pound do? A nickel a pound on hams and loins would boost the value difference per 100 pounds between grades from $1.00 to $2.50 on carcasses, from 50 cents to $1.25 on live hogs. What if we could also get an extra nickel a pound for the picnics, butts, and bellies from No. 1 carcasses? Then the value difference between grades would be increased to $4.00 on the carcass and $2.00 on the live hog.[8]

This hypothetical figure of a nickel a pound is probably conservative. In a research project at the University of Illinois in 1954, loins from meat-type hogs were placed in packages in a tray alongside regular "mine run" chops. When they were priced at 10 cents a pound premium, they all sold before any appreciable quantities of the regular pork chops moved. It was not until the premium was increased to 18 cents that the regular chops sold in about equal quantities with the chops from the meat-type hogs.[9]

## Grading Improves Pricing Accuracy

One of the important jobs expected of grade standards is the more accurate pricing of different lots of hogs according to their value to the packer. Research conducted by the University of Minnesota some years ago throws some light on the relative pricing accuracy of alternative methods of buying hogs.[10]

In this research some 32 separate lots of hogs were priced in different ways. Carcasses were weighed and graded. Each carcass was cut into the basic wholesale cuts to determine the value of the carcass and the value of the live hog from which it originated. This way it was possible to determine the actual value of each lot of hogs and to compare this actual value with the price that would have been paid for the lot under different alternative pricing methods. To measure the pricing accuracy of these several alternative methods, we have a statistical measure that we call the variance of pricing errors. To use more familiar words, we call this variance the "variation of pricing errors" in Table 22.6.

[8] Gerald Engelman, *The Economics of Marketing Meat-Type Hogs*, North Central Livestock Marketing and Production Specialists Regional Extension Conference, Austin, Minn., May 12, 1954, p. 9.

[9] M. B. Kirtley, "Consumer Acceptance of Lean Pork Chops," *Illinois Farm Economics Journal*, No. 233 (June, 1955), pp. 1580–82.

[10] Gerald Engelman, Austin A. Dowell, and Robert E. Olson, *Relative Accuracy of Pricing Butcher Hogs on Foot and by Carcass Weight and Grade*, Univ. of Minn. Agr. Exp. Sta. Tech. Bul. 208, June, 1953.

**TABLE 22.6: Pricing Methods for Four Alternative Methods of Pricing Hogs**

| Error | Pricing Method | | | |
|---|---|---|---|---|
| | Live weight | | | |
| | Flat price within weight groups | Live grading: 80 per cent accuracy | Live grading: 100 per cent accuracy | Carcass weight and grade |
| Variation of pricing errors ........ | .223 | .117 | .106 | .040 |
| Percentage of weight group pricing errors* ........................ | 100 | 52 | 47 | 18 |
| Pricing errors as compared with carcass weight and grade† ......... | 5.5 | 2.9 | 2.6 | 1.0 |

Source: Gerald Engelman, Austin A. Dowell, and Robert E. Olson, *Relative Accuracy of Pricing Butcher Hogs on Foot and by Carcass Weight and Grade,* Univ. of Minn. Agr. Exp. Sta. Bul. 208, June, 1953, p. 25.

* .233 = 100 per cent.

† .040 = 1.0.

Table 22.6 indicates that the pricing errors on a live-weight flat-price method were 5½ times the pricing errors under the carcass weight and grade method. With perfect accuracy of live grading the pricing errors would be about 2½ times the pricing errors under the carcass system. With 80 per cent accuracy of live grading, about what we expect in commercial practice, the live grade method had pricing errors almost 3 times those of the carcass method.

Figure 22.8 from this research compares the pricing accuracies of the flat-price weight-group system and the carcass system. Each dot represents the price of one lot of hogs. The length of the vertical line connecting the dot to the diagonal represents the pricing error—the difference between price and cutout value. With perfect pricing all the dots would lie on the diagonal line. The contrast is striking. With live-weight pricing, the dots arrange themselves on three horizontal lines—one for each of three weight groups. Under the carcass system the dots (or prices) arrange themselves much closer to the diagonal line that represents actual cutout value.

There are several points we can make on the basis of the table and the figure:

1. Carcass grading is not completely accurate. It does not eliminate all of the pricing errors present in the live-weight flat-price method of buying hogs. Pricing errors for this system still show up on Figure 22.8. But it does substantially improve the pricing accuracy. It does a most effective job of carrying the price incentive all the way to the producer.

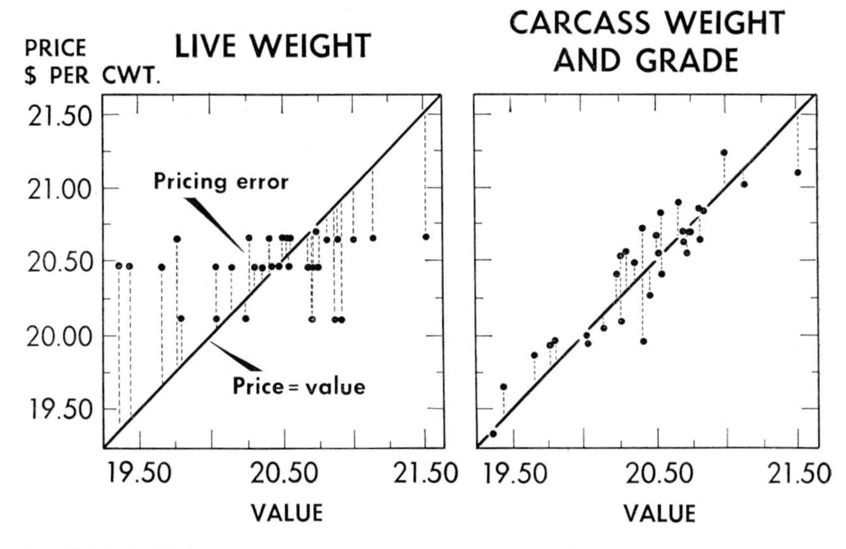


FIG. 22.8—Pricing hogs according to value by live weight and by carcass weight and grade.

2. Buying by live grade also improved pricing accuracy substantially over the live-weight flat-price method of buying hogs. It removed about half of the pricing errors inherent in the live-weight pricing system.
3. There are two reasons why the carcass method is a more accurate system of pricing hogs. The first is because the carcass is one step closer to the hams, pork chops, and pork roasts that ultimately determine the value of the hog. The second reason is because variations in yield no longer affect value. From the producer's vantage point this means that the amount of shrink, or the amount of fill, does not count under the carcass method. It has no effect on final returns. It is completely circumvented. The farmer is only paid for the pounds of meat and meat products he delivers to the packer.

We can get some idea of the relative importance of the two reasons given in (3) by again looking at Table 22.6. As we move from 80 per cent grading accuracy to 100 per cent grading accuracy we do improve the accuracy of pricing somewhat. But the big improvement between the live grading and the carcass method comes because we have eliminated the yield variable (the shrink and fill factors) as a value-determining element.

### CARCASS METHOD

To be sure, there are some operational problems associated with the carcass method. Some of the larger packers in the Midwest have automated this operation, however. As each carcass is weighed and graded, the weight, grade, and tattoo number are punched on a card which is fed into a computing machine. The computer "knows" the seller of the hogs to whom this tattoo number was assigned. It also "knows" the prices which were agreed to for the various weights and grades of carcasses before the seller relinquished possession of his hogs. The machine sorts out all the cards from one owner and computes the total value of the shipment. It then prints an invoice automatically, showing the farmer the number of grade 1, grade 2, and grade 3 carcasses he delivered and the price he received for each grade, the total value of each category, and the total value of the shipment.

Farmers taking advantage of this method of selling receive a report almost identical to that received by the farmers in Canada. This system is more economical than live grading. The machine can sort cards a lot easier than buyers can sort hogs, nor are cards as independent minded as hogs.

Another problem of the carcass method in this country is the fact that the farmer must have absolute confidence in the integrity of the packer with whom he is dealing. In Canada this problem is circumvented because the grading staff also has regulatory responsibilities. The grading staff checks the accuracy of the scales and maintains general supervision over the disbursement of the returns to the producer, so that the producers have complete confidence in their system. In this country such regulatory activities are delegated to the Packers and Stockyard Division.

### CUTABILITY METHOD

Another method of buying hogs on the basis of quality or merit has been developed during the last several years. It has been called the per cent lean cut system, the merit buying system, and more recently, the cutability system. Rather than a carcass grade concept, the system uses the basic value-determining variable—the percentage of live weight that is made up of the four lean cuts. A 33 hog is one estimated to yield 33 per cent of its live weight in lean cuts, a 35 hog is expected to yield 35 per cent, etc. The greater the estimated lean cuts, the higher the price that can be paid for the hogs. In this system a 2 per cent range of lean cuts is about equivalent to the range within one carcass or live-hog federal grade.

For those buyers who use the per cent lean cut system, it

represents a substantial improvement over the flat-price live-weight system. Although no comparable research data are available to compare pricing accuracy, it appears reasonable to believe that this system is roughly comparable with the live-grade system of pricing.

However, the system has some limitations for use as a national or across-the-board system of buying. The language by which the marketing system tells the farmer what kind of hogs he is selling becomes a bit unprecise. Because packers differ in the cutting and trimming of pork cuts, a given hog might turn out to be a 34 at one plant while the same hog would have a cut-out to a 35 at another. Even different plants within the same firm experience this same problem.

Another limitation stems from the reputed simplifying advantage of the system. It combines the two important value determinants, (1) the carcass characteristics and (2) the dressing percentage of carcass yield, into one grade. A load of hogs with carcasses cutting out 50 per cent lean cuts and dressing out 66 per cent would be 33's (50 $\times$ 66 per cent) on the live-weight basis. However, a load of hogs with a 47 per cent carcass cutout in four lean cuts, but dressing out 70.2 per cent carcass weight, would also be 33's on the live basis. Both lots of hogs gave the producer the same grade and price signal under this buying system; and in each case they may have been priced accurately. Yet these two loads represent the product of entirely different breeding, different feeding, or a different management program.

In another situation, hogs with carcasses yielding 50 per cent lean cuts might be sold at one market with a 66 per cent carcass yield or dressing percentage and be called 33's. At another market the same hogs might carry less fill (or more shrink) to dress 70 per cent. Here they would be 35's—the same hogs, but quite a different signal to the producer as to what he should do about his breeding program.

A number of carcass and cutout contests at barrow shows use cutout value on the live-weight basis to determine the prize winner. But they meet this yield problem head-on. They weigh the contents of the alimentary tract on the killing floor and adjust or standardize the carcass yield for each entry to equalize the differences in fill between different hogs. This is not practicable in a commercial marketing situation. Differences in the carcass yield variable allow some outside noise to distort the price and grade signals that we want the pricing and marketing system to relay to the hog producer. The price and grade signals are clearer and more distinct when they are more positively geared to carcass characteristics—even when hogs are sold on a live-weight basis.

### Grading To Improve Hog Quality

We have made a good start in improving hog quality. The carcass evaluation and cutout results at the various barrow shows and at the swine evaluation stations over the country have made a substantial contribution. However, much more progress is needed. The Canadian experience indicates that much more progress is possible.

Relatively few U.S. hog producers have an opportunity to know how many of grade No. 1, No. 2, and No. 3 hogs they market or to be aware of the price differentials between these grades. If most of our American hog farmers received such reports on the hogs they marketed, we probably could make much faster progress in the United States than Canada made after they adopted their grading system. This is because most of our swine producers raise hogs as a major enterprise, while in Canada most of the hogs are produced as a sideline enterprise.

If farmers got a complete report on the hogs they sold, those farmers having a high proportion of No. 2 and No. 3 hogs would ask themselves how they could improve their consist. Instead of paying a uniform $60 price for boars, commercial producers would be more willing to pay a substantial premium for herd sires having testing-station records indicating that they carry superior genes. Purebred breeders could expect to receive a much greater premium for breeding stock carrying these superior genes for meatier carcass characteristics. Purebred breeders have a big stake in the existence of informed commercial producers, aware and concerned about the proportions of the No. 1's, No. 2's, and No. 3's they bring to the market place.

## BEEF CATTLE[11]

The use of federal grades for beef has seriously handicapped the large national packers in their efforts to develop nationally recognized brand names for their fresh beef product. Federal grades are widely recognized over the entire country. Beef sold under a packer brand is usually sold at a discount below the corresponding federal grades these packer brands attempt to emulate. Federal grade standards have contributed to the sharp reduction in nonslaughtering packer-owned branch houses operated by the large brand-name packers. Since World War II the portion of the total beef supply handled by national packers has declined. Medium volume and specialized independent packers

[11] Adapted from Gerald Engelman, *Issues and Problems in Beef Grading*, USDA, 1961.

have tended to increase their relative importance in the slaughtering of beef.

Whether these effects appear to be "good" or "bad" to any individual in the industry depends upon the position he occupies. Nevertheless, these structural adjustments have been associated with substantial improvements in operational and pricing efficiency in the marketing, processing, and distributing system.

### Arguments Against Federal Beef Grading

Because grading has been a matter of such intense controversy, it is worthwhile to examine some of the elements—some of the arguments that have been raised against the official grading of beef.

Examination of these arguments is not intended to discredit the segments of the meat industry that have advanced them. But it is perfectly proper for some of the rest of us to examine these arguments and appraise them in light of the public interest.

1. *Federal meat grading is said to be an improper government intervention or encroachment on the prerogatives of business. Some say it interferes with free enterprise, or that it is another form of government socialism.*

For years the government has maintained standards of length, weight, and measure. A pound includes 16 ounces all over the country—not 15 ounces in the state of Washington and 17 ounces in New England. Nor is it 14 ounces for packer A and 15 ounces for packer B. These standards add to confidence in the language of trading.

The federal grading system is not forced on anybody. The only reason any beef carcass is graded is because someone in the marketing and distribution system wants to have it graded. The use of the service is strictly voluntary. It is not even financed by tax revenue. Those using the service must pay for it. But because it is a nationally recognized system, it creates confidence in the trade. It does contribute to the effectiveness with which the decentralized, free-market, free-pricing system operates within a free-enterprise economy.

2. *Beef grading is said to be a form of price control because the grader actually prices the product when he puts the grade stamp on it.*

It would be more nearly proper to say that the grader defines the product. He determines which carcasses are Choice, which carcasses are Good, and which are Standard. He applies the limits within which each of these kinds of beef is classified. He does not determine the supply of these grades of beef, nor does he determine the demand for them.

Price differentials between grades change from time to time as the supplies of various grades change in relation to demand for them. There are times when Prime beef sells for less than Choice—when the *supply* of Prime beef is momentarily much larger than the rather thin or narrow, although highly selective, *demand* for Prime beef among hotel and restaurant operators. This situation could not prevail for a very long period of time, however, because it costs more to bring cattle up to the Prime grade.

Meat grading does not determine values. It places the carcasses within relatively broad categories of quality and helps the formation of relative prices and values based on the supply and demand conditions for these various categories of beef.

3. *It is sometimes argued that private packer brands can be more easily adjusted and more carefully attuned to the needs of the market place.*

This is technically possible. Private packer brands *could* be used to meet the particular specifications of certain buyers within the federal grading system. The evidence of history, however, indicates that they have not been used essentially for that purpose. Private packer brands are sold in competition with government grades, usually at a discount. If their use were applied within the federal grading system to account for the special needs of certain types of demands, the packer brands would be expected to sell at a premium above the corresponding federal grades.

An important problem associated with the use of private grades concerns the language for price quotations in trading. Each system of private grades is a separate language. It may be possible for some traders to understand two different grading systems and their relation to each other very well. It becomes more difficult when there are seven or eight, or even ten or a dozen, different grading systems or different languages for price quotations. Remember the Tower of Babel. It never got up to Heaven. Too many languages killed the whole project.

Would the public interest be best served if federal grading were removed and numerous private brand and grading systems substituted for it? The test for the public interest is the effect on the level of knowledge. Would traders generally know more, or less, about the beef on which they are negotiating prices? Would the levels of information between buyer and seller be more nearly equalized, or less so?

That federal grading enlarges the area of informed, intelligent decision making in the price-making process seems fairly clear. Withdrawing federal grades would enlarge the area of ignorance. Profits gained from the ignorance of others do not get passed back to the farmer. Markets would inevitably be narrowed, competition would be less effective, and market news would be made virtually ineffective.

4. *Some have argued that although they accept the functions of the federal government in setting up the grade standards, the actual application of these standards is a job for employees of the packing firm where meat is slaughtered.*

It is understandable that some packers resent having an outsider—in this case a civil service federal employee—apply the grade on company-owned beef.

The grader's position is something like that of an umpire. The grader interprets the grade specifications, the umpire interprets the rules—and some of the calls are very close. Nevertheless, it seems to be the experience of professional baseball that having umpires hired by the league is generally more satisfactory than using regular employees of the home team. The federal grader has no financial interest in the meat he is called on to grade. For the same reason, meat inspectors are either state or federally employed. And those individuals charged with enforcement of accurate weights and measures are employees of some governmental agency.

### Yield Grading

The quality of lean meat—that predicts or estimates the expected eating satisfaction—is not the only important variable factor affecting value in beef carcasses. The yield of lean meat—the proportion of the carcass weight which the retailer can sell as trimmed and retail cuts at the meat counter—is another major factor affecting the value of beef carcasses. This yield factor is called "cutability."

Beef standards historically have tried to measure both factors within the same grade; therefore a grade sometimes represents a compromise. A carcass showing evidence of Prime quality and Good grade conformation (the only factor in the conventional system which relates to the cutting yield) might be graded Choice. This continues to be the predominant grading procedure in this country. However, it is not fully satisfactory for several reasons.

Within the same grade, carcasses can vary as much as $150 in retail value because of differences in the yield of high-value retail cuts. A $50 difference is not at all unusual. When grades represent a compromise, they cannot be as accurate indicators either of eating satisfaction or of cutability as they might be if these factors were separated in the grading process.

As a result of these problems, alternate systems have been developed. USDA researchers learned in studies of a large number of beef carcasses that differences in yield or cutability can be predicted quite accurately by using four physical indicators of cutability only:

1. Thickness of fat over the rib eye.
2. Size of rib eye muscle.
3. Amount of kidney and pelvic fat.
4. Carcass weight.

These studies indicated that it would be possible to set up a "dual" grading system, providing two separate identifications affecting value for every carcass—a quality grade and a yield or cutability grade. A dual grading system was subsequently offered to packers on an optional basis for a one-year trial period beginning July 1, 1962. Conventional grading services were also continued. Existing grade names—Prime, Choice, Good, etc.—were used for the quality grade. Cutability grades were indicated by a numerical scale, No. 1 representing the highest yield and No. 10 the lowest. Under this system, price differentials of up to $4 per hundredweight developed in some areas to reflect differences in yield.

Dual grading was not widely used in the trial period, but there was sufficient interest in it to encourage further study and consideration of some dual system for grading beef. This resulted in the addition of "yield" grading to the federal grading system on a continuing basis beginning in June, 1965. Yield grading is performed in conjunction with conventional grading upon request from the packer. Quality is designated by the grade names Prime, Choice, Good, Standard, etc., while cutability or yield is indicated by numbers ranging from 1 to 5. No. 1 represents the highest yield and No. 5 the lowest.

The two grades are determined separately and independently of each other. This enables grade standards to sort out beef carcasses and live animals much more accurately and precisely according to the important value-determining attributes—quality or eating satisfaction and cutting yield or cutability—at the same time. Under yield grading the overlap should be less than for the conventional grading system.

Under yield grading retailers can order the yield and quality grades they want. If carcasses of a particular yield grade are not available they can order a substitute lower yield grade, within the same quality designation, at a proper price differential reflecting the actual cutting differences between the two yield grades.

Yield grading provides a much more accurate language for price quotations and for conducting trading activities. It helps the market place provide more effective price incentives for ranchers and feeders to produce beef animals yielding a higher proportion of the lean meat that consumers want, at the several different levels of beef quality they find acceptable. Yield grading represents the greatest improvement in beef grade standards that has ever been implemented during the 35-year history of beef grading.

### Buying Beef Cattle by Carcass Weight and Grade

Beef cattle can be sold by carcass weight and grade, with less change in existing marketing methods than in the case of hogs. A well-established system of government beef carcass grading has been in effect in the United States for many years for substantial percentages of the total beef cattle slaughtered. All that is necessary is to hitch the basis of settlement on to this already established system of government carcass grading.

A start has been made in the direction of setting up objective specifications for beef-carcass grades. Research has indicated that carcass weight and length, and the thickness of the backfat over the eye *(longissimus dorsi)* muscle (called "eyefat" thickness) at points *L*, *M*, and *N* in Figure 22.9 show a high

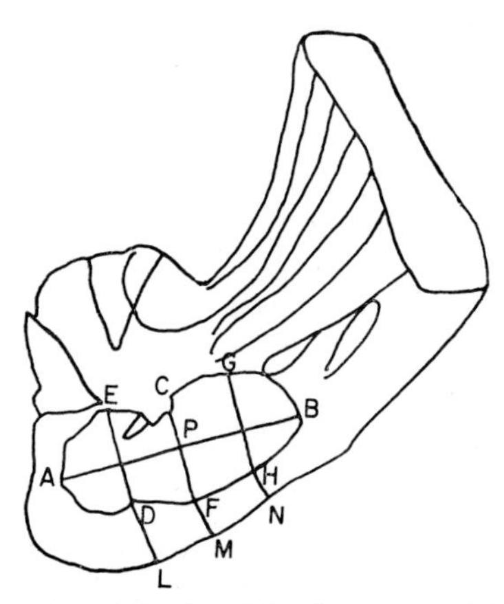


FIG. 22.9—Face of twelfth rib of beef carcass (Prime grade), illustrating measurements taken.

correlation with carcass grade. A tentative set of objective beef carcass grade specifications, based on these measurements, for 500–549-pound carcasses, is shown in Table 22.7.

A number of packers are buying some of their beef cattle by carcass weight and grade. Further research and extension work to establish objective beef-carcass grade specifications is helping the movement to spread.

In 1961, in the United States 4.5 per cent of the cattle slaughtered were purchased by the packers on the carcass grade and weight basis. By 1968, the percentage had risen to 17.2. The data for beef cattle and the other kinds of livestock from 1961 to 1966 are given in Table 22.8.

Several benefits would follow if the basis of sale in the United States were shifted completely from the live animal to the carcass. This step would come close to solving both the market reporting problem and the grading problem. It would thus greatly improve the conditions under which farmers in decentralized markets could sell their livestock themselves. At present, packers either have to quote prices per 100 pounds live weight in fairly wide ranges (to cover the fairly wide range of values that exist among livestock of equal live weight), or pay too nearly a flat price for all animals of a given weight. Both of these alternatives are bad. Shifting to the carcass weight and grade basis would reduce the range of values within a given carcass weight and grade and would permit prices to be quoted in much narrower ranges, or in single figures for each carcass

**TABLE 22.7: Tentative Objective Carcass Grade Specifications for Slaughter Steers, Carcass Weights, 500–549 Pounds**

| | Carcass Grades | | | | |
|---|---|---|---|---|---|
| | Prime | Choice | Good | Commercial | Utility |
| Length of Carcass | Eyefat thickness at margin | Eyefat thickness at margin | Eyefat thickness at margin | Eyefat thickness at margin | Eyefat thickness at margin |
| *(mm.)* | *(mm.)* | *(mm.)* | *(mm.)* | *(mm.)* | *(mm.)* |
| Less than 1800 | 44 | 20 | 0 | ... | ... |
| 1800–1849 | 47 | 23 | 0 | ... | ... |
| 1850–1899 | 53 | 29 | 5 | 0 | ... |
| 1900–1949 | 59 | 35 | 11 | 0 | ... |
| 1950–1999 | 65 | 41 | 17 | 0 | ... |
| 2000–2049 | 71 | 47 | 23 | 0 | ... |
| 2050–2099 | 77 | 53 | 29 | 5 | 0 |
| 2100–2150 | 83 | 59 | 35 | 11 | 0 |
| More than 2150 | 89 | 65 | 41 | 17 | 0 |

Source: E. S. Clifton and Geoffrey Shepherd, *Objective Grade Specifications for Slaughter Steer Carcasses,* Iowa State Univ. Agr. Exp. Sta. Res. Bul. 402, Nov., 1953, p. 552.

**TABLE 22.8: Livestock Purchased on Carcass Grade and Weight Basis With Comparisons, 1961–68**

| Type of Packer and Year | Cattle | | Calves | | Hogs | | Sheep and Lambs | |
|---|---|---|---|---|---|---|---|---|
| | 1,000 head | % of commercial slaughter | 1,000 head | % of commercial slaughter | 1,000 head | % of commercial slaughter | 1,000 head | % of commercial slaughter |
| *1961* | | | | | | | | |
| 10 Major packers .... | 587 | 2.3 | 52 | 0.7 | 1,673 | 2.2 | 745 | 4.3 |
| Other packers ....... | 558 | 2.2 | 91 | 1.2 | 117 | 0.1 | 253 | 1.5 |
| Total ............... | 1,145 | 4.5 | 143 | 1.9 | 1,790 | 2.3 | 998 | 5.8 |
| *1963* | | | | | | | | |
| 10 Major packers .... | 667 | 2.4 | 94 | 1.4 | 1,529 | 1.8 | 590 | 3.7 |
| Other packers ....... | 1,254 | 4.6 | 49 | 0.7 | 538 | 0.7 | 190 | 1.3 |
| Total (295 firms) .... | 1,921 | 7.0 | 143 | 2.1 | 2,067 | 2.5 | 789 | 5.0 |
| *1965* | | | | | | | | |
| 10 Major packers .... | 1,240 | 3.8 | 186 | 2.5 | 1,453 | 2.0 | 379 | 2.9 |
| Other packers ....... | 2,143 | 6.6 | 128 | 1.7 | 489 | 0.6 | 277 | 2.1 |
| Total (339 firms) ..... | 3,383 | 10.4 | 314 | 4.2 | 1,942 | 2.6 | 656 | 5.0 |
| *1967* | | | | | | | | |
| 10 Major packers .... | 1,680 | 5.0 | 96 | 1.6 | 1,332 | 1.6 | 571 | 4.5 |
| Other packers ........ | 2,705 | 8.0 | 82 | 1.4 | 1,164 | 1.4 | 288 | 2.3 |
| Total (firms) ........ | 4,385 | 13.0 | 178 | 3.0 | 2,496 | 3.0 | 859 | 6.8 |
| *1968* | | | | | | | | |
| 10 Major packers .... | 2,057 | 5.9 | 76 | 1.4 | 2,159 | 2.5 | 679 | 5.7 |
| Other packers ....... | 3,328 | 9.5 | 105 | 1.9 | 904 | 1.1 | 322 | 2.7 |
| Total ............... | 5,385 | 15.4 | 181 | 3.3 | 3,063 | 3.6 | 1,001 | 8.4 |

Source: Summarized from annual reports of packers filed with the Packers and Stockyards Administration, USDA.

Note: Data includes livestock, where the amount of settlement was determined after slaughter on basis of carcass grade, carcass weight, or carcass grade and weight.

weight and grade as in the case of hogs in Canada. Farmers then could compare bids by carcass weight and grade at different markets far more accurately than they can on the present live-weight basis and could be free of any need to dicker with the buyer about the grade. The government grader would settle the grade for both parties. A new step forward thus would be taken in livestock marketing efficiency.

# 23

# LIVESTOCK AND MEAT: SUPPLY AND COSTS

BY AND LARGE, livestock is produced where the feed is. In most cases it is cheaper to feed livestock near where the feed is grown, and then ship the livestock or meat to the consumer, than it is to ship the feed long distances to the livestock.

Hogs, for example, are heavy grain-consuming animals. Accordingly, they are produced mostly in the eastern half of the United States—east of the 100th meridian—in the area that is best suited to feed crop production. This is shown in Figure 23.1. The figure also shows that within the eastern half of the United States, hog production is heavily concentrated in the Corn Belt, where the supplies of feed are the greatest.

Beef cattle and sheep are primarily range and hay-consuming animals. Their production, therefore, is spread more evenly over the United States than is hog production, as shown in Figures 23.2 and 23.3.

## RELATION BETWEEN PRODUCTION AND CONSUMPTION AREAS

If meat consumption per capita were uniform over the United States, the meat-consuming areas would be shown accurately by the human population data. Actually, however, there are some geographical differences in the per capita consumption of meat. Results of a household food consumption survey in 1965 indicated per capita consumption of beef in the western states averages about 13 per cent greater than in the rest of the United States (Table 23.1). Pork consumption in the same region is below the U.S. average. The reverse is true in the South. Beef consumption is lower there than in other parts of the country, while pork consumption averages higher.

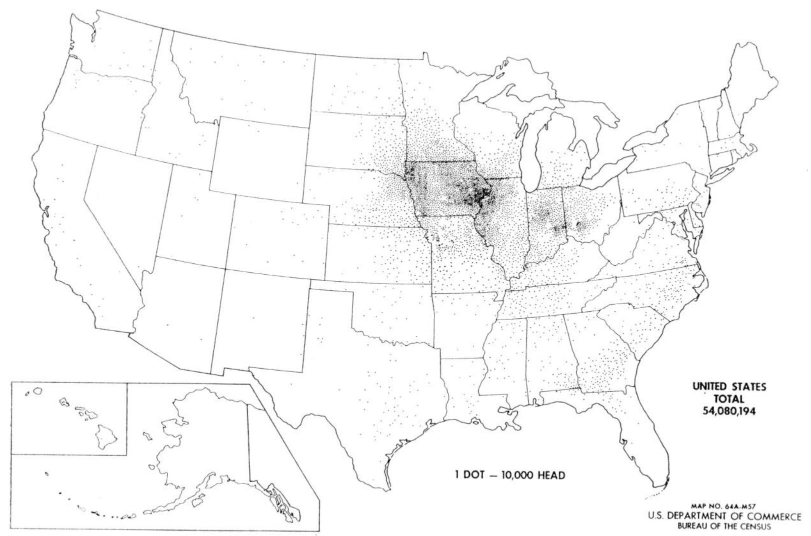


FIG. 23.1—Number of hogs and pigs on farms, 1964.

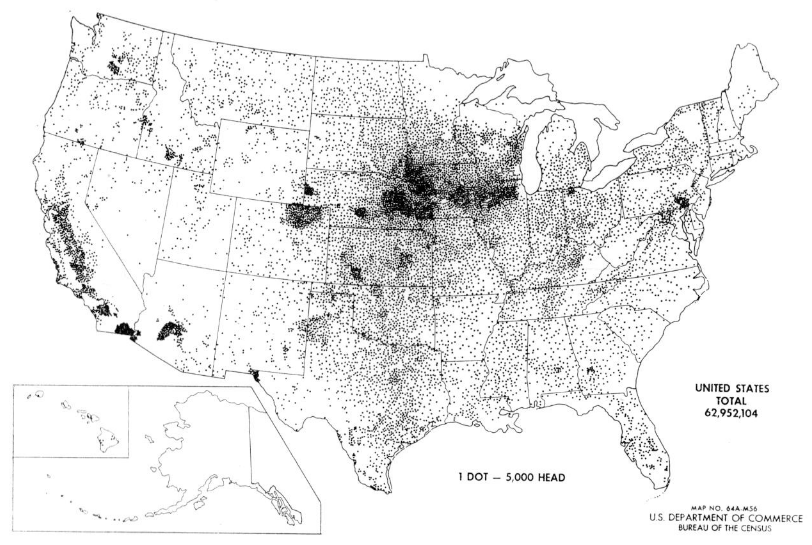


FIG. 23.2—Number of cattle and calves sold alive, 1964.

**TABLE 23.1: Per Capita Meat Consumption by Regions, United States, All Households, Spring, 1965**

| | Quantity Used at Home Per Week | | | |
|---|---|---|---|---|
| | All meat | Beef | Pork | Chicken |
| | *(lbs.)* | *(lbs.)* | *(lbs.)* | *(lbs.)* |
| Northeast ........ | 3.34 | 1.63 | .98 | .80 |
| North Central .... | 3.62 | 1.81 | 1.17 | .73 |
| South ........... | 3.11 | 1.43 | 1.18 | .87 |
| West ............ | 3.43 | 1.86 | .96 | .76 |
| United States .... | 3.35 | 1.65 | 1.10 | .80 |

Source: Based on data published in *Food Consumption of Households in the United States, Spring, 1965,* USDA, ARS-62-16, Aug., 1967, p. 14.

Human population is heavily concentrated east of the Mississippi River and west of the Rocky Mountains in the Pacific states, where population has been increasing rapidly. Both of these areas consume more beef than they produce. They pull beef cattle and beef east and west from the heavy production areas in the center of the United States shown in Figure 23.2.

The "watershed" or "continental divide" between eastward and westward shipments of beef cattle has been moving east as human population has increased in the Pacific states. Figure 23.4 shows the approximate "lines of balance" between eastward and westward shipment of beef cattle from 1925 to 1955. These lines are based on the calculated production and requirements of beef cattle by states, together with information on interstate

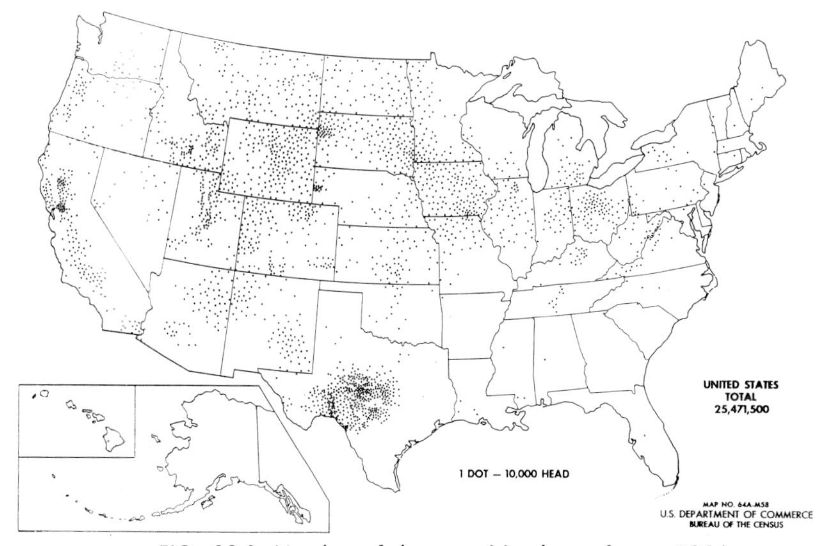


FIG. 23.3—Number of sheep and lambs on farms, 1964.

shipments. Shipments of livestock at various times cross these lines from considerable distances in both directions. The dividing line has moved farther east in recent years, as human population in the West has continued to increase faster than beef cattle production.

A similar shift to the east has been taking place in the dividing line between eastern and western shipments for sheep, although the lines lie farther west than the lines for beef cattle. The lines for hogs lie farther east than the lines for beef cattle. Their location is shown in the other parts of Figure 23.4.

## VARIED LIVESTOCK MARKETS

Let us follow the livestock and meat marketing process from producer to consumer, studying the costs involved and the possibilities of reducing those costs at each step on the way.

The markets for livestock are more varied than the markets for grain. Most grain either moves short distances by truck direct from farm to farm or is loaded into local elevators for shipment by rail or truck to mills that are usually located some distance away. But livestock is sold through half a dozen different kinds of markets, and sometimes through two or three of them in series. These different kinds of markets have their own characteristics; they require separate discussion for each.

The most important kinds of livestock markets are (1) terminal public markets, (2) local or country markets, and (3) auction markets. The percentages of livestock purchased by

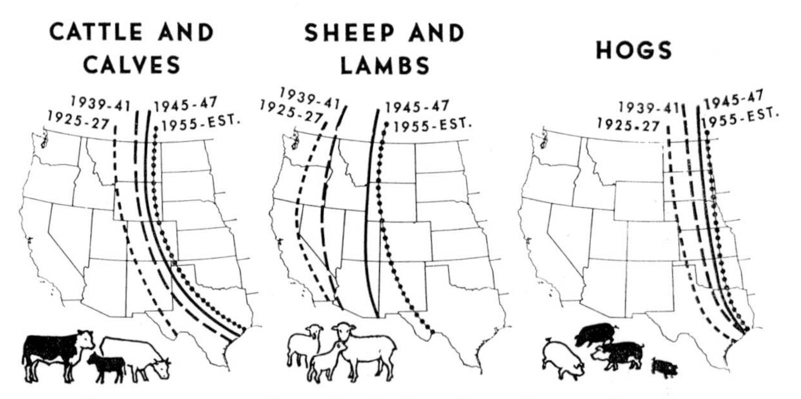


FIG. 23.4—Lines between eastward and westward shipment of cattle and calves, sheep and lambs, and hogs.

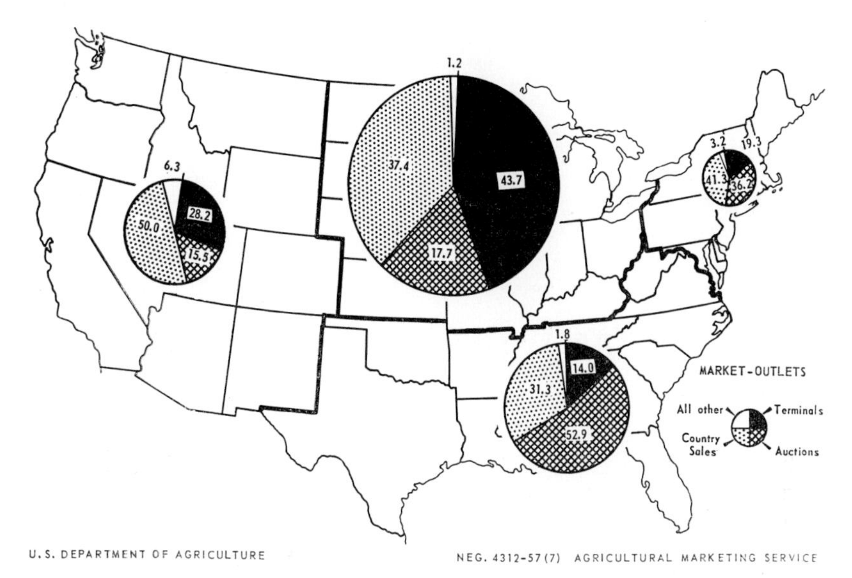


FIG. 23.5—Livestock sold by farmers through different market outlets, by geographic regions, 1955. Measurement in terms of marketing equivalents, equal to 1 head of cattle, 3 calves, 4 hogs, or 10 sheep.

packers at these three different kinds of markets in 1968 are given in Table 23.2. The percentages by regions in 1955 are given in Figure 23.5.

### Terminal Public Markets[1]

Terminal public markets (also referred to as terminal markets, central markets, public stockyards, and public markets) are livestock trading centers having complete facilities for receiving, caring for, handling, and selling livestock on a "private treaty basis." Various numbers of commission firms, depending on size of market, sell livestock at these markets. All buyers and sellers of livestock are free to use these facilities.

Through World War I the majority of slaughter livestock in the United States was sold through terminal public markets directly by farmers or by local buyers shipping to them. Since then, the importance of these markets has declined in relation to other outlets. The decline was illustrated earlier in Figure 7.1, which shows the changing percentages of animals that were bought at public markets from 1923 to 1951 and slaughtered in federally inspected plants. In 1923 federally

[1] The next two sections are adapted from V. B. Phillips and G. Engelman, *Market Outlets for Livestock Producers*, USDA, Marketing Res. Rept. 216, Mar., 1958, pp. 5–10, and from *Agricultural Markets in Change*, USDA, AER-95, 1966, pp. 261–92.

**TABLE 23.2: Packer Purchases of Livestock, by Type of Market Outlet, and Type of Packer, 1968**

| Type of Packer and Market Outlet | Cattle | | Calves | | Hogs | | Sheep | |
|---|---|---|---|---|---|---|---|---|
| | 1,000 Head | Per cent | 1,000 Head | Per cent | 1,000 Head | Per cent | 1,000 Head | Per cent |
| *Ten major packers* (10) | | | | | | | | |
| Direct, country dealers, etc. | 6,577 | 65.1 | 536 | 38.5 | 29,744 | 73.2 | 4,820 | 73.1 |
| Terminal markets ........ | 2,435 | 24.1 | 268 | 19.2 | 7,481 | 18.4 | 1,192 | 18.1 |
| Auction markets ......... | 1,094 | 10.8 | 589 | 42.3 | 3,426 | 8.4 | 583 | 8.8 |
| Total ................. | 10,106 | 100.0 | 1,393 | 100.0 | 40,651 | 100.0 | 6,595 | 100.0 |
| *Food chains* (5) | | | | | | | | |
| Direct, country dealers, etc. | 541 | 72.7 | 159 | 74.0 | 126 | 96.9 | 419 | 84.7 |
| Terminal markets ........ | 156 | 21.0 | 5 | 2.3 | 1 | 0.8 | 71 | 14.3 |
| Auction markets ......... | 47 | 6.3 | 51 | 23.7 | 3 | 2.3 | 5 | 1.0 |
| Total ................. | 744 | 100.0 | 215 | 100.0 | 130 | 100.0 | 495 | 100.0 |
| *Other packers* (1,285)* | | | | | | | | |
| Direct, country dealers, etc. | 10,788 | 52.5 | 1,012 | 29.5 | 23,308 | 59.6 | 2,212 | 53.6 |
| Terminal markets ........ | 5,147 | 25.0 | 433 | 12.6 | 7,939 | 20.3 | 821 | 19.9 |
| Auction markets .......... | 4,614 | 22.5 | 1,991 | 57.9 | 7,855 | 20.1 | 1,094 | 26.5 |
| Total .................. | 20,549 | 100.0 | 3,436 | 100.0 | 39,102 | 100.0 | 4,127 | 100.0 |
| *All packers* (1,300) | | | | | | | | |
| Direct, country dealers, etc. | 17,906 | 57.0 | 1,707 | 33.8 | 53,178 | 66.6 | 7,451 | 66.4 |
| Terminal markets ........ | 7,738 | 24.7 | 706 | 14.0 | 15,421 | 19.3 | 2,084 | 18.6 |
| Auction markets ......... | 5,755 | 18.3 | 2,631 | 52.2 | 11,284 | 14.1 | 1,682 | 15.0 |
| Total ................. | 31,399 | 100.0 | 5,044 | 100.0 | 79,883 | 100.0 | 11,217 | 100.0 |

Source: *Packers and Stockyards Resumé*, USDA, Vol. VII, No. 13, Dec., 1969.
* All 1968 reports not received.

inspected slaughterers purchased 90 per cent of their cattle in central markets; in 1951, 73 per cent; and in 1964, only 37 per cent. The percentage of federally inspected slaughter of calves and of sheep and lambs sold through terminal markets declined from about 86 per cent in 1923 to 56 per cent in 1951 down to 19 per cent in 1964 for calves, while for sheep and lambs these percentages declined from 51 per cent in 1951 to 29 per cent in 1964. The percentage of hogs that federally inspected plants bought from central markets dropped from 77 per cent in 1923 to 42 per cent in 1951 and to 24 per cent in 1964.

Public markets differ greatly in size. In 1969 the 10 largest public markets handled nearly three-fourths of the combined total of various species of livestock sold through 38 public markets that year.

Most of the large public markets are located in or adjacent to the Corn Belt. However, several large markets for calves are in Texas and Oklahoma, while large lamb markets exist in Texas, Colorado, and Utah.

Chicago was the largest cattle market during the first half of the 1950's, followed by Omaha, Sioux City, Kansas City, and St. Paul. These markets have rather consistently been the largest cattle markets since World War I. Chicago was first in volume of receipts for many years; however, the relative importance of markets other than Chicago has been increasing greatly. In 1969 Omaha stood in first place, Chicago second, and St. Paul third. In some years St. Paul has ranked second ahead of Chicago.

South St. Paul, the largest calf market, is primarily an outlet for veal calves from neighboring dairy areas. Oklahoma City, Forth Worth, Sioux City, and West Fargo follow in importance, mainly as outlets for beef calves. At the time of World War I, Chicago was more than twice as large a calf market as any of its nearest competitors. Since that time this supremacy has declined substantially, and in 1966 Chicago ranked near the bottom in calf receipts at terminal markets.

Sioux City was first in hog receipts in 1969, followed by Omaha, East St. Louis, South St. Paul, and St. Joseph. For many years Chicago was the leading market for hogs. With the growth of direct marketing, however, hog receipts dropped more rapidly at Chicago than at other terminal markets, and in 1969 it ranked eighth in volume. Chicago's role as a leading hog market ended in May, 1970, when the hog division at the Chicago Union Stockyards was closed.

Chicago and Omaha were the leading sheep markets during the 1920's. By the 1951–55 period, Denver had become the largest sheep market, followed by Omaha, Fort Worth, Ogden,

St. Paul, and Chicago. Other markets have gained in relative importance in more recent years. In 1969 the market with the largest receipts of sheep and lambs was San Angelo, Texas, followed by Sioux Falls, St. Paul, West Fargo, and Sioux City.

At the central or terminal livestock market, as at local markets, livestock is inherently more difficult to handle than grain. Animals are perishable, not durable; they are difficult to grade by objective methods; and they cannot be sampled.

Accordingly, while grain is bought by sample on the trading floor of the terminal grain market, livestock has to be bought by inspection out in the yards. Rain or shine, hot or cold, the livestock buyers have to walk or ride from pen to pen to see the livestock firsthand before they buy.

As the railroads opened up the West and the terminal markets developed at such cities as Chicago, Kansas City, etc., the markets at those cities went through a period when railroads and other interests would set up several different competing livestock markets in the same city.

The advantages of having only one central market for livestock at each city soon became so apparent, however, that the railroads and other interests pooled their forces and set up one modern union or central market in each city in place of the several scattered markets. This was done first at Chicago, with the opening of the present Union Stockyards in 1865 and later was accomplished at most of the other large cities.

The livestock arriving at these terminal markets are usually fed, watered, and rested overnight before being exposed for sale the next morning, when the buyers go through the yards and bargain with the commission men who represent the owners of the stock. The terminal markets have been aptly described as "hotels for transient livestock." Ordinarily, they provide supper, bed, and breakfast for the livestock on their way to the packer.

From a physical point of view most of the central or terminal markets for livestock operate at about as high a level of efficiency as the characteristics of the livestock permit. The stockyards are usually well located, well laid out, and well organized. Most of them were built for railroad transportation, but they have been adapted to truck transportation without too much difficulty.

## COSTS AND SERVICES AT TERMINAL PUBLIC MARKETS

Livestock sold at terminal public markets is generally consigned to commission agencies that do the selling, receive payment from the buyers, and remit to the owners of the livestock after deducting for marketing expenses and transportation. A commission is paid for this work. The stockyards company undertakes to yard, feed, and care for the animals, and deliver them to the buyer; and for this the consignor pays a fee. Feeding is common, and the shipper pays for the feed. In addition, small charges are made for such services as inspection, insurance, and switching fees for rail shipments.

Commission rates are on a per head basis and vary with the size of the consignment, being higher per head for small lots than for larger lots. Yardage charges are higher for livestock received by motor truck than by rail. Feed cost varies among markets. The cost of feeding varies among consignments at the same market because the quantity of feed differs. Some livestock is sold without being fed.

The commission rates and other charges at the terminal markets are set after hearings by the Packers and Stockyards Administration of the USDA. Average marketing charges for the salable livestock received at public markets are shown in Table 23.3. These figures include both the charges which are levied directly against the producer, or other marketing agents who may "initially" ship the livestock to the market, and the indirect costs incurred by resales through livestock dealers active on the market. Commission fees are the major charges paid by producers or other shippers at terminal markets. These usually account for about one-half of the total charge. Yardage charges roughly account for about one-third of the total charges paid by the initial

**TABLE 23.3: Average Marketing Costs Per Head for Salable Livestock at Posted Terminal Markets (Dollars Per Head)***

| | Initial Sales Charges | | | | | Dealer | |
|---|---|---|---|---|---|---|---|
| Species | Initial yard-age | Feed† | Initial sales commis-sion | Serv-ices‡ | Total charges for initial sale§ | Han-dlings Average Costs for Resales‖ | Total Market-ing Costs¶ |
| Cattle .... | 0.82 | 0.26 | 1.18 | 0.07 | 2.33 | 3.48 | 2.74 |
| Calves .... | .46 | .10 | .65 | .04 | 1.25 | 2.34 | 1.61 |
| Hogs ..... | .28 | .08 | .38 | .03 | .77 | .71 | .88 |
| Sheep and lambs ... | .17 | .05 | .25 | .03 | .50 | 1.05 | .58 |

Source: E. Uvacek and D. L. Wilson, *Livestock Terminal Markets in the United States,* USDA, Marketing Res. Rept. 299, 1959, p. 31.

* These include charges levied against producers and indirect costs of livestock dealer handlings at terminal markets, 1954 data.

† Producer's feed costs from USDA producer's expenditure survey 1955.

‡ Includes bedding.

§ Charges paid by shipper or producer.

‖ Weighted averages include resale yardage, resale commission, and dealer's adjusted gross margin.

¶ Includes total charges for livestock initially sold plus the indirect costs of dealer handlings allocated to these livestock.

consignor of the livestock. Feed and service charges are among the minor charges for livestock. Much livestock moves through terminals without receiving either feed or any special services.

These marketing charges include all charges which are deducted from the producer's, or other "initial" shipper's, check for the animals they sell at the terminal markets.

The advantage of the terminal public market is the experienced salesmanship and the concentration of livestock buyers there. The development of packing plants at country points, the provision of more adequate market news by the federal government, the development of trucks and good roads which give each farmer access to several buyers at different markets, and the development of auction markets at country points have given country markets some degree of the same advantages; and this, plus the stronger bargaining position that farmers hold while their hogs are still on their farms, may equal or surpass the advantages of the terminal market.

The outcome of the competition between the terminal public markets and the country markets for livestock will depend upon two things—upon comparative costs and comparative prices. In general, it costs less to bring the buyer to the product than to bring the product to the buyer—that is, it costs less to decentralize the livestock buyers in the country than to centralize the livestock in the terminal public market. With respect to prices, it used to be possible for many buyers in country markets to outsmart farmers because the buyers had better market information than farmers. This advantage is rapidly disappearing, and it seems likely that the trend toward more direct marketing will continue in the future.

### Country Markets

In addition to market outlets such as the terminals and auctions, "country selling" has become relatively important as a method of marketing livestock.[2]

Country selling accounted for virtually all sales of livestock prior to the beginning of the public stockyard development before 1900. Sales of livestock in the country declined thereafter and increasing numbers were sold at public market until this method reached its peak of selling at the time of World War I. But a new uptrend of country selling began after that. Its expansion, either as direct buying by packers or sale from farm and ranch through dealers to packers, came at the expense of terminal markets. The decline in proportion of all livestock

[2] "Country selling," as used here, refers to producers' sales of livestock direct to packers, local dealers, or farmers without the support of commission men, selling agents, buying agents, or brokers.

moving through terminal public markets was largely accounted for by growth in country selling until the later 1930's and by growth in auctions since. Both direct and auction selling have a certain appeal, inasmuch as they permit producers to observe and exercise some control over selling while it takes place. Consignment to distant terminal markets usually represents an irreversible commitment to sell. Many of the larger and more specialized livestock farmers feel competent to sell their livestock direct.

As the extension of the railroad network across the country in the nineteenth century had an important part to play in the terminal market development, so the later development of trucking and improved highways facilitated the growth of market channels other than the established terminal markets. Farmers were no longer tied to outlets located at important railroad terminals or river crossings. Livestock could move in any direction. Improved communications, such as the radio and telephone, and an expanded market information service also aided in the development of country selling of livestock, especially in sales direct to packers.

Direct selling is the dominant means of marketing hogs in many areas of the north central states. It is also an important outlet for slaughter cattle in many areas, especially in the Pacific coast states and parts of the north central states.

Some of the packers buy livestock direct from producers at the packers' plants and at their country buying points. These country buying points have fixed places of business including yards and scales where livestock are delivered directly by farmers. Cattle and hogs are often bought by packer-buyers who travel from farm to farm and from feedlot to feedlot, making their bids on the livestock that they inspect.

### Auction Markets[3]

An auction is a market at which goods are offered for sale simultaneously to several prospective buyers and are sold to the buyer making the highest bid.

Livestock auctions are well adapted to small lots and odd weights or grades of livestock. Livestock consigned at auctions are sold either by weight on a price-per-pound basis or by the head.

Two different methods are used for selling livestock on a weight basis. In one method, the animals appearing in the ring are all consigned by the same person and are sold either singly,

---

[3] This section is adapted from D. Wilson, B. Pense, and V. Phillips, *Marketing Costs and Margins for Livestock and Meats*, USDA, Marketing Res. Rept. 418, 1960, pp. 32–35.

in pairs, or in small lots that are fairly uniform in size, condition, and quality. When this method is used, the animals are weighed either prior to or immediately following the sale, depending upon the established practice of the market.

Auctions selling livestock by the other method combine consignments from a number of owners to make up rather large lots containing animals of uniform grade and weight. Animals in these pooled lots are weighed only at the time they are sorted. This method is most frequently used at large auctions selling a predominant amount of slaughter livestock. Animals sold per head may be auctioned individually, in pairs, or in small lots. Selling by the head is generally more common in areas where substantial numbers of breeding stock are sold. Many auctions, however, use both methods.

The rates charged for marketing livestock vary at different auctions. Services for which charges are levied may include selling, yardage, weighing, insurance, brand inspection, and health inspection. Many auctions do not provide all these services. A commission or selling fee, however, is charged at all markets and is the primary source of income to auction operators. At some auctions, the commission covers yardage and weighing in addition to the selling service. Some operators levy a separate charge for each service provided, while others charge a single rate to cover all services.

Auction operators levy their charges on a percentage of gross value, on a per head basis, or by a combination of the two methods. Methods of assessing charges on livestock sales are classified into the following four categories:

1. Straight per head—all charges levied per head.
2. Per head combination—per head commissions, with other charges based on a percentage of gross value.
3. Straight percentage—all charges assessed on a percentage of gross value.
4. Percentage combination—percentage commissions, with other charges levied per head.

In 1955 more auctions used the straight per head method as a basis for levying charges on all species than any other method (Table 23.4).[4] Among regions this method was used by the largest proportion of North Central and Southwest Central auctions. In the Western Region, the straight assessment per head was most important for cattle, calves, and sheep and lambs.

[4] The authors know of no more recent data on auction charges.

**TABLE 23.4: Distribution of Auctions Reporting, According to Method of Assessing Charges, 1955**

| Method of Assessing Charges | Number and Proportion of Auctions Reporting Charges on: | | | | | | | |
|---|---|---|---|---|---|---|---|---|
| | Cattle | | Calves | | Hogs | | Sheep and lambs | |
| | Number reporting | Per cent | Number reporting | Per cent | Number reporting | Per cent | Number reporting | Per cent |
| Commission charges on per head basis: | | | | | | | | |
| Straight per head .. | 332 | 40 | 324 | 42 | 276 | 37 | 307 | 46 |
| Per head combination* .. | 75 | 9 | 71 | 9 | 64 | 9 | 70 | 10 |
| Commission charges based on percentage of sales: | | | | | | | | |
| Straight percentage . | 161 | 20 | 159 | 20 | 188 | 25 | 125 | 19 |
| Percentage combination† .. | 255 | 31 | 222 | 29 | 217 | 29 | 167 | 25 |
| Total ......... | 823 | 100 | 776 | 100 | 745 | 100 | 669 | 100 |

* Other charges including yardage, insurance, brand inspection, health inspection, etc., are based on percentage of value.
† Other charges are assessed on a per head basis.

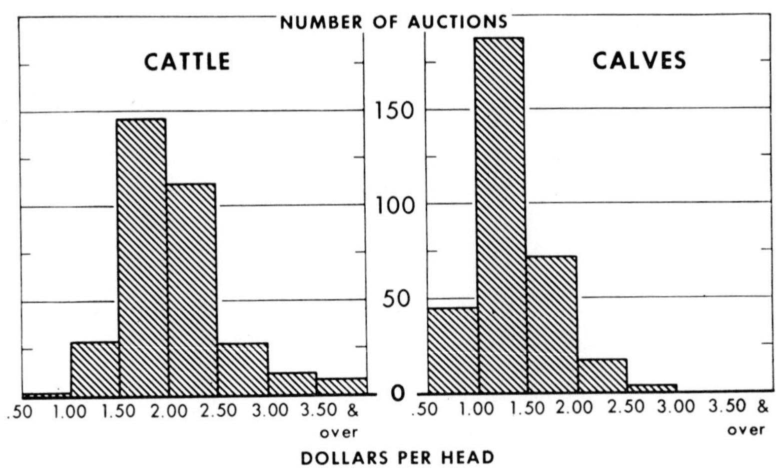


FIG. 23.6—Marketing charges at livestock auctions, cattle and calves, 1955.

Straight charges per head on cattle and calves varied considerably among auctions reporting this type of assessment (Fig. 23.6). However, the most usual charges for cattle ranged from \$1.50 to \$2 per head, and over three-fourths of the auctions levied rates between \$1.50 and \$2.50. Straight charges per head on calves tended to be less than on cattle and were predominantly set at amounts ranging from \$1 to \$1.50. No assessments on calves of over \$3 were reported by these auctions, and only 6 per cent of the markets levied fees of more than \$2.

While ranges in charges per head on hogs and sheep and lambs were generally smaller than those on cattle and calves, rates varied substantially (Fig. 23.7). Charges per head most frequently levied on hogs ranged from 50 to 60 cents. However, another smaller grouping of charges occurred within the range of \$1 to \$1.10. This may be partially due to the fact that many auctions levy separate rates on the different classes—particularly butcher hogs and feeders. More than half of the assessments on sheep and lambs were within the range of 40 to 60 cents, only a few auctions reporting charges over 70 cents in 1955.

Comparatively few markets used the per head combination method in which commissions were assessed per head and other charges were based on a percentage of value. The only region in which this method was significant was the South, where about a third of the auctions reported per head combination charges on sheep and lambs.

Commissions on cattle and calves were relatively low at auctions levying per head combination charges. Over four-fifths of these auctions reported commissions per head on cattle within the range of $1 to $2. Commissions of 50 cents to $1 per head on calves were assessed by almost four-fifths of the markets using this system, and none reported amounts over $1.50. More than 95 per cent of these auction operators levied other charges on cattle and calves at the rate of 1 per cent or less.

Two major groupings were noted in the distribution of hog commissions per head—between 20 and 30 cents and between 50 and 60 cents. Over three-fourths of the sheep and lamb commissions were levied at rates within the range of 20 to 40 cents. Again, over 95 per cent of the other charges reported by these auctions were assessed at 1 per cent or less both on hogs and on sheep and lambs.

About a fifth of the auction operators reported straight percentage charges on cattle, calves, and sheep and lambs, while a fourth of the auctions used this method for levying charges on hogs. In the Northeastern Region most of the auctions used the straight percentage method for all livestock.

The most usual charge on cattle, calves, and hogs for auctions reporting straight percentage charges was 3 per cent (Fig. 23.8). Five per cent was the most usual charge for sheep and lambs at these markets. The 5 per cent rate, however, was more than twice as widespread as the intermediate 4 per cent rate for all species.

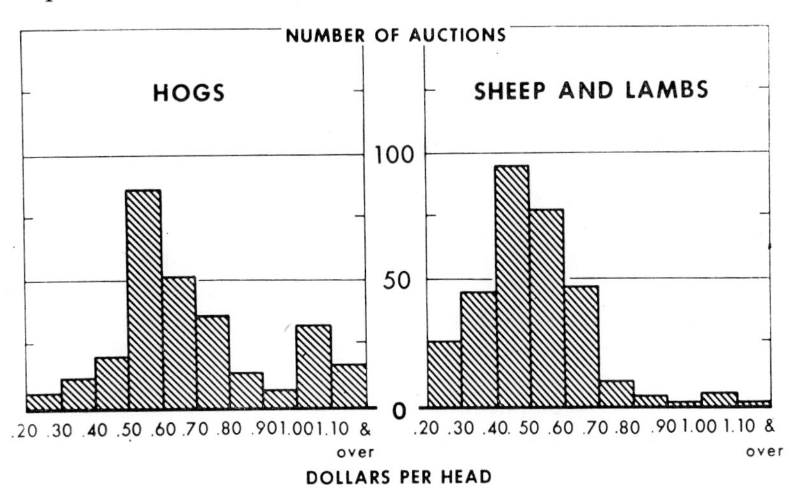


FIG. 23.7—Marketing charges at livestock auctions, hogs and sheep and lambs, 1955.

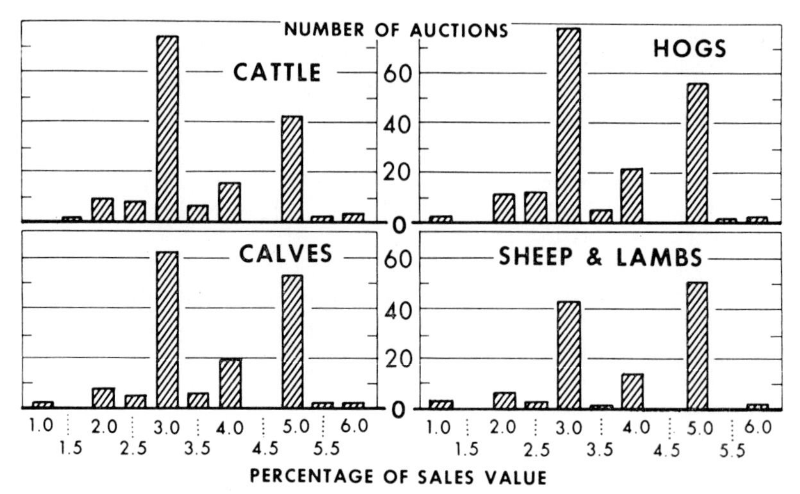


FIG. 23.8—Marketing charges at livestock auctions, as a percentage of the value of the livestock sold, cattle, calves, hogs, and sheep and lambs, 1955.

The percentage combination charge (percentage commission, with other charges levied per head) was used by more auction operators than was the straight percentage assessment. Among regions, the percentage combination method was most important at southern auctions. This method of assessment was second in importance in the North Central Region for all species, and ranked second also in the Western Region for cattle, calves, and sheep and lambs.

Commissions for auctions assessing percentage combination charges were generally lower, as would be expected, than the charges levied by auctions using the straight percentage method. Commissions of 3 and 3.5 per cent were most common for all species. Less than a fourth of these markets charged commissions of over 3.5 per cent. The most usual charge per head for other services at these markets ranged from 10 to 20 cents for cattle, calves, and hogs, and from 0 to 10 cents for sheep and lambs.

The rates charged at most auctions are lower than the rates at public markets for animals of low value and for small lots, but higher for animals of high value and for those sold in large lots. The reason for this is that commission rates at public markets are set on a per head basis and decrease sharply as the number of head per lot increases.

## COMPETITION IN AUCTION MARKETS

One of the advantages of local livestock markets is that they provide a place where livestock can be exposed to the direct competition of several buyers who are physically present in the same ring. This traditional form of competition is more reassuring to many livestock producers than the modern decentralized form, where the competition exists between several buyers a number of miles apart, exercising their competition through the newspaper and over the radio and long-distance telephone.

But in many local livestock auctions, the competition is not as well informed and sharp as the physical form of the competition would permit. We saw earlier that the excellence of a market depends upon the excellence of the market news concerning supplies, demands, and prices possessed by the buyers and sellers in the market, rather than whether they are close enough together to rub elbows or are miles apart. In actual fact, the market information concerning what is going on in many local livestock auction markets is deficient. Many lots are sold without the prices being known to all the buyers and sellers present. The obscurity that surrounds the transactions in many cases is well reflected in the following descriptive account:

> The local livestock auction market, still and practically lifeless for five days a week, takes on a circus atmosphere on sales day. Animals and men move about the yards at a fast pace and often in a pattern confusing to the occasional visitor. Once the sale begins, the excitement and tempo increase.
>
> The auctioneer's chant, the calls and exclamations of the ring men, together with the movements of buyers indicating bids in their own peculiar manner, create a sense of mystery and intrigue that is not always confined to the occasional observer but often is shared by farmers consigning livestock for sale. Frequently it is difficult for the experienced observer to determine the final sales price and even more difficult to determine the purchaser's name.
>
> The "ring man," calling bids to the auctioneer, may be bidding for two or more buyers as he catches their signals. Some buyers do not like for certain other buyers to know that they are bidding on a particular lot of animals. Partly because of this and the fact that a single buyer may be buying for several accounts, the actual name of the buyer or the firm he represents may not always be understandable.
>
> The buyer's name frequently is called in shorthand terms such as P-1, K-5, Scotty, etc. Failure to announce the buyer's name clearly does not mean that any "undercover work" is going on. Rather, the practice is followed because of the desire of some buyers to remain anonymous and the fact that it shortens the recording time of the clerk who is hard pressed to keep everything properly identified, par-

ticularly if the sale proceeds at a fast pace. Most, if not all, auction managers do not object to disclosing the buyer's name on request.[5]

### Livestock Futures Markets

A relatively new development in livestock marketing is trading in live cattle and hog futures contracts on organized commodity exchanges. Futures trading in live beef steers was initiated by the Chicago Mercantile Exchange on November 30, 1964. This was the first time that futures contracts in a live commodity had been traded on an organized exchange. As a result the market attracted considerable interest, and the early trading was sufficient to create more optimism about the potential for this type of futures market.

Encouraged by initial response to the live cattle futures market, futures trading in live hog contracts was added by the Mercantile Exchange in February, 1966. A few months later, in October, 1966, the Chicago Board of Trade added live beef steers to the list of commodities offered for futures trading on that exchange. Another effort at futures trading in live cattle, however, was short-lived. In June of 1966, the Kansas City Board of Trade initiated futures trading in a live feeder cattle contract. Trading was discontinued in 1967, however, due to limited interest and trading in the contract.

Futures contracts in live cattle and hogs provide a way for producers to hedge their production and feeding operations and thereby remove some of the price uncertainty that normally exists. In this respect the major hedging use of livestock futures may be somewhat different than for some of the more conventional futures markets. In other futures markets, hedging has more often been related to storage, handling, or product procurement operations. The markets have been used most often by handlers and processors rather than producers.[6]

It may be some time before the potential of livestock futures markets for hedging purposes is fully known. The early years of trading in these contracts recorded substantial increases in volume traded, especially in live beef futures, where, at the end of the first year's trading, there were 3,324 open contracts. By the end of 1969 the number of open contracts had increased to 20,654—19,796 on the Chicago Mercantile Exchange and 858 on the Chicago Board of Trade.

[5] Jack D. Johnson, "Who Buys Your Cattle?" *Virginia Farm Economics*, Va. Pol. Inst., No. 139 (Aug., 1954), pp. 7–8.

[6] For more discussion on livestock futures markets, see J. M. Skadberg and G. A. Futrell, "An Economic Appraisal of Futures Trading in Livestock," *Jour. of Farm Econ.*, Vol. 48, No. 5 (Dec., 1966), pp. 1845–89.

## THE MEAT-PACKING INDUSTRY

Meat packing is a term applied to the industry whose principal functions are slaughtering livestock and processing meat, although it may handle other products or perform other functions. The term was descriptive of the industry during its early period when the packing of pork was its principal operation. The early name of the industry persists, although the packing of meat now has largely been replaced by other processing.

### Number of Packing Plants and Their Operations

Meat-packing plants are distributed throughout the United States, but the volume of slaughter is largest in the north central states. Slaughtering plants are most numerous in Pennsylvania, Ohio, Michigan, and Texas, but many are relatively small. Packing plants range in size from small establishments in which livestock is slaughtered for local distribution only to large establishments in which more than a million hogs (in addition to considerable other livestock) are slaughtered annually. The four largest meat-packing concerns, sometimes referred to as national packers or as the "Big Four," operated 91 slaughtering establishments in 1963. The next four in size operated 18 slaughtering plants. The national packers operate many of the larger packing plants, but some others have individual plants that are among the largest in the country. In addition to those where slaughtering is done, some packing plants are engaged principally in the manufacture of sausage and specialty meats.

Packing plants that distribute products interstate and abroad slaughter and prepare their meat and meat products under federal inspection. This inspection is not required of plants that distribute their products within the borders of the state where they are located. Some plants not under federal inspection, however, have meat-inspection service provided by the state or municipality. The inspection of meat and the supervision of slaughtering are carried on to guard against the sale of products that are diseased or otherwise unfit for human consumption.

Amendments to the Meat Inspection Act in December, 1967, authorized federal inspection of slaughtering and processing plants not engaged in interstate trade, under certain conditions. The legislation specified that state and local inspection requirements must be equal to federal requirements within two years—or by approximately December, 1969. If inspection standards and enforcement are not brought up to that level, federal inspection is authorized.

The location of the federally inspected plants is shown in Figure 23.9.

FIG. 23.9—Federally inspected livestock slaughtering plants, Mar. 1, 1970.

The number of livestock slaughtering plants in the United States in 1950, 1955, 1960, 1965, and 1970, as reported by the USDA, are given in several categories in Table 23.5. These plants slaughtered 99 per cent of the total commercial slaughter. The rest of the slaughter was handled by about 3,845 plants slaughtering less than 300,000 pounds each.

Between 1950 and 1970 there was a substantial increase in the number of federally inspected slaughter plants, from 455 to 725. Considerably more movement of *firms* into and out of the slaughter industry occurred than is indicated by the net change in number of plants. However, the data on the number of firms is less recent.

The total number of federally inspected firms slaughtering livestock increased by 105 (from 336 to 441) between 1950 and 1962; yet 130 of the firms in the industry in 1950 had exited by 1962, and 234 of the 440 firms slaughtering in 1962 had entered the industry since 1950. Therefore, over one-third of the firms in the industry in 1962 had entered since 1950.[7] Differences be-

[7] These data are taken from *Structural Changes in the Federally Inspected Livestock Slaughter Industry, 1950–62*, USDA, Agr. Econ. Rept. 83, Apr., 1966, pp. 5–6.

**TABLE 23.5: Number of Livestock-Slaughtering Plants by Class, 1950–70, United States**

| Class of Plant | 1950 | 1955 | 1960 | 1965 | 1970 | Percentage Change 1960–70 |
|---|---|---|---|---|---|---|
| | *(number)* | *(number)* | *(number)* | *(number)* | *(number)* | *(per cent)* |
| Federally inspected ... | 455 | 441 | 530 | 570 | 725 | +37 |
| Other commercial | | | | | | |
| Large* ............ | 952 | 725 | 902 | 849 | 562 | −38 |
| Medium† .......... | 1,810 | 2,072 | 1,712 | 1,538 | 2,582 | +51 |
| Total ............ | 2,762 | 2,797 | 2,614 | 2,387 | 3,144 | +20 |
| Total plants ......... | 3,217 | 3,238 | 3,144 | 2,957 | 3,869 | +23 |

Source: *Number of Livestock Slaughter Establishments,* USDA, Mar. 1, 1955; *Number of Livestock-Slaughtering Plants,* March 1, 1965, USDA, SRS-8, June, 1965, and SRS-8 (Revised), May, 1970.

* Includes nonfederally inspected plants slaughtering over 2 million pounds live weight annually.

† Includes nonfederally inspected plants slaughtering less than 2 million pounds live weight but more than 300,000 pounds annually.

tween number of firms and number of plants reflects the fact that many firms operate more than one plant.

## Changing Industry Organization[8]

There are two dimensions of the slaughter industry in which economic organization has decentralized. One of these is the functional structure of the industry; the other is the size structure. Functional structure refers to the way in which the various functions or processes in meat packing are organized within and among packing plants. Both horizontal and vertical integration are measurements of functional structure.

### FUNCTIONAL STRUCTURE

There are two characteristics of functional structure in the livestock slaughter industry: (1) horizontal organization—the number of different livestock species slaughtered and (2) vertical organization—the number of different meat-packing processes performed. The fully centralized slaughter plant could be described as one slaughtering all livestock species and completely processing all meat products. The fully decentralized plant would slaughter only a single livestock species and would conduct no further processing. Since 1950 there has been decentralization in both vertical and horizontal dimensions. Livestock slaughter plants have become more specialized in the slaughter of a single livestock species. In other words, there has been a tendency toward horizontal decentralization.

[8] This section is based on *Decentralization in the Livestock Slaughter Industry,* USDA, Agr. Econ. Rept. 83, Suppl., Apr., 1966, pp. 2–5.

In addition to the trend toward species specialization, plants have also become more specialized in the vertical dimension. Rather than engaging in both slaughter and processing, they are tending to become more specialized in one of the functions. The data series for meat processing by federally inspected plants is less complete than for livestock slaughter. Only 1961 data were available for this study. These do not show a time trend in slaughter-processing specialization. However, a trend toward slaughter specialization began before 1961 and has continued.

In 1961, 49 federally inspected slaughter plants were doing no meat processing. A rather high proportion of the slaughter plants were doing a limited amount of processing. Half of the slaughter plants which did engage in meat-processing activities processed only an average of 14 per cent of their slaughter production. These limited processing activities tended to consist of some boning, carcass breaking, and other meat operations. Specialization in meat processing, which includes curing, smoking, fabricating, and so forth, appears to be greater than in slaughtering; 65 per cent of the processing plants performed no slaughtering.

The trend toward functional specialization in the slaughter industry differs from the trend in many other agricultural processing industries, such as dairy and flour, which are becoming centralized and integrated. Why is this functional decentralization occurring in livestock slaughter? The answer is not simple. A complex set of economic variables is shaping the reorganization.

Increased specialization by species has resulted from changing patterns of livestock production, changing marketing channels, and developments in slaughter-plant technology. These factors have been coupled with a transportation and freight-rate structure which has fostered and facilitated functional reorganization.

In recent years, there has been increased geographic specialization in livestock production. This has been rather recent in fed-cattle production, while it occurred much earlier in hog production. However, the relative geographic specialization has not been the same for all species. For example, beef-cattle feeding has expanded in the West, but hog feeding has not. Consequently, if a new slaughter plant is built in a cattle-feeding area, other livestock species must be shipped in from some distance, or the plant must specialize. To avoid long-distance shipping of one species (and a high transportation bill), one would expect that slaughter plants located near specialized cattle-feeding areas would tend to specialize in cattle slaughter, providing production costs do not affect the procurement economies. A similar specialized pattern would tend to develop in hog-slaughter plants if there were no diseconomies of specialization. Important developments in technology have permitted production specialization. On-the-rail dressing, mechanical knives, and more efficient refrigeration have permitted relatively small plants to operate efficiently. Thus it is possible to take advantage of procurement savings in species specialization over a relatively small geographic area.

While these considerations would explain plant specialization in a completely specialized pattern of livestock production, the pace of change has been faster than the pace of production specialization. Other factors explain this.

The trend toward specialization has been from a pattern of highly diversified plants. The fact that a large proportion of all species of livestock was marketed at the terminals was one of the factors contributing to the early construction of the diversified terminal plants. Since power sources (steam) could be efficiently used in large plants and there were no particular disadvantages in slaughtering all species of livestock under one roof, plants were horizontally diversified to slaughter all species at the terminal.

As new transportation techniques developed and roads were improved and as livestock production has shifted to new areas and larger production units, there has been a relative decline in terminal marketing. When all species are not already assembled in one spot, as at a terminal, it becomes less efficient to bring all species to one point solely for slaughter. Unless all species are produced in equal numbers in an area, there will be disadvantages from excessive transportation costs if full-line plants are used. Thus new nonterminal plants have been specialized in one or two livestock species.

Other factors can be cited for the trend toward more specialization in slaughter and meat processing. There appears to be no particular cost advantage in slaughtering and processing under the same roof. Some advantage exists in maintaining processing plants in and around consumption areas (often near large cities), rather than locating them with slaughter, near livestock production areas. Several factors account for consumption-point orientation in meat processing. First, since product differentiation is important in processed meat, it is often an advantage to cultivate the "home-town" product especially tailored for local tastes. Second, by limiting their sales to one metropolitan area, many processing firms can be operated without federal inspection. Third, because of communications and merchandising programs, service of retail stores may be provided more effectively when plants are near consumption points.

Fourth, many of the "old" plants, formerly used for both slaughter and processing, can be maintained for meat processing. Fifth, the source of raw materials for processing is often public warehouses located in cities. Thus these plants actually may be near their principal sources of supply. As long as economic factors affecting the location of slaughter relative to processing are different, this specialization trend is likely to continue.

### SIZE STRUCTURE

Size structure refers to the degree to which a small proportion of slaughter firms dominate the output of the entire industry. For example, it is thought that an industry controlled by a small number of large firms is more likely to exhibit collusion and noncompetitive action than one in which many firms are of approximately equal size.

Concentration of slaughter in the hands of the largest firms is one measure of the degree of dominance of large firms. Dominance by a few large firms has declined. The 4 largest firms did 51 per cent of total federally inspected slaughter in 1950; by 1962 their share had decreased to 35 per cent (Table 23.6). Decreases occurred not only for total slaughter but also

**TABLE 23.6: Percentage of Federally Inspected Slaughter by the Largest Slaughter Firms, United States, by Species, 1950, 1954, 1958, and 1962**

| Size Rank of Firms | Year | | | |
|---|---|---|---|---|
| | 1950 | 1954 | 1958 | 1962 |
| | | *Cattle* | | |
| 1–4 | 51.5 | 45.2 | 35.7 | 29.5 |
| 5–10 | 8.7 | 10.0 | 10.5 | 10.4 |
| 1–10 | 60.2 | 55.2 | 46.2 | 39.9 |
| | | *Calves* | | |
| 1–4 | 58.0 | 59.3 | 49.7 | 39.9 |
| 5–10 | 12.9 | 11.7 | 13.9 | 16.3 |
| 1–10 | 70.9 | 71.0 | 63.6 | 56.2 |
| | | *Sheep* | | |
| 1–4 | 69.6 | 68.7 | 64.4 | 58.9 |
| 5–10 | 15.9 | 16.1 | 17.2 | 17.1 |
| 1–10 | 85.5 | 84.8 | 81.6 | 76.0 |
| | | *Hogs* | | |
| 1–4 | 48.5 | 48.4 | 41.3 | 39.0 |
| 5–10 | 22.1 | 23.0 | 23.4 | 21.5 |
| 1–10 | 70.6 | 71.4 | 64.7 | 60.5 |
| | | *Total* | | |
| 1–4 | 50.8 | 46.6 | 38.9 | 35.0 |
| 5–10 | 15.8 | 16.1 | 15.9 | 14.1 |
| 1–10 | 66.6 | 62.7 | 54.8 | 49.1 |

Source: *Decentralization in the Livestock Slaughter Industry,* USDA, Agr. Econ. Rept. 83, Suppl., Apr., 1966, p. 8.

for slaughter of each species. The share of slaughter by the 4 largest firms decreased from 52 to 30 per cent for cattle, from 58 to 40 per cent for calves, from 70 to 59 per cent for sheep, and from 49 to 39 per cent for hogs.

Concentration of slaughter in the 4 largest firms is not extremely high, but the 10 largest federally inspected slaughter firms do have a substantial proportion of the total slaughter. Although their share decreased from two-thirds in 1950, they controlled nearly one-half of total federally inspected slaughter in 1962. It is interesting to note that, while the share by the 4 largest firms declined, the share by the next 6 large firms remained relatively constant. These firms grew at about the same rate as total slaughter increased, thus their share remained constant. But the 4 largest firms sustained a very small growth, thus their share decreased.

Two developments have produced the declining concentration. First, new firms have entered the industry and are slaughtering an increasing portion of the increased livestock production. As noted earlier, between 1950 and 1962, the number of federally inspected slaughter firms increased from 336 to 441, and 88 per cent of the firms were larger than the mean size in 1950. Secondly, small firms which stayed in the industry have been growing in size at an average rate more than eight times greater than large firms. Thus they have taken an increasing share of slaughter, and the largest firms have had a decreasing share.

Many of the same factors producing specialization in slaughter have also been instrumental in changing the size structure of the industry. Technological developments have made the entry of relatively small plants economically feasible because they can now be as efficient as large ones. Further, costs of slaughtering in a specialized plant are apparently no greater than in a diversified plant. Thus it is advantageous for an entering firm with limited capital to construct a specialized slaughter plant of sufficient size to achieve scale economies, rather than a diversified plant which might be too small.

Transportation technology and freight rates, coupled with increased specialization of livestock producers, have made nonterminal plant locations economically feasible. Thus it has been possible for small firms to enter the industry without the necessity of jockeying for a terminal plant location and a share of terminal market receipts.

Further, federal inspection and grading have also facilitated growth of small firms. They are able to enter the national dressed-meat market on the same basis as large firms with heavy investment in sales organizations and brand names.

The growing predominance of chain stores in the retail

meat trade also appears to have facilitated the growth of small slaughter firms. Retail chains have generally not been interested in merchandising packer-branded fresh meats. Hence, small slaughter firms have been able to compete for fresh meat sales without advertising campaigns or sales organizations. With newer and more efficient plants, they often have had a cost advantage relative to the large, older firms. Consequently, they have been able to secure increasing shares of the fresh meat business.

Finally, large slaughter firms may have been expanding at a slower rate than small firms because they have other investment possibilities. Often, a large meat-packing firm has opportunities to invest in meat processing or in other industries such as chemicals and fertilizers. The large firm has these investment opportunities because it has a larger "purse" and access to national financial markets. (Profit rates in other industries have often been greater than in meat packing in recent years.) On the other hand, a small slaughter firm interested in reinvesting its capital may not have a more profitable alternative.

### IMPLICATIONS OF DECENTRALIZED SLAUGHTER

Decentralization in the livestock slaughter industry has implications for rural communities, for livestock producers, for livestock slaughter, and for livestock service agencies.

It is apparent that a successful plant need not integrate all slaughtering and processing functions. Thus, the relative capital requirement for a successful specialized plant is less than for the older type full-line plant. Further, federal inspection and grading have enhanced the probability of success of a small, independent slaughter plant. As a result of these factors, it may now be easier for a small community to attract or organize a slaughter plant than once was the case.

On the other hand, decentralization in the industry has been accompanied by a great deal of organizational and promotional activity for slaughter plants. Many developers and community development groups have proposed and built slaughter plants. Some of the proposals have not been carefully considered beforehand, and the plants have failed. Hence, in the flurry of promotional activity, a small community should analyze carefully all the conditions that might affect the success of a proposed slaughter plant. Such an analysis is particularly important in an environment where many plants have been successful, for success in one community is no guarantee that a slaughter plant will be successful in every community.

The trends identified here also have implications for livestock producers. The increased number of small firms locating at the point of livestock production means increased outlets for livestock at interior points. Since livestock do not have to move so far, net returns can be increased by reducing transportation costs.

However, reduced transportation costs do not necessarily mean increased net returns to producers. Many of these new plants are highly specialized by species and by class. Hence, the market may not have been broadened in some geographic areas for certain types of livestock. Some producers may still wish to move livestock for sale elsewhere in order to use selling services available at other points.

Assuming that the factors which generate these trends continue in the future, livestock slaughter firms will have to continue specializing in both horizontal and vertical functions to take advantage of locational and functional economies. These adjustments will in turn have implications for both the location and the type of market service agencies handling livestock.

## MARKETING AND PROCESSING MARGINS AND COSTS

Figure 23.10 and Table 23.7 show where the consumer's dollar spent for beef, pork, and lamb goes. They also show that the distribution of the retail price per pound of meat differs for pork, beef, and lamb. The retailing margins per pound for beef and lamb are larger than for pork. In 1969 retail margins per pound took 28 cents for beef and 27.0 cents for lamb, compared

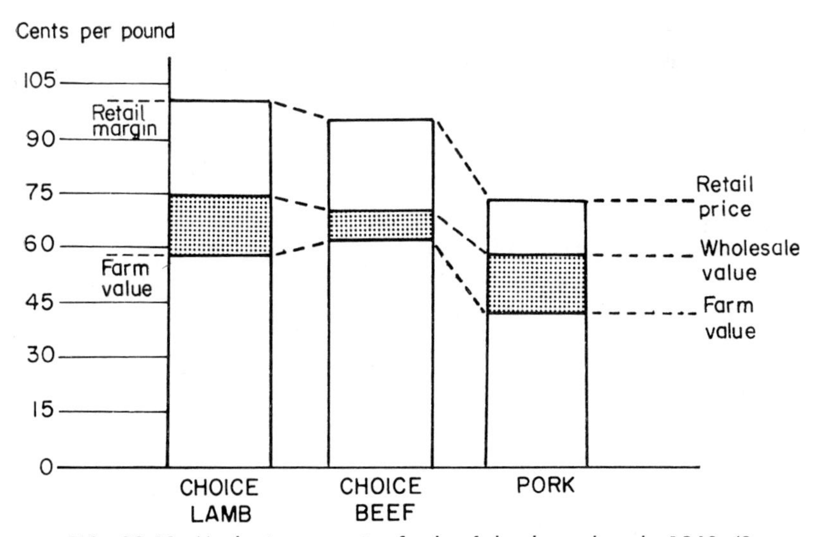


FIG. 23.10—Marketing margins for beef, lamb, and pork, 1969. (Source: Based on data in **The Marketing and Transportation Situation,** USDA, Feb., 1970, p. 10.)

**TABLE 23.7: Distribution of Retail Price of Beef, Pork, and Lamb, 1969**

| Function | Beef, Choice | Pork | Lamb, Choice |
|---|---|---|---|
| | *(cents/lb)* | *(cents/lb)* | *(cents/lb)* |
| Farm value | 62.2 | 42.3 | 59.3 |
| Assembly, processing, and wholesaling | 26.5 | 16.2 | 15.5 |
| Retailing | 27.6 | 15.8 | 27.0 |
| Retail price | 96.3 | 74.3 | 101.8 |

Source: *Marketing and Transportation Situation,* USDA, May, 1970, p. 8.

with 15.8 cents for pork. This is partly because more labor is required to retail beef and lamb than pork. Retailers generally buy carcasses and primal cuts of beef and lamb from packer-wholesalers, which they make into retail cuts such as roasts and steaks. They trim off excess fat, bone some cuts, and make a portion into ground meat. Retailers buy pork products which require comparatively little further cutting and trimming, such as hams, picnics, Boston butts, and sliced bacon. The marketing margin for retailing covers the services performed by the retailer.

The packer-wholesaler margin is larger per pound for pork than for beef and lamb. In 1969 it amounted to 16.2 cents for pork compared with 6.5 cents for beef and 15.5 cents for lamb. This is because the packer-wholesaler normally performs on hogs a much larger share of the total marketing services necessary to move live animals from the farm to the ultimate consumer than he performs on cattle and lambs. For "block beef" and lamb, the packer-wholesaler's functions are usually confined to slaughtering the live animals and wholesaling the dressed meat as whole or quarter carcasses.[9] For pork, meat packers slaughter the hog, cut the carcass into its component parts—hams, bacon, picnics, Boston butts, spareribs, loins, and others—and cure, process, and package some of these pork products.

In percentage terms, about 25 per cent of the retail dollar spent for beef, pork, and lamb goes, in each case, for retailing costs. Processing costs, however, make up a larger part of the retail pork dollar than for beef and lamb. One reason for this is that the pork carcass is usually cut into wholesale cuts at the processing plant before it is moved into retail channels. Also, many of the pork cuts receive additional processing, such as

[9] "Block beef" is beef which ordinarily moves into fresh meat consumption channels rather than to processors or boners. It is fresh beef which moves across the cutting block of the retail butcher and includes qualities of beef sold to restaurants and other dining establishments.

curing of hams, picnics, and bacon. Costs of assembling the livestock are somewhat smaller on hogs than for cattle and lambs and make up a smaller percentage of the retail pork dollar.

These variations in the distribution of the consumer's dollar spent for meat reflect in part differences in kinds and costs of services performed at different levels in the marketing system. They do not measure or indicate in any way the relative operational or functional efficiencies.

### Changes in the Marketing Margin for Beef

Figure 23.11 shows the irregular but persistent upward trend of the marketing margin between the farm price of beef cattle and the retail price of beef, by months from 1954 to 1966. The margin between the two prices rose 38 per cent over the period, but the farm price of beef cattle was hardly any higher at the end of the period than it was at the beginning.

This upward trend in the marketing margin between farm and retail beef prices appears to have been caused chiefly by increases in marketing costs. There was no significant upward trend in the profits of packers or retailers.

Operating expenses for both packers and retailers appear to have increased more rapidly than productivity; it cost more to handle

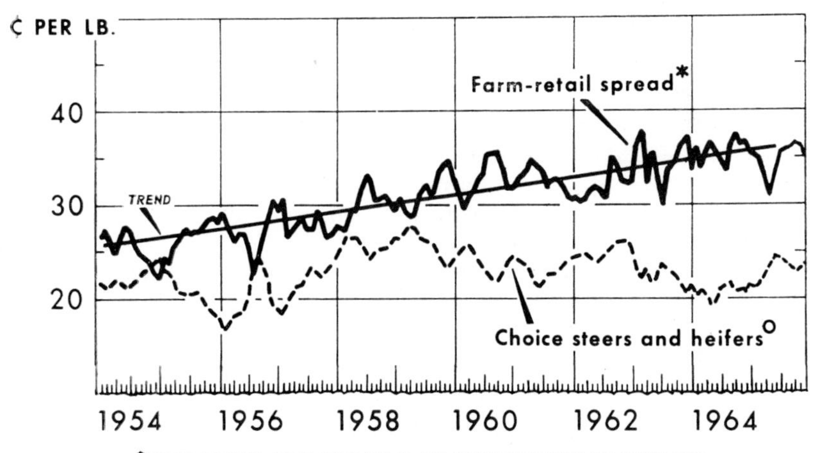


U. S. DEPARTMENT OF AGRICULTURE NEG. ERS 3485-66 (2) ECONOMIC RESEARCH SERVICE

FIG. 23.11—Farm-retail spreads for beef and beef-cattle prices, 1954–66.

a pound of beef in 1969 than in 1955 or 1960. More beef cuts are prepackaged now and retailers seem to trim beef more closely and to sell more of it in boneless cuts. These changes affect product quality as well as cost. Both the packer and retailer now pay considerably more for their labor than they did in 1955—probably 70 to 80 per cent more per hour. However, they probably use 10 to 15 per cent less labor, and correspondingly more equipment, which also costs more now than it did in 1955. Packers and retailers operate more efficiently today than they did 10 years ago. Thus, better location, organization, and equipment of packing plants and retail stores have offset at least part of the increased input costs.

Short-term changes in the spread are closely associated with short-term changes in cattle prices. The 1-month lag between changes in cattle and beef prices causes the price spread to be a comparison between a cattle price that is adjusting to the supply change and a beef price that has not yet reacted to this change. Cattle prices change first, because supply increases are first felt at the live market level. By the time the impact of a given supply change is felt at retail, cattle prices may be responding to a later supply change. Thus, in the very short run, changes in spreads are dominated by changes in cattle prices. Monthly price spreads tend to widen as cattle prices fall, and narrow as cattle prices rise.

The lag between cattle and beef price changes and its consequent impact on the spread are observed both when prices rise and when they fall. Its cause appears to be mainly the length of time required for a change in supply to move from live level to the retail level. Other factors may be important, including the preference retailers have shown for stable regular prices and their dependence on special sales to move increases in supply that may be of short duration.

The short-run lag in retail price responses, combined with changes in cattle prices, appears to explain a large proportion of the month-to-month changes in the price spread, but not the long-run trend. As the price spread moved up and down in 1954–65, it usually did not go quite as far down as it had gone up. The result was an upward trend not explained by changes in cattle prices, which had a definite long-term pattern of nearly equal up-and-down movements.

Cattle prices begin to increase about a month before retail prices and retail prices continue to rise about a month after this trend in cattle prices has ended. In periods of falling prices, cattle prices go down for about a month before beef prices follow. Furthermore, beef prices continue this trend for about a month, on the average, after cattle prices have stopped falling. On the whole, retailers have lagged about the same in following cattle price rises as they have in following cattle price declines.[10]

---

[10] *Agricultural Markets in Change,* USDA, Agr. Econ. Rept. 95, July, 1966, p. 274.

## Breakdown of Retail Cuts

The way a typical 1,000-pound Choice steer carcass breaks down into retail cuts is shown in Figure 23.12. The figure is based on USDA data on yield of retail cuts and on Chicago prices for Choice steers, Choice beef carcasses at wholesale, and Bureau of Labor Statistics retail price estimates at chain and independent stores in Chicago in mid-March, 1970.

The 1,000-pound steer at 30.0 cents per pound cost the packer $300. The value of the by-products, such as hides, fats, hair, animal feeds, fertilizer, etc., in part offsets the packer's processing and selling expenses, so that the beef from a steer generally sells at wholesale for less than the live animal cost. In this case, the steer yielded 600 pounds of carcass, which at 48.5 cents per pound cost the retailer $291. The retailer cut the carcass up and sold 444 pounds of retail cuts as shown in Figure 23.12, receiving a total of $413. The other 156 pounds were fat, bones, and shrinkage. The retailer in this example

444 LBS. RETAIL CUTS

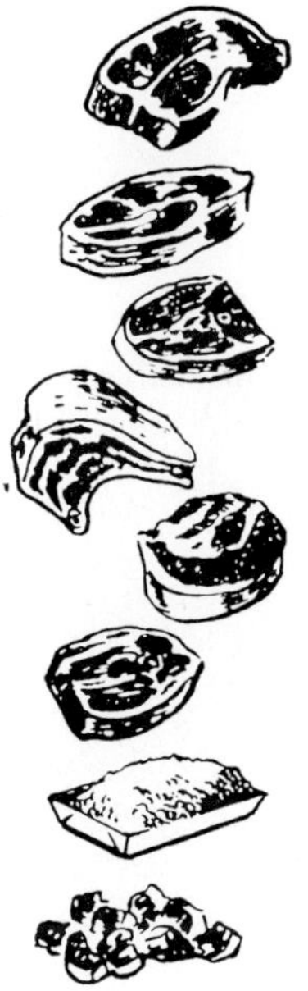

| | POUNDS | PRICE | TOTAL |
|---|---|---|---|
| PORTERHOUSE, T-BONE & CLUB STEAK | 31 | 1.56 | $48.00 |
| SIRLOIN STEAK | 50 | 1.30 | 65.00 |
| ROUND STEAK | 68 | 1.07 | 74.00 |
| RIB ROAST | 38 | 1.09 | 41.00 |
| BONELESS RUMP ROAST | 20 | 1.10 | 22.00 |
| CHUCK ROAST | 90 | .69 | 62.00 |
| HAMBURGER | 98 | .66 | 65.00 |
| STEW MEAT & MISC. CUTS | 49 | .73 | 36.00 |
| | | | $413.00 |

FIG. 23.12—Value of retail cuts from 1,000-pound Choice grade steer, Chicago, Mar., 1970.

received $122, or 42 per cent more for the retail cuts than he paid for the carcass. This represents his gross margin to cover costs of retailing and profits.

The prices for each cut shown in Figure 23.12 reflect the demand and supply for that cut. Since consumers like some retail cuts of meat better than others, retailers price the different cuts in such a way as to keep them moving in the same proportion as they occur in the carcass. If one cut does not move fast enough, the retailer reduces its price; if another moves too fast, he raises its price.

A similar example showing the retail value of a pork carcass is shown in Figure 23.13. A 220-pound hog at 26 cents per pound cost the packer $57.20. It yielded 173 pounds of carcass, including 144 pounds of wholesale cuts and 29 pounds of lard.

132 LBS. RETAIL CUTS

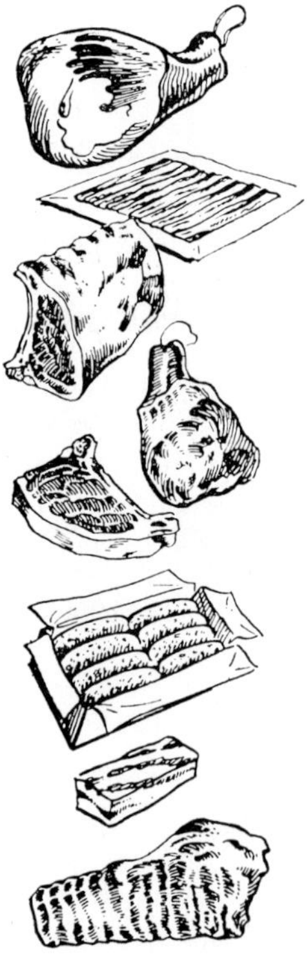

| | POUNDS | PRICE | TOTAL |
|---|---|---|---|
| HAM | 31 | .76 | $23.50 |
| BACON | 26 | 1.05 | 27.30 |
| LOIN ROAST | 17 | .81 | 13.80 |
| PICNICS | 14 | .61 | 8.50 |
| BUTTS | 10 | .80 | 8.00 |
| PORK CHOPS | 9 | 1.07 | 9.60 |
| SAUSAGE | 14 | .76 | 10.60 |
| MISC. CUTS | 11 | .52 | 5.70 |
| | | | $107.00 |

FIG 23.13—Value of retail cuts from a 230-pound hog, Chicago, Mar., 1970.

At an average of 54 cents per pound, the wholesale cuts cost the retailer $77.75. The retailer sold 132 pounds of retail cuts at the prices shown in Figure 23.13, for a total value of $107.[11]

Actual retail margins are generally not this wide, as was shown earlier in Table 23.7. The retail prices used in these examples are estimates by the Bureau of Labor Statistics and do not reflect prices of meat sold on "special" at reduced prices. Meat department gross margins in 1969 for one of the largest affiliated independent grocers in the United States averaged 21.3 per cent.[12]

## MEAT RETAILING

Table 23.7 earlier in this chapter showed that farmers get about 60 cents of the consumer's meat dollar. Processing and distribution take the other 40 cents. And over half of the latter goes to retailing—the largest single cost item in meat distribution. Self-service has reduced retailing costs for a large number of grocery items. A major part of the meat sold at retail is by self-service. Which costs less—self-service or salesman-service meat retailing? Which is the more efficient?

A study of the operations of 26 salesman-service meat departments and 23 self-service meat departments, which ranged in size from sales of $500 to $11,000 per week, provides a basis for an answer.[13] It found that the self-service method cost less for labor but more for wrapping supplies than the salesman-service method. These two differences cancelled out, so that the total costs per dollar of sales were about the same for both types of service. But in both cases, costs decreased with volume, as shown in Figure 23.14.

But—and this is important—most stores which switched to self-service increased their volume of sales. Thus, converting to self-service pushed their cost farther to the right and down along the cost curve. Their cost per pound went down as their volume increased. Their cost decreased because of the larger volume of sales that came with the switch to self-service—not because self-service in itself is a lower-cost method of retailing.

### Consolidation of Some Marketing and Processing Functions

The preceding discussion has dealt with the individual

---

[11] For a more detailed discussion, see *Price Spreads for Beef*, USDA, Misc. Publ. 992, Feb., 1965; and *Price Spreads for Pork*, USDA, Misc. Publ. 1051, Jan., 1967.

[12] "37th Annual Report of the Grocery Industry," *Progressive Grocer*, Apr., 1970, p. 69.

[13] F. H. Wiegmann, E. S. Clifton, and G. S. Shepherd, "Self-Service or Salesman-Service Meat Retailing?" *Iowa Farm Science*, Iowa State Univ., Vol. 8 (Aug., 1953), pp. 23–24.

FIG. 23.14—Relationship of combined costs per dollar sales to meat department sales for one week.

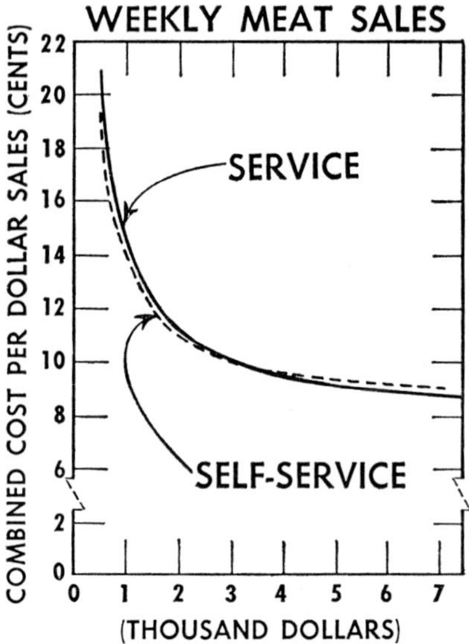


marketing and processing functions as now generally performed. The question may be raised as to how the consolidation of some functions might contribute to more efficient operation and to the reduction in operation costs.

A change that might be important would be to have some of the processing now done in the retail store transferred to the packing plant. If packers could complete the preparation of meat in consumer-style units of sale, and put up the meat in suitable packages, the entire structure of present-day meat retailing might be changed. This could be done through the medium of precut frozen meat, or cooked meats wrapped or placed in cartons which would furnish protection and make economical handling possible.

## Marketing Frozen Meat

The preparation, distribution, and sale of fresh meat in frozen form to consumers would cause great changes in processing and meat distribution. Adoption of this method of merchandising would expand operations at the packing plant; some changes would be required in the refrigeration of meat in transit, in storage, in the retail market, and in the homes; and some changes would be made in the retail distribution of meat. It is likely that these changes would result in a net reduction of the aggregate marketing and processing margin between the packing plant and the customer. In any event, some shifts would take place in the relative margins of different agencies handling the product owing to modifications of their functions.

If more fresh meat were sold in frozen form, services performed at packing plants would be greatly increased. They would include the preparation of retail cuts, which would involve a large amount of boning and trimming. The cuts would be wrapped, packaged, graded, labeled, and frozen at the plant. Trimmings from the cutting could be made into ground meat, sausage, or other prepared meats, and these also would be frozen at the plant. Shifting the preparation of consumer cuts from the retail market to the packing plant would permit the work to be done more efficiently and more economically. Professional retail meatcutters operating in the packing plant could then devote all their time to boning meat and preparing cuts. Trimmings from cutting operations could be utilized to better advantage because of the greater volume, and because the products made from trimmings could be sorted, graded, and standardized. Bones, waste fat, and other inedible products could be more fully salvaged in the plant than in retail markets.

The cost of transporting frozen, boned, and packaged meat under refrigeration should be materially less than that of unboned carcasses and wholesale cuts, primarily on account of the reduced weight, even after allowing for the increased cost of maintaining lower temperatures. The bone, ligament, and tendon in a beef steer carcass of Good grade is about 18 per cent, and in a lamb carcass of the same grade, 24 per cent. In the carcass of a hog weighing 200 pounds alive, bone and skin equal about 21 per cent of the weight. Then too, frozen packaged meat could be loaded much more advantageously for transportation in refrigerator cars and motor trucks than fresh carcasses and wholesale cuts. The loss from spoilage and deterioration in quality of meat in the frozen form, and from shrinkage in weight, should be negligible.

Reduction in the cost of retailing frozen fresh meat compared with present methods of handling fresh meat should be substantial. If meat were prepared and packaged at the packing plant, the services of professional meatcutters would not be needed in retail stores. Packaged meats could be retailed through either self-service or service stores in about the same manner as dairy and poultry products. The reduction in retailing costs might more than offset the added cost of processing. On the other hand, low-temperature refrigeration equipment for the storage and display of frozen packaged meat would be needed, and this would add to both capital investment and operating cost for refrigeration in most stores; although this is not a large item over a period of years. Opposition to such arrangement from the unions of meatcutters might be encountered.

Freezing meat and selling it in frozen form to consumers should facilitate the more uniform distribution of meat throughout the year. In this regard it would serve the same purpose as that of curing and smoking hams, shoulders, and bellies. Some of these pork cuts, after being processed, are withdrawn from the market during periods of heavy slaughter and are added to the current meat supply during periods of light slaughter. This makes the supply more even throughout the year, and reduces fluctuations in price.

It should be recognized that if fresh meat is to be sold at retail in frozen form, many changes will need to be made in its preparation and distribution. Technical problems pertaining to preparing frozen meat, grading, grade labeling, wrapping, packaging, refrigeration, storage, and distribution have received considerable study by the packing industry and by some distribution agencies in recent years. Consumer reaction to frozen meat will need to be given careful consideration. Moreover, the price relationships among cuts of meat may be materially changed, as some cuts when boned will have a high selling price per pound as compared with other cuts.

This centralization of cutting and freezing in the packing house is being developed. Self-service meat in the retail store has become more and more popular, but the cutting is done in the retail store. Frozen meat remains less popular with homemakers than fresh meat, and the technical problems involved in keeping fresh meat that is cut in the packing house in good condition through the retailing operation remains unsolved.

# 24

# DAIRY MARKETING: MILK

MILK is consumed in a number of different forms—fresh fluid milk, butter, cheese, and so forth. The consumption of these different forms has been changing rapidly—Figure 24.1 shows the changes from 1958 to 1968 and indicates that per capita sales of milkfat in butter declined more than 30 per cent in that period. This was due to greater competition from products made from lower-priced vegetable oils and to a conscious effort on the part of consumers to restrict their intake of certain fats. These changes occurred despite rising real incomes and declining real prices for dairy products.

Table 24.1 is made up from a different source—a survey of food consumption in 1965. It divides milk products into smaller categories but tells much the same story as Figure 24.1, however the greater detail enables indication of the changes in consumption of specific products.

Both sources show the same approximately 30 per cent decline in the demand for butter. This is discussed in the next chapter on butter marketing. In the present chapter we will deal with milk.

## THE DEMAND FOR MILK

The per capita consumption of fluid milk by the civilian population in 1969, 296 pounds for the year, amounted to nearly

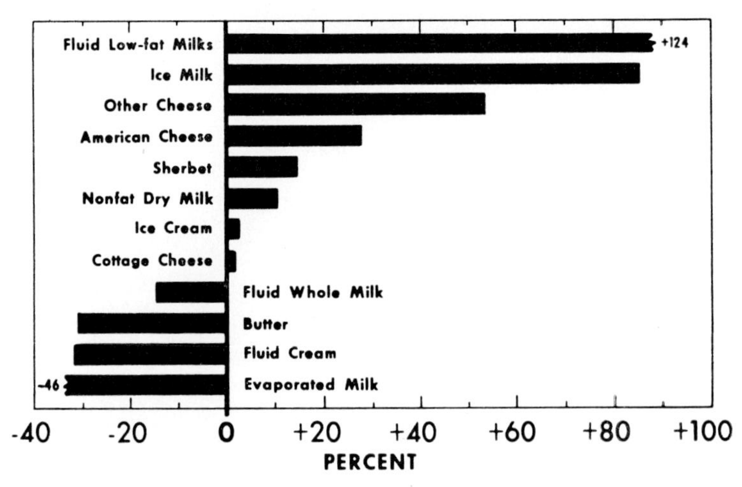


FIG. 24.1—Per capita sales of selected dairy products, 1958–68.

one pint per day. This is close to the consumption recommended by nutritionists of one pint per day for adults and up to one quart per day for children.[1] Thus if milk consumption were distributed evenly, there would not be much farther to go to meet nutritional requirements.

Milk consumption, of course, is not distributed evenly. Table 5.1 has shown that the lowest income group in 1965 consumed only 3.6 quarts of milk in all its forms—cheese, ice cream, etc., as well as fluid milk—per week, while the upper income groups consumed 4.5 quarts. Individual differences in consumption within income groups are larger than the differences among groups. The greatest opportunities for increasing the demand for milk apparently lie at the low end of the dispersion behind the average. Efforts directed at that point are likely to be more successful than attempts to increase the general demand by all consumers. Progress in any case is likely to be slow and steady rather than spectacular.

The value of the minerals and vitamins in milk has been generally recognized for some time, but the value of milk as a source of low-cost, high-quality animal protein is still not generally known. The comparative cost of animal protein from different sources in 1970 is indicated approximately in Table 24.2.

Quite apart from the question of nutrition is the matter of taste. Some people may drink more milk than they require

[1] *Recommended Dietary Allowances,* National Research Council, Reprint and Circular Series, 1958.

**TABLE 24.1: Selected Dairy Products: Civilian Annual Per Capita Consumption, Total and in Households, United States, 1965 With Comparisons**

| Item | Annual 1965 Per Capita Consumption | | Percentage Change, 1955–65 | |
|---|---|---|---|---|
| | Households* | Total† | Households | Total |
| | *(pounds)* | *(pounds)* | *(per cent)* | *(per cent)* |
| Fresh fluid milk‡ | 303 | 305 | −18 | −9 |
| Cream§ | 4.4 | 7.5 | −33 | −24 |
| Evaporated milk | 9.9 | 8.4 | −35 | −41 |
| Nonfat dry milk | 2.1 | 5.6 | +100 | +2 |
| Frozen desserts | 26.5 | 28.1 | +24 | +20 |
| Cottage cheese | 7.8 | 4.6 | +15 | +18 |
| All other cheese ‖ | 10.4 | 9.5 | +5 | +20 |
| Butter | 6.8 | 6.4 | −35 | −29 |

Source: *The Dairy Situation,* USDA, DS-318, Nov., 1967, p. 36. (Based on USDA 1965 household food consumption survey.)

* Includes only products used directly in homes. Weekly per capita consumption expanded to annual level.

† Includes products used in restaurants, schools, and institutions, as well as those used in home.

‡ Includes product weight of whole, skim, and chocolate milk and buttermilk.

§ Includes half and half.

‖ Includes cheese spreads.

simply because they like the taste of it. However, average per capita use of fluid milk has declined in recent years. In the future, prospects are that total human demand for fluid milk in the United States will not rise as rapidly as population.

## MILK PRICE DETERMINATION

About half the total production of milk in the United States is sold as fresh fluid milk. The prices of fresh fluid milk are determined under specialized conditions that are markedly different from the conditions for most other farm products. The prices for most farm products are, in general, open-market prices, determined under conditions approximating those of atomistic competition. The price of milk, however, is determined under conditions that depart considerably from atomistic competition. Milk prices are determined by negotiation between two groups—the producers and the distributors—each of which has some degree of geographical monopoly.

The reasons for milk being taken out of the open competitive market system are clear enough. The competitive system requires the existence of certain conditions if it is to work well—large numbers of buyers and sellers (no one large enough to affect prices appreciably by his own actions, and each free to deal with any other seller or buyer) and adequate information as to supply, demand, and prices. But these conditions are not met in milk marketing. The producers of milk are large in num-

**TABLE 24.2: Cost of Proteins in Specified Foods, 1970**

| Product | Unit | Protein Content* | Assumed Cost† | Cost Per 10 Grams of Protein |
|---|---|---|---|---|
| | | *(grams)* | *(cents)* | *(cents)* |
| Whole Milk | qt. | 33.8 | 28.7 | 8.5 |
| Skim Milk | qt. | 34.6 | 25.5 | 7.4 |
| Poultry and Eggs | | | | |
| Eggs, large grade A | doz. | 104.2 | 67.8 | 6.5 |
| Chicken, ready-to-eat fryer | lb. | 57.4 | 41.5 | 7.2 |
| Red Meats | | | | |
| Beef | | | | |
| Round, without bone | lb. | 88.5 | 129.0 | 14.6 |
| Sirloin steak, with bone | lb. | 71.1 | 132.4 | 18.6 |
| Chuck roast, with bone | lb. | 71.6 | 72.6 | 10.1 |
| Rib roast, with bone | lb. | 61.8 | 110.7 | 17.9 |
| Hamburger | lb. | 81.2 | 65.5 | 8.1 |
| Veal | | | | |
| Cutlets | lb. | 88.5 | 214.6 | 24.2 |
| Pork | | | | |
| Pork chops, center cut | lb. | 61.1 | 120.8 | 19.8 |
| Roast pork, loin half, with bone | lb. | 61.1 | 85.0 | 13.9 |
| Lamb | | | | |
| Loin chops, with bone | lb. | 63.7 | 185.1 | 29.1 |
| Frankfurters | lb. | 64.5 | 82.8 | 12.8 |
| Fish | | | | |
| Haddock, fillet, frozen | lb. | 83.0 | 85.3 | 10.3 |
| Other Commodities | | | | |
| Beans, dry | lb. | 101.2 | 19.1 | 1.9 |

Sources:
* *Composition of Foods, Raw, Processed and Prepared,* USDA, Handbook 8, Dec., 1963.
† *U.S. Retail Food Prices,* BLS, Mar., 1970.

ber and small in size, but the distributors are usually small in number and large in size. The economies of large-scale operation in milk distribution are so great that milk distribution soon becomes concentrated in the hands of a few large distributors. The small number of these distributors, coupled with the fact that milk is bulky and perishable so that a milk producer can usually sell his milk only in the one city market adjacent to him, puts the *distribution* of milk in the monopoly category. And when you have a monopoly (the distributors)[2] dealing with a competitive group (the milk producers), you are likely to have trouble.

The trouble is accentuated in this case by the nature of the commodity itself. Milk is highly perishable; it must reach the market fresh every day in the year. It is so excellent a medium for the growth of disease bacteria that it must meet rigid sani-

[2] In this case operating as a monopsony (a single buyer) or more accurately, as an oligopsony (a few buyers).

tary standards. It is produced in markedly varying amounts from season to season throughout the year. The demand for fluid milk is more nearly constant throughout the year than the supply, so that any group of producers with enough milk to supply the market in the winter will have more than enough milk to supply the demand in the summer. The demand for fluid milk is so inelastic that this "surplus" milk cannot easily be disposed of simply by lowering this price. If, as in the traditional competitive market, the price for all the product fell to the level of the marginal uses (in this case butter, ice cream, and cheese), summer production would be so reduced that winter production would be expensive (either because of producers being out of milk entirely, or producing it in fairly constant amounts throughout the year). Milk prices then would be low in the summer and high in the winter.

As a result of this complicated situation, a system has been worked out by which a surplus of milk (over fluid milk consumption) is not choked off nor allowed to pull all milk prices down to butterfat levels, but is segregated and paid for at manufactured milk product levels. The price paid for that part of the milk which is used for fluid milk purposes remains at a more constant level throughout the year. Thus arises the phenomenon of two different prices being paid for milk out of the same cow—perhaps $5.25 per 100 pounds for the milk that is used for fluid purposes, and $4.00 per 100 pounds for the "surplus."

## ROLE OF FEDERAL GOVERNMENT IN PRICING FLUID MILK

Milk price systems have been set up to remove milk prices from the open-market category and to put them into the administered category. Any advantage in milk pricing has historically been on the side of the distributors, who usually were small in number and large enough in size to possess considerable monopolistic (actually, oligopsonistic) power. When the competitive producers realized the weakness of their bargaining position, they organized into cooperative bargaining associations and met oligopsony with monopoly. In this situation the price is determined by bargaining between the two groups. Federal and state governments were called upon to intervene in the early stages of the pull and haul between the bargaining groups, and with time have become involved in an increasing number of cases.

The process of setting minimum prices to be paid to farmers for milk is therefore fairly well regularized in most large cities today through the operation of federal milk marketing orders. These orders can be established upon approval by two-thirds or more of the producers, representing at least half the milk in the area, under the authority of the Agricultural Marketing Agreement Act of 1937.

Where these orders are in effect, whenever there is dissatisfaction with the price of milk, the Secretary of Agriculture is authorized to call a hearing at which all interested parties may present their evidence. After the hearing, the milk price officials of the Department of Agriculture must weigh the evidence from all parties to the hearing and make a decision on the question. Their decision may be incorporated into a proposed marketing agreement, which then goes back to the producers and handlers for their vote. If at least two-thirds of the producers and half of the handlers vote for the agreement, it goes into effect and is binding upon all producers and handlers in the marketing area. More commonly, these decisions are incorporated into a proposed order and marketing agreement. In this case the provisions may be put into effect as a marketing order even if handlers vote against it, providing that at least two-thirds of the producers representing at least half of the milk in the area have voted for it. Subsequent amendments to the order go through a similar hearing and voting procedure before adoption.

A milk marketing order applies to a specified local area and requires all milk dealers (usually called *milk handlers*) to pay certain minimum prices for the different use classifications and to observe certain terms of sale with respect to milk purchased from milk producers.

The marketing areas covered by the federal orders are shown in Figure 24.2. The supply area covers the eastern half of the United States almost completely with the exception of the southeastern seaboard.

A number of states have enacted legislation and established administrative agencies with power to set retail prices as well as minimum prices payable to producers. These laws differ from state to state and the number having such laws varies from time to time. In 1969, 20 states had laws authorizing regulation of milk prices at the farm; 25 states also had some authority to regulate wholesale and retail prices.

### Purpose of Federal Marketing Orders[3]

The general objective of the Agricultural Marketing Agreement Act of 1937 was "to establish and maintain such orderly marketing conditions for agricultural commodities in interstate

[3] The section on federal marketing draws on information presented in *The Dairy Situation*, USDA, Apr., 1954, and later issues; also, "Summary of Major Provisions," *Federal Milk Marketing Orders*, USDA, Jan., 1970; and *Organization and Competition in the Dairy Industry*, National Commission on Food Marketing, Tech. Study 3, June, 1966.

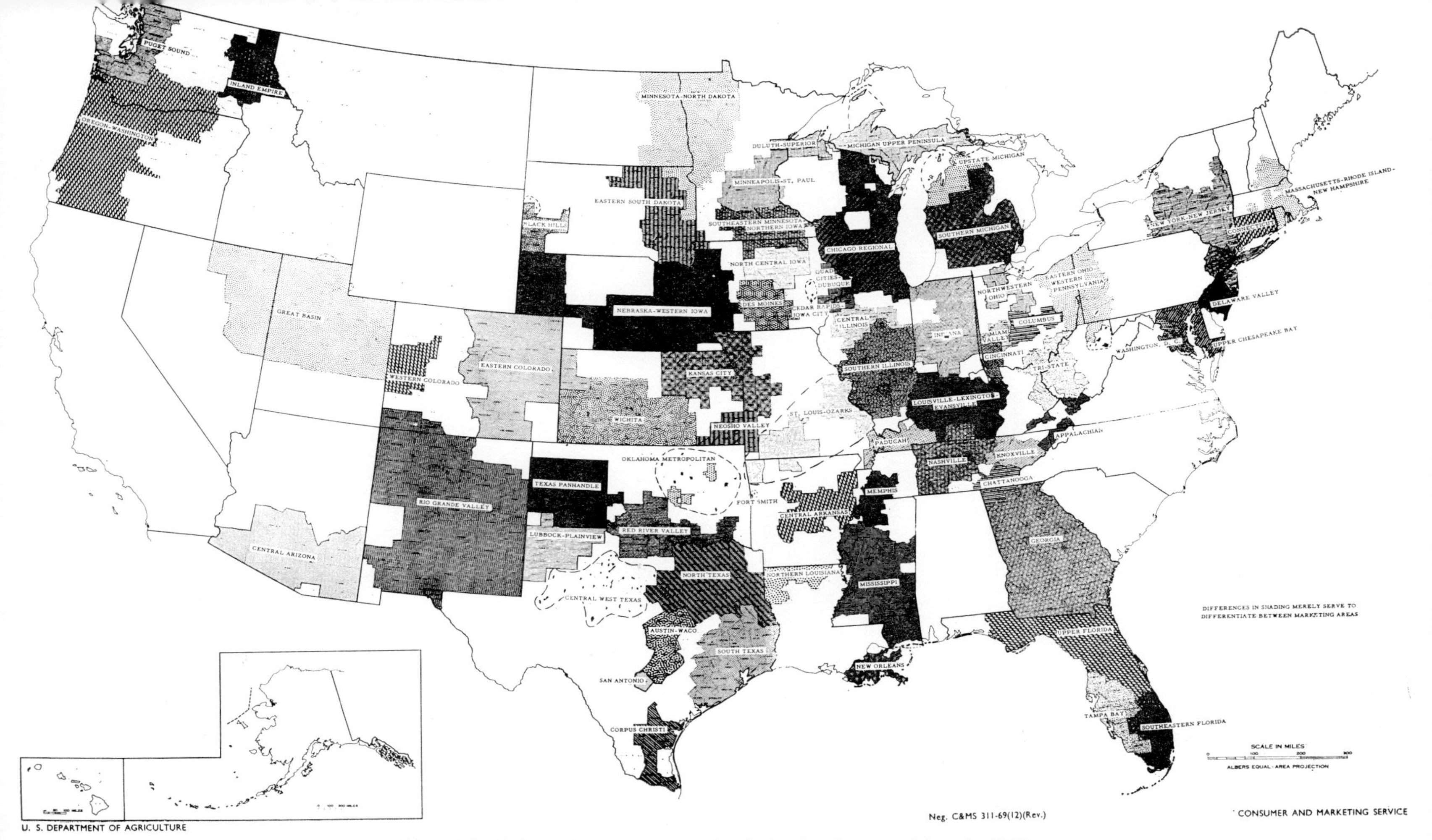


FIG. 24.2—Milk marketing areas under federal orders as of Jan. 1, 1970.

commerce as will establish" parity prices for such commodities. In the case of milk, however, the Secretary of Agriculture is directed by the act to establish minimum prices different from the parity price if such parity price does not appear reasonable in view of the price of feeds, the available supplies of feeds, and other economic conditions which affect market supply and demand for milk and its products in the marketing area to which the contemplated order program relates. The actual minimum price so established shall be such as to "reflect such factors, insure a sufficient quantity of pure and wholesome milk, and be in the public interest." More recently, the Food and Agricultural Act of 1965 specifically authorized marketing orders for manufacturing milk.

Under the federal marketing orders, only the milk handlers are regulated. The handlers are directed to pay not less than the minimum prices established in the order and to comply with certain rules regulating the handling of milk in the market. Federal orders do not fix resale prices for milk.

The number of federal milk marketing orders in effect increased steadily from 1936 to 1960, when there were over 80. Consolidation of federal orders during the next few years, however, reduced the number to 68 by 1970, as shown in Figure 24.2.

#### The Classified Pricing Plan

The Marketing Agreement Act of 1937 requires the Secretary of Agriculture to use the "classified use" basis for setting the minimum prices to be paid to producers for their milk. This means that the distributors pay for milk according to the use they make of it.

Under this plan a relatively high price is paid for the amount a dealer sells as fluid milk; but for the milk sold as cream, a lower price is paid, and for that which is manufactured into butter, cheese, or evaporated milk, a still lower price is paid. The prices for these various classes are then averaged so that the same price is paid to all farmer-shippers, selling to one dealer, for the milk of a given test and grade.

Every dealer, of course, pays the same price for milk going to a particular use, such as fluid milk, but different dealers sell different proportions of milk for the various uses. One dealer may sell 75 per cent of his total milk receipts for fluid uses; another may sell only 50 per cent for this use. Thus, the one dealer will not pay the same average, or composite, price to his patrons as will the other.

In order that all dealers do pay the same average or composite price, some producers' associations have formed market pools. Under this arrangement every dealer turns his total payments over to the pool instead of paying his shippers direct, and the pool in turn pays the producers. Thus, every producer receives the same average or composite price for his milk regardless of the dealer to whom he sells. In some other markets an adjustment is made whereby distributors who have a small proportion of surplus pay an amount to the market pool, and those with a large proportion receive an amount from the pool so that, while every distributor pays his producers direct, all producers receive the same average price.

Some markets employ individual handler pool arrangements; the uniform price to individual farmers is computed on the basis of the use made of the milk by the handler to whom it was sold. The others use market-wide pools. In 1970, 5 markets employed the individual handler pool device and 63 used the market-wide pool arrangement.

### Milk Price Formulas

In the early years of federal order regulation, Class I milk prices were established at a fixed minimum, based on testimony received at public hearings in each market; and these fixed minimums remained effective until modified by amendment to the order.

The Agricultural Market Agreement Act of 1937 established detailed regulations for the promulgation and amendment of federal orders. These procedures require considerable time, whereas changes in Class I prices have to be made quickly to keep them in line with changing market conditions. In order to avoid delay in changing Class I prices in line with changing economic conditions, formulas for determining Class I prices have been developed. These formulas make Class I prices respond automatically to changes in the market situation. All the federal orders provide for some kind of formula pricing for Class I milk.

The early formulas were based on butter and milk-powder prices. Later, "economic index" formulas were developed and used for pricing Class I milk (milk used for fresh fluid consumption) in northeastern United States. These economic-index formulas use indexes such as U.S. wholesale commodity prices, prices paid by dairy farmers, disposable personal income, and manufacturing milk prices, thus reflecting changes in demand as well as in supply.

Still later, in 1960, the USDA adopted the Minnesota-Wisconsin manufacturing milk price series as a better basis for reflecting the value of milk in the marginal supply area for fluid markets. This was the average price for manufacturing-grade milk, f.o.b. plants in Minnesota and Wisconsin, where about one-half the manufacturing-grade milk is produced. Changing economic conditions are quickly reflected in this index. By 1969, all but six of the orders used this series.[4]

Some orders include a "supply-demand adjuster." This device increases the Class I price when supplies of milk relative to Class I sales are less than normal and decreases Class I prices when supplies are greater than normal.

Supply-demand adjusters usually provide for a comparison of the percentage of producer receipts utilized as Class I milk, with a standard or ideal level of utilization. The difference between the current percentage and the standard percentage is expressed as a net utilization percentage, which is then converted to a price adjustment for the period.

Some orders also incorporate seasonal adjustment factors to reflect seasonal changes in the level of milk production into the pricing formula.

### EXAMPLE OF "ECONOMIC-TYPE" FORMULA

The order for the Massachusetts-Rhode Island market may be used to illustrate pricing by formula based on general economic factors (Table 24.3). The first step in determining the Class I price for any month is calculation of an "economic index." To do this, the U.S. monthly wholesale price index for all commodities (as reported by the Bureau of Labor Statistics, U.S. Department of Labor) is multiplied by the factor 1.0025. Then a New England consumer income index is calculated to reflect the current relationship between New England per capita personal income and national per capita income. A New England grain-labor cost index is calculated from USDA data on the average price paid by New England farmers for mixed dairy feed and New England farm wage rates. The final "economic index" is obtained by adding three times the adjusted U.S. wholesale commodity price index, the New England consumer income index, and three times the New England grain-labor cost index and dividing by seven.

An "economic index price" is obtained by multiplying the economic index by $5.57 (1958 adjusted base price) and adjusting this to within 5 cents of the New York-New Jersey Class I-A price (before supply-demand and seasonal adjustments). The

---

[4] By 1970, these six orders had the economic index deleted and a Class I price specified in the order, to be adjusted upward by the amount the Minnesota-Wisconsin price series exceeds $4.33 per 100 pounds. However, hearings were held early in 1970 to consider putting all federal orders on economic index Class I pricing formulas. This illustrates the changing nature of federal order provisions.

**TABLE 24.3: Computation of Massachusetts-Rhode Island Class I Prices for December, 1966. Index Numbers, 1958 = 100**

*(prices per cwt. for 3.5 per cent milk)*

*Economic Index:*

United States Wholesale Commodity Price Index:
Index for all commodities October 1966, 106.2;
divided by 1.0025 .......... 105.94

New England Consumer Income Index:
U.S. per capita disposable income, 3rd quarter 1966, $2,576 a year;
times 109.7 (New England adjustment percentage) $2,810 a year;
divided by 20.50 .......... 137.07

New England Grain-Labor Cost Index:
New England dairy ration index:
Average price for 100 pounds of dairy ration, Oct. 15, $4.07;
divided by 0.03884 = 104.79; times 0.6 .......... 62.874

New England farm wage rate index:
Weighted average farm wage rate, Oct. 1, $257.06;
divided by 1.9833 = 129.61; times 0.4 .......... 51.844

Grain-Labor Cost Index (sum of grain and labor components): .. 114.72

Economic Index (above indexes weighted by 3, 1, and 3, respectively) .......... 114.15

*Economic Index Price:*

1958 adjusted base price of $5.57, times Economic Index percentage, 114.15% .......... $6.358

New York-New Jersey December 1966 Class I-A price for 3.5% milk, $6.15, divided by product of Order 2 utilization adjustment percentage, 94.1, and seasonal adjustment factor, 1.07 ...... 6.108

Difference .......... $ .250

Difference in excess of $.05 .......... .200

Economic Index Price ($6.358 adjusted for difference in excess of $.05) .......... 6.158

*Supply-Demand Adjustment:*

| 1966 | Class I Producer Milk N.E. Federal Order Mkts. (1,000 lbs.) | Base Class I Percentage | Base Supply (Col. 1 ÷ Col. 2) | Producer Receipts N.E. Federal Order Mkts. (1,000 lbs.) | Percentage of Base Supply (Col. 4 ÷ Col. 3) |
|---|---|---|---|---|---|
| Aug. | 235,746 | 69.8 | 337,745 | 338,260 | 100.15 |
| Sept. | 241,199 | 74.1 | 325,505 | 333,000 | 102.30 |
| Oct. | 246,532 | 77.8 | 316,879 | 338,761 | 106.91 |
| Average | | | | | 103.12 |
| Supply-demand adjustment factor | | | | | 0.98 |

*Seasonal Adjustment:* Factor for December .......... 1.08

*Unbracketed Price:* Economic Index Price, $6.158, times 0.98 times 1.08 $6.518

*Class I Price Schedule:*

| Range: At least, but | Range: Less than | Class I Prices: Zone 21 | Class I Prices: Nearby (city) plants |
|---|---|---|---|
| $6.26 | $6.48 | $6.37 | $6.84 |
| 6.48 | 6.70 | **6.59** | **7.06** |
| 6.70 | 6.92 | 6.81 | 7.28 |

Source: Provided by the Dairy Division, USDA, Consumer and Marketing Service, Washington, D.C.

**TABLE 24.4: Computation of Kansas City Class I Price, November, 1967**

|  |  |
|---|---|
| Minnesota-Wisconsin manufacturing milk price* | $4.05 |
| Class I differential† | 1.50 |
| | $5.55 |
| Supply-demand adjustment‡ | —.07 |
| Class I Price for November, 1967 | $5.48 |

Source: *Market Administration Bulletin,* Greater Kansas City Marketing Area, Vol. 23, No. 11, Nov., 1967.

* The actual Minnesota-Wisconsin manufacturing milk price for November, 1967 was $3.98/cwt. However, under temporary price increase amendments it was provided that the basic formula price should not be less than $4.05/cwt. beginning April, 1967.

† Prior to April, 1967, the Class I differential was $1.10 in April, May, June, and July and $1.40 in all other months. This seasonal variation was suspended at that time and a constant differential of $1.50 was established.

‡ The supply-demand adjustment was suspended (at least temporarily) in December, 1967.

final Class I price is determined by multiplying this "economic index price" by a supply-demand adjustment factor, multiplying by a seasonal adjustment factor, then adjusting to the nearest 22-cent increment above or below $5.49 and adding 47 cents.[5]

The supply-demand adjustment factor is based on current production of milk in New England order markets as a percentage of a specified "base" or normal supply. The supply-demand adjustment factor varies with changes in the relationship of current production to base supply according to a schedule contained in the federal order for that market.

#### EXAMPLE OF "MINNESOTA-WISCONSIN-TYPE" FORMULA

The order for the Kansas City market is an example of the Minnesota-Wisconsin-type pricing formula (Table 24.4). The Class I price is based on the Minnesota-Wisconsin monthly average price per hundredweight for manufacturing-grade milk, f.o.b. plants in Minnesota and Wisconsin, as reported by the USDA. This manufacturing milk price is adjusted to a 3.5 per cent butterfat basis by using a butterfat differential computed by multiplying the Chicago 92-score butter price by 0.12 and rounding to the nearest one-tenth cent.

In the Kansas City market, the Minnesota-Wisconsin manufacturing milk price is adjusted by a Class I differential, which varies seasonally according to the following schedule:

[5] The seasonal adjustment was suspended April 1, 1967 and the bracket system was suspended December 1, 1967.

| Month | Price | Month | Price |
|---|---|---|---|
| January | $1.40 | July | $1.10 |
| February | 1.40 | August | 1.40 |
| March | 1.40 | September | 1.40 |
| April | 1.10 | October | 1.40 |
| May | 1.10 | November | 1.40 |
| June | 1.10 | December | 1.40 |

In addition a supply-demand adjustment factor is applied, the amount depending upon the relationship of current utilization and production to specified "normal" relationships. The supply-demand adjustment is based on the percentage which total producer receipts are of Class I utilization in the two months preceding the delivery period. A price adjustment (plus or minus) is made whenever such utilization percentage differs by specified amounts from standard percentages listed in the order for the corresponding months. The maximum supply-demand adjustment is plus or minus 45 cents.

### The Base-Excess Plan

The classified pricing plan applies to the dealers and determines the prices they pay for the different classes of milk. In a number of cases this plan is combined with what is called the *base-excess* plan, which determines the distribution of the payments to individual farmers.

The base-excess plan, as first used in many markets, was designed primarily to encourage farmers to produce milk uniformly throughout the year. This feature of the plan has not been materially changed, and the usual method is to pay each individual farmer a higher price for an amount of milk produced in the spring, which is equal to his average monthly production during the previous fall months—this amount is called his base. For all milk in excess of this basic amount (surplus milk) the farmer is paid a lower price. Many variations exist, but the fundamental feature of discouraging high summer production relative to the winter production by paying each farmer according to the seasonality of his volume is common to all.

Confusion often arises over the use of the base-excess plan because the term "excess" is sometimes used with reference to the amount of milk produced by the farmer over and above his basic quantity, and at other times "excess" applies to the milk used by the dealer for cream and manufactured products. This might be clarified by using two terms: *farmer's excess* and *market excess*. There is also a dual meaning for "base." The word is sometimes used to describe the basic amount of production of an individual farmer and in other cases to describe the amount of milk used in the market for fluid purposes. This might also be clarified by the use of two terms: *farmer's base* and *market base.*

The amount of milk a producer ships during the fall months establishes what is known as his "basic" quantity upon which his individual surplus will be determined. Specifically, suppose a producer shipped the following amounts of milk: August—4,620 pounds; September—4,600 pounds; October—5,130 pounds; and November—5,650 pounds. Adding these amounts and dividing by four it is found that on an average, this shipper produced 5,000 pounds of milk per month during this so-called base period. This 5,000 pounds becomes his base for the following eight months beginning December 1. In some markets this base is used for a period of twelve months instead of eight; in others, it may apply for only four to six months in the spring.

According to an agreement entered into between the producers' association and the distributors, the individual producers may be allowed during the following eight months a certain "tolerance." This tolerance is the amount by which a producer is permitted to exceed his basic quantity in any month and still receive the basic price. If the producer exceeds his tolerance, he will receive only the manufactured price for the excess. This tolerance may run as high as 50 per cent of the amount established during the base period. Thus, the above producer would receive the average price for all milk shipped during any of the eight months following, up to 7,500 pounds. If he shipped an amount greater than this, he would receive only the manufacturing price for the excess. For example, if this producer shipped 7,800 pounds of milk during the month of June, he would receive the average price for 7,500 pounds and the manufactured price for 300 pounds. In some markets if the total amount of base milk of all farmers plus any tolerance allowed is not sufficient to provide the market needs of fluid milk and cream, the additional amount needed will be obtained from the farmers' surplus. This will raise the surplus price paid to farmers to a level somewhat above that of milk used for manufacturing purposes.

Usually, however, the situation is the opposite of this; the total amount of the base milk of all the producers—the total farmer's base—exceeds the total fluid needs of the market—the market base. For this reason producers in some markets are allowed the base price for only 90 per cent of their base quantity.

The total farmer's base is likely to exceed the total market base because the base price is set high enough above the everyday butterfat equivalent price to cover the extra cost of meeting the fluid milk sanitation requirements and still make it worthwhile for the farmer to belong to the association. This higher price attracts other farmers' attention, and they apply for membership in the association. The officers of the association then have a difficult question to decide. If they let the new applicants join the association and give them a base quantity, this amount added to the previous total farmer's base will make the new total farmer's base exceed the market base. If they meet this situation by making, let us say, a 10 per cent cut in the existing farmers' bases, they will hear complaints from those farmers; or if instead they reduce the base price because they cannot sell all the base milk at the fluid milk price, they will also have trouble. So they may be tempted to refuse to admit the new applicants into the association. But if they do that, the applicants may set up a new association or start in as individual producer-distributors, in either case taking some of the market away from the original association.

To meet these difficulties, milk-cooperative administrators have adopted policies ranging all the way from an *open base* at one extreme to a *closed base* at the other. Under the open base policy, each producer earns an entirely new base each year, unrelated to the bases he held in former years. Under the closed base policy the same base assignments may remain in effect with only minor adjustments, for ten or fifteen years at a stretch. Under policies between these two extremes, bases may be held for two or three years at a time. In 1970 base-excess plans were in use in 14 milk markets.

### Effects of Federal Marketing Orders on Milk Prices

A 1964–65 report[6] compared the farm prices of milk in regulated markets (that is, markets with milk orders) and unregulated markets in the United States. It found that most of the unregulated market prices were lower. The Springfield, Illinois, unregulated price was $4.09 per 100 pounds, compared to $4.26 for the regulated Chicago price, although Springfield was 100 miles farther from the center of production at Eau Claire, Wisconsin.

The unregulated Bemidji and Winona prices in Minnesota were $3.55 and $3.68, respectively, compared to $4.13 and $3.99 for regulated Duluth and St. Paul prices, respectively (all four cities are roughly equidistant from Eau Claire). The unregulated Eau Claire price, the lowest in the country, was $3.53. Prices in regulated Madison and Milwaukee were $4.20 and in Green Bay,

[6] Reuben A. Kessel, "Economic Effects of Federal Regulation of Milk Markets," *Journal of Law and Economics*, Vol. X (Oct., 1967), pp. 51–78.

$3.75. The prices in four other unregulated markets were about the same (adjusted for distance) as regulated prices.

The author concluded his study with this summary:

In summary, present legislation constitutes class legislation. It favors the suppliers of fluid milk markets and injures the suppliers of milk for manufacturing. The proliferation of orders following World War II led to an increase in the supply of milk for manufacturing as a result of the use of blend prices in making output decisions by order producers. Consequently, the higher prices obtained by fluid market suppliers were associated with lower prices for manufacturing milk suppliers. The economic gains of the fluid milk suppliers are considerably smaller than the economic costs incurred by society as a result of orders.

Orders constitute a monopolistic pricing arrangement that produces, not too small, but too large, an output. Typically, monopolists have marginal costs that are less than the price at which their marginal output is sold; the economic costs of monopoly arise because output is too small. In contrast, order producers sell their marginal output at prices below marginal costs. Hence, some of their gains in monopolizing the fluid milk market are dissipated in excessive production of milk at costs that exceed marginal returns. Consequently, if the output of order producers were reduced, the resources relinquished could be used to produce goods and services whose market value would exceed the value of the milk in fact produced. One method of achieving this objective is the replacement of orders with competition. Another is to establish Class I production quotas and sell all other milk at the market, and this is apparently the purpose of the Food and Agriculture Act of 1965.[7]

There is some difference of opinion regarding the effect of federal marketing orders on milk prices. This represents one viewpoint; others may reach somewhat different conclusions.

## EFFECTS OF STATE LAWS ON RETAIL MILK PRICES

The milk markets under federal orders set the prices that milk distributors pay to milk producers, but they do not set the prices that distributors charge consumers. Most of the states with state milk price legislation, however, do fix retail prices too.

What effect has this state legislation had on consumer milk prices?

A 1966 report of the National Commission on Food Marketing provided a general comment on this question.[8]

States which set farm and retail prices have tended to price at a higher level than in adjoining areas. This has caused outside milk

[7] *Ibid.*, p. 71.

[8] *Organization and Competition in the Dairy Industry*, National Commission on Food Marketing, Tech. Study 3, June, 1966, p. 169.

plants to seek ways of sharing in the higher prices in the controlled State markets. States with milk control have tried to discourage the entry of milk from outside markets, but with only limited success, since they cannot control interstate commerce. Improved transportation facilities and increased pressure on sanitary barriers have also made it easier for outside suppliers to sell in State regulated markets.

An earlier study covering selected periods from 1929 through 1953 reached similar conclusions.[9] This study also showed that consumers in cities under state control were forced to pay higher prices for milk than prevailed in cities where competition existed.

## DEVELOPMENT AND CHANGES IN THE MARKETING SYSTEM

In the late 1940's the whole effect of milk pricing and marketing arrangements was to build up a milk producers' monopoly in each city milk area, to match the distributors' monopoly that was inherent in the large size and small number of distributors in each city area. Both kinds of monopolies were reinforced by the natural and artificial barriers protecting one city area from invasion by another. The situation is similar to the workmen (the producers) in the old feudal castle organizing to bargain with the feudal lord on more nearly equal terms. This represented a step forward, even though the walls hindered movement between castles and the whole castle system was inefficient.

In the early 1950's the trend in this direction began to be reversed. New technological developments in milk handling at the farm, in processing, and in distributing began to breach the walls around the separate city areas and permit the invasion of one domain by another, much as the invention and use of gunpowder breached the walls of the old feudal castles.

The next few sections show briefly how technological developments are changing the milk marketing system.

### The Grade A Ordinance

One of the developments that has brought more competition into milk distribution is the wider use of the Grade A ordinance—a set of specifications for milk production equipment and practices designed to bring milk up to a high standard of cleanliness. In 1924, when Alabama asked the United States Public Health Service for help in raising the quality of its milk, the USPHS developed what it called the Grade A ordinance, and Alabama adopted this regulation. Several other southern states followed suit. During the 1930's a large number of states

[9] R. W. Bartlett, "Is State Control of Consumer Prices of Milk in the Public Interest?" *Illinois Farm Economics,* Univ. of Ill., No. 219 (Mar., 1954), pp. 1509–13.

adopted the ordinance, while the northeastern states developed their own.

Originally, it was possible for one state or milkshed to adopt the Grade A ordinance and use it not only to raise the quality of its milk but also to keep out milk from other areas. With the widespread adoption of the ordinance, however, the situation suddenly was reversed. A city milkshed that had the Grade A ordinance could not keep out milk from another milkshed that had the same ordinance. Thus the monopolistic positions of many areas began to break down; they were exposed to competition from any other areas that could deliver Grade A milk below their prices.

In their attempts to keep out this invasion of cheaper milk, several communities took drastic measures. One such instance is the case of Waukegan, which went so far as to specify in Section 577 of its milk ordinance, that "no milk or milk products shall be sold in the City of Waukegan unless the same is produced and pasteurized in Lake County, Illinois" (where Waukegan is located). This section was contested by the Dean Milk Company in 1949. The supreme court of Illinois in 1951 declared the section invalid, stating that a city cannot keep out milk from other areas that meets its own quality standards.

Under this ruling, the increasing use of the Grade A ordinance permits a distributor in one Grade A area to invade other Grade A areas. Accordingly, distributors' sales areas, instead of being confined to one city as they were previously, have spread out into neighboring cities and towns. In some cases the area covers a major part of a state and includes dozens of small towns and cities.

Other changes in milk legislation, as well as technological advances in milk packaging and transportation, have also caused milk to break out of its traditional local market structure. The passing of compulsory pasteurization laws in a number of states has had significant effects, by squeezing out milk distributors whose volume was too small to support pasteurization equipment. The widespread use of the paper container has had a similar effect.

### The Paper Container

The paper container for retail milk has grown rapidly in popularity. In 1940 only 5 per cent of the fluid milk and cream sold in cities and towns in the United States was put up in paper. By 1952 the percentage had risen to 39 per cent,[10] and by 1958

[10] George D. Scott, *Development of Paper Milk Containers,* Dairy Marketing Conference, Univ. of Ill., AE 2939, Feb. 3, 1953, p. 24.

to 54 per cent.[11] In 1966, 68 per cent of the fluid milk sold in 68 federal order markets was distributed in paper cartons.[12]

The increasing use of the paper container for milk favors large-volume operation. Distributors with a large volume of business can buy paper containers knocked down and shipped in carload lots, set them up in their own machines, and use them at a cost of 2 cents or less per quart container. Smaller distributors either have to use smaller and less efficient machines, or to buy containers already set up, necessarily more bulky to ship, store, and handle, at a cost of nearly 3 cents. This gives the larger distributor about a 1-cent advantage over the smaller distributor.

The increased use of paper containers has been a factor in causing milk-plant operators to expand their distribution areas. Milk packaged in paper and handled in wood or wire cases weighs much less than milk in glass bottles in the same type of case. It also requires less space and stays cold longer than milk in glass bottles. These characteristics, plus the fact that return of empty bottles to the plant is eliminated, make it easier and cheaper to distribute milk over wide areas in paper cartons than in glass bottles.

The paper container has made possible the shipment of large loads of milk for long distances and at little more expense than delivering the same quantities of milk in bulk. In the North Central Region, outer-market shipments of milk in paper containers have become commonplace. This has increased the amount of overlapping in markets for fluid milk. Separate and distinct markets for packaged milk have practically disappeared.

Use of paper has also opened up a new distribution technique—the milk-vending machine. Located in such places as schools, offices, and factories, these machines dispense half-pint paper containers of milk upon the insertion of a coin.

### The Tank Truck Pickup

Another technological development is the farm milk tank and the tank truck pickup. This development has altered milkshed *supply* areas. Under this system, the dairy farmer puts his milk into a mechanically refrigerated stainless steel tank in his farmyard milk house instead of into 40-quart milk cans. The milk dealer's bulk tank truck then comes, pumps the cooled milk out of the farm tank into the truck tank, and hauls it to the distributor's milk plant. The truck tank is refrigerated too, and the milk can safely be hauled for long distances.

---

[11] *Highlights Study No. 10*, Alfred Politz Research, Inc., 1959, p. 37.

[12] *The Dairy Situation, USDA*, March, 1968, p. 32.

The whole system is clean and efficient, but the mechanically refrigerated farm tank represents a considerable investment for the dairy farmer. Even so, the adoption of bulk milk farm tanks has been rapid. One third of the approximately 600,000 farms that sold milk or cream in 1964 were equipped with bulk tanks.

The farm tank milk pickup system provides a high degree of flexibility as to the distances over which milk may be delivered directly from farms. This means that in many instances different markets can be supplied directly from a given farming area.

All this adds up to an expansion of each local milkshed and market. These expansions will bring new problems for producer cooperative associations—particularly those formed to work in an isolated market with a given group of distributors. The position of local associations in region-wide markets may be similar to the position of unorganized producers in the days before cooperatives. Their problem will be to evolve marketing plans in keeping with the technological progress that has brought about this market expansion.[13]

## REDUCING MILK DISTRIBUTION COSTS

Earlier in this chapter the total demand for milk in the United States was shown as likely to increase in the future, although not as fast as the increase in United States population.

The total human consumption of milk, however, could rise a good deal faster than the increase in population if technological developments in milk processing and distribution reduced costs and permitted the price to cut the demand curve at a lower point.

Figure 24.3 shows that in recent years increases in marketing costs have about offset increases in technological efficiency in milk distribution. In 1954 farmers received 49 per cent of what the consumers paid for milk sold at stores; by 1964 this had declined to 46 per cent, but it was up to 50 per cent in 1969.

One of the most expensive items in milk distribution is the delivery of milk to the consumer's doorstep. This cost has been reduced by every-other-day delivery, but the overlapping and duplication of milk routes and the basically expensive nature of personal distribution services still keep it high. Door-to-door delivery is, in fact, steadily being replaced by selling milk through stores and passing the reduction in delivery cost on to the con-

[13] A. Swantz and L. Herrmann, "Expanding Fluid Milk Markets," *Marketing Activities*, USDA, Mar., 1953, pp. 4–5.

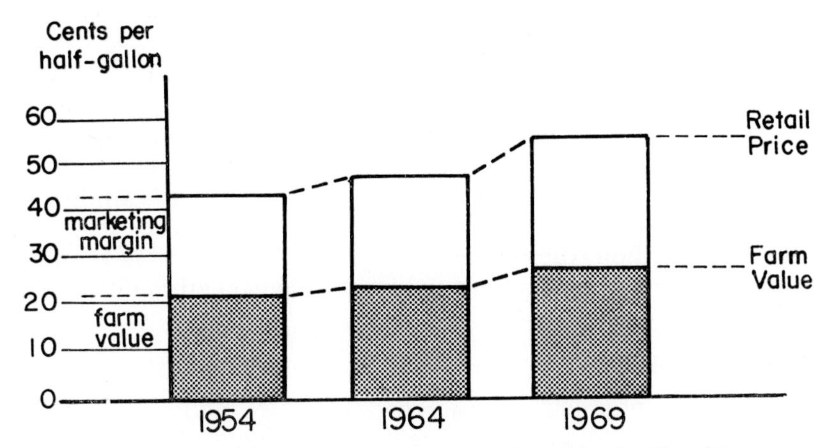


FIG. 24.3—Marketing margin and farm value of fluid milk sold at stores, 1954, 1964, and 1969.

sumer. Today, only about 30 per cent of the fluid milk in the United States is delivered to homes.[14]

### Home Delivery Versus Sales Through Retail Stores

Several developments have contributed to the shift from home delivery of milk to sale through retail stores. A major factor has been the rise in supermarkets, which have provided milk distributors with outlets for large quantities of milk at a single point of distribution. Increased use of paper containers and improved self-service refrigeration cases for milk display have facilitated the growth of retail store distribution.

Large-volume distribution through retail stores is somewhat less costly than delivery to homes. Indications are that 400–500 delivery points are needed to make home delivery profitable. Typically, savings in distribution costs are great enough to enable retail stores to sell somewhat below home-delivered rates. In 1969 the prevailing price paid by consumers for whole milk per half-gallon at retail stores in 25 cities averaged 54.5 cents. This compared with an average of 62.0 cents per half-gallon for home-delivered milk in the same cities.[15]

[14] *Agricultural Markets in Change*, USDA, AER Rept. 95, 1966, p. 152.
[15] *Fluid Milk and Cream Report*, SRS, USDA, Feb., 1970, pp. 28–29.

There is probably substantial opportunity for lowering milk distribution costs by further shifts from home delivery. However, there are other considerations that may cause home delivery to continue as an important distribution method. It is a good way to introduce new products to consumers and to develop and maintain loyalty to a particular brand of dairy product. Home delivery also provides an opportunity to offer milk to families in larger containers and in some cases through bulk dispensing devices. In addition, there is evidence that higher-income families prefer home delivery and are willing to pay something extra for this service.

### Skim Milk Powder

Another promising possibility for cost reduction lies in the increased use of skim milk. The nutritive value of skim milk is as high as or higher than that of whole milk in an ordinary mixed diet. The elasticity of the demand for fluid skim milk at substantially lower prices than whole milk is about —4.0. This means that a reduction of 10 per cent in the price of skim milk would result in an increase in consumption of 40 per cent.

Substantial reductions in price could be made if the biggest item of cost, the cost of door or store delivery in fluid form, could be avoided by distributing the skim milk in powder rather than in liquid form. Milk is 85 per cent water, and water is heavy to carry around. Drying milk to powder costs about 1 cent per quart. Delivering bottled fluid milk to the doorstep costs at least 4 cents per quart. The costs of bottling must be added to this. In 1969, the prices of half-gallons delivered to homes in 25 major cities averaged 62.0 cents. The prices paid to farmers for fluid milk averaged $6.70 per 100 pounds. Assuming 42 quarts per 100 pounds, the distributors paid farmers 16.0 cents per quart or 32.0 cents per half-gallon. Thus the distributors' margin was 15.0 cents per quart. Drying milk is a far less expensive operation than delivering fluid milk in bottles.

Recent improvements in technology of milk drying have produced skim milk powder of excellent keeping quality and flavor, available for home consumption well below the cost of fluid whole milk. For example, in Ames, Iowa, in 1970, fresh fluid whole milk delivered to the consumer's door was 33 cents per quart or 58 cents per half-gallon. Prices in retail stores were 33 cents per quart and 56 cents per half-gallon; skim milk was 30 cents per quart. But skim milk powder, at $1.85 for a package that would make 14 quarts, was equivalent to 13.2 cents per quart of milk. This lower price may encourage greater consumption of skim milk powder, depending upon how readily consumers will give up the convenience of obtaining milk in the fluid form, in order to obtain the savings that are possible.

### Sterile Milk

Still another technical innovation is sterile milk, made by heating fresh whole milk to a high enough temperature to kill the bacteria which ordinarily cause milk to spoil. The product is then concentrated to about a third of its original bulk. It will keep about six months on the pantry shelf or about a year in the refrigerator.

Sterile milk can be shipped anywhere, like a can of beans. This permits bypassing various state and local sanitary restrictions. The big economic factor is that the sterilizing and concentrating takes the product out of the fluid milk classification. This, plus the low costs of transportation resulting from the small bulk of the concentrated product, should enable states like Wisconsin, for example, to sell sterile milk in high-cost areas like Florida at relatively low prices.

### The Elasticity of the Demand for Milk

Early studies of the short-run elasticity of the demand for fresh fluid milk showed a considerable range of elasticities, averaging about —0.25. The average long-run elasticity was about —0.51.

More recent statistical analyses of the long-run elasticity, in which retail prices, 1949–59, in 55 markets broken down into three groups, were plotted against per capita consumption, 1957–61, with per capita disposable income and per cent of nonwhites also taken into account, yielded the results shown in Figure 24.4. The price elasticities in this case ranged from —0.574 to —2.229.[16]

## MARKET CONCENTRATION IN THE FLUID MILK DISTRIBUTION INDUSTRY[17]

The number and size of handlers in a given market influences the way in which competitors react toward their rivals. It also affects the method of pricing milk and the level of milk prices. In most markets the number of milk distributors declined during the 1950's, but the volume of milk handled increased.

[16] R. W. Bartlett, "Potential Expansion of Sales of Fluid Milk as Related to Demand Elasticities," *Expanding Markets for Milk*, Univ. of Ill. Agr. Econ. Bul. 7, 1963, pp. 25–33.

[17] Adapted from W. H. Alexander, "Market Concentration in the Fluid Milk Distribution Industry," *Louisiana Rural Economist*, Vol. 24 (Feb., 1962), pp. 2–8 and *Organization and Competition in the Dairy Industry*, National Commission on Food Marketing, Tech. Study 3, June, 1966.

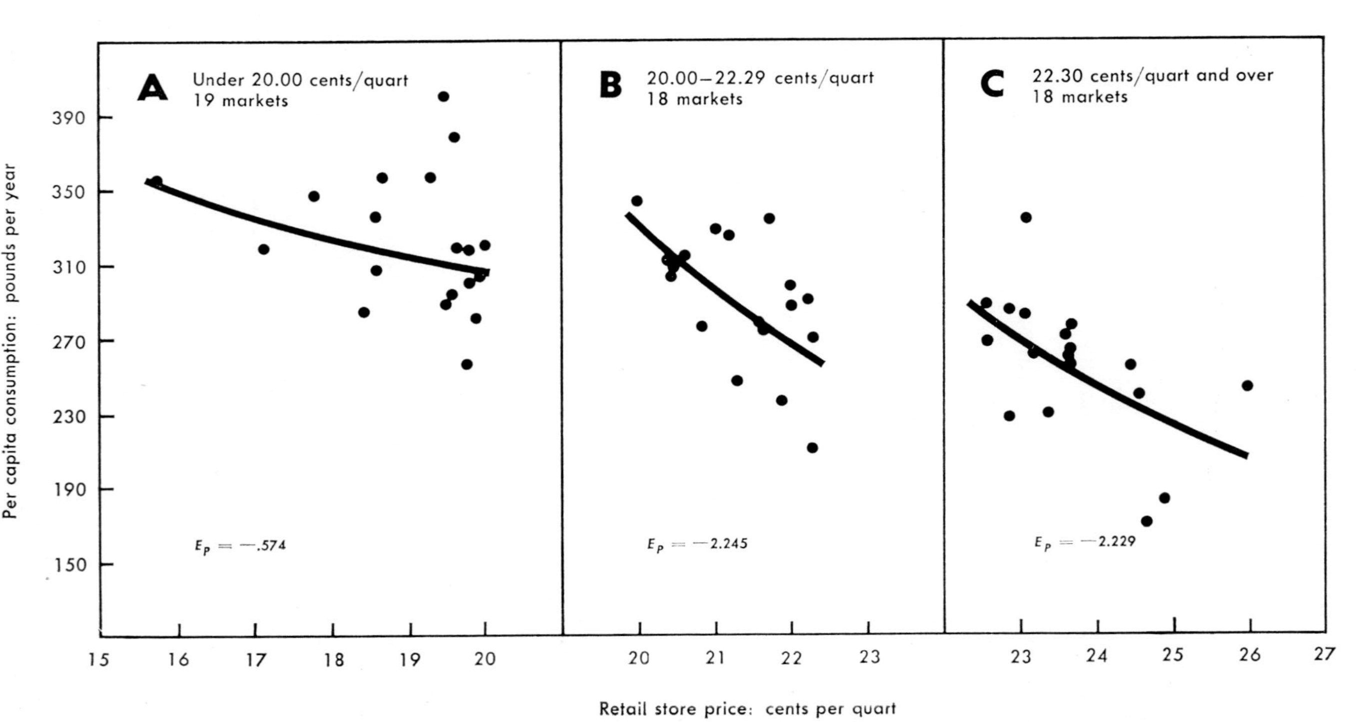


FIG. 24.4—Regression of per capita milk consumption on retail store price, three specific groups of markets.

This trend will continue if it is necessary to increase the size of firms to achieve lower distribution costs.

As firms become larger, their control over the market is increased. Geographic expansion into one another's marketing areas by the large competitors, however, has been a stimulant to competition and price wars during the last decade. In markets where there are relatively few sellers, each firm has a definite policy with respect to price and nonprice behavior of its rivals. Each firm's presence and actions in the market affects the decisions and actions of his competitors. In markets where the bulk of milk sales are handled by a small number of handlers, price policy seems to be one of "live and let live." The attitude of certain federal agencies seems to be in accord with this policy.

The primary methods of growth of large firms have been mergers and acquisitions. Between 1925 and 1959, more than 2,200 independent dairy companies were absorbed by the nation's eight largest dairy companies. These included firms handling fluid milk as well as manufactured dairy products. An additional 67 acquisitions were made by the eight companies between 1960 and 1964. Mergers have continued to play an important role in increasing both area and product extension. Firms making horizontal acquisitions in new areas are engaging in market extension. Firms adding new but related products in areas previously served are making product extension.

### At the National Level

Market concentration in the fluid milk industry at the national level is an important structural consideration. It shows the relative size of the nation's largest competitors who sell milk and dairy products in the national market. It also influences the method and level of price formation.

A declining number of dairy companies are doing an increasingly larger share of the total milk business in the United States. We can observe two methods of growth and concentration: (1) internal—by expansion of present facilities and (2) external—by mergers and acquisitions. Growth in size of dairy firms at the national level is reflected by the value of total assets and total sales accounted for by the eight largest dairy companies who distribute milk on a nation-wide basis. The value of total assets of the eight largest dairy companies in the United States increased from $1.3 billion in 1955 to $1.6 billion in 1959, an increase of more than 20 per cent. Total sales by these companies were thirteen times greater in 1969 than in 1940 and more than twice as large in 1969 than in 1959 (Table 24.5).

Dairy firms have also acquired assets in distinctly different

**TABLE 24.5: Total Sales by the Eight Largest Dairy Companies in the United States, 1940–69**

| | Net Sales | | | | | | | |
|---|---|---|---|---|---|---|---|---|
| Year | Kraftco Corp.* | The Borden Co. | Fore-most Dairies, Inc. | Carna-tion Co. | Beatrice Foods Co. | Arden-Mayfair, Inc. | Pet Milk Co. | Fair-mont Foods |
| | *($ mil.)* | *($ mil.)* | *($ mil.)* | *($ mil.)* | *($ mil.)* | *($ mil.)* | *($ mil.)* | *($ mil.)* |
| 1940 | 347.4 | 216.8 | 2.8 | 62.7 | 63.7 | 19.9 | 34.9 | 39.2 |
| 1945 | 632.8 | 459.4 | 12.8 | 168.8 | 110.3 | 57.9 | 114.8 | 79.2 |
| 1950 | 906.6 | 631.1 | 48.2 | 256.3 | 190.5 | 101.0 | 137.5 | 107.0 |
| 1954 | 1,210.0 | 777.0 | 247.0 | 310.0 | 287.0 | 195.0 | 167.0 | 94.0 |
| 1959 | 1,603.7 | 941.3 | 440.1 | 396.3 | 385.4 | 322.6 | 190.3 | 98.5 |
| 1964 | 1,920.0 | 1,293.0 | 415.0 | 477.0 | 681.0 | 467.0 | 347.0 | 190.0 |
| 1969 | 2,581.0 | 1,740.2 | 1,780.0 | 964.4 | 1,550.0 | 588.1 | 650.0 | 315.0 |
| | *Per cent increase in sales 1959–69* | | | | | | | |
| | 61 | 85 | 304 | 143 | 302 | 82 | 242 | 220 |

Source: *Industrial Manual,* Moody's Investment Service, New York, 1947, 1959, and 1969; and *Organization and Competition in the Dairy Industry,* National Commission on Food Marketing, Tech. Study 3, June, 1966, p. 68.
* Formerly National Dairy Products.

industries. This accounts for the very large gains in net sales by some of the firms listed in Table 24.5.

When concentration is measured by the percentage of total milk sales handled by the four largest firms in the market, it is even greater than when measured by the number of firms. This is especially true for local markets.

### At the Local Level

In terms of competition among firms in the distribution of fluid milk, the local market is most important. Firms that are relatively insignificant in terms of national sales can be very important competitors in local markets. Thus fluid milk markets are more concentrated locally than data for national markets suggest.

Market concentration in terms of the percentage of total fluid milk sales accounted for by the four largest handlers in a market is a good measure of concentration for which data are available. A typical fluid milk market in the United States is characterized by a small number of milk handlers. Usually the bulk of milk sales is accounted for by the four largest handlers in the market and the remainder distributed among varying numbers of smaller handlers.

Data in Table 24.6 show market concentration in terms of the percentage of total processing accounted for by the four largest handlers in 79 federal order markets from 1950 through 1964. The degree of concentration increased during that period, although the change in the larger markets was relatively small. The degree of concentration was considerably greater in smaller-size markets than in large-volume markets. In markets with under 8 million pounds of milk processed per month, the four largest dealers handled 87 per cent of the volume. As the size of the market increased, the percentage of processing accounted for by the four largest dealers decreased to 53 per cent for markets processing over 60 million pounds per month.

## WHAT OF THE FUTURE

Where are all these technological developments, and those that are bound to continue to come in the future, going to lead milk marketing? Are they going to lead to freer and fuller competition, or are they going to lead to wider monopoly areas, organized on a regional and, for that matter, national basis?

That is to say: Are distributors going to lose their local monopoly powers and compete actively among themselves? And if they do, are we going to have overlapping and duplication of delivery routes among cities as well as within cities? Or are distributors going to grow larger, along with the increase in the size of the market area, and regain their monopoly powers on a wider geographical basis? And if they do, will they allocate territories among themselves to avoid wasteful overlapping and duplication of services—and if so, will they pass the gains from this efficient distribution back to producers or forward to consumers or both, or will they keep them for themselves, plus other

**TABLE 24.6: Average Share of the Four Largest Fluid Milk Dealers, Based on Volume of Milk Processed, 79 Federal Milk Order Markets, Specified Years, 1950–64**

| Size of Market (millions of pounds a month) | Share of Volume Processed, in Per Cent* | | | | | |
|---|---|---|---|---|---|---|
| | 1950 | 1953 | 1956 | 1959 | 1962 | 1964 |
| Under 8 | 67 | 71 | 77 | 81 | 84 | 87 |
| 8–15.9 | 55 | 62 | 65 | 75 | 78 | 78 |
| 16–23.9 | 59 | 65 | 67 | 65 | 69 | 74 |
| 24–59.9 | 56 | 57 | 58 | 57 | 58 | 60 |
| 60 or more | 52 | 50 | 51 | 47 | 50 | 53 |

Source: *Organization and Competition in the Dairy Industry,* National Commission on Food Marketing, Tech. Study 3, June, 1966, p. 78.

* Calculated as a link index from available data. Excludes three Colorado markets. Based on volume processed by pool handlers regulated by the particular federal order. Includes volume of products moving out of the market area and excludes volume of products coming into the area from other processors.

gains that they can extort because of their monopoly position? If they do the latter, can producers organize on a regional or national basis to deal with them? If this is done, will the producers and distributors both gang up on the consumer? And if so, will the federal government then have to step in, as it has in Great Britain, Norway, and a number of other countries, to "rationalize" and control the whole system?

These questions can hardly be answered in an introductory chapter. But they should be raised to be kept in mind, at least, by those who go no further into the subject, and to be explored by those who go on into advanced study.

# 25

## DAIRY MARKETING: BUTTER

IN THE PRECEDING CHAPTER, Table 24.1 showed that the per capita consumption of butter declined nearly 30 per cent from 1955 to 1965. The consumption of butter declined for several reasons, one of which is shown in Table 25.1 and in Figure 25.1. The consumption of margarine increased from only 2 or 3 pounds per capita before 1940 to 10.8 pounds—almost double butter consumption—in 1969.

Table 25.1 shows that the price of margarine was 53.9 per cent as high as the price of butter in 1930. This price gradually declined to 50 per cent, to 40 per cent, and finally, in 1969, to 33 per cent of the price of butter. Since the two products, according to research, are about equal in nutritional value in a mixed diet,[1] the decline in the price of margarine relative to butter has been a potent reason for the increase in margarine consumption. Also a factor was the improvement in the quality of margarine, including fortification with vitamin A.

The increase in the consumption of margarine has not been the only reason for the decline in butter use. The sum of the consumption of the two products has declined—from 19.8 pounds in 1930 to 15 or 17 pounds in the 1960's. Influencing this decline is the drop in the per capita consumption of potatoes

[1] *A Report on Margarine,* Report of the Food and Nutrition Board, National Research Council, Reprint and Circular Series, 118, 1943, p. 18.

**TABLE 25.1: Butter and Margarine: Consumption Per Person, Retail Price, and Price of Margarine as a Percentage of Price of Butter, United States, 1930–69**

| Year | Consumption Per Person | | Retail Price Per Pound* | | Margarine Price as Percentage of Butter Price |
|---|---|---|---|---|---|
| | Butter | Margarine | Butter | Margarine | |
| | *(pounds)* | *(pounds)* | *(cents)* | *(cents)* | *(per cent)* |
| 1930 .......... | 17.6 | 2.6 | 46.4 | 25.0 | 53.9 |
| 1940 .......... | 17.0 | 2.4 | 36.0 | 15.9 | 44.2 |
| 1950 .......... | 10.7 | 6.1 | 72.9 | 30.9 | 42.9 |
| 1955 .......... | 9.0 | 8.2 | 70.9 | 28.9 | 40.4 |
| 1960 .......... | 7.5 | 9.4 | 74.9 | 26.9 | 36.0 |
| 1961 .......... | 7.4 | 9.4 | 76.3 | 28.6 | 37.3 |
| 1962 .......... | 7.3 | 9.3 | 75.2 | 28.4 | 37.8 |
| 1963 .......... | 6.9 | 9.6 | 75.0 | 27.5 | 36.7 |
| 1964 .......... | 6.8 | 9.7 | 74.4 | 26.1 | 35.1 |
| 1965 .......... | 6.4 | 9.9 | 75.4 | 27.9 | 37.0 |
| 1966 .......... | 5.7 | 10.5 | 82.2 | 28.7 | 34.9 |
| 1967 .......... | 5.5 | 10.5 | 83.7 | 28.6 | 34.2 |
| 1968 .......... | 5.6 | 10.8 | 83.6 | 27.9 | 33.4 |
| 1969† ......... | 5.4 | 10.8 | 84.6 | 27.8 | 32.9 |

Source: *U.S. Food Consumption,* USDA, Stat. Bul. 364, June, 1965; *The Dairy Situation,* USDA, Nov., 1961, p. 38 and selected later issues; and *The National Food Situation,* USDA, May, 1970, p. 14.

* Average of 56 cities, from Bureau of Labor Statistics. Beginning January, 1951, price for colored margarine; prior to that time, uncolored.

† Preliminary.

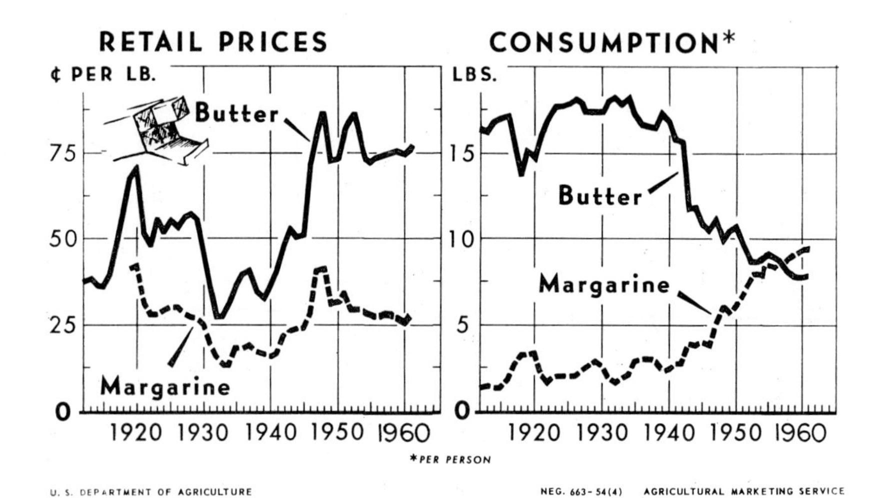


FIG. 25.1—Retail prices and per capita consumption of butter and margarine, 1912–61.

and cereal products, both of which require use of substantial quantities of butter or margarine. It seems likely that these trends will persist for some time in the future.

## BUTTER PRICES

The bulk of the butter produced in the United States is sold direct; only a small percentage is sold through wholesalers located at the central markets. Butter distributors fall into several groups. Ranked in the order of their volume of business in butter, they are: marketing cooperatives (such as Land O' Lakes Creameries and Consolidated Dairy Products), wholesalers, chain stores (such as A & P), meat packers, and large dairy corporations (such as Borden's). The relative importance of these different distributors has changed greatly, as shown in Table 25.2. In 1951 large dairy corporations, wholesalers, and meat packers handled the largest volume and were nearly equal in importance. Marketing cooperatives, which handled nearly half the volume in 1965, had only 15 per cent of the business in 1951.

Except when butter prices are being supported above open-market levels by federal price-support and storage levels, butter prices are open-market prices, varying freely from day to day and from area to area with short-run and local variations in supply and demand, like livestock prices, for example. They are more dependent on central market quotations, however, than livestock prices because of the method of selling butter that is used by most local creameries—the use of a standing agreement to sell

**TABLE 25.2: Butter Shipments to Major Types of Primary Receivers as a Proportion of Total Shipments to Major Receivers, United States, 1951, and 542 Manufacturing Plants, May, 1965**

| Type of Receiver | Per Cent 1951 | Per Cent 1965 |
|---|---|---|
| Wholesalers | 22 | 22 |
| Large dairy corporations | 24 | 8 |
| Meat packers | 23 | 11 |
| Marketing cooperatives | 15 | 48 |
| Chain stores | 16 | 11 |
| Total shipments to major receivers* | 100 | 100 |

Source: *Organization and Competition in the Dairy Industry,* National Commission on Food Marketing, Tech. Study 3, June, 1966, p. 281.

* Excludes shipments to Commodity Credit Corporation and other than major receivers.

at so much over the Chicago or New York wholesale market quotation, as explained in Chapter 15.

Country creamery butter prices fail to reflect accurately to the producer the price differentials for quality that consumers pay in retail stores. This is the same defect that we found in the case of hog prices. It is, in fact, common to most farm products. The differentials in butter prices are reflected fairly well to the wholesale markets. But less than 1 per cent of the butter is sold through these markets, and the grade price differentials paid to country creameries are much smaller than the differentials paid in the wholesale market. They are also much less closely related to grade. The influence of decentralized marketing on the price level of butter is discussed in Chapter 15.

## REDUCING MARKETING COSTS FOR BUTTERFAT AND BUTTER

The processing and marketing of butter is a relatively simple and inexpensive operation. At a time when farmers were getting only 41 cents of the consumer's food dollar for farm products on the average, in 1969 they were getting 73 cents of the consumer's dollar spent for butter.

What are the opportunities for reducing butter marketing

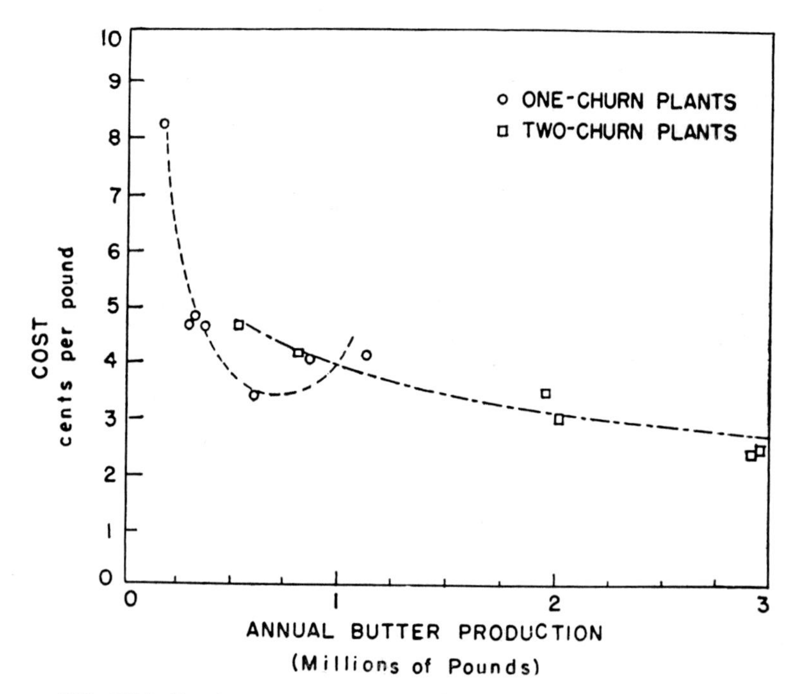


FIG. 25.2—Total unit costs to manufacture bulk butter in 13 sample plants.

**TABLE 25.3: Relation Between Plant Size and Cost Per Pound of Butter, 1961, for a Sample of Butter Plants in Iowa**

| Plant Number | Annual Butter Production (1,000 pounds) | Cost Per Pound of Butter |
|---|---|---|
| 1 | 360 | 7.0 |
| 2 | 720 | 5.3 |
| 3 | 1,080 | 5.4 |
| 4 | 1,440 | 5.4 |
| 5 | 2,160 | 4.9 |
| 6 | 3,880 | 4.5 |
| 7 | 4,500 | 3.0 |
| 8 | 8,000 | 2.5 |

Source: Unpublished data compiled by J. R. Strain, Iowa State University, Ames.

costs still further? One place to look is at the costs of assembling cream and processing it into butter in country creameries.

A study of a sample of Iowa plants in 1949 showed the costs of processing butter separately for one-churn plants and for plants with two churns or more.[2] The relation between cost and volume is shown in Figure 25.2.

This figure shows that the costs for one-churn plants decline rapidly until they reach a minimum of about 3.5 cents per pound at an annual volume of about 700,000 pounds. Beyond this point, costs begin to rise with volume until they exceed the costs of two-churn plants. Costs of two-churn plants decline continuously from nearly 5 cents a pound down to less than 3 cents for an annual volume of 3 million pounds.

These were the costs in 1949. More recent data, based on a smaller sample of plants, given in Table 25.3, show the same overall picture of declining costs with increasing size. The more recent costs run a little higher than the earlier costs; the general price level is higher.

## Very Small Creameries

Most of the creameries in the United States are too small for efficient operation. Table 25.4 shows that in 1963 more than a quarter of them made less than 10,000 pounds of butter apiece.

Nearly 40 per cent of the creameries in the United States make less than 250,000 pounds each. These creameries are much smaller, and therefore incur much higher costs than one-churn creameries with the optimum volume of 700,000 pounds. In these small creameries it is not unusual to have costs as high

[2] J. R. Frazer, V. H. Nielsen, and J. D. Nord, *The Cost of Manufacturing Butter*, Iowa State Univ. Agr. Exp. Sta. Res. Bul. 389, 1952.

**TABLE 25.4: Distribution of Butter Plants in the United States by Production-Size Groups, 1957 and 1963**

| Annual Production (1,000 pounds) | Number of Plants 1957 | Number of Plants 1963 |
|---|---|---|
| 0–100 | 576 | 340 |
| 100–249 | 412 | 180 |
| 250–499 | 340 | 194 |
| 500–749 | 211 | 131 |
| 750–999 | 126 | 90 |
| 1,000–1,499 | 131 | 109 |
| 1,500–1,999 | 93 | 58 |
| 2,000–2,999 | 82 | 89 |
| 3,000–3,999 | 43 | 60 |
| 4,000 and over | 48 | 70 |
| Total | 2,062 | 1,321 |

Source: *Organization and Competition in the Dairy Industry,* National Commission on Food Marketing, Tech. Study 3, June, 1966, p. 270.

as 8 to 10 cents per pound of butter—more than twice the cost of 3.5 cents for a 700,000-pound creamery.

These small creameries are in very poor competitive position with respect to plants producing 400,000 pounds of butter with costs of less than 5 cents per pound and plants producing 700,000 pounds with costs less than 4 cents per pound.

### 300,000- to 350,000-Pound Creameries

It is possible to manufacture from 300,000 to 350,000 pounds of butter annually in a creamery operated by one man. A plant with this volume can achieve costs of less than 5 cents per pound and is in a fair competitive position. However, in this plant the physical and mental demands on the operator tend to be excessive and are greater than in any other plant. Manual work alone will frequently require more than an eight-hour day, leaving no time for managerial duties. This plant is particularly inflexible in time of emergency, whether the emergency is due to illness of the operator or breakdown of equipment.

### 600,000- to 700,000-Pound Creameries

In a creamery producing from 600,000 to 700,000 pounds of butter annually, costs of less than 4 cents per pound can be achieved. This represents the lowest unit cost for a small one-churn plant.

The building space required for this volume is essentially the same as that required for a much smaller volume. Only slightly more equipment is necessary. The labor efficiency in this plant is better than in a plant with a smaller volume, even though the total labor force is increased.

This plant is in a good competitive position, in that its unit cost of manufacturing is only slightly higher than that of a plant with a very large volume.

### 1 Million-Pound Creameries

In creameries producing from ¾ million to 1½ million pounds of butter annually, the unit costs are somewhat higher than in creameries producing either smaller or larger volumes.

It is not possible to produce this volume with the same equipment as that required by smaller creameries without suffering substantial losses in labor efficiency. Even with additional equipment, it is not possible to reduce the unit labor cost. The chief reason for this is the necessity of segregating buttermaking and management functions, both of which require fairly well-paid employees. In addition, there is a tendency for the churning and cream-receiving operations to overlap, thereby necessitating a large labor force to handle this peak load when it occurs.

### Very Large Creameries

Creameries having an annual production of 2 million pounds of butter or more can achieve the lowest operating costs. These plants have sufficiently large volumes to permit the use of full-time crews in the major operations. Because of this, the equipment and building are used more efficiently than in the smaller plants.

Plants producing 2 million pounds annually have essentially the same costs as plants producing 700,000 pounds, while plants producing 3 million pounds have costs nearly ¾ cent lower.

### Costs of Assembling Cream

The preceding section shows that large 2 million-pound creameries have about the same costs as one-churn 700,000-pound creameries—about 3.5 cents per pound. The volume has to be up around 3 million pounds to achieve costs below 3 cents.

In most areas these larger volumes reduce the costs of processing butter, but they increase the costs of assembling the cream to make the butter. We need to know how *total* costs—costs of processing plus assembly—vary with volume before we can determine the most efficient size of creamery.

### Trend Toward Whole Milk Creameries

The preceding section is based on farm-gathered cream plants, where farmers skim the cream off the milk on the farm and the creamery gathers the cream to make it into butter.

There is a strong trend away from this system and toward the system where the plants gather whole milk and skim off the cream in the plant. This trend is shown in Table 25.5, which shows that the bulk of the butter today is made from cream that is skimmed from whole milk in whole milk creameries.

The costs in these whole milk creameries decline with increasing scale of operation, much as the costs do for the farm-gathered cream plants. Table 25.6 shows the costs for a sample of different-size Iowa and Minnesota plants in 1961.

## CONSOLIDATION CONSIDERATIONS

The amount of butterfat available in a particular area will greatly influence the production volume of a consolidated plant. From the standpoint of plant costs, there are two production volumes that warrant primary consideration. The lowest costs are found in plants with an annual butter production of 3 million pounds. However, plants with an annual volume of from 600,000 to 700,000 pounds represent the low cost point for a small one-churn plant. The difference in manufacturing costs between these two production volumes approximates ¾ cent per pound. In planning a consolidation, it appears that a choice exists between a consolidation effecting a production of 600,000 to 700,000 pounds annually and a consolidation that will result in a production approaching 3 million pounds.

There are factors other than manufacturing costs that influence creamery organization. Many of these factors would also influence plant consolidation. Sociological factors which

**TABLE 25.5: Percentage of All Marketings as Whole Milk, 1940–69**

| Year | Iowa | United States |
|---|---|---|
| 1940 | 12.4 | 54.7 |
| 1945 | 16.9 | 70.0 |
| 1950 | 20.5 | 75.4 |
| 1955 | 34.7 | 83.8 |
| 1960 | 68.1 | 91.2 |
| 1965 | 85.5 | 95.3 |
| 1968 | 92.6 | 96.7 |
| 1969 | 93.0 | 97.0 |

Source: *Milk Production, Disposition and Income, 1968–69,* USDA, Apr., 1970, and earlier issues.

are largely built upon community considerations would tend to favor a smaller consolidation. In addition, if assembly costs (farm-to-plant shipment of cream) increase substantially with an increase in volume, the smaller consolidation would be favored. On the other hand, the larger creameries, because of their large volumes, normally process buttermilk into dried or semisolid buttermilk. These by-products often may be marketed at prices which make this operation a profitable one. In creameries producing less than 1 million pounds, the buttermilk is normally disposed of in fluid form on a day-to-day basis.

## IMPROVING CREAMERY EFFICIENCY

Individual creameries can do much to improve their efficiency. They independently can reorganize cream routes, obtain better control of them, and minimize hauling costs. The creamery that succeeds in drawing even its present small volume of business from the smallest possible trade area gains a competitive advantage through lower hauling costs.

**TABLE 25.6: Costs of Making Butter in Whole Milk Creameries, With All Costs Assigned to Butter Only, Based on a Sample of Plants in Iowa and Minnesota, 1961**

| Plant Number | Annual Butter Output | Cost Per Lb. of Butter | Equivalent Cost Per Cwt. of Milk |
|---|---|---|---|
| 1................ | 200,000 | 22.69–25.60 | 112.64 |
| | 300,000 | 17.45–17.93 | 76.89 |
| | 400,000 | 13.74 | 60.46 |
| | 500,000 | 11.22 | 49.37 |
| 2................ | 500,000 | 15.21 | 66.92 |
| | 600,000 | 12.86–13.52 | 59.49 |
| | 700,000 | 11.75 | 51.70 |
| | 800,000 | 10.41 | 45.80 |
| | 900,000 | 9.36 | 41.18 |
| | 1,000,000 | 8.56 | 37.66 |
| 3................ | 1,000,000 | 10.25–10.37 | 45.63 |
| | 1,100,000 | 9.52 | 41.89 |
| | 1,200,000 | 8.82 | 38.82 |
| | 1,300,000 | 8.23 | 36.21 |
| | 1,400,000 | 7.75–7.93 | 34.81 |
| | 1,500,000 | 7.45 | 32.78 |
| 4................ | 1,500,000 | 8.29–8.56 | 37.66 |
| | 1,600,000 | 8.07 | 35.51 |
| | 1,700,000 | 7.68 | 33.79 |
| | 1,800,000 | 7.29 | 32.08 |
| | 1,900,000 | 6.99 | 30.76 |
| | 2,000,000 | 6.69 | 29.44 |
| | 2,200,000 | 6.19 | 27.24 |

Source: J. R. Strain, Iowa State University, Ames.

The prevailing system of paying truckers on a commission basis without designating the territory or the farmers they shall serve, the confusing methods of charging hauling costs to patrons, and the lack of effective control over hauling practices explain much of the inefficiency in obtaining cream by local creameries.

To the extent that scrambling of patrons and creameries is the result of methods of quoting prices, methods of charging hauling costs, and other competitive practices that make it difficult for producers to determine the best outlet, a greater amount of uniformity in business and accounting methods and a higher standard of business ethics would place competition more definitely on a basis of relative efficiency. Many self-governing measures might be adopted voluntarily by the creameries. It might be desirable to supplement such industry action with appropriate legislation.

## COOPERATIVE ACTION AMONG CREAMERIES

Although anything that can be done to place competition more definitely on the basis of efficiency is desirable, the concentration of butter manufacturing in fewer and more efficient plants would even then involve considerable time. The least efficient creameries would sooner or later be forced out of business, in most cases at considerable cost to present owners. Farmers patronizing such creameries in the meantime would be burdened with high costs.

Since a reduction in the number of creameries seems inevitable, a quicker and more economical way of bringing about the adjustment in most cases would be by deliberate cooperative action on the part of farmers and creameries. The members or owners of two or three creameries in a given area might set up a new organization which would purchase the assets of several existing units. The new organization would make the most advantageous use of all facilities under its control and liquidate the surplus facilities.

On a larger scale, creameries in several counties might go together and, on the basis of a careful survey and analysis of the whole area, establish several economic units. Still another plan would be for the dairy industry of the state to sponsor legislation which might provide for the voluntary establishment of districts for surveying and appraising the most economical butterfat marketing system. These districts might issue bonds which could be liquidated by means of a butterfat tax levied in the district for this purpose. Each of these different plans is being followed in various parts of the United States or in other countries.

The decision is in the hands of farmers and creamery operators—whether they permit nature to take its painful and long-drawn-out course or whether they deliberately reorganize their butterfat marketing system through a carefully planned program.

# 26

# POULTRY AND EGGS

THE MOST IMPORTANT poultry product in the United States is eggs. The rapidly growing broiler industry ranks next, while turkeys come third and farm chickens, fourth.

The per capita consumption of eggs in the United States has declined since the early 1950's, after rising sharply during the 1940's. The per capita consumption of poultry meat (chicken, turkey, duck, and so forth) has more than doubled since 1940, increasing more than any other farm product.

The recent changes in poultry and egg consumption are shown in Figure 26.1 and Table 26.1. The per capita consumption of farm chickens was only 4 pounds in 1969, contrasted to 9.1 pounds in 1954. But the consumption of broilers has risen from 13.7 pounds to 35.3 pounds per capita. The consumption of the two together has risen from 22.8 to 39.3 pounds. Turkey consumption has also increased, from 5.3 pounds per capita in 1954 to 8.4 pounds in 1969. Egg consumption has declined from an average of 376 eggs per person in 1954 to 316 in 1969.

## CHANGES IN DEMAND AND SUPPLY

The increase in consumption of chicken and turkey is the result of an increase in per capita demand and supply for those products. The demand for poultry has increased, partly due to the development of broilers, small young tender chickens which

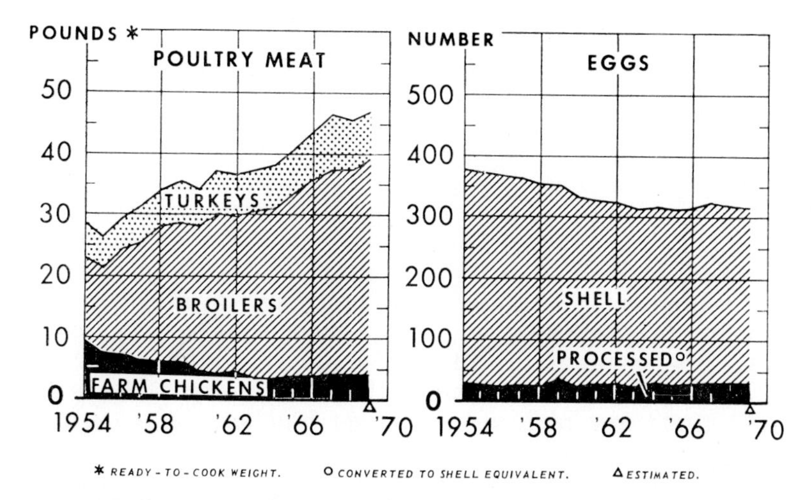


FIG. 26.1—Per capita consumption of poultry and eggs, United States, annually, 1954–69.

**TABLE 26.1: Per Capita Consumption of Poultry and Eggs, United States, Annually, 1954–69***

| Year | Chicken: Broilers | Chicken: Other† | Chicken: Total | Turkey | Total Poultry | Eggs: Shell† | Eggs: Processed‡ | Eggs: Total |
|---|---|---|---|---|---|---|---|---|
| | *(pounds)* | *(pounds)* | *(pounds)* | *(pounds)* | *(pounds)* | *(number)* | *(number)* | *(number)* |
| 1954... | 13.7 | 9.1 | 22.8 | 5.3 | 28.1 | 351 | 25 | 376 |
| 1955... | 13.8 | 7.5 | 21.3 | 5.0 | 26.3 | 346 | 25 | 371 |
| 1956... | 17.3 | 7.1 | 24.4 | 5.2 | 29.6 | 345 | 24 | 369 |
| 1957... | 19.1 | 6.4 | 25.5 | 5.9 | 31.4 | 335 | 27 | 362 |
| 1958... | 22.0 | 6.1 | 28.1 | 5.9 | 34.0 | 328 | 26 | 354 |
| 1959... | 22.8 | 6.1 | 28.9 | 6.3 | 35.2 | 319 | 33 | 352 |
| 1960... | 23.4 | 4.6 | 28.1 | 6.1 | 34.1 | 306 | 28 | 334 |
| 1961... | 25.9 | 4.1 | 30.0 | 7.4 | 37.4 | 298 | 30 | 328 |
| 1962... | 25.6 | 4.3 | 29.9 | 7.0 | 36.9 | 296 | 30 | 326 |
| 1963... | 27.0 | 3.7 | 30.7 | 6.8 | 37.5 | 290 | 27 | 317 |
| 1964... | 27.5 | 3.5 | 31.0 | 7.3 | 38.3 | 287 | 31 | 318 |
| 1965... | 29.4 | 3.9 | 33.3 | 7.5 | 40.8 | 285 | 29 | 314 |
| 1966... | 32.2 | 3.8 | 36.0 | 7.8 | 43.8 | 283 | 30 | 313 |
| 1967... | 32.7 | 4.4 | 37.1 | 8.6 | 45.7 | 289 | 34 | 323 |
| 1968... | 32.8 | 4.3 | 37.1 | 7.9 | 45.0 | 289 | 31 | 320 |
| 1969§.. | 35.3 | 4.0 | 39.3 | 8.4 | 47.7 | 286 | 30 | 316 |

Source: *Handbook of Agricultural Charts, 1969,* USDA, Agr. Handbook 373, Nov., 1969, p. 87.

* Includes data for Alaska and Hawaii beginning in 1961.

† Includes an allowance for consumption of output from backyard flocks, 1950–63.

‡ Shell equivalent of processed eggs.

§ Estimated.

appeal to consumers more than the traditional farm chickens (as indicated by the fact that broiler prices run higher). The demand has increased also because of the reduction in the seasonality of production, which makes the product readily available all through the year.

But the main reason for the increase in consumption of poultry is the marked increase that has taken place in supply. The supply has increased more than production (in numbers of birds) and more than demand. Technological improvements in poultry production and marketing practices—in nutrition, management, breeding, and so forth—have substantially reduced costs. Broiler producers in 1967 used substantially less feed units per unit of poultry than in 1940, as shown in Figure 26.2.

A trend toward fewer but larger hatcheries has been continuous since official estimates were begun in 1934. In 1969 there were 1,486 chick hatcheries in the United States, compared with 6,000 in 1953. The decline in hatchery numbers in recent years has been only partly offset by an increase in the size of the remaining units, so that total hatchery capacity has declined. Expansion in poultry production has been achieved through a fuller utilization of existing hatchery capacity.

These improvements in production practices have reduced production costs, stimulating an increase in production that has reduced prices. These lower costs plus the increase in demand

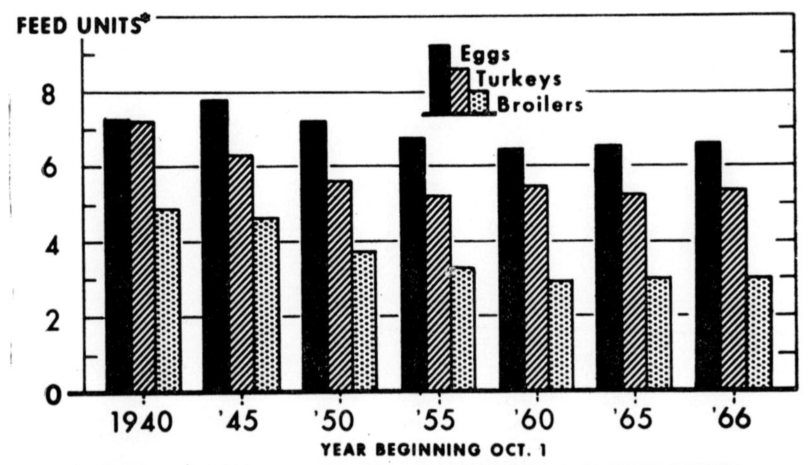


FIG. 26.2—Feed per unit of eggs and poultry produced, United States, 1940–66.

have moved the whole demand curve to the right. Prices fell, in spite of the increase in demand, because the supply increased more than the demand—the supply curve moved farther to the right than the demand curve. The relatively low prices for poultry, therefore, are not the result of a decrease in demand such as took place for butter. The supply increased because reduction in costs increased profits. Thus the declining prices have not meant declining profits. Profits have varied from year to year, but have averaged about the same as before.

Similar improvements in production and marketing technology have also taken place in the egg industry, although to a lesser degree than for poultry. But the demand for eggs has not increased as it has for chicken and turkey. The rate of lay (egg production per bird), for example, increased more than 60 per cent between 1940 and 1961. Further moderate gains have taken place since that time, as shown in Figure 26.3. Many of the technological improvements have been most practical for the owners of large flocks. Accordingly, the number of small flocks has declined sharply and the trend is toward fewer and larger flocks.

While egg production has become more efficient, the demand for eggs has not increased as it has for chicken and turkey. One reason is probably a decline in egg use for the breakfast meal, as more people eat a lighter breakfast now than in the

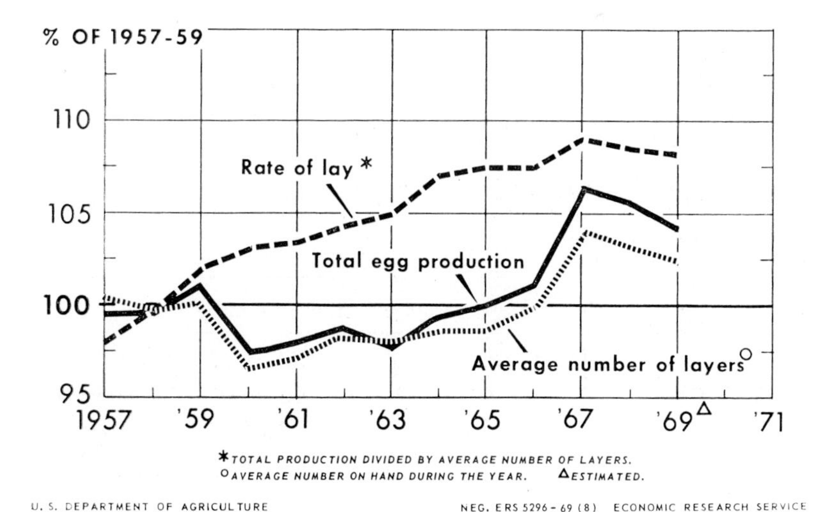


FIG. 26.3—Total egg production, rate of lay, and average number of layers, United States, 1957–69.

past. Medical and dietary considerations may also be a factor in decreased egg use.

## LOCATION OF EGG PRODUCTION

Poultry and egg production is a widely scattered industry. About one-third of the farms in the United States raise poultry of one type or another—either for egg production or poultry meat.

The geographic location of egg production has shifted considerably during the past couple of decades. Production is much more uniformly located throughout the country than formerly, as shown in Table 26.2. The North Central Region (east and west combined) is still the largest egg-producing area of the country. But the level of production has declined in this region; and the proportion of total U.S. production dropped from 48.3 per cent in 1950 to 27.2 per cent in 1969. In the same period, production increased greatly in the south Atlantic, south central, and western states. Major surplus states in egg production are in the North Central Region and in the South. California also produces more eggs than are used in the state, while the chief deficit states are in the East, the Southwest, and parts of the eastern Corn Belt. (See Figure 26.4.)

## EGG PRICES

The seasonal variation in egg prices has been decreasing, as shown in Chapter 11 on seasonal price movements, because the seasonal variation in egg production has been decreasing. In 1933–37 egg production in the peak month of April was about four times as great as it was in the low month of December. After that time the seasonal variation in egg production steadily

**TABLE 26.2: Regional Distribution of Egg Production, United States, 1950, 1960, and 1969**

| | 1950 | | 1960 | | 1969 | |
|---|---|---|---|---|---|---|
| Region | Quantity | Percentage | Quantity | Percentage | Quantity | Percentage |
| | *(mil.)* | | *(mil.)* | | *(mil.)* | |
| North Atlantic | 10,137 | 17.2 | 9,995 | 16.3 | 9,772 | 14.2 |
| East North Central | 11,743 | 20.0 | 10,787 | 17.6 | 9,311 | 13.5 |
| West North Central | 16,690 | 28.3 | 15,067 | 24.5 | 9,457 | 13.7 |
| South Atlantic | 5,165 | 8.7 | 8,036 | 13.1 | 14,402 | 20.9 |
| South Central | 8,786 | 14.9 | 8,745 | 14.2 | 14,398 | 20.9 |
| Western | 6,442 | 10.9 | 8,737 | 14.3 | 11,585 | 16.8 |
| United States | 58,954 | 100.0 | 61,377 | 100.0 | 68,925 | 100.0 |

Source: *Agricultural Markets in Change,* USDA, Agr. Econ. Rept. 95, July, 1966, p. 360; and *Chicken and Eggs,* USDA, Apr., 1970.

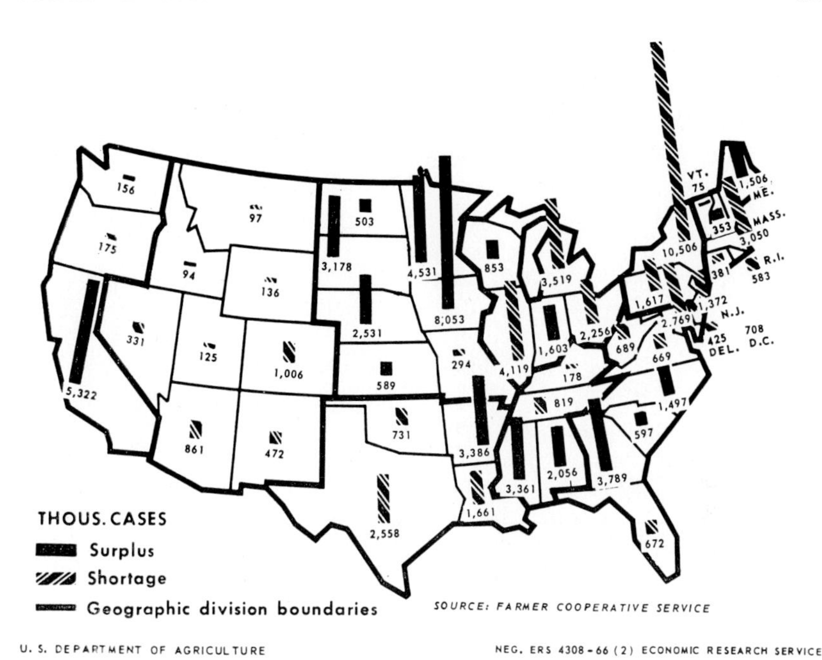


FIG. 26.4—Surplus and deficit states in egg production, 1964.

decreased. In 1948 egg production in the peak month of April was only *about twice* as great as it was in the low month of November. By 1953 the seasonal variation decreased further; egg production in the peak month, March, was only *50 per cent* greater than in the low month, September. By 1969 production had become fairly evenly distributed throughout the year. The peak month, May, was only 15 per cent above the low month, February, and 10 per cent above the next lowest production month, September.[1]

Shell eggs in storage lose grade, and a small percentage of the eggs may, in fact, become inedible. Frozen eggs do not suffer this loss. Table 26.3 shows how the quantity of shell eggs in storage has declined, while the quantity of frozen eggs in storage, expressed in terms of case equivalent (38.5 pounds to the 30-dozen egg case), has shown less change. In 1969 the storage stocks of shell eggs were only 18 per cent as large as the stocks of frozen eggs. The total quantity of eggs stored declined from 16.6 million cases equivalent in 1946 to 2 million in 1969.

The smoothing out of egg production through the year has

[1] *The Poultry and Egg Situation,* USDA, Apr., 1970, p. 21, and earlier issues.

**TABLE 26.3: Peak Commercial Storage Stocks of Eggs, United States, 1946–69 (Million Cases)**

| Year | Shell | Frozen (shell equivalent) |
|---|---|---|
| 1946 | 9.7 | 6.9 |
| 1948 | 5.6 | 6.0 |
| 1950 | 3.7 | 5.0 |
| 1952 | 3.4 | 4.3 |
| 1954 | 1.6 | 4.8 |
| 1956 | 1.5 | 4.5 |
| 1958 | 0.9 | 3.4 |
| 1960 | 1.1 | 4.0 |
| 1962 | 0.4 | 3.2 |
| 1964 | 0.2 | 3.0 |
| 1966 | 0.1 | 1.6 |
| 1967 | 0.4 | 2.6 |
| 1968 | 0.3 | 2.8 |
| 1969 | 0.3 | 1.7 |

Source: *Summary of Regional Cold Storage Holdings, 1969,* USDA, Mar., 1970, p. 8, and earlier issues.

reduced the quantity of eggs needing to be stored, and the resulting reduction in the seasonal price change has made shell egg storage less profitable, so fewer eggs are being stored. The relationship between egg prices and egg production on an annual basis is shown graphically in Figure 26.5.

### Egg Price Reports

Egg buyers at country points buy eggs on a shipping differential under the wholesale price quotation at New York in much the same way that wholesale butter buyers base their bids on the Chicago or New York quotation. But whereas the wholesale butter buyers pay country creameries on the basis of the wholesale price when the butter arrives at Chicago or New York, the country egg buyers pay farmers on the basis of the current quotation. They take the risk of a loss if the price in New York drops before their shipment arrives several days later, but they stand to gain if the price rises. Over a period of time, presumably, the gains and losses cancel out.

The same sort of problems are encountered with wholesale egg price quotations as with wholesale butter price quotations, which were discussed earlier in Chapter 15. The Urner-Barry price report at New York quotes the base price for eggs, with a statement of the premiums that were paid for unusually high quality. The Urner family has been reporting prices since 1858, and their quotations have been used as the basis of settlement for generations. Since October, 1953, the USDA also has been

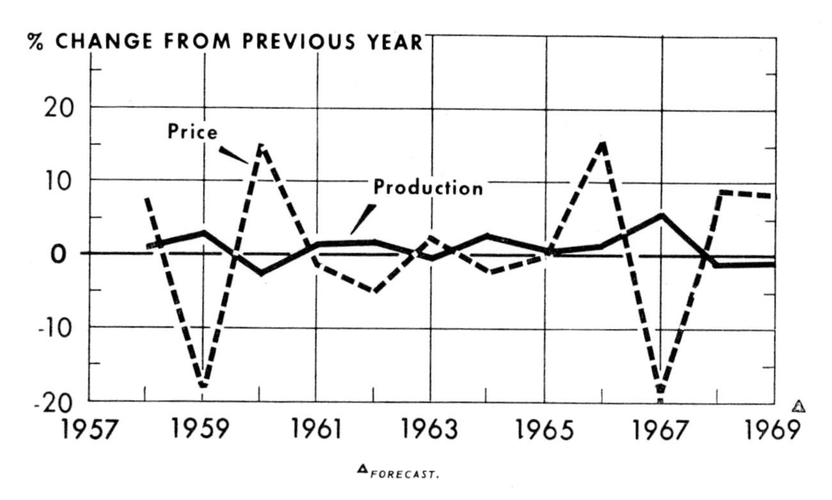


FIG. 26.5—Changes in annual egg production and average price received by producers, United States, 1957–69.

reporting New York wholesale egg prices. The USDA reports the prices at which sales were made, including the premium sales; their prices accordingly run higher than the Urner-Barry prices. This creates confusion in the trade and leads to recriminations from producers who do not get the higher prices reported by the USDA.

The USDA market news service quite properly maintains that it

> has never had as a purpose the establishing of a price which would serve primarily to fix a base for trading, nor to "make the market." On the contrary, every effort is made to avoid that position. . . . The function of the market news service is to report the results of . . . transactions on a market-wide basis. . . . One may occasionally hear a federal market reporter referred to as the man who "makes the market."

Nothing could be further from accuracy than such a statement. Federal reporters do not "make the market." They report prices, and their reports follows, rather than precede, trading.

## EGG MARKETING CHANNELS[2]

Eggs move from producers to consumers through a variety of market channels. The simplest way is for eggs to be sold by

[2] Adapted from *Agricultural Markets in Change*, Agr. Econ. Rept. 95, USDA, July, 1966, pp. 330–31; and *Changing Marketing Channels for Farm Foods*, USDA, AMS-350, 1959, pp. 26–27.

the producer directly to the consumer. The predominant process, however, is for eggs to be assembled from producers by assembler-shippers who ship in truckload lots to wholesale distributors. The wholesale distributors then sell to food chains and independent retailers. An increasing volume of eggs is being distributed by producer-marketing groups called producer-distributors, who have replaced the assembler-shipper in some areas. There is also a trend for more eggs to bypass the wholesale distributor and to move directly to retailers from either assembler-shippers or producer-distributors.

Smaller chains and independent retailers generally buy eggs from wholesale distributors, while larger chains tend to buy eggs directly from assembler-shippers or producer-distributors. This direct buying provides retailers a fresher product, reduces procurement costs, and offers greater assurance of obtaining the desired quality and volume when needed.

Changes in the location for grading and cartoning eggs have influenced the changes in egg-marketing channels. These functions used to be performed mainly by wholesalers at the central markets. As food chains increased in size, many of them began performing these operations in their own warehouses. More recently, however, a growing proportion of the eggs are being graded and cartoned at country points by assembler-shippers or producer-distributors.

More of the eggs are graded and cartoned at country points because these functions can be done more cheaply there than in city plants or warehouses. This is due in part to lower wage rates, taxes, and other costs. More important, however, is the fact that grading and cartoning eggs at country points lowers the total cost of labor and equipment, reduces the number of times the eggs are handled between producer and consumer, and permits direct delivery of eggs to retail stores.

Egg production has become more concentrated in recent years, with a higher proportion of the eggs coming from specialized, large-volume operations. This has enabled plants in the producing areas to assemble a large volume of eggs directly from producers and to perform the handling, grading, and cartoning operations more economically than would be possible in smaller plants. Assembly costs are also reduced, since the eggs are obtained from a smaller number of producers. In order to improve operational efficiency, many of the country assembler-shippers or producer-distributors have production or marketing contracts with producers. These agreements may specify the minimum size of flock, standards for feeding and care of hens and for handling the eggs, and the marketing and pricing terms.

A look back will illustrate how the egg-marketing system has changed. Twenty-five years ago retail stores in the larger cities usually bought eggs from jobbers who, in turn, bought bulk eggs from city wholesalers. Jobbers candled the eggs, packed them in retail-size containers, and made deliveries to retail stores. City wholesalers who sold to jobbers received carlot or trucklot shipments from country shippers. Many of the eggs were produced in areas where individual farmers had only small volumes to sell, so shippers generally had to assemble eggs from a wide area. They bought eggs from country stores, feed stores, and other local buyers and maintained their own buying stations at various points to buy directly from farmers and other buyers.

## INTEGRATING EGG PRODUCTION AND MARKETING[3]

As already noted, the dominant pattern of egg marketing in recent years has been sale by producers to country-point buyers or assemblers who sell in turn to city wholesale distributors or directly to retail chains. Prices arrived at through open-market trading direct the allocation of eggs through marketing channels. Quality is encouraged through price premiums based upon federal, state, or private grades or upon the reputation of the handler and the producers supplying him.

But this open-market pricing of eggs has failed to solve many of the problems of quality control and seasonal distribution of production. Conventional production and distribution methods also result in higher costs of production and marketing than appear possible with more highly integrated operations.

New methods of handling eggs, in which production and marketing are coordinated under a single management, have spread rapidly in the last few years.

The many different programs being used to coordinate the production and marketing of eggs can be roughly classified into three categories: (1) contract marketing and quality control, (2) contract production, and (3) owner-integrated operations.

### Contract Marketing and Quality Control Programs

Under the contract marketing and quality control programs, the producer agrees to market eggs under certain conditions. Practices to be followed by the producer generally are specified in writing. The buyer employs field personnel to check adherence to details. In several of these programs egg quality is

[3] From Ralph L. Baker, *Integrating Egg Production and Marketing*, USDA, Marketing Res. Rept. 332, June, 1959.

checked by breaking out samples. The producer is generally paid a premium over prices received by nonquality control producers.

Contract egg quality control programs contain provisions similar to those long used in other businesses. In contracting with another firm for parts of a total assembly, the buyer specifies the materials and processes which go into the parts and their final form. The ownership of each firm is separate. The supplier generally is responsible for his own financing. The major issue is whether he wishes to supply the product according to the buyer's specifications. Similarly, in contract quality control programs for eggs, the buyer specifies production practices and sets minimum standards for the product.

Probably the major difference between the specifications in egg quality control contracts and in most industrial operations is the method of setting prices. Industrial contracts usually specify absolute prices, whereas most contract quality control programs for eggs specify a differential from a fluctuating base price such as a well-known market report or quotation. As a result, the egg producer bears price uncertainties in addition to production cost risks.

For example, Baker's study indicated that in 1958 prices paid producers by independent operators of contract quality control programs were generally based on a specific quotation. Cooperative organizations generally paid premiums above regular pool prices.

In the Northeast, one contract quality control program buyer paid a net price to producers of either 2 or 2½ cents a dozen, depending on the number of dozens delivered, over the New York Urner-Barry Extra Fancy Heavy-Weight White Egg quotation for AA and A large eggs if the yield of AA eggs was 60 per cent or more. The paying price for eggs yielding 30 to 59.9 per cent AA eggs was 1 cent a dozen less than for those yielding 60 per cent or more AA eggs. A cooperative organization paid 1 cent a dozen more to contract producers than to other producers with the same grades of eggs.

In the Midwest, producers were generally paid a net price for Grade A large eggs of either 4 or 5 cents under the New York Urner-Barry Midwest Fancy Heavy-Weight Mixed Color quotation. Two midwestern cooperative organizations guaranteed no specific differential. Premiums were based on added returns from the sale of the program eggs. Another midwestern cooperative guaranteed quality control producers a minimum of 1 cent a dozen premium plus any additional amount realized from the sale of the eggs. Independent organizations in the Midwest indicated that program producers received about 3 cents more per dozen for Grade A large eggs than nonprogram producers received for the same grade.

The southeastern programs included only quality control producers and, therefore, premiums were not paid as such. One organization was a cooperative and the other did not pay producers on a specific quotation basis.

On the West Coast, prices for quality control eggs were tied closely to USDA reports of prices to retailers.

### Contract Egg Production

Contract egg production involves a contract to produce eggs for a specific firm. The producer is paid a given number of cents per dozen eggs, or per hen per specified time period, for supplying the facilities and labor of producing eggs. All eggs produced are the property of the contractor.[4] Another variation is one in which the producer rents hens from the contractor for specified amounts per dozen, depending upon prices received for the eggs. The pullets, all feed, and medications or similar items are supplied by the contractor. In most instances, quality control requirements are similar to those of contract quality control programs. In addition, contract production programs require specific housing and other facilities and stipulate more management details.

The contractor carries most of the price and production cost risks in contract egg production. However, he is able to reduce as well as to spread production risks by contracting with many producers. Field supervision is much closer in contract production than in most contract quality control programs.

Contract production marketing and quality control programs accounted for about 35 per cent of all eggs sold from farms in 1968.

### Owner-Integrated Operations

Owner-integrated operations are those in which the facilities for egg production as well as the birds are under one ownership and the eggs are marketed to retailers or consumers, or facilities are provided for performing the grading and cartoning operations. The integration of production operations or production and marketing is controlled by a single firm. Control over production and quality maintenance practices is direct. There

[4] The term "contractor" is used to refer to the program developer and operator who owns the hens. The term "producer" is used to refer to the person on whose farm the eggs are produced.

are thousands of owner-integrated operations but nearly all are small.

### Probable Impacts of Egg Programs

Integration of production and marketing operations affects all segments of the egg industry.

Egg production costs probably will be lowered by contract production and large owner-integrated operations. Total egg production may increase faster than population increases. Because of the low price elasticity of demand for eggs, increased production per person could result in proportionately greater declines in egg prices than the increases in egg production per person. Unless there is a major change in consumption habits, methods developed for making eggs more convenient to use, or new markets developed, egg prices may decline in the years ahead. It does not appear realistic to expect egg consumption per person to increase the way broiler consumption has in recent years. Broilers substitute directly for other meats; the elasticity of substitution is high. Substitution between eggs and other foods is less direct and less elastic.

Despite lower egg prices, many operators who are able to dovetail their production and marketing operations and take advantage of the cost-lowering possibilities of an integrated operation may have fairly good net income. But many small unintegrated producers and market operators may go out of the egg business.

## BROILERS

One of the most spectacular changes in the poultry industry has been the rapid development of commercial broiler production.

The rise of the broiler industry is a striking illustration of an adaptation of a product to consumer demand, involving a revolution in production methods. It is a clear demonstration that the field of marketing does not merely begin at the farm gate—that marketing does not merely consist of disposing of whatever farmers produce, but reaches back into the choice of breeds to produce in the first place and carries through to the weight and grade of the product and the form in which it is put up for the consumer. The consumer wanted young, tender meat-type chickens of the right size for her needs, rather than older, tougher, egg-type chickens that were chiefly a by-product of the egg industry. The broiler industry gave her what she wanted and has prospered accordingly.

Broilers are young chickens of heavy breeds raised solely for meat. The USDA defines a broiler as "a young chicken (usually under 16 weeks of age) of either sex that is tender-meated with soft, pliable, smooth-textured skin and flexible breastbone cartilage." A large share of the broilers is produced in specialized broiler "factories" (broiler production is not included in the farm production data). No pullets from broiler flocks are kept for egg production. Most broilers are marketed at 2.5 to 3.5 pounds live weight; farm chickens average about 4.5 pounds.

Broiler production in the United States, virtually nonexistent in 1930, increased from 34 million head in 1934, when figures were first compiled, to nearly 2.6 billion head in 1969. Broiler production now substantially exceeds the production of chickens on farms.

### Broiler Areas, Old and New

Broiler production is heavily concentrated in the south Atlantic and south central states, as shown in Figure 26.6. In 1969 these areas produced 87 per cent of the U.S. total and shipped broilers to nearly all other parts of the country.

Large-scale broiler production had its birthplace in the Del-Mar-Va (Delaware, Maryland, Virginia) peninsula in the early 1930's. This area has continued to be important in broiler production, although several states have since surpassed it in volume. Georgia has been the leading broiler state since the early 1950's and in 1969 produced nearly 450,000 birds. Early production in Georgia was in localities characterized by small farms, low incomes, and few other sources of earnings. While these operations are still important, more of the production now is in the hands of large integrated units.

Arkansas now ranks second in broiler production, followed by Alabama, North Carolina, Mississippi, Texas, and Maryland. Broiler expansion in Arkansas was encouraged by the closeness of midwestern feed supplies and the comparative proximity to the West Coast. In Alabama and other southern states, increases in broiler production resulted in part from cutbacks in cotton allotments. This led to a search for new ways to utilize labor on many of the relatively small farms.

While broilers are grown mainly in the South, a few northern states have sizable numbers. These include Maine, Pennsylvania, Indiana, Missouri, and on the West Coast, California.

### Broiler Marketing

Around 95 per cent of the commercial broiler production is under contractual arrangements between producers and either processors or suppliers of inputs. This, along with mass-merchandising of broilers at retail, has tended to shorten the marketing channel from producer to consumer. In recent years, over

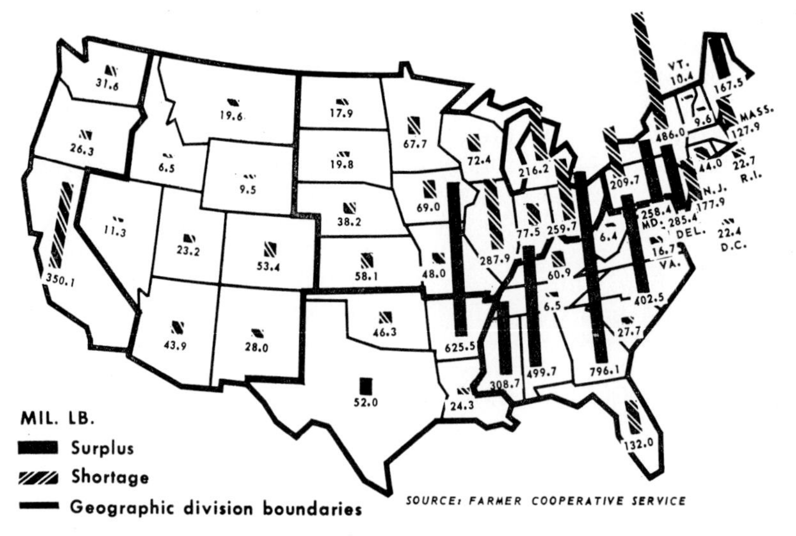


FIG. 26.6—Surplus and deficit states in broiler production, 1964.

half of the broilers have moved directly from processors to retailers, bypassing wholesale distributors and jobbers.

Broiler pricing is largely on a ready-to-cook basis, reflecting levels at which processors sell to wholesalers or retailers. Movement of live birds is mainly a transfer from one part of an integrated firm to another part, so that pricing on a live basis is limited. Prices at major terminal markets are usually used as a base, with values in producing areas adjusted to reflect transportation and handling costs.

## TURKEYS

Turkey production is more widely distributed than broiler production but is concentrated most heavily in the north central states. This area increased its share of the national crop from 37.6 per cent in 1950 to 42.9 per cent in 1969. The relative importance of the southern states in turkey production has also increased, while in the West it has declined. In 1950, the south Atlantic states produced 12.6 per cent of the U.S. turkey crop, the south central states, 11 per cent and the western states 29.6 per cent. In 1969, the proportions were 17.6 per cent, 13.6 per cent, and 21.8 per cent, respectively.

An increasing proportion of turkey production is under contractual or pricing arrangements of some type. By 1969 at least two-thirds of the crop was produced in this way. Contracts provide processors with some control over volume, quality, and time of processing. For producers, it assures an outlet for the birds and usually an approximate price or return.

The marketing channel for turkeys is very similar to that for broilers, with a large volume moving directly from processors to retailers. Most of the turkeys leave processing plants in frozen form.

# 27

## GRAIN MARKETING

THE DEMAND for grain falls into two main groups—the demand for direct human consumption and the demand for livestock feed. Many grains are used to meet both types of demand, although one is normally more important than the other. Grains classed primarily as food grains include wheat, rice, and rye. Major feed grains are corn, grain sorghum, oats, and barley. Soybeans are included in the grain discussion, although the crop is actually a legume. It is also classed as an oilseed crop, along with cotton and flaxseed.

Corn is the most valuable crop grown in the United States, with the 1969 crop worth $5.1 billion. The next most valuable crop, soybeans, was worth $2.6 billion, while the wheat crop was valued at nearly $2.0 billion.[1]

### CORN

Corn is by far the most important of the feed grains and makes up around three-fourths of total feed grain production in the United States. Production of corn is concentrated in the Midwest, as shown in Figure 27.1, even though it is grown to some extent throughout much of the eastern half of the country.

[1] *Field and Seed Crops; Production, Farm Use, Sales, Value,* SRS, USDA, May, 1970.

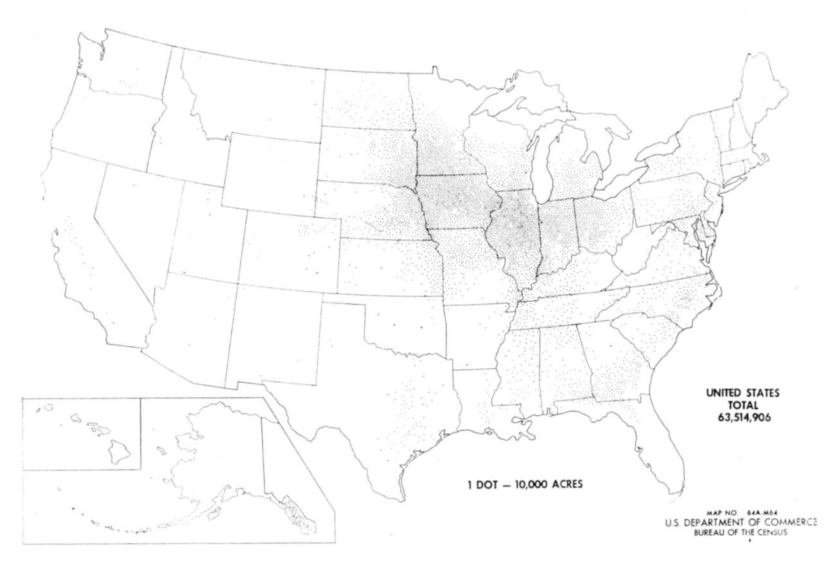


FIG. 27.1—Corn harvested for all purposes, acreage, 1964.

Illinois and Iowa are the top corn states and have shifted back and forth between the number one and two positions.

Most of the corn crop is fed to livestock—about half of it on the same farm where it is grown. The amount and percentages of the corn crop used for feed and other uses in the 1968–69 marketing year are shown in Table 27.1[2]

Exports have been increasing although they vary sharply from year to year, taking 11.7 per cent of the 1968 crop and 12.9 per cent of the 1967 crop. By contrast, corn exports in 1960 were only 7.5 per cent of the crop. For the most part, the volume of corn exports depends upon factors outside the United States, such as need, ability to pay, and production in competing countries. Domestic supplies are a factor only when we have a short crop. In 1947–48, a short crop year, we exported only 7 million bushels.

Corn used directly for human food took over 3 per cent of the 1968 crop; the quantity used is fairly stable from year to year. Included in this use are manufacture of corn meal, grits, and breakfast foods and direct farm household use.

The wet-processing industry is the third most important outlet for corn and has taken around 5 per cent of the crop in recent years. This industry makes cornstarch, corn syrup, corn oil, and gluten feed and meal. Most of its products go into foods. The use of corn by the wet-processing industry has been increasing, although year-to-year changes have not been large.

---

[2] *The Feed Situation*, USDA, FdS-234, May, 1970, p. 8.

**TABLE 27.1: Percentage of Corn Utilization for Feed and Other Uses, 1968–69**

| Use | Bushels | Per cent |
|---|---|---|
| | *(millions)* | |
| Livestock feed | 3,522 | 79.3 |
| Exports | 521 | 11.7 |
| Food and industrial: | | |
| Wet processing | 219 | 4.9 |
| Dry processing | 136 | 3.1 |
| Alcohol | 33 | 0.7 |
| Seed | 12 | 0.3 |
| Total | 4,443 | 100.0 |

The production of alcohol by distilleries takes less than 1 per cent of our corn. Alcohol production from corn has been quite variable since World War II. The peak year was 1946–47, when 56 million bushels of corn were used, and the low year was 1952–53, with 17 million.

Seed use of corn is very small in relation to other outlets and changes little from year to year.

## Utilization of Corn by Livestock

Far and away the most important outlet for corn is livestock feed, which accounts for around 80 per cent of the total disappearance. In recent years, this consumption has averaged around 3.5 billion bushels. Of this amount, about 2.1 billion bushels were fed on the farms where the corn was grown, and nearly 1.5 billion bushels were sold for feed.

Hogs consume around two-fifths of the total corn fed to livestock. Poultry and beef cattle are next with about 20 per cent each, and dairy cattle account for about 14 per cent.

Variations in the supply of corn from year to year do not have much effect on the numbers of these different kinds of livestock except hogs. There is a close relation between the production of corn from year to year and the number of hogs raised. The chief reason for this close dependence of the number of hogs upon corn supplies is that corn constitutes over 75 per cent of the feed they consume. This is a far higher percentage of total feed consumption than for any other kind of livestock.

The demand for feed grains for livestock feeding is moderately inelastic. The elasticity of the demand for corn is about —0.6. With respect to feed grains as a group, it is about —0.5. The demand is fairly stable, except for the variations in hog numbers caused by variations in the size of the corn crop from year to year. A short corn crop increases the price of corn and reduces the farmer's incentive to produce hogs. This reduction in hog numbers reduces the demand for corn next year. By that time, the next corn crop comes on the market. It is usually larger than the preceding short crop. The combination of reduced demand and increased supplies reduces corn prices, while the reduction in the number of hogs causes hog prices to rise. The increase in the ratio between the price of hogs and the price of corn (the hog-corn price ratio) makes it more profitable for farmers to feed hogs, and hog production expands. When that larger production of hogs reaches the market, it depresses hog prices, and this reduces hog production, and so on in a cyclic fashion.

## WHEAT

Wheat, of course, is the principal grain used for direct human consumption in the United States. The quantity used for human food in this country remains almost constant, close to 500 million bushels, year after year.[3]

The demand for wheat for human food in the United States apparently is very inelastic and stable. The population of the United States has been increasing about 1.5 per cent per year, but the total direct human consumption of wheat has remained almost stationary; the per capita demand has been declining at about the same rate as the total population has been increasing.

An amount that usually ranges between 50 and 100 million bushels of wheat per year is fed to livestock, the trend remaining practically constant. This demand for wheat for livestock feed is relatively elastic, at least in the lower price ranges where wheat can be substituted for livestock feeds such as corn.

The demand for wheat, therefore, consists of three separate elements: (1) the demand for direct human food, inelastic and stable; (2) the demand for livestock feed, relatively elastic in the lower price ranges; (3) the export demand, probably elastic but rather unstable, depending on variable conditions abroad.

The areas in which winter wheat and spring wheat are grown are shown in Figures 27.2 and 27.3. Wheat production in the United States has been running between 1 and 1.6 billion bushels over the past 20 years. Between one-third and one-half of the crop was exported up to 1960; exports rose to nearly two-thirds of the crop in the mid-sixties, but dropped back to the 35 to 50 per cent range during 1967–69.

In spite of considerable elements of instability, the price of wheat was rather stable from 1949 through 1963. During this time, the season average price received by farmers ranged

[3] The statistical information on this page is taken from *Agricultural Statistics*, USDA, 1967, pp. 1, 2, 12; and *The Wheat Situation*, USDA, Feb., 1970.

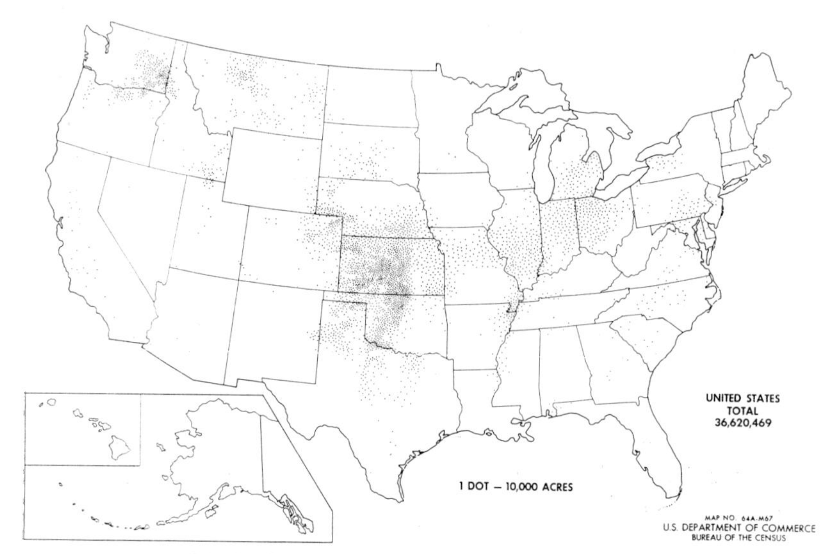


FIG. 27.2—Winter wheat harvested, acreage, 1964.

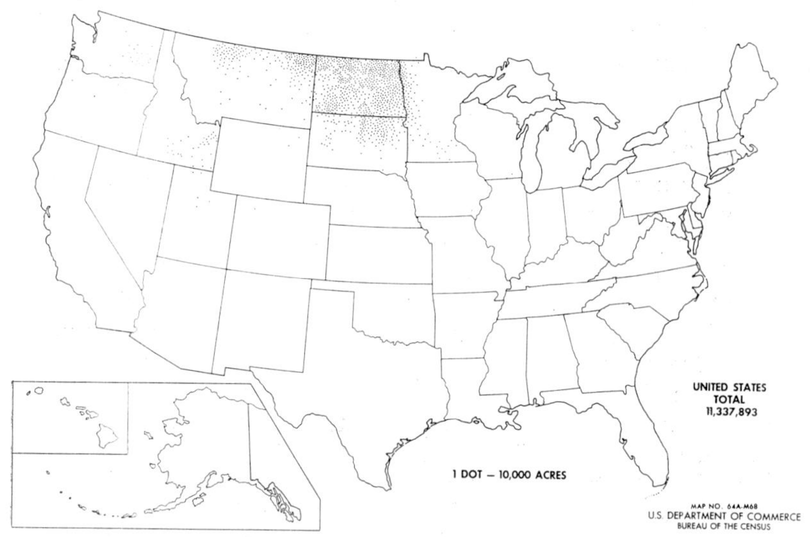


FIG. 27.3—Spring wheat harvested, acreage, 1964.

between $1.74 and $2.12 per bushel.[4] In all but three of those years the average price was above $1.83. The chief reason for this stability was a succession of good crop years, plus the storage activities of the Commodity Credit Corporation. The good years kept wheat prices from rising, and the loan and storage activities of the CCC kept them from falling sharply.

[4] *Agricultural Statistics*, USDA, 1967, p. 23.

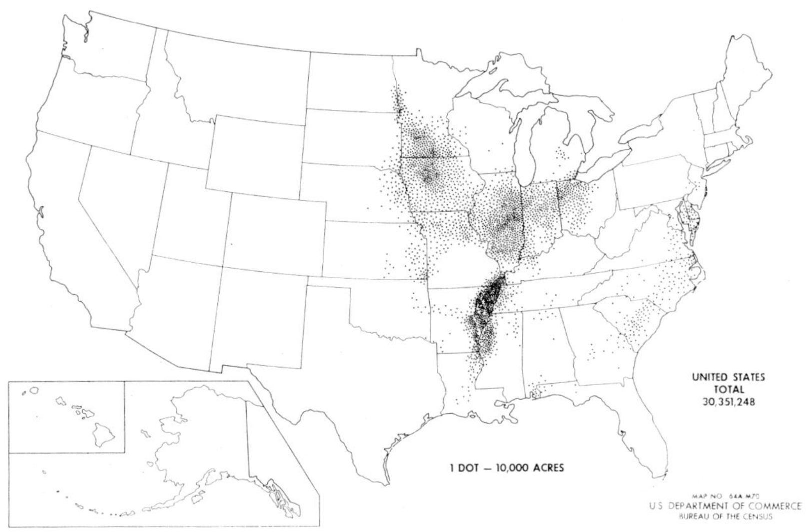


FIG. 27.4—Soybeans harvested for all purposes, acreage, 1964.

A change in the government wheat program beginning in 1964 resulted in sharply lower market prices for wheat, with 1964–69 prices within a range of $1.15 to $1.74 per bushel. The total price to farmers for wheat was higher than this, however, since participants in the wheat program also received direct marketing certificate payments. For example, in 1968 and 1969 the average payments on marketing certificates were 55 and 65 cents per bushel respectively.

## SOYBEANS[5]

Soybean acreage and production have increased rapidly in the United States during the past 30 years. In 1939 only 4.3 million acres were harvested, and the crop totaled 90.1 million bushels. By 1949, 10.5 million acres were harvested, and production rose to 234.2 million bushels. Production continued to move up sharply in the fifties and sixties. The 1969 crop of 1,117 million bushels came from 40.9 million harvested acres.

Soybean production is concentrated in the Corn Belt and in several southern states, as shown in Figure 27.4. In recent years, production has shown the largest relative gains in Iowa and several of the southern states, including Mississippi, Tennessee, North Carolina, South Carolina, and Louisiana. The leading states in production in 1969 were Illinois, Iowa, Indiana, Arkansas, Missouri, and Minnesota.

[5] Data on soybean production and utilization is from *Agricultural Statistics*, USDA, 1967; *The Fats and Oils Situation*, USDA, Apr., 1970; and *Crop Production, 1969 Annual Summary*, USDA, Dec., 1969.

### Utilization of Soybeans

Soybeans provide protein meal for use in livestock and poultry feeds and oil for use in a variety of food products. Each bushel of soybeans yields approximately 11 pounds of soybean oil and 48 pounds of soybean meal. So the price of soybeans is determined by the respective values of these joint products.

The largest part of the crop goes to domestic processors, although the quantity exported has increased sharply in recent years. In the 1968–69 marketing year soybean utilization was distributed as follows:

| | *million bushels* | *per cent* |
|---|---|---|
| Domestic crush | 606 | 64 |
| Exports | 287 | 30 |
| Seed, feed, and residual | 52 | 6 |
| Total | 945 | 100 |

Domestic demand for soybean meal has shown substantial growth over the years. Feed usage has continued to rise, although strong competition from other protein sources such as urea and fish meal has slowed the increase somewhat in recent years. In 1949 the amount fed to livestock and poultry in this country totaled 4.5 million tons. By 1969 domestic feed use had increased to 12.9 million tons.

While past uses of soybean meal have been primarily in livestock feeds, soybean protein appears to have considerable potential as a food for humans. Synthetic food products similar in appearance, texture, and taste to certain meat and poultry products have been developed from soybean protein. Use of soybeans for these foods and in other food products will probably increase.

Domestic use of soybean oil has also increased a great deal. Main uses are in shortening, margarine, and cooking and salad oils, where it has increasingly replaced cottonseed oil. About 10 per cent of the domestic disappearance of soybean oil is in nonfood products such as paints and plastics. Total soybean oil usage in the United States increased from 1.6 billion pounds in 1949 to 5.8 billion pounds in 1968–69.

As noted earlier, exports of soybeans have gone up steadily—from 13 million bushels in 1949 to 287 million bushels in the 1968–69 marketing year. In addition to soybeans, large quantities of soybean meal and oil are also exported, mostly commercial sales to western Europe and Japan. Soybean meal exports amounted to 3.1 million tons in 1968–69.

Soybean oil exports are quite variable from year to year.

Commercial sales are especially dependent upon the supply of other vegetable oils in Europe, including the olive oil supply in the Mediterannean countries and sunflowerseed oil in eastern Europe. A smaller than normal supply of these oils tends to increase U.S. shipments of soybean oil. Sizable quantities of soybean oil have been exported under government aid programs, such as the P.L. 480 program. These amounts have also varied, depending upon supply and price levels in this country and the need and amount of aid authorized for the recipient countries.

## OTHER GRAINS[6]

Oat production has declined in this country, due to changes in crop cultural practices and to greater returns in many areas from corn and soybean production. Oats are used often as a nurse crop for legume and hay crop seedings; a shift to more intensive use of land for corn and soybeans has reduced the acreage in hay crops—thereby contributing to smaller oat acreage. The 1969 crop of 950 million bushels compared with 1.5 billion bushels produced in 1955.

Production of oats is concentrated in the Midwest, with Minnesota, South Dakota, Wisconsin, Iowa, and North Dakota the largest producing states. In the 1968–69 marketing year, 86.5 per cent of the oats used were fed to livestock. Breakfast foods accounted for 5.2 per cent of the total usage, seed 6.3 per cent, and exports 1.0 per cent.

Grain sorghum production has increased substantially in the past 20 years. The 1969 crop totaled 743 million bushels, compared with only 131 million bushels in 1948. Most of the grain sorghum is grown in Texas, Nebraska, and Kansas, with these three states accounting for 82 per cent of the 1969 crop. In recent years, about four-fifths of the grain sorghum use has been for livestock feed and about one-fifth has been exports.

Barley production has been fairly stable in recent years. Annual crops between 1955 and 1969 ranged from 377 to 477 million bushels, but only two years were above 430 million bushels. North Dakota, California, Minnesota, Montana, and Idaho are the main producing states. In the 1968–69 marketing year, 61 per cent of the barley used was for livestock feed; 29 per cent was used in the production of industrial alcohol and alcoholic beverages, 3.5 per cent was exported, and the balance was used for food and seed.

Rye production is relatively small in the United States, to-

[6] Production and utilization data in this section are from *Feed Statistics,* USDA, Stat. Bul. 410, Oct., 1969, and *The Feed Situation,* USDA, May, 1970.

taling only 31.4 million bushels in 1969. South Dakota and North Dakota are the leading states in production, with Minnesota, Nebraska, and Georgia other major producing states. While rye is considered a food grain, over a third of the crop is usually fed to livestock. Food and industrial uses account for another third of the disappearance, seed use nearly one-fifth, and a small volume is exported.

Rice is grown in only a few states, including Texas, Louisiana, Arkansas, and California. Production has increased in this country, with the 1969 crop of 91 million hundredweight more than double the 1957 crop. Around two-fifths of the rice is exported and one-fifth is used domestically for food. Other uses, including seed, use by breweries, and residual loss account for the balance.

Flaxseed production is also limited to a small number of states, with most of the crop grown in North Dakota, South Dakota, and Minnesota. A large percentage of the crop is crushed to obtain linseed oil and meal; exports vary widely but usually account for 10 to 25 per cent of total disappearance. Linseed meal is a high-quality protein feed for livestock, but makes up only a small part of the total protein-meal supply. Linseed oil is used primarily in drying-oil products.

## THE GRAIN-MARKETING SYSTEM

For grain that enters commercial channels, the usual starting point is sale by the producer to a local country elevator. This may be at harvesttime or later in the year after a period of storage. Local elevators hold some of the grain purchased in an effort to utilize storage space and to earn a profit from price changes or grain-merchandising operations. Much of the grain is moved on to subterminal or terminal elevators and to processors and exporters.

Movement of grain from the farm is normally by truck. From country elevator points it is shipped to subterminal and terminal markets either by rail or truck. Grain also moves by barge, especially to port locations for export or to river terminals for other distribution.

Continued expansion of broiler and turkey production in the South and increased cattle feeding in the West, Southwest, and South have brought greater movement of feed grains from the Midwest to these areas. Movement of feed grains and wheat to port locations for export has also increased. In order to be more competitive for this larger grain business, railroads have developed large "Big John" hopper cars designed especially for grain transport. Freight rates have also been adjusted downward in many cases.

The elevators which handle and store grains cover a wide range in size. The smallest are most numerous—20,000-bushel to 200,000-bushel local elevators that break the skyline at small country towns throughout the midwestern and western plains. Many of the country elevators are larger, ranging from 200,000 bushels or so to 600,000- or 700,000-bushel capacity. Elevators at subterminal markets—country assembly and dispersal points, such as Wellington, Kansas; Fremont, Nebraska; or Des Moines, Iowa—vary greatly in size but tend to be larger than most local elevators. They may range in size from 400,000 or 500,000 bushels to several million bushels. At the terminal markets, the largest elevators range up to 50 million bushels or more capacity.

Each year these grain warehouses or elevators handle on the average about 3 billion bushels of grain. Much of this grain comes on the market during the first few months after harvest each year, especially in the case of wheat, oats, and soybeans. One indication of this is the monthly distribution of grain receipts at primary markets. The percentages for the 1968–69 marketing year for corn, wheat, oats, and soybeans are shown in Table 27.2.

The channels of distribution for wheat and feed grains for 1963–64 are shown in Figures 27.5 and 27.6. The channels for soybeans are similar. Practically all of the soybean supply moves from local elevators to either subterminals or terminals or directly to processors and exporters.

The soybean processing industry has grown rapidly in capacity in order to handle the larger volume of beans produced. The number of processors increased during the late 1930's and the 1940's, but has declined in recent years. The size of individual mills has gone up sharply, however. There were only 47 soybean processors in the United States in 1939, with an average annual capacity of 1.2 million bushels. In 1951 there were 193 processors with average capacity of 1.6 million bushels. By

**TABLE 27.2: Monthly Distribution of Inspected Receipts of Grain at Selected Markets, 1968–69,* Percentages**

| | July | Aug. | Sept. | Oct. | Nov. | Dec. | Jan. | Feb. | Mar. | Apr. | May | June |
|---|---|---|---|---|---|---|---|---|---|---|---|---|
| Wheat ...... | 13.7 | 10.9 | 7.8 | 8.0 | 7.0 | 6.2 | 5.7 | 5.3 | 6.8 | 7.7 | 8.0 | 12.9 |
| Oats ....... | 7.9 | 22.2 | 12.2 | 7.5 | 5.1 | 7.3 | 3.8 | 6.6 | 6.2 | 5.0 | 5.5 | 10.7 |
| | Oct. | Nov. | Dec. | Jan. | Feb. | Mar. | Apr. | May | June | July | Aug. | Sept. |
| Corn ....... | 8.5 | 15.0 | 10.3 | 4.4 | 5.9 | 7.0 | 5.9 | 6.4 | 8.1 | 8.8 | 10.0 | 9.7 |
| Soybeans .... | 25.9 | 15.8 | 7.4 | 4.2 | 5.5 | 7.3 | 7.5 | 5.0 | 4.9 | 5.4 | 4.6 | 6.5 |

Source: Derived from data published in *Grain Market News, Weekly Summary and Statistics,* USDA, selected issues, Aug., 1968–Oct., 1969.

* Includes receipts at over 63 markets throughout the United States; however, not all markets handle each grain.

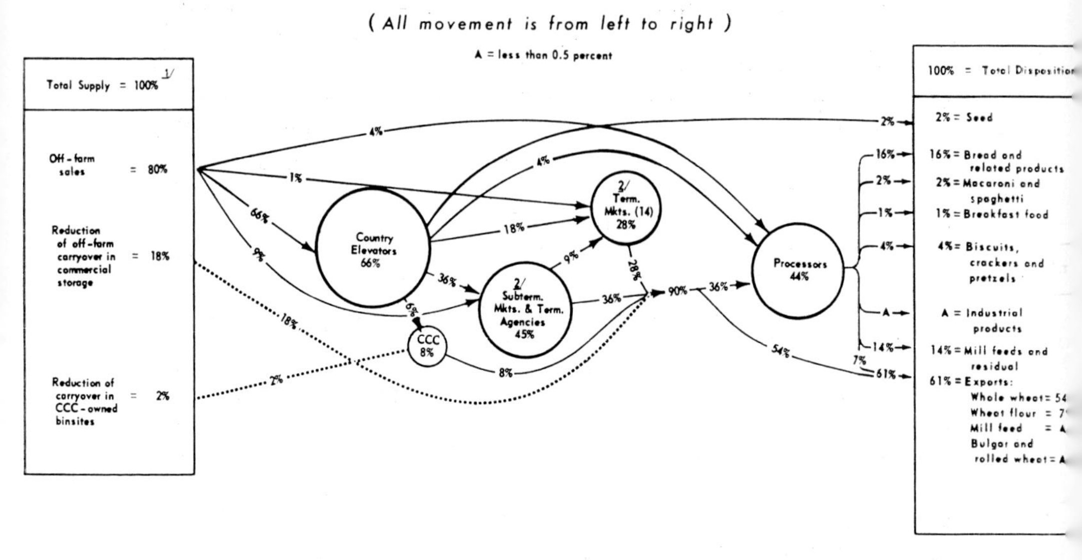


1/ TOTAL SUPPLY DURING THE 1963-64 MARKETING YEAR WAS 1,378 MILLION BUSHELS. OFF-FARM SALES (97 PERCENT OF TOTAL PRODUCTION) TOTALED 1,103 MILLION BUSHELS, OR 80 PERCENT OF THE TOTAL SUPPLY. REDUCTION OF OFF-FARM CARRYOVER IN COMMERCIAL STORAGE TOTALED 249 MILLION BUSHELS, OR 18 PERCENT OF THE TOTAL SUPPLY, AND ENTERED THE MARKETING CHANNELS FROM THE TERMINAL AND SUBTERMINAL ELEVATORS. REDUCTION OF CARRYOVER IN CCC-OWNED BINSITES TOTALED 26 MILLION BUSHELS, OR 2 PERCENT OF THE TOTAL SUPPLY, AND ENTERED THE MARKETING CHANNELS FROM CCC STORAGE SITES.

2/ TERMINAL RECEIPTS ARE BASED ON THE VOLUME OF INSPECTED RECEIPTS. FOURTEEN TERMINAL MARKETS INCLUDE CHICAGO, DULUTH, HUTCHINSON, INDIANAPOLIS, KANSAS CITY, MILWAUKEE, MINNEAPOLIS, OMAHA, PEORIA, SIOUX CITY, ST. JOSEPH, ST. LOUIS, TOLEDO AND WICHITA.

U.S. DEPARTMENT OF AGRICULTURE NEG. ERS 3535-65 (2) ECONOMIC RESEARCH SERVIC

FIG. 27.5—Channels of distribution for wheat in the United States, 1963–64.

1969 the number of processors had declined to 132, but average capacity per plant had zoomed to 5.8 million bushels. Total industry capacity at that time was estimated at 770 million bushels per year.[7]

## Grain Storage Problems

Much of the grain that flows through commercial channels is shipped from the farm soon after harvest; but it is consumed in fairly constant quantities each month through the year. The excess grain coming to market at harvesttime has to be held in storage somewhere along the line and released later on through the year when receipts are light. This grain is held in storage for periods ranging from a day to several months—in some cases, for more than a year.

Grain storage capacity in the United States has been increasing rapidly. The total capacity of off-farm commercial

[7] *The Fats and Oils Situation,* USDA, Nov., 1969, p. 9.

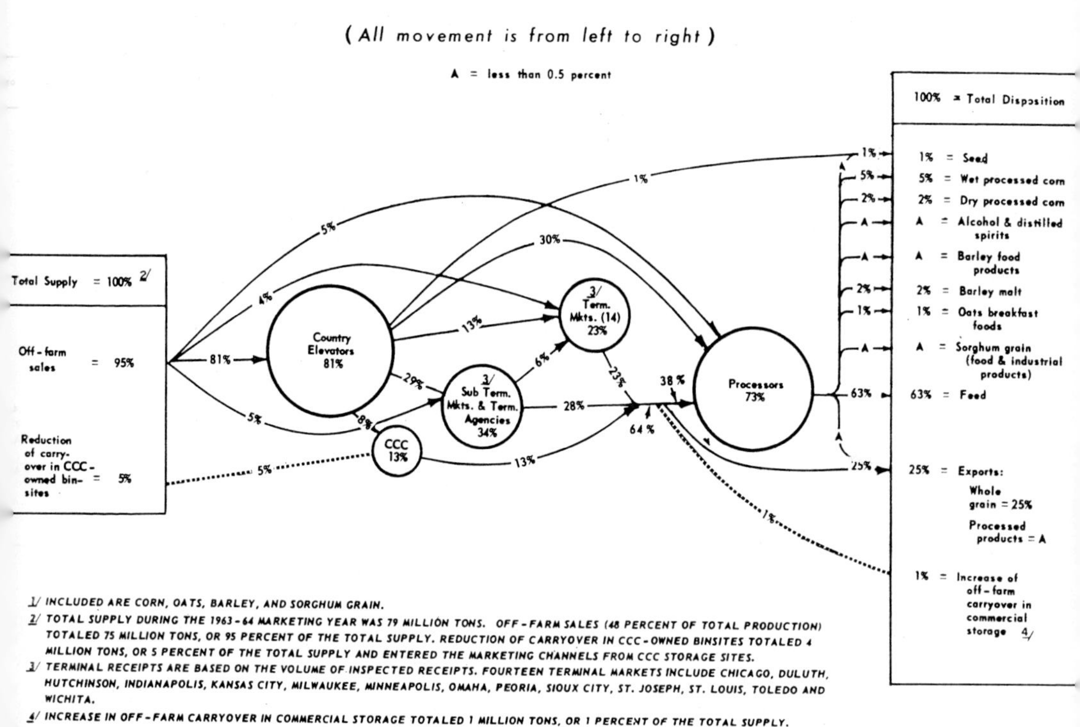


FIG. 27.6—Channels of distribution for feed grains in the United States, 1963–64.

grain storage establishments in the United States on January 1, 1970, was estimated at 5,637 million bushels. This was more than twice as great as the capacity in 1951—2,176 million bushels. It was over a half billion bushels greater than the capacity on January 1, 1961.

Table 27.3 shows that Texas ranked as the state with the largest capacity, followed by Kansas and Illinois. The combined storage amounted to 2.1 billion bushels, nearly 40 per cent of the nation's total storage capacity in off-farm positions.

The wide use of modern cultural and harvesting methods has accentuated the grain storage problem. Improved varieties, increased use of commercial fertilizers, and more effective methods of insect and weed control have combined to boost yields and production, especially in the case of corn. This in itself has increased total storage requirements. Government price support and storage programs for grain have also affected the amount of storage capacity needed, both on and off farms.

**TABLE 27.3: Capacity of Off-Farm Grain Storage Facilities, by States, January 1, 1970***

| State | Rated Off-Farm Storage Capacity | State | Rated Off-Farm Storage Capacity |
|---|---|---|---|
| | *(1,000 bushels)* | | *(1,000 bushels)* |
| N. Eng. | 4,160 | Ga. | 32,000 |
| N.Y. | 66,950 | Fla. | 5,550 |
| N.J. | 2,180 | Ky. | 28,790 |
| Pa. | 25,010 | Tenn. | 40,070 |
| Ohio | 165,000 | Ala. | 18,150 |
| Ind. | 149,470 | Miss. | 50,050 |
| Ill. | 521,000 | Ark. | 150,700 |
| Mich. | 55,600 | La. | 71,200 |
| Wis. | 109,200 | Okla. | 187,570 |
| Minn. | 328,140 | Tex. | 845,080 |
| Iowa | 437,600 | Mont. | 47,100 |
| Mo. | 173,500 | Idaho | 45,680 |
| N. Dak. | 139,000 | Wyo. | 6,540 |
| S. Dak. | 82,880 | Colo. | 82,000 |
| Nebr. | 477,630 | N. Mex. | 15,910 |
| Kans. | 767,000 | Ariz. | 27,910 |
| Del. | 13,660 | Utah | 17,470 |
| Md. | 30,600 | Nev. | 340 |
| Va. | 20,660 | Wash. | 151,240 |
| W. Va. | 280 | Oreg. | 58,700 |
| N.C | 33,200 | Calif. | 123,860 |
| S.C. | 27,730 | U.S. | 5,636,990 |

Source: *Stocks of Grains in All Positions,* USDA, Jan. 22, 1970, p. 27.

* The capacity data, by states, include all elevators, warehouses, terminals, merchant mills, ships under private control, other storages, and oilseed crushers which store grains or soybeans. Capacity data exclude CCC bins, mothball ships under government control used to store grain, warehouses used to store only rice or peanuts, oilseed crushers processing only cottonseed or peanuts, tobacco warehouses, and storages that handle only dry beans or dry peas.

Maintaining the quality of grain in storage has also become a bigger problem. By and large, the corn varieties that require the longest growing season produce the highest yields and are therefore most widely used. This increases the probability that corn will be high in moisture content at harvesttime and will require conditioning or special attention in storage. This continues to be a problem with that portion of the corn that is harvested by mechanical picker and stored in ear form in cribs.

A rapid shift to field-shelling methods of harvesting corn has modified this problem somewhat, however. With field-shelling equipment, corn is usually harvested at 22 to 28 per cent moisture in order to minimize field losses and to permit earlier harvest. This is well above the 14 or 15 per cent moisture level necessary for extended storage and means that most of the corn that is field shelled must be artificially dried to a storable moisture level. An exception is corn that is stored in silos or other facilities for feeding to livestock as "high-moisture" corn. Field-shelling harvesting methods have also changed the type of storage facilities needed in many cases—both to facilitate drying and to hold the shelled grain.

Before the federal government undertook market stabilization operations in grain, storage problems were primarily intraseasonal. The quantities of grain that were carried over from one year to another were comparatively small. But after the "ever-normal granary" programs were set in operation, the quantities increased. More grain was carried over to smooth out the effects of yearly fluctuations in production.

The build-up of grain carryover stocks was especially rapid during the 1950's and reached a peak in 1961. By that time, carryover stocks of wheat and feed grains had become excessive; wheat carryover amounted to nearly 1.5 billion bushels and corn stocks were over 2 billion bushels. Changes in the government wheat and feed grain programs after 1961 held annual production below utilization of these grains during the 1962–66 period; and carryover stocks declined sharply. By 1967 the wheat carryover was down to 425 million bushels but it increased to about 800 million bushels by 1969. The corn carryover had been reduced to a little over 800 million bushels by 1967 but rose to about 1.1 billion bushels in 1969.

These wide changes in carryover levels have affected the grain business greatly. Storing grain for government account became a major new activity during the 1950's and early 1960's. Many country elevators constructed new facilities to handle government grain and received a sizable part of their revenue from this activity. The sharp reduction in Commodity Credit Corporation grain holdings by the mid-sixties left many country elevators with unused storage capacity and with a substantial drop in income. Some offset has been provided by the shift to field shelling of grain and by the trend to specialization in grain production on many farms in the Midwest. These developments have expanded the demand for commercial grain-storage facilities in many areas and have also increased the demand for drying services at the local elevator level.

### LOCATION OF STORED GRAIN

Table 27.3 shows the total off-farm grain-storage capacity in the different states. About four-fifths of this capacity is located at country elevator and subterminal locations, with the balance at inland and port terminals. Government-owned storage facilities are not included in the total.

Stocks of the individual grains are concentrated in different areas, usually corresponding to areas of heaviest production. Thus, wheat stocks are usually largest in Kansas, North Dakota,

Nebraska, Montana, South Dakota, and Oklahoma. Illinois, Iowa, Nebraska, and Minnesota account for a large share of the corn stocks in most years, while most of the grain sorghum is stored in Texas, Nebraska, and Kansas. Soybean stocks are concentrated in Illinois, Iowa, and a small number of other states in the Midwest and South.

Grain owned by the Commodity Credit Corporation is stored in a combination of commercial and government-owned facilities. And the relative importance of the different types of storage varies for different grains. The bulk of the wheat owned by CCC has typically been stored in commercial facilities, especially at country elevators and subterminals. On January 1, 1970, only 6 per cent of the wheat owned by the government was stored at CCC bin sites.

By contrast, a much larger proportion of the corn owned by the CCC has been stored in government-owned facilities. Prior to 1956 commercial facilities were used to only a limited extent. The use of commercial storage increased sharply in the late fifties, however, during the period of rapid buildup of CCC corn stocks. In 1958 the proportion of CCC-owned corn stored in CCC-owned or controlled facilities was 56 per cent, with the balance in commercial storage. By 1970, with total stocks lower, 49 per cent was stored at CCC bin sites.

Storage of CCC-owned grain sorghum is largely in commercial facilities; in 1970 less than 1 per cent was in government-owned storage.

## METHODS OF SELLING GRAIN

Two methods of selling grain are available to elevator operators. One is the consignment method; the other is selling for deferred delivery either on "to arrive" or "on track" bids.

### Selling by the Consignment Method

Under the consignment method, grain is shipped to a terminal market or other point and consigned to a commission merchant who acts as the elevator's agent in selling the grain. The elevator retains ownership of the grain and incurs any loss due to damage or price changes while the grain is in transit. He does not know what price the grain will bring until it reaches the market, is inspected, and is offered for sale.

The commission charge for selling grain at Chicago and most other markets is 1 per cent of the gross price received for the grain, delivered at the market where sold. In return for this charge, the commission merchant sells the grain at the highest price he can get, deducts his commission, and remits the proceeds to the consignor.

Commission houses also perform other services. They permit country elevator men to draw against them for a portion of the value of the grain consigned to them. They thus constitute a source of credit for the country elevators. In some cases they go as far as to advance money to the country elevator on open account, simply on the implied condition that all, or at least a major part, of that country elevator's grain be consigned to them.

Farmers sell most of their grain outright to local elevators. An elevator operator who buys corn, for example, intending to consign it to a commission man at a terminal market, will not be able to get it to that market for several days. If he wishes to protect himself against a possible decline in price while the grain is en route to the terminal market, the local elevator man bases the price he pays the farmer on the current price of grain at the terminal market, less the commission, freight, and his own local handling charge (the latter charge in most cases is about 3 cents a bushel for corn and oats and about 4 cents for wheat and soybeans), and hedges his purchase by the sale of an equivalent amount of grain on the futures market. Thus if the price of cash grain has declined by the time his grain arrives at the terminal market, the price of futures usually will have declined by about the same amount, and he will recoup his own loss on the cash grain by his gain on the futures transaction.

### "On Track" and "To Arrive"

Hedging on the futures market is not the only method by which the local elevator operator can protect himself against a decline in the price of grain. Instead of consigning his grain and hedging it en route, he may sell it on a deferred shipment basis under either "to arrive" or "on track" terms. Bids on this basis quote a current price but give the elevator man a number of days time to get the grain to the terminal market or interior mill. The price agreed upon will be paid if the grain arrives during the time specified, unaffected by changes that may take place in market prices. In this case, the buyer assumes the risk of price changes either by carrying that risk himself or by hedging in the futures market. In some ways this is an advantage. Large buyers with headquarters at the terminal markets are frequently in a position to perform hedging operations more skillfully with respect to possible changes in "basis" (the relation between cash and futures prices), than small-scale local elevator men.

"To arrive" sales are made on the basis of bid cards sent out by brokers or elevators or manufacturers. These cards name price offers (on the basis of the terminal or manufacturing market from which the cards are mailed) that hold good only until

9:15 the morning after mailing, the grain to be delivered any time within 10 or 15 days, or sometimes longer. The price is the amount the terminal buyer pays on the arrival of the grain, so the local elevators must pay the freight to the terminal market.

"On track" sales (on track at the country elevator point; also called track country station) are made on the basis of prices bid f.o.b. country elevator points. The elevator agrees to load the car within a specified time. The buyer pays all charges from the local elevator to the destination point.

After the price is settled and the deal is made, the country elevator man is not affected by subsequent changes in price when he is selling on either the "to arrive" or the "on track" basis. Suppose that he has accepted an "on track" bid of $1.25 a bushel for a carload of corn, and that by the time he delivers the grain, say in ten days, the price has fallen to $1.15. That makes no difference; he still gets the original price of $1.25 a bushel. Similarly, if the price rises to $1.35, he still gets only the original price of $1.25 a bushel.

The elevator may not always be able to cover its price risk effectively by "to arrive" and "on track" sales. Sometimes the "to arrive" price is out of line with cash prices being paid currently for grain by the elevator. When this happens, one of the things the local elevator can do is to hedge in the futures market to obtain price protection.

## COUNTRY ELEVATOR OPERATING COSTS

A USDA study indicated that grain storage and handling costs at country elevators in the United States averaged 10.4 cents per bushel in 1964–65.[8] This included one year's storage, plus receiving grain by truck and shipping by rail. Depreciation and interest costs as carried on the elevator's books were also included. Out-of-pocket costs (excluding depreciation and interest on investment) averaged 6.9 cents per bushel. The breakdown of this total included 5.4 cents for storage, 2.1 cents for receiving the grain by truck, and 2.9 cents for loading-out by rail. In the same study, average costs for commercial drying of grain at country elevators was estimated at 4.6 cents per bushel; cleaning costs averaged 2.1 cents per bushel. For handling only, costs averaged 2.2 cents per bushel.

### Factors Affecting Country Elevator Operating Costs

Two of the most important factors affecting country elevator operating costs are the size of the elevator and the percentage of its capacity used.

[8] *Costs of Storing and Handling Grain in Commercial Elevators, 1964–65*, USDA, ERS-288, Apr., 1966.

A study of the costs of operating different-sized country elevators at different percentages of their capacity reached the following conclusions with respect to (1) merchandising or handling costs and (2) storage costs.[9]

### MERCHANDISING OR HANDLING COSTS

When a large country elevator has sufficient volume to operate near its maximum practical volume level, it has an important competitive advantage over smaller elevators.

At the maximum practical volume level, costs for merchandising or handling grain, including shrinkage and quality deterioration, ranged from 5.08 cents a bushel in the new 20,000-bushel model to 2.63 cents a bushel in the 600,000-bushel model. This was on the basis of a 250,000-bushel annual volume in the 20,000-bushel model and 1.5 million bushels in the 600,000-bushel model.

The larger the elevator the higher the unit costs at the same volume, however. This is because of higher fixed costs in the larger models.

For example, at a 200,000-bushel annual volume, the new 20,000-bushel elevator had per bushel costs of 5.32 cents. At the same volume, per bushel costs were 10.47 cents in the new 600,000-bushel elevator.

The curved lines in Figure 27.7 show these costs graphically for the six elevator models. By intersecting the curved line with a horizontal line at the unit cost of operating the new 20,000-bushel elevator at a 250,000-bushel annual volume—5.08 cents—you can readily see what additional volume would be necessary to operate the larger elevators at the same per unit cost. It took 500,000 bushels, or double the annual volume of the small model, to operate the 600,000-bushel model at the 5.08-cent unit cost. The old 200,000-bushel elevator required only a 185,000-bushel volume to operate at the same cost.

To operate at the same per bushel costs, the additional volume required for each 100,000 bushels of elevator capacity decreased as the elevator size increased. This general relationship will hold whether the horizontal line in Figure 27.7 is drawn at the 5.08-cent level or at some other lower unit cost level.

The 600,000-bushel model could merchandise or handle grain at one-third its maximum practical volume and still be competitive with the new 20,000-bushel model merchandising or handling its maximum volume, or 250,000 bushels annually.

This also indicates the advantage of an elevator located in

[9] Thomas E. Hall, *New Country Elevators, Influence of Size and Volume on Operating Costs*, U.S. Farmers Cooperative Serv. Circ. 10, June 1955, pp. 3–5, 25.

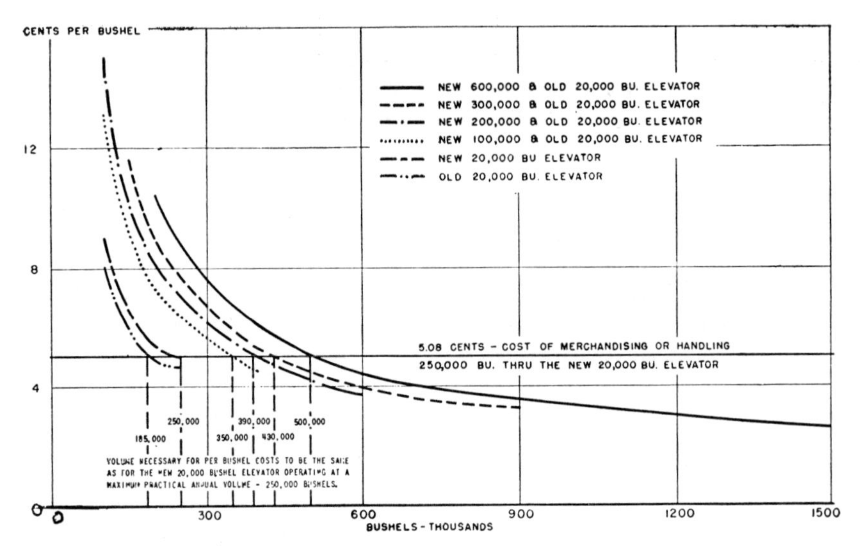


FIG. 27.7—Costs of handling different volumes of grain in six elevators of different sizes.

a trade territory that will give it an average of a million bushels or more annually over competing elevators with small trade territories and correspondingly small annual volume merchandised or handled.

Furthermore, these data point to the advantage of adequate siding for spotting and loading cars, and fast receiving and loading-out equipment. Shipping wheat on to subterminal or terminal storage rather than storing it in country elevators also adds to volume merchandised or handled. Thus, lower unit costs result, regardless of elevator size, for the merchandising or handling function.

To minimize grain merchandising or handling costs, the study recommends:

1. Build as large an elevator as needed to handle the average volume but no larger. Add elevator storage capacity only when what appear to be average conditions make it impossible to ship grain, including that for terminal storage, as fast as it is received during the harvest season.
2. Provide enough equipment and railroad siding to ship grain as fast as terminal elevator capacity and rail facilities will permit. This will reduce unit costs because of the high volume merchandised or handled in relation to the capacity of the local elevator.

## STORAGE COSTS

No elevator can use all its capacity for storing grain. Some space must be reserved for grain owned by the elevator and for turning stored stocks. In the study models, capacity used for storage beyond the harvest season was as follows: In both the 20,000-bushel models—15,000 bushels; in the new 100,000-bushel model plus the old 20,000-bushel model—90,000 bushels; in the new 200,000-bushel model plus the old 20,000-bushel model—180,000 bushels; in the new 300,000-bushel model plus the old 20,000-bushel model—270,000 bushels; and in the 600,-000-bushel model—540,000 bushels.

The findings are based mainly on the models with new elevators and deal with costs in terms of per bushel capacity used.

Annual storage costs per bushel of capacity, when all available capacity was used, were less than half as high in the 600,000-bushel model as in the new 20,000-bushel model—5.14 cents compared with 11.44 cents.

But storage unit costs at identical amounts of capacity used were considerably higher as the size of the elevator increased. For example, using 90,000 bushels of elevator capacity, costs per bushel of capacity used were 7.32 cents, 10.92 cents, and 14.46 cents for the 100,000-bushel, 200,000-bushel, and 300,000-bushel models respectively.

Costs were not budgeted for storing as little as 90,000 bushels in the 600,000-bushel elevator. They were 20.4 cents per bushel of capacity used, when storing a higher proportion of available capacity—120,000 bushels.

Figure 27.8 shows the number of bushels and the per cent of capacity the 200,000-bushel, 300,000-bushel, and 600,000-bushel elevators have to use to bring their costs per bushel of capacity occupied down low enough to equal those of the 100,000-bushel model using all its available storage space.

The horizontal line in Figure 27.8 intersects the curved unit-cost line at full use of storage capacity in the 100,000-bushel model plus the old 20,000-bushel model. The new 200,-000-bushel model will operate at that cost or lower when using from 145,000 to 180,000 bushels of capacity. The 600,000-bushel model will have the same or lower costs in the range between 345,000 bushels—or 58 per cent capacity use—and 540,000 bushels, or 90 per cent available capacity use.

There will be a substantial advantage if the size of the elevator is planned so that it will operate year after year with about all the available storage capacity in use, regardless of the size of elevator needed for the territory.

## Appraisal

Changes in the nature of grain production, harvesting, and marketing and continued improvements in transportation are creating strong pressures for adjustment in the number and size of local grain-handling facilities and in the services provided. The storage, handling, and conditioning services that producers will demand, along with many related farm supply services, can probably be provided efficiently and profitably only if the number of firms is reduced substantially.

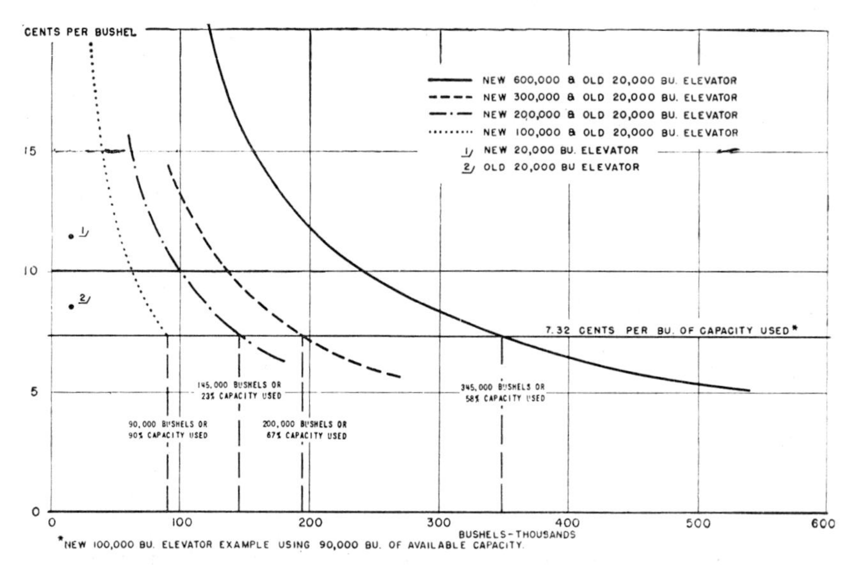


FIG. 27.8—Annual costs of storing grain, per bushel of capacity used, in elevators of different sizes.

# 28

# GRAIN PRICES AND COSTS OF STORAGE

DOES IT PAY farmers to sell grain right after harvest, or is it better to put it into storage and sell it later in the year? And what are the comparative costs and advantages of storing grain in elevators and on farms?

Chapter 11 on seasonal price movements showed that the average seasonal rise in Iowa farm prices for the period 1955–69 was 14 cents per bushel for corn, 6 cents for oats, 13 cents for wheat, and 36 cents for soybeans. These are the average revenues that farmers can expect to realize from storing these grains from harvest time to the month later in the season when prices ordinarily reach their seasonal peak.

We need now to compare these average revenues with the costs of storage. These costs are discussed below.

## FARM STORAGE COSTS[1]

The costs of storing grain on the farm can be divided into fixed and variable costs. Fixed costs are those that are related to the investment in buildings and equipment—interest, property

[1] This section is based largely on T. A. Hieronymus, *When To Sell Corn, Soybeans, Oats, Wheat,* Univ. of Ill. Coop. Ext. Serv., Circ. 948, Oct., 1966.

tax, depreciation, insurance, and maintenance. These costs are incurred even if the storage space is not used.

Variable costs are those related to the grain itself. They include the cost of moving the grain into and out of storage, insurance on the grain, shrinkage and deterioration, and in some cases, property tax on the grain.

If the grain is artificially dried on the farm, the costs of owning and operating the drying equipment should also be included. This has become an increasingly important item in on-farm storage of corn in recent years, due to the rapid shift to field-shelling methods of harvesting.

On-farm storage is most prevalent in the case of corn and grain sorghums; a major part of the oats crop is also stored on the farm as well as a sizable amount of wheat. In recent years the amount of wheat stored on U.S. farms October 1 has been equal to about 40 per cent of the annual crop. The volume of soybeans stored on farms varies quite a bit from year to year, but indications are that from one-third to one-half of the crop is usually stored on the farm for at least some period after harvest.

### Corn

The fixed costs of on-farm storage facilities for corn vary a good deal depending upon the type of storage and whether the storage has alternate uses at a particular time. Metal storage bins of 10,000-bushel capacity, including a batch-in-bin drying system, cost about 60 cents per bushel of capacity to buy. Good wood storage facilities for either ear or shelled corn (without drying equipment) cost around 85 cents per bushel of capacity. Annual fixed costs connected with grain storage facilities and equipment are around 10 per cent of the initial cost, assuming a 20-year depreciation schedule.

Variable costs are influenced by the length of time the corn is stored as well as by the type of storage. Costs are somewhat greater for on-farm drying and storage of shelled corn than for ear corn storage, due mainly to the costs of artificial drying. Annual fixed costs, however, are usually greater for ear corn storage.

Estimates of on-farm storage costs for corn in Illinois are summarized in Tables 28.1 and 28.2 For a six-month storage period, variable costs of storing ear corn are about 4 cents per bushel. Corresponding costs for drying and storing shelled corn are about 8 cents per bushel. When fixed costs are included, the total costs are about 12.5 cents per bushel for ear corn and 14 cents for shelled corn.

**TABLE 28.1: Costs of Storing Ear Corn on Farms***

| Cost | 1 Month | 3 Months | 6 Months | 9 Months |
|---|---|---|---|---|
| | | (cents per bushel) | | |
| Annual fixed crib cost | 8.50 | 8.50 | 8.50 | 8.50 |
| Interest at 6 per cent | .55 | 1.65 | 3.30 | 4.95 |
| Insurance | .15 | .27 | .46 | .62 |
| Taxes | .00 | .00 | 1.50 | 1.50 |
| Extra handling and dry-matter loss | 1.55 | 1.55 | 1.55 | 1.55 |
| Natural drying (deduct)† | —.36 | —.60 | —2.83 | —.98 |
| Total without crib cost | 1.89 | 2.87 | 3.98 | 7.64 |
| Total including crib cost | 10.39 | 11.37 | 12.48 | 16.14 |

* Assuming a corn price of $1.10 per bushel and beginning moisture of 20.5 per cent.

† The moisture loss due to natural drying raises the grade of the corn until it reaches 14 per cent if other grading factors permit; this raises the value per bushel. Therefore, these amounts should be deducted from the costs of storage.

## Soybeans

The fixed costs of on-farm storage of soybeans are similar to those for ear corn if the storage bin is a part of a combination ear corn and tight bin facility. The initial cost is around 85 cents per bushel of capacity, with annual charges of about 8.5 cents per bushel. If storage is in metal bins, the initial cost is around 40 cents per bushel of capacity and the annual charge about 4 cents per bushel. The main variable costs are interest, insurance, and taxes on the grain itself. These costs are greater than for corn, since the value per bushel is considerably higher

**TABLE 28.2: Costs of Storing and Drying Shelled Corn on Farms***

| Cost | 1 Month | 3 Months | 6 Months | 9 Months |
|---|---|---|---|---|
| | | (cents per bushel) | | |
| Drying, fixed costs | 2.80 | 2.80 | 2.80 | 2.80 |
| Storage, fixed costs | 3.20 | 3.20 | 3.20 | 3.20 |
| Drying, operating costs | 2.80 | 2.80 | 2.80 | 2.80 |
| Interest at 6 per cent | .55 | 1.65 | 3.30 | 4.95 |
| Insurance | .15 | .27 | .46 | .62 |
| Extra handling and dry-matter loss | 1.55 | 1.55 | 1.55 | 1.55 |
| Market discount minus weight loss (deduct)† | — 1.62 | — 1.62 | — 1.62 | — 1.62 |
| Total without fixed costs | 3.43 | 4.65 | 7.99 | 9.80 |
| Total including fixed costs | 9.43 | 10.65 | 13.99 | 15.80 |

* Assuming a corn price of $1.10 per bushel, beginning moisture of 22 per cent, and moisture discount of 1 cent per ½ point.

† The remaining quantity at 1.10 is worth 98.62 cents per bushel of the original quantity, while the original quantity would have been discounted 13 cents and thus be worth 97 cents per bushel of original weight. Therefore 1.62 cents should be credited to the drying process.

on soybeans. Estimated costs for on-farm storage of soybeans are shown in Table 28.3.

### Oats

Costs of on-farm storage of oats are less than for corn or soybeans. The fixed costs are essentially the same as for soybeans; however, the lower value per bushel means lower charges for insurance, interest, and taxes. Estimates of these costs range from .38 cents per bushel for one month to 3.9 cents per bushel for nine months of storage.

### Wheat

The costs of storing wheat on farms are somewhat greater than for oats or soybeans. The fixed costs are similar, but costs related to shrinkage and quality loss raise the variable costs. Recent studies on wheat storage costs are not available. However, past research has estimated variable costs of storing wheat on farms in three different states as shown in Table 28.4. The costs shown are averages; actual costs vary with the length of storage.

Costs of interest and taxes on the grain are not included in Table 28.4. These costs vary with the price of wheat and the length of storage. At $2 per bushel, the interest cost would be around 1 cent per bushel per month; at $1.50 per bushel, around two-thirds of a cent. Tax costs were probably incurred only when the wheat was stored for more than six months.

## COST OF OFF-FARM STORAGE

The cost of storing grain off the farm includes the elevator charges as well as interest and taxes on the grain. Interest and tax costs are on the same basis as shown for on-farm storage of corn in Table 28.2. If corn is artificially dried at the elevator, the total costs of drying and storage should also reflect the change

**TABLE 28.3: Costs of Storing Soybeans on Farms***

| Cost | 1 Month | 3 Months | 6 Months | 9 Months |
|---|---|---|---|---|
| | *(cents per bushel)* | | | |
| Annual bin cost | 8.50 | 8.50 | 8.50 | 8.50 |
| Interest at 6 per cent | 1.25 | 3.75 | 7.50 | 11.25 |
| Insurance | .35 | .60 | 1.05 | 1.40 |
| Taxes | .00 | .00 | 3.00 | 3.00 |
| Total without bin | 1.60 | 4.35 | 11.55 | 15.65 |
| Total including bin | 10.10 | 12.85 | 20.05 | 24.15 |

* Assuming a soybean price of $2.50 per bushel and storage in bin space that is part of an ear corn-tight bin space combination facility.

in value due to drying compared with taking a discount for moisture. This varies with the moisture discount rate but would normally be a credit against the storage and drying costs.

To illustrate, assume corn with 15.5 per cent moisture is priced at $1.10 per bushel and the discount is 1 cent for each .5 per cent of extra moisture. Corn with 22 per cent moisture would bring 97 cents a bushel or $970 for 1,000 bushels. After drying to 15.5 per cent, the original 1,000 bushels would be down to 923 bushels; allowing another .5 per cent for invisible shrink from dry-matter loss leaves 918 bushels. At $1.10 per bushel the 918 bushels are worth $1,009.80, or the equivalent of $1.0098 per bushel based on the original 1,000 bushels. The difference between $1.0098 and 97 cents (3.98 cents) is the increase in value because of moisture loss.

### Elevator Storage Charges

The rates farmers pay for elevator storage are based on managers' estimates of their operating costs, their experience with storage, and the degree of competition that exists for the farmer's storage patronage. Rates for neighboring competing elevators are usually rather uniform. Rates in areas far removed from one another, however, may differ considerably because of differences in costs, competition, and state regulations.

Most elevators use one of two main methods to determine storage charges. One method is to charge a minimum rate for storage up to a specified maximum time period; then a monthly rate is added for any additional storage time. Minimum charges typically apply for a three- or four-month period of storage, al-

**TABLE 28.4: Variable Costs of Storing Wheat on Farms in Oklahoma, North Dakota, and Indiana***

| Cost | Average Cost Per Bushel Stored† | | |
|---|---|---|---|
| | Oklahoma | North Dakota | Indiana |
| | *(cents)* | *(cents)* | *(cents)* |
| Shrinkage and loss in quality | 5.6 | 2.9 | 7.1 |
| Insurance on grain | 1.3 | 1.0 | 0.7 |
| Treating and conditioning | 0.4 | 0.4 | 0.5 |
| Risk not insurable (nominal) | 0.5 | 0.5 | 0.5 |
| Extra transportation and labor | 3.1 | 2.9 | 3.1 |
| | 10.9 | 7.7 | 11.9 |

* Based on data in Farm Credit Administration Bulletins 58, 61, and 68 published in cooperation with Agricultural Experiment Stations in Oklahoma, North Dakota, and Indiana. Storage years were: Oklahoma, 1947–48; North Dakota, 1948–49; and Indiana, 1949–50. Facilities were new 1,000-bushel steel bins on recommended foundations, with mechanical loaders.

† Based on 60 per cent utilization of available farm storage capacity and assuming wheat valued at $2 per bushel.

though both longer and shorter terms are also used. The other primary method is to charge a flat daily or monthly rate, with no minimum charge.

An Illinois study, based on the 1964–65 marketing year, indicated that 75 per cent of the elevators in that state based storage charges for corn on a minimum charge, plus a monthly rate.[2] For elevators using this method, the minimum charge averaged 5.1 cents per bushel. Monthly rates for storage beyond the period covered by the minimum charge averaged 1.2 cents per bushel. Most of the monthly rates were within a range of 1 to 1.5 cents.

A survey of elevators in Iowa showed a somewhat different distribution between the two methods of setting corn storage charges.[3] About 65 per cent of the elevators used a minimum charge. For those using a minimum, most of the charges were in a range of 3 to 6 cents. A fairly common arrangement is for the elevator to charge a minimum of 5 cents per bushel for up to three months storage, with charges of either 1 cent per month or 1/20 cent per day for additional storage. These charges are also common for elevators which do not have a minimum.

A charge of 1/20 cent per day is a fairly common rate for elevator storage of wheat, oats, and soybeans.

### Elevator Drying Charges

Elevator charges for drying services are usually based on a minimum charge plus an additional rate per bushel per point of moisture removed. In an Iowa study a minimum of 5 cents per bushel for up to 5 points of moisture removal was the most common charge.[4] The charge for additional moisture removed was usually either 1 cent per point or ½ cent per point. Each charge was used by 28 per cent of the elevators responding to the survey.

In a smaller number of cases the drying charges are based on a minimum with a graduated rate for additional moisture removal, or a flat rate per bushel per point of moisture removed, without a minimum charge. An example of the first method would be a 5 cent per bushel minimum for the first 5 points of moisture removed, ½ cent per point for the next 5 points, and 1 cent per point for all additional moisture removed.

## COMPARISON OF ON-FARM AND OFF-FARM STORAGE AND DRYING COSTS

The relative costs of storing grain off the farm versus on-farm storage may vary widely depending upon the type and size

[2] Lowell D. Hill, *Elevator Charges for Drying, Storing, and Merchandising Corn,* Univ. of Ill. Agr. Exp. Sta., AERR-80, Apr., 1966.

[3] R. W. Wisner, *Corn Handling Facilities and Charges in Iowa Elevators,* 1967, Iowa State Univ. Coop. Ext. Serv., M-1059, Aug., 1968.

[4] *Ibid.*

of equipment available, the volume of grain involved, and other factors. Usually these costs can be readily compared for a particular situation. If suitable storage facilities are already available on the farm and do not have alternative uses, on-farm storage will probably be the most economical. But the decision is often not so simple. A farmer may have more than one kind of grain that can be stored in available facilities and must decide which one is the better alternative use of the space. In other situations the decision may be whether to build new storage facilities or to buy custom storage and drying services.

A decision on which of two grains to place in available storage requires a careful comparison of on-farm and off-farm storage costs for each. The main consideration is the amount of variable costs in on-farm storage of each grain compared with the total off-farm storage costs. Another consideration is the potential seasonal change in price of each grain.

Both fixed and variable costs must be considered in decisions on whether to build new storage or to pay for commercial storage. Costs of owning and operating drying equipment are an integral part of this decision in many cases. Table 28.2 indicates the annual fixed and variable costs for on-farm drying and storage of corn are about 14 cents per bushel. This assumes a six-month storage period, 22 per cent initial moisture, metal storage bins of 10,000-bushel capacity, a batch-in-bin dryer, and corn price of $1.10 per bushel.

Under the same initial moisture condition, elevator charges for drying the corn and storing it for six months would be around 14.5 cents. This is computed as follows: Drying charges = 5 cents for the first 5 points of moisture removed, plus 1 cent × 1½ points of additional moisture, or a total of 6.5 cents per bushel; storage charges = 5 cents for the first three months of storage plus 1 cent × 3 months of additional storage, or a total of 8 cents per bushel. But this is only a part of the off-farm storage cost. Interest on the corn adds another 3.3 cents per bushel, and taxes add 1.5 cents. These add up to a total of 19.3 cents per bushel. Subtracted from this, however, is the increase in value per bushel due to lower moisture content. This would amount to 3.98 cents per bushel, under the price and moisture discounts assumed, leaving a net cost of 15.32 cents per bushel for drying and storage. (See discussion under "Cost of Farm Storage" earlier in this chapter.)

In this illustration the costs of off-farm storage are slightly higher than on-farm costs. If on-farm drying and storage equipment is already available and fixed costs are excluded from the decision, the advantage would be strongly for storing on the farm. The variable costs of on-farm storage amount to about 8

**TABLE 28.5: Grade Requirements for Yellow Corn, White Corn, and Mixed Corn (U.S. Department of Agriculture Standards)**

| Grade Number | Minimum Test Weight Per Bushel | Maximum Limits of— Moisture | Cracked corn and foreign material | Damaged kernels Total | Damaged kernels Heat-damaged |
|---|---|---|---|---|---|
| | *(lb.)* | *(per cent)* | *(per cent)* | *(per cent)* | *(per cent)* |
| 1 | 56 | 14 | 2 | 3 | .1 |
| 2 | 54 | 15.5 | 3 | 5 | .2 |
| 3 | 52 | 17.5 | 4 | 7 | .5 |
| 4 | 49 | 20 | 5 | 10 | 1.0 |
| 5 | 46 | 23 | 7 | 15 | 3.0 |

Sample grade: Sample grade shall include corn of the class Yellow corn, or White corn, or Mixed corn, which does not come within the requirements of any of the grades from No. 1 to No. 5, inclusive; or which contains stones; or which is musty, or sour, or heating; or which has any commercially objectionable foreign odor; or which is otherwise of distinctly low quality.

cents per bushel, compared with 15.3 cents for off-farm drying and storage. While costs and charges vary somewhat in different areas or for individual farm situations, these examples illustrate the general approach to the problem.

## CORN SHRINKAGE AND DISCOUNTS[5]

The loss of excess moisture from corn improves the grade if the corn is otherwise good in the first place. The grade requirements for shelled corn are listed in Table 28.5. A reduction in moisture content from 20 per cent to 14 per cent raises the grade from No. 5 to No. 1 if the corn meets other specifications for No. 1 corn.

When ear corn is cribbed, it usually is fairly high in moisture content. During the winter it may dry out a little if the weather is dry and cold. As warmer weather comes in April and May, it dries out rapidly. The moisture content reaches a low point in the summer. Corn with 18–19 per cent moisture when cribbed may be down to 15 per cent in April and to 13–14 per cent in July. As the corn loses moisture, it loses weight, so that there are fewer bushels; but it grades higher, and progressively smaller discounts will be taken. Unless the grade is lowered by damage or some other factor besides moisture, the bushel price will be higher for drier corn.

Table 28.6 shows how many bushels of corn will be left after corn has dried out to different degrees. No allowance is made in this table for any loss in weight except what is caused by loss of water. The table shows that if a farmer has 1,000

[5] This section is based partly on L. J. Norton, *When To Market Grain*, Univ. of Ill., Circ. 711, 1953, p. 11.

**TABLE 28.6: Weight Loss in Shelled Corn Dried Naturally to Specified Moisture Contents, Assuming 1,000 Bushels When Cribbed**

| Moisture in Corn When Cribbed | Amount of Corn Remaining When Moisture Is Reduced to the Following Percentages* | | | | | | | | |
|---|---|---|---|---|---|---|---|---|---|
| | 19 | 18 | 17 | 16 | 15.5 | 15 | 14 | 13 | 12 |
| *(per cent)* | *(bushels)* | | | | | | | | |
| 28.......... | 889 | 878 | 867 | 857 | 852 | 847 | 837 | 828 | 818 |
| 26.......... | 914 | 902 | 892 | 881 | 876 | 871 | 860 | 851 | 841 |
| 24.......... | 938 | 927 | 916 | 905 | 899 | 894 | 884 | 874 | 864 |
| 23.......... | 951 | 939 | 928 | 917 | 911 | 906 | 895 | 885 | 875 |
| 22.......... | 963 | 951 | 940 | 929 | 923 | 918 | 907 | 897 | 886 |
| 21.......... | 975 | 963 | 952 | 940 | 935 | 929 | 919 | 908 | 898 |
| 20.......... | 988 | 976 | 964 | 952 | 946 | 941 | 930 | 920 | 909 |
| 19.......... | 1,000 | 988 | 976 | 964 | 959 | 953 | 942 | 931 | 920 |
| 17.5 ........ | — | — | 994 | 982 | 976 | 971 | 959 | 948 | 938 |

Source: T. A. Hieronymus, *When To Sell Corn, Soybeans, Oats, Wheat,* Univ. of Ill. Agr. Exp. Sta., Circ. 948, Oct., 1966, p. 6.

* The quantities listed were obtained by dividing the percentage of dry matter in the corn at the beginning of storage (100 minus original percentage of moisture) by the percentage of dry matter remaining at the end of the storage period (100 minus final percentage of moisture) and multiplying by 1,000.

bushels of corn with 19 per cent moisture, and carries it until it is down to 15 per cent, he will have 953 bushels left. Or if he carries the corn until it is down to 13 per cent moisture, he will have 931 bushels. The amount of shrinkage is not simply the difference between the original moisture and the final moisture but is based on the difference in dry matter at the two times (see footnote, Table 28.6).

The cost of shrinkage from moisture loss depends both on the price of corn and on the discount taken for extra moisture. Discounts vary somewhat between areas and from year to year. They are influenced by the supply of high moisture corn, the availability of conditioning facilities, the quality needs of merchandisers and processors, and the level of corn prices.

A common discount scale applied by buyers for the 1969 corn crop was 1 cent for each .5 per cent of moisture above 15.5 per cent. Some elevators apply a 1½-cent discount per .5 per cent of moisture, while still others use a variable discount scale. An example of the latter would be a discount of 1 cent per .5 per cent of moisture between the 15.5 per cent standard and 20 per cent; then a 1½-cent discount for each additional .5 per cent of moisture above 20 per cent.

With No. 2 corn at $1.30 per bushel, the arithmetic works out this way. Nineteen per cent corn has 3.5 per cent of moisture over 15.5 per cent, or seven .5 per cents; $7 \times 1 = 7$ cents. If No. 2 corn is $1.30, then 19 per cent corn is worth

$1.23. No premiums are normally paid for corn with less than 15.5 per cent moisture so the 13 per cent moisture corn will also be worth $1.30. The values for this lot of corn at different stages of dryness would be:

| | | |
|---|---|---|
| 1,000 bushels of 19 per cent corn at $1.23 a bushel | = | $1,230.00 |
| 959 bushels of 15.5 per cent corn at $1.30 a bushel | = | $1,246.70 |
| 931 bushels of 13 per cent corn at $1.30 a bushel | = | $1,210.30 |

Under this discount scale, this lot of corn will bring the highest returns when sold as No. 2 corn (15.5 per cent). The increase in value is approximately $17 for 1,000 bushels. This $17 or 1.7 cents a bushel is the return for storing it until it is down to No. 2 moisture. Since no premiums are paid for individual lots of corn below 15.5 per cent moisture, any further drying does not add to the price per bushel and so will reduce total returns.

This example assumes the corn dries naturally. If it is artificially dried, an additional .5 per cent shrink should be included to account for the dry-matter loss (invisible shrink). The cost of drying must also be considered in determining which moisture level will bring the highest return.

The problem is the same with corn that is field-shelled at a relatively high moisture content, perhaps from 22 to 28 per cent. If the corn is a cash crop, the producer must decide whether to sell the corn at harvest and take a discount for extra moisture or to dry the corn artificially (on or off the farm) either for immediate or later sale.

Why should there be discounts for moisture? There are three reasons. First, there is less dry matter per bushel; and water is not worth as much as dry matter. Second, with higher moisture the risk of spoilage in storage increases. When the moisture is too high, the corn must be artificially dried if it is to be stored. This leads to the third reason for discounts; artificial drying costs money.

#### Does Artificial Drying Pay?

Artificial drying pays only if the cost, which includes investment and maintenance of equipment, fuel, and operation and the "invisible" loss in weight which occurs when corn is subjected to heat, is less than the increase in value plus the value of advantages which may be associated with the storage of dried shelled corn.

When 1,000 bushels of 19 per cent corn are dried to 15.5 per cent, they are worth about $17 more, or 1.7 cents a bushel, as shown above. If we start with 22 per cent corn, the problem is the same. At the 1-cent discount scale, the discount on such corn would be 13 cents a bushel, calculated as follows: 13 × 1, or 13 cents for the thirteen .5 per cents between 22 and 15.5 per cent.

One thousand bushels of 22 per cent corn are equivalent to 923 bushels of naturally dried 15.5 per cent corn (Table 28.6). The comparative values are:

1,000 bushels at $1.17 ($1.30 less $.13 discount) = $1,170.00
923 bushels at $1.30 = $1,199.90

The increase in value, under these discounts, would be $29.90 or about 3 cents a bushel. In this case drying would also reduce the possibility of damage developing if the 22 per cent corn were stored.

Artificial drying of corn has other advantages besides the increase in value. It permits early harvesting, when weather and ground conditions are good and field losses are at a minimum. Dried shelled corn can be stored more cheaply than ear corn; if new storage space is a consideration, the difference would be about 5 cents a bushel in the annual cost of providing space. Drying may permit storage in some years and places when corn moisture is too high to be considered safe.

As noted earlier, an increasing proportion of the corn is field shelled. It is harvested at a relatively high moisture content in order to minimize field losses and to permit early harvest. As a result, artificial drying is a necessity for most of this corn—unless it is held at high moisture in a silo or similar storage for livestock feed.

### Sale of Ear Corn

When corn is sold on the ear the main problem is how many pounds are taken for a bushel. High-moisture corn has more water in the cobs than dry corn, so more pounds per bushel of ear corn are required to yield a bushel of ear corn at harvest-time or early in the winter than later in the year.

The pounds taken for a bushel should be such as to yield 56 pounds of shelled corn. The true market value of a bushel of ear corn is obviously equal to the value of the shelled corn less the cost of shelling. An equivalent weight can be determined only by a test. Shell a good sample and calculate the weight of ear corn that yields 56 pounds of shelled corn. For example, if 75,000 pounds of ear corn shells out 56,000 pounds of corn, then 75 pounds of ear corn is equivalent to a bushel of shelled corn. Such tests should be made each year and each season as various factors, particularly moisture, will determine this ratio.

## COSTS COMPARED WITH SEASONAL PRICE INCREASES

We are now ready to compare the costs of seasonal storage for the different grains with the seasonal increase in prices that can be expected.

The costs of storing corn for a six-month period were shown earlier in this chapter to be around 14 or 15 cents a bushel for both on-farm and off-farm storage. When fixed costs were excluded, on-farm storage costs were around 8 cents. Wheat storage is estimated at around 15 cents a bushel off the farm and 15 to 20 cents for on-farm storage when fixed costs are included; soybean storage is from 15 to 20 cents a bushel when fixed costs are included or around 12 cents for variable costs; and for oats, 8 to 12 cents for all costs or about 4 cents for variable costs.

When these costs are compared with the seasonal rise in prices shown in Chapter 11—14 cents per bushel for corn, 6 cents for oats, 13 cents for wheat, and 36 cents for soybeans—it becomes evident that farmers cannot expect to make much money storing wheat and oats for the seasonal price rise. The 1955–69 average seasonal price rises for oats and wheat (6 and 13 cents) were less than the costs of storing these grains on the farm, although the rise did exceed the variable costs.

The average seasonal price rise for corn more than covers the cost of farm storage, but is about equal to off-farm storage costs; it is, however, well above variable costs.

The average seasonal price rise for soybeans is more than twice as great as needed to cover the cost of farm storage in metal bins and is well above the costs of storing in other facilities either on or off the farm.

The years when storage will pay better than average are hard to predict. Usually, it is more profitable to store after a big crop than after a small crop. But if you store only in those years when it looks as if storage will be profitable, this increases the overhead or fixed costs per year when the grain is stored. And it is difficult to predict the years when prices will rise enough to cover these higher costs.

The general conclusion emerges that farmers cannot expect to do much more than break even by storing grain, except in the case of soybeans, and to a lesser extent corn. This indicates that the grain market approaches the criterion of market perfection with respect to time (within the season) that we set up earlier in this book. The seasonal rise in prices is about equal to the seasonal costs of storage.

Elevator storage costs less in some cases than farm storage. This indicates that elevator operators can make somewhat more money storing grain than farmers. Presumably, they make enough to keep them in business. The large scale of their operations is one thing that keeps their storage costs low relative to farm storage costs. Their additional income from mixing and blending grain of different grades is another. Still another factor is their frequent hedging, spreading, and straddling operations in the futures market. Their operations are likely to keep the seasonal rise in the prices of the different grains at about the levels of recent years if the demand remains fairly constant.

# 29

## COTTON

FOR CENTURIES, cotton has been an important article of consumption and world trade. It is one of the world's major raw materials, and almost all industrial nations spin and weave large quantities into textiles.[1]

The world's production of cotton was rising slowly, from about 44 million bales in 1955–59 to a peak of 53 million in 1965, when it suddenly declined to only 47.6 million in 1967. Figure 29.1 shows that this decrease resulted from a sudden decline of cotton production in the United States.

Figure 29.2 shows that cotton production in the United States ran at about 15 million bales until 1965. Then in 1966 it dropped one-third to less than 10 million bales. The next year it declined further to only 7.6 million. The sharp declines in U.S. cotton production in 1966 and 1967 resulted mainly from direct efforts by the Department of Agriculture to divert land from cotton production and to reduce carryover stocks to desired levels. Unfavorable weather also contributed to the decline, as yields were below average in both years. Production moved back up to over 10 million bales in 1968 and 1969.

---

[1] This chapter is adapted from C. C. Cable, "Marketing Cotton and Cotton Textiles," *Agricultural Markets in Change*, USDA, Agr. Econ. Rept. 95, July, 1966, pp. 112–41.

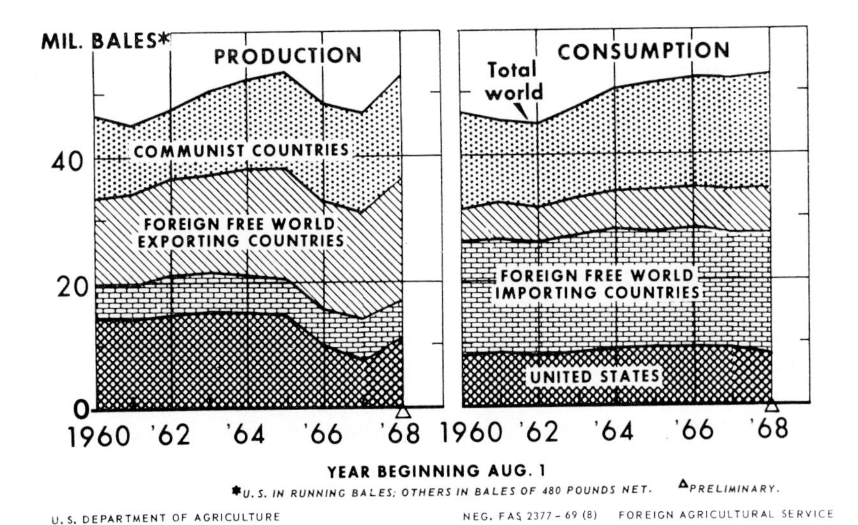


FIG. 29.1—World cotton production and consumption, 1960–68.

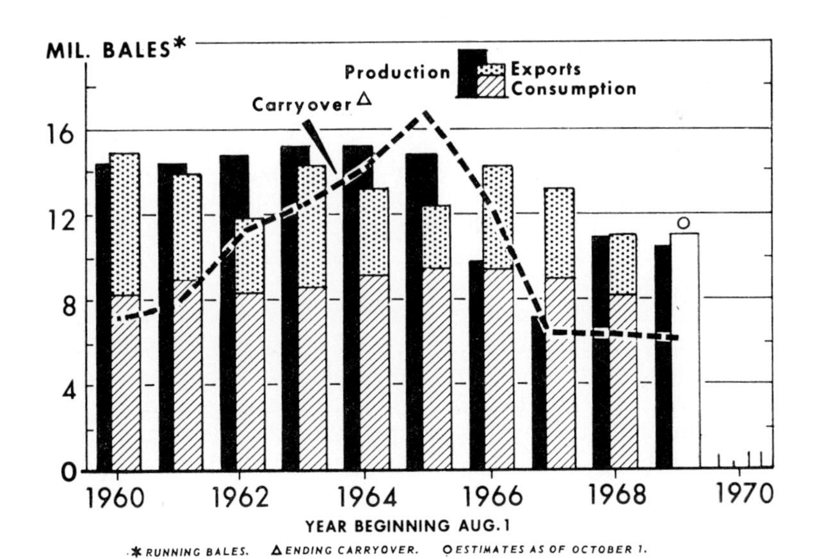


FIG. 29.2—Cotton production and use, United States, 1958–69.

## CHANGES IN COTTON PRODUCTION

During the past two decades, cotton acreage and production have gradually moved westward to the higher yielding states of New Mexico, Arizona, and California.[2] Yields of about two bales per acre in the West are double the average for the remainder of the Cotton Belt and have increased more rapidly. Up to the end of World War II, about 5 per cent of the total U.S. crop was grown in the West; by the late fifties and to the late sixties, this area accounted for roughly 20 per cent of the total crop. In comparison, the proportion of the total grown in the Southeast declined from 30 per cent in 1945 to about 15 per cent by the late sixties. The present location of cotton production is shown in Figure 29.3.

Mechanization of production and harvesting, and larger and fewer production units also have contributed to the present upward trend in yields and production. In 1947–48, only about 2 per cent of the total crop was harvested with machines; by 1964–65 approximately 78 per cent was mechanically harvested. Machine harvesting, as compared to hand harvesting, permits producers to gather their entire crop during optimum harvesting conditions in the fall and reduces field losses resulting from adverse winter weather.

In 1939 there were almost 1.6 million farms producing cotton in the United States. Twenty years later the number of farms growing cotton had declined to 0.5 million. For the same period the total number of farms in the Cotton Belt declined from 3.5 million to 2 million.

Labor required to produce a bale of cotton has also been declining for many years. In 1930, 274 man-hours were needed to produce a bale; by the mid-sixties, less than 58 man-hours were needed. Within the same period, production per man-hour increased from 1.8 pounds to 8.6 pounds. This increased productivity resulted primarily from higher yields, larger farm units, and mechanization.

Since 1930 the quantity of cotton in the carryover, another major component of the U.S. annual supply of raw cotton, has ranged from a low of 2.3 million bales in 1951 to an all-time high of over 16.5 million in 1966 and has exceeded 10 million bales for twelve of the years during 1930–69. The small crops in 1966 and 1967 reduced the carryover to 6.5 million bales in 1969.

[2] Major cotton-growing states are commonly divided into the following four areas: West—Arizona, California, and New Mexico; Southwest—Oklahoma and Texas; mid-South—Arkansas, Louisiana, Mississippi, Missouri, and Tennessee; Southeast—Alabama, Georgia, North Carolina, South Carolina, and Virginia.

Stocks held by the Commodity Credit Corporation are usually several times as large as the stocks held by private establishments.

## VALUE OF COTTON IN THE UNITED STATES

Annual cash receipts from farm marketings of cotton lint and cottonseed in the United States approximated $2.5 billion annually during 1960–65; but they dropped to the $1.1–$1.6 billion range in 1966–68. Cotton lint accounts for about 85 to 90 per cent of the farm income received from cotton; cottonseed and other by-products account for from 10 to 15 per cent. Value added by textile mill processing and the manufacturing of cotton apparel and other items is estimated at from $7 to $7.5 billion annually.

Over half the cotton crop is grown in the Southwest and the West, and only about 15 per cent in the southeastern states where the textile mill industry is concentrated. Thus, the cotton-marketing system is responsible for transporting a large proportion of the crop several hundred miles to domestic mills or to port warehouses for export. U.S. cotton is harvested in late summer and early fall but is processed by domestic and foreign mills on a year-round basis. Hence, storage is another major function of the cotton-marketing system.

The yarns, woven goods, and other products of domestic mills are shipped to manufacturers of cotton apparel and house-

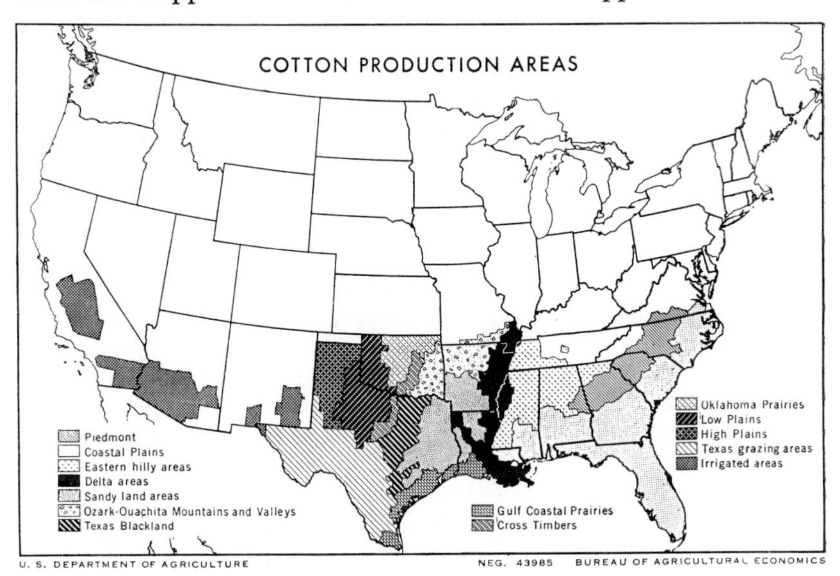


FIG. 29.3—Cotton production areas in the United States.

hold articles who are located principally in the industrial northeastern and mid-Atlantic states, or to foreign manufacturers. Finally, finished cotton items are packaged, stored, and shipped through wholesalers to retail outlets throughout the United States, or through exporters to foreign retail outlets.

Changes in technology are being made constantly at all stages of the marketing systems for cotton and cotton textile products. Associated with these developments are changes in market structure and organization and in the efficiencies of marketing services. In addition, the ever-changing character of consumer demand for textile products greatly influences the cotton and cotton-products industries.

## PHYSICAL FLOW AND PROCESSING

Except for farm producers, firms directly involved in handling, processing, and transporting raw cotton from farm to textile mills do not usually own or buy and sell cotton; they render services—as directed by buyers and sellers—which facilitate ownership transactions. Thus, a discussion of the marketing of raw cotton involves its physical movement, changes in ownership, and the services performed by marketing agencies.

### Transportation of Seed Cotton

As seed cotton is harvested, it is hauled from the field to nearby cotton gins in trailers pulled by farm-type tractors or pickup trucks. In almost all areas of the Cotton Belt, this initial step in the physical flow of cotton is performed by the producer. In some areas, producers provide their own trailers; in others, the ginning firms provide seed-cotton trailers as a competitive means of obtaining additional ginning volume. In major producing areas, trailers used today hold enough seed cotton to yield from four to eight bales of ginned lint.

### Ginning

At the gin the seed cotton is conditioned and cleaned; then the lint is separated from the seed and packaged into bales weighing roughly 500 pounds. This is the first major process in the cotton-marketing system. Some gin owners may also grow cotton, merchandise cotton, operate cottonseed oil mills, or have other related business interests. Both vertical and horizontal integration at various stages of the marketing system are becoming increasingly evident.

Fifty years ago, there were some 25,000 gins in the United States; in 1964 there were only about 5,000 gins processing approximately the same total volume. The steady decline in number of gins, and the increase in volume handled per gin have been accompanied by a sharp rise in the cost of constructing a modern gin plant. Large modern plants erected in the early sixties required investments of $250,000 to $350,000, whereas in the early fifties an up-to-date gin cost only $50,000 to $75,000. By the early 70's, capital outlays for new high-capacity gins exceeded a half-million dollars. The cost of gins has increased because of the increase in mechanized harvesting and because of the rise in the general price level.

Seed cotton which has been machine harvested is delivered to gins in a rough and trashy condition. Additional seed-cotton cleaning and conditioning equipment and lint-cleaning machinery have been added in almost all gins in recent years to facilitate ginning the roughly harvested crop. Machine harvesting also has accelerated the rate of cotton harvest and delivery to gins. To keep pace with the rate of harvest, many ginners have increased their rate of ginning either by adding gin stands and other equipment or by installing new higher-capacity machinery.

To meet rising fixed costs and corresponding increases in operating costs, charges for ginning service have been increasing. The average charge in the United States for ginning in 1964–65 was $16.78 per bale, equivalent to more than 3 cents per pound.

Possibilities for reducing the cost of ginning appear limited, in view of the trend to more elaborately equipped gins and the common practice of ginning the crop simultaneously with harvesting. A few gins have constructed storage facilities to receive seed cotton as it is harvested and to increase their total ginning volume. However, the cost of storing seed cotton may, in some cases, more than offset the reduction in fixed cost of ginning resulting from larger seasonal volume.

### Warehousing and Compressing

Storing and compressing baled lint are necessary functions for the efficient marketing and handling of U.S. cotton. In the southeastern states, a substantial amount of cotton moves directly from gin to local mills; in other areas of the Cotton Belt, the crop moves from gins through warehouses with compresses. As packaged at almost all gins, the bales are pressed to a density of about 12 pounds per cubic foot. Compression reduces the volume and increases the density of bales and decreases the space required for storage and transportation. For domestic shipment, bales are compressed to standard density of about 23 pounds per cubic foot; for export shipments, they are compressed to high density, about 33 pounds per cubic foot. Pressing to standard density at the gin eliminates extra handling and compressing at warehouses. But only a very low percentage of the total crop is handled that way. Most of the gins equipped with standard density presses are located in the West.

In addition to compressing and storing baled lint, the cotton warehouse industry performs other services necessary to merchandise the crop. Some of these services are weighing; reconditioning bales; issuing negotiable warehouse receipts; sampling, sorting, and assembling cotton in even-running lots for shipment at the direction of merchants; and loading rail cars and other carriers.

Half of the total cotton storage capacity is accounted for by about 205, or 17 per cent, of the warehouse establishments. This capacity, located throughout the Cotton Belt, is under the control of only 14 separate business organizations. Over a third of the total capacity, which is controlled by the five largest business firms, is concentrated in 155 warehouses, 13 per cent of the total number.

Only about one-fourth of the warehouses have compress facilities, but these have some two-thirds of the total U.S. storage capacity for cotton. Less than 1 per cent of the warehouses in the Southeast have compresses, whereas approximately 60, 55, and 85 per cent of those in the mid-South, Southwest, and West, respectively, have compresses.

Since the late thirties, the number of warehouses with compresses has declined about 15 per cent. However, in the West, the number has almost tripled. The number of warehouses without compresses also has declined some 15 per cent since 1945. Much of this decline occurred in the Southwest and the mid-South. Formerly these small warehouses were available to farmers and local buyers for storing bales during and immediately after harvest. After the cotton was purchased by a central market firm, it was moved from the country point to a larger facility located at a transportation center. However, with the improvement in roads and the adoption of flatbed semitrailer trucks, an increasing proportion of the nation's crop moves directly from gins to centrally located storage facilities.

Charges for warehousing and related services in the United States have trended upward since the early forties, following a period of fairly stable charges during the thirties. Charges for receiving (which generally includes unloading of bales arriving for storage, tagging, weighing, sampling, issuing a warehouse receipt, and movement of bales to a temporary block preparatory to storing) increased from averages of 27 cents a bale in 1942–43 to 74 cents in 1964–65.

Storage charges per month increased from 20 cents to 52 cents a bale during the same period. Charges for compressing also increased—from $.65 to $1.56 for compressing to standard density and from $.78 to $1.89 for compressing to high density.

### Transportation

The transportation of baled lint from the gin to the warehouse is generally arranged for by the ginner. The cost of this service is usually included in the ginning charges.

Reconcentrating cotton in warehouses at strategic transportation centers and moving it from these points to domestic mills or dockside accounts for the greatest proportion of the total transportation cost for cotton. During the early sixties, the southeastern mill area was the destination of about 8 million bales of cotton, and over 4 million bales were transported to ports. Shipments to Alabama and Georgia represented about equal proportions from the Southwest, mid-South, and Southeast, but only 5 per cent from the West. The mid-South was a much heavier shipper to the Carolinas and Virginia and also to the Northeast and Canada than other regions. The Southwest Region was the lightest shipping region to the Carolinas and Virginia. About 90 per cent of shipments to the port destinations originated in the Southwest and the West. U.S. cotton exports go primarily from ports in Louisiana, Texas, and California.

Except in the Southeast, the volume of cotton hauled by rail greatly exceeds the volume transported by trucks. Approximately 78 to 80 per cent of the cotton originating in the other three areas was moved by rail in 1961–62.

Rail transportation is the major component of the cost of moving cotton from warehouses to domestic mills. From the early thirties to the end of World War II, rail freight rates for cotton increased only slightly, then increased sharply to a peak in the mid-fifties. From this peak they gradually declined, and by the mid-sixties they had dropped to the lowest level since the early fifties.

## MARKETING AGENCIES AND PRACTICES

Almost all sales by producers, and the government loan rates, are based on the grade and staple length of each bale. The U.S. Department of Agriculture provides a quality classification service—at no charge to growers who qualify for the service as members of cotton improvement associations—through its cotton classifying offices throughout the Cotton Belt. Cotton is classed —that is, its grade and staple length determined—on the basis of a sample taken from each bale, usually at the warehouse or gin.

This service helps the producer determine the value of his cotton before offering it for sale to local marketing agencies. Beginning with the 1966 crop, the mike reading, along with grade and staple, was provided by cotton classing offices. The mike reading, a measure of fiber fineness and maturity in combination, is an important quality attribute from the standpoint of spinning performance and end-use value; it is rapidly becoming an important element in pricing cotton.

Depending on functions performed and methods of operation, central market firms may be classified as shippers, local merchants, mill buyers, commission buyers, and brokers. Most of these firms, regardless of type, have some common characteristics. Normally, they handle no other commodity and few are allied with any other business, although several produce, gin, and store cotton and process cottonseed.

Central market firms operating as shippers are the major link between the farm producer and the mill consumer of raw cotton. Through their competitive trading and selling to mills, price differentials for different classes (grade and staple length combinations) of cotton are established on the basis of mill demands and market supplies. Shippers buy baled cotton in lots of mixed qualities as near the points of growth and as soon after it enters marketing channels as practicable. Bales are then concentrated and stored at locations that provide economical distribution. After determining quality and sorting the bales into lots of "even-running quality," they are ready for sale under terms suitable to the needs of the textile mills. In selling, shippers generally arrange for, and pay the costs of, transportation. Most of the costs and risks associated with other marketing services—including assembly, sampling, quality classification, storage, price risks, and selling—are also assumed by shippers.

Brokers, local merchants, and commission buyers function chiefly in aiding cotton shippers in acquiring or selling cotton. Brokers are agents who sell on commission for various types of owners. Changes in the movement of cotton in recent years have greatly reduced the number of brokers and the need for their services. Considerable quantities of cotton, which once would have been handled by brokers for producers and local market buyers, now move directly into government loan stocks or are purchased directly by mill buyers.

Commission buyers purchase cotton primarily for shippers and mills; most of their purchases are made at country points from growers, ginners, and local buyers. Their numbers have declined during the past decade.

Local merchants, who buy cotton in local markets or at gin points, resell in mixed lots within a short time to shippers or mill-buying agencies in nearby central markets. Like shippers, they take title to the cotton, but they assume fewer risks and perform fewer services.

Several of the larger textile mill firms maintain buying offices in central markets rather than using the services provided by other types of central market firms. Direct mill buying, which is becoming more prevalent in marketing raw cotton, is a clear-cut example of vertical integration in the cotton industry.

Cooperative marketing associations in many areas of the Cotton Belt act as shippers for their members. In the 1960's, the volume handled by these organizations has increased rapidly and no doubt has contributed to the decline in the number of brokers, local merchants, and other types of central market firms. This expansion in the cooperative marketing of cotton by producers is another example of economic integration in the cotton industry.

Fifteen of the central markets are "designated spot cotton markets." A quotations committee in each of these markets issues cotton price quotations, as required by U.S. cotton futures legislation. The markets are designated by the Secretary of Agriculture, and the committees are supervised by the Department of Agriculture.

For a cotton shipper to service his mill customers effectively, he must abide by highly standardized mill rules. In the mill area in the Southeast, these rules are known as "Southern Mill Rules for Buying and Selling American Cotton." The rules cover the nature and form of contract to be used; shipping terms; the use of standards and other methods for classification of cotton; and determination of weight, excess tare, damage to cotton, density of bales, and similar items. In addition, they specify when contracts become binding, when cotton may be rejected and when it must be made good, how and when prices are to be fixed, and means of settling disputes.

To better provide the service required by mill customers, many shippers have an office or broker representative in several strategically located cities and towns in the mill area. To expedite the purchasing of cotton, many mills have salaried buyers or agents who can readily contact local and central market firms or their agents by telephone or telegraph. Because mills are located in many small communities, mill markets may be described as unassembled markets. This is in contrast with the more highly organized exchanges at the central market level. However, from the time cotton manufacturing was mechanized and operated in large factory units, shippers and other central market firms have customarily catered to the wishes of mills in selling cottons to them. Thus for many decades, mills and their representatives have usually been the strongest element in the market. This market strength of mills is of increasing importance to the U.S. cotton industry because competition and technology have made man-made fibers and foreign cottons substitutable for American cotton.

## MANUFACTURING AND DISTRIBUTING COTTON TEXTILE AND APPAREL PRODUCTS

Converting raw cotton into the form demanded by ultimate consumers requires numerous manufacturing processes and changes in ownership. These include making yarn and cloth, finishing cloth, and making consumer items from finished cloth. Firms performing these processes are generally referred to in the trade as textile mills, finishing plants, and cutters, respectively.

### Textile Mills

The primary functions of textile mills are to spin yarns and to weave and knit cloth. Some mills produce yarns only; others specialize in weaving and knitting cloth and fabrics. However, there is a trend toward greater integration and diversification of functions performed by textile mills.

The initial steps of cotton textile manufacturing are opening bales and cleaning the lint, then carding (also combing for fine yarns) and spinning the lint into yarn. On an average, about 15 per cent of a 500-pound bale is waste and tare (bagging and ties), and 85 per cent is made into yarn.

### Converters and Finishing Plants

Converters are the major intermediary between producers of unfinished cloth (mills) and users of finished cloth (garment makers and industrial users). Their prime function is to buy gray cloth from the most favorable mill source, move it through finishing plants, and then sell the finished cloth to the highest bidder. Because these firms handle the bulk of gray cloth, they hold a key position in textile marketing. Even with the best of knowledge, they must outguess the market if their operations are to be profitable. Their profit is a residual—the difference between the initial costs of gray goods plus the costs of finishing and the selling price received for finished cloth.

### Cutters and Industrial Users

The major function of cutters is buying finished cloth from converters and mills, manufacturing the cloth into such apparel items as shirts and dresses, and selling these items to retailers. Hence, the cutter's demand for finished cloth is a derived demand dependent on the demand for the products he manufactures. In turn, the cutter's demand for cloth is reflected back to the textile mill through converters' orders for unfinished cloth.

Many firms in the garment industry are small, employing fewer than 50 people and requiring a small capital investment relative to the capital required by textile mills and finishing plants. Hence, entry into the industry is easy. As a result, it is highly competitive, and there is a high turnover of establishments in apparel manufacturing.

### Wholesaling Textile Products

Textile products are wholesaled by merchant wholesalers, manufacturers' sales branches and offices, and merchandise agents and brokers. Merchant wholesalers take title to the merchandise, buying from manufacturers and reselling principally to retail outlets. They may extend credit to customers, make deliveries, and serve as a source of market information for retailers. Manufacturers' sales branches and offices are usually separate establishments owned and maintained by manufacturers primarily for selling their products. Merchandise agents and brokers are independent firms that buy and sell for others rather than buying for their own account.

### Retail Outlets

Retail stores and mail-order houses are the major market outlets for the apparel manufacturing industry. Department stores, clothing specialty shops, and chain stores are the major retail outlets, and they have increased in importance relative to small independent and general stores. However, many food, drug, and other types of stores now stock apparel items.

The larger chain stores buy almost all their stock directly from garment manufacturers; smaller chains and some of the independents do most of their buying from wholesalers. Although the sources, buying practices, and inventory policies of different types of retail establishments differ, as a group these firms do not wish to be caught with excessive inventory. This is particularly true in regard to outerwear, since styles and fashions may change drastically from one season to the next. When caught with excessive stocks, retailers may have to resort to unprofitable price-cutting sales to unload their surpluses. In other instances, retailers may be caught short; then they ask for rapid delivery of garments. Such failures to anticipate consumer demand correctly can set off a chain reaction which is reflected back to the cutter, the converter, and eventually to the textile mill. As a result, prices for garments, finished and unfinished cloth, and yarn may at times fluctuate violently.

### Production and Supply of Competing Fibers

Wool, silk, and such man-made fibers as rayon, acetate, and noncellulosic fibers compete with cotton as raw materials for manufacturing textiles. In recent years, especially since World War II, competition from man-made fibers has greatly increased. For the world as a whole, production of rayons, acetates, and noncellulosics combined increased about eightfold from 1945 to 1964. In cotton equivalents, this 20-year increase was from 4 million to slightly more than 32 million bales (see Figure 29.4). In 1945 world production of cotton was 5 times as large as world production of man-made fibers; by the mid-sixties, it was only about 1.5 times as large. Production of man-made fibers in the United States accounted for more than half of the world total in 1945; by the mid-sixties, U.S. production accounted for less than a third.

Man-made synthetic fibers have been replacing both cotton and wool in the United States. Figure 29.5 shows that consumers in the United States now use almost as many pounds of these man-made fibers as they do of cotton.

### Prices of Competing Fibers

In the early years of the man-made fiber industry, the price of rayon greatly exceeded the price of cotton. In 1930 the equivalent price per pound of usable fiber for rayon staple was about 5

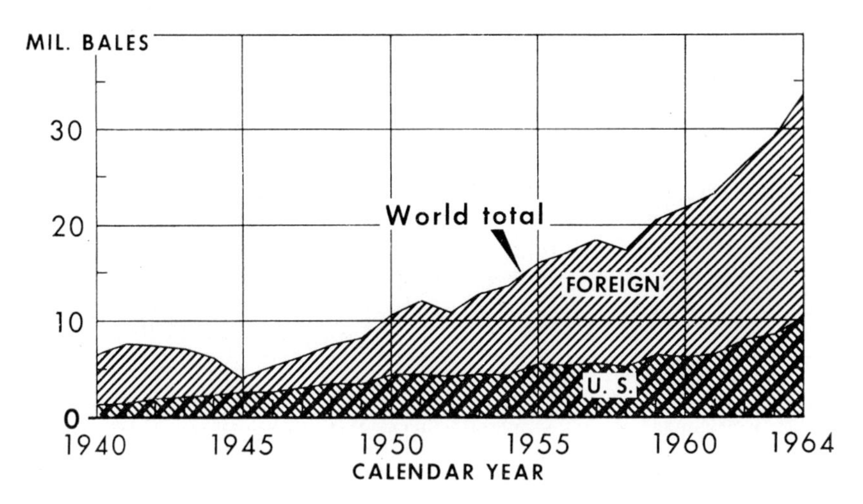


FIG. 29.4—World production of rayon, acetate, and noncellulosic fibers, 1940–64.

times the price of Middling 15/16-inch cotton; by 1940 the price of rayon was still about double that of cotton (see Figure 29.6). After another five years, prices for these two fibers were approximately the same, and beginning in 1945, the price of rayon has been below that of Middling 15/16-inch cotton. Prices for both have trended downward since 1950; however, the price of rayon is declining more rapidly than the price of cotton. In the early sixties, the rayon staple price was about three-fourths of the price of Middling 15/16-inch cotton. The increasing price advantage for rayon probably accounts for its relatively steady consumption compared with the gradual decline in cotton consumption since the early fifties.

## DIVISION OF THE CONSUMER'S COTTON DOLLAR

The many processes and services rendered from the time producers deliver their seed cotton to gins until consumers purchase cotton apparel and household items in retail stores involve considerable cost. Manufacturing yarn and finished cloth at the mill and manufacturing and distributing the final product account for more than four-fifths of the total retail cost of 25 representative articles of cotton clothing and house furnishings. Retailing alone accounts for approximately 33 per cent of the consumer's dollar, wholesaling 8 per cent, manufacturing the finished article 30 per cent, and manufacturing and finishing cloth about 12 per cent.

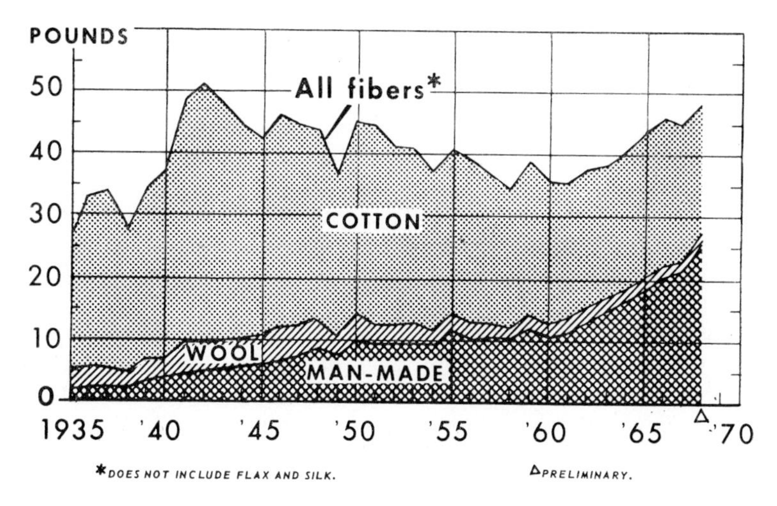


FIG. 29.5—Mill consumption of fibers, per capita, United States, 1935–68.

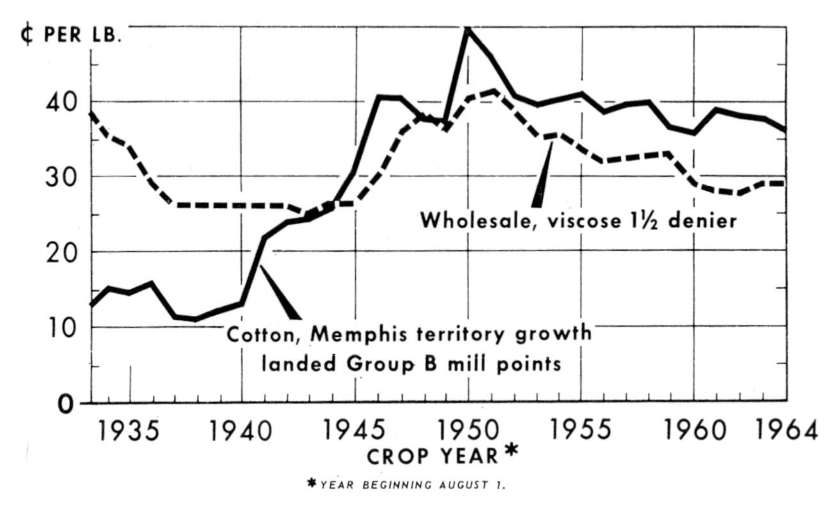


FIG. 29.6—U.S. equivalent price of usable Middling 15/16 cotton, rayon staple, 1935–64.

On the average, the farmer receives between 14 and 15 per cent of the consumer's retail dollar for these representative articles of clothing and house furnishings, and between 3 and 4 per cent goes to ginning, compressing, storing, transporting, and various merchandising agencies required to move raw cotton from production areas to textile mill centers.

## COTTON'S PROBLEMS AND PROSPECTS

The U.S. cotton industry has been confronted with a variety of problems during the past 30 to 35 years. These problems have ranged from low farm prices and incomes in the early thirties to the present loss of markets to man-made fibers and foreign cottons. It was generally conceded that prices for cotton were disastrously low during the early thirties; and, because of declining consumption and mounting surpluses in the sixties, it is believed by many that prices now are too high.

Prices and price legislation and their effects on industry have been a major concern of all segments of the cotton industry. There is apparently no general agreement as to the basic cause of cotton problems. Similarly, there is lack of agreement as to the effects of both tried and proposed solutions on firms at all stages of the producing-marketing system. Universally satisfactory short-run solutions are probably impossible because of the varying extent and degree of their economic impact on different segments of the industry.

Numerous federal programs have been enacted for the purpose of aiding the cotton industry. Most of this legislation has been directed to solving immediate short-run problems of low prices and surpluses. Research can provide some guides as to the effects of alternative solutions for the trade and for society to consider in making decisions.

Although the most controversial problems of the U.S. cotton industry revolve around prices, there are other problems confronting the industry. Many of these problems arose partly as the result of short-term solutions to pricing problems; others came about primarily as a result of technological developments. The development, mass production, and aggressive promotion of man-made fibers, the increase in mechanical harvesting and accompanying problems in ginning, the effects of various changes in processing and marketing practices on quality and end-use value, and similar problems are of equal concern to all segments of the industry. Solutions that are generally acceptable to all are needed if U.S. cotton is to maintain, let alone improve, its current status in the world fiber market.

### Loss of Markets

Declines in cotton's proportionate share of the total U.S. fiber market, in the absolute quantity of cotton consumed, and in per capita consumption are ample evidence that cotton has lost domestic markets. In addition, the volatile fluctuations in exports reveal the lack of stability in foreign markets. Basically, loss of markets—regardless of the contributing causes—is the most crucial problem of the industry. All other problems are secondary, their solutions depending on the reversal or at least the checking of the downward trend in cotton sales.

Research to develop new markets for cotton is under way at the U.S. Department of Agriculture's utilization laboratory in New Orleans. New finishing processes, new uses, and other developments are under investigation. Whether the volume going to new market uses will offset cotton's losses in older established outlets is a challenge to the U.S. cotton industry. In one domestic end use alone—the tire cord and fabric market—the quantity of U.S. cotton used declined from about 600,000 bales in 1939 to 32,000 bales in 1963. For this period, cotton's share of total fibers used in this specific end use dropped from 96 to 2 per cent. Cotton has lost this important industrial outlet to man-made fibers. Similar losses have occurred in some apparel and household outlets.

An analysis of the causes of U.S. cotton's loss of markets to man-made fibers and foreign-produced cottons is immensely complicated. Wartime shortages of natural fibers; competitive prices; rising costs of production, processing, and marketing; durability in various end uses; consumer acceptance and satisfaction—these and many other factors have all contributed. For a complete appraisal, the price and cost relationships of U.S. cotton to its most significant competitors in each end use should be analyzed.

U.S. cotton has lost export markets primarily to foreign-grown cotton and to man-made fibers. Production of man-made fibers was stimulated by the increased demand for fibers during World War II and has been encouraged since then by a decline in prices relative to the prices for natural fibers.

The downward movement of rayon prices during the sixties, coupled with the slight decline in production, suggest that the U.S. market for rayon may be saturated and further inroads into traditional outlets for cotton may be negligible. However, the continued expansion of noncellulosic fibers remains a challenge to both U.S. and foreign-grown cottons.

### Maintaining and Evaluating Cotton Quality

Twenty years ago, the quality of cotton was described by its grade, staple length, and "character." This was before the introduction of mechanical harvesting, and these measures of quality were generally satisfactory for merchandising purposes and for decisions relative to spinning operations. Since the late fifties, as the proportion of the U.S. crop harvested mechanically has increased, mills have had increasing difficulties with cotton's spinnability, especially in plants with newer and faster machinery.

Gins have installed additional drying and cleaning equipment to clean the rougher machine-harvested seed cottons to maintain high grades. These efforts have been generally successful, but in achieving this goal other components of quality have been adversely affected by defoliation for harvesting and excessive gin drying and cleaning in some areas.

Fiber length, length distribution, fineness, strength, and many other properties significantly affect mill operating costs and quality and value of the finished product. Considerable attention recently has been focused upon length uniformity in evaluating cotton quality and in predicting yarn quality.

By following pricing and loan policies that emphasize grade, both textile manufacturers and the Commodity Credit Corporation encourage ginning practices that improve grade but at the same time may damage length and other inherent qualities of cotton. Improved means of evaluating cotton that will better reflect its end-use value and permit more effective pricing is urgently needed. In modern textile manufacturing, one of the first requisites is length and length distribution that has not been altered significantly from its basic nature. Any pricing structure used now or later must preserve these characteristics if cotton is to compete more effectively.

### Packaging, Sampling, and Trading Improvements

As a result of sampling, compressing, and handling, U.S. cotton may arrive at U.S. and foreign mills in an unsightly condition, and the protection provided by the bagging may no longer be adequate. These adverse effects and possible means for overcoming them have been known for years; however, the problem is more prevalent and the need for correction more urgent today than ever before.

Mechanically drawn samples obtained during ginning are equal to cut samples for evaluating the initial quality of cotton. In addition, mechanically drawn samples are more representative of the contents of a bale than cut samples, which are made up of only two portions taken from each side of the bale. Stored portions of mechanically drawn samples are also reliable up to about six months for subsequent merchandising purposes. Increased acceptance of this method of sampling would help improve the appearance of bales as they are moved to the mill, and would also reduce contamination of bale contents.

If all segments of the trade, including domestic mills and exporters, would adopt only one density for bales, warehouse compressing could be greatly reduced and possibly eliminated in some areas of the Cotton Belt. Gins could install presses which economically could produce bales of the desired dimensions and density. However, institutional factors, custom, and lack of acceptance must be overcome and changes in trading rules adopted before such improvements can be made.

Other changes in trading rules and practices would have to be adopted for the industry to realize the full benefits of mechanical sampling and one bale density. Net-weight trading and standards for tare appear to offer opportunities for more efficient pricing and marketing of cotton. The advantages, limitations, and necessary adjustments in trade rules associated with net-weight trading were summarized for the industry more than 25 years ago. However, cotton remains the only major agricultural commodity traded on a gross-weight basis.

Improvements in bale-covering materials and methods of wrapping are closely associated with net-weight trading; standards for tare; and general improvements in packaging, quality maintenance, and marketing efficiency. Lighter-weight bagging and ties would reduce the total transportation costs of marketing cotton in both domestic and foreign outlets. More selective use of bale-covering materials and ties offers some possibilities for saving in packaging cost at the gin and preprocessing costs in the opening rooms of textile mills.

Incorporating standardized moisture content into the trading rules may also contribute to more efficient marketing practices. However, the advantages and limitations of trading on the basis of standardized moisture content and its effects on costs and quality maintenance should be thoroughly evaluated before the practice is adopted.

Similarly, all these suggested improvements should be appraised carefully as to their combined contributions for reducing the cost of marketing cotton and maintaining its quality during storage and while in transit to domestic mills and foreign markets. It is generally agreed that production and marketing costs must be greatly reduced and quality improved or maintained if cotton is to keep pace in the competitive textile market.

### Effects of Public Control

Prices of U.S. cotton and some other farm products have been greatly influenced by legislation. For example, the availability of crop-support loans greatly reduces the risk of price fluctuations. Since the risks of price fluctuations have been almost completely eliminated, there is much less need for the "inventory insurance" provided by futures contracts. As a result, the New Orleans Cotton Exchange, after almost 100 years of business, suspended trading in 1964. The gross business of the New York Cotton Exchange dropped from over 325,000 contracts a year to less than 10,000 during the sixties.

For several years, the domestic price of cotton has exceeded the world price. Since 1956 exporters have been given a direct payment to offset the supported farm price. However, this action put U.S. cotton mills, which had to buy U.S. cotton at supported prices, at a competitive disadvantage with foreign textile manufacturers, who paid the lower world price even for U.S. cotton. Not only were U.S. mills having to pay a higher price than foreign mills for raw cotton from the same point of origin but the foreign mills were also reselling the cotton in the United States in the form of finished products in competition with domestic mills.

On a raw-cotton-equivalent basis, imports of cotton textile products in the mid-sixties exceeded 600,000 bales annually. Ten years earlier imports of cotton textiles were equivalent to less than 100,000 bales.

During most of this ten-year period, there was an equalization payment on cotton products exports. However, in contrast to the sixfold increase in imports, U.S. exports of cotton textile products decreased from about 580,000 bales in the mid-fifties to less than 450,000 bales in the mid-sixties.

To correct this situation, and to increase the domestic consumption of cotton, the 1964 farm bill provided an equalization payment to domestic users of U.S. raw cotton. Although total domestic consumption was up slightly in 1964 and 1965, cotton's proportion of the total fiber market continued to decline; and prices for unfinished cloth rose, on an average, 4 to 5 cents per pound.

Meanwhile, the number of cotton farmers continues to decline, the average size of production units continues to get larger, and cotton in the carryover is approaching record levels. Per capita consumption of cotton in the United States in 1963 and 1964 was the lowest since the mid-thirties, whereas the per capita use of man-made fibers in 1964 was the highest on record.

It appears that competition from man-made fibers and foreign-grown cottons, changes in consumer demand, and public programs associated with these developments are adversely affecting the status of cotton in the national economy. The reduction in number of gins and active merchandising firms and cotton's declining share of the U.S. fiber market are just a few examples of the problems confronting the U.S. cotton industry in the mid-sixties.

# 30

## FRUITS AND VEGETABLES

THE PER CAPITA CONSUMPTION of fruits and vegetables in the United States increased rapidly up to World War II, and projections of future demand made in the 1950's extrapolated this rising trend all the way to 1980.

Alas for the poor forecaster! His life is hard. Figure 30.1 shows that after 1950, the rising trend of per capita vegetable consumption practically flattened out. And Figures 30.2 and 30.3 show that after 1957 the per capita consumption of citrus and of noncitrus fruit both declined.

These charts show further that the decline was concentrated in *fresh* fruits and vegetables. The processed forms—frozen, canned, or dried—mostly increased. The annual per capita consumption of processed vegetables increased from 84 pounds in 1950 to 95 in 1957 to 116 in 1969; they now provide about half the total supply. The increase in the use of processed forms was dramatic in some cases. Figure 30.4 shows that by 1968, more than a third of the total consumption of even the commonplace potato was processed.

These charts show how the per capita consumption of fresh fruits and vegetables has been declining in the United States. But this does not mean at all that the fresh fruit and vegetable business as a whole is declining also. As a matter of fact, it is increasing and becoming more important and more complicated every year.

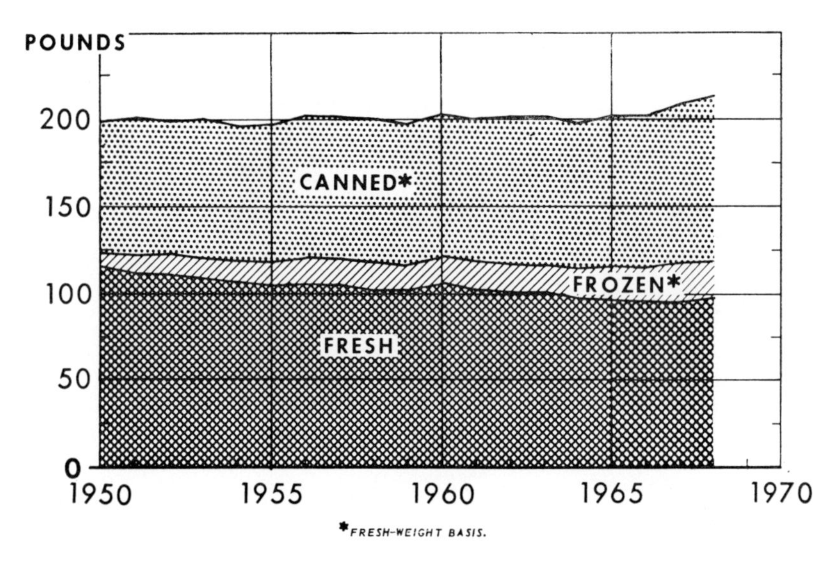


FIG. 30.1—Vegetable consumption per person, United States, 1950–68.

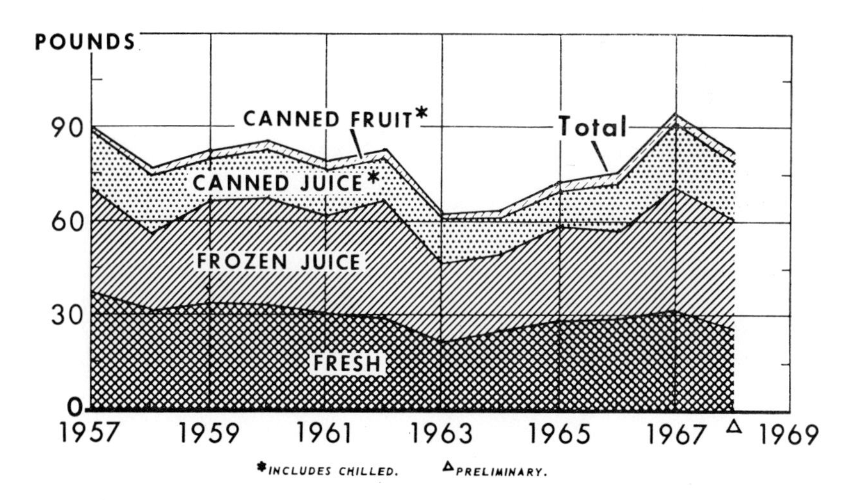


FIG. 30.2—U.S. citrus fruit consumption per person, fresh-equivalent basis, 1957–68.

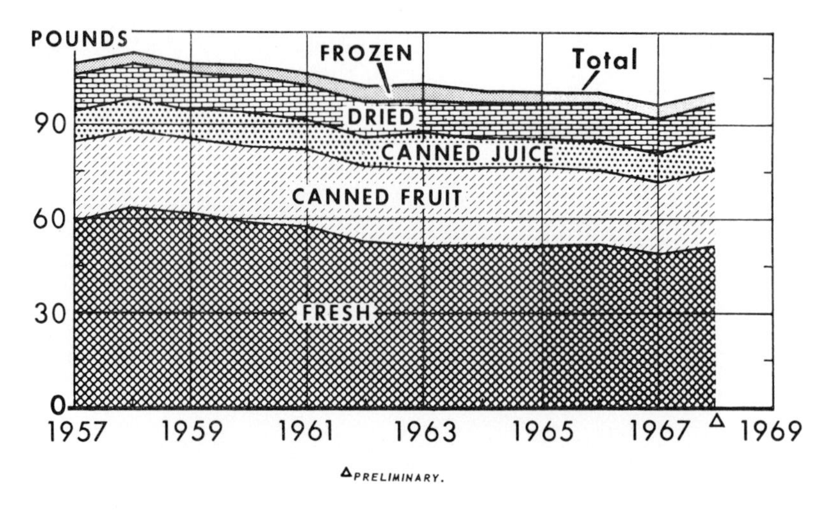


FIG. 30.3—U.S. noncitrus fruit consumption per person, fresh-equivalent basis, 1957–68.

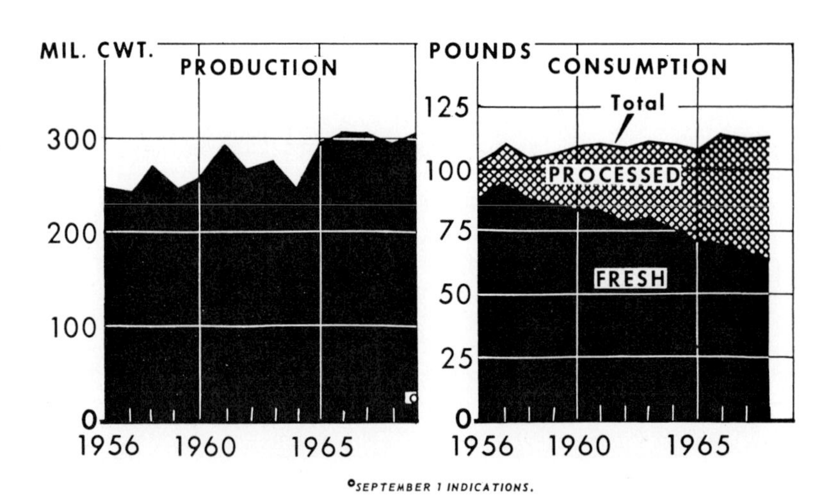


FIG. 30.4—Potato production and per capita consumption, United States, 1956–68.

There are several reasons for this. The first reason is obvious—the rapid growth of population in the United States more than offsets the declining consumption per capita. The second reason is also quantitative, but less obvious—the continuing concentration of the increasing population in the cities of the United States, especially in the larger ones. The fresh fruit and vegetable markets in the big cities are expanding much faster than the growth of total population in the country as a whole.

The third reason is qualitative—consumer tastes are becoming more exacting. Consumers are demanding higher quality, fresher fruits and vegetables. The produce needs to be handled faster and kept in better condition than in the past. The task of marketing fresh fruits and vegetables is not only greater but is more exacting also.

## MARKETING COSTS

Most fresh fruits and vegetables are bulky and perishable, and many are shipped long distances. Their marketing costs therefore are high. The processed forms also involve high marketing margins because the costs of processing are usually high.

The overall marketing margin for fresh and processed fruits and vegetables has increased in recent years as shown in Figure 30.5. The farm value of the fruits and vegetables included in

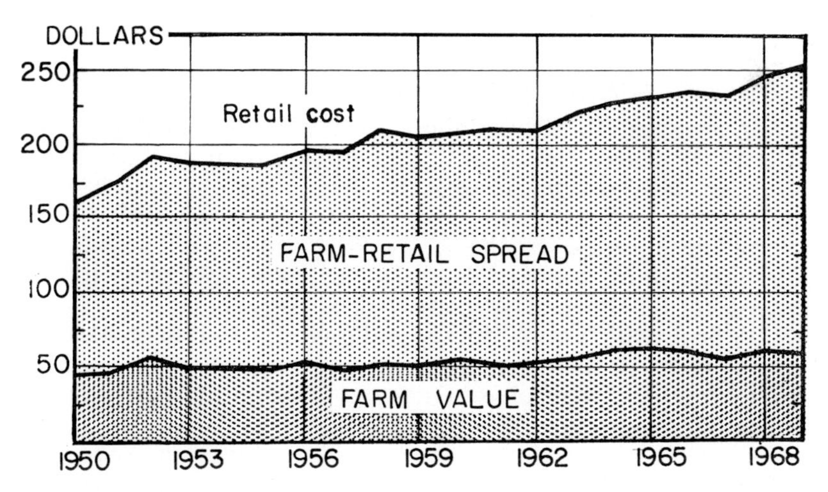


FIG. 30.5—Marketing bill for fresh and processed fruits and vegetables, United States, 1947–69.

this "market basket" statistic has remained quite stable, while the marketing bill has trended upward. In percentage terms, the marketing margin in 1969 was 73 per cent of the retail cost, compared with 69 per cent in 1950. The marketing margin on all fresh fruits and vegetables in 1969 averaged 67 per cent of the retail value; the margin on processed fruits and vegetables was somewhat larger, averaging 79 per cent.

A more detailed look at the marketing bill for fresh fruits and vegetables is provided by Table 30.1. A similar breakdown of marketing costs for more recent years is not available, but the overall distribution between the producer and the marketing system has remained about the same as in 1964.

**TABLE 30.1: Farm Value and Marketing Costs for Fresh Fruits and Vegetables, 1964***

| | Per Cent of Retail Dollar |
|---|---|
| Farm value | 33.07 |
| Harvesting, hauling, packing, selling | 12.80 |
| Intercity transportation | 13.40 |
| Wholesaling | 8.90 |
| Delivery to retailer | 1.73 |
| Retailing | 30.10 |
| Total | 100.00 |

Source: *Cost Components of Farm-Retail Price Spreads for Foods,* National Commission on Food Marketing, Tech. Study 9, June, 1966, p. 46.

* Based on the weighted value of a market basket of fresh fruits and vegetables.

## WHOLESALE TERMINAL MARKETS[1]

In contrast to industrial markets where production tends toward geographic concentration and the pricing process is diffused, food marketing historically has been characterized by spatially diffused production and a central market trading and pricing mechanism. In the fresh fruit and vegetable industry this central market served as the focal point for supply and demand forces. The market consisted of the wholesale terminal market firms which qualitatively and quantitatively matched producer supplies with buyer demands and performed such wholesaling functions as receiving, storage, and the forward physical distribution of products.

These fresh fruit and vegetable terminal markets were, and still are, the major source of information for industry marketing

[1] This section is based on *Organization and Competition in the Fruit and Vegetable Industry,* National Commission on Food Marketing, Tech. Study 4, June, 1966, pp. 103–10.

decisions. As the locus of intersecting supply and demand forces, these markets generate industry prices which serve as guidelines for fresh fruit and vegetable marketing operations all over the country. Public and private market information on wholesale receipts, unloads, holdings, and prices in the central terminal markets is used extensively by producers and shippers as well as terminal firms as the basis for marketing decisions.

The terminal market complex of a large metropolitan area includes the full range of firms and physical facilities involved in fresh fruit and vegetable wholesaling. It is described better as a metropolitan area than as a particular street or district. These markets are composed of chain store warehouses, wholesaler-receivers, jobbers, auctions, and other types of wholesaling firms. Varying degrees of interdependence exist between these firms and they represent alternative means of terminal market distribution.

Terminal market wholesaling in the fresh fruit and vegetable industry is made up of a group of specialized marketing firms performing break-bulk and local distribution services for supplies received from shipping-point markets. Changes in the market structure of food retailing as well as fresh fruit and vegetable distribution patterns have modified the role and importance of these markets since the early 1950's. Many firms have ceased operations, others have made major adjustments in their organization and the functions they perform, and there has been a general change in the structure of the terminal market complex.

All firms, regardless of their location within the market area or the nature of their business organization, have the common goal of facilitating the distribution of fresh fruits and vegetables. Within the terminal market complex, however, there are two distinct though related sectors—integrated and nonintegrated. Changes in the relative importance of these sectors since the 1950's have had significant effects on the entire fruit and vegetable industry. They are discussed separately in the next few sections.

## THE INTEGRATED SECTOR OF TERMINAL MARKETS

### Food-Retailing Operations

The most striking change in the food industry affecting fresh fruit and vegetable terminal markets has been the integration of retailing and wholesaling marketing functions. Substantially all national, most regional, and many local chain store organizations today operate integrated warehousing and distribution systems.

Moves toward vertically integrated distribution systems

were initiated by large chain store organizations but were by no means limited to them. The process has been promoted further by the growth of cooperative and wholesale-sponsored procurement, warehousing, and distribution systems. Individual retail stores no longer rely on local wholesale terminal markets for the bulk of their fresh fruit and vegetable supplies. Instead, each retail store is serviced by the wholesaling plant of the parent firm. Thus, such firms have become a separate part of the wholesale terminal market complex.

### Integrated Buying

In the early days of their development, when the chain stores accounted for a smaller proportion of retail food sales, they purchased their supplies in wholesale terminal markets from carlot receivers, commission merchants, auctions, and jobbers. But now, under integrated retail-wholesale arrangements, most chain store organizations buy the bulk of their fresh fruit and vegetable supplies by description direct from shipping-point markets in the producing areas. With a large share of the retail food market and larger organizations, chain stores have increased their purchases from shipping-point markets and decreased their purchases in the traditional central wholesale terminal markets. They do their wholesaling themselves.

These integrated retailers do not completely bypass the remainder of the fresh fruit and vegetable terminal market complex. Since shipping-point supplies cannot be perfectly matched with retail store needs, all chain stores find it necessary to make some purchases from other firms in the terminal markets, particularly for specialty items. But there are indications that purchasing from such firms will continue to decline.

Transportation and communication conditions once made it difficult for retailers to purchase direct from certain shipping-point markets, but recent improvements make it easier now. In addition, many fresh fruit and vegetable shippers and shipping-point brokers have reached forward along the marketing chain and assumed quasiwholesaling functions which aid retailer shipping-point procurement. One such service is the mixed-car shipment, whereby an assortment of fruits and vegetables is made up into a single unit at the shipping point. Another is the pool shipment, in which supplies for several buyers are consolidated at shipping points. Both services replace the traditional wholesaling functions of terminal market firms, shifting these functions back to the shipping point. This has further freed the chain store organizations and buying groups from dependence on other terminal market firms.

### Plant Location

As chain stores have integrated into wholesaling, they have not physically entered the central terminal market district. To facilitate rapid delivery and avoid the congestion of these districts (many of which are located in the hearts of major cities) chain store organizations have located their receiving and warehousing facilities elsewhere. They have usually located on the periphery of cities where it is possible to obtain a better ratio of parking, loading, and unloading space to building space than in the central market districts. Moreover, buildings in central markets are not well suited to efficient materials-handling techniques.

With these fringe locations, fresh fruits and vegetables arrive at the chain store warehouse without passing through the central terminal market districts. Hence, the development of integrated systems of retailing has brought about a physical as well as a structural division of the terminal market complex: structural, in that the integrated firms are less dependent upon the remainder of the market complex; physical, in that these integrated firms have not located in the central market districts, and consequently even less of the supply of fresh produce will move physically through those central markets in the future.

### Emerging Integration Patterns

The institutional market for food, consisting of restaurants, cafeterias, hospitals, and other public institutions, is served principally by the nonintegrated sector of the terminal market. But integration in this institutional food market is growing rapidly. In particular, chain restaurants and cafeterias, which first went through extensive horizontal integration, are now integrating vertically into wholesaling as well.

This integration has much the same effect on the role of the terminal market as chain store integration into wholesaling. The vertically integrated institutions purchase direct from shipping-point markets, and there is also a tendency for these firms to relocate their receiving and distribution facilities in outlying sections of the metropolitan areas which they serve. This contributes to the structural and physical cleavage in the central market complex.

As the density of chain institution feeding units increases, more vertical integration on the part of these firms will develop. Multiunit institutional firms with centrally determined menus and quality standards will find it increasingly advantageous to integrate into wholesaling in order to control product quality through direct shipping-point purchases.

Not only are horizontal and vertical integration of chain stores and institutions increasing but there is evidence of cross-integration between the two markets. In some areas, chain stores are beginning to service the institutional market from their warehouses. In addition, a few chain store organizations operate chain cafeterias, and indications are that they will integrate further into institutional food retailing in the future.

#### Implications of the Growth of the Integrated Sector

The growth and dominance of the integrated sector has led to a decline in business for the nonintegrated sector. So now there are too many nonintegrated wholesaling firms, and overcapacity in some terminal markets. There is a declining need for wholesalers, particularly for those who perform a limited number of specialized marketing functions. Moreover, direct shipping-point purchases by the integrated sector have altered the nature of the wholesaling business.

Integration of retailing and wholesaling marketing functions and direct purchases from the shipping point have the effect of concealing price and movement data for a large and increasing quantity of fresh fruit and vegetable supplies. Since buyers who purchase direct from the shipping point do not reveal their operations to other buyers or to shippers and growers, pricing and movement data are no longer public as they were in the earlier terminal markets. As a result, the small buyer who purchases from only a few areas has less market information than the large buyer. Furthermore, the integrated sector has access to public marketing data generated in the nonintegrated sector, but the reverse is not the case.

The growth of the integrated sector has, most importantly, affected industry pricing procedures. Earlier, much produce was sold at auction or in central markets where many buyers and sellers were assembled. Prices were made public, and these centrally determined prices were accurate reflections of local market supply and demand conditions. But now, with direct buying from the shipping point and decentralized wholesaling, there are not so many central markets where forces of total supply and demand interact. Instead, there are a large number of shipping-point markets in which only a portion of total supply and demand for fresh fruits and vegetables meet. While terminal market statistics continue to serve as industry pricing guides, this information becomes a less and less valid representation of industry market conditions as the volume of purchases direct from the shipping point increases, the number of buyers in the terminal market declines, and shippers employ these markets for their lower quality products or distressed sales.

## THE NONINTEGRATED SECTOR OF TERMINAL MARKETS

The nonintegrated sector of terminal markets consists of carlot receivers, merchant wholesalers, jobbers, purveyors, commission merchants, repackers and prepackers, and auction companies. These firms perform specialized and complementary market functions. Carlot receivers, merchant wholesalers, commission merchants, and auction companies primarily acquire supplies from shipping-point markets and sell to jobbers and purveyors who in turn meet the small-lot requirements of the retail and institutional market.

The growth of the integrated sector of terminal markets has resulted in a decline in the importance of the nonintegrated sector. Central market districts comprised of nonintegrated firms are still important in many cities; but their importance is declining in all instances, and they have almost disappeared from the smaller cities. In the larger cities, particularly those with ports and large suburban trading areas, well-defined central market districts still exist, primarily to serve the nonintegrated retail and institutional trade. However, the growth of the integrated sector has imposed many changes and adjustments even in these markets.

### Combining Central Market Functions

Before the dominance of the integrated sector, terminal market wholesalers for the most part specialized in one (or a few) marketing function. These were primarily carlot receiving and initial break-bulk functions involved in selling to jobbers and purveyors. The interdependence fostered by this specialization required jobbers and purveyors to locate in physical proximity to wholesalers. It was this firm specialization and dependence which initially produced the central terminal market district for fresh fruits and vegetables. Firm adjustments to the growth of the integrated sector have had the effect of lessening this interdependence.

Receiving, wholesaling, and jobbing functions in small- and medium-sized markets have been almost entirely consolidated into single-firm operations. Only in larger terminal markets are these marketing functions still separate to any extent, and even in these considerable functional combination has occurred.

The service wholesaler performing the combined distributing, receiving, and jobbing functions is in the best position to serve the growing institutional food market and the shrinking number of independent retail firms. Service wholesalers are also best equipped to provide those items which integrated retailers do not procure directly from shipping points.

In order to survive, firms in the nonintegrated sector of the wholesale terminal markets will need to adjust toward performing more wholesaling functions and providing additional buyer services. Thus, nonintegrated terminal market firms will no longer be specialized and interdependent as in the past. There will be less need for physical proximity of the firms except for the retailing function, and possibly packaging.

### Changes in Clientele and Product Lines

Another adjustment by the nonintegrated sector to changing wholesale market conditions has been the change in jobbers' clientele. Many jobbing firms which once serviced retail stores only are now servicing both retail stores and institutions. A similar trend is much in evidence for service wholesaling firms. In contrast, purveyors (or firms normally servicing the institutional food market) have not undertaken to service retail stores because the size of the retail food market declined with the growth of direct shipping-point purchases by integrated firms.

Still another terminal market adjustment, precipitated by changes in retail procurement, has been the tendency for jobbers and service wholesalers to add processed items to their product lines. The addition of processed products reduces both sellers' and buyers' procurement costs, besides enhancing their ability to service more needs of the independent retail and institutional market. However, facility, delivery, and refrigeration requirements have limited this adjustment to the larger jobbers and service wholesalers.

### Decrease in Consignment and Auction Selling

Consignment and auction selling, once important means by which shippers marketed fresh fruits and vegetables, now account for only a small portion of total sales in terminal markets. In imitation of chain store and buying-group operations, nonintegrated wholesalers, including jobbers and purveyors, now secure supplies direct from the shipping point under FOB or delivered sales arrangements. Consignment sales of fresh fruits and vegetables still persist in most terminal markets, but their importance is small and declining. Moreover, the preponderance of such sales at the present involves distressed merchandise or supplies unsold from the direct-sales operations of shipping-point firms.

Terminal auction markets have historically been a major means of marketing citrus and certain deciduous fruits. At one time, these auctions operated in 15 major U.S. cities. Over the last 15 years several auctions have failed, due to loss of trade, and most of the remaining auctions will probably cease operations in the near future. Few shippers sell consistently at auction today, and most major buyers have deserted the auction markets for direct purchasing from the shipping point.

### Decentralization

Because of the increase of direct purchasing from the shipping point, the exodus of major buyers from the terminal market district, the combining of wholesaling functions into one firm, and the lessening of dependence between wholesalers, many nonintegrated terminal market firms have moved their operations away from the central market district. Aside from the congestion and outmoded facilities that exist in many terminal market districts, there simply is no longer any reason why these firms should locate in physical proximity to one another. Continued movements to the fringe of cities can be expected on the part of wholesalers. In the past, such moves have involved the complete relocation of central fruit and vegetable market districts in major cities, and further major relocations are anticipated.

## PRODUCT PACKAGING

Fresh fruits and vegetables may be packed at the shipping point by terminal market packers or in chain store warehouses. It is estimated that about 40 per cent of fresh fruit and vegetable supplies are now prepackaged at the shipping point or in terminal markets, and the trend is to offer more products at retail in consumer packs.

At present, the terminal market prepacker performs substantial packing services for both chain stores and nonintegrated firms. Thus prepacking, like fill-in buying, results in an interdependence between the integrated and the nonintegrated sectors of the terminal market complex. However, as chain stores increase their volume in owned or affiliated warehouses, they will purchase less from terminal market packers. Today many chain stores perform their own packing services for the supplies that are not packed at the shipping point; others are moving toward integrated packing operations. Under these circumstances the integrated sector will divert still more supplies from these nonintegrated terminal market firms.

The declining dependence of chain stores on central market packers has been facilitated by increased prepackaging at the shipping point. Shipping-point consumer packaging is developing rapidly for such crops as citrus fruits, potatoes, onions, and carrots. Furthermore, the central market repacker is being bypassed by increasing prepacking of vine-ripe tomatoes at the shipping point and unit packaging of bananas by importing firms.

Because of their specialized marketing services in the past, terminal market repackers and prepackers suffered the least market displacement with the growth of the integrated sector. Today, however, chain store as well as shipping-point prepackaging is eroding the market position of these firms. To improve their competitive positions, some wholesalers and jobbers have assumed the packaging function.

## EVALUATION OF PRESENT MARKET SYSTEM

The chief improvement that many of these terminal or central markets need to make, however, is all too obvious to those who use them. Many of the markets need complete physical reorganization.

In a number of cities there are too many wholesale fruit and vegetable markets, poorly coordinated with one another and inadequately equipped to handle motor truck receipts. Reorganization would substantially reduce the cost of city wholesaling and distribution and provide better service to farmers, retailers, and consumers.

Most of the markets "just growed" without any over-all plan. Their facilities are antiquated. Many of the new markets, built as the cities expanded, were not properly designed; some were built for the benefit of certain elements in the trade or for individual railroads, not for the benefit of the efficiency of the market as a whole. The New York City market, before its reorganization, was a prime example of the result of haphazard growth.

The New York market is one of the largest in the world for fresh fruits and vegetables. Its annual supplies, arriving by all forms of transportation, average about one carload a minute for the daylight time of each working day in the year. About one-tenth of the total commercial production in the entire United States finds its way to this one great market, and values established there influence the prices of hundreds of thousands of carloads sold in other parts of the country. The New York market is in every sense of national importance.

In the past, fruits and vegetables in New York City were marketed in an antiquated, congested, downtown Manhattan, Washington Street area that was everything that a big city market should not be.

The only way to get railroad cars of produce into the old market was to move them across the river by barge. A produce truck could only drive to within four blocks of the market; then the trailer had to be unloaded into small hand trucks, which men pushed to the market. Just to unload a trailer in this manner cost $140.

Finally, in 1966 New York City built at its own expense a new $40-million market, big enough to hold 25 football fields, in a 128-acre area at Hunt's Point near the Bronx River. The market includes 4 miles of railroad sidings and more than 4 miles of paved roads for trucks. It opened October 1, 1966, fully leased to 135 tenants.

Each of the four main buildings is two stories high and one-third of a mile long, with 200 feet of space between them. The second story consists of offices, with a long corridor running the full length of the building to connect them. The lower story contains the markets. In each, the produce comes in at one side and is sold from the other.

Every tenant in the market has a front platform directly on a railroad siding and a back platform at truck tail-gate height, and each tenant arranges for his own heating or cooling needs according to the kind of produce he handles.

# 31

# PATTERNS OF MARKETING PROGRESS

Do THE HETEROGENEOUS CHARACTERISTICS of agricultural marketing revealed in this book make up any coherent pattern? We have uncovered the hieroglyphics. Can we decipher their meaning? What story do they tell? Do they mean anything in an over-all sense? Or are they just a mass of indiscriminate and independent marks on crumbling stone, each interesting in itself but unrelated to the others, soon to be obliterated, and useless as a guide to the future?

The interpretation of hieroglyphics involves judgment and experience as well as simple factual observation. In this concluding chapter, then, we will trace the patterns as we see them dimly in the half-light of our present knowledge, making use of scraps of information in one part of the field to piece together the scraps in another.

We will start with demand, and then go on to prices and costs.

## CONSUMER DEMAND FOR MORE HIGHLY PROCESSED FOODS

One common feature of the demand for most farm products is readily apparent and is commented on in Chapters 1 and 3. It is the change in demand that has been taking place toward more highly processed foods—foods that have been brought to a form more nearly ready for the table. This feature is common to practically all foods.

The change in demand toward more highly processed foods is the result of the general desire of housewives—and husbands—to spend less time in the kitchen. This arises from several things. One is the increasing cost and difficulty of hiring cooks and housemaids. Another is the increase in the number of two-income families, in which both the husband and wife work and do not have much time to spend in preparing meals. Another is the continued shift in population from rural to urban areas. All these things contribute to the increasing demand for foods with "built-in maid service."

These conditions seem likely to persist in the future, at least while prosperity continues. Accordingly, the trend toward more processed foods, with the increased variety of choice which they afford, seems likely to continue also. This means that work will continue to be transferred from the kitchen to the food-processing factory. Most of this transfer represents a net saving of labor for the economy as a whole—an increase in efficiency which permits a fuller satisfaction of wants in the economy as a whole. It is one evidence of economic progress.

## NARROWING PRICE DIFFERENTIALS

In the price part of the field of agricultural marketing, a prominent common characteristic is the tendency for the price differentials that reflect consumers' preferences for different grades of product to narrow down on their way back to the producer. We saw in Chapter 16 on grades, values, and prices and in several of the commodity chapters how this occurs with hogs, eggs, and cotton; it is common with most farm products. Many price differentials of several cents a pound at the retail store narrow down to one or two cents, or to zero, by the time they get back to the producer.

This tendency results from the natural inclination of country buyers of farm products, when it is difficult to determine differences in value, to play it safe and pay close to the average for all lots. When producers cannot tell very accurately what the grade of their eggs or poultry or grain or hogs or cream is, they are more displeased by a discount they do receive for a low-grade product than they are by a premium they do not receive for a high-grade product. Country buyers have found by experience that where the factors that determine grade are difficult to ascertain on an objective basis, they can keep their clientele happier by paying small premiums and discounts, or none at all, than by paying full premiums and discounts.

This feature of agricultural marketing has adverse effects on the economy. It overpays the producer of the product with the least desirable qualities, and underpays the producer of the product with the most desirable qualities. The price system does not reflect consumers' desires accurately to producers.

This leads producers to misallocate productive resources among the different grades of products. They produce more than consumers want of the products with the least desired qualities and less of the products with the more desired qualities. Consumer satisfaction and producer returns are not maximized. Constant effort is required to overcome this tendency of the agricultural marketing system.

## NEED FOR MORE MARKET NEWS ON PRICES AND GRADES

Another prominent characteristic in the field of prices is the need for more market news about prices and grades. The decentralization of the market for farm products that has been taking place at the farmer's end of the marketing system has increased the need for accurate and detailed market news at the farmer level.

When farmers turned the job of selling their products over to commission men at the terminal markets, they could leave the job in their hands. The commission men sold the products to buyers at the yards by personal inspection. But today a farmer with opportunities to sell direct at several different interior markets within reach of his truck needs to know before he selects his market what prices the different markets are paying for the different grades of his product. He is his own salesman and, at that stage of the game, he is selling by description, not by inspection. For that purpose, he needs accurate and detailed price information, by grades, so that he can select the best market for his product before it leaves the farm. The market news system, primarily a central market system originally, lags behind the movement toward more decentralized marketing. It needs to be brought more closely up to date.

A revolutionary change has also taken place at the other end of the marketing system, in retailing, from personal service in the small corner grocery store to self-service in the large supermarket. This has depersonalized the housewife's shopping almost completely. She no longer relies on the advice of the store clerk that he has a good buy on beans this week or that the Colorado peach crop is coming next week. Instead, she confronts racks of packaged goods from which she makes her own selections, relying entirely on what she sees on the package and what knowledge she has herself.

She is her own buy-woman, much as the farmer in the decentralized market is his own sales-man. Both she and he have dispensed with an army of clerks and salesmen, and have saved the expense of maintaining them. But both of them now have to do these displaced intermediaries' work themselves.

Accordingly, both the farmer's market and the housewife's retail market have changed in character and function. Previously, both had a social aspect as well as an economic aspect. Farmers in their markets and housewives in theirs would bargain with their neighbors and dicker with different tradespeople for sociable as well as economic reasons. That was half the fun of going to town. Saturday afternoon and evening was a grand social occasion as well as a busy market day. But now, most lumberyards and garages close at noon on Saturday, and most of the stores close at 5:30 P.M. To a considerable extent, the farm market has moved right into the farmer's home; it comes in over the radio and the television set, and he dickers with several buyers, not at the market, but over his own telephone. And the dickering is less and less a matter of argument or cajolery and more and more a simple inquiry about what different buyer's prices for the particular grade and weight of product are, followed by a simple yes or no decision.

So it is with the housewife. She no longer shops about from store to store, gossiping with her neighbors in each one and all along the way. She likes one-stop service. To a considerable extent, the retail market has moved into her home; and it comes in, not only over the radio and the television set but also through state college and USDA reports on new products and processes and *Consumer Research* and other such publications, or direct from the original source or popularized in women's magazines. She gets a good deal of information from advertisements. She studies the qualities of the different new products that keep coming on the market, and goes to the supermarket with her head full of facts and figures. She is kept busy balancing prices against qualities and quantities and has little time for socializing.

This is all to the good. But to get the best out of it, the housewife needs to be provided with full objective, accurate, and detailed market information. She cannot keep up on the constant stream of new brands and products, compare one firm's "Jumbo" with another firm's "Colossal," or, still less, keep track of company "grades," such as "Cool Spring" or "Star," or properly evaluate brand names that have no accurate connotation of size or quality at all. However much these names may appeal to the manufacturer who thinks them up, most of them do not make much sense to the housewife. "Give me simple ABC or other self-evident grades," she asks. At the self-serve meat counter she picks up a "U.S. Choice" or "U.S. Good" piece of meat, without feeling any urge to cut it with her thumbnail to test its tenderness, as housewives do in France. She wishes that some still more self-explanatory and objective set of grades could be applied to her other purchases and that still more standardization could be attained in package size.

Some distributors express the fear that buyers would be reluctant to buy the lower grades if the designations A, B, and C or 1, 2, and 3 were used. They fear that customers' pride, in their relations with store clerks and other customers, would not permit them to buy the lower grades, even if they had no reservations about how good a buy the lower grades were. The need for this professed solicitude for the consumer's feelings is totally without foundation in fact. Sales of C grade products accounted for 60 per cent of the sales of grade-labeled products of the Great Atlantic and Pacific Tea Company between 1934 and 1941. Consumers evidently were not reluctant to buy the lower grades. They are still less reluctant now in self-serve stores.

One of the mail-order houses uses words which clearly indicate the quality or grade of the product. Montgomery Ward describes the general cut and character of a garment, and lists three prices. One price is for its "Good quality," or simply "Good," along with the specifications for that quality (percentage of wool, etc.). A higher price is quoted for its "Better" quality, with its specifications; and a still higher pricc is listed for its "Best" quality or grade. Why could not the same sort of thing be done more widely with food, and the standards made uniform?

Country markets for farm products have come a long way from their earlier stages. In those markets in the past, and in some parts of the world today, buyers and sellers agree on prices through an intermediary who holds the buyer's hand in one hand and the seller's hand in the other under a blanket and conducts secret negotiations by finger language until, after an hour or more, a price is reached—both buyer and seller then exploding into imprecations to hide their real satisfaction with the deal. In the words of the Bible, " 'It is naught, it is naught,' saith the buyer. But when he is gone his way, then he boasteth." Retail stores have come a long way too from the primitive markets where both buyers and sellers would be disappointed if they could not haggle for a long time about prices. The savings in time and energy in modern markets are very great.

But both kinds of markets need to go further. Farmers and housewives are all busy doing other things more worthwhile than spending their time trying to outwit buyers and sellers.

In livestock markets, for example, price quotations for objectively determined carcass grades would reduce the need for livestock market intermediaries and would permit farmers to ascertain the best markets for their livestock with the maximum accuracy and the minimum cost. In retail markets there is no haggling about prices; retail prices now are marked right on the package. But they are prices for what? Just what does the package contain? We have abolished the arguments about prices, but the housewife is still not very well informed as to the contents of the package. Objective grade specifications would give her the help she needs. She knows whether she wants first, second, third, or fourth grades of this and that product. She can pick out her U.S. grades of meat at a glance. But how can she make intelligent choices between different brands of fancy names for the hundreds of other products she buys? Someday the same sort of retailer who figured out how to give her what she wanted in the way of supermarket self-service will be able to provide her satisfactory objective and unequivocal grades and standardized packages.

## REDUCING COSTS WITH LARGER OPERATING UNITS

In the field of marketing costs, a prominent feature is the trend toward larger operating units. Milk production, milk processing, and milk distribution are all becoming large-scale operations, as shown in Chapters 24 and 25 on milk and butter. Cotton gins are getting larger, as shown in Chapter 29; so are grain elevators, as shown in Chapter 27. Supermarkets are replacing the little corner grocery, as shown in Chapter 21 on retailing.

The average production of cheese per plant in 1964 was 239 per cent greater than in 1944. During the same period, percentage increases in the average output per plant of other principal products were: creamery butter, 218 per cent; evaporated milk, 34 per cent; ice cream, 54 per cent; and nonfat dry milk solids, 292 per cent. Each of these products was manufactured by fewer plants in 1964 than in 1944, although the total output of each product, except butter, was greater.[1]

The average volume of cotton ginned per plant increased from 965 bales in the 1939–40 season to about 3,060 in the 1964–65 season. In the soybean-processing industry, the average annual capacity per mill increased from 1.6 million bushels in 1951 to 5.8 million by 1969.

The average size of new supermarkets (in square feet) provides an indication of the change at the retail level. From 1953 to 1964, the average size of new supermarkets increased by 47 per cent—from 13,600 square feet to 20,000 square feet.[2]

---

[1] *Organization and Competition in the Dairy Industry,* National Commission on Food Marketing, Tech. Study 3, June, 1966.

[2] *Organization and Competition in Food Retailing,* National Commission on Food Marketing, Tech. Study 7, June, 1966, p. 16.

**Reasons for Increase in Size**

Several different forces have been responsible for this general increase in size.

One force is the internal economies that go with large size, up to a point that varies from case to case. The inverse relation between size of plant and cost per unit is shown in Chapter 18 on costs and in several of the commodity chapters. The costs of a pasteurizing unit are prohibitive unless they can be spread over a good-sized volume of business. Large-size creameries can operate at lower cost per unit than small creameries. The same thing is true of cottonseed mills and most other processing plants. Many economies of scale that previously could not be attained because of difficulties with accounting and internal communication are becoming attainable, as methods are being worked out to handle these difficulties.

The second force responsible for the increase in size is the increase that has taken place in the speed and range of the trucks that bring the product to the plant. Improved trucks and roads have increased the radius of the supply area around most plants. Since the area increases as the square of the radius, a modern truck with twice the radius of an earlier model can cover four times the area and bring in four times as much volume. This in itself can lead to lower procurement costs as well as to larger volume.

**Increase in Monopoly?**

Has this increase in size of operating unit led to an increase in monopoly power?

In some cases, perhaps it has. In most cases, probably it has not—at least, not proportionately. In many cases, probably there has been no increase in monoply at all.[3] There are reasons for this.

1. The total volume of business has increased. The percentage of the total business handled by the larger plant may be no greater than before.

2. The greater mobility of sellers and buyers resulting from the increased range of cars and trucks has increased the range of competition as well as the size of the operating unit. There is as much competition now among large elevators, creameries, etc., 50 or 100 miles apart as there used to be among small plants 5 or 10 miles apart.

[3] See A. D. H. Kaplan, *Big Enterprise in a Competitive System*, Brookings Institution, Washington, D.C., 1954.

### Which Serves Society Best—Atomistic or Monopolistic Competition?

Is society served better by a large number of small units actively competing under conditions of atomistic competition or by a small number of large units under conditions of monopolistic competition?

It is difficult to give this question any single simple answer. The question needs to be considered separately for each case, where the economies of large scale in that particular case can be measured and compared with the effects of monopolistic control of production in that particular case.[4]

In the automobile industry, for example, most of the production has gradually become concentrated in the hands of three large manufacturers—General Motors, Ford, and Chrysler. In the absence of any unfair practices of the early Standard Oil variety, this is convincing empirical evidence that the economies of large scale exceed the benefits that would result from atomistic competition. The few large manufacturers evidently can produce cars at lower cost than the more numerous small producers, who have been forced by their higher costs either to merge or to go out of business.

It is an open question whether the same thing is true of milk distribution or meat packing or retail distribution, to name only a few agricultural marketing industries. Nicholls' studies of the meat-packing industry and the cigarette industry raise questions of this sort but stop short of answering them.[5] The constant percentages into which the Big Four packers divide their purchases at certain markets imply, not necessarily monopoly, but the existence of something other than atomistic competition. But that is only a first step. It is really not the important point. The important question is not whether the industry operates under conditions of atomistic or monopolistic competition, but whether the conditions under which it does operate enable it to produce and sell at the lowest prices permitted by existing technology. The Department of Justice has kept a watchful eye on the Big Four, but decided in 1954 that there was not enough evidence to support an indictment under the Sherman Anti-Trust Act, particularly since a federal court had ruled out evidence pertaining to the years before 1937.

Some elements of the milk distribution industry have been in and out of the courts on charges of restraint of trade, as in the case of Dean versus Milwaukee. The point at issue in that

---

[4] *Ibid.*

[5] William H. Nicholls, *Imperfect Competition Within Agricultural Industries,* Iowa State Univ. Press, 1941; and *Price Policies in the Cigarette Industry,* Vanderbilt Univ., Nashville, 1951.

case was not the behavior of a distributor, but the legality of a city ordinance protecting local distributors; and the court decided that the ordinance was illegal. On the more general level, the fact that large distributors have been invading small markets implies that they operate at lower cost than the small distributors in those markets.

In retail distribution, competition among large units in selling is clearly wide open. But competition in wholesale buying is more suspect. Antitrust action a few years ago was directed against the Atlantic Commission Company, a purchasing subsidiary of the Atlantic and Pacific chain store company, for its purchasing activities, not against the A & P itself for its selling activities.

Of major commodities essential to farming, where production or distribution is concentrated in so few firms that a monopolistic collusion could develop, there is no clear evidence that any exploitation has been practiced to the detriment of agriculture. Table 31.1 shows price changes, both short-run and long-run, for a few selected items purchased from nonconcentrated and relatively concentrated industries. Prices of items produced in the former category such as lumbering (represented by building and fencing materials) show a short-run increase of 18 per cent and a long-run increase of 48 per cent; while prices in

**TABLE 31.1: Price Changes for Farm Products and Selected Groups of Farm Inputs, United States, 1960–69 and 1950–69**

| Product Group | Per Cent Changes in Prices | |
|---|---|---|
| | 1960–69* | 1950–69* |
| All farm products | 18 | 9 |
| Inputs purchased from nonconcentrated industries: | | |
| Feed | 7 | —1 |
| Hired farm labor | 65 | 144 |
| Buildings and fencing materials | 18 | 48 |
| Land | 65 | 182 |
| Inputs purchased from relatively concentrated industries | | |
| Motor vehicles | 32 | 73 |
| Machinery | 36 | 87 |
| Fertilizer | —7 | —1 |
| Motor supplies (oil, tires, etc.) | 10 | 30 |

Sources: *Agricultural Prices,* USDA, 1968 Annual Summary and Dec., 1969, issue.

* Annual averages for 1950 and 1960 compared with prices during the final quarter of 1969.

the latter category such as fertilizer (chemical industry) and oil, tires, etc. (motor supplies), show changes ranging from small decreases for fertilizer to increases of 32 to 73 per cent on motor supplies. From this it appears that changes in demand or production costs have influenced price changes more than has the structure of the market.[6]

These examples illustrate the point we made at the beginning of this section. There is no single, simple, general answer to the question of whether monopolistic competition is better or worse than atomistic competition. What is needed is separate investigation in each case. This type of study is difficult to conduct. The operating units to be studied are understandably reluctant to cooperate when the results of the study may show the need for breaking them up. But this problem of the nature of the competition is one of the large, neglected fields in agricultural marketing; it needs to be explored.

## CONCLUSIONS ON NEEDED CHANGES IN PUBLIC POLICIES, STATUTES, AND GOVERNMENT SERVICES

What more does the government need to do about marketing? New marketing developments in the past required a good deal of government action to keep them in line with the long-run interests of producers and consumers. Present developments require still further government action.

The specific actions that are required are quoted below from the conclusions reached by a National Commission on Food Marketing appointed by the President of the United States and published in a 1966 report entitled *Food From Farmer to Consumer:*[7]

## STRUCTURE OF THE INDUSTRY

Competition requires competitors. It works best when the number of competitors is sufficiently large so that they impose mutual restraints on each other, with the result that their collective activities are guided along paths consistent with the public interest. The numbers, sizes, and types of firms, and the potential ease of entry by new firms, profoundly affect the competitive environment in which each operates.

---

[6] For further discussion, see K. L. Robinson, "Market Structure—How Important in Explaining Long-run Price and Output Behavior?" *Journal of Farm Economics*, Vol. 45, Nov., 1963, No. 4, p. 878.

[7] *Food From Farmer to Consumer*, Report of the National Commission on Food Marketing, June, 1966, pp. 105–13. The commission also issued 10 technical studies and 12 supplements prepared by its staff or under contract. These constitute a mine of up-to-date marketing information. Some of them are drawn upon at several points in this book.

## Concentration in Individual Fields of the Food Industry

There is a tendency for business in the several fields of the food industry to become more concentrated in the hands of a few large firms except where special circumstances prevail—for example, in meat packing. In neither food processing nor distribution do economies of operation resulting from large size necessitate high concentration in national markets. The United States is fortunate in being large enough to permit both high efficiency and effective competition in foods. But as indicated . . . firms tend to grow, especially by merger and acquisition, well beyond the size needed to attain full operating efficiency. In the absence of restraint, concentration is expected to increase in most fields of the food industry.

Concentration of purchasing power by food retailers is especially significant. The increasing market orientation of the food industry and changes in the organization of buying have transferred market power from processors and manufacturers to retailers. Prospective developments in the industry are likely to further enhance their position. Increasing concentration of purchases restricts the alternatives open to suppliers, stimulates compensating concentration on their part, and weakens the effectiveness of competition as a self-regulating device throughout the industry.

Concentration of much of the food industry is not yet high enough to impair seriously the effectiveness of competition, and we do not suggest divestiture of current holdings even where concentration is highest unless future conduct demonstrates the need for it. Nor do we believe that internal growth should be restrained if achieved fairly. The principal danger of impairment of competition appears to be merger and acquisition by dominant firms.

*It is our conclusion that acquisitions or mergers by the largest firms in any concentrated branch of the food industry, which result in a significant increase in their market shares or the geographic extension of their markets, probably will result in a substantial lessening of competition in violation of the Clayton Act. In this connection, we believe accumulations of buying power have a significant effect on the competitive process and that food firms should not be permitted to form buying groups representing a greater sales volume than a single firm would be permitted to gain by merger or acquisition.*

An urgent need, as we see it, is positive action by the regulatory agencies to make clear and effective the policy of Congress as declared in the Clayton Act, and we favor development of guidelines by the Department of Justice and the Federal Trade Commission to make the policy specific in those food fields to which its application is most significant.

There is at present no regular method by which responsible Government agencies are advised of mergers and acquisitions. Neither are the regulatory agencies afforded any opportunity to evaluate the legality of mergers and acquisitions before they are effected. It often happens that mergers and acquisitions are completed without any clear indication of the Government's position, and too frequently this results in unnecessary litigation. Moreover, assets may become intermingled before the Government can act, and if divestiture is ordered, "unscrambling" is difficult and expensive. If advance notice were required, safeguards might be adopted to avoid jeopardizing legitimate mergers and acquisitions.

*We conclude that legislation requiring some form of premerger notification is desirable.*

The work of the regulatory agencies in dealing with mergers and trade practices would be made more effective if firms were to refrain from objected-to actions until a decision was reached as to their legality. *In order to accomplish this purpose, we consider it necessary to give the regulatory agencies power to issue temporary cease and desist orders, to be effective for a limited time and from which appeals can be taken to the courts.*

### Vertical Integration and Conglomerate Firms

Vertical integration and the combining of diverse lines of business within one company may result in significant operating economies or significant increments of market power. Guidelines as to when growth through vertical integration and diversification is not warranted are difficult to establish. We emphasize, however, that concentration policy should be applied to vertically integrated and conglomerate firms as vigorously as to any other, and that business practices of such firms (which may be more complicated than those of simply structured firms) should be scrutinized to insure that competition is not restricted in particular lines.

We also believe that the diverse activities of conglomerate and integrated firms will be less likely to be contrary to fair competition if information is made publicly available about their operations in the various fields in which they do business. Under present arrangements, conglomerate and integrated firms publish financial data only for their total activities and thus disclose no information about operations in particular fields such as their specialized competitors regularly publish. Competitors would be more nearly on an equal footing, so far as information about each other is concerned, if conglomerate and integrated firms published financial data for each major field in which they operate. Information is a necessary component of a viable competitive system.

*We conclude that each public corporation having annual sales in excess of a specified amount should be required to report annually to the Securities and Exchange Commission, for publication, its sales, expenses, and profits in each field of operations in which the annual value of shipments is larger than a given minimum.*

"Value of shipments" means both sales by the firm and transfer from one field to another within the firm. The definition of fields should be administratively determined to achieve the objective of enhanced information without excessive detail.

## INFORMATION ABOUT MARKET STRUCTURE AND COMPETITION

The food industry will continue to change in ways that cannot be fully anticipated. In the past, both failure to be aware of actual developments and erroneous beliefs about presumed developments have led to inaccurate appraisals of regulatory needs. In addition, some regulatory programs are rendered obsolete and unworkable by evolving changes in industry structure.

*In order that the Congress, the executive branch, and the public will be fully informed, we believe that the Federal Trade Commission should be charged with making a continuing review of market structure and competition in the food industry and report annually thereon to the Congress.*

The value of these reports will be enhanced if the appropriate committees of the Senate and the House of Representatives hold public hearings as necessary to inquire into the cause and implications of the developments revealed by such reports and other current information. We also think it would be helpful if the Federal Trade Commission would provide in its administrative structure for specialization in the economics of the food industry.

## DISCRIMINATORY PRACTICES

Price discrimination continues to be a threat in the food industry to fair competition among buyers, and in some cases among sellers. Concentration in many fields has decreased the number of business alternatives to both buyers and sellers, and has increased the pressures for favoritism. While the Robinson-Patman Act is widely viewed in the food industry as an important and necessary statute, it has shortcomings which endanger its effectiveness.

The single most serious deficiency of the act is the unenforceability of its section 2(f) ban on the inducement of discriminations by buyers. Although inducement by buyers may be the most important factor in present day price discrimination, enforcement is almost solely against sellers who grant the discriminations. This is true because of the great difficulty in satisfying the statutory requirement of proof of the buyer's knowledge. A more effective way of reaching practices originating with the buyer would make the act substantially more useful.

Other troublesome matters in the food industry are area price discrimination and the difficulty of preventing price discrimination when the "meeting competition" defense is available to sellers. Concepts of competitive injury should be kept abreast of changing business practices, and the enforcement agencies should avoid routine use of statutes without regard to the significance of discrimination.

*We conclude, therefore, that a study and reappraisal of the Robinson-Patman Act and its administration is now appropriate, in order to determine needed revisions in light of current economic conditions and overall antitrust policies.*

## REGULATORY RESPONSIBILITIES FOR FOODS

In view of the changing structural characteristics of the food industry, a major realignment of regulatory responsibilities and activities for food products is needed. Review of these activities should be a continuing effort to insure that the functions are necessary and are being efficiently performed.

## Sales of Meat and Dressed Poultry

Meat and dressed poultry are major products to which should be applied the same antitrust policies and administrative procedures as are applied to the economy at large. Changes in the structure of firms processing these products and in marketing practices reduce the apparent earlier need to correlate regulatory and technical activities. Firms processing the products are becoming increasingly conglomerate in character.

*We conclude that regulatory jurisdiction over transactions in meats, dressed poultry, and products processed from them should be removed from the Department of Agriculture and exercised only by the Department of Justice and the Federal Trade Commission.*

## Perishable Farm Food Products

By perishable farm foods, we mean livestock, live poultry, eggs, and fruits and vegetables in unprocessed form. Their perishability reduces to a short span the time in which buyers and sellers can seek their best alternatives. Lack of organization among producers makes them vulnerable to objectionable trade practices under some market conditions. Regulatory responsibility for livestock, poultry, and fresh fruits and vegetables has been assigned to units of the Department of Agriculture administratively associated with units engaged in nonregulatory work. It appears desirable to separate more distinctly the regulatory from the nonregulatory in the Department of Agriculture for the effective functioning of regulatory activities.

*We believe it important that an agency reporting directly to the Secretary should be established within the Department of Agriculture to administer the laws regulating competition in the marketing of perishable farm foods.*

The agency should have its own legal and investigative staff. The Department's adjudicatory function, for which adequate staff should be available, should remain distinct from the agency's regulatory function.

To give full effect to the program intended for such agency, we propose the following:

1. Regulatory responsibility for eggs should be assigned by statute to the Department of Agriculture without removing the jurisdiction of the Federal Trade Commission and the Department of Justice.

2. The obvious intent of the Packers and Stockyards Act should be made explicit by amending the act to make live poultry dealers and handlers subject to the complaint, order, and penalty provisions of title II.

3. Terminal markets for livestock are still the focal points of livestock trading in many areas, play an important role in all pricing, and are especially important sales outlets for smaller producers. In order that these markets have every opportunity to serve the changing needs of the livestock industry, and in view of increased competition from other marketing methods, the Packers and Stockyards Act should be administered, and if necessary amended, to give stockyard

owners and marketing agencies the greatest flexibility and control over their operations consistent with protecting the interests of buyers and sellers. Where a terminal livestock market ceases to be the dominant market in its area, upon request and with proper notification it should be subject to the same regulations as the other public livestock markets in the area.

4. The Perishable Agricultural Commodities Act should be amended as required to accomplish the objectives described below.

### Perishable Agricultural Commodities Act

The extreme perishability of fruits and vegetables and the lack of organization of the growers of many of them warrant more attention to trade practices in these commodities than in any other group of foods.

*We conclude that the Perishable Agricultural Commodities Act should be strengthened and administered in a positive fashion to bring about orderly and equitable trading in fresh fruits and vegetables.*

Among the ways in which we think this might be done are the following:

1. Require all shippers, packers, receivers, and sellers acting as agents for others to keep, for their total operations, records that account for the disposal of products, funds received and paid out, prices, services performed, charges therefor, and other information required for accurate identification of all transactions.
2. Provide that firms acting as agents supply the parties for whom they act with final settlement statements giving at least as much information about prices, charges, packouts, and similar matters as prescribed by the regulatory agency.
3. Require written confirmation of all interstate transactions in fresh fruits and vegetables within a stated time after agreements have been made, and require written notice of all subsequent modifications of agreements.
4. If the regulatory agency has reason to believe that unwarranted rejections of shipments are being made, it should require, for a trial period or longer, submission of notice of any rejection, by both receiver and shipper, to the regulatory agency.
5. Similarly, if the regulatory agency has reason to believe that discriminatory or other unwarranted concessions are taking place in the sale of fresh fruits and vegetables, it should require, for a trial period or longer, submission of copies of all notices of modifications of agreements made in interstate transactions.
6. The act should be amended to authorize the regulatory agency to examine records and accounts for any purpose consistent with the act, including but not restricted to the investigation of complaints.

Enforcement of the act should not be limited by funds received from license fees, and we question the financing of trade practice regulation by assessing the regulated industry.

*We are of the view that regulatory activities relating to perish-*

*able farm foods should be adequately supported by appropriations from general funds and not wholly dependent upon fees for licenses required of handlers or sellers.*

## SERVICES TO CONSUMERS

The central purpose of the following proposals is to provide consumers with the choices and unbiased information they need to get the most satisfaction for their money. Given such choices and information, individual consumers are responsible for their own decisions. Collectively, these will guide the production of goods and services by the food industry. Toward this end, we make the following suggestions:

1. *Consumer grades should be developed and required to appear on all foods for which such grades are feasible, that are sold in substantial volume to consumers, and that belong to a recognized product category.*

The grades should prominently appear on consumer packages if the product is ordinarily sold in such packages by manufacturers. Except for foods for which other nomenclature is well established, the grades should be in the form A, B, C . . . as established by the responsible Government agency.

It is not intended that genuinely new products should carry consumer grades when first put on the market. If a new product becomes widely used and takes on an identity of its own, it should then be considered for consumer grading. Nor is it intended that products sold in highly heterogeneous or perishable form should be consumer graded. In our view, rigid rules should not be laid down in this field but, rather, a flexible program of consumer grading should be adopted.

Although the principal purpose of this suggestion is to inform consumers, it may also serve to reduce the excessive use of promotion, thus contributing to a better performance of the food industry.

To carry out the program, the Department of Agriculture could be authorized to promulgate consumer grades, determine the products for which they are feasible and required to be used, and check on compliance. The unit charged with this work would have ready access to the technical skills available in the Department. Provision should be made for hearing the views of the food industry before new grades are put into effect.

2. *The Food and Drug Administration should establish standards of identity for all foods recognized by the public as belonging to a definite product category and for which standards are practicable.*

Standards of identity define what a given food product is, so that consumers will not be misled and reputable processors will not be exposed to unfair competition.

In numerous instances where either standards of identity or consumer grades are not in use, it would be practicable to give consumers needed information by requiring labels on processed foods to state certain facts determined to be especially indicative of quality.

For example, butterfat content and overrun (indicating the air in the product) are important measures of quality in ice cream and should be shown on labels as long as grades are not used.

3. *Packages and their labels should assist consumers in gaining an accurate impression of the contents and in making price comparisons.*

These are positive values for consumers, to be sought wherever they do not necessitate unreasonable cost. They are distinct from but merge into another matter, that of preventing deception through packaging and labeling. We urge the Federal Trade Commission and the Food and Drug Administration to give more attention to this area, and we favor further legislation if needed to give them authority they lack.

4. *A centralized consumer agency should be established in the executive branch of the Government by statute.*

Such an agency should assume the primary consumer protection roles now held by other Government agencies, such as the Special Assistant to the President for Consumer Affairs, the Department of Agriculture, Office of Economic Opportunity, Department of Labor, etc.

Although such an agency would represent consumers in areas other than food, the food industry is so large and so important to consumers that it justifies and requires this action.

With respect to food, such an agency should not only speak on legislative matters, but it should make a major effort to educate the consumer to play a more intelligent role in purchasing food. It would thus effectuate our earlier suggestions by informing consumers as to grades, standards, and packaging. Further, it should educate consumers in the more efficient and economic use of food. This might be accomplished through all types of media and by use of the services of all segments of the food industry, the country's educational facilities, and existing organizations, both private and public, whether local or national.

## POSITION OF FARMERS

The marketing and pricing problems in agriculture differ, sometimes dramatically, from those found in food processing and distribution. Contributing to the difference are the large number of farmers, the lack of product differentiation, the frequent oversupply resulting in part from rising farm productivity, unplanned variations in yields arising from weather and other natural hazards, and the extreme perishability of many products. Farm markets lacking the firming influence of group action are volatile, often depressed, and highly sensitive to downward pressures originating further along in marketing channels. Farmers as independent operators have not been able to coordinate quality improvement programs or to schedule more even flows of products to the extent demanded by today's food industry.

We believe, therefore, that there is frequent need for group action by farmers to adjust sales more uniformly to market demands at reasonable prices, to improve product quality and uniformity, to negotiate with buyers, and to protect themselves against trade practices and abuses of market power to which they are otherwise vulnerable. We see three approaches by which this might be done.

### Cooperatives and Bargaining Associations

The first is through producers' marketing cooperatives and bargaining associations, which already play a prominent part in food marketing. We believe that farmers do not yet fully appreciate the importance of cooperative action in marketing their products. We support all assistance government can reasonably give to producer cooperation.

### Marketing Agreements and Orders

The second and often complementary approach is through marketing agreements and orders, which have been available for use for certain products for about 30 years.

*We conclude that Federal marketing agreements and orders should be authorized for any agricultural commodity produced in a local area or regional subdivision of the United States.*

Since marketing orders and agreements may outlive their usefulness, it follows that they should be periodically reviewed by the Secretary of Agriculture, and we think that the reviews should be made public.

### Agricultural Marketing Boards

Producers frequently are not able to coordinate sufficiently their individual production efforts, or to negotiate effectively with buyers, by means of cooperatives or under the usual marketing order or agreement.

*We therefore conclude that a third and new approach is needed. Legislation should be enacted enabling Agricultural Marketing Boards to be brought into being upon vote of producers for the purpose of joining in the sale of products as they first enter into channels of trade.*

By an Agricultural Marketing Board is meant a body having specific powers in group marketing activities in the farm sale of a particular commodity. Such activities should be in the immediate charge of an Administrator appointed by and representing the Secretary of Agriculture. Powers that may be exercised under a board include those granted under Federal marketing orders and, in addition, regulating production or marketing and negotiating prices and other terms of trades. The board should also be empowered to engage in other activities necessary to accomplish these purposes.

While the main purpose of our proposal is to strengthen the bargaining position of farmers, we also see opportunities to increase efficiency in the marketing of farm products. Group action by producers permits advance planning of production, greater assurance for both farmers and buyers that enough but not too much product will be available, lower procurement costs for buyers, more control of quality and shipping schedules, and, in general, less disorganized marketing than now commonly exists.

To insure that the powers granted to a board are not misused, the body's membership should include representatives of handlers and the public as well as producers, and all policies should be subject to the approval of the Secretary of Agriculture. Criteria for boards should preclude their use by any group other than all growers of a product over a substantial producing area. Provision should be made for periodic public review of each board's purpose and operations.

### Protection of the Right To Organize

Special efforts appear necessary to protect the right of farmers to organize bargaining associations, to approve marketing orders, and to engage in other group efforts.

*We believe that specific legislation should be enacted providing that all processors, shippers, and buyers of farm products, engaging in or affecting interstate trade, are prohibited from obstructing the formation or operation of a producers' bargaining association or cooperative, and from inflencing producers' understanding of or voting on marketing orders or similar programs, by disseminating false or misleading information, discriminating among producers in any manner, boycotts, or other deceptive or coercive methods.*

The enforcement of this statute should be assigned to the agency responsible for regulation of trade in perishable farm foods.

We expect that the foregoing proposals to strengthen the position of producers will have most application to the more specialized branches of agriculture, e.g., fruits and vegetables, poultry, and fluid milk production for local markets. Problems faced in types of production widely distributed over the Nation and engaged in by scores of thousands of producers must be approached mainly by other means.

## MARKET INFORMATION ABOUT PRICES AND SUPPLIES

Collection of market data by price reporters from voluntarily cooperating traders on terminal markets was once adequate and economical. As marketing has become more decentralized, such means of collecting adequate price information have become less feasible, while the need for price information on the part of bargainers has increased. New approaches should be tried and then developed as experience is gained.

*In order to make better price reporting possible, we believe that the Department of Agriculture should be authorized to require submission of prices, quantities bought or sold, grades, and similar information by firms transacting business in foods, including growers, in such forms as is essential to the prompt publication of news about market prices and product movement.*

This would permit the Department to gather complete and reliable information, to summarize it to assure confidentiality, to publish it quickly, and to provide more service per dollar spent. Processing data by computer would often be possible. Spot checks of the records of reporting firms should be made as an additional safeguard of the data's reliability. Given this access to data, the Department could work out the procedures that best suited the needs of particular products and markets.

Producers of fresh fruits and vegetables frequently are less well informed than buyers about conditions in different producing areas that will affect market supplies and prices in the immediate future.

*We therefore are of the opinion that the Department of Agriculture should give high priority to developing timely reports of prospective market supplies of selected perishable farm food products.*

Traders regularly doing business with each other are turning to formula pricing, by which they tie their prices to well-known price quotations assumed to reflect current market conditions. But as formula pricing and vertical integration become more common, prices independently established by the interplay of supply and demand tend to disappear.

A more comprehensive price reporting system will help with this problem by utilizing all available information.

*In view of the increasing importance of sales arrangements made well in advance of delivery, we suggest that the Department of Agriculture should explore means of reporting forward prices, contract terms, and other potential successors of ordinary spot prices.*

## UNIFORMITY OF STATE AND FEDERAL REGULATIONS

The conflicts among the profusion of State regulations bearing on containers, grades, labels, product nomenclature, and the like are a significant burden on interstate trade in food products.

*We therefore believe that a concerted effort should be made to effect uniformity among State regulations that obstruct trade in foods across State lines.*

In this connection, it may be noted that in some instances particular State regulations have been outstandingly successful and provide an example for uniform State codes or for Federal regulation.

Section 203(d) of the Research and Marketing Act charges the U.S. Department of Agriculture with the positive responsibility of studying and devising programs to eliminate artificial barriers to the free movement of agricultural products.

*In view of the significance of such barriers, we are of the view that the Department of Agriculture should actively carry out its responsibility under the Research and Marketing Act to study the economic efforts of interstate barriers and means of eliminating them.*

Changing technology and transportation facilities have greatly reduced the former need for local inspection of milk supplies for sanitation purposes. Duplicate inspection of plants and farms and unreasonable barriers to the movement of milk increase industry costs and tend to raise prices to consumers. There is ample evidence that the U.S. Public Health Service Standard Milk Ordinance and Code affords adequate protection to consumers.

*We therefore suggest that State and local governments should adopt the U.S. Public Health Service Code and accept reciprocal inspection by all qualified agencies.*

Fluid milk markets tend to be especially unstable because of their local character, the small number of buyers and sellers often in each market, and the upsetting influence of new plant technology and improved transportation. Trade practices such as interest-free loans are common, and price wars repeatedly occur. The problem is best dealt with by the States, and a number have dairy trade practice laws.

*We are hopeful that the States will give careful study to defining and preventing practices detrimental to fair competition in the sale of fluid milk, and that consideration will also be given to developing uniform trade practice regulation among the States.*

The proliferation of packer buying stations, livestock dealers, and auction markets is creating wasteful duplication in many areas and invites unfair trading practices.

*We believe that the U.S. Department of Agriculture should develop, in cooperation with affected States, a model code for the licensing and operation of local livestock markets to foster efficient and fair methods of marketing livestock.*

## OTHER TOPICS

1. We were unable to study whether discounts given by advertising media to food advertisers are cost justified, as would be required in the sale of physical products. Variations in advertising costs have an important bearing upon competition among firms in the food industry.

*Therefore we believe that it would be appropriate for the Federal Trade Commission to investigate advertising rates for the purpose of examining discounts, other variations in charges, their justifications, and ratemaking methods.*

2. Changes in transportation rates are importantly affecting the location of agricultural production and food manufacturing. *We therefore believe that the Department of Agriculture or other appropriate agency should undertake a study of changes in methods and costs of transporting food products, the effects on prices and the locations of production, probable future trends, and their implications.*

3. Prices of certain food products collected by the Bureau of Labor Statistics for its Consumer Price Index, especially prices of red and poultry meats, do not adequately reflect the influence of price "specials" advertised by retailers. The resulting overstatement of average retail prices is not itself important for the Bureau's purpose of measuring changes in prices, but price changes are also misrepresented, since the frequency and depth of price specials tend to vary with supplies. While it is not practicable to obtain wholly accurate average prices, the Bureau's food price data would be better if different weights were assigned to first-of-week prices and end-of-week prices to reflect the volume of food normally purchased in each half-week. The Bureau probably could obtain prices inexpensively

from food chains' local headquarters and visit chain stores only to confirm reported prices.

*We suggest that the Bureau of Labor Statistics should study means by which it might improve the accuracy of its reports of changes in food prices without unduly increasing collection costs.*

4. Information published by the Department of Agriculture about farm-retail price spreads would be improved by more accurate basic data and by more information about the costs and profits that comprise the price spreads. It will be necessary for the Department to obtain supplementary data from the food industry for this purpose.

*We believe that the Department of Agriculture should improve the accuracy of its price-spread data and its information about the costs and profits that comprise them; and that the food industry should assist the Department by supplying such data as might reasonably be necessary.*

5. Commissions or similar bodies established by the States to increase market demands for farm products have become a significant part of the food marketing system. We suggest that there be periodic review of their purposes and accomplishments, and that consideration should be given in some instances to joining forces in the interests of economy and effectiveness.

6. Futures markets for meats and livestock are not directly supervised by any Government agency. *In order to prevent abuses to which futures markets repeatedly have been demonstrated to be vulnerable, it is our view that futures trading in meats and livestock should be under the supervision of the Commodity Exchange Authority.*

If there is established in the Department of Agriculture a separate regulatory agency for perishable farm foods, that agency and the Commodity Exchange Authority might well be administratively associated under one head.

We made no study of coffee or sugar marketing, but we suggest that consideration be given to including futures trading in these two commodities under the Commodity Exchange Authority as well.

# INDEX

## C